Women Writing Africa
THE SOUTHERN REGION

The Women Writing Africa Project

A Project of the Feminist Press at the City University of New York
Funded by the Ford Foundation and the Rockefeller Foundation

Women Writing Africa, a project of cultural reconstruction, aims to restore African women's voices to the public sphere. Through the publication of a series of regional anthologies, each collecting oral and written narratives as well as a variety of historical and literary texts, the project will make visible the oral and written literary expression of African women. The definition of "writing" has been broadened to include songs, praise poems, and significant oral texts, as well as fiction, poetry, letters, journals, journalism, and historical and legal documents. The project has been undertaken with the expectation that the publication of these texts will allow for new readings of African women's history.

PROJECT CO-DIRECTORS AND SERIES EDITORS
Tuzyline Jita Allan, Department of English, Baruch College, CUNY
Abena P. A. Busia, Department of Literatures in English, Rutgers University
Florence Howe, emerita, Department of English, The Graduate Center, CUNY, and publisher/
    director emerita, The Feminist Press at CUNY

EXECUTIVE COMMITTEE

Anne Adams, Cornell University
Diedre L. Badejo, Kent State University
Ann Biersteker, Yale University
Debra Boyd, Winston-Salem State College
Judith Byfield, Dartmouth College
Frieda Ekotto, University of Michigan
Thomas A. Hale, Pennsylvania State University
Peter Hitchcock, Baruch College, CUNY

Nancy Rose Hunt, University of Michigan
Marjolijn de Jager, New York University
Eileen Julien, Indiana University
Judith Miller, New York University
Angelita D. Reyes, University of Minnesota
Joyce Hope Scott, Wheelock College
Marcia Wright, Columbia University
Louise Allen Zak, Marlboro College

BOARD OF ADVISORS

Jacqui Alexander, Barbados
Belinda Bozzoli, South Africa
Boutheina Cheriet, Algeria
Johnnetta B. Cole, United States
Carolyn Cooper, Jamaica
Fatoumata Sire Daikite, Mali
Nawal El Saadawi, Egypt
Aminata Sow Fall, Senegal
Wanguiwa Goro, Kenya
Asma Abdel Halim, Sudan
Charlayne Hunter-Gault, United States
Adama Ba Konaré, Mali
Joy Kwesiga, Uganda
Françoise Lionnet, United States
Marjorie Oludhe Macgoye, Kenya

Fatma Moussa, Egypt
Mbulelo Mzamane, South Africa
Lauretta Ngcobo, South Africa
Kimani Njogu, Kenya
Asenath Bole Odaga, Kenya
Mamphela Ramphele, South Africa
Sandra Richards, United States
Fatou Sow, Senegal
Filomena Steady, Sierra Leone
Margaret Strobel, United States
Susie Tharu, India
Nahid Toubia, Sudan
Ngugi wa Thiong'o, Kenya
Aminata Traore, Mali

◆

Volume 1: The Southern Region (Botswana, Lesotho, Namibia, South Africa, Swaziland, Zimbabwe)

Women Writing Africa

THE SOUTHERN REGION

The Women Writing Africa Project, Volume 1

Edited by M. J. Daymond, Dorothy Driver, Sheila Meintjes, Leloba Molema, Chiedza Musengezi, Margie Orford, and Nobantu Rasebotsa

ASSOCIATE EDITORS: Heike Becker, Devarkshanam Govinden, Mary Lederer, V. M. Sisi Maqagi, Virginia Phiri, and Cristiana Pugliese

CONSULTING EDITORS: Tuzyline Jita Allan and Marcia Wright

TEXT EDITOR: Florence Howe

The Feminist Press at the City University of New York
New York

Published by the Feminist Press at the City University of New York
The Graduate Center, 365 Fifth Avenue, New York, NY 10016
feministpress.org

First edition, 2003

09 08 07 06 05 04 03 02 01   5 4 3 2 1

Library of Congress Cataloging-in-Publication Data
  Women writing Africa : the southern region / edited by M.J. Daymond . . . [et al.].
    p. cm. — (The women writing Africa project ; v. 1)
    Includes bibliographical references and index.
    ISBN 1-55861-406-0 (acid-free paper) — ISBN 1-55861-407-9 (pbk. : acid-free paper)
    1. Southern African literature (English)—Women authors. 2. Women—Africa, Southern—
Literary collections. 3. Women—Africa, Southern—History—Sources. 4. Africa, Southern—
Literary collections. 5. Africa, Southern—History—Sources. I. Daymond, M. J. (Margaret J.)
II. Series.

PR9345 . W66 2002
820.9'9287'0968—dc21
                                                                          2002029483

Publication of this volume is made possible, in part, by funds from the Ford Foundation and the
Rockefeller Foundation.

Text and cover design by Dayna Navaro
Cover art: Celebration. Copyright © 1989 by Gertrude Fester. (See page 555 for further information.)
Printed in Canada on acid-free paper by Transcontinental Printing

To the women of Southern Africa who fought and continue to fight for democracy: in admiration and with thanks. And to the memory of the thousands of women whose voices remain unheard, as well as those whose voices are presented here.

CONTENTS

1960s and 1970s

A Note on the Women Writing Africa Project

The first conversation about this project took place when Tuzyline Jita Allan spoke with Florence Howe at the 1990 meeting of the Modern Language Association. Allan was responding to the recent publication by the Feminist Press of the first volume of *Women Writing in India: 600 B.C. to the Present*, edited by Susie Tharu and K. Lalita. Referring to this landmark publication as a striking example of the untapped potential of international feminist scholarship, Allan pointed to the need for similar work in Africa. Both Allan and Howe knew that a project for Africa like that the press had begun for India could offer significant testimony to the literary presence and historical activity of African women. While Howe did not want to assume responsibility for such a project, she agreed to discuss it at a meeting of the Publications and Policies Committee of the Feminist Press held in February 1991. All present understood that so massive a project would need funding.

Initially, a small exploratory group including Chikwenye Ogunyemi, Peter Hitchcock, Allan, and Howe, began to discuss the merits and scope of the project. Later that year, when Howe was delivering the volume of *Women Writing in India* to the Ford Foundation to thank them for their grant in support of that project, Alison Bernstein said, "Africa has to be next." Members of the exploratory group, now including Abena P. A. Busia, recently elected president of the African Literature Association (ALA), met with Bernstein to discuss the possibility of and support for a planning meeting to follow the ALA conference in Accra, Ghana, in April 1994.

We are grateful to Johnnetta B. Cole, then president of Spelman College, who opened that meeting and testified to the need for a project focusing on the writing and history of African women and to the commitment of the Feminist Press to publishing women's lost voices. Susie Tharu, who grew up in Uganda, Abena P. A. Busia, and Florence Howe also spoke with enthusiasm about the importance of such a project. Some forty members of the ALA attended these two-day meetings, including Judith Miller, who has been an important member of the committee for the West/Sahel region ever since.

Three primary considerations guided the preliminary discussions of the project. First, in spite of their overlapping agendas, Women Writing Africa could not be an exact replication of Women Writing in India. Africa's entrenched oral traditions called for a different response to the discursive modes of expression on the continent. Reconceiving the notion of "writing" marked a conceptual breakthrough in determining how to name a project aimed at capturing African women's creative landscape. "Writing" in Women Writing Africa metonymically suggests a blend of verbal and written forms of expression embodying the experience of African women in envisioning their lives in relation to their societies. The project's matrix of spoken and scripted words represents the creative interaction between live women in the actual world and the flux of history: in short, African women "making" a world.

Women Writing Africa, therefore, became a project of cultural reconstruction that aims to restore African women's voices to the public sphere. We will publish several volumes documenting the history of self-conscious expression by African women throughout the continent. This expression is both oral and written, ritual and quotidian, sacred and profane. We became as interested in dance songs and private letters as in legal depositions and public declamations. We hoped to foster new readings of African history by shedding light on the dailiness of women's lives as well as their rich contributions to culture. In the end, seeing through women's eyes, we expect to locate the fault lines of memory and so change assumptions about the shaping of African knowledge, culture, and history.

A second consideration focused on the establishment of a framework for conducting research on the continent, and here two hard questions presented themselves: how to think of Africa regionally rather than nationally, and how to set up working groups in those regions and also in the United States. Eventually we undertook work in twenty-five countries within four regions, to produce four representative, rather than all-inclusive, volumes—from Southern Africa, from West Africa and the Sahel, from East Africa, and from North Africa.

Following the Ghanaian planning conference, Abena P. A. Busia had joined Allan and Howe as co-directors of the project. Together we formed an Executive Committee of U.S.-based Africanist scholars to serve as a resource and review board for the project's articulated goals and an Advisory Committee of prominent scholars and writers in the field. Together we planned how to organize both regionally and nationally in the field: Allan would find the scholars in the Southern region; Busia would do the same in the West/Sahel region. For their help with this phase of the project, thanks are due to Deborah Boyd and Joyce Hope Scott, who attended the Accra meeting and have continued to make contributions to our endeavor. Then, with African-based colleagues, both Allan and Busia began the work of developing research teams in their assigned regions, first by locating national coordinators who would work together with their regional counterparts. Later, we would proceed in a somewhat similar manner in the East and the North.

The third consideration essential to realizing the project's promise was funding. The three co-directors wrote the first grant proposal to the Ford Foundation, and within two years, another to the Rockefeller Foundation. At Ford, we wish to acknowledge specifically the instigating interest of Alison Bernstein and the support of our several program officers—Janice

Petrovitch, Margaret Wilkerson, and Geraldine Fraser. At Rockefeller, we wish to acknowledge the interest and support of Lynn Szwaja, our program officer. We are also grateful to the Rockefeller Foundation for two Team Awards to the Bellagio Study and Conference Center, where we worked with the editorial team and translators of the West/Sahel volume, and where we wrote drafts for this note. We want to thank especially Susan Garfield for her administrative support and Gianna Celli, the director in Bellagio, for her special interest in our work.

Without the commitment of the staff and Board of Directors of the Feminist Press we could not have done this work. Florence Howe wants to thank Helene D. Goldfarb, chairperson of the board, and acknowledge the whole staff during the years 1993 to 2000, when she was publisher/director of the Feminist Press, for their support in keeping the press running when she had to be away working in Africa. Tuzyline Jita Allan would like to thank Adam Ashford at Princeton University for his help in identifying the scholars to contact in Southern Africa in preparation for the first regional meeting in 1997. She also acknowledges the kindness and aid of the director and staff at the National English Literary Museum in Grahamstown, South Africa. Both Allan and Howe would like to thank the Zimbabwe Women Writers and the organizers of the Zimbabwe Book Fair for their hospitality and interest in the project during the pair's trips to the region between 1996 and 1999.

Abena P. A. Busia wishes to acknowledge the support of the Department of English at Rutgers University, especially chairpersons Dr. Barry V. Qualls and Dr. Cheryl A. Wall, not only for the purchase of essential equipment, but also for flexible teaching schedules that allowed for extensive travel in Africa. In addition, two graduate students were particularly helpful: Carol Allen, now in the English Department at Long Island University, who helped plan the ALA meeting in Accra at which Women Writing Africa was launched, and Krista Johnson, now at De Paul University, who helped with the preparation for the second Bellagio meeting.

All of us want to acknowledge the support of Jean Casella, the new publisher/director of the Feminist Press, the permissions work of Meg Samuelson, Deirdre Mahoney, Wendy Williams, and Shaun Southworth, the editorial work of Livia Tenzer, the design and production work of Dayna Navaro, and the marketing work of Lisa London and Franklin Dennis. We are also grateful for the work of several project assistants: Kim Mallett, Rona Peligal, Sandra Vernet, and Jean Murley. Feminist Press Board of Directors member Laura Brown, president of Oxford University Press, has been especially helpful; we want to note the work of our accountant, Paul Pombo, for his attention to the myriad financial details of this project. Finally, we wish to express our thanks to friends and colleagues in the African Literature Association for their continuing interest and support.

In the summer of 2000, the seven editors of the Southern regional volume spent a month in residence at Brown University. We wish to acknowledge the hospitality of the university, and especially Feminist Press Board member Nancy Hoffman, who was then professor of education at Brown. Merrily Taylor, Joukowsky Family University Librarian, and Samuel Streit, Associate University Librarian for Special Collections, were particularly welcoming and supportive.

We are aware that Women Writing Africa represents the largest undertaking of our lives, a responsibility to set the reality of African women's lives in history and in the present before a world that is only just waking up to their importance. We would like to see this first volume—on the Southern region—give birth to hundreds of other volumes.

Tuzyline Jita Allan
Abena P. A. Busia
Florence Howe

Project Co-Directors and Series Editors

PREFACE

For five years, working part-time, seven editors from four countries in Southern Africa worked locally in different ways to produce this volume. We will describe these briefly, as well as the regional meetings organized by the co-directors of Women Writing Africa and funded by the Ford and Rockefeller foundations. Although the process was lengthy and often arduous, it has also been, for us, a unique experience whose outcome we hope will be useful to a wide audience.

To begin with, Nobantu Rasebotsa in Gaborone, Botswana, agreed to assume, with Tuzyline Jita Allan in New York, the job of regional coordinator. Sheila Meintjes became secretary-treasurer, took notes at all meetings, and kept accounts with the aid of a firm of auditors in Johannesburg, South Africa.

Because of the size and complexity of South Africa, and the amount of available material in libraries and archives, three editors divided responsibilities. In Cape Town, with the help first of Angelo Fick and later of Meg Samuelson, and assisted by Sisi Maqagi's knowledge of Xhosa writing, Dorothy Driver communicated with many academics, first asking for suggestions of texts, and then doing primary research into writing by women across the entire southern region. Later, when texts had been chosen, Driver then asked many younger as well as more seasoned academics to write headnotes. Sisi Maqagi, one of the associate editors for the project, researched Xhosa writing and performance in libraries, archives, and local communities, and arranged a broadcast interview on the project in the hope of attracting lost or forgotten material.

In Johannesburg, Sheila Meintjes worked closely with Susan Maloka to find texts by women in journals and archives. Their committee responsible for choosing materials included Professor Nhlanhla Maake.

In Durban, Margaret Daymond wrote to some twenty-five academics in her region, inviting them to a workshop to discuss ideas and possible texts. From the group came many suggestions as well as a smaller committee that continued to work with her, including Devarkshanam Govinden and Liz Gunner, both of whom helped to refine the selections. Later, Daymond called on other individuals to write headnotes.

Zimbabwe's pattern was different, since two members of Zimbabwe Women Writers (ZWW) had attended the 1994 organizing meeting of Women Writing Africa in Accra, Ghana. Hence, all material related to Women Writing Africa in Zimbabwe was housed in their Harare offices, under the leadership of Chiedza Musengezi. From the first, women writers were interested in participating, and later, academics, publishers, and friends of ZWW became more involved as advisers and researchers.

Headed by Margie Orford, and meeting in homes, restaurants, and at the University of Namibia, the Namibian research team for Women Writing Africa was diverse. Without E-mail and the Internet, the research would have been less fruitful, since many important archives—recorded in Oshiwambo and Finnish—are housed in Finland. Simon le Roux, a patient architect with a smattering of both languages, sifted through countless microfiche, searching for women's names in a large collection dating from the 1930s. He turned up more than forty records, some of which proved useful. Many other researchers in Namibia, notably Heike Becker, shared information and offered suggestions to the local team. Later the team brought their discussions to a wider audience, some of them on national radio.

The two Botswana coordinators, Leloba Molema and Nobantu Rasebotsa, wrote to scholars and received many suggestions for sources. Ultimately, Molema and Rasebotsa worked as a team with Mary Lederer, all three based in the English department of the University of Botswana. They relied on the assistance of students, including Alpheons Moroke, as well as other colleagues for leads to useful texts. They also worked in the archives and, later, took responsibility for the work in Lesotho and Swaziland (in the latter with the help of Sarah Dupont-Mkhonza).

These searches were not intended to be comprehensive. For one thing, with few exceptions, we were using only Southern African libraries and resources. For another, we had no paid leaves from our regular jobs in order to do research, nor did we receive remuneration for our work. What kept us going, at least in part, was the knowledge that we were breaking new ground for women in Africa. Over time, the support of a wider group of assistant editors was critical to the progress of the project. Their contributions towards the selection of texts and the initial conceptualization and drafting of the introduction provided an invaluable foundation for the final anthology.

That our work was groundbreaking became especially evident as regional meetings began to occur regularly—in Johannesburg, Cape Town, Harare, and Windhoek—at first with the U.S.-based coordinators present. These group meetings allowed all of us to share not only the various texts we were finding, but also to debate and define the overarching goals of the project. Without these meetings we would not have been able to select specific texts for inclusion and discard others, agreeing on criteria not only of historical significance but also of literary value.

In 1998, we met following the Zimbabwe Book Fair, in part for the convenience of the Feminist Press as publisher. The press exhibited at the fair, and we were part of a panel presentation on Women Writing Africa in which we discussed texts we had already located and saw as important finds. To our own meeting the co-directors had invited four scholars from East African countries, so that they might begin to observe the methods and consider the purposes of Women Writing Africa as a project. This meeting was dominated by discussions about ideology and class, and helped to focus us as compilers of the anthology and as participants in a pioneering project. We left this meeting strengthened in our resolve to proceed, whatever the difficulties of ideological positioning, to say nothing of the extraordinary amount of time we knew that this project would consume.

In 1999, when the African Literature Association (ALA) met in Fez, Morocco, the co-directors of Women Writing Africa invited us to attend a larger-than-regional meeting to which the West/Sahelian African team had also been invited, along with prospective members of a North African team. First we contributed to the annual conference of the ALA by reading some of our selected texts and discussing their contexts and significance with other scholars gathered there. Then, at our own meetings, as we compared our selections with those of the West Africans and Sahelians, we began to agonize about questions of dating and chronology.

At all of these regional meetings, and in Fez, as we discussed texts and selected some of them for inclusion, and as we discussed drafts of headnotes, we considered the under- or overrepresentations of kinds of texts, of nations, of language groups, and we began to theorize about the shape of the introduction. But of course we never had more than four days of time together for intense discussion. There was never any time to review more than a segment of what was to be a volume of 120 texts. Nor was there writing time during these meetings. In 2000, therefore, the project co-directors invited us to a month in residence at Brown University, in Providence, Rhode Island. There we decided first to review the final selection of texts, then to rewrite headnotes, and, most significantly, to determine the shape of the introduction, to divide responsibilities for its writing, and to map out first drafts. We also made time for a brief visit to New York City, where we accepted two luncheon invitations to meet our funders: first, Margaret Wilkerson, our program officer at the Ford Foundation, along with Vice President Alison Bernstein, and then Lynn Szwaja, our program officer at the Rockefeller Foundation, joined by other staff and officers.

In general, the richest sources for research were in South Africa, Namibia, and Zimbabwe—the former settler colonies. Though Botswana had escaped settler colonialism by becoming a British Protectorate, the country was isolated from early influence leading to the emergence of literacy. Hence, selections from Botswana in this volume do not begin until 1926. In contrast, from Morija, the site in Lesotho of an early Christian mission station, we have a text collected in 1836 by Thomas Arbousset, among the first missionaries to work in Lesotho. From Swaziland, where the indigenous aristocracy resisted mission education unless they also controlled it, we have the full text of a 1921 speech made by a queen regent who could neither read nor write. Regretfully, we had to let go of the oldest text of all, court testimony from a slave woman in Cape Town in 1709, since the court record did not offer an account in the first person.

The question of borders in Africa generally, as well as in Southern Africa, remains a vexed and vexing one. For practical purposes, we have limited the volume dealing with the southern region to coverage of the following countries: Botswana, Lesotho, and Swaziland, which were historically protectorates of the British crown; and Namibia, South Africa, and Zimbabwe. Other nearby countries will be included in subsequent volumes in the series.

Additionally, the sheer volume of material from South Africa threatened to overwhelm the collection from other countries. Because of South Africa's large population, early literacy, and powerful economy, it would have been easy to devote the entire volume to its texts. Hence, it became important to find a balance between South Africa and other countries we agreed to include. Our route lay through orality and the radical reduction of the number of literary texts produced by South African women.

It was important to us to begin and end the volume with texts by black women. We also wanted to make clear that orature, an art form in which black women dominate, is not frozen in some particular period of time but a continuous tradition with roots going back many hundreds of years. Oral texts appear throughout the anthology, placed according to the date of collection or publication. Thus their location insists that oral composition, although utilizing ancient techniques, always re-creates itself in the present.

Because of high rates of illiteracy, great numbers of African women have remained "invisible" and "inaudible." One of our aims has been to seek the testimony of women who have limited access to the written and published word. The volume includes several oral testimonies that allow the reader privileged insight into experiences rarely made public.

Working towards the compilation of the volume meant involving teachers, literary critics, historians, political scientists, archivists, anthropologists, translators, and creative writers in English, Afrikaans, and the indigenous languages. The research that we all carried out involved finding texts, selecting texts for final inclusion that would make sense according to the history and relationships of the region, translating texts or selecting translators, writing headnotes or selecting headnote writers to provide needed context for the entries, and writing the introduction. Published texts appear here as they were originally printed. Only very obvious typographical errors have been corrected. In the case of handwritten manuscripts, no changes have been made at all.

Although working within a group of seven editors occasionally posed problems, there have been many advantages, not least in the continuing pressure on us to take into account other points of view, and to maintain the essentially heterogenous nature of this anthology as a positive rather than negative fact. Moreover, the presence of many different headnote writers serves usefully to interrupt the relation between ourselves as editors and the selected texts. Headnotes sometimes offer readings different from those of one or another of the editors. We chose headnote writers for various reasons. Often the writer found the text or was chosen by the person who found the text. Sometimes the choice of headnote writer was determined by a decision to turn to a noted authority or a representative of the group to which the author belonged. Often we were motivated by a desire to include in this anthology a greater range of voices, and to draw younger scholars in as well, especially from previously disenfranchised communities. Sometimes, too, our choice was determined by a specific historical coincidence: Mary Simons, for example, who wrote the headnote on Hilda Bernstein, was also a banned person in the 1970s. Early in her life, she read the journal *Africa South in Exile*, and recalls the impact on her of finding there Bernstein's prison diary, smuggled out of South Africa. In almost all cases, the headnotes have had to be radically shortened, to make space for more texts. We apologize to the headnote writers for this and trust they understand.

Gendering the history of the Southern African region has been central to the organization of the introduction, which, to some extent, strives to work against the rigorously chronological order of the anthology. For chronologies must always be reminiscent of the masculinist imperial history from which women have been occluded. A strictly chronological "master" history flattens out the unevenness of the process of change that has convulsed the Southern African region, and the lives of women, in the period covered by the texts of this anthology. It also masks the great differences in local articulations of historical change, complicity, and resistance. For example, the Cape had been largely brought within the expanding British colonial ambit by the early 1800s, while northern Namibia was only brought under colonial administration by the 1940s. The women's texts we have included here subvert the accepted sense of linear, imperial chronological history (of wars and laws) and foreground an understanding of women organized around contestations to do with fertility, bride-wealth, and land. The rights over, and access to, women and to women's bodies were and remain key to Southern African societies because of the central importance of women's reproductive and productive capacities. And then central, too, has been women's cultural production, both orally and in writing.

Although we originally thought we would include only unknown, unpublished, lost, and unheard voices in order to produce a unique anthology, later, we decided also to include at least some of the established voices. Generally, we chose lesser-known works to represent well-known writers, but even here we did not work to rule. We made decisions on individual texts with an eye to overall balance of historical significance with general interest and reading pleasure, and in selecting any one text we often had to juggle and nimbly re-sort others. The experience was difficult, but often exhilarating, as we came to develop what we see as a new shape to the Southern African cultural scene.

With regard to the terminology of naming groups and languages, although we may seem inconsistent, we have tried as much as possible to use the names and spellings that the people concerned use for themselves. Thus the reader will see words like isiZulu for the Zulu language, but Setswana for the language spoken by Tswana people. The greatest difficulty and most complex discussion concerned appropriate terminology for the people known variously as Khoesan, San, Bushman, or Basarwa. Because most of the names used by government agencies, anthropologists, and the people themselves have been contested over many years (some groups see certain terms as derogatory, while others find them acceptable), we have used in the headnotes the terms that the groups concerned use to refer to themselves, e.g., Bugakhwe, Ju/'hoansi, and so on. The political implications of such terms are quite far-reaching and have given rise to heated disputes. Many groups oppose the term Bushman, but others find that it has recognition value internationally and so do not find it objectionable. In Botswana, the people previously known as Masarwa, a potentially derogatory term, are now known as Basarwa. The change in prefix indicates changing attitudes towards the people themselves, as the prefix "ba-" indicates insider status, while "ma-" indicates outsider status and was possibly introduced to encourage the lower, debased, position of these groups among the dominant groups in Botswana society. The term Basarwa is currently in use in Botswana as a general term to indicate people who have a common political agenda but who otherwise differ culturally and linguistically. Such difficulties also exist in other countries regarding how to designate people who have similar political concerns, and so one will find different terms used supportively in different sources.

People in Southern Africa speak many different languages (South Africa alone has eleven official languages), and hence in this volume many languages are represented at least slightly, though some not at all. Throughout, we have been aware of the perils of translation. In so far as it has been possible, we have checked the translations in this anthology several times for accuracy and faithfulness to the original.

The logistical difficulties of producing a volume such as this have been both extremely exciting and extremely challenging and we owe many, many people our gratitude for their assistance, including in ways that cannot be captured by the lists that follow. We thank the following individuals for various kinds of assistance: with translation, research, locating texts; for the following kinds of advice: selecting texts, identifying headnote writers, locating authors and information on texts. We also thank friends and colleagues who made suggestions we were not always able to take up, and who offered texts, and wrote headnotes, that were not ultimately published.

Nahas Angula; Carol Archibald; David Attwell; Diedre Badejo; Gabeba Baderoon; Megan Biesele; Veronica Belling; Bruce Bennett;

Jane Bennett; Iris Berger; Debbie Bonnin; Barbara Bowen; Duncan Brown; Raymond Brown; James T. Campbell; Michael Chapman; Keresia Chateuka; Anthony Chennells; Henrietta Dax; Jenny de Reuck; Sarah Dupont-Mkhonza; Elizabeth Gant; Angelo Fick; Ingrid Fiske; Sadie Forman; Willie Haacke; Patricia Hayes; Werner Hillebrecht; Dag Hinrichson; Eva Hunter; Angela Impey; G. Kahari; Russell Kaschula; Adrian Koopman; Jochen Kutzner; Margaret Lenta; Simon le Roux; Nhlanhla Maake; Lily Mafela; Thenji Magwaza; Cathrine Mahaja; Stoffel Mahlabe; Zandile Makahamadze; Susan Maloka; Phiwe Mankayi; Alice Maponya; Andrew Martin; Nhlanhla Mathonsi; Meredith McKitterick; Alpheons Moroke; Gilbert Mpolokeng; Peter Mtuze; Beverley Muller; Ellen Ndeshi Namhila; Mary Ndlovu; Sihawu Ngubane; Barbara Nkala (Makalisa); Abner Nyamende; Anthony O'Brien; Andries Olifant; Kenny Parker; Elaine Pearson; Nigel Penn; Juliet Perumal; Roy Pheiffer; Michele Pickover; Terence Ranger; Natalie Ridgard; Daniel Roux; Sonja Rowan; Elaine Salo; Waleska Saltori; Harold Scheub; Karel Schoeman; Erastus Shamena; A.Z. Simelane; SISTER Namibia; Wim Smit; Yolisa Kambule Soul; Irene Staunton; Shirley Stewart; Jeremy Sylvester; Mary Tandon; Ann Torlesse; Phillipa Tucker; Annalet van Schalkwyk; Randolph Vigne; Dennis Walder; Cherryl Walker; Marion Wallace; Peggy Watson; Julia Wells and Rose Zwi.

We thank the following libraries, archives, and organizations for their assistance:

Botswana: Botswana National Archives and Records Service

England: Rhodes House, Oxford; School of Oriental and African Studies Library, London

Lesotho: Morija Museum and Archives

Namibia: National Archives of Namibia; National Library of Namibia

South Africa: African Studies Library, Inter-Library Loans, and Manuscripts and Archives, all of University of Cape Town Libraries; Anglo-Boer War Museum; Cape Town Archives Repository; Free State Archives; Historical Papers, William Cullen Library, University of the Witwatersrand; Killie Campbell Collections, University of Natal-Durban; Kimberley Africana Library; Kwa Muhle Museum, Durban; KwaZulu-Natal Archives, Durban; National English Literary Museum, Grahamstown;

Pretoria Central State Archives; South African Chinese History Project; South African Library, Cape Town; State Library, Pretoria; University Library, University of Fort Hare; Cory Library for Historical Research, Rhodes University, Grahamstown; Clarkes Bookshop, Cape Town
Swaziland: Swaziland National Archives

United States: Harry Ransom Humanities Research Center, University of Texas; Mission College, Grantham, Pennsylvania

Zimbabwe: Brethren in Christ Church Archives in Bulawayo; Curriculum Development Unit under the Zimbabwean Ministry of Education and Culture; National Archives, Harare; Zimbabwe Women Writers

We thank the accounting firm of Douglas and Velcich, in Johannesburg, where Nerine Butler kept our finances in order.

Megan Biesele gratefully acknowledges the support of the United States' National Endowment for the Humanities (grants RL 21441-89, RL 22066-93, and RZ 20925-02) during collection and preparation of certain texts.

We are much indebted to Iris Berger, Ann Biersteker, and Helen Bradford for reading and commenting on the whole introduction in an early draft, to Diedre Badejo for comments on and corrections to an early draft of the section on orature and orality, and to Heike Becker for some specific and very useful comments on certain aspects of the introduction at two different stages of its composition. Berger and Biersteker also offered comments on the anthology as a whole with regards to the selection of texts. To Marcia Wright, too, our thanks for very useful comments on some key aspects of the introduction, and for general encouragement through the project. Our particular thanks to Jane Bennett, who not only read and commented on the introduction in an early draft but also worked closely with us in giving shape to the final draft. Her understanding of what needed to be done in the introduction was based on a knowledge of the texts we had selected, and was thus all the more time-consuming for her, and all the more invaluable to us. Tuzyline Jita Allan provided valuable guidance and advice at critical moments in the process of assembling this anthology.

Florence Howe edited the entire volume, and, with Livia Tenzer, prepared it for the copyeditors and the proofreaders; Tenzer had ultimate responsibility for preparing the manuscript for publication. Without Florence Howe, the project would not have seen the light of day, not only because of her pioneering and continuing involvement in the history of the U.S. feminist movement, an involvement that led to the establishment of the Feminist Press, but also because of her tireless fundraising, her interest in Africa, and the direction, advice, and encouragement she offered at so many of the meetings she made possible for us. For all this, we are deeply grateful.

We owe a special debt to Meg Samuelson, whose significant work as Southern African regional administrative assistant has kept the countless texts, headnotes, comments, and communications from going astray and who has managed to keep order in a logistically difficult situation in which the publishers, editors, and associate editors have been often on different continents. We owe her warm thanks also for helping to chase up both early and last-minute references and for generally going well beyond the call of duty, both in relation to the introduction and to the project as a whole.

Archival sources sometimes give a greater sense of women's presence than do most essays and books on Southern African history and literary history. While it is true that the authors of government reports, church records, early travel diaries, newspaper articles, and so on, have been predominantly white, and male, they have often made reference to, or given accounts of, women that Southern Africanist historians have not always been quick to use, although recently some key essays and books on Southern Africa have appeared that focus either entirely or in part on women or gender. In preparing the anthology and in writing the introduction, we have been painfully aware of not always having the research support we needed in readily accessible form, which sometimes meant that we did not always hadve the time to find and comb through journal essays, theses, conference papers, government reports, and so on, for the information we needed. In addition, it is fair to mention that published research is not evenly distributed over the different countries that make up the Southern region. We offer this volume, then, with this awareness, but trust that it will extend readers' knowledge of Southern African women, knowledge which we hope will be amended, debated, and further expanded by the readers themselves.

In collaborating on this volume, we relied heavily on E-mail for communicating with one another, but we would not have been able to achieve any consensus without meeting each other face-to-face and working out particular problems by talking to each other across the table. These meetings (especially the argumentative ones at which we justified the inclusion or exclusion of texts from the perspective of our various social, national, and academic backgrounds) enabled us to create this volume. They also allowed us to forge relationships and networks that we will be able to build on and nurture. We derived great pleasure from working with one another and together developed confidence that what we were doing was very important. Juggling our Women Writing Africa lives and our academic and personal lives was not easy. But we were on the trail of something exciting, and we had fun on the side. With one of us at the wheel, we drove to Cape Point, where the Atlantic and Indian Oceans meet. At Brown we danced to Congolese music in one of our bedrooms. We engaged in quiet conversations about politics, our careers, and our families. We made and received countless gestures of friendship. These and other moments leavened our meetings.

In sum, this project generated excitement and produced fresh intellectual challenges. We enjoyed meeting our peers in the region and we relished discovering previously unavailable documents. We were pleased to invite young scholars to work with us on texts they found. We are proud to have produced a significant, scholarly volume that promises to enhance cultural, historical, and literary studies of Africa as well as to provide teachers and students with a valuable resource for the classroom.

M. J. Daymond
Dorothy Driver
Sheila Meintjes
Leloba Molema
Chiedza Musengezi
Margie Orford
Nobantu Rasebotsa

INTRODUCTION

What does it mean, at the beginning of the twenty-first century, to be creating an anthology called *Women Writing Africa*, focusing on the region of Southern Africa? This volume is the first in a series intended to represent women's oral and literary production through most of the African continent. In it our focus is on women, and in broad terms we aim to redress what is generally recognized as an imbalance in Southern African literary and historical anthologies and accounts, given that male writers and performers have been more widely published than women, and that historical agency is generally taken to be male. Widening the focus to include a greater generic variety of material than usually appears in literary anthologies, and to pay attention to women's voices, and in many cases, their agency, changes the contours of Southern African literary and political history. A temptation might be to see the anthology as a history of resistance to colonization or apartheid or "patriarchy," but appreciation of women's heterogeneity undermines any such monologic account, although the anthology certainly includes many instances of resistance. Women engage with social and political forces in such a variety of ways that even using a deft combination of two or more of the spectrum of standard terms in feminist and postcolonial literary criticism—acceptance, refusal, complicity, revolt, among others—cannot cover the complexity of responses that individual women make to the different situations around them.

The term "women" of our title serves in a political project where naming oneself as part of a group is a necessary move in the face of enormous and complex struggles that still await us. For us, the term is not yet under erasure, and it is used in our title only in the most provisional, precarious, and hypothetical way. Women need to place themselves as "women" in order to function politically as part of such a grouping, even while they may not actually share among themselves the same conception of "womanhood." Some of our readers will see in the term only the deep fractures of Southern African history, knowing that gender must always be defined through race, class, ethnicity, culture, and other coordinates in order to achieve any meaning. Others will not want the term problematized, but will see a commonality of experience even under what has been defined as a "patchwork quilt of patriarchies" (Bozzoli 1983: 149, 155). Another perspective would see in "women" something as yet undiscovered, always in the process of becoming, something promising transcendence over the social divisions that have hitherto kept women apart, both from one another and from men. Understandings vary, and it is perhaps best to assert simply that the texts selected for the anthology are spoken by "women" only in the sense that they are not spoken by "men," although—as some of our anthology selections will show—women often speak along-side men and perhaps even give their voices over to men. (Men, it should be kept in mind, are as heterogeneous as women in both their relations to women and their relations to social and political forces.) Nevertheless, even where gender is silenced by race, as it so often is in Southern Africa because of nationalism, apartheid, and colonialism, creating an under-standing of the specificities of women's positions has been important to the assembling of this anthology. Gender is crucial to the articulations of iden-tity, social aspiration, and voice. What it is to be a "woman" continually fluctuates, depending on the historical context and even on the projected audience. Whether people become women in the acts of speaking or writ-ing, or what kind of women they become, depends not only on the specific ways they place themselves—or are placed—through the linguistic gestures they make, but also on the shape given them in the acts of listening and reading. Writing, reading, and oral performance are mediated by their his-torical contexts, which include the political situation and the political expedience of the time and place.

This anthology offers a multitude of actual voices in its one hundred and twenty entries, and nearly twice that when the count includes the headnotes, which are mostly written by women. Despite this multiplicity, and the theoretical heterogeneity of women, women's voices in this anthol-ogy often cluster in class categories. The second term in our title—"writ-ing"—helps us address this. In sub-Saharan Africa, until very recently, European culture virtually monopolized the production of written and printed material, and it was the thinking of a particular segment of the European population that first controlled what went into print. Christian missionaries brought with them prescriptive notions of civilization and the primitive, which played a major role in determining what was acceptable for publication, and even within the European population relatively few had access to print. Many women might not have wished to enter, or did not consider entering, the world of print; print culture is "modern" in more ways than one. There is a need to offer redress to colonial ignorance of black cultural performance, women's and men's. There is a need also for another kind of redress. In this deeply divided and richly diverse region, women form an extraordinarily heterogeneous group. Not only have black women been silenced much more than white women, but the term "black" can, moreover, obscure other silencings within that grouping.[1] In selecting from the texts available to us, we represent only those women whose voices someone before us has recorded (or, on very few occasions, those whom one of us has recorded) or those who have had their own access to print.

As our anthology will continually show, writing signifies both empow-erment and entrapment to women. Literacy was central to colonization and inseparable from the various Christian missionary enterprises across the Southern African region. In assuming certain class, race, and gender divisions, literacy created new elites, and, up to the 1950s, writing by black Southern African women was most often produced by those few who wished, or were able, to take up educational opportunities provided by Christian missions. Usually signaling rupture between newly educated women and the wider community, literacy tended to mark a division between what have been called "school people" and "ochre people" (this is an Eastern Cape term; formulations vary from region to region). But even this generalization is contradicted in our anthology: Nontsizi Mgqwetho (1924), for instance, uses writing not only to produce what reads like oral poetry, but also to assert a non-school status and moral sensibility.

Oral texts—a phrase that covers a wider range here than is commonly understood by "orature," with its literary significance—are centrally important to our anthology and may be likelier than printed texts to detail experiences and perspectives partially impermeable to the colonial gaze. Performers may sometimes belong to the struggling, oppressed class that Walter Benjamin calls the depository of historical knowledge (1970: 260), or that Gayatri Spivak, following Antonio Gramsci, calls "subaltern" (1987: 197). Over a third of the texts we selected are originally oral: some, like the praise songs and wedding songs, are orature; some are as-told-to stories or essays; some are close to being interviews, spoken—perhaps under prompting and other direction—to an interlocutor, transcribed, and perhaps also translated; some are court records or affidavits; some are petitions. Petitions are often hard to locate in either the oral or the written. They may have been put into written form by lawyers, as in the case of the Petition of the Native and Coloured Women of the Orange Free State (1912).[2] In petition writing, simply to keep to this example, whether a legal advisor shapes the voice of the women, or whether they determine their own stance, the question of hegemony arises to destabilize the notion of a woman's "own" voice. As anthology editors, we have sometimes had to live with the uncertainty of authorship, knowing that a central point we need to make through this anthology has to do with the production—through the signature of women—of what have come to be known as "women's voices." The question of mediation, and specifically of white cultural domination, arises particularly strongly in the case of the transcriptions and translations undertaken by well-meaning missionaries in the nineteenth century. In literary matters, mediation takes many forms and occurs at many stages of the process of cultural interaction: from recording to transcribing, translating, editing, and publishing. At all of these stages, cultural intervention occurs, and at its center is a question of power.

Although the power of speaking is potentially open to all women, and may serve to give them dissident space, it exists within the peculiarly doubled patriarchalism of "racism" and "sexism," meager terms, we feel, for the complex of forces at work within their practices. In the real world, says Zimbabwean novelist and short story writer Yvonne Vera, women's speech is often blocked by "interruption" and "shocked reaction," and speaking is "still difficult to negotiate." The book, in contrast, "retains its autonomy" (Vera 1999: 3). This does not mean that speaking cannot and has not offered moments of political and personal intervention for women, both under colonial hegemony and today. However, the notion of the book's autonomy is a useful one, for the agency of these texts is palpable.

In addition, acts of writing project acts of reading. The transformation of the spoken word into writing means that the word enters the at least potentially democratic space of interpretation.[3] Although literacy in English is not available to all Southern Africans, and although writing, as South African writer and critic Zoë Wicomb maintains, cannot alleviate the hunger of those "beating at our doors for food" (1992: 19), the book nonetheless invites others to enter it. Writing passes over to others the power of re-creating that writing in a potentially democratic exchange about the meaning making, value debating, and identity formation in constant process in and around us. Our anthology, moreover, invites its international readership to take account of the ways Southern African women transform neocolonial assumptions and stereotypes.

In our title, the verb "writing" points in two directions, not only to the women who seize or are accorded agency, but also to the "Africa"—or in this case, the "Southern Africa"—under inscription. Writing turns space into place. Creating a country, a nation, or a region was not necessarily in the consciousness of the women whose voices we have here, but we nonetheless see them as, together, offering a new way of reading and understanding the vast, varied, interlinked, and independent set of places we call Southern Africa. This anthology challenges colonial habits of mapping (for European colonization arbitrarily mapped identities under territories), in that many of our texts cross borders or thematize border-crossing. It also transgresses modernity's distinctions between the urban and the rural, for the experience of migrant labor means that in the lives of many people, including women recorded in the anthology, the two are continually combined. If space becomes place by being named (Carter et al. 1993: xii), by becoming the focus for specific forms of social and psychic identification (Daymond 2001), and by generating cultural markers that allow its definition, perhaps a new kind of Southern Africa is being created here. If that were so, it would be one that strives to incorporate and manifest—without obscuring, without repressing—the historical and current divisions that keep coming to light, especially and most recently through South Africa's Truth and Reconciliation Commission. Speaking of political transformation as an embrace of fracture, the South African poet Ingrid de Kok uses a lyrical phrasing from the speech made by Caribbean writer Derek Walcott when he accepted the 1993 Nobel Prize for Literature: "Break a vase, and the love that reassembles the fragments is stronger than that love which took its symmetry for granted when it was whole" (de Kok 1998: 62).

If the act of writing transforms space into place, so too does it transform time into history. In one of our texts (Qedabakwabo Moyo's "Going to

School," 1921), a young Christian convert notes the conversion of time into days and weeks, the rhythms of her experience now being placed into a system measuring others' time as well. Time is differentially experienced and ordered, and many of our anthologized texts subvert the accepted sense of a linear, imperial chronological history (of wars and laws) and develop an understanding of women organized around other contestations, for instance, those to do with fertility, bride-wealth, and land. Indeed, the variety of texts also serves to disrupt the chronological ordering we decided on for this anthology, by foregrounding the unevenness of the processes of change both over the whole Southern African region and in the lives of specific women. Southern African countries have different histories of colonialism and independence.[4] Their temporalities, in other words, are varied, not in the sense that they are the same societies at different stages of "development," to use the European post-Enlightenment term, but in the sense of being nonsynchronic (Fabian 1983: 155). Southern African historians have written of the way in which what might otherwise be thought of as a specific historical moment can be made up of different notions of temporality and periodization, so that "different historical narratives" come "into closer dialogue with each other," although they never become "a single history" (Sylvester, Wallace, and Hayes 1998: 12).

Ultimately, despite the possible binding forces provided by the term "women," and despite the promise within the anthology's new understandings of time and place, and the integration offered through the many different interlinkings and interdependencies that characterize the southern region, we do not offer "Southern Africa" as a new entity. Instead, our intention is to open up the archives of Southern African women's cultural and political history to different ways of understanding the region, an understanding which will focus now on homogeneity, now on heterogeneity, now on sameness, now on difference, and allow for entirely new connections and insights.

In the pages that follow, we justify some of our selections, and especially our focus on the political and creative output of the black majority rather than the white minority. Despite the apparent stranglehold of colonialism, and of apartheid in South Africa and Namibia, along with South Africa's economic domination of the countries in the region, Southern African women have continued to look through and beyond these forces for their voices and cultural identities. In the context of a predominantly patriarchal organization of women's productive and reproductive capacities, whether colonial or indigenous, the rights over, access to, and attempted control of, women's bodies, minds, and voices are key to an understanding of Southern African history and literary history, and so is their capacity to negotiate the terms of their social and psychological existence: hence the presentation, in this introduction, of a sometimes extended discussion of certain historical moments in Southern African oral and written production. Our discussion does not cover the entire history but is keyed to the anthology's contents, as we draw readers' attention to some aspects of the history of gender in Southern Africa.

WOMEN AND ORALITY

Women's communal performances, vital to cultural life in Southern Africa, include fables, legends, and songs (both ritual and occasional), as well as proverbs and riddles. Passed from generation to generation, these genres and their contents evolve over time, as individual texts are created afresh with each performance. That over half of our texts in the 1980s and 1990s are orature or oral testimony attests to the continuing significance of the oral in women's lives.

While songs and stories do not provide unbroken access to the past, they do provide information about how women were—and still are—expected to behave as daughters, wives, and mothers. Experiencing orature as informative does not diminish it. We thus stand at an angle to the important cautionary arguments of Spivak and others about the appropriation by academic, "first-world" women of "third-world" women's voices (Spivak 1985; Mohanty 1988; Lewis 1996).

Women compose songs for different occasions, for instance, to mark declarations of war, to announce political resistance, or to lament military loss (see, for instance, "Song of the Afflicted," 1842). Women's songs also celebrate particular moments in life, including generational passage (see, for example, "*Intonjane*—Xhosa Initation Songs" and "*Mutondo*—Nyemba Initiation Songs," 1999) and marriage (for example, "Setswana Wedding Songs," 1999). While the function of women's orature is partly to conserve, encouraging compliance with social requirements, women find ways to use songs, dances, and storytelling in counterpoint to conventional maxims.[5] As suggested by the Nyemba initiation song that opens "We found a man collecting honey, he had large testicles" (1999), women often elect to convey potentially subversive views of masculinity. The apparently playful mockery demarcates a realm men may not enter, an uncontestable space in which women sing and dance in a manner defining complex, sometimes ambivalent, self-locations. The dances and the call-and-response structure of songs offer individuals an opportunity to comment upon orthodoxies without diminishing the songs' potential to maintain collectivity. The songs' hortatory notes do not preclude a poignant and even robust recognition of the difficulties, for example, of puberty and marriage. Since on marriage a young woman leaves her family, one of the singers of the "Swazi Wedding Songs" observes that marriage "is like throwing away your own bones [. . .] like throwing yourself away" (1993). In their initiation songs, the Nyemba speakers, who are refugees from Angola, now residing in Namibia, greet a girl's first menstruation as a "force" which comes to "destroy the house." The secret of the mukula tree which features in Nyemba ritual is, it seems, to teach female obedience, and specifically the endurance of menstrual pain. Even as the older singers induct the novice, they warn her of the demands of a patriarchal social system.

Knowledge of the earliest oral production and the groups producing it is still slight. Archaeological evidence about the first people in Southern Africa, known collectively as the San/Bushmen,[6] goes back 14,000 years and suggests that they once occupied the whole region represented in this volume. From about 2,300 years ago, a related people—the Khoekhoe—then living as pastoralists in what is now known as northern Botswana, are thought to have begun moving to the south, and eventually also up the east coast (Wilson and Thompson 1969: 40–47). The Khoekhoe were the first people at the Cape to encounter the Dutch traders in the seventeenth century, as they had encountered Portuguese explorers in the fifteenth and sixteenth centuries.

Archaeology also suggests that a different, third group of people—agriculturalists, pastoralists, and smelters—were gradually moving southwards from west and central Africa, settling in the northeastern part of South Africa from about the third century A.D. They are thought to have spoken "Bantu"[7] languages and possibly to have been the ancestors of the Shona people in Zimbabwe. "Bantu" language speakers branched into the Nguni, who settled the eastern and southern regions, and the Sotho-Tswana, who settled on the central plateau of Southern Africa. Despite dialectical differences, speakers of the Sesotho and Setswana languages are mutually intelligible, as are the Nguni speakers of siNdebele, isiZulu, and isiXhosa. Today the "Bantu" language family "covers approximately the whole of the southern half of the continent of Africa, and consists of well over two hundred languages" (A. C. Jordan 1973: 2). The living patterns and kinship structures of each linguistic group show variations, but also comparability, as linguistic grouping alone does not define culture. Indeed, language, locality, and economic modalities are not consistently related to each other (Wilson and Thompson 1969: 43; Omer-Cooper 1987: 10).

In both Nguni and Sotho-Tswana societies, a patrilineal and patrilocal social organization underwrote the authority of male elders and rested on the sexual division of labor. Patriarchal control of women's fertility was pervasive and often continues to influence the present, as "Citizenship: An Open Letter to the Attorney-General" (1985) indicates for Botswana.[8] Senior men arranged marriages at all levels, and bride-wealth—*lobola* (isiXhosa and isiZulu), *bogadi* (Setswana), *roora* (chiShona)[9]—articulated a relation of alliance between the families and polities involved. The practice of *lobola* is still honored in many African societies but is increasingly contested, many women (and men) arguing that it makes women mere commodities. However, as Bessie Head (1981: 56–65) says in the case of Botswana, when Khama the Great, influenced by his own conversion to Christianity in the late nineteenth century, abolished *bogadi,* women found that neither law nor custom could be invoked to protect them against neglect and abuse.[10]

Owambo, in northern Namibia, forms the northern boundary of the geographical area covered by this anthology. It is also the western-most boundary of the central African matrilineal belt. The prevalence of patrilineal societies in this collection does not occlude "the particular meshing with male authority" that occurs in matrilineal societies, where "matrilineal forms of organization and ideology tend to give greater social and political space to women" (Orford and Becker 2001: 293).

The genres of orature are deeply gendered,[11] although the idea of generic division and the evaluative hierarchy attendant on such division may owe more to the assumptions of colonial ethnographers than to actual practice. Usually men performed the genealogical history of the clan, often as part of a praise poem, but the example of Nongenile Masithatu Zenani, both a renowned storyteller ("A Man Hides Food from His Family," 1972) and a widely respected Xhosa historian, suggests that narrating history was not always closed to women. Zenani was celebrated for her knowledge, memory, sense of humor and irony, linguistic skills, and endurance. Her performances often took days: one lasted two and a half weeks (see Scheub 1996: 78). While most early collectors of orature were men, some women—Lucy Lloyd and Dorothea Bleek, for example[12]—left enduring legacies of collaborative work with their informants. It was mostly /Xam men who recounted Khoesan tales to Lucy Lloyd and her brother-in-law, but the young woman !Kweiten ta//ken was also one of her sources (see the selection dated 1874). Lydia Umkasetemba's narrative in our anthology (1868) is not the only one by a woman in Bishop Henry Callaway's collection, although Umkasetemba is generally considered an outstanding narrator.[13] Usually, senior women, often grandmothers, were noted performers of such tales as "The Story of Ngangezwe and Mnyamana" (1879).

Orature has evolved in a cultural setting that values the spoken word as humanity's most distinguishing and most valuable possession.[14] Fables have deep-rooted origins, and while their motifs are common property, the individual performer's selection and choreography of the commonly known elements allow for significant variation, and audiences relish the skill with which this is done. Moreover, each performance is shaped through audience interjection. (Communal responsibility for meaning is usually lost in the early records, but today oral performance can be captured on video and film, media that bring new kinds of interventions, depending on who is shooting, editing, distributing, and viewing ethnographic material.) Members of the audience interact with the composer-performer by signaling delight, curiosity, surprise, or dismay as the performance unfolds. Intense discussion between audience members and with the performer often follows, or an answering performance may be the response.[15]

In many oral tales, the performers choreograph a rapid passage from the familiar world to the realm of the marvelous and back. In the realistic aspect of "The Story of Ngangezwe and Mnyamana" (1879) there are signs of the tension experienced by women in the social system of polygyny, such as in the wives' competing ambition. When read less realistically, the tale's component women are subordinated to a purpose beyond themselves. In the end, the wives' rivalry seems to be a motif needed to trigger a chain of events, and once the focus of the tale has transferred from the women to their sons' conflict and its eventual resolution, the fate of the women becomes relatively unimportant.

Missionary Attitudes to Songs and Stories

The boldly erotic content of some ritual songs sometimes earned missionary disapproval. In Namibia, Finnish Lutheran missionaries insisted that the initiation rites of young Owambo women were something of which "no decent person could even speak" (Becker 1998a: 9), thereby bringing their notions of shame and sin to bear on songs and rituals which had the socially vital function of giving meaning to and legitimizing sexual behavior. The personally divisive effects of such disapproval can be seen in a comment made in about 1930 by Paulina Dlamini when, after her conversion to Christianity, she related her life story to a Lutheran colleague and explained her inability to speak of her time in the court of the Zulu king, Cetshwayo: "About the king's nightlife with his isigodlo [harem] girls I must remain silent; because as a Christian, who has now learnt to kneel before the King of all Kings, the Lord Jesus Christ, I can no longer speak about such things" (Dlamini 1986: 82; see also our selection from Dlamini's story "Flight of the Royal Household," 1939).

Missionary attitudes were contradictory. Although they banned certain initiation and marriage songs, missionaries were active early collectors. For example, "Unanana-bosele" (1868) and "Two Lions Who Changed Themselves into People" (1886) have survived in their nineteenth-century form because missionaries recorded and published them. Most other ritual songs in this anthology were performed and transcribed more recently, however deeply rooted they might be. Since fables were transcribed because they accorded in some way with missionary purposes, the orature collected in the nineteenth and early twentieth centuries is not necessarily representative. What survives must to some extent speak of missionary interest and prejudice. The "Two Lions" story was deemed useful as an appendix to an otjiHerero grammar. Henry Callaway, who recorded "Unanana-bosele," wanted to encourage what he called "a close communion of mind with mind" (1868: i) by helping others to learn the language and customs of the Zulu people. In collecting their stories and histories, he did not, however, envisage an equality of cultures.

It may well be, then, that the angriest or most resistant of women's voices were occluded and so unavailable to this anthology. As has been said in another context: "Historically, the native woman who 'speaks' does so at the prompting of colonial officials, missionaries, and anthropologists" (Sharpe 1993: 33). Occasionally, however, in travelers' accounts, we have access to the kinds of voices that colonizers could not retrieve (see, for example, Pringle 1835: 15–16). The nineteenth-century traveler George Stow passes on the following instructive message from a woman known to him simply as Kou'ke:

> Kou'ke stated that all the men of these tribes were shot without mercy by the different commandos that came to attack them. When the writer was trying to persuade her and her husband to

accompany him on his travels for a short time, that he might have an opportunity of learning more of their history, she said: "Do you see where the mountain comes down to the river?" pointing to where its steep shoulder formed the left bank of the Caledon, in the Jammerberg Poort. "There," she continued, "were all the best of our tribe shot down; there all our brave men's bones were left in a heap: my captain's, my brothers', and those of every friend that I had. Do you think I could live in the land of the men who did me that evil? No! not for a single night would I sleep on their accursed ground!" Her reasons were unanswerable. She departed, and the opportunity to obtain their unrecorded history was lost. (Stow 1905: 188–189)

Issues of Cultural Mediation in Oral Texts

In recording orality, a potentially hegemonic mediation may be at work from the moment of the spoken encounter to the final (written) product. It can seep into all attempts to understand diverse cultures, their products and their history. It is in the nature of reproducing and translating orature that intervening presences—interviewer, transcriber, translator—shape, and misshape, the text that we read. Court records, for instance, present a single perspective on the court encounter, and the views and purpose of the person creating the document color its content, "whether he was a European judge, African clerk, or local ruler" (Roberts and Mann 1991: 47). Many of the documents in our anthology are mediated by men; many, too, are mediated by whites. !Unn/obe Morethlwa's words, reproduced in our anthology, were gathered in 1971 by a white researcher, Megan Biesele, who had western technological resources, her education, and her institutional position to empower her. Biesele's appreciation of what it meant for her interviewee to choose to live apart from western influence indicates her own awareness of the imbalances—material, political, and discursive—between those who perform and those who report. In her book about Ju/'hoan storytelling, *Women Like Meat*, Biesele indicates that she also found gender affecting the balance and shape of material (1993: 2; see also Hofmeyr 1993). By no means is all orature collected by white researchers, as our anthology shows. In Zimbabwe in the 1960s, under state encouragement, tales in the vernacular were collected by such women as Jane Chifamba (1964) as a way of countering the linguistic and cultural domination of English.

Feminist and postcolonial studies often focus on the meaning of intercultural translation and its theory (von Flotow 1998). The power relations that shape these transactions have been explored by Spivak, among others. Her essay "The Politics of Translation" (1992) observes that a translation into a colonial language of colonized women's texts that forced the source language into the discourse of the target group might coerce the interests of the source voices. Therefore, Spivak argues, a translator's attempt to render a text completely accessible constitutes a betrayal of that text. This argument is of particular importance for the translation and reception of orature. In orality the performer is in direct, primary communication with the community. The rhetorical and structural processes through which written texts interpellate readers are assumed in orature, and because these processes cannot be transcribed (and therefore cannot be translated), must be inferred and reconstructed by the reader of the translation.

Given these various problems, our anthology reminds readers that they are reading mediated and translated texts. In order to ensure that readers register the strangeness of what they encounter in translations, the headnote writers have illuminated, through as much detail as possible, the distance of the translator's text from the original. Such illumination of distance suggests both the analytic and the interpretative nature of translation and refutes the idea of translation as pure access to a source text.

Colonized Women: Forms of Resistance

The gendered economy of Southern Africa was unevenly but profoundly changed through colonization and initially, at the Cape, through the introduction of slavery.[16] Early colonial economies had employed male and female agricultural labor, but, with abolition, male migrants were increasingly sought and coerced. After the discovery of mineral wealth, the growth of mining in the region led to still greater male migrancy. As women's labor in the homestead was reordered, new ideological constructions of indigenous and subject women were imposed.

The experiences of two women—Krotoa in the seventeenth century and Sara Baartman in the nineteenth—illuminate particularly destructive effects of colonial projections. Krotoa, whose own narrative is not recorded in history but who is celebrated in this volume by Karen Press (1990), was a young Khoe woman who lived for a time in the Dutch station where she acted as interpreter.[17] She converted to Christianity and subsequently married a Danish military surgeon, Pieter van Meerhoff. The Dutch called her Eva, in a renaming which foreshadows much of the gendered apparatus that imperialism would use in justifying its conquest of the region. The Dutch read Southern Africa through Christian myths, assuming that the story of the Garden of Eden applied, and that Cape women were a reminder of man's Fall.[18]

The narrative of the young Khoe woman Sara Baartman illustrates the profound hostility of nineteenth-century European thought to colonized women, who were depicted in literature, medical discourse, and art as excessively and aberrantly sexual. Baartman was taken to Europe in 1810 as an ethnological curiosity and displayed in a cage as the "Hottentot Venus." Even after her death, her body remained an emblem of "primitive" sexuality, preserved at the Musée de l'Homme, Paris, until her remains were returned to South Africa in 2002.[19]

Without a revolution in epistemology it is impossible to trace women's direct resistance to such colonial gendering. However, the available orature shows that Khoesan women had a very different attitude to their sexuality than that assigned them by early travelers. This can be glimpsed in the story told by !Kweiten ta//ken (1874) in this anthology about the maidens who adorn themselves with ochre so that the springs, and the men, do not "dry up." Helen Bradford's rereading of the story of Nongqawuse, the young Xhosa woman whose prophesies directed her people to kill their cattle in 1856–1857, offers further insight into African women's views on sexual propriety and license. While some would see Nongqawuse as merely the mouthpiece for a male prophet (see Peires 1989), Bradford (1996) emphasizes her status as a sexual adult, having undergone initiation rites, and as someone well aware of the turmoil within Xhosa families due to colonial war and predation. In particular, the carrying off of herds from the defeated Xhosa thwarted the completion of marriage through bride-wealth payments. Bradford also identifies intensely female elements in Nongqawuse's call for purification and redemption through sacrifice, especially her pointing to such male transgressions as incest and rape as displeasing to the ancestral spirits. While Nongqawuse apparently instructed the Xhosa that, if they killed their cattle and ceased to cultivate crops, their ancestors would arise and drive the colonial invaders from their lands, other women, as the documents in this anthology suggest, resisted colonial patriarchy with great determination from within colonial institutions themselves.

The Early Court Records

As Roberts and Mann have written, "Laws and courts, police and prisons formed essential elements in European efforts to establish political domination" (1991: 3). Colonial legal systems affected moral education and discipline, as well as the economic order, especially with regard to mobilizing and controlling labor. While the law gave occasion for battle between Africans and Europeans, it could be, and often was, used by Africans against Europeans and among Africans themselves. Women used law as a resource in struggles over property, in particular, and also over authority over their own bodies, invoking symbols and ideas, negotiating meanings, asserting positions, and reconstructing understandings of gender. Correspondingly, law was used against African women, criminalizing them in ways indigenous legal traditions did not.[20]

While colonial law empowered some Africans and not others, creating asymmetries of power and also often buttressing patriarchal control, customary law was constructed in the process of contact between the indigenous and the colonial.[21] This meant that women sometimes found ways to adjust their social situations. Customary law did not, for instance, usually see women as entitled to land (Chanock 1985: 172–216). In the nineteenth century, especially in "buffer" communities, conflicts about property rights and resurgent customary inheritance propelled some women into court. Appearing before a Cape government commission in 1858, and arguing that her land was being redistributed to rival claimants, Kaatje Nieuwveldt ("Testimony," 1858) asserted her right as a daughter and a widow to own and farm arable land in the Kat River valley in the Eastern Cape. She positioned herself in the economy primarily as an independent farmer, able to enlist men to help her, and determined to use the land commission, the colonial state's apparatus, to seek justice for herself. It was a step that Emma Sandile, too, would take in her 1883 "Land Submission." Almost twenty years after this, farther north, Tryn Isaac gave evidence to a commission investigating disputes over diamond-bearing land involving the Boers, the British, and the Griqua. Her account of how people come to regard land as theirs is both gendered and anticolonial. Her brother's gravestone is a marker of personal connection with terrain that belongs to her family through its link with life and death. Her ancestral land claim draws attention to the specific symbolic order within which she operates, for her view is significantly different from that of the encroaching colonial state, which stakes its claims by setting up demarcated boundaries (fences) through which the official record of ownership is then justified.

The establishment of new religious authority and the importation of law brought in new ideas about individual rights, and women were often attracted both to the missions and to magistrates' and district commissioners' courts for ways of escaping unhappy marriages, thus challenging the authority of their husbands and male elders. Christian religious authorities introduced into Southern Africa beliefs regarding the relation between law and sin; as the point of judicial proceedings was to determine legal guilt, new notions of Christian guilt were transplanted as well (Roberts and Mann 1991: 15). The court documents in our anthology generate information about the daily lives of African women not available elsewhere, both as regards their sense of their own rights and as regards the imposition of guilt and sin. Courts were crucial sites for gender and generational struggle, and thus for the reconstruction of patriarchal authority as well as its entrenchment. Yet court records are always to be read within their specific historical contexts, for colonial legal administrations, their relation with indigenous authorities, and the particular practices of European officers varied enormously from region to region and court to court.[22]

WOMEN AND WRITING

Our anthology contains many examples of the way women took power through engagement with colonial literacies, trying to turn available resources to their own advantage. Nieuwveldt and Isaacs indicate that women with little or no literacy could most certainly understand their circumstances and voice needs, and their efforts point forward to a variety of women across the whole span of this anthology, such as Louisa Mvemve in 1916 and

Keamogetswe and Lesie Kwere in 1997. Compelled to live in a context where colonial authorities relied on written documents and reorganized society through the power bestowed on those who could write, these and other women who made depositions provide an instance of the "jagged, unpredictable and uneven" interaction between orality and writing (Hofmeyr 1993: 12) that characterizes the long colonial encounter in Southern Africa. Their endeavors encourage a rethinking of the rigidly dichotomous view of the colonial encounter. The binary oppositions of Manichean thought were undoubtedly part of colonial discourse (culture/nature, civilized/primitive, and so on) and were used by colonists to justify their practices, but many actual examples of how women lived and what they said suggest that such oppositions are naïve as philosophical approaches to gendered experience in Southern Africa.

The history of education and of literacy for Southern African women stands as a further context for the written texts chosen for this anthology, for education and literacy had major impact on the history of gender. Like court practices, educational practices varied across region and time, and only some general suggestions can be given, both of the practice itself and its impact on gender. The earliest educational institutions available to Southern Africans were the Christian missions, and the history of education speaks volubly both of inequality and of access to new rights and new ways of imagining the self. This section of the introduction points almost exclusively to key moments in the education for black rather than white Southern African women, but it should be noted that even among white settlers, for most of the nineteenth century, the available schooling was usually rudimentary and illiteracy was frequent. Once colonies such as Natal were granted responsible government (in 1893), education for white children was more single-mindedly pursued (Hughes 1990: 198). The advantages to white girls are obvious, and yet it must be remembered that theirs was a cramped education, which, in the few "ladies' academies" they could attend, consisted of dressmaking, music, drawing, and some grammar (Vietzen 1980: 17–18).

After the formation of the Union of South Africa, access to education varied from one province to another as much as did property rights, voting rights, and governmental representation, but in general terms it is fair to say that the education of European children was at the expense of Africans and other "non-whites," including Indians, particularly in Natal, with its dependence on Indian immigration. Racial segregation started replacing class differentiation, while at the same time education was instrumental in new class formations within once relatively homogeneous groups among both the indigenous peoples and the non-white settler population. Racist policies controlled education also in Namibia and Zimbabwe.

Conceptions of gender as well as race and class were changing. Initially, transformation included differential access to education, since boys rather than girls were singled out to be educated, thus demarcating gender in new ways. Whereas women in pastoral communities had traditionally been responsible for agricultural tasks, under colonial rule young men in the mixed agro-pastoral societies were admitted to agricultural colleges. As Bradford has pointed out for Xhosa society, doctors in the nineteenth century were predominantly female (1996: 29 n. 42). In many, if not the majority, of the other societies in the region, women doctors were numerous. Colonial representational practices, however, held that medicine was a male occupation, and under colonial rule, therefore, black women were fortunate to achieve the status of nurses (Marks 1994: 10–11 et passim). In Botswana, the three women whose testimonies are collected under the title "Lend Me a Dress" (1991) agree that girls were allowed education more readily if there were no boys in the family, but in families of one girl there would be no relief from time-consuming domestic work or from being "lent out" to the extended family (Mafela 1993). It is difficult to make generalized gender comparisons across the whole region, although we know for example that among Indians the gap between female and male attendance at school was wide until World War II (Hughes 1990: 199). In general, during the latter part of the twentieth century girls' access to education began to match that of boys in primary and secondary schools, although in some contexts more girls were educated than boys, given demands made on boys to herd cattle and family dependence on male migrant labor.

Converting people to Christianity had started in the early eighteenth century, although—again—the timing of the various conversions differs according to the region and the local reception of missionaries.[23] Often, the processes of conversion were syncretic: a community of converts might continue customary practices even while absorbing and adapting the new religion, thus complicating any analysis of missionaries' impact on cultural practice and gender (Comaroff and Comaroff 1986). Nevertheless, it is clear that the advent of Christianity changed the cultural imagination of Africa. New standards and even a new mode of being were imposed on all aspects of social life, in particular as regards gender and family relations. Positioned by missionaries as the "bearers of culture," women (as mothers, wives, and primary school teachers) became pivotal to the conversion process: converted women would—it was believed—ensure and maintain the Christianization of whole families and were essentially suited to teaching the young. In particular, the missionaries' radically new cultural tools—literacy, school education, printing, and books—had a profound impact on girls and women, on their social positioning, and more generally on gender relations. It was with the use of these tools, however, that women negotiated and resisted, even as they sometimes complied with, the new world in the making. In this new world, the colonial stratification of Christian and non-Christian became more explicitly racial as the nineteenth century wore on.

The missionaries instituted changes that now lie so deep in gendered behavior and experience that they are often hard to identify. In creating orthographies for indigenous languages, missionaries determined racial demarcations and empowerments; indeed some linguistic—and, hence, "tribal"—divisions were purely products of nineteenth-century European discourse (Harries 1988: 26). However, what is only recently starting to become clear is the impact of orthography and translation on gender. For instance, Benedicta Egbo refers to "the wide use of gender-neutral pronouns in many living African languages" (2000: 2), but translations were sometimes skewed to the extent of effacing the female gender. Speaking of Sesotho, Marc Epprecht notes that the term translated into English as "headman," and thus gendered as male, may refer in Sotho to both female and male (2000: 5).

Letters and Mission School Essays

Besides Europeans, the first people in Southern Africa to read and write were probably not Christian converts but Muslim slaves or political prisoners who were literate on arrival in the eighteenth century.[24] African women of the region took up opportunities to acquire literacy mainly in the nineteenth century, and especially in the eastern Cape: "[Xhosa] women became involved in Western-style education to a far greater degree than African women did elsewhere in southern Africa" (Wilson and Mafeje 1963: 71). It is from this part of the region that we draw the first writing by black Southern African women, in the form of letters and school essays. These are soon followed by mission-derived writings originating in Natal and Namibia.

Missionaries were aghast at conditions that they defined, crudely and through Eurocentric paradigms, as a state in which girls and women were "practically slaves to the other sex" (Young 1902: 123), and they focused on creating new structures for domestic life founded on the nuclear family rather than polygyny. Their emphasis on the basic training of women for domesticity is evident even in an essay in this anthology written from a seminary that prided itself on offering secondary education for girls (see "The War in Zululand," 1884).[25] The domestic training of women became such a standard feature of school education that in KwaZulu-Natal, in 1879, an inspector for schools said openly that "industrial education for women was simply a euphemism for the training of domestic servants" (Meintjes 1990: 138).[26] As Jacklyn Cock points out in *Maids and Madams*, "[d]omestic work constituted an important initial point of incorporation whereby the conquered population was absorbed into the colonial economy" (1980: 197).

Missionaries were, furthermore, intent on educating not only the future leaders (male) of the African people, but also the royal women they would marry, and thus, for instance, was Zonnebloem College established in Cape Town in 1858. Here Emma Sandile was sent, the (less important) daughter of the Xhosa chief. Sandile's *nkosikazi*, or primary wife (usually called "first" wife in historical literature, but this temporality is misleading), refused to let her daughter be educated at Zonnebloem.[27] As Emma's letters show (1860–1883), the missionaries' marriage plans for her came to naught, and for a time, like other girls sent both to this and to other institutions, she became a teacher.

Given the need for their "evangelical work to spread and bear fruit," the missionaries needed locally trained converts—"teachers, lay preachers, clergy, community leaders" (Hughes 1990: 199)—but they usually appear to have made accessible to women only the more subordinate roles. Qedabakwabo Moyo's account in this anthology of going to school in Zimbabwe (1921) refers to her being trained as a "helper." The letter sent in 1861 by the Herero woman Urieta Kazahendike to her mentors, the missionaries Carl and Emma Hahn, gives us a glimpse of the dependence of missionaries on converted women. Urieta Kazahendike's life story is one of considerable linguistic and scholarly accomplishment, which Carl Hahn appropriated for his own advancement as a scholar and writer. Used not only as domestic servant/foster-mother and linguistic informant, she accompanied the Hahns on a return visit to Germany, where they displayed her as living proof of the success of their evangelizing, thus ensuring the raising of substantial funds.

We referred earlier to the abuse of black women's bodies through reference to Sara Baartman in the early nineteenth century. It was this context of abusive prurience that Urieta Kazahendike entered in 1863. Standing before white German audiences, functioning as the sign of the Hahns' successful mission work, she becomes another version of display, and her nightmare before boarding ship home is one of the more haunting moments in this anthology. Neither she, nor her missionary-madam, can find the words to write out what she had had to experience, and so it remains a matter of speculation. In some ways this selection reaches forward historically into a time when such horrors can be voiced more fully—and it is worth breaking chronology once again to point to Zoë Wicomb's "Another Story" near the end of our volume. Wicomb's character cannot speak of the "shame" attached to Khoe bodies, but perhaps her story exorcises it.[28]

Urieta Kazahendike's letter has survived because it is preserved in the Hahn papers, and some discussion of the preservation of writing will help explain some of our early anthology selections. In the case of Emma Sandile, all but one of her extant letters have survived because of the status of their recipient, either Bishop Robert Gray, whose papers have been preserved in the Archives of the United Society for the Propagation of the Gospel in London, or Sir George Grey, whose papers are in the Grey Collection in the South African Library (Hodgson 1987: 18, 22). Her last extant letter has been preserved in the Government Archives in Cape Town as part of policy records. It is possible that the letter by Noneko Toney (1875) was written, let alone preserved, because she knew how important it was for women such as Anne Mackenzie to gather and publish accounts of the successes of the mission schools. Early in the twentieth century, in Namibia, another letter survived only because it was intercepted by colonial police. In it a young Herero woman attempts to warn her brother of his danger and urges him to destroy his papers. In a comparable context, the central character in Tsitsi Dangarembga's "The Letter" (1985) preserves a personal letter from her husband only to have it lead to her imprisonment in apartheid South Africa. In Botswana, in a context of patriarchal rather than colonial restraint, Motshabi Molefhe writes: "You can never keep letters. You have to throw them away because sometimes they will land you in trouble" ("Lend Me A Dress," 1991). The material found in the archival searches we undertook suggests that the letters, diaries, journals, and other recorded thoughts of early African women are most often preserved because they served the interests of colonial authorities.

The same may be said of Eliza M.'s writing in 1863. African newspapers were beginning in the late nineteenth century to offer black women some opportunity to publish, and scholars are now starting to uncover more publication both then and in the early years of the twentieth century. Eliza M.'s account of a visit to Cape Town was, like "The War in Zululand" (1884), probably written in the first instance as a school exercise but was seen, presumably by a missionary teacher, to warrant translation and newspaper publication. Probably Eliza M. did not herself decide on publication, and it is instructive that neither the translator nor the newspaper editor recorded her family name. Two decades later, as we will discuss in a later section, a black woman went into print in newspaper form, in a voice directly and clearly antagonistic to missionary edicts and colonial rule: Adelaide Charles Dube, with her poem "Africa: My Native Land" (1913). In the following decade, Nontsizi Mgqwetho began publishing in newspapers an extensive body of poetry, and some essays, sometimes under her clan name and sometimes under her mother's name.[29]

Settler Fiction and Memoirs

Mission wives saw themselves sometimes as the rescuers of women entrapped in "primitive" polygynous structures, but they rarely questioned the state of subordination—political, economic, and psychological—into which entire nations were being placed, nor did they question the impact of their alien and profoundly disempowering attitudes toward women. As in British women's responses to *sati*, or "widow burning," in nineteenth-century India, their posturing was narcissistic. White colonial women saw themselves as "saviors," but usually failed to address the social and material contexts of African women's lives, or even to hear their voices. They operated in, and reproduced, a discourse founded on a symbolic of "civilized" and "primitive," "agent" and "victim," and oblivious to the nuanced and diverse speaking positions of African women. For example, Eliza Feilden writes of her servant Louisa: "If we can only have patience with her she may turn out a fine creature and learn to be very useful, but you cannot reason with one of another language, who has no ideas upon daily duties" (Feilden, "Portrait of Louisa," 1887).

We have placed Olive Schreiner as the first white woman writer in our anthology.[30] Although she was, by her own account, ambivalently poised between South Africa, her "native land," and England, her "mother land" (1923: 13, 15), Schreiner is generally named as South Africa's first novelist, an assessment based on her first published novel, *The Story of an African Farm* (1883). In the standard accounts, it is usually her unprecedented ability to depict a South African landscape that gives her prominence or first mention (see Gray 1997; J. M. Coetzee 1998; van Wyk Smith 1990; Schoeman 1991; Chapman 1996), although it was her feminism that brought her immediate fame. Her major novel, *From Man to Man*, receives far less critical attention than *African Farm*, is called "melodramatic and didactic" (Chapman 1996: 134; see also Schoeman 1991; First and Scott 1980), has never been published in South Africa, and in editions abroad has not been kept in print. Our excerpt, which we have given the title "Leaving the Farm" (1886–1887), is from this book. It shows neither the feminism nor the anti-imperialism many readers might expect Schreiner to be remembered by[31]—or at least not in any direct way—but instead portrays the character Rebekah in what we take to be a crucial moment in white colonial gender formation. Rebekah weighs up her life's possibilities and yearns for what also drove the character Lyndall in *African Farm* to leave the farm: an escape from the version of femininity on offer in bourgeois colonial life. This early writing reveals the profoundest unease at the source of the white South African English novel: unease at bourgeois definitions of femininity which were already directing not only colonial women's lives but also their fiction. Ironically, too, our title "Leaving the Farm" might allude not only to Rebekah's leaving, but also to the departure, mentioned briefly by Rebekah later in the novel, of black farm-laborers and a domestic worker.

In colonial discourse, modern gender—saturated with eugenicist hierarchies of class and race—is produced through the role of authorship given to the white narrator, who exhibits her particular kind of colonial "mastery" over the bodies of black women, women whom she trains in the kitchen and about whom she writes. Later in Schreiner's novel, Rebekah's "whiteness" means she is incapable of behaving sympathetically towards a black servant, despite her original intention, showing much the same colonial limit as does Feilden, writing from Natal. The white woman in Feilden's text is positioned as the virtuous and hardworking wife, the black woman as the figure of brute-like strength. If either text describes a sympathetic connection between two women, it is a sympathy emanating from a domain proclaimed as superior.[32] In white writing of this time and place, white identity needs to be constantly reaffirmed, and—since the process of such identification involves recognition by the black "other" of white superiority—subordinate black characters abound. In an 1888 text, this time from Lesotho, offering Adèle Mabille's contrasting portrait of Penelopa Lienguane, the black woman asserts her own power as a woman and a human being—giving gifts to the white children, offering her labor as a friend, acting as a missionary herself, and thus subverting Mabille's production of her, through writing, as the object of conversion and a sign of Mabille's own superiority and success.[33] Seeing these black characters inserted thus, between the lines of white women's texts, critics are tempted to ask whether there is any way to hear the black women *themselves* speak out.

Eliza M.'s 1863 account is worth returning to here, specifically regarding race and voice, in order to help develop our argument about some of the complexities of textual power relations and the production of the voice of the "other." Eliza M. is struck by seeing in Cape Town the performance of racial difference by whites in the Mayday practice of "black face."[34] Here whites stage as a theatrical display the fantasy of "going native," appropriating the place of the other, and acting out what they see as the typical or essential gestures—in this case, street begging. Eliza's voice mediates this event for us, framing with her own voice—and thereby subverting—any existing mediation of blacks by whites. Yet her account also allows us to consider the complexity of the white experience of "black face." In *White Skins/Black Masks* Gail Ching-Liang Low sees the white colonial fantasy of going native as both the affirmation and disavowal of difference between white and black. Using the voices of black characters, white writers fantasize the ability to become the other without actually needing to engage in any more practical (but socially difficult) way in that process of becoming. Southern African fiction would not have been possible without writers' attempts at a sympathetic connection across the chasms of difference, and there is a danger, in the analysis of their writing, of seeing only fixed or hostile stereotypes and overlooking the complex situations that writers strive to address or to produce.[35]

Instead of, or as well as, using stereotypes, writers sometimes represent the "other" in ways that reveal not only hostility but also anxiety, fear, yearning, or desire. (See Bhabha 1994: 66–84 for important discussion on the act of writing in this regard.) In white Southern African women's writing, sympathetic connections across race are often shot through with considerable ambivalence—sexual jealousy, fear of black male sexuality, anxiety at losing their own limited social positions as custodians of the white family, homestead, and nation. The women sometimes also provide critiques of a male double standard where white men can cross a racial divide that is taboo for white women. Their ambivalence often gives a richness to their acts of writing, whose figurative language takes on a certain life of its own, even providing a depth of textured prose that serves to release the stereotype from its apparent fixity. Thus it is—to turn back to Feilden's text— that Feilden's Louisa seems, through the ambivalence of the white writer's voice, to take on her "own" voice. The "hybrid" construction of black and white voices is a crucial topic throughout our anthology.

This kind of moment, along with other questions regarding representation and voice, is pursued and complicated in Zoë Wicomb's "Another Story" (1990), a black woman writer's response to an early twentieth-century white woman's novel. Wicomb explores whether the story about so-called coloured characters can be more safely told by a so-called coloured rather than a white woman.[36]

Textual Interactions and Hybridities

Throughout this anthology, and stressed by means of our continual juxta-positions of one voice against another, issues are raised about the roles of gender and race in the way responsibility and accountability are constructed, and about how representation and mediation operate. "Speaking for" may sometimes transform itself into the possibility of "speaking to," in the sense that one text may speak not always past or across another, but in a manner that may be read as one woman speaking to another. These juxta-positions are couched within a range of stances. Some texts in this anthology suggest that the practitioners of oral and written modes have developed ways of coexistence and even of mutual support, and there are at least some indications of intimacy across racial divisions, whether women unite in common cause or simply make use of one another in a benevolent way. These interactions can take many forms, and it is useful once again to range across the anthology's chronology for a moment to look at some of them.

Poets and storytellers adapt traditional forms for use on new occasions and, in the process, create new kinds of written work, as Nontsizi Mgqwetho's 1924 poem reveals or, differently, Minnie Martin's "Moliege's Vengeance" (1906). Nise Malange ("I, the Unemployed," 1985) is an example of a cross-over poet who first composes in writing the poems that she performs.[37] In contrast, Elizabeth Ncube (1993), who could read and write both Shona and English, chose to remain wholly within orature; her circumstances in post-independence Zimbabwe may have motivated this, and orature clearly offers her linguistic and culturally nuanced possibilities of voice. The pieces by Antjie Krog (1998) and Sindiwe Magona (1990) indicate how, for writers, style can depend on and reproduce the power of originally spoken material (Daymond 2002). Krog incorporates into her writing the voices of white and black, male and female; and in a later text than the piece selected here, Magona adopts the voice of a semiliterate, working-class woman in order to address the white mother of a political murder victim (Samuelson 2000). Gcina Mhlophe's work inhabits both oral and written modes ("Praise to Our Mothers," 1989). Mhlophe is a well-known poet, short story writer and playwright who, since 2000, has chosen to work chiefly as a creator and performer of *iintsomi*, drawing on isiXhosa and isiZulu orature, and performing before black and white audiences. These examples suggest various and complex kinds of cultural coordinations: voices develop as hybrid entities, as well as apart from one another. Far from being subordinated to writing, Southern African orality functions outside, alongside, and in interaction with the written. The interaction between orality and writing might then stand for us—not in parallel but chiastically—as an analogy to the race and class interactions that other texts, and the anthology as a whole, depict.

EARLY TWENTIETH-CENTURY TRANSITIONS

In *Take Care of Your Children* (1962), the first novel by a black Zimbabwean woman, written in siNdebele and excerpted in our anthology under the title "Past and Present," Lassie Ndondo looks back to the late nineteenth century. Conceptualizing this period in terms of its double offering—the Bible and those small "pieces of metal" that translated into money—she understands the massive social transformation brought about by colonization less in terms of the spiritual conversion missionaries believed they were instituting, and rather more in terms of the social and personal changes ushered in through the radical shift in economic life. Old forms of authority, manners, and communal relations were destabilized by the new needs and desires brought about by the entry, however partial, into a capitalist economy. The taxes imposed under colonial regimes compelled large numbers of people—primarily men—to engage in migrant labor, which itself brought radical changes to gender and to gender relations. The gradual entry into a capitalist culture meant an entry into the almost altogether new "man"/"woman" divisions signified by consumerism. New definitions were given, and new hierarchies made, with respect not only to gender and race, but also to genealogy and generation. New distinctions emerged—the urban and rural, the civilized and savage. All of these meant changes both to external markers of gender and internal experiences of it, as first the Khoe, and then the Xhosa and Zulu, and later other indigenous groups as well, began to enter the colonial economy. At the same time, even as the various systems of education in the different regions demanded a degree of acculturation, education and literacy also provided some of the tools whereby the processes of acculturation might be resisted, just as orality did, in its different forms. The texts in our anthology represent, negotiate, assimilate, comply with, adapt, refuse, and resist the wide-ranging processes of late nineteenth- and early twentieth-century colonialism, whether material or ideological.

The political and economic position of women changed radically in the early twentieth century as a colonial-capitalist economy was forcibly imposed. Land was expropriated, and sociopolitical rights were increasingly denied or removed. Value was placed on male (migrant) labor for its production of goods, and female labor—producing crops and children—was subordinated. Women were given a geopolitical place. Capitalism required that the reserves (land demarcated for black inhabitation and farming) function as a labor pool, to supply the industrializing cities and—to whatever extent possible—to feed their own populations. This demand produced a profound tension within the ideology, and between it and reality. Women's oral skills continued to be important as a means of negotiating the contradictory demands of modernity. Expression of their consciousness became carefully considered analysis, often interventionist, and ranged from verbal testimony (Nosente of the Umgqwashe, c. 1930), orature (Nekwaya Shikongo, known locally as Mother Loide, 1953) and speech making (Charlotte Maxeke, 1930, and Lilian Ngoyi, 1956) to a continued assertion of the power of performance.

By 1902 and the end of the Anglo-Boer War, European rule extended over the region that would, in 1910, be declared the Union of South Africa. Industrialization made South Africa the dominant economic power in the entire Southern African region, particularly through the practice of migrant labor. With this came cultural dominance (hence the greater number of South African texts in this anthology). The expanding, modernizing economy and white power brought an increased burden of work and responsibility for women. Wage earning was first undertaken by young, unmarried men (Walker 1990a: 173, 179) in order to meet colonial measures of control such as "hut tax," which hit hard at a polygynous social system in which each wife had a separate dwelling. As migrant labor took more men to the cities for long periods, women took sole responsibility for their own agricultural labor, for herding, and for maintenance of the home. When they found work on the white farms in rural areas, women were paid less than men. In Zimbabwe, for example, women and children hired on a seasonal basis were often paid in kind at very low rates (Schmidt 1992: 72). The development of a cash economy gave men a new basis for exerting power and authority over women. On the one hand, then, the demand for and social dependence on women's productivity gave women more control over their own resources, but on the other hand migrant labor led to greater impoverishment and psychological and moral social disruption. In the cities, the only employment available to women was as domestic labor in white suburbs or, from home, as washerwomen, brewers of beer,[38] and providers of services, including sexual ones. The social problems were matters of concern not only to literate African Christian women—as shown in the speeches by Maxeke (1930) and Ngoyi (1956)—but also to rural women without formal education (like Nosente in c. 1930).

Prompted by anthropologist Monica Hunter (later known as Monica Wilson), Nosente explains in the early 1930s the customs within which she was raised and married, and then laments the modern ways adopted by young wives, particularly their disturbance of maternal hierarchies. For her, the gender differences of her own upbringing were not demeaning to women; rather she fears changes such as the "softening" or feminization that men risked by entering the house of a nursing mother. Through her children's experiences as "school people" and her own as a domestic worker, she is certain that the system in which she was raised is not giving way to one which brings equality to women.

Approaches to Public Discourse: Letters, Diaries, Pamphlets

The letters and essays of later generations were very different from those of the late nineteenth-century schoolgirls and young women teachers. Writing gave women opportunities to negotiate indigenous patriarchal hierarchies, and it gave women more specific political opportunities as well. From the concentration camps of the Anglo-Boer War of 1899–1902, where Afrikaner women and black women were detained (van Heyningen 1999), to the apartheid prison cells that held black and (fewer) white women dissidents, very different women use the diary form to document the historical salience of their experience (see "Journal of the War," 1900, and "Diary of a Detainee," 1961). Further, writing enabled women to enter the professional world. Our anthology includes a rare example of secular self-publication, where the herbalist Louisa Mvemve (1916)—without having had a mission education—wrote pamphlets advertising her medical knowledge, boldly entering and exploiting a print culture to her own commercial advantage.

In her pathbreaking research on missionary education and "maid-madam" relations, Cock points out that missionary-educators were blind to the way Western influences weakened "women's role within precolonial society" and did not allow them significant "alternative roles of power or autonomy" (1990: 95). In 1892, in Natal, the young Susiwe Bengu fled to the mission to escape the authority of her father and the old man chosen to take her as his wife ("Testimony of Susiwe Bengu," 1892). But the missionary world did not always offer women the lives they sought, and the register at Susiwe Bengu's school is sprinkled with the words "Ran Away." For a story of the profoundest disappointment about the mid-twentieth-century constraints of mission education, there is no better illustration than the letters of the pseudonymous "Lily Moya," not excerpted here (they are readily available; see Marks 1987). Many school-educated women saw the missions more positively. Writing in chiShona in Zimbabwe in 1974, Joyce Simango stages Christianity as a refuge from patriarchal abuse ("Women are Wealth"). And over this entire period many school-educated women achieved some access to power.

In the process of inserting themselves into the domestic structures created for them, and into a symbolic system which placed so much weight on oppositional and hierarchized distinctions, these women often renegotiated definitions of the domestic, rejecting modern demarcations between the domestic and the social, and developing voices for themselves from within this subtly transformed ideology of domesticity. Many women may have accepted at least some of the terms within the hierarchical symbolic ordering of colonialism, but they sometimes destabilized it as well. Their often sharply directed responses give an ironic spin to the missionary expectations of African women. For instance, in the case of the Xhosa it was said in the early twentieth century that the women showed "more docility and proficiency than the male scholars" and "more immediate prospect of improvement, because of their greater readiness to receive instruction" (Young 1902: 128). Yet, as we have seen, Emma Sandile had by no means been "docile." In her demand for land, she challenged the state through the very legislation designed to curtail her authority, doing much more than simply rehearsing Caliban's curse.[39] In Botswana some forty years later, the daughters of the former president, Seretse Khama, appealed to the higher authority of the British High Commission in order to assert their case against a grasping uncle ("Letter to the High Commissioner," 1926). Significantly, they drew on the discourse of equal rights for women derived from European feminism, repeating the moves that were made also by early twentieth-century, mission-educated Xhosa women. This European influence would later be conceptualized as cataclysmic in the Southern African discourse of politics and human rights—the public articulation of women's needs would be seen as rupturing the African community.

Early Political Speeches and Essays: Women's Assessments of Modernity

As suggested above, the conceptual construction of domesticity was at the forefront of missionary education of girls and women. Domesticity shaped notions of "labor and time, architecture and space, consumption and accumulation, body and clothing, diet and hygiene, and sexuality and gender" (Hansen 1992: 5) in ways crucial to understanding the cultural ordering of Southern African history. The focus on domesticity, deeply imbricated with class and racial hierarchies in some of the early political essays, enters into many of our anthology selections. In South Africa and to some extent in Zimbabwe, the emergence of an African middle class was defined primarily in terms of the gendered separation between "social" and "domestic," "public" and "private," which had been fundamental to the emergence of the middle class in Europe during the period of industrialization (Armstrong 1987). Whereas African men and women had arranged homestead life and gender relations in differential ways that both accorded and limited power to women, the Western-derived colonial definition of domesticity radically redefined Southern African women's positions. Historically, women had taken their self-validation in large part from their diverse family positions as wives, mothers, co-wives, mothers-in-law, sisters and aunts, but now domesticity (as a primary relation to a husband, children, and a place outside the wage economy) was meant singly to define women's identity (Hansen 1992: 6). At the same time, under the racist hierarchies first of colonialism and then of apartheid, the class aspirations produced through the ideology of domesticity were simultaneously made impossible to fulfill. The poverty of many urban households, which prompted African women to work outside the home, meant that the middle-class domestic ideal of the good mother and housewife was constantly out of reach (Gaitskell 1983). In any event, the black women represented in our anthology see themselves as much more than the "domestic" figures that mission education had intended to create.

Some remarkable early political speeches by women converts, deeply revealing about the new class relations of the time, have been collected in missionary publications. Typically, this class of women combined a distinguished genealogy with mission school education, followed by further education in Britain or the United States of America. School-educated women and men tended to marry one another, founding a small black middle class from which came the newspaper editors, essayists, biographers, and political leaders who, with their wives, would have a marked impact on early African history and politics. The emergence of women leaders in their own right was relatively rare. Our anthology includes Nolwandle Jabavu (1928) and Charlotte Maxeke (1930) from among the only nineteen women who receive entries in T. D. Mweli Skota's *African Yearly Register*, a local Who's Who, published in 1931. Besides the other seventeen women who received entries of their own, many more were named as wives. In a related text, a Mrs. Sesing is celebrated for being a "cheerful and hospitable" hostess, a sign of progress quite as worthy as the Sesings' house, "artistically furnished according to modern European style" (Mancoe 1934: 55).

In the 1880s Southern African women and men were sent to American universities to study, largely at Wilberforce University under the auspices of the African Methodist Episcopal (A.M.E.) Church. Charlotte Maxeke (then Charlotte Manye) was among the first to be admitted to Wilberforce and graduated in 1901 with a B.S. degree. Other women studying in the United States were Adelaide Tantsi Dube (later taking on the name Adelaide Charles Dube, and represented in our anthology); Hannah Gow; Sibusisiwe "Violet" Makhanya, whose sister Katie Makhanya would later produce her life story;[40] Amelia Njongwana; Eva Mahuma; and Pearl Ntsiko (see Campbell 1995: 249–295).[41] Hence the emergence, from the early twentieth century, of a group of outspoken and, albeit politely, angry women, who were at least partially empowered by their access to the North American feminist discourse of the time. Maxeke, who wrote some of the biographies in Skota's *African Yearly Register*, and Jabavu senior, who was also speech making and writing in the early twentieth century, are the forerunners of a long line of political spokeswomen and activists—Phyllis Ntantala, Lilian Ngoyi, Ellen Kuzwayo, and others, in this anthology, and many more whom we might have included.

Several of these women had been educated at Lovedale[42] as part of a larger group called "School Xhosa" (as opposed to the "ochre people" who would form the subject of Noni Jabavu's later writing, such as "Bus Journey to Tsolo," 1963). Their ideological positioning was derived in part from the Presbyterian missionaries of the Free Church of Scotland, whose views coincided with those of the A.M.E. Church circles in which they moved once they arrived in the United States. The establishment of the Native University College of Fort Hare in the Eastern Cape partly stemmed the flow of black South African students to universities in the United States, and homegrown university graduates began to emerge, including those from the neighboring countries of Botswana, Lesotho, and Swaziland in the 1930s. In the British Protectorates, the pattern was for women to attend secondary school in South Africa (usually Tigerkloof, but also

Inanda, Zonnebloem, and Lovedale) and thereafter to go to Fort Hare for degree work. In Namibia, the pattern was similar, but emerged later, because of its uneven colonization and the later incorporation of Owambo women into mission education. Thus, to illustrate from selections in this anthology, Nehambo Magdalena Shamena, who became an activist in the 1960s, was the product of an education similar to Phyllis Ntantala's but started writing at a much later date.

Charlotte Maxeke, speaking at much the same time as the rural woman Nosente of the Umgqwashe, presents more ambivalent views. Part of an emerging African middle class, she voices considerable concern about the destructive effect of urbanization and modernity on family life, contrasting the freedom that "progress" offered women with the actual lives of women and children in cities such as Johannesburg. The conflicting forces with which women had to contend, which often included the authority of and abuse of power by black males as well as "white government and industrializing power-brokers," led Bozzoli to comment on the complexities of the terms "resistance" and "opposition": "[When people are] so intricately enmeshed in different types of domination . . . opposition to one type may involve collaboration with another" (1991: 14). To some extent Maxeke masks these conflicts by voicing optimism about the opportunities available for educated African women of her class. However, she acknowledges that for uneducated and unskilled urban women there was little legitimate employment. (In most regions domestic service was dominated by men until the secondary, manufacturing industry expanded after the Great Depression of the 1930s.) Maxeke, like others of her class, adopted the colonial image of Africa as "a slumbering continent, just stirring to life"— all counting themselves among "the awakened" (Campbell 1995: 266). Embedded in their discourse is the now familiar dichotomy of the civilized and the primitive; but there is much that is different as well, for they did not miss the ambiguities contained within the dyad "Christianity and Civilization." As a leader in the Joint Councils Movement, which sought to improve the quality of life of urban Africans from the mid-1920s onward, Maxeke was held in considerable awe in South Africa. She was a renowned public speaker. A generation later, but writing in the same intellectual tradition, Ellen Kuzwayo recalls Maxeke as a major influence and quotes her 1938 advice to women (she was the first national president of the National Council of African Women):

> This work is not for yourselves—kill that spirit of "self" and do not live above your people, but live with them. If you can rise, bring someone with you. Do away with that fearful animal of jealousy— kill that spirit, and love one another as brothers and sisters. The other animal that will tear us to pieces is *tribalism*. (original emphasis; Kuzwayo 1985: 103)

This call for selflessness in the common interest is one that would resurface in the 1970s in the emphasis placed on *ubuntu* in Black Consciousness.

The narrow construction of a domesticated and disempowered femininity was not acceptable to women who could assess it both through their own alternative positioning, from within their community life, and through their liberal education, based as it was on an ideology of individual rights, including rights for women. Accepting "Christian civilization" did not mean they were the dupes of Southern African Christian practice, and if a Christian conception of femininity as it pertained to girls and young married women, the future "motherhood of the nation," remained as a partial source of their own thinking about femininity, so, too, did their belief that Christians should mean what they said when they spoke about humans being equal before God. Femininity was delivered to them—if one might put it this way—in so obviously a racialized form that it could not but be reimagined, as we see, albeit differently, in Maxeke's, Nolwandle Jabavu's, and—later—Phyllis Ntantala's thinking. Nevertheless, whether because of the demands of the occasion and her consciousness of address, or because of a contamination of her thinking by Christians who operated in terms of race-class hierarchies, or because of incipient notions of superiority embedded in Xhosa genealogical rankings, Maxeke shifts some part of those hierarchies onto the "Natives" and even "domestic servants," those not school-educated like her. On the other hand, it is this "Native" perspective she adopts when she wishes to voice antagonism to Christian practice—speaking through a mask, as so many women have done before and since.

Nolwandle Jabavu's rhetorical skill and deft cultural negotiation are similarly evident. She takes the nineteenth-century British feminist dictum "No people can rise above the standard of its own women" seamlessly into her own cultural context as "a saying which is very old" and uses it to draw attention to her own perspectives on women, different from those of local males and missionaries. Refusing to see precolonial women as "chattels," she refuses them, and herself, a position as victim. Like Maxeke, she insists that British modernity interferes with the stabilizing patterns of domestic life and with existing gender structures.

In sum, in these important political essays, we hear a skillfully orchestrated resistance to colonialism and a deft, if also sometimes clearly compromised, management of a profoundly ambiguous historical moment. These women weave together the discourses of Christianity, modernity, class, gender, and race in subtle and intricate ways. Throughout the twentieth century, Southern Africanized versions of Christianity will remain the organizing principle of the newly racialized nation-in-formation, and will continue to inflect notions of femininity in their relation to national survival.[43]

Through the 1960s and later, questions of gender will persist, but will be increasingly voiced as issues not between women and men but primarily between black and white women. Maxeke's suggestion in 1930 for cooperation between "Bantu and White women" came only four years after a shameful moment in the history of white South African women, when most suffragists dropped their demand for votes for all women and asked for votes for "European women only."[44] In these early political essays, women couch their resistance in the discourse available to them, including the discourse of courtesy, which may make them seem less angry than, for example, the poet Nontsizi Mgqwetho, who was not converted, wrote in isiXhosa, and commonly addressed "Africans," not "Europeans."

By the 1950s the civic rights which concerned women (the right to choose one's place of abode and to seek work) had become politicized with a new intensity in the face of the National Party government's legislation further entrenching white domination. In her famous "Presidential Address to the African National Congress Women's League, Transvaal" (1956), Lilian Ngoyi identifies the extension of the pass laws as being of primary concern to African women, but calls on "women of all races throughout the length and breadth of our country" to unite in "the sacred struggle for justice, peace and freedom." Unity was not realized in any significant degree either in her generation or beyond it, but with Ngoyi on the organizing team was Helen Joseph, who saw herself as not "a white woman doing things *for* black people but a member of a mixed committee headed by a black woman" (original emphasis, 1986: 5). It was in this spirit that four women of different races led the anti-pass march: "Lilian Ngoyi, the African, Rahima Moosa, the Indian, Sophie Williams, the coloured and I, the white" (Joseph 1986: 12).[45] The time for such public gestures was coming to an end. Political efforts had once been towards moral persuasion, such as in the Defiance Campaign, but once these were rebuffed through repressive tactics such as the Treason Trial, political opposition in South Africa was forced underground. From the beginning of the 1960s, it was rare for women, or men, to unite publicly across the races in the way Ngoyi envisaged.

Like others before her, Ngoyi draws on formal education in making her public political analysis, but Nekwaya Loide Shikongo, in her performance of the "Song of King Iipumbu" (1953), deploys also the resources of orature, with its strong tradition of sociopolitical commentary, to chide delinquencies of chiefdom. Referring to "staybehinders," she reflects on the intricacy of living in and between two cultures (Becker 2000a). Similarly, the forthright self-expression of the Sesotho song "Aunt, Stretch out the Blanket" (1959) indicates the singer's confidence in asserting personal needs and choices, as well as the ability of women in her community to adapt to the requirements of migrant labor—both for the sake of those who leave for the city and for those who stay behind.

Fiction and Poetry by Black Women in the 1920s and 1930s

Protestant missionaries soon after their arrival began to want converts to study not only the Bible, but also key civilizing texts. *Pilgrim's Progress*, John Bunyan's seventeenth-century religious allegory, was much favored

(Hofmeyr 2001 and 2002). Missionaries began to translate religious or "uplifting" texts into indigenous languages, their newly imported printing presses disseminating this material along with their dictionaries and grammars. The first translations were by the missionaries themselves, but by the end of the nineteenth century in South Africa, and early in the twentieth century in Lesotho, texts translated by Christian converts began to be published. The earliest translators were men, and when they began producing exemplary biographies of black Southern Africans, their subjects were men. The first fiction was also written by men (some palpably indebted to *Pilgrim's Progress*).[46] Production was sparse, and sparser still by women. (The corpus of writing by black women is further depleted by the inexplicable "loss" of two of the texts after they had been the subject of summary or analysis by male researchers and critics.[47]) Thus, in the region's first writing, women were shifted from their central place in the storytelling tradition, despite the missionaries' stated interest in the education of women as the bearers of culture to future generations.

Under missionary direction, the early novels and novellas were infused with Christian didacticism. It is significant, then, that in our excerpt from Victoria Swaartbooi's 1934 novella the young teacher, Mandisa, deploys orature in the classroom and thus identifies herself as a social commentator in the more oblique mode appropriate to the *intsomi* rather than to the parable. However, by assuming—as a young, modern woman—the educative function that was conventionally the prerogative of older women, Mandisa disturbs the standard hierarchy in Xhosa life. In her characterization as a single woman and a teacher—not as a wife and mother—she occupies, as Peter Mtuze's study shows, an almost unique position throughout four decades of Xhosa fiction. Swaartbooi's text negotiates both missionary and indigenous conventions of womanhood, defining for the central character the status and dignity of a modern, autonomous African woman, and making pointed reference, too, to the code of hospitality so fundamental to African conceptions of home. Early Xhosa writing is replete with references to the homestead as a space which the good wife and mother keeps open to the stranger. In one of the oral tales that Mandisa presents this code is broken; in effect, what her anti-heroine lacks is *ubuntu*, which is what white South Africans, too, are said by black South Africans to lack. The reconstruction of the African community would come increasingly to depend on women's function as moral custodians for the family and community, and—as addressed in the context of Black Consciousness writing—on a revaluation of Africanness through the concept of *ubuntu*. Swaartbooi's promotion of *ubuntu*, then, has profound social significance.

In poetry, as in fiction, the leading figures have been named as male. How accurate such gendered assessments are remains to be seen, for on the early literary scene there has very recently been acknowledged a truly explosive female voice, that of Nontsizi Mgqwetho, who wrote and published in the 1920s and 1930s hundreds of poems and some essays in the newspapers of the time. Cutting sharply across all statements about the "traditional" preserves of women, whether in the invented traditions[48] of indigenous life or in those of Western Christian life, Mgqwetho's voice takes on the male-dominated political establishment and usurps the male role of public poet. Her work is not referred to in any standard Southern African literary history, nor is it collected in any standard literary anthology, and her biography remains to be fully researched and written.[49] This scholarly belatedness perhaps throws some light on why it is that copies of some of the early novellas and novels written by women are no longer extant.

Adelaide Dube's "Africa: My Native Land" (1913) is included in our anthology as the earliest example yet unearthed of a published poem written in English by a black Southern African woman. Unlike Mgqwetho's, Dube's voice is culturally syncretic. Just as—to take an instance from some later orature—Nekwaya Loide Shikongo from Owambo uses Christian language to criticize the king's abuse of power ("Song of King Iipumbu," 1953), so Dube uses it to criticize colonial power. Her gendered stance is interesting, too. In a way that anticipates later debates about nationalism and gender, the speaker's voice is at one with the voice of the land and nation. Her "troubled bones" signify national disturbance, but without alluding either to a feminized land or a passively nurturant Mother country. The female voice is heroic, bearing no trace of the bourgeois. In adopting poetry rather than narrative as the vehicle for their voices, both Mgqwetho and Dube sidestep the ideology of domesticity to which converted women were being subjected.

Fuller understanding of early black Southern African women's writing would need detailed analysis of their diverse and complex contexts, both with regard to the material conditions of life and to different symbolic systems of belief. While we draw on existing research, further work is needed in all areas. What we will focus on here, as a hitherto insufficiently researched issue in the Southern African region, and one that connects many of our anthology entries, is gender's deep implication in the violence of colonial relations. In this regard, white and black women were "tethered to" one another rather than simply opposed (Bhabha 1994: 44), but in a fraught and profoundly ambiguous way.

The White Peril

In Britain at the end of the nineteenth century and into the twentieth, definitions of masculinity and femininity were in crisis. Feminist and bourgeois domestic discourses meant that patriarchy was all the more rigorously produced in the colonies (McClintock 1990). Carefully defined and circumscribed within what was an avowedly masculine enterprise, the place of white women depended on their participation and ambivalent cooperation (Driver 1988). Within the colonial project itself, at least as it was manifested in Southern Africa, masculinity and femininity were being reconstructed in the context of race, and the relation between femininity and imperialism became as crucial as that between masculinity and imperialism. White settler women needed to negotiate different types of femininity, and above all that supreme signifier of civilization, the middle-class British and—in Namibia—German ideal of femininity,[50] whose virtues were motherhood, homemaking, and racial purity. Early colonial autobiography and bourgeois romance written by women flirted with other female types—boyish heroines, wild pioneer women, for instance—and often founded these competing fictional images on metaphors of racial otherness. The "proper lady" had a lily-white skin, for instance, whereas the "new woman" might be likened to a "Hottentot."[51] In the context of imperial concerns about racial degeneration, however, European standards of femininity and domesticity won the day.[52] But they remained hedged with anxieties about household authority and racial purity.

Such anxieties issued in what critics term a "moral panic" about male and female sexuality, marriage, prostitution, and immorality (Davin 1978, McClintock 1994, Low 1996, Stoler 1997). Modern racism was predicated on what Michel Foucault called the "eugenic ordering of society" of the second half of the nineteenth century, and was closely focused on the body and sexuality, with sexual regulation integral to the organization of race (Foucault 1978: 143). In the colonies, where the concept of femininity was often harnessed to the discourses of empire and nationalism, this moral panic developed into an obsession first with notions of feminine purity—which suddenly became particularly powerful in South Africa during the debate over the Contagious Diseases Act (1868–1872) (Schoeman 1991: 217; van Heyningen 1999)—and then with black male sexuality, known as the "black peril."[53]

The social creation of fears about black male sexuality went hand in hand with the patriarchal injunction to white women to participate in the formation of the white nation. Rape and the threat of rape by black men became regularly occurring moments in colonial discourse, and served as occasions for the expression of white female patriotic subjectivity. The discourse of rape was a major means through which notions of gender were constructed. Legislation aimed at controlling sexuality dated from the nineteenth century and through the twentieth century exercised greater and greater control over interracial sexuality and especially over interracial marriage.

This is the context that frames "Ominous Weather" (1907) by Margarethe von Eckenbrecher, a German South West African settler. Her body is poised—if we read the text ideologically—to become the icon of a white female martyrdom to sanctity, her voice mustering all it can of white superiority, teaching those who threaten her "how to behave towards a white woman." There is, in early white writing, a large body of discourse—captivity narratives, travel accounts, political documents, conduct books, as well as fiction and memoirs—which defines and promotes certain qualities of gender, race, and nation by displaying these qualities in the figure of a single white English woman. The discourse of rape set value on the white woman's body, that is, made her—rather than black women—worthy of protection. The colonial economy depended on the relative values of the populace and the relative value of female bodies; the distinction between them is an important and founding moment of colonial discourse. As both the legislation and the practice of sentencing suggest, it was only white women's safety and "purity" that were at stake. Black women were not able to be "raped."[54]

However, for black women the "peril" was decidedly white. As hinted at in the political speeches made by Nowandle Jabavu and Charlotte Maxeke, black female domestic workers were the prey of white men and boys in their place of work.[55] Our anthology's texts note the sexual danger posed to young black women venturing into white areas, whether as domestic workers or as activists.[56] White women attempted to criminalize sexual relations between white men and black women—in 1921, for example, over half the white female population in then Rhodesia signed a petition to this effect (Pape 1990)—and wrote fiction that laid bare the manner in which white men strayed into the rooms or "compounds" of the black domestic workers. This kind of stance has readily been taken by at least one white male critic as the sign of so autonomous a racism in white women that it is single-handedly responsible for sexual regulations such as South Africa's Immorality Act (Glenn 1996: 145–46). However, white women were not simply fearful and jealous of black women; they were aware also of the double standard exercised by white men, who allowed themselves but not their wives the freedom to have cross-racial sexual relations. Moreover, sexual relations between white men and black women were often forced and always conducted across differences in power (Stoler 1997). Paradoxically, the situation was turned to ambiguous advantage by at least one group of women in their struggle against racism. The Indian women who petitioned in 1908 for tax relief made oblique threats about resorting to prostitution if their demands were not met ("Domestic Unhappiness"); these threats gather considerable force when seen in the context of white women's anxieties about their white husbands.

In "Ominous Weather," the song of Margarethe von Eckenbrecher's "poetically inclined washerwoman, Emma" signifies the depth of the gender rupture between the white and black woman, madam and maid, as Emma speaks across the context in which white and black women's bodies have been so differently valued. Other anthology selections that refer to the gender dynamics between black and white women, such as "Meeting of the Herero Women" (1939), do not directly mention the deep betrayals on the part of white women towards black women, but it is clear that their rights regarding sexual reproduction, health, and legal status were being ignored. It is not entirely surprising, then, that when a group of Herero women referred to the "poison" that had taken over their land (i.e., the disruption of traditional ways of life and the attendant social problems this caused), it was they themselves—rather than the white authorities—who were investigated as the source ("Nation Is Going to Ruinaion, 1936). In a petition, "Letter from Keetmanshoop" (1939), eight angry Herero women group together to protest the policy of forced physical examinations, thus rejecting the discourse of "diseased" black women's bodies that had haunted Southern African women since the "Hottentot Venus." At the same time the women demand the medical and spiritual authority that is being denied them. Other women's petitions in our anthology address this denial of value and describe clearly, if sometimes obliquely, the sexual violence that has been at the center of Southern African race-gender relations. In later Southern African fiction, gender dynamics often pivot on the differences between white and black women's control over their own bodies, their sexuality, and their reproductive potential. Lauretta Ngcobo's *And They Didn't Die* (1990) portrays the failure of interracial sisterhood precisely over the kind of distinction made between the "value" of white femininity and that of black femininity. Ngcobo's main character, Jezile, comforts a white woman after she has been beaten by her husband, but the white woman does not, in turn, either protect Jezile from rape or assist her afterwards.

Much of the writing chosen for this anthology refers to a modern, bourgeois world dominated by an ideology of domesticity, where women are assigned a certain position in relation to the family and, through that, a certain social role. The ideology of domesticity is markedly racial, with white and black women each being assigned their specific place, and gender taking on somewhat different meanings as it crosses the racial line. Lurking within this modern, domestic world exists what may have seemed to missionaries and colonial authorities and racist administrators the primitive world of African sexuality. But to others, and to us, this "primitive" world is defined primarily by the male ownership, control, and rape of women, a world not archaic but a product of the peculiar kind of "modernity" born of the conjunction of colonial and indigenous patriarchies. There are in Southern African literature many different manifestations of such a world, and readers are likely to want to attend to the ways in which various women's affidavits, petitions, and testimonies make their own kinds of gestures to this profoundly "uncivilized" world, to the obsessive colonial greed, the sexual control and rape, bizarre forms of policing, and the law, all of which women attempt to redefine, ward off, and control for themselves. South Africa's Truth and Reconciliation Commission—as will be discussed in a later section—gave many Southern Africans their first sustained and verbalized glimpse of this world.

Black peril, white peril: what, then, about love? Cross-racial love—or its romantic failure—has been a dominating theme in Southern African literature. To cast forward briefly to later writing, texts in the 1960s and 1970s make frequent reference to the legislation that criminalized sexual intercourse between black and white people. Joyce Sikhakhane's piece "Working on the Mail" (1977) neatly juxtaposes, and connects with the prison arrest of a black woman under the Terrorism Act, two sociosexual moments whose roots lie in colonial race-gender attitudes and the distortion of desire: a white man's hysterical response to a black woman's entering a white domain "by the front door," and white men's hysterical response to a black woman's sitting in the front seat of a car driven by a white man. Besides the obsessive sexual anxiety of the abusive white men who drag her from the car, the second incident points silently to the hypocrisy and prurience of South African police officials in their hunt for contravening couples. The atmosphere is shot through with sexual fear and tabooed desire. While Sikhakhane is able to turn her narrative into a story about love, what dominates her text is the increasing pessimism, in South Africa, of an apartheid era whose effects spread through the region.

MID-CENTURY POLITICAL AND CULTURAL TRANSITIONS

Women's writing and speech making in the 1950s reveal their courageous repudiations of apartheid legislation. Colonial education had to a large degree already ruptured access to history (Wilentz 1992) and had skewed engagement with the writing of the metropolitan world, while at the same time holding it out as a model. This peculiarly combined gesture—challenge plus handicap—worsened under apartheid, which was established in South Africa and Namibia through a set of laws passed mostly in the 1950s. Apartheid kept black South Africans out of most libraries and delivered to them an inferior education intended to create subordinates, especially of black women. Language and literacy training under the Bantu Education Act disempowered those having to deal with apartheid's bureaucracies, let alone those aspiring to write. The language policies of the other countries' educational systems, as well as the limited publishing opportunities, meant that publication by black women in Southern Africa was slow and sporadic relative to that by white women and even to that by black men.

Mission education, despite its limitations and hypocrisies, may have been preferable to apartheid state education, although the latter brought mass schooling. From Phyllis Ntantala's *A Life's Mosaic* and Ellen Kuzwayo's *Call Me Woman*, both autobiographical texts that partly deal with girls' and women's education in the 1920s, 1930s and 1940s,[57] one gains a sense of generations of black women intellectuals whose lives were unnaturally curtailed by colonial prohibition against career aspirations. Yet both authors state clearly that their education was better than that given to the generation after them. As Kuzwayo says: "The detested Bantu Education (and its successors) introduced by the Nationalist Government of South Africa in 1953, in contrast, provides no education at all; it seeks only to suppress talent, to lower morale, and to produce obedient servants to carry out instructions without question, even when urgently needed. When I see the quality of teachers provided by Bantu Education and training, I bow my head in shame; that an Act like this can come from a so-called 'Christian' government!" (1985: 94).

In her 1958 essay "The Widows of the Reserves," Ntantala addresses the calculated disintegration of families, focusing her rhetorical skill as an English writer on the situation of women left behind in the rural areas of the Transkei while their husbands engaged in migrant work, women working themselves to the bone to pay for the education they still believe will "free them from poverty, the education that has given the other races so much knowledge and power." Most women by this time had to carry passes, like the men, and Cherry Stephana Mogolo Sibeko's "African Women Do Not Want Passes" (1958) is a last-ditch protest. Critics often name the 1950s the "*Drum* decade" or the "fabulous decade" (Chapman 1989, Nkosi 1983), but these terms obscure the political tempestuousness and desperation of these years, which were so strongly marked by women's continuing political protest in an ultimately unsuccessful struggle against the pass system, and by the coming to an end of women's public interracial political action.

Political opposition was severely punished. Many were imprisoned for anti-apartheid work during this time, and Hilda Bernstein's description of a prison hunger strike ("Diary of a Detainee," 1961), stands as one of two examples in this anthology of writing about prison conditions for women.[58] Bernstein's subsequent exile exemplifies the loss to Southern Africa of many significant women intellectuals, white and black, through bannings, censorship, exile, and—in the case of Ruth First—murder.[59] It is worth noting both Bernstein's and First's Jewish heritage, for, although many Jewish South African women were as acquiescent to apartheid policy as other whites, they also formed a disproportionate number in revolutionary organizations such as the Communist Party of South Africa (CPSA) and the African Resistance Movement.[60] During her short, intense career as a newspaper journalist and editor (she was probably the most influential investigative journalist between the late 1940s and the early 1960s), First produced various essays, including "Pretoria Conquered by the Women" about the famous women's march of 1956. In such essays, she gave definition to the concept of protest journalism (Pinnock 1997: 29)) that would filter into Southern African creative writing. Both in the production of various nonfiction books, which included analysis of the wider Southern African region, and in her life, First exemplifies the courage of many women dissidents of the time who, like Bernstein, strove to bring about judicial and economic equality for black Southern Africans, and in the process to forge the kind of world in which white and black South Africans could coexist more easily. In South Africa, both First and her writings were banned, but in London, where recruits were prepared to join the Umkhonto weSizwe troops, her prison memoir *117 Days* was prescribed reading during the 1970s (Kasrils 1993).

Despite our insistence that writing of the 1950s be remembered as more turbulent than the "*Drum* decade" would suggest, it must be said that the writing of these years is distinguished by feminist assertions that began to emerge in the work of women loosely associated with *Drum* magazine. Producing a female consciousness that wanted to have nothing to do with the West, they publicly vocalize, very briefly, a self-confident, even joyous, women's protest against demeaning treatment and representation.

Women's Sexuality and the "*Drum* Decade"

At the end of the 1950s Marie Kathleen Jeffreys began publishing a series of controversial essays on interracial families and racial passing for *Drum* magazine, but it is one of her poems that we reproduce in this anthology instead, and that we associate with the *Drum* ethos. "Though I Am Black, I Am Comely" (1947) directly confronts the contemporary discursive representation of black women's bodies, placing it in the Judeo-Christian tradition which dominated colonial thinking. The poem's reference is to the Old Testament's Song of Solomon ("I am black, but comely"). Jeffreys's rephrasing draws attention to that problematic connector "but," and also asserts "comeliness" by placing it in the main clause, thereby rejecting the degradation of black women's bodies. For Jeffreys, both here and in her *Drum* essays, racial mixing signifies the positive rather than the shameful. Positioned ambiguously as a mixed-race woman passing for white, yet drawing proudly on an Asian heritage both for her pen-name "Hamsi" and many of her metaphors, Jeffreys is an important new presence in this anthology. She attests to the complexity of racial affiliation and suggests a creative direction more South African writers might have followed if the iron hand of the law had not come down so heavily on imaginative expression.[61]

The "*Drum* decade" has been discussed in South African literary history largely for its class/race ambiguities (Visser 1976, Sole 1979, Chapman 1989, Nixon 1994), although some later critics refer to the construction of gender and the short-lived airing of an interest in sexual transvestism (Driver 1996). In the context of a postwar liberal humanism that promised much to black South Africans even while apartheid capitalism kept material benefits beyond their reach, *Drum* subjected African women to European models of beauty and to a code of ethics dependent on the ideology of domesticity, the nuclear family, and romantic love. Negotiating their modernity in relation to sexuality, the black male journalists, in contrast, sometimes emphasized an African model of self-determined female sexuality. At the same time they depicted "beauty queens" and models as their property, "on offer" to readers, and ran sensationalist essays in which rape was euphemistically known as "abduction" or "love by martial law." In this fraught, ambiguous, and hostile context Bessie Head began a career in writing which would flourish only after her arrival in Botswana in 1964. And it is to this context that Marion Morel's *Drum* essay speaks.[62] Morel's "It's Gotta Be Cash for a Cookie" (1959) puts *Drum*'s beauty contests in perspective by focusing on the violence and abusiveness of male behavior towards the competitors, and by referring also to the poverty and degradation of apartheid that these women were striving to escape.

Dorothy Masuka, one of the most famous local composers and jazz singers of this time, was often featured in *Drum*. During her time in Johannesburg in the 1950s she incorporated much domestic, social, and political comment into her songs; it was the recording of her song "UDr Malan unomteth' onsima'" (Dr. Malan has made a terrible law) which made her friends advise her to return to Bulawayo. A few years later, a song in which she blamed Mobuto for the murder of Patrice Lumumba forced her to leave the then Southern Rhodesia (Chitauro, Dube, and Gunner 1994: 124–5). The two songs from the 1950s reproduced here are sharp retorts to the ethos of domestication promulgated in the pages of *Drum*. In Masuka's first song, "Nolitshwa" (1956), the woman singer takes on a male voice, thus subverting the *Drum* convention of male journalists speaking for women. Her fantasized man is not simply punitive of wayward women but loves them all the more. Reaching for its metaphors not to racial mixing, as Jeffreys's poem does, but to gender switching, and alluding to *Drum*'s occasional alternative model of femininity, Masuka's song is similarly antagonistic to the discourse of domesticated desire.

During this period, despite this vital writing, various inhibiting forces were at work to limit literary production by black Southern African women: the combined patriarchy of indigenous and colonial structures, unequal access to material resources, lack of leisure time, and psychological disempowerment. With regard to genre, too, there were barriers. With its focus on the individual, the narrow understanding given to the domestication of women, and the racializing of gender, the European, or Western, novel was an inhospitable form, whatever language women wrote in. Although Bantu education spread literacy in South Africa and Namibia, the kind of literacy it offered was inimical to the production of writing as a creative engagement with language and the world. And it had adverse if complicated effects on vernacular writing.

Vernacular Literature in the 1960s and Later

African-language writing—whether by women or men—did not flourish in regions in which the official languages—and, usually, the languages of education—were not indigenous.[63] Each of the Southern African vernacular languages has served a relatively small audience; in 2002, great unevenness in literacy in all languages persists.[64] In Namibia and South Africa, Bantu Education purported to encourage indigenous cultural traditions, but the overall atmosphere was too dismissive of local forms not to split most educated people from the oral traditions. In South Africa, vernacular-language literature (particularly in Sesotho, isiXhosa, and isiZulu) was commissioned for school prescription, but the context of literary and linguistic policing curtailed the emergence in print of independent or vigorous vernacular expression (see Maake 2000).[65] Authorities were fearful of the influence of a vibrant and engaging literature on those meant to remain a slave race.

In Botswana, Swaziland, and Lesotho, the official languages and the language of education were mostly shared as mother tongue by the entire population, and the broad political climate offered a more conducive educational atmosphere up to high levels of school education, in the African vernacular as well as English. However, major publishing opportunities— apart from books meant for schools—still exist only in English, and even from these independent countries, selections of literary material for this anthology were hard to find. A major figure in the 1950s and 1960s, whom we could not include because translations reached us too late, is the Lesotho writer Ntseling Masechele Khaketla, who published several plays and numerous poems in Sesotho about the difficulties for women of love and marriage (see Lenake 1983). Called by Dan Kunene "one of the best poets I know," she was not interviewed by "any of the numerous white self-styled experts on African literature," with the dual result that "even a mediocre piece of writing" in English is given "a prominence way out of proportion to its merit" in the white dominated field of literary criticism (Kunene 1992: 506–507), and that her writing is not used as an inspiration for younger writers.

In Zimbabwe, the overall picture appears much better, given the amount of fiction and poetry we have been able to include here from the 1960s through to the 1990s, although more research on vernacular writing in other regions may adjust the comparison. English was the medium of education in Zimbabwe, but publication was encouraged in the vernacular chiShona and siNdebele. While the political climate was less repressive than in South Africa, it nonetheless cramped black intellectual development, in women particularly, and any literary encouragement went hand in hand with the censoring and banning of politically or socially critical work (Veit-Wild 1992). Vernacular writing was largely restricted to folklore, romance, and entertainment, and its promotion geared to state notions of the "happy" colonized subject. Nonetheless, during the 1960s Lassie Ndondo and Jane Chifamba produced fiction; a novel by Ndondo is excerpted here ("Past and Present," 1962), and a story by Chifamba is included ("The Widow and the Baboons," 1964).

In the politics of literature, vernacular writing—and particularly vernacular broadcasting, a powerful medium across the region—stands as an area of complex production too little explored by this anthology, but vital to the full understanding of Southern African voices. Only in relation to Xhosa literature has there been substantial research into women's writing.[66] Although the vernacular languages remained vigorously alive throughout the Southern African region, both mission and state education, along with other forces, have continued to curtail what might otherwise have been a far richer continuity between a thriving oral culture and its written forms. Greater continuity would have enabled women writers to develop with greater force sites for literary self-representation other than those derived from English. Xhosa novels and poetry by both women and men during the 1970s and 1980s did begin to give more focus and sometimes more voice to independent female characters.[67] Particularly notable is Gertrude Belebesi's portrayal of the complex indigenous and colonial constraints on women; her novel *Unongxaki nezakhe* (1976)—not included in the anthology—opens by referring to the "itching of an old sore" that prompted her to write her book. The "sore" is caused by the belief (an old saw) that "The place of a woman is in the kitchen," and Belebesi adds, "This spear stabbed her when she was still a child but its wound does not heal" (1976: Preface; trans. Mtuze 1990: 119). That Belebesi uses the English original for the statement about women draws attention to the edict's colonial origin, while the reference to the spear incorporates Xhosa patriarchal decrees as well.[68]

The field begs for further research in representations and foundations of gender in vernacular writing and publication. That such publication was heavily directed by educational demands under an apartheid government does not mean that alternative manuscripts never reached the publishers' desks, nor that texts critical of apartheid, especially poetry, "did not 'slip' through" (Ntuli and Swanepoel 1993: 139). During the mid-1980s, for instance, poems that question apartheid's construction of women appear: the Xhosa poet, Nobantu Ndlazulwana, produced a poem called "Ubufazi" (Womanhood), thematically similar to Zimbabwean poet Kristina Rungano's "The Woman" (1984), written in English. The tone of resignation at the end echoes Rungano's:

> All my efforts are in vain,
> My injunctions none will fulfill,
> My struggles none will take heed of
> Just because they say I am weak, I am a woman.
> (Ndlazulwana 1986: 27; trans. Mtuze 130)[69]

RESISTANCE, CONTINUITIES, RUPTURE, AND RENEWAL: 1960S TO 2000S

In South Africa the 1960 Sharpeville massacre against pass protesters heralded a period of increasing repression; the two major organizations of political opposition, the Pan African Congress (PAC) and African National Congress (ANC) were banned (this included the ANC Women's League, led by Lilian Ngoyi and with which Winnie Madikizela Mandela—also in this anthology—would later be associated). By the late 1960s apartheid was even more deeply entrenched in the legislation than in the 1950s, and black South Africans had virtually no recourse to the law in their struggle against exploitation, oppression, and psychological subordination.

The texts from the 1940s and 1950s breathed inexorable political changes beginning to take place, although the optimism of those years waned during the 1960s and 1970s. Yet, despite the power and increasing ruthlessness of a reactionary white state, leading to a condition of unrest bordering on civil war in some areas, the prospect of liberty and democracy continued to bring forth some assertively interventionist speeches and texts from women. Women activists and writers drew on the cultural strengths maintained in their communities. Significantly, however, as the period unfolded, any recovery of the resources of this "past" could not simply and easily be liberatory, for, while on the one hand the apartheid regime had exploited re-ethnicized cultural traditions in the interests of separateness, on the other hand the African political elite of the 1970s and 1980s used tradition to create and command political loyalty in patriarchal terms. While the rise of localized nationalisms became an issue for women, ultimately social and cultural stratification was less significant to black communities than the wide economic gap between black and white.

Political repressions in South Africa, Namibia, and Zimbabwe, the realities of poverty, and the limited access to education across the entire Southern African region produced an environment particularly inhospitable to black women's voices. Nonetheless, literary production increased in relative terms, largely in English, and orature continued to engage changing circumstances. The most important and best-known writer of this period is Bessie Head, who left South Africa for Botswana in 1964, and from whose corpus of work we take a relatively unknown early piece (1965). Her writing testifies to the resources provided by an oral community, as well as to the border-crossing with which this anthology is so deeply concerned. Another major figure of this period is Nongenile Masithathu Zenani, whose oral work manifests philosophical and spiritual depth on par with Head's. The work of both these women invites the speculation that had other aspirant women writers of this period had access to a community, even an adopted one, as in Head's case, or the kind of community that an anthology such as this offers to young writers today, they might have achieved something comparable in writing to what Zenani and Head, in their different ways, did.

The factors that affect the continuity of cultural performance are an important matter for enquiry. In her study of the songs and dances (*kiba*) performed by migrant women from the region of South Africa known as Leboa (the North), Deborah James (1999) contextualizes them through migrant men's related performances. Men performed songs and dances in township competitions, and hostel-dwellers would gather for the day-long events. But because women were usually precluded from participation by their employment as live-in domestic workers in the white suburbs, it was much less easy for them to meet. It was not until the growth of the taxi industry in the late 1970s that transport to and from townships became possible and women could then form their own *kiba* teams and participate (James 1999: 52.) Their songs, and their performance identities, became important means of creating ideas of "home" for the city-dwellers, thus holding together groups of women from diverse districts and lineages in Leboa. Unlike the men's performances, which did not include songs, theirs blended ritual songs from "home" and lyrics representing their urban experience (James 1994). In the following example, Paulina Mphoka, adding new lyrics to an existing song, addresses women's responses to police harassment:

> Woman who wears a skin, woman of beer
> She sells beer
> The police of Lebowa are looking for her.
> Tsodio is thin, he does not sleep
> He is troubled by [the ghost of] his uncle
> Who is called Matshabataga
> Tsodio has killed Matshabataga
> He is also troubled by police.
> Women have now joined the soldiers
> They are getting passes just like men.[70]

Like other self-employed beer-selling women, Mphoka had experienced police harassment, which was linked to the political resistance to pass laws. Such interactions between urban and rural life, and between the past and the present, recall earlier songs in our anthology, such as "Aunt, Stretch Out the Blanket" from Lesotho (1959), that also offer a heritage of resistance to a later generation of women. The resilience of orature continues to challenge totalizing theoretical positions that hold to colonialism's complete destruction of cultural, religious, and intellectual traditions (Boomer 1995: 245). Features normally taken as negative—the rural-urban divide, enforced illiteracy, patriarchal disapproval of educated women, and women's exclusion from publication (especially in languages other than English, German, or Afrikaans)—paradoxically contributed to this endurance. In addition, in situations where war and conflict determined everyday options, keeping diaries and writing letters or even novels were dangerous occupations, but the ephemeral nature of oral performance made censorship more difficult and also accounts for its generic survival. In some cases, oral forms that have been recently revived are ones that had been publicly repressed during colonialism and anticolonial resistance, as when military activity in Namibia made impossible the continuing performance of the *mutondo* (see "*Mutondo*: Nyemba Initiation Songs," 1999).

Exile and Excommunication

Apartheid produced increasingly deep social division, ethnic, linguistic, political, and geographic. Many women writers were silenced through bannings, house arrest, imprisonment, and exile. Loss and fracture as well as endurance defined the times. Even in the literature that could be produced at home, much was censored or embargoed, and some was from the start produced underground. For example, Doris Lessing, who had been living abroad since 1950, found her *African Stories* (1964) banned, as were Nadine Gordimer's *Burger's Daughter* (1981), and Miriam Tlali's *Amandla* (1980) as well as an early short story. *Cry Rage!* (1972), the first volume of poems written in English by a black woman—the volume is shared by James Matthews and Gladys Thomas—was the first poetry to be banned.

South Africa had already started losing generations of women intellectuals, women who left the country in chosen or forced exile, sometimes to join the liberation struggle. After 1976, with the further wave of repression—which included detentions, disappearances, and deaths—many more young women left the country. Driven out of the country were the journalist Maureen Kim Sing ("What of the Future?" 1965), the poet Jennifer Davids ("Poem for my Mother," 1974), prose writers Zoë Wicomb ("Another Story," 1990), Agnes Sam ("Jesus Is Indian," 1989), and the Namibian Ellen Ndeshi Namhila ("The Price of Freedom," 1997), and many others, including those whose writing we have not been able to reprint here.[71]

Although it was to a large extent published abroad, anti-apartheid writing continued to be produced locally by women writers within the country.[72] Alongside the dissident white Afrikaans male writers known as the "sestigers," the Afrikaans term for the decade, was Ingrid Jonker. She is represented here not by her most celebrated poem, "Die kind wat doodgeskiet is deur soldate in Nyanga" (The child shot dead by soldiers in Nyanga), which was published in the heat of the Sharpeville crisis of 1960, but by a less familiar poem ("I Drift in the Wind," 1966) in a new translation by the well-known poet and journalist Antjie Krog. The Afrikaner community produced a number of important writers, who attempt in their work to distance themselves from the orthodoxies of race and gender in the 1960s and later.[73]

Hilda Bernstein's nom-de-plume "Tandi" (see "Diary of a Detainee," 1961) signals cross-racial identification with the black women whose conditions in prison were far worse than those experienced by white middle-class women. Winnie Madikizela Mandela's piece ("Detention Alone Is a Trial in Itself," 1975) is an important early work in this area. Black women ran special risks in prison; without political representation, they had no protection against abuse, including sexual abuse, by policemen, warders, and Special Branch interrogators. (Except for a Federation of Transvaal Women document of this period, the narrative about rape in apartheid prisons was never mentioned at this time.[74]) More narratives of resistance have emerged in the late 1980s and in post-independence days about the women who risked imprisonment and death by working underground or engaging in the armed struggle.

The written literature of the 1960s and early 1970s was more diverse than that of the earlier decades, even before the effects of mass education. On the one hand, Noni Jabavu's autobiographical writing (excerpted here as "Bus Journey to Tsolo," 1963)—written after a long residence in East

Africa and Britain—gestures towards the conventions of rural patriarchy for its preferred social model and rejects the "new woman" cast loose from the patriarchal family, who so deftly negotiates the bleak choices delivered her in the name of modernity. On the other hand, Bessie Head, who only properly began her writing career in Botswana after she had left South Africa, addresses the difficulties encountered by educated women within a community not only defined by rural patriarchal conventions, but also by the tensions and suspicions wrought by the historical upheavals of colonization and apartheid.[75] Given Jabavu's and Head's (different) literary empowerments outside South Africa, moving away from the apartheid South was apparently encouraging to South African women writing in English. Jabavu marks herself as an outsider in her use of cultural comparisons, yet, as our excerpt shows, she also forges a more complex position for herself than the conventional binary outside/inside suggests. All of the other major writers in this anthology (and many others not included) had the opportunity to travel, even if often occasioned by exile: Miriam Tlali, Lauretta Ngcobo, Agnes Sam, Sindiwe Magona, and Zoë Wicomb, for instance, whose post-travel writings are marked by a measure of distance from local ideological positionings of women. The anthology entries for this period chart complex longings for home, even when the writers are positioned within the country—longings for continuity, security, and hospitality that have as much to do with the encroachments and brutalities of colonization and/or apartheid as with local male domination.

Apartheid did not provide the only muzzle on women's voices, nor was it the only oppressive force addressed. Tlali talks of her grandmother's shock "to find me picking up a book" instead of "cooking for my husband" (Tlali 1989: 83). In other countries, too, local patriarchal attitudes inhibited women's writing, a situation exacerbated by the atmosphere of militarization, for these were countries at war. In Zimbabwe, for instance, Jane Chifamba's "The Widow and the Baboons" (1964) notes the unfair handicaps placed on widows by the men who should, rather, be supportive, and Joyce Simango ("Women Are Wealth," 1974) addresses also from Zimbabwe the brutality consequent on the patriarchal exchange of women.[76] In its own ways Black Consciousness asserted control over black women's bodies and voices, and thus had profound implications for gender.

Black Consciousness Writing

From the mid-1970s, a radical new movement was underway, deeply affected by both women and children. Responding to the increasingly repressive political measures of the 1950s and 1960s, Black Consciousness established itself from the mid-1970s through the 1980s as the dominant rejuvenating political and cultural force in South Africa and, to a lesser extent, Namibia, with some influence as well over cultural politics in the other countries. Black history, agency, and language were stressed, through a new conception of the importance of the black community in the formation of personal and social identity.

The feminist voices of the early political essays and petitions as well as those literary voices beginning to be audible through *Drum* magazine, and through writing by women associated with *Drum*, changed direction under the demands of Black Consciousness, so that during the 1970s and 1980s women often displayed an ambivalent relation to their own power, on the one hand asserting themselves, and on the other hand re-establishing male authority. Yet the overall heritage from this literary period is one of black women's solidarity and assertion of political power within, and stretching, the imposed limits. Over and again, women manifested their ability to mobilize and act. Women's committees proliferated. In our anthology, the Crossroads Women's Committee, established in 1976, gives voice to Regina Ntongana, whose testimony "Crossroads" (1984) tells of her group's courageous opposition to the destruction of home and community.[77] Women's maternal positioning combined with street activism, and other activism outside the home, rather than contradicting it as in much Euro-centric feminist thinking, even if the male-dominated movements often refused to take women seriously as activists in their own right. All women are mothers and men are their children, said Gcina Mhlophe (1980: 44), making a subversive and important intervention into a patriarchal ideology which privileged age and seniority. Her phrasing invites us to look more closely at the nuanced political and cultural positions taken up by women of the 1970s and 1980s, for it gives a new spin to the phrase "mothers of the nation," offered as an ambiguous heritage to a later generation of women.

The Black Consciousness Movement urged a revival of African traditions half-destroyed or distorted by colonization and apartheid, attempting to negotiate the difference between the movement's vision of tradition and apartheid's "tribalism," drawing to some extent on the vernacular languages and the generic strategies and rhetorical devices of oral forms, and charting a movement from colonized to activist or revolutionary. In the refusal of European standards, the movement posed a new notion of culture in which aesthetic value became not a property essential to the text but "a social relation between a work and its audience, constituted rather than revealed" (McClintock 1994: 331).

The political climate continued to be shaped by the solidarities among mature women, and between them and their communities. Through the 1980s especially, women's writing from an older generation suggests continuity with the practical and spiritual strength manifested in women's political activism during the early decades of the twentieth century, as well as the traditions of *manyano* (church groups) and the *stokvels* (economic support groups), which continued to function actively. They also drew on their continued access to a community-oriented world and to oral traditions.

But another generational force was also at work. Standard vertical structures of authority were being replaced by the horizontal alliances among peers forged at least partially across gender divisions. The usual marker for this shift is the schoolchildren's uprising in 1976, commonly called "Soweto 1976," since this was its spatio-temporal starting point, although it quickly spread to other parts of South Africa and Namibia.

Black Consciousness was in different ways antagonistic to both white and black structures of authority. The younger generation reacted to what it saw as the assimilationist political quietism of its elders over the past decades. It reacted as well to the massive increase in political repression, a key feature of which was the increased militarization and masculinization of the white political and social environment. From these starting points, Black Consciousness produced a nationalist discourse based on masculinized militaristic strength. Asserting itself in these masculinist terms, the youth rebellion offered an ambiguous opportunity to young women activists, whose challenges to patriarchy would have no place.[78] Women did not generally position themselves as "feminist" but nonetheless began to give definition to the development of a specifically South African feminist theory and practice, as traced by Mamphela Ramphele, for example, who writes of herself: "I became quite an aggressive debater and was known for not suffering fools gladly. Moreover, I intimidated men who did not expect aggression from women. Soon a group of similarly inclined women, Vuyelwa Mashalaba, Nomsisi Kraai, Deborah Matshoba and Thenjiwe Mtintso, became a force to be reckoned with at annual SASO [South African Students' Organisation] meetings. Ours was not a feminist cause at that time—feminism was a later development in my political consciousness—but an insistence on being taken seriously as activists in our own right amongst our peers" (Ramphele 1995: 66). Women, then, began to speak publicly as part of a larger group of young, single people engaged in street politics, and at least in the generational sense were detached from black patriarchal and hierarchically organized structures.

Identifications tended to be with "the children," as suggested in Mavis Smallberg's 1988 poem "For Willy Nyathele," reprinted in this anthology. Women among the older generation often strove to reassert authority over the family, both participating in the struggle and constructing themselves as "mothers" of the militant youth, concerned about the irreversibility of "the children's" rejection of school structures (Magona 1992: 148–164), but without supporting the Bantu education that, as Lilian Ngoyi put it, "makes African women like fowls laying eggs for others to take away and do what they like with" (qtd. in Joseph 1986: 4). Speaking out across the masculinist rhetoric of Black Consciousness, but using its strategies of empowerment, the differences among the women writers and performers of this time depended on their age and social location. Key members of the older generation were Ellen Kuzwayo and Emma Mashinini, whose (respectively) *Call Me Woman* (1985) and *Strikes Have Followed Me All My Life* (1989) were important political memoirs of the 1980s. These women and others inflected the Black Consciousness discourse of motherhood with a communal focus and affiliation which simultaneously extended their own power and voice. Speaking not in the name of motherhood, and further removed from the immediate political context of Black Consciousness by being outside the country, Bessie Head nonetheless connected the notion of community with specifically female capacities whose function was to restore to men the "unconscious masculine generosity" (Head 1993: 142) lost to them under colonialism (see Daymond 1996b). Thus women writers often drew on the kind of vision evident in Zenani's tale ("A Man Hides Food from His Family," 1972), where the morality of the "house of birth" infuses the "house of marriage." The generational division was not hard and fast, and some of the period's younger spokeswomen were not single. Gladys Thomas ("Fall Tomorrow," 1972) is a case in point. Although the dustcover of one of her collections describes her as a "housewife," her voice ranges from family and home into the street.

Under Black Consciousness, women aligned themselves with a nationalist, rather than an explicitly feminist, struggle, yet even in the context of its masculinism, women found space for their "own" voices. As noted earlier, the "Women's Charter" of 1954, reprinted in our anthology, and the famous women's march of 1956 had been partially multiracial affairs. While some such groupings persisted, overall racial divisions hardened during the period, and women and schoolgirls took their identification from the black community. "Doubly oppressed" black women may have been, but the recognition of these race and class oppressions gave black women recourse to dual identifications and redefined feminism in terms of a political struggle of race and class. In this way Black Consciousness led readily, if not smoothly, into a feminist consciousness (the word "womanist" also began to be used). Although a later generation of writer-critics would rebel against the discourse of motherhood, seeing it as limiting and insulting rather than enabling, women's alignment with Black Consciousness was with a Black Consciousness constantly redefined through their presence. They further adjusted its masculinist focus by drawing metaphors from the racial situation to address their own experience of gender inequality. Emma Mashinini, for instance, writes in *Strikes Have Followed Me All My Life* (1989) that her husband is as lazy as a white man.

Under Black Consciousness, then, gender dynamics were often muted through gestures of political and psychological solidarity between men and women, and public critiques of sexist behavior were minimal. Part of the new social relation between text and community to which McClintock (1994) alludes involved an exhortation to action in which women participated, yet whose discourse often explicitly relegated them to a passive, maternal, and nurturant role. Later, out of the contradictions of Black Consciousness, other writers developed a different political and aesthetic position. Zoë Wicomb, for instance, grew up under Black Consciousness, and—writing some years after she had left South Africa—adopts Black Consciousness and feminism as strategic positions of mutual destabilization (see Wicomb 1996).

Young aspiring writers who remained within South Africa during the 1970s and 1980s formed their voices amid the dissident political energy of the time. Political resurgence created conditions for cultural renewal, as meetings offered a venue for poets, and, after 1976, when funerals became increasingly politicized, women as well as men recited or performed at the graveside. Cultural activists organized themselves into theater groups, dance groups, music groups, and poetry groups and performed in the townships, announcing their separation from bourgeois or elitist aesthetic values and their alignment with communalism rather than individualism (see Malange's "I, the Unemployed," 1985). Many new organizations were founded during the 1970s, and although they were mostly banned by 1977, by this time the movement had made a cultural impression. Established and aspirant writers were brought together in adult education programs and trade union organizations and, a little later, in writers' groups, notably the Congress of South African Writers (COSAW) and the African Writers' Association. Links were established with cultural organizations across national borders, too, especially in Botswana.

Because of the political climate, only after black leadership came forward did local black theater begin to thrive. During the 1950s and 1960s, white-run organizations had tried to encourage South African drama. But after the establishment of the South African Black Theatre Union in 1972, black theater developed. Groups producing plays and musicals in the "townships" (using schools, churches, municipal halls, garages, and often the outdoors) took confidence from Black Consciousness's promotion of black history and black destiny. The preferred mode was epic. Plays were rarely scripted (partly because of censorship) and thus they changed from one performance to the next. In contrast to the 1950s, when women actors and singers had achieved some prominence—the composers and singers Dorothy Masuka, Miriam Makeba, and Dolly Rathebe, most notably—here few roles were scripted for women (Kruger 1999). In the phenomenon critics have called "Soweto poetry," male poets achieved prominence and notice. Soweto poetry drew on the traditions of the Xhosa *izibongo*, the Sotho genres of *lithoko* and *sefela*, as well as on township jazz, referencing "history, myth and legend" (Barnett 1985: 33) in an epic mode not fundamentally hospitable to women's accepted social stances.[79] But in the Western Cape, to take one example, women poets achieved some visibility, stepping forward to speak in community-based events. Our representative selection is Gladys Thomas's "Fall Tomorrow" (1972), a poem produced for public performance, which takes up the military metaphors characteristic of the time.[80] Other prominent figures were Christine Douts and Ilva Mackay, who spoke out in verse during the University of the Western Cape student crisis of 1973. Their work was included in the volume *Black Voices Shout!* (Matthews 1974), which was promptly banned.

These young Black Consciousness women writers or performers usually depended on generational rather than gendered difference for their subject positions, as in Jennifer Davids's "Poem for My Mother" (1974) in our anthology.[81] The generational conflict is domestic and personal, but also addresses maternal authority over writing, and implicitly gestures towards the more general social antagonisms to women's writing against which writers like Davids struggled. However, as the headnote to Davids's poem suggests, the poet herself now resists such a reading, thus drawing our attention to the question of meaning in different historical, political formations.

In sum then, during the Black Consciousness era, women's voices, actions, and political courage were directed towards black solidarity, a masculinist movement in that men elevated themselves to the executive level of Black Consciousness, and relegated women to a culturally and politically marginal role, while at the same time, motherhood was represented as central, both iconically and as practice. Furthermore, the concept of *ubuntu*, invoked throughout Black Consciousness writing as an African virtue, was founded on the ideology of hospitality, which was conventionally seen as the preserve of women. Women were the custodians of familial and communal morality, continually enjoined to open up the homestead to the stranger and thus to keep *ubuntu* alive. This is why Ellen Kuzwayo, for instance, hears her mother's voice when she remembers the proverbs through which she teaches her children hospitality and other virtues associated with the feminine and domestic. In other words, Black Consciousness depended fundamentally on women's cultural agency. Women maintained the communal connections to which Black Consciousness was striving. Their continuing agency—too often simply explained away as "resilience" or "endurance"—is evident in their visibility as politically active figures, whether in the small, local collectives known as *stokvels*, or in the *manyano* movement, a country-wide church union for women, or in the drives to collect and present affidavits and petitions, or in the anti-pass-law campaign.

Against the standard view, therefore, that women writers were marginalized by Black Consciousness, some of our anthology entries suggest that Black Consciousness's central tenet, *ubuntu*, drew from women's continuing community connections, including oral tradition. The positioning of the mother and the home in Black Consciousness writing by men, along with images of birth, illuminates the central importance for African political philosophy of femininity in a patriarchal formulation, although women's actual cultural and political positioning exceeds this.

Speaking for a younger generation, Boitumelo Mofokeng testifies to the curtailment among younger women activists of their literary careers, for they had to leave the country or go underground (1988: 6–7). Using Miriam Tlali as an example, Mofokeng points to the crucial difference made by age. Tlali herself suggests that she was "fortunate to have been born at a time when most of these restrictive measures imposed by Bantu education did not yet exist" (1981: 43). Most of the books published in the 1970s and 1980s were indeed written by women of Tlali's generation or older. Tlali's writing reflects, in an exemplary way, the participation in and formulation of Black Consciousness thinking of women of a certain generation. Writing in 1980, Tlali spoke of apartheid's impact on writing: "They say writers learn from their predecessors. When I searched frantically for mine there was nothing but a void." Tlali is referring here both to the lack of availability of books through censorship and cost, and to cultural disempowerment. She traces the kind of direction being taken by other Black Consciousness intellectuals and activists of the time: "I had to change and find inspiration from within myself. I could not divorce myself from my peculiar status in an 'artificial' society which refuses to recognize even my existence. It was while in this dilemma that I found myself: that I finally drew the line and retraced my steps. Only then could I come to terms with myself and walk upright again" (1980: 45).

Tlali had published her first novel, *Muriel at Metropolitan*, in the 1970s. Later, in *Staffrider* magazine, generally understood as a Black Consciousness vehicle, she offered a column, "Soweto Speaking," in which she told stories about various people.[82] Through this column, and her subsequent writing, she stressed the need for black women to join Black Consciousness' self-identification as black, rather than "non-white." According to Tlali, few black women attended readings and writers' workshops in the late 1970s and early 1980s (Tlali 1989: 79), and few were educationally, economically, politically, or culturally empowered to become writers.[83] But the invitation proffered by *Staffrider* was crucial. It was here that the young writer Gcina Mhlophe, whose poem "Praise to Our Mothers" (1989) is included in our anthology, began publishing. Then writing under the name Nokugcina Sigwili, she produced a story called "My Dear Madam,"[84] thereby inaugurating a new voice in black writing, the voice of the black "maid" making her retort to the white "madam." This voice would be taken up by Sindiwe Magona in stories published in the 1990s, one of which is reprinted in our anthology ("Stella," 1991).

The Resilience of Orality: Life Stories and Women's Legacies

In Southern Africa in the 1980s, the gathering of autobiographical testimony became a part of a vigorous cultural-political agenda and many writers sought ways of listening to women, often using recorded interviews.[85] In Zimbabwe, the Zimbabwe Women's Writers Association, affiliated with the Zimbabwe Writers Union, was formed in 1990 in order to support women's literary production in both urban and rural areas, in English and vernacular languages. Groups formed also in Namibia and Botswana. Part of the overall project has been the historical retrieval of stories of outstanding women, part has been to encourage and teach aspirant writers. In two entries in our anthology, one from Zimbabwe and one from South Africa, Elizabeth Ncube ("Praise to Mbuya Nehanda," 1993) and Karen Press ("Krotoa's Story," 1990) recreate the lives of famous women whose stories—so often left out or minimized or misunderstood in the dominant accounts—change the shape of Southern African history. Ncube and Press thus transform representation itself, and extend the possibilities of writing. Colette Mutan-gadura has, in our anthology, re-presented her maternal grandmother, a rural woman caught up in the violent colonial appropriation of land and labor. Her story, "Ngonya's Bride-Price" (1997), explores the gendered logic of colonial power through the narrative of an appropriated woman. Mutangadura's family story is collaboratively produced, fashioned in English from accounts given in chiShona by the author's mother and great-aunt.

The *manyano*, or women's Church Union, continues as the site of collective oral production. Prayer and preaching are creatively and spontaneously offered. Within established churches and in independent, syncretic churches, oral texts reflect the absorption of Christianity into African traditions. As suggested by our entry "Two Dream-Miracle Stories" (1992), syncretic churches may be a site of resistance for women, who counter both the racism and the male dominance of, at least, the ministry in Western-affiliated churches. The interculturalism in the Nazarite ceremonies and their texts becomes an intracultural process in Gcina Mhlophe's "Praise to Our Mothers" (1989) and Thoko Remigia Makhanya's "A Noble Woman of Africa" (1993), both praise poems composed and performed to honor Nokukhanya Luthuli. Here the poets draw on one cultural tradition—Zulu women's composing and performing their own and their children's praises—and extend it to meet a new purpose: to intervene actively in public, political matters. Echoing and changing the male recitation of patriarchal lineage in royal praises, Mhlophe draws into her poem the lineage of women, both famous and unknown, who formed the bedrock of activism in the struggle against apartheid. Mhlophe demands honor be given to Nokukhanya Luthuli as "mother of the nation," but shifts conventional iconic representation to her everyday political influence.

Writing in the 1990s Kuzwayo turns not to school education for solutions to what she sees as social and ethical community disintegration but to proverbs for the alternative education they provide, or might provide, black youth. Her book *African Wisdom* (1998)—excerpted for this anthology—stands as an act of retrieval and reconstruction in the aftermath of Bantu education. She also invokes *ubuntu*, emphasizing the respect for others binding together individual and community, seeing it as a resource capable of addressing theft, killings, and rapes. Many other African women writers of this period and later turn to the spiritual and ethical resources offered by a world that resists or transcends the Christian word. Sometimes the focus is on the ethical codes within vernacular language, as in Noni Jabavu's writing; sometimes it is on the generosity of rural communities, as in Bessie Head's writing; sometimes it will be on a cosmological system, as in Yvonne Vera's *Under the Tongue* (1996) and *Nehanda* (1993).

The resilience of orality lies partly in its flexibility, its ability to incorporate new possibilities of feminist rebellion while tapping well-developed narrative motifs. Maria Munsaka's version of "Nhamiwa's Magic Stick," recorded in 1991, is prefaced by the comment that "Women are the stone houses of our culture." The metaphor recognizes women's pivotal function in the communication of ritual symbolic forms and motifs to young and old alike. Women thus safeguard African representational forms against the myriad of assaults inflicted by nineteenth- and twentieth-century colonialism. Munsaka is in fact the stone mason: She builds, rather than speaking as a timeless repository of frozen or conserved culture. In her feminist reworking of a trickster story, she refuses to collaborate any longer with the patriarchy that oppresses her. She takes her magic stick, symbol of her power, and uses it for her own liberation. We take this magic stick as a signifier of women's writing, as a means whereby writing exceeds the given social situation.

Still, women's authority, power, and autonomy continue to be curtailed, while at the same time there is more public attention given to their situation. In Zimbabwe, only now, after as many as twenty years have separated them from the actual events, have women begun to refer publicly to their specific sexual abuse. Marevasei Kachere's account in chiShona of her participation in the liberation war, excerpted in our anthology ("War Memoir," 1998), is one among several other recently aired examples of rape and sexual service (see Zimbabwe Women Writers 2000). Women's accounts of post-independence brutalities are also beginning to emerge, among them the massacre of innocent civilians in Zimbabwe's Matabeleland. This happened in the early 1980s when the specially trained Fifth Brigade was sent to the area. It targeted civilian communities, as is evident in Elizabeth Dube's personal account ("Good as Dead," 2000). In Yvonne Vera's most recent novel, *The Stone Virgins* (2002), the descent of the Fifth Brigade on a village called Kezi and the devastating consequences for the women is represented—including rape and forced participation in murder.

In South Africa, only recently, in testimonies to the Truth and Reconciliation Commission, have the deepest horrors of the apartheid years been aired publicly. Women have, for instance, begun to describe—if still hesitantly—the "sexual terrorism" of prison life.[86] Although many narratives are emerging from women who risked imprisonment and death by working underground or engaging in the armed struggle, or who experienced the traumas of apartheid through the torture and loss of family members, we expect that many women's stories are still to emerge, many silences still to be broken.

Of these many silences, it is nearly impossible to select one that is more painful, more imprisoning, or more urgent than the others. And yet one scourge—newly present and overwhelming the region—compels public action and recognition here. The selection from Unity Dow's novel on HIV-AIDS ("Caring for the Dying," 2000) offers a portrait of the suffering of a mother and child in Botswana. The circumstances Dow describes are ubiquitous and occur countless times each day. The toll that HIV-AIDS will take on Southern Africa defies comprehension. Still, without diminishing individual tragedy or collective grief—everyone in the region has lost at least one beloved family member or friend—one can discern a note of grim hope from the pain and the deaths. For confusion, dread, and despair are not the only responses to this catastrophe. Especially when one considers another crisis facing Southern Africa—famine—one sees that communities are fighting HIV-AIDS courageously and constructively. While people can do little to counter drought, and while it is appropriate to expect governments to supply emergency food, individuals and communities are not leaving action on HIV-AIDS solely to the authorities.

In some places, local and national groups have organized volunteers to help in education and in caring for the sick. In South Africa, this has happened because the government's response to HIV-AIDS has seemed inadequate and confused, especially with regard to prevarication on AZT and the prevention of mother-to-child transmission. Into the vacuum thus created has stepped grassroots activism, including the Treatment Action Campaign (TAC). Prevarication has also, of course, served as a counsel of despair, and even the terrible rape of infants and children may be seen as part of this confusion. But as local communities take up the challenge of HIV-AIDS, the protests and the counseling are often led by women. In this way, another generation of women—and some men as well—are leading the way in both civic responsibility and the process of asserting individual rights in a context of democratic rule.

In a documentary shown in the *Special Assignment* series on South African television on 18 June 2002, a young woman who is HIV-positive and who works with the TAC said that while her parents' generation had fought for freedom from racial oppression, her generation must struggle for the right to proper treatment against HIV-AIDS. This was her way of noting that she has had to learn to take her rightful place in the world. We would add to her comment that this volume of Women Writing Africa testifies to the lengthy and continuous history through which women in Africa have been learning to work for freedom, not only for themselves but for the whole society. Yvette Christiansë's poem (2001), the concluding selection in this anthology, reminds us of "those who have tried to find their Jerusalems"—the generations of struggle—and speaks in the voice of a present in which people remain "chained / to the walls of our childhood." And yet, the poem continues:

> . . . we set off again. We press on,
> deep into the destination of the past.

Like Ingrid de Kok ("Our Sharpeville," 1987), who reads the impact of the past on individual identity through one of the most famous political events in South African history, Christiansë recalls the complex history that makes up her generation's sense of self. We read her poem's concluding lines as full of energy and a persistent hope, not only for Africa, but indeed for the world:

Extreme are our ways and our lives are blown
by the idea of horizons that lie deep in scriptures
that are the measure of dreams. *We beseech thee,*
we beseech thee and thy generations. For you are ours
and our lives have been laid down in the trenches
of the past as we chain ourselves to the wake
of such ships that storm seas, these seas
that ring and link themselves to such rhymes
that circle the world and clip the wings of birds.

NOTES

1. Like other categorizing terms, "black" needs continual interrogation. It has a complex history and uses; in the 1970s and 1980s it was adopted for purposes of solidarity in resistance by most of those who had been victimized by white racist domination in Southern Africa.

2. Research into petition drafting may often be politically fraught. During the late 1970s fear of police reprisals severely constrained Julia Wells's research on the Orange Free State Native and Coloured Women's Association and the process whereby this petition was drafted (see Wells 1993: vii). For further information on the background to this petition, see Sol T. Plaatje's chapter "Persecution of Coloured Women in the Orange Free State" in *Native Life in South Africa* (1916: 91–101).

3. See, for example, Florence Howe's *Myths of Coeducation: Selected Essays, 1964–1983* (1984). In "Feminism, Fiction, and the Classroom" (1970: 47–64), she describes the ways in which black inner city youth understand Bigger Thomas's motives in *Native Son,* even as their own black and white teachers (and some critics) remain baffled. In addition to revealing how race and class can shape new interpretations, she discusses "the maleness" of Joyce's and Lawrence's art "rather than [their] alleged universality," thus indicating how gender inflects writing and its reception. As Annette Kolodny points out: "[R]eading is a learned activity which, like many other learned interpretive strategies in our society, is inevitably sex-coded and gender inflected" (1980: 588). See also Culler (1983: 43–64) and Jacobus (1986). There are of course other coordinates which inflect reading. On writing, see, for example, Jacques Derrida: "The semantic horizon which habitually governs the notion of communication is exceeded or punctured by the intervention of writing, that is of a *dissemination* which cannot be reduced to a *polysemia.* Writing is read, and 'in the last analysis' does not give rise to a hermeneutic deciphering, to the decoding of a meaning or truth" (1982: 329). See also note 14.

4. The Cape, for example, had been largely brought within the expanding British colonial ambit by the early 1800s, while northern Namibia came under colonial administration only by the 1940s. Referring to South Africa in a comment that can apply to the whole Southern African region, Elaine Unterhalter (1995: 208 ff.) delineates four historical phases, seeing them as overlapping rather than sequential processes, with, for instance, the national projects characteristic of late eighteenth-century and nineteenth-century African kingdoms reaching into the settler nationalist period of the twentieth century, but in different form.

5. Thenjiwe Magwanza (2001: 26) notes that amongst rural Zulu women dress style could be used to express personal difference, while Deborah James (1999: 110–142) notes the use of dress by urban women performers to convey female solidarity.

6. As we note in the preface, the collective appellation for these peoples is a contested one. While "Bushmen" may have negative connotations, including gender bias, "San" is also problematic. Megan Biesele reports that two Ju/'hoan brothers argued over the two terms in 1991, one saying that his preferred term, "Bushmen," could "be ennobled by the way in which they themselves now chose to use it." When she wrote, Biesele was still awaiting consensus, and decided in the interim to use "Bushmen" (1993: Author's Note.). It is in the same spirit of provisionality that all such terms in this anthology are being used.

7. During the apartheid years, "Bantu" was made the official term for black Africans in South Africa, but was much disliked. It is used here in its earlier, linguistic, sense only, as the name of "a category of languages" (Wilson and Thompson 1969: xi).

8. See Guy (1990). There are a few instances of matrilineal descent structures in Southern Africa, from the Owambo in northern Namibia to the Tonga in Zimbabwe (Jacobs 1995: 243). In Owambo society, the authority of men is not completely replaced, in that "authority flows through the mother's brother rather than the father," but this form of organization and ideology seems to give greater social and political space to women. Since the 1940s, socioeconomic change has put the matrilineal inheritance of culture amongst the Owambo under pressure (Orford and Becker 2001: 291). Belinda Bozzoli notes that many families became matrifocal after capitalist disruption of gender relations (1983: 165).

9. The practice of paying bride-wealth in cattle began to alter when a money economy was introduced after the arrival of colonists, and since the early twentieth century it has been increasingly "commercialised" (Walker 1990a: 184).

10. Khama the Great also abolished male initiation and circumcision (*bogwera*).

11. For example, Isabel Hofmeyr found that in the community she studied "women tended to tell fictional stories, while men told historical stories, although this division was never watertight" (1993: 9), and she suggests that the gendering of the household spaces "served to differentiate what were, in effect, cognate narrative skills" (1993: 6–7).

12. The German linguist Dr. W. H. I. Bleek and his family arrived in South Africa in the 1850s with Bishop Colenso's team in Natal. The group included Bleek's sister-in-law, Lucy Lloyd, also a linguist. They settled in Cape Town ten years later and there heard about the /Xam prisoners, from the northern Cape, who were working on the new breakwater in the Cape Town harbour. Bleek and Lloyd arranged to have some of these prisoners (who had been found guilty of crimes such as stock theft) moved to their employ, and they spent five years interviewing them. They learned the /Xam language and devised a phonetic script for its notation. Their 12,000–page collection is now in the archives of the University of Cape Town. Bleek's daughter, Dorothea, also worked on a grammar and dictionary, and translated and edited /Xam texts. Today no one can speak the /Xam language: "/Xam, once spoken in the western half of South Africa, is now extinct and known to us only from the written material preserved by linguists and folklorists" (Biesele 1993: xix).

13. For further discussion of Umkasetemba's skill, see Chapman (1996: 47) and Scheub (1985: 506–508).

14. In *Nehanda* (1993), Yvonne Vera imagines the Shona people's angry response to their first experience of written documents, which the invading colonists used to take away their land, in this way:

> Our people know the power of words. It is because of this that they desire to have words continuously spoken and kept alive. We do not believe that words can become independent of the speech that bore them, of the humans who controlled and gave birth to them. . . . Words surrendered to the stranger, like the abandoned child, will become alien—a stranger to our tongues.
>
> The paper is the stranger's own peculiar custom, a trick he employs against time. Among ourselves, speech is not like a rock. Words are as malleable as the minds of the people who create them. (39–40)

15. The ontological impossibility of actual audience response as part of the production of written texts offers a definitive difference between oral performance and written literature.

16. Because the Khoekhoe were unwilling to work for the first free burgers or for the Dutch East India Company, slaves were first purchased at the Cape in 1658–1659. They came from Dahomey and were taken from a Portuguese ship going from Angola (Davenport 1987: 26). Until the early nineteenth century, slaves were imported in large numbers from Madagascar, India, Indonesia, Malaysia, Zanzibar, and Mozambique. In 1860 the first indentured laborers were brought from India to work on the sugar farms in Natal. For a short period, mineworkers were imported from China. Robert Ross (1983) gives some information on the conditions of women slaves at the Cape; some of this is extended by Helen Bradford (1996). While white women sometimes went on record for their abhorrence of slavery, others were in support (see note 18 below). In a recent comment on the historical silence around slavery Kerry Ward and Nigel Worden note that "images and representations of slavery had been firmly submerged in the Cape. In part this was the result of the suppression of this history of South Africa's marginalized and working-class people which pervaded the public history of the apartheid era" (1998: 201). Slavery "was also 'forgotten' by many of the slave descendants themselves" (207). Some "distanc[ed] themselves from their slave past in order to claim a more privileged position in the colony than indigenous Africans who were being increasingly marginalized" (205), while for others the history of slavery was seen as divisive, as "a history that separated 'Coloured' South Africans from their brothers and sisters in the struggle who were descended from indigenous inhabitants of the land" (208). For recent fictional references to slavery see Rayda Jacob's historical romance, *The Slave Book* (1998), and her bildungsroman, *Sachs Street* (2001), and Zoë Wicomb's *David's Story* (2000), where the suppressed slave figure reemerges to remind the male protagonist about other forgotten "truths."

17. The Dutch East India Company established a station at the Cape in 1652 in order to supply fresh food and water to its trading ships. The first commander of this station was Jan van Riebeeck, who brought his wife, Johanna Maria Queillerie, and son with him. As the Company and then the free burgers established farms, the Khoe found themselves trespassers on land they had once occupied (Reader's Digest 1992: 36–7). For further information on Krotoa, see Malherbe (1990), Abrahams (1996), Landman (1996), Wells (1998), Bloem (1999), and Karttunen (1994: 248–252).

18. See J. M. Coetzee (1988). One of the reasons for the Boer Great Trek from the Cape was the freedom to own slaves, a right which the settlers saw as based on Christian principle. For example, in an essay first published in the *Cape Monthly Magazine*, Sept. 1876, Anna Elizabeth Steenekamp refers to "[t]he shameful and unjust proceedings with reference to the freedom of our slaves: and yet it is not so much their freedom that drove us to such lengths, as their being placed on an equal footing with Christians, contrary to the laws of God and the natural distinction of race and religion, so that it was intolerable for any decent Christian to bow down beneath such a yoke; wherefore we rather withdrew in order thus to preserve our doctrines in purity" (Steenekamp 1888: 459).

19. Baartman's treatment has been discussed by Sander Gilman (1985) and a film documentary of her story has been made by Zola Maseko (1998). More recently Abrahams (1997: 46; 1998: 222) has suggested that Gilman's reading reenacts Baartman's historical mistreatment. See also Wicomb (1998). For background information, see Noël Mostert (1992: 113–114), who details the sexual prurience of seventeenth-century European travelers towards both Khoe men and women.

20. See, for instance, Sandra Burman's extended discussion of and quotation from a court case in 1874 in which a woman named only as Maseboko pleaded guilty to infanticide after giving stillbirth to a seven- or eight-month-old foetus; infanticide was not a crime in Sesotho law but had just been declared so in colonial law (Burman 1990: 48–51). The essay is generally informative on the status of nineteenth-century Basotho women.

21. "The unfamiliarity of British officials with local property, labor, gender, and power relations" meant that they often upheld "in the name of custom practices that were not customary at all" (Roberts and Mann 1991: 14).

22. See, for instance, Hay and Wright (1982) for discussion of women's court records, and Marks (1985) for discussion of the relation between the Tswana chiefs and British law.

23. Moravian missionaries were the first to come to Southern Africa. They were followed at the end of the eighteenth century by missionaries from the South African Missionary Society (Dutch Reformed Church) and from the London Missionary Society (interdenominational). Early in the nineteenth century, Methodists followed the 1820 Settlers into Xhosa territory and also worked amongst the Sotho and Rolong on the Caledon River; the American Board Mission sent workers to Mzilikazi's Ndebele (in present-day Zimbabwe) and to Dingane's Zulu; and the Paris Evangelical Society began work amongst the Sotho in 1833 (Davenport 1978: 34). Sustainable missionary efforts in Mashonaland (now Zimbabwe) began after European occupation in 1890. Some leaders (such as Moshoeshoe in Lesotho and Khama the Great in Botswana) and some groups (such as the Basters in Namibia) found it useful to have a resident missionary who was literate and could interpret, negotiate, and even advise. Some leaders who did not themselves convert to Christianity were interested by the missionaries' teachings and did not prevent their followers from attending the missions. Among the Tswana and the Sotho, rulers and other male aristocrats became the first converts. This was in contrast to many other Southern African societies where Christianity first attracted the marginal and powerless—young men, the poor, and women of all ranks—people who attempted to use the new religion and the mission to enhance their opportunities (see de Kock 1995).

The missionaries sometimes also played a significant role in trade. In Namibia, for example, traders (in guns, ivory, and other goods) made use of the missions as trading posts. Later in the century, some missionaries were able to foster profit-making farming amongst peasant communities which grew up around the mission station; by mid-century several such communities owned freehold land in Natal (Maylam 1986: 71, 86–77; Meintjes 1990: 126–130).

24. One of the earliest prisoners brought to the Cape was the "Radja of Tambora . . . [who] was banished from Bima and arrived at the Cape in chains in 1667." He and his wife (who had followed him) were later housed at Vergelegen, the residence of Governor Simon van der Stel. A visitor to Vergelegen in 1706 found that the Radja was "writing a Quran in Arabic from memory as a gift for Simon van der Stel" (Davids 1987: 40). The Afrikaans language began in the Cape as a Creole spoken not only by the Dutch, but also by the slaves and the prisoners who were brought from Indonesia. Among the prisoners, and perhaps also the slaves, were Islamic scholars, and the first examples of writing in the Creole that would become Afrikaans are in Arabic script, and contain religious instruction. Given the subsequent links between literacy and power, and the disenfranchisement of South

Africans of Asian heritage, there is an historical irony in this. In an article in *Drum* titled "Afrikaner Owes the Coloured," Marie Kathleen Jeffreys (author of "Though I Am Black, I Am Comely," 1947) uses archival evidence to argue that it was not only the slaves, but also "the freed slave women who married among the whites," who brought this "newly-emerging language to the white settlers at the Cape" (Jeffreys 1959: 34).

25. The Inanda Girls' Seminary, established near Durban in 1869 by the American Mission Board, was a first in providing secondary education for women without educating them "for economic subservience"; in this, it was "nothing short of revolutionary" (Hughes 1990: 197–198).

26. Ten years earlier Theophilus Shepstone, the Secretary for Native Affairs in Natal, had suggested the establishment of separate schools for girls so that educated men would not have to marry "ignorant, half heathenish girl[s]" (qtd. in Meintjes 1990: 138).

27. There is no adequate translation of *nkosikazi*; "first," "great," and "senior" have been used, but these words cannot convey the complex meanings of the hierarchy of wives. The *nkosikazi*, the most important wife, was not necessarily the first woman to be married to a chief, but she was the one nominated to bear his heir. In Sandile's case, Janet Hodgson explains: "In the polygamous household of a chief each wife and her offspring composed a distinct unit called a 'House,' and it was ranked according to the seniority of the wife. The Great wife was highest in rank and she bore the heir. The wife of the right-hand house was next in line, and then came the supporting wives in both houses. . . . Emma was the daughter of the Right-Hand Wife" (1987: 33). Hodgson adds, "Sandile's Great Wife, [was] Noposi, and [her daughter] Victoria was his favourite daughter. . . . [When Noposi could not be induced to let her daughter go to Zonnebloem] Sandile refused to make an issue of the matter with his Great Wife" (85).

28. For further discussion of "Another Story," see Driver (1999). Wicomb returns in different ways to the representation of black women's bodies in two later texts: "Shame and Identity" (1998) and *David's Story* (2000).

29. Mission presses had since the late nineteenth century been expanding their activities to produce newspapers that reported on secular as well as church matters. The earliest of these was the *Kaffir Express*, first issued in 1870 by the Lovedale Press (Switzer and Switzer 1979: 270). Other early, mission-published newspapers of long standing include *Leselinyana La Lesotho* (The Little Light of Lesotho), started in 1863 by Adolphe Mabille at Morija (see "Penelopa Lienguane," 1888), and *Umafrica*, started in 1910 and published at Mariannhill near Durban. This period also saw the beginnings of purely secular publishing in Southern Africa, and of African efforts to finance and control the companies responsible. The writer and political activist Sol T. Plaatje was, for example, engaged between 1901 and 1915 in editing, publishing, and seeking finance for two newspapers—*Koranta Ea Becoana* (The Bechuana Gazette) and *Tsala ea Batho* (The People's Friend)—both of which were important organs of black political news and opinion. Between them, these early, indigenous-language newspapers (which usually also had items in English) attracted a wide range of contributions, articles, regular columns, and sometimes single poems or short stories from the major black intellectuals of the early years of the century. These were women as well as men who were gradually to be silenced as apartheid policies curtailed their hard-won opportunities. Probably the two most important African vernacular newspapers were *Ilanga laseNatal* (The Sun of Natal),

now called *Ilanga*, which was founded by John L. Dube in 1903 and published in isiZulu, and *Imvo Zabantsundu* (African Opinion), which was founded by John Tengo Jabavu in 1884 and published in isiXhosa. *Umteteli wa Bantu* (The Mouthpiece of the People) was founded in 1920 (see our text by Nontsizi Mgqwetho from 1924) and, although it was financed and published by the Chamber of Mines in the Transvaal, "covered an enormous range of black political, social and cultural activities" in its early years (Switzer and Switzer 1979: 110). In Zimbabwe it was not until the 1930s that small newspapers and magazines which targeted black readers appeared, for instance, *The Native Mirror* in 1936 (later renamed *Bantu Mirror*) and *African Weekly* in 1944. These were, however, white-owned publications and always sensitive to any criticism of the colonial government. In Namibia several German language newspapers were established at the end of the nineteenth century, and *The Windhoek Advertiser*, the first English-language paper, was founded in 1911.

30. Eliza Feilden's excerpt might have been positioned first, for her manuscript was written in 1852, but as the manuscript appears not to be extant, we have positioned the excerpt according to the 1887 publication date. In our decision to open the anthology's selection of early white women writers with Schreiner and Feilden, we miss much early colonial writing from travelers and settlers, both English and Dutch. The earliest extant writing from Southern African women is in fact Dutch: the letters written by Johanna Maria Queillerie (later van Riebeeck), wife of the first Dutch official in the Cape, which cover the years 1709 to 1711.

31. See, for instance, Lauretta Ngcobo: "The reason why Olive Schreiner continues to engage the minds of South Africans and women and scholars alike is that she not only fathoms and explores her own times with great insight, but she has penetrating foresight into her future, which is our present" (1991: 191).

32. That there is also a class factor within this "superior domain" is evident when the letters of Ellen McLeod are compared with Feilden's writing. McLeod arrived penniless in Natal with her family in 1850 after they lost all their possessions in the wreck of their ship at the entrance to Port Natal. At least during her first few years in the colony, McLeod expressed appreciation for her occasional African domestic helpers as fellow workers. In 1859 she wrote to her sister Louisa about a woman who, with her husband, was a refugee from the fighting in Zululand, saying that she "comes to assist me in my washing one day a week, of which I can assure you I am very glad. She washes and cleans my room with her little baby always tied to her back" (McLeod 1970: 101). Her attitude changed to a simpler, racialized sense of having a right to certain labor as the family's circumstances improved, and as she, perhaps, had more time to absorb colonial attitudes (Daymond 2000). McLeod's letters were preserved by her family in England and not published until 1970.

33. Burman (1990: 51) discusses the sympathetic attitudes of the early missionaries in then Basutoland, noting that they spoke Sesotho fluently and let their children mingle with Basotho children since no settler society was allowed to develop there.

34. We are indebted for the terminology on performance to Judith Butler's *Gender Trouble* (1990).

35. Jane Tompkins argues that the "popular domestic novel of the nineteenth century represents a monumental effort to reorganize culture from the woman's point of view" by expressing a belief in social redemption through sentimental values, "salvation through motherly love" (1986: 83). For Tompkins, the sentimental and domestic focus of this female tradition presents a powerful alternative to patriarchalism.

See Ann Douglas (1988) and Nancy Armstrong (1987) for somewhat different discussions.

36. In South Africa, the racial category "coloured" was applied to people of certain mixtures of descent since colonial times. Gradually it was formalized to serve apartheid and white domination; officially the South African government declared it to include all people of "mixed race," but the category soon came to include the many peoples who could not be placed in the rest of the irrational system. Thus San, Khoe, and Griqua people, as well as those of "Malay" origin (the descendants of slaves brought to the Cape from Java and neighboring islands), were categorized as coloured, as were Chinese people. Commenting on the meaning that "coloured" can be given now, Zimitri Erasmus has said: "In re-imagining coloured identities we need to move beyond the notion that coloured identities are 'mixed-race' identities. Rather, we need to see them as cultural identities comprising detailed bodies of knowledge, specific cultural practices, memories, rituals and modes of being" (2001: 21).

37. Some male praise poets have said that they follow a similar practice (Kaschula 1997: 178, 182).

38. Women brewers in the cities have been an important part of resistance to government and municipal attempts to monopolize the production of beer and the income it generated. Lauretta Ngcobo's second novel, *And They Didn't Die* (1990), depicts the uprising of women in Durban against municipal beer halls; these women were noted for their public disapproval of the African men who drank there.

39. See Loomba (1998: 90–93) on the limitations of suggestions that those who resist colonialism are simply taking up Caliban's curse: "You gave me language / And my profit on't is I know how to curse."

40. Some of Sibusisiwe Makhanya's letters are reprinted in Marks (1987); for her sister's autobiography, see McCord (1995); the extensive and incompletely discussed mediation by McCord of this account (despite the recentness of its publication) was one of the reasons for our deciding not to include it in our anthology, although of course we have other, earlier, mediated texts.

41. The writings of some of these women await collection and research.

42. Lovedale was founded in 1841; an "industrial" (domestic skills) department opened at the Lovedale Girls' School in 1871 (Cock 1990: 90). While Lovedale College, like most other mission-run institutions, put its emphasis on teaching women domestic skills rather than the three R's, it appears that the presence there of women teachers such as Jane Waterston made considerable difference (see the letters of Jane Waterston, published in 1983).

43. Ian Fairweather (2001: 149–150) has argued that the Christian myth of a "passage" from savagery to civilization has been reappropriated by rural people in the Finnish mission's heartland in Owambo. The local museum established in the first Finnish missionary's house in the area reproduces this myth in its reconstruction of the early days of mission work and does so in such a way that it valorizes local people's participation in the "passage."

44. Cherryl Walker (1982: 24), quoting a speaker at the 1926 select committee hearing on women's suffrage.

45. Helen Joseph's account of women's refusal to accept passes and of their organized protests refers only to urban women (1986: 15); Lilian Ngoyi refers only to the town of Winburg outside the Transvaal. For evidence that some rural women were deeply involved, see Hooper (1960), who gives a detailed, first-hand

account of the Bafurutse women's refusal to accept passes and of the brutal methods by which they and the men were subdued. This was on the border of Botswana, near Zeerust; for similar resistance in Natal, see Ngcobo (1990), who postulates cooperation between rural and urban women.

46. Peter Mtuze (1990: 24) refers to H. M. Ndawo's *Uhambo lukaGqobhoka* (1909), the first-full length Xhosa novel.

47. For a list of the male critics who saw these now no longer extant works, and for a listing of the works themselves, see Mtuze (1990).

48. See Terence Ranger's work on invented tradition (1983, 1993).

49. See the work of Jeff Opland (1995, 1998, 1999). See also Kaschula (2002: 164–170).

50. For German colonial femininity and masculinity, see Wildenthal (2001).

51. See Walton (1997: 86, 91, 93–4). In Gertrude Page's *Love in the Wilderness* (1907), Nan, as the "new woman," displays characteristics borrowed not only from men (she is tomboyish, sporty, domesticated) but also from Africans: the headmistress of the British school she goes to sends her home, saying, "I think you are almost as out of place here as an aborigine" (55). In *The Claw* (1911), Cynthia Stockley refers to how her heroine might live under a tree, as if like "natives." In Olive Schreiner's *From Man to Man* (1926), the child Rebekah bitterly notes the need to keep her white skin from getting sunburnt.

52. For important preliminary discussion, see Chennells (1982), and, more generally, Mitchell (1995) and Stoler (1997).

53. For discussion of "black peril" in Zimbabwe, see Schmidt (1992: 157–158, 169–173); in South Africa, Dubow (1995: 180–181), and Cornwell (1996). For one among many fictional treatments of the subject, see Lessing (1950).

54. In Western societies, social attitudes to rape are fractured, and it is not possible to speak of a single "white" attitude. In feudal societies, rape was sometimes regarded as an infringement of the honour of the father or husband, to be avenged; at other times marriage would put it right. By the mid-eighteenth century, rape was looked on as an event in a woman's life of an ontological order that she might not survive. Arguably, white and black women often functioned as signifiers of these different temporalities.

55. Writing about colonial Rhodesia in the early decades of the twentieth century, Susie Jacobs refers to the use of black male domestic workers rather than female, and suggests that it reflects settlers' true fears as to which "peril" was greater, that of black men raping white women, or white men raping black women (Jacobs 1995: 249–250; see also Kennedy 1987: 140; Schmidt 1992:158, 173 ff.)

56. See also Plaatje (1921).

57. See also *The Wrath of the Ancestors* (1980) by A. C. Jordan, Phyllis Ntantala's husband, which adds to Ntantala's and Ellen Kuzwayo's largely sympathetic portrayal of the relationship between white female teachers and their black female students. However, Kuzwayo hints at the autocratic, perhaps even sexually jealous, behavior towards her of one of the nuns (1985: 82). And in that important nonfiction depiction of school education in the 1940s, *Not Either an Experimental Doll*, "Lily Moya" to a considerably greater degree problematizes the relationship with her white female educational benefactor (this text is available in Marks 1987).

58. Further examples of prison writing are Caesarina Makhoere's prison memoir *No Child's Play* (1988) and the important autobiography by trade unionist Emma Mashinini, *Strikes Have Followed Me All My Life* (1989), which has moving chapters on her experiences in Pretoria Central Prison and Jeppe Central Prison

(see especially pp. 61–65). Barbara Schreiner, herself an activist (and Olive Schreiner's great-grandniece), put together an important collection of prison writings by women, *Snake with Ice Water* (1992), and Diana Russell's *Lives of Courage: Women for a New South Africa* (1989) has several interviews conducted in 1987 with women about prison. Ruth First's memoir, like others of the time and later, is reticent about the sexual and gender dimensions of imprisonment and torture. *117 Days* refers to a sexual tension between herself and one of her warders (see pp. 139–141, for instance), but this did not involve physical abuse.

59. First fled to Swaziland in 1960 but then decided to return; she was banned, then arrested and jailed, and on her release she fled again, finally being killed in Mozambique in 1982 by a letter bomb sent either to her or her husband by the South African security branch. First's writing is not in our anthology because of our constantly pressing need to limit inclusions by white women writers, and because the essay we would have chosen repeats a theme well-covered elsewhere— the pass campaign—and her most appropriate book from which to take an excerpt is about imprisonment, also covered in our anthology. Besides her extensive political journalism, First also wrote numerous books of revisionist history, including a co-written biography of Olive Schreiner (First and Scott 1980) and a history of South West Africa, based quite extensively on oral interviews with local people.

60. Among this group were several outstanding women (only one of whom is included in our anthology), notably Ray Alexander, Mary Benson, Hilda Bernstein, Helen Joseph, Norma Kitson, and AnnMarie Wolpe. See Shain and Frankental (1999), Suttner (1997), Frankel (1999), Leveson (1996).

61. Meg Samuelson, assistant for this project, found the Jeffreys material at the South African Library and the Cape Town Archives Repository; see her forthcoming essay "Marie Kathleen Jeffreys, alias 'Hamsi' (1893–1968): A Literary Historical Retrieval." The single poem reprinted here indicates a vast body of Jeffreys's writing still waiting to be "discovered." Two of her poems have hitherto been anthologized, but in only two of the many anthologies of Southern African writing, and she is altogether left out of literary histories.

62. It is worth noting that while some 1950s *Drum* columns were written by women, Mavis Kwankwa (who was also an occasional poet), Priscilla Mtimkulu, and Dolly Hassim, the fictional stories that appeared under the signatures of "Doris Sello," "Rita Sefora," and "Joan Mokwena" were written by male journalists (a few others were by non–Southern African women). Sello's is unfortunately included in Annemarié van Niekerk's otherwise impressive short story anthology, *Raising the Blinds: A Century of South African Women's Stories* (1990).

63. In Zimbabwe the official language was English, as was the language of education. In Namibia they were English, Afrikaans, and German; and in South Africa both English and Afrikaans.

64. Although Sesotho, Setswana, and siSwati cross the borders between the former British Protectorates and South Africa, they are spoken by only between two to four million people. SiSwati was developed as a written language only from the late 1960s, with Swazi independence; until this time the Swazis used Zulu books at school (see Mkhonza 2000: 34). IsiXhosa and isiZulu are spoken by between six and seven million people. TshiVenda is spoken by fewer than two million people. See N. A. Milubi (1988). One of the texts we had reluctantly to drop because of space was a tshiVenda text written by a woman under the pseudonym Dora Magidi and translated by anthropologist John Blacking (1964).

65. Moreover, African-language publishing was riddled with corruption, deals being made between publishing companies, schoolteachers, and authorities in charge of prescribing schoolbooks. The secondary school teachers and school inspectors from whom texts were usually commissioned were mostly men. Local and multinational companies exploited a lucrative market but rarely invested in training. The South African Broadcasting Corporation's introduction in 1960 of radio service in the nine local African languages meant that some women started writing serials and radio plays, but the political restrictions, along with the class and gender constraints otherwise placed on women's voices, severely hampered the emergence of interesting work. Patronizing attention was given writers who toed the line.

66. We are deeply indebted to Mtuze (1990) for our discussion of Xhosa women's writing, although some of the interpretation is our own. In Zulu fiction, Jessie Gwayi produced three historical novels in the 1970s, one of them on the female leader Mmanthathisi, and E. M. Damane produced radio plays, but these have yet to be given scholarly attention.

67. Writing in 1952, Xhosa novelist Liziwe Tsotsi asserted girls' right to education, as Letitia Kakaza and Victoria Swaartbooi had done before her. She spoke of the days when "most people thought that it was a waste of money to educate girls because they did not realize the purpose of educating children. They believed that it was enough if a girl could just write her name and was able to write a letter. They said that education delayed girls from marrying. Secondly, girls hardly finished studying before someone wanted to marry them even before they could work and repay their parents' expenses" (26; translated by Mtuze 1990: 65).

68. Much of the general information here on vernacular writing has been taken from Ntuli and Swanepoel (1993).

69. Ndlazulwana's poem was published at a time when the demands for a visible black solidarity between women and men no longer held so firm a dominion over women's voices, but in any event its publication in Xhosa meant that it would not have been seen as available to English speakers wishing to identify fracture in black South African solidarity.

70. This song is included in James's collection *Songs of the Women Migrants* (1999: 89). The references to Tsodio come from a song by a famous male musician, Johannes Mokgwadi, and from a "hugely popular radio serial of the same name which has been broadcast by Radio Lebowa. It is the topicality and popularity of the radio serial and the song on which it is based which enables listeners to attach to this brief reference a range of meanings not set down in the text itself" (James 1994: 99). "Leboa" is Sesotho for "the North" and "Lebowa" is the name given to the apartheid homeland.

71. Amelia House, for example. Christine Douts and Ilva Mackay, two poets of the struggle, left the country after a period of imprisonment to train as guerrillas. Yvette Christiansë ("Generations," 2001) left as part of a family group relocating to a more hospitable place and has stayed abroad. Some women, however, returned as democracy began to establish itself, for example, the journalist Joyce Sikhakhane ("Working on the *Mail*," 1977), the fiction writer Farida Karodia, and the poet Baleka Kgositsile. Although her work is not represented in this anthology, the career of the South African writer Lindiwe Mabuza may be usefully outlined. Unlike most of her contemporaries, but like earlier generations of South African women (Charlotte Maxeke and Nolwandle Jabavu, for instance), Mabuza was able to go abroad for her education. She joined the ANC in exile in 1977, publishing

revolutionary poetry in the major dissident magazines of the time. On her return to post-apartheid South Africa she entered the diplomatic corps. Mabuza edited the collection *One Never Knows: An Anthology of Black South African Women Writers in Exile* (1989), which gathers the writing of six women, besides a story of her own, and includes two stories by Dulcie September, killed in 1988 at the age of thirty-three when she was chief ANC representative in France.

Many white South African writers and writer-critics also left permanently: Sheila Roberts, Jeni Couzyn, Sheila Kohler, Mary Benson, Jillian Becker, Rose Moss, Lyndall Gordon, and Norma Kitson. See also Bernstein (1994). Hilda Kuper made a life for herself in exile in Swaziland. Here she published a novel, *Bite of Hunger: A Novel of Africa* (1965). Later her play, *A Witch in My Heart* (1970), was a standard school textbook in its Swazi translation (see Vincent 2000). A significant amount of South African writing is still produced by such writers in exile, along with a group of younger white women writers whom the country is now hard put to claim as its own, even when the focus of their work remains local: Elleke Boehmer, Ann Landsman, Marion Molteno, and Jenefer Shute, for instance.

72. Besides the well-known Nadine Gordimer, one may cite Sheila Roberts, who before leaving the country established herself as a fiction writer (and, to a lesser extent, a poet) during the 1970s. Her novel *He's My Brother* (1977) was banned. Sheila Fugard published books of poetry and fiction; Yvonne Burgess produced three novels in the 1970s.

73. In the following decade, two young writers, Rosa Keet and Welma Odendaal, started the magazine *Donga* (1976). Carrying work in English, Afrikaans, and Setswana, it aimed to give voice to young writers being turned down by the established journals. It was banned two years after it started, Odendaal losing her job at the government-controlled South African Broadcasting Corporation.

For further information on women writing in Afrikaans, see Viljoen (1996). While more than half of all people who speak Afrikaans as a first language were classified coloured under apartheid, Afrikaans-language publication used, until very recently, to be almost entirely by whites. Exceptions include a recent anthology called *WEAVE's Ink @ Boiling Point* (WEAVE 2000), produced by a group of women writing in English and Afrikaans, and two recent life-narratives by women: *My Storie Loop So* (Mfengu 1997) and *Umzabalazo* (Mroxisa 1997). In 1996 E. K. M. Dido became the first black woman to publish a novel in Afrikaans, *Die Storie van Monica Peters*. Since then she has published *Rugdraai en Stilbly* (1997) and *'n Stingetjie Blou Krale* (2000). Apart from Adam Small, other Afrikaans male authors of color, all recent, are to be found in the anthology *I Qabane Labantu: Poetry in the Emergency* (Coetzee and Willemse 1989), *Vatmaar—'n Lewendagge verhaal van 'n tyd wat nie meer is nie* (Scholtz 1995), and *Deur die oog van 'n naald* (Phosa 1996).

74. FEDTRAW (1988). See also *Truth and Reconciliation Commission Final Report* (1998), especially chapter 10 on the Women's Hearings.

75. See, for instance, her short story collection *The Collector of Treasures* (1977). In *When Rainclouds Gather* (1969), Head first indicates the power, economic and political, that South Africa exerted over Botswana.

76. In texts other than those selected for this anthology, both Gcina Mhlophe and Tsitsi Dangarembga show their main characters having to deal with the following question, "Can you cook books and feed them to your husband?" (Mhlophe 1987: 1; Dangarembga 1987: 15). Zimbabwean writer Ketinah Muringaniza told Flora Veit-Wild in 1987: "My first manuscript was complete when my husband

burnt it saying I wasn't giving him due attention" (Veit-Wild 1993: 101).

77. Josette Cole's important book *Crossroads: The Politics of Reform and Repression 1976–1986* (1987) focuses on the activism of the courageous women engaged in fighting the destruction of their homes and community, including that of Regina Ntongana.

78. Referring to the late 1950s, Juby Mayet, one of the journalists at *Drum,* spoke of her perception at the time that she had been treated in a degrading way by male *Drum* writers; but in the era of Black Consciousness she effectively denied this response (see Nicol 1991: 146).

79. For much of the general information on Black Consciousness, we are indebted to Sole (1994), and for some to Chapman (1980, 1996). No women are included in Chapman's account of "Soweto Poetry" (1980). Little critical attention has been paid to women's poetry of the time, but see Gunner (1979) and Lockett (1990).

80. Mafika Gwala (1979; reprinted in Chapman 1980: 171) singles out Ilva Mackay for her poem "Powerful Thoughts for All." In another poem simply called ". . . and liberty," Mackay offers a battle cry in incantatory rhythms—"There will be / bangs, blood, bruises, bodies / corpses, children crying, clenched / fists, furious, fervent fighting"—that are similar to those found in Gladys Thomas's poem in this anthology.

81. For another example, see Ilva Mackay's "Beware" in *Black Voices Shout!* (Matthews 1974), where she writes against the smothering of ideas by "eager fretting parents."

82. The column was published under various titles, "Soweto Speaking" and "Voices from the Ghetto" among them. Miriam Tlali interviewed old-age pensioners, shopkeepers, hawkers, and so on. Significantly, although this mode of retrieval of voice had already been practiced in South Africa, but in one-on-one encounters, and would become an especially important genre (the "as-told-to" story) in the 1980s, it would continue to be mostly white women who would act as scribes. In *Muriel at Metropolitan* Tlali signals the need for black solidarity, over and above anti-sexist protest, and is in this sense instrumental in formulating Black Consciousness. "I regard raising the level of consciousness of blacks as my prime responsibility [. . .] I must go deeper into [. . .] their feelings, try to make them understand their hopes, desires and aspirations, as a people" (qtd. in Lockett 1989: 277).

83. When she was forced to leave University of Witwatersrand under the Extension of University Education Act of 1959, which closed the doors of white universities in South Africa to black students, and which meant, further, that most of the black academics (amounting to a handful of men) either left or lost their jobs, Tlali went to the University of Botswana, Lesotho, and Swaziland. (Situated at first in Lesotho, the university later expanded to the other two independent states.)

84. "My Dear Madam" would later extend into a fuller short story (published in *Reconstruction*). Mhlophe also published some poems in *Staffrider*.

85. Several books appeared in the 1980s, see for example Hermer (1980), Lipman (1984), Gordon (1985), Bond-Stewart (1987), and Griesel, Manqele, and Wilson (1987). A decade later, interviews form the basis of important historical/anthropological/literary studies by Bozzoli (1991) and Hofmeyr (1993); in these studies the politics of the solicited testimony is carefully considered. See also Griesel (1991).

86. The term "sexual terrorism" is Diana Russell's. She used it to head a 1987 interview with Elaine Mohamed, who was imprisoned for seven months between 1981 and 1982, and sexually threatened (Russell 1989: 31–44).

WORKS CITED AND SELECT BIBLIOGRAPHY

Abrahams, Yvette. 1996. "Was Eva Raped? An Exercise in Speculative History." *Kronos: A Journal of Cape History* 23: 3–21.

———. 1997. "The Great Long National Insult: 'Science,' Sexuality and the Khoisan in the 18th and early 19th century." *Agenda* 32: 34–48.

———. 1998. "Images of Sara Baartman: Sexuality, Race, and Gender in Early Nineteenth-Century Britain" in Ruth Roach Pierson and Nupir Chaudhuri, eds. *Nation, Empire, Colony: Historicizing Gender and Race*. Bloomington and Indianapolis: Indiana University Press. 221–236.

ANC Women's League. 1993. *Status of South African Women*. Marshalltown: ANC Women's League Policy Division.

Armstrong, Nancy. 1987. *Desire and Domestic Fiction: A Political History of the Novel*. New York: Oxford University Press.

Attwell, David and Barbara Harlow with Joan Attwell. 2000. "Interview with Sindiwe Magona." *Modern Fiction Studies* 46(1): 282–295.

Barnes, Teresa. 1999. *"We Women Worked So Hard": Gender, Urbanization, and Social Reproduction in Colonial Harare, Zimbabwe, 1930–1956*. Portsmouth, NH: Heinemann; London: James Currey.

Barnett, Ursula A. 1985. *A Vision of Order: A Study of Black South African Literature in English (1914–1980)*. Cape Town: Maskew Miller Longman.

Beall, Jo. 1990. "Women Under Indentured Labour in Colonial Natal, 1860–1911" in Cherryl Walker, ed. *Women and Gender in Southern Africa to 1945*. Cape Town: David Philip; London: James Currey. 146–167.

Becker, Heike. 1992. "Towards Empowerment: Gender, Power and Strategies of Women in Namibia." Paper presented at Namibia Peace Plan Conference on Women, Power, and Violence. Windhoek, 16 May.

———. 1995. *The Namibian Women's Movement 1980-1992: From Anti-Colonial Resistance to Reconstruction*. Frankfurt: IKO—Verlag für Interkulturelle Kommunikation.

———. 1998a. "Efundula Past and Present: Female Initiation, Gender and Customary Law in Northern Namibia." Paper presented at Conference on Gender, Sexuality and Law. Keele University, 19–21 June.

———. 1998b. "Gender Aspects of Traditional Authorities and Customary Courts in Northern Namibia: 'This New Thing That Came with Independence'" in Marina d'Engelbronner-Kolff, Manfred Hinz, and John Sindano, eds. *Traditional Authority and Democracy in Southern Africa*. Windhoek: New Namibia Books. 257–88.

———. 1998c. "Premarital Female Sexuality and Customary Law in Northern Namibia" in Karin Fischer-Bude, ed. *Human Rights and Democracy in Southern Africa*. Windhoek: University of Namibia and New Namibia Books. 215–245.

———. 1999. "'Women in Power': Gender and 'Traditional' Politics in Northern Namibia, 1800–1997." Paper presented at the African Studies Association Conference. Philadelphia, 11–14 November.

———. 2000a. "A Concise History of Gender, 'Tradition' and the State in Namibia" in Christiaan Keulder, ed. *State, Society and Democracy: A Reader in Namibian Politics*. Windhoek: Gamsberg Macmillan. 171–199.

———. 2000b. "Meekulu's Children—A Tale of War and Survival from Northern Namibia." *Agenda* 46: 105–108.

———. 2001. "The Least Sexist Society? Perspectives on Gender, Change and

Violence among Southern African San." Paper presented at The Association for Anthropology in Southern Africa and the South Africa Society for Cultural Anthropologists Joint Conference, Anthropology's Challenge for Southern Africa. Pretoria, 9–11 April.

———. 2002a. "'We Want That Women Be Given an Equal Chance': Post-independence Rural Politics in Northern Namibia" in Meredeth Turshen, Sheila Meintjes, and Anu Pillay, eds. *The Aftermath: Women in Postconflict Societies.* London and New York: Zed Press. 225–242.

———. 2002b. "Eengoma: When the Drums Call. Female Initiation and the Politics of Gender and Sexuality in Colonial and Postcolonial Northern Namibia." Paper presented at Workshop on Contexts of Gender in Africa. Uppsala, 21–24 February. Forthcoming in Signe Arnfred and Ulla Vuorela, eds., *Thinking Sexualities in Contexts of Gender in Africa* (working title). Uppsala: Nordic Africa Institute.

Becker, Heike and Silke Felton. 2001. *A Gender Perspective on the Status of the San in Southern Africa.* Windhoek: Legal Assistance Centre.

Belebesi, Gertrude. 1976. *UNongxaki nezakhe.* Pretoria: Van Schaik.

Benjamin, Walter. 1970. *Illuminations.* London: Jonathan Cape.

Berger, Iris and E. Frances White. 1999. *Women in Sub-Saharan Africa: Restoring Women to History.* Bloomington and Indianapolis: Indiana University Press.

Bernstein, Hilda. 1994. *The Rift: The Exile Experience of South Africans.* London: Jonathan Cape.

Bhabha, Homi K. 1994. "The Other Question: Stereotype, Discrimination and the Discourse of Colonialism" in *The Location of Culture.* London and New York: Routledge. 66–84.

Biesele, Megan. 1993. *Women Like Meat: The Folklore and Foraging Ideology of the Kalahari Ju/'hoan.* Johannesburg: Witwatersrand University Press; Bloomington and Indianapolis: Indiana University Press.

Blacking, John. 1964. *Black Background: The Childhood of a South African Girl.* New York, London, and Toronto: Abelard-Schuman.

Bloem, Trudie. 1999. *Krotoa-Eva: The Woman from Robben Island.* Cape Town: Kwela.

Bond-Stewart, Kathy, ed. 1987. *Independence Is Not Only For One Sex.* Harare: Zimbabwe Publishing House.

Bozzoli, Belinda. 1983. "Marxism, Feminism and South African Studies." *Journal of Southern African Studies* 9(2): 139–171.

Bozzoli, Belinda, assisted by Mmantho Nkotsoe. 1991. *Women of Phokeng.* Johannesburg: Ravan Press.

Bradford, Helen. 1996. "Women, Gender and Colonialism: Rethinking the History of the British Cape Colony and Its Frontier Zones, c. 1806–70." *Journal of African History* 37: 351–370.

Brink, Elsabe. 1990. "Man-Made Women: Gender, Class and the Ideology of the *Volksmoeder*" in Cherryl Walker, ed. *Women and Gender in Southern Africa to 1945.* Cape Town: David Philip. 273–312.

Brown, Duncan. 1998. *Voicing the Text: South African Oral Poetry and Performance.* Cape Town: Oxford University Press.

———, ed. 1999. *Oral Literature and Performance in Southern Africa.* Oxford: James Currey; Cape Town: David Philip; Athens: Ohio University Press.

Burman, Sandra. 1990. "Fighting a Two-Pronged Attack: The Changing Legal Status of Women in Cape-Ruled Basutoland, 1872–1884" in Cherryl Walker, ed. *Women and Gender in Southern Africa to 1945*. Cape Town: David Philip; London: James Currey. 48–75.

Butler, Judith P. 1990. *Gender Trouble: Feminism and the Subversion of Identity*. New York and London: Routledge.

Callaway, Henry. 1868. *Nursery Tales, Traditions and Histories of the Zulus in Their Own Words with a Translation into English and Notes by The Rev. Canon Callaway M. D.* Natal: John A. Blair; Springvale and Pietermaritzburg: Davis and Sons; London: Trubner and Co.

Campbell, James T. 1995. *Songs of Zion: The African Methodist Episcopal Church in the United States and South Africa*. New York and Oxford: Oxford University Press.

Carter, Erica, James Donald, and Judith Squires, eds. 1993. *Space and Place: Theories of Identity and Location*. London: Lawrence and Wishart.

Chanock, Martin. 1985. *Law, Custom and Social Order: The Colonial Experience in Malawi and Zambia*. Cambridge: Cambridge University Press.

Chapman, Michael, ed. 1980. *Soweto Poetry*. Johannesburg: McGraw-Hill.

———. 1989. "More than Telling a Story: *Drum* and Its Significance in Black South African Writing" in M. Chapman, ed. *The Drum Decade: Stories from the 1950s*. Pietermaritzburg: University of Natal Press. 183–232.

———. 1996. *Southern African Literatures*. London: Longman.

———, ed. 2002. *The New Century of South African Poetry*. Johannesburg and Cape Town: AD Donker.

Chennells, A. J. 1982. *Settler Myths and the Southern Rhodesian Novel*. Unpublished Ph.D. thesis. University of Zimbabwe, Harare.

Chitauro, Moreblessings, Caleb Dube, and Liz Gunner. 1994. "Song, Story and Nation: Women as Singers and Actresses in Zimbabwe" in Liz Gunner, ed. *Politics and Performance: Theatre, Poetry and Song in Southern Africa*. Johannesburg: Witwatersrand University Press. 111–138.

Cock, Jacklyn. 1980. *Maids and Madams: A Study in the Politics of Exploitation*. Johannesburg: Ravan Press.

———. 1990. "Domestic Service and Education for Domesticity: The Incorporation of Xhosa Women into Colonial Society" in Cherryl Walker, ed. *Women and Gender in Southern Africa to 1945*. Cape Town: David Philip; London: James Currey. 76–96.

Cock, Jacklyn, M. Favis, A. Joffe, S. Miller, K. Satchwell, J. Schreiner, G. Volbrecht, and J. Yawitch. 1982. "Women and Changing Relations of Control." *South African Review One*. Johannesburg: Ravan Press.

Coetzee, Ampie and Hein Willemse. 1989. *I Qabane Labantu: Poetry in the Emergency*. Bramley: Taurus.

Coetzee, J. M. 1988. *White Writing: On the Culture of Letters in South Africa*. New Haven and London: Yale University Press.

Cole, Josette. 1987. *Crossroads: The Politics of Reform and Repression 1976–1986*, Johannesburg: Ravan Press.

Colenso, Frances. 1958. *Colenso Letters from Natal*. Wyn Rees, ed. Pietermaritzburg: Shuter and Shooter.

———. 1994. *My Chief and I* (by Atherton Wylde). Introduction by M. J. Daymond. Pietermaritzburg: University of Natal Press.

Comaroff, Jean and John Comaroff. 1986. "Christianity and Colonialism in South Africa." *American Ethnologist* 13(1): 1–22.

————. 1991. *Of Revelation and Revolution. Vol. 1: Christianity, Colonialism, and Consciousness in South Africa; Vol. 2: The Dialectics of Modernity on a South African Frontier*. Chicago: University of Chicago Press.

Cornwell, Gareth. 1996. "George Webb Hardy's *The Black Peril* and the Social Meaning of 'Black Peril' in Early Twentieth-Century South Africa." *Journal of Southern African Studies* 22(3): 441–453.

Couzens, Tim. 1985. *The New African: A Study of the Life and Work of H. I. E. Dhlomo*. Johannesburg: Ravan Press.

Culler, Jonathan. 1983. *On Deconstruction: Theory and Criticism after Structuralism*. London: Routledge and Kegan Paul.

Dangarembga, Tsitsi. 1988. *Nervous Conditions*. London: The Women's Press.

Davenport, T. R. H. 1978. *South Africa: A Modern History*. 2nd ed. London: Macmillan.

————. 1987. *South Africa: A Modern History*. 3rd ed. London: Macmillan.

Davids, Achmat. 1987. "The Role of Afrikaans in the History of the Cape Muslim Community" in Hans du Plessis and Theo du Plessis, eds. *Afrikaans en Taal Politiek*. Pretoria: H.A.U.M. 37–59.

Davin, Anna. 1978. "Imperialism and Motherhood." *History Workshop Journal* 5: 9–65.

Daymond, M. J., ed. 1996a. *South African Feminisms: Writing, Theory, and Criticism, 1990-1994*. New York and London: Garland.

————. 1996b. "Inventing Gendered Traditions: The Short Stories of Bessie Head and Miriam Tlali" in M. J. Daymond, ed. *South African Feminisms: Writing, Theory, and Criticism*. New York and London: Garland. 223–239.

————. 2000. "Natal Women's Letters in the 1850s: Ellen McLeod, Eliza Feilden, Gender and 'Second-World' Ambi/valence" in Rowland Smith, ed. *Postcolonizing the Commonwealth: Studies in Literature and Culture*. Waterloo, Ontario: Wilfrid Laurier University Press. 99–114.

————. 2001. "'Nowhere Yet Everywhere': Bessie Head's Question of Place in the 'Meditations' of 1964–5" in Jacqueline Bardolph, ed. *Telling Stories: Postcolonial Short Fiction in English*. Amsterdam and Atlanta: Rodopi. 183–196.

————. 2002. "Complementary Oral and Written Narrative Conventions: Sindiwe Magona's Autobiography and Short Story Sequence, 'Women at Work.'" *Journal of Southern African Studies* 28(2): 331–346.

de Kok, Ingrid. 1998. "Cracked Heirlooms: Memory on Exhibition" in Sarah Nuttall and Carli Coetzee, eds. *Negotiating the Past: The Making of Memory in South Africa*. Cape Town: Oxford University Press. 57–71.

de Kock, Leon. 1995. *Civilising Barbarians: Missionary Narrative and African Textual Response in Nineteenth-century South Africa*. Johannesburg: Witwatersrand University Press; Alice: Lovedale Press.

de Mist, Augusta. n.d. *Diary of a Journey to the Cape of Good Hope and the Interior of Africa in 1802 and 1803*. Cape Town and Amsterdam: A. A. Balkema.

Derrida, Jacques. 1982. "Signature Event Context" in *Margins of Philosophy*. Trans. Alan Bass. Brighton: Harvester Press. 307–330.

Dido, E. K. M. 1996. *Die Storie van Monica Peters*. Cape Town: Kwela Books.

————. 1997 *Rugdraai en Stilbly*. Cape Town: Kwela Books.

————. 2000. *'n Stringetjie Blou Krale*. Cape Town: Kwela Books.

Dlamini, Paulina. 1986. *Paulina Dlamini, Servant of Two Kings*. Comp. Heinrich Filter, trans. and ed. S. Bourquin. Pietermaritzburg: University of Natal Press.

Douglas, Ann. 1988. *The Feminization of American Culture*. New York: Doubleday.
Driver, Dorothy. 1988. "'Woman' as Sign in the South African Colonial Enterprise." *Journal of Literary Studies* 4(1): 3–20.
———. 1996. "*Drum* Magazine (1951–99) and the Spatial Configurations of Gender" in Kate Darian-Smith, Liz Gunner, and Sarah Nuttall, eds. *Text, Theory, Space: Land, Literature and History in South Africa and Australia*. London and New York: Routledge. 231–242.
———. 1999. "Hybridity, Mutability, and Difference in South African Writing: *God's Stepchildren* and 'Another Story.'" *Marang* (Special Issue: *Language, Literature and Society: A Conference in Honour of Bessie Head, 16–19 June 1998*. Ed. Leloba S. Molema): 93–100.
Dubow, Saul. 1995. *Illicit Union: Scientific Racism in Modern South Africa*. Cambridge: Cambridge University Press; Johannesburg: University of Witwatersrand Press.
Egbo, Benedicta. 2000. *Gender, Literacy and Life Chances in Sub-Saharan Africa*. Clevedon: Multilingual Matters.
Ellenberger, D. Fred. 1912. *History of the Basuto: Ancient and Modern*. Trans. J. C. MacGregor. Morija, Lesotho: Morija Museum and Archives, 1997.
Epprecht, Marc. 2000. *"This Matter of Women Is Getting Very Bad": Gender, Development and Politics in Colonial Lesotho*. Pietermaritzburg: University of Natal Press.
Erasmus, Zimitri. 2001. "Introduction: Re-imagining Coloured Identities in Post-Apartheid South Africa" in Zimitri Erasmus, ed. *Coloured by History, Shaped by Place: New Perspectives on Coloured Identities in Cape Town*. Cape Town: Kwela Books and South African History Online. 13–28.
Fabian, Johannes. 1983. *Time and the Other: How Anthropology Makes Its Object*. New York: Columbia University Press.
Fairweather, Ian S. 2001. *Identity Politics and the Heritage Industry in Post-Apartheid Northern Namibia*. Unpublished Ph.D. Thesis, University of Manchester, Department of Social Anthropology.
FEDTRAW (Federation of Transvaal Women). 1988. *A Woman's Place Is in the Struggle, Not Behind Bars!* Johannesburg: FEDTRAW.
First, Ruth. 1963. *South West Africa*. Harmondsworth: Penguin.
———. 1965. *117 Days: An Account of Confinement and Interrogation under the South African Ninety-Day Detention Law*. Harmondsworth: Penguin.
First, Ruth and Ann Scott. 1980. *Olive Schreiner*. New York: Schocken Books.
Foucault, Michel. 1978. *The History of Sexuality*. New York: Pantheon.
Frankel, Glenn. 1999. *Rivonia's Children: Three Families and the Cost of Conscience in White South Africa*. New York: Farrar, Straus and Giroux.
Frankental, Sally and Milton Shain. 1993. "Accommodation, Apathy and Activism: Jewish Political Behaviour in South Africa." *Jewish Quarterly* (Spring): 5–12.
FSAW (Federation of South African Women). "Report by FSAW on the Anti-Pass Campaign." FSAW document C1 6, 6. FSAW Collection, University of Witwatersrand.
Gaitskell, Deborah. 1983. "Housewives, Maids or Mothers: Some Contradictions of Domesticity for Christian Women in Johannesburg, 1903–39." *Journal of African History* 24: 241–256.
Gelfand, Michael. 1978. *A Non-Racial Island of Learning: A History of the University College of Rhodesia from Its Inception to 1966*. Gwelo: Mambo Press.

Gilman, Sander. 1985. "Black Bodies, White Bodies: Toward an Iconography of Female Sexuality in Late Nineteenth-Century Art, Medicine and Literature." *Critical Inquiry* 12(1): 204–242.

Glenn, Ian. 1996. "Legislating Women." *Journal of Literary Studies* 12(1/2): 145–170.

Goldblatt, Beth and Sheila Meintjes. 1997. "Dealing with the Aftermath—Sexual Violence and the Truth and Reconciliation Commission." *Agenda* 36: 7–18.

——. 1998. "South African Women Demand the Truth" in Meredeth Turshen and Clotilde Twagiramariya, eds. *What Women Do in Wartime: Gender and Conflict in Africa*. London and New York: Zed Press. 27–61.

Gordimer, Nadine. 1979. *Burger's Daughter*. London: Jonathan Cape.

Gordon, Suzanne, ed. 1985. *A Talent For Tomorrow: Life Stories of South African Servants*. Johannesburg: Ravan Press.

Gqola, Pumla Dineo. 1999. *Black Woman, You Are on Your Own: Images of Black Women in Staffrider Short Stories, 1978–1982*. Unpublished MA thesis, Dept. of English Language and Literature, University of Cape Town.

Gray, Stephen. 1979. *Southern African Literature: An Introduction*. Cape Town: David Philip; London: Rex Collings.

Griesel, Hanlie. 1991. "Text and Expression of Being at Mboza." *Current Writing* 3: 50–56.

Griesel, Hanlie, E. Manqele, and R. Wilson. 1987. *Sibambene: The Voices of Women at Mboza*. Johannesburg: Ravan Press.

Gunner, Liz. 1979. "Songs of Innocence and Experience: Women as Composers and Performers of *Izibongo*, Zulu Praise Poetry." *Research in African Literatures* 10(2): 239–267.

——. 2000. "Wrestling with the Present, Beckoning to the Past: Contemporary Zulu Radio Drama." *Journal of Southern African Studies* 26(2): 223–237.

Gunner, Liz and Mafika Gwala, trans. and eds. 1991. *Musho: Zulu Popular Praises*. Johannesburg: Witwatersrand University Press.

Guy, Jeff. 1990. "Gender Oppression in Southern Africa's Precapitalist Societies" in Cherryl Walker, ed. *Women and Gender in Southern Africa to 1945*. Cape Town: David Philip; London: James Currey. 33–47.

Gwala, Mafika. 1979. "Black Writing Today." *Staffrider* 2(3) (July-August); reprinted in Michael Chapman, ed. *Soweto Poetry*. Johannesburg: McGraw-Hill, 1982: 169–175.

Haarhoff, Dorian. 1991. *The Wild South-West: Frontier Myths and Metaphors in Literature Set in Namibia, 1760-1988*. Johannesburg: Witwatersrand University Press.

Hansen, Karen Tranberg, ed. 1992. *African Encounters with Domesticity*. New Brunswick, N.J.: Rutgers University Press.

Harries, Patrick. 1988. "The Roots of Ethnicity: Discourse and the Politics of Language Construction in South-East Africa." *African Affairs* (Jan): 25–52.

Hassim, S., Metelerkamp, J. and Todes, A. 1985. "A Bit on the Side: Gender Struggles in the Politics of Transformation." *Transformation* 5: 3–32.

Hay, Margaret Jean and Marcia Wright, eds. 1982. *African Women and the Law: Historical Perspectives*. Boston: Boston University, African Studies Center.

Head, Bessie. 1969. *When Rain Clouds Gather*. London: Victor Gollancz.

——. 1977. *The Collector of Treasures*. London: Heinemann Educational.

——. 1981. *Serowe, Village of the Rain Wind*. Cape Town: David Philip.

———. 1993. "Africa" in *The Cardinals with Meditations and Short Stories.* (Daymond, M. J., ed. and intro.) Cape Town: David Philip. 141–144.

Hermer, Carol. 1980. *The Diary of Maria Tholo.* Johannesburg: Ravan Press.

Hishongwa, Ndeutala. 1996. *Marrying Apartheid.* Abbotsford, Victoria, Australia: IMPRENTA.

Hodgson, Janet. 1987. *Princess Emma.* Johannesburg: AD Donker.

Hofmeyr, Isabel. 1989. "Turning Region into Narrative: English Storytelling in the Waterberg" in Philip Bonner, Isabel Hofmeyr, Deborah James, and Tom Lodge, eds. *Holding their Ground: Class, Locality and Culture in 19th and 20th Century South Africa.* Johannesburg: Witwatersrand University Press and Ravan Press. 259–283.

———. 1993. *"We Spend Our Years as a Tale That Is Told": Oral Historical Narrative in a South African Chiefdom.* Johannesburg: Witwatersrand University Press.

———. 2001. "Bunyan in Africa: Text and Transition." *Interventions* 3(3): 322–335.

———. 2002. "How Bunyan became English: Missionaries, Translation and the Disciplines of English Literature." *Journal of British Studies* 41(1): 84–119.

Hooper, Charles. 1960. *Brief Authority.* Cape Town: David Philip, 1989.

Howe, Florence. 1984. *Myths of Coeducation: Selected Essays, 1964–1983.* Bloomington and Indianapolis: Indiana University Press.

Hughes, Heather. 1990. "'A Lighthouse for African Womanhood': Inanda Seminary, 1869–1945" in Cherryl Walker, ed. *Women and Gender in Southern Africa to 1945.* Cape Town: David Philip; London: James Currey. 197–220.

Israel, Mark and Simon Adams. 2000. "'That Spells Trouble': Jews and the Communist Party of South African." *Journal of Southern African Studies* 26(1): 145–162.

Jabavu, Noni. 1963. *The Ochre People.* London: John Murray.

Jacobs, Rayda. 1998. *The Slave Book.* Cape Town: Kwela Books.

———. 2002. *Sachs Street.* Cape Town: Kwela Books.

Jacobs, Susie. 1995. "Gender Divisions and the Formation of Ethnicities in Zimbabwe" in Daiva Stasiulis and Nira Yuval-Davis, eds. *Unsettling Settler Societies: Articulations of Gender, Race, Ethnicity and Class.* London: Sage. 240–262.

Jacobus, Mary. 1986. *Reading Woman: Essays in Feminist Criticism.* London: Methuen.

James, Deborah. 1994. *"Basadi ba baeng*/Visiting Women: Female Migrant Performance from the Northern Transvaal" in Liz Gunner, ed. *Politics and Performance: Theatre, Poetry and Song in Southern Africa.* Johannesburg: Witwatersrand University Press. 81–110.

———. 1999. *Songs of the Women Migrants: Performance and Identity in South Africa.* Johannesburg: Witwatersrand University Press.

Jeffreys, M. K. 1959. "Afrikaner Owes the Coloured." *Drum* (Dec.): 34–5, 37, 39.

Jordan, A. C. 1973. *Tales from Southern Africa.* Berkeley: University of California Press.

———. 1980. *The Wrath of the Ancestors: A Novel.* Alice: Lovedale. (First published as *Ingqumbo yeminyanya.* Lovedale: Lovedale Press, 1940.)

Jordan, Z. Pallo. 1973. "Foreword" in A. C. Jordan. *Tales from Southern Africa.* Berkeley: University of California Press. ix-xxiii.

Joseph, Helen. 1986. *Side By Side: The Autobiography of Helen Joseph.* Johannesburg: Ravan Press.

Joubert, Elsa. 1980. *The Long Journey of Poppie Nongena.* Johannesburg: Jonathan Ball. (First published in Afrikaans as *Die Swerfjare van Poppie Nongena* in 1978; later published in paperback as *Poppie.*)

Karttunen, Frances. 1994. *Between Worlds: Interpreters, Guides, and Survivors*. New Brunswick, N. J.: Rutgers University Press.

Kaschula, Russell H. 1997. "Exploring the Oral-Written Interface with Particular Reference to Xhosa Oral Poetry." *Research in African Literatures* 28(1): 173–191.

———. 2002. *The Bones of the Ancestors are Shaking: Xhosa Oral Poetry in Context*. Cape Town: Juta.

Kasrils, Ronald. 1993. *Armed and Dangerous: My Undercover Struggle Against Apartheid*. Oxford: Heinemann Educational.

Kennedy, D. 1987. *Islands of White: Settler Society and Culture in Kenya and Southern Rhodesia, 1890–1939*. Durham: Duke University Press.

Kezilahabi, E. 2001. "Dramatic Performance of Gaoditswe Shao's Story-Telling and the Location of Culture" in Brian Harlech-Jones, Ismail Mbise, and Helen Vale, eds. *Guardian of the Word: Literature, Language and Politics in SADC Countries*. Windhoek: Association of University Teachers of Literature and Language. 49–56.

Kinsman, M. 1983. "Beasts of Burden." *Journal of Southern African Studies*, 10(1): 39–54.

Kolodny, Annette. 1980. "Reply to Commentaries: Women Writers, Literary Historians, and Martian Readers." *New Literary History* 11: 587–92.

Kruger, Loren. 1999. *The Drama of South Africa: Plays, Pageants and Publics since 1910*. London and New York: Routledge.

Kunene, Daniel P. 1992. "Language, Literature and the Struggle for Liberation in South Africa" in Michael Chapman, Colin Gardner, and Es'kia Mphahlele, eds. *Perspectives on South African English Literature*. Johannesburg: AD Donker. 497–513.

Kuper, Hilda. 1965. *Bite of Hunger: A Novel of Africa*. New York: Harcourt Brace.

———.1970. *A Witch in My Heart: A Play Set in Swaziland in the 1930s*. London: Oxford University Press for the International African Institute.

Kuzwayo, Ellen. 1985. *Call Me Woman*. London: The Women's Press.

———. 1998. *African Wisdom: A Personal Collection of Setswana Proverbs*. Cape Town: Kwela Books.

Landman, Christina. 1996. "The Religious Krotoa (c. 1652-1674)." *Kronos: Journal of Cape History* 23: 22–35.

Lenake, J. M. 1983. "Southern Sotho Literature: The Development Between 1960 and 1990" in Albert S. Gérard, ed. *Comparative Literature and African Literature*. Goodwood: Via Afrika. 129–138.

Lenta, Margaret and Basil le Cordeur. 1998. *The Cape Diaries of Lady Anne Barnard 1799–1800*. (2 vols.). Cape Town: Van Riebeeck Society.

Lessing, Doris. 1950. *The Grass Is Singing*. London: Michael Joseph.

———. 1951. *This Was The Old Chief's Country*. London: Michael Joseph.

———. 1964. *African Stories*. London: Michael Joseph.

Leveson, Marcia. 1996. *People of the Book: Images of the Jew in South African English Fiction 1880–1992*. Johannesburg: Witwatersrand University Press.

Lewis, Desirée. 1996. "The Politics of Feminism in South Africa" in M. J. Daymond, ed. *South African Feminisms: Writing, Theory, and Criticism, 1990–1994*. New York and London: Garland. 91–104.

Lipman, Beata, ed. 1984. *We Make Freedom: Women in South Africa*. London and New York: Pandora.

Lockett, Cecily. 1989. "The Fabric of Experience: A Critical Perspective on the

Writing of Miriam Tlali" in Cherry Clayton, ed. *Women and Writing in South Africa: A Critical Anthology*. Marshalltown: Heinemann. 275–286.

———. 1990. *Breaking the Silence: A Century of South African Women's Poetry*. Johannesburg: AD Donker.

Loomba, Ania. 1998. *Colonialism/Postcolonialism*. London and New York: Routledge.

Low, Gail Ching-Liang. 1996. *White Skins/Black Masks: Representation and Colonialism*. London and New York: Routledge.

McClintock, Anne. 1990. "Maidens, Maps and Mines: King Solomon's Mines and the Reinvention of Patriarchy in Colonial South Africa" in Cherryl Walker, ed. *Women and Gender in Southern Africa to 1945*. Cape Town: David Phillip. 97–124 and 354–357.

———. 1994. *Imperial Leather: Race, Gender, and Sexuality in the Colonial Conquest*. London and New York: Routledge.

McCord, Margaret. 1995. *The Calling of Katie Makanya*. Cape Town: David Philip.

Mackenzie, Craig and Cherry Clayton, eds. 1989. *Between the Lines: Interviews with Bessie Head, Sheila Roberts, Ellen Kuzwayo and Miriam Tlali*. Grahamstown: National English Literary Museum.

McLeod, Ellen. 1970. *Dear Louisa: History of a Pioneer Family in Natal, 1850–1888*. Edited by Ruth Gordon. Pietermaritzburg: Shuter and Shooter.

Maake, Nhlanhla. 2000. "Publishing and Perishing: Books, People and Reading in African Languages in South Africa" in Nicholas Evans and Monica Seeber, eds. *The Politics of Publishing in South Africa*. London: Holger Ehling Publishing. 127–156.

Mabuza, Lindiwe. 1989. *One Never Knows: An Anthology of Black South African Women Writers in Exile*. Johannesburg: Skotaville Press.

Mafela, Lily. 1993. *Competing Gender Ideologies in Education Among Batswana of the Bechuanaland Protectorate, 1840–1966*. Unpublished Ph.D. Thesis, Northwestern University, Evanston, Illinois.

Mager, Anne Kelk. 1999. *Gender and the Making of a South African Bantustan: A Social History of the Ciskei. 1945–1959*. Portsmouth, N.H.: Heinemann; Oxford: James Currey; Cape Town: David Philip.

Magona, Sindiwe. 1990. *To My Children's Children*. Cape Town: David Philip.

———. 1992. *Forced to Grow*. Cape Town: David Philip.

———. 1998. *Mother to Mother*. Cape Town: David Philip.

Magwanza, Thenjiwe. 2001. "Private Transgressions: The Visual Voice of Zulu Women." *Agenda* 49: 25–32.

Makhoere, Caesarina Kona. 1988. *No Child's Play: In Prison Under Apartheid*. London: The Women's Press.

Malherbe, V. C. 1990. *Krotoa, Called "Eva": A Woman Between*. Cape Town: Centre for African Studies, University of Cape Town.

Mancoe, J. X. 1934. *The Bloemfontein Bantu and Coloured People's Directory*. Bloemfontein: A. C. White.

Marks, Shula. 1985. "Southern Africa, 1867–1886" in Roland Oliver and G. N. Sanderson, eds. *The Cambridge History of Africa*. Vol. 6. Cambridge: Cambridge University Press. 359–421.

———. ed. 1987. *"Not Either an Experimental Doll": The Separate Worlds of Three South African Women*. Durban: Killie Campbell Africana Library; Pietermaritzburg: University of Natal Press.

————. 1994. *Divided Sisterhood: Race, Class, and Gender in the South African Nursing Profession*. Basingstoke: Macmillan; New York: St. Martin's Press.

Maseko, Zola. 1998. *The Life and Times of Sara Baartman—The Hottentot Venus*. Johannesburg: Film Resource Unit (fru@wn.apc.org).

Mashinini, Emma. 1989. *Strikes Have Followed Me All My Life: A South African Autobiography*. London: The Womens Press.

Matthews, James, ed. 1974. *Black Voices Shout! An Anthology of Poetry*. Athlone: BLAC.

Matthews, James and Gladys Thomas. 1972. *Cry Rage!* Johannesburg: Spro-Cas.

Maylam, Paul. 1986. *A History of the African People of South Africa: From the Early Iron Age to the 1970s*. London: Croom Helm; Cape Town: David Philip.

Meer, Fatima. 1975. "The Black Woman in South Africa" in T. Thoahlane, ed. *Black Renaissance: Papers from the Black Renaissance Convention*. Johannesburg: Ravan Press. 34–46.

Meintjes, Sheila. 1990. "Family and Gender in the Christian Community at Edendale, Natal, in Colonial Times" in Cherryl Walker, ed. *Women and Gender in Southern Africa to 1945*. Cape Town: David Philip; London: James Currey. 125–145.

————. 1998. "Gender, Nationalism and Transformation: Difference and Commonality in South Africa's Past and Present" in R. Wilford and R. L. Miller, eds. *Women, Ethnicity and Nationalism: The Politics of Transition*. London and New York: Routledge. 62–86.

Mfengu, Nongeteni. 1997. *My Storie Loop So*. Mowbray: Kagiso.

Mhlophe, Gcina [writing as Nokugcina Sigwili]. 1980. "Women Writers: Men Are Always Women's Children." *Staffrider* 3(1): 44.

—— [writing as Nokugcina Sigwili]. 1981a. "My Dear Madam . . ." *Staffrider* 3(4): 11–12, 14.

—— [writing as Nokugcina Mhlope]. 1981b. "My Dear Madam" in Mothobi Mutloatse, ed. *Reconstruction: 90 Years of Black Historical Literature*. Johannesburg: Ravan Press. 180–198.

————. 1987. "The Toilet" in Ann Oosthuizen, ed. *Sometimes When It Rains: Writings by South African Women*. London and New York: Pandora. 1–7.

————. 2002. "My Dear Madam" in *Love Child*. Pietermaritzburg: University of Natal Press. 29–44.

Mill, John Stuart. 1869. *The Subjection of Women*. Indianapolis: Harket Publishing Company, 1988.

Milubi, N. A. 1988. *Aspects of Venda Poetry: A Reflection on the Development of Poetry from the Oral Tradition to the Modern Forms*. Unpublished D. Litt. Thesis, University of the North.

Mitchell, Sally. 1995. *The New Girl: Girls' Culture in England, 1880–1915*. New York: Columbia University Press.

Mkhonza, Sarah. 2000. "The Writer as Woman: Experiences in Swaziland" in *Women and Activism: Women Writers Conference, Harare, 29–30 July 1999*. Harare: Zimbabwe International Book Fair and Zimbabwe Women Writers. 50–57.

Mnthali, Felix. 1983. "Letter to a Feminist Friend." *Marang* 4: 32–34.

Mofokeng, Boitumelo. 1988. "Breaking the Silence" in *Buang Basadi—Khulumani Makhosikazi—Women Speak: Conference on Women and Writing*. Johannesburg: COSAW Transvaal Region. 6–10.

Mogwe, Gaele. 1999. "Experiences of Batswana Women during the Second World War." *Pula: Botswana Journal of African Studies* 13(1-2): 93–107.

Mohanty, Chandra. 1988. "Under Western Eyes: Feminist Scholarship and Colonial Discourses." *Feminist Review* 30: 61–88.

Moitse, Sindile. 1994. *The Ethnomusicology of the Basotho.* Roma, Lesotho: Institute of Southern African Studies, National University of Lesotho.

Molema, Leloba S. 1989. *The Image of Christianity in Sesotho Literature: Thomas Mofolo and His Contemporaries.* Hamburg: Helmut Busker Verlag.

Morton, Barry. 1998. "The Evolution of Women's Property Rights in Colonial Botswana, 1890–1966." *Pula: Botswana Journal of African Studies* 21(1–2): 5–21.

Mostert, Noël. 1992. *Frontiers: The Epic of South Africa's Creation and the Tragedy of the Xhosa People.* New York: Knopf.

Motlotle, Ntikwe P. 1998a. "*Bojale*—Girls Initiation School." *The Zebra's Voice* 25(2): 19–21.

———. 1998b. "*Bojale* in Kgatleng." *The Zebra's Voice* 25(3–4): 22–25.

Mroxisa, Neliswa. 1997. *Umzabalazo.* Mowbray: Kagiso.

Mtuze, Peter. 1990. *A Feminist Critique of the Image of Woman in the Prose Works of Selected Xhosa Writers (1909-1980).* Unpublished Ph.D. Thesis, University of Cape Town.

Ndawo, H. M. 1909. *Uhambo lukaGqobhoka.* Lovedale: Lovedale Institution Press.

Ndlazulwana, Thelminah Nobantu. 1986. *Iingxangxasi.* Cape Town: Maskew Miller Longman.

Ngcobo, Lauretta. 1988. "African Motherhood—Myth and Reality" in Kirsten Holst Petersen, ed. *Criticism and Ideology: Second African Writers Conference, Stockholm, 1986.* Uppsala: Scandinavian Institute of African Studies. 141–151.

———. 1990. *And They Didn't Die.* Johannesburg: Skotaville Press; London: Virago. Reprinted 1999 with "Afterword" by M. J. Daymond. New York: Feminist Press; Pietermaritzburg: Natal University Press.

———. 1991. "A Black South African Writing Long After Schreiner" in Itala Vivan, ed. *The Flawed Diamond: Essays on Olive Schreiner.* Sydney: Dangaroo. 189–199.

Nicol, Mike. 1991. *A Good-Looking Corpse.* London: Secker and Warburg.

Nixon, Rob. 1994. *Homelands, Harlem and Hollywood: Southern African Culture and the World Beyond.* New York and London: Routledge.

Nkosi, Lewis. 1983. "The Fabulous Decade: The Fifties" in *Home and Exile and Other Selections.* London and New York: Longman. 3–24.

Ntuli, D. B. and C. F. Swanepoel. 1993. *Southern African Literature in African Languages: A Concise Historical Perspective.* Pretoria: Acacia.

Omer-Cooper, J. D. 1987. *History of Southern Africa.* London: James Currey; Portsmouth, N.H.: Heinemann.

Opland, Jeff. 1983. *Xhosa Oral Poetry: Aspects of a Black South African Tradition.* Johannesburg: Ravan Press.

———. 1995. "Nontsizi Mgqwetho: Stranger in Town" in Graham Furniss and Liz Gunner, eds. *Power, Marginality and African Oral Literature.* Cambridge: Cambridge University Press; Johannesburg: Witwatersrand University Press. 162–184.

———. 1998. *Xhosa Poets and Poetry.* Cape Town: David Philip.

———. 1999. "Nontsizi Mgqwetho (Cizama, Imbongikazi yakwaCizama): Xhosa Poet" in Nelly E. Sonderling, ed. *New Dictionary of South African Biography.* Vol. 2. Pretoria: Vista University Press. 108–109.

Orford, Margie. 2001. "Women's Voices: Weaving a New Body Through Language" in Brian Harlech-Jones, Ismael Mbise, and Helen Vale, eds. *Guardian of the*

Word: Literature, Language and Politics in SADC Countries. Windhoek: Gamsberg Macmillan. 39–48.

Orford, Margie and Heike Becker. 2001. "Homes and Exiles: Owambo Women's Literature" in Barbara Bender and Margot Winer, eds. *Contested Landscapes: Movement, Exile and Place.* Oxford: Berg. 289–302.

Orford, Margie and Nepeti Nicanor. 1996. *Coming on Strong: Writing by Namibian Women.* Windhoek: New Namibia Books.

Page, Gertrude. 1907. *Love in the Wilderness: The Story of Another African Farm.* London: Hurst and Blackett.

Pape, J. 1990. "Black and White: The 'Perils of Sex' in Colonial Zimbabwe." *Journal of Southern African Studies* 16(4): 699–720.

Peires, J. B. 1989. *The Dead Will Arise: Nongqawuse and the Great Xhosa Cattle-Killing Movement of 1856–7.* Johannesburg: Ravan Press; Bloomington and Indianapolis: Indiana University Press; London: James Currey.

Penn, Nigel. 1999. *Rogues, Rebels and Runaways: Eighteenth-Century Cape Characters.* Cape Town: David Philip.

Petlane, T. and M. Mapetla 1998. "Gender Aspects of Female Chieftainship in Lesotho" in F. M. d'Engelbronner-Kolff, M. O. Hinz, and J. L. Sindano, eds. *Traditional Authority and Democracy in Southern Africa.* Windhoek: New Namibia Books. 247–256.

Phosa, Mathews. 1996. *Deur die oog van 'n naald.* Cape Town: Tafelberg.

Pinnock, Don. 1997. *Ruth First.* Pretoria: HSRC.

Plaatje, Sol T. 1916. *Native Life in South Africa.* London: P. S. King.

———. 1921. *The Mote and the Beam: An Epic on Sex-relationship 'twixt White and Black in British South Africa.* Kimberley: Tsala ea Batho; New York: Young's Book Exchange.

Pringle, Thomas. 1835. *Narrative of a Residence in South Africa.* Edited by A. M. Lewin Robinson. Cape Town: Struik, 1966.

Ramphele, Mamphela. 1995. *A Life.* Cape Town and Johannesburg: David Philip.

Ranger, Terence 1983. "The Invention of Tradition in Colonial Africa" in E. J. Hobsbawn and Terence Ranger, eds. *The Invention of Tradition.* Cambridge and New York: Cambridge University Press. 211–262.

———. 1993. "The Invention of Tradition Revisited: The Case of Colonial Africa" in Terence Ranger and Olufemi Vaughan, eds. *Legitimacy and the State in Twentieth-Century Africa: Essays in Honour of A. H. M. Kirk-Greene.* Basingstoke: Macmillan. 62–111.

Rasebotsa, Nobantu and Leloba Molema. 1998. *Women Creating the Future: An Anthology of Women's Writing in Southern Africa.* Florida Hills: Vivlia.

Reader's Digest. 1992. *Reader's Digest Illustrated History of South Africa.* Cape Town, London, New York, Sydney, Montreal: Reader's Digest Association Ltd.

Reiner, Peter, Werner Hillebrecht, and Jane Katjavivi. 1994. *Books in Namibia: Past Trends and Future Prospects.* Windhoek: Association of Namibian Publishers.

Roberts, Richard and Kristin Mann, eds. 1991. *Law in Colonial Africa.* Portsmouth, N.H.: Heinemann; London: James Currey.

Roberts, Sheila. 1977. *He's My Brother: A Novel.* Johannesburg: AD Donker.

Robinson, A. M. Lewin. 1993. *The Cape Journals of Lady Anne Barnard 1797–1798.* Cape Town: Van Riebeeck Society.

Ross, Robert. 1983. *Cape of Torments: Slavery and Resistance in South Africa.* London: Routledge and Kegan Paul.

———. 1999. *A Concise History of South Africa*. Cambridge: Cambridge University Press.

Russell, Diana. 1989. *Lives of Courage: Women for a New South Africa*. New York: Basic Books.

Samuelson, Meg. 2000. "Reading the Maternal Voice in Sindiwe Magona's *To My Children's Children* and *Mother to Mother*." *Modern Fiction Studies* 46(1): 227–245.

Schapera, Isaac. 1965. *"In Praise of Molefi Kgafela": Praise-Poems of Tswana Chiefs*. Oxford: Clarendon.

Scheub, Harold. 1985. "Zulu Oral Tradition and Literature" in B. W. Andrzejewski, Stanislaw S. Pilaszewicz, and Witold Tyloch, eds. *Literatures in African Languages, Theoretical Issues and Sample Surveys*. New York and Cambridge: Cambridge University Press. 493–528.

———. ed. 1996. *The Tongue Is Fire: South African Storytellers and Apartheid*. Madison: University of Wisconsin Press.

Schmidt, Elizabeth. 1992. *Peasants, Traders and Wives: Shona Women in the History of Zimbabwe, 1870–1939*. Portsmouth, N.H.: Heinemann; Harare: Baobab.

Schoeman, Karel. 1991. *Olive Schreiner: A Woman in South Africa, 1855–1881*. Johannesburg: Jonathan Ball.

Scholtz, A. H. M. 1995. *Vatmaar—'n Lewendagge verhaal van 'n tyd wat nie meer is nie*. Cape Town: Kwela Books. 2000. *A Place Called Vatmaar*. Translated by Chris van Wyk. Cape Town: Kwela Books.

Schreiner, Barbara. 1992. *Snake with Ice Water: Prison Writings by South African Women*. Johannesburg: COSAW.

Schreiner, Olive. 1883. *The Story of an African Farm*. London: Chapman & Hall.

———. 1897. *Trooper Peter Halket of Mashonaland*. London: T. Fisher Unwin.

———. 1911. *Woman and Labour*. London: T. Fisher Unwin.

———. 1923. *Thoughts on South Africa*. London: T. Fisher Unwin.

———. 1926. *From Man to Man; Or, Perhaps Only . . . .* London: T. Fisher Unwin.

Seda, Owen S. 2001. "The Female Character in Post-Independence Zimbabwean Theatre—Some Case Studies" in L. Losambe and D. Sarinjeive, eds. *Pre-Colonial and Post-Colonial Drama and Theatre in Africa*. Cape Town: New Africa Books. 120–127.

Shain, Milton and Sally Frankental. 1999. "Community with a Conscience: Myth or Reality" in Glenda Abrahamson, ed. *Modern Jewish Mythologies*. Cincinnati: Hebrew Union College. 57–67.

Sharpe, Jenny. 1993. *Allegories of Empire: The Figure of Woman in the Colonial Text*. Minneapolis: University of Minnesota Press.

Skota, T. D. Mweli. 1931. *The African Yearly Register: Being an Illustrated National Biographical Dictionary (Who's Who) of Black Folks in Africa*. Johannesburg: R. L Esson.

Smith, Edwin W. 1939. *The Mabilles of Basutoland*. Morija, Lesotho: Morija Museum and Archives.

Smithers, Elsa. 1935. *March Hare: The Autobiography of Elsa Smithers*. London: Oxford University Press.

Sole, Kelwyn. 1979. "Class, Continuity and Change in Black South African Literature 1948–1960" in B. Bozzoli, ed. *Labour, Townships and Protest: Studies in the Social History of the Witwatersrand*. Johannesburg: Ravan Press. 143–182.

———. 1994. *Authority, Authenticity and the Black Writer: Depictions of Politics and Community in Selected Fictional Black Consciousness Texts*. Unpublished Ph.D. Thesis, University of Witwatersrand.

Spivak, Gayatri Chakravorty. 1985. "Three Women's Texts and a Critique of Imperialism." *Critical Inquiry* 12(1): 243–261.

———. 1987. *In Other Worlds: Essays in Cultural Politics.* London and New York: Methuen.

———. 1992. "The Politics of Translation" in Michèle Barrett and Anne Phillips, eds. *Destabilizing Theory: Contemporary Feminist Debates.* Stanford: Stanford University Press. 177–200.

Steenekamp, Anna Elizabeth. 1888. "Record or Journal of Our Migration from Our Mother Country to Port Natal" in John Bird. *The Annals of Natal, 1495–1845.* Vol. 1. Pietermaritzburg: P. Davis and Sons. 457–468.

Stockley, Cynthia. 1911. *The Claw.* London: Hurst and Blackett.

Stoler, Ann Laura. 1997. "Making Empire Respectable: The Politics of Race and Sexual Morality in Twentieth-Century Colonial Cultures" in Anne McClintock, Aamir Mufti, and Ella Shohat, eds. *Dangerous Liaisons: Gender, Nation, and Postcolonial Perspectives.* London and Minneapolis: University of Minneapolis Press. 344–373.

Stow, George W. 1905. *The Native Races of South Africa: A History of the Intrusion of the Hottentots and Bantu into the Hunting Grounds of the Bushmen, the Aborigines of the Country.* Ed. George McCall Theal. London: Swan Sonnenschein; New York: Macmillan.

Suttner, Immanuel. 1997. *Cutting through the Mountain: Interviews with South African Jewish Activists.* London: Viking.

Switzer, Les and Donna Switzer. 1979. *The Black Press in South Africa and Lesotho: A Descriptive Bibliographic Guide to African, Coloured, and Indian Newspapers, Newsletters, and Magazines, 1836-1976.* Boston: G. K. Hall.

Sylvester, Jeremy, Marion Wallace, and Patricia Hayes. 1998. "'Trees Never Meet': Mobility and Containment: An Overview, 1915–1946" in Patricia Hayes, Jeremy Sylvester, Marion Wallace, Wolfram Hartmann with Ben Fuller, Jr., eds. *Namibia under South African Rule, Mobility and Containment 1915–46.* Oxford: James Currey; Windhoek: Out of Africa; Athens: Ohio University Press. 3–48.

Tlali, Miriam. 1975. *Muriel at Metropolitan.* Johannesburg: Ravan Press.

———. 1978. "Soweto Speaking." *Staffrider* 1(1): 2–6.

———. 1980. "In Search of Books." *The Star* (July 30): 16; reprinted in Michael Chapman, ed. *Soweto Poetry.* 44–45.

———. 1981. Interview. Staffrider 4(3): 41–43.

———. 1984. "Remove the Chains: South African Censorship and the Black Writer." *Index on Censorship* 6: 22–26.

———. 1988. "Miriam Tlali" in *Women Speak: Conference on Women and Writing.* Johannesburg: COSAW. 56–57.

———. 1989. "Interviewed by Cecily Lockett" in Mackenzie, Craig and Cherry Clayton, eds. *Between the Lines: Interviews with Bessie Head, Sheila Roberts, Ellen Kuzwayo and Miriam Tlali.* Grahamstown: National English Literary Museum. 69–85.

Tompkins, Jane. 1986. "Sentimental Power: *Uncle Tom's Cabin* and the Politics of Literary History" in Elaine Showalter, ed. *The New Feminist Criticism: Essays on Women, Literature, and Theory.* London: Virago. 81–104.

Truth and Reconciliation Commission Final Report. 1998. Cape Town: Juta.

Tsotsi, Liziwe. 1952. *UNtabaziyaduma.* Lovedale: Lovedale Press.

Unterhalter, Elaine. 1995. "Constructing Race, Class, Gender and Ethnicity: State and Opposition Strategies in South Africa" in Daiva Stasiulis and Nira Yuval-Davis, eds. *Unsettling Settler Societies: Articulations of Gender, Race, Ethnicity and Class.* London, Thousand Oaks; New Delhi: Sage. 207–240.

van Heyningen, Elizabeth. 1999. "The Voices of Women in the South African War." *South African Historical Journal* 41 (Nov.): 22–43.

van Niekerk, Annemarié, ed. 1990. *Raising the Blinds: A Century of South African Women's Stories.* Johannesburg: AD Donker.

van Wyk Smith, M. 1990. *Grounds of Contest: A Survey of Southern African Literature.* Kenwyn: Juta.

Veit-Wild, Flora. 1992. *Teachers, Preachers, Non-Believers: A Social History of Zimbabwean Literature.* London: Hans Zell Publishers.

———. 1993. *Survey of Zimbabwean Writers: Educational and Literary Careers.* Bayreuth African Studies Series, no. 27. Bayreuth: E. Breitinger.

Vera, Yvonne. 1993. *Nehanda.* Harare: Baobab Books.

———. 1996. *Under the Tongue.* Harare: Baobab Books.

———. 1998. *Butterfly Burning.* Harare: Baobab Books.

———. 1999. "Preface" in Yvonne Vera, ed. *Opening Spaces: An Anthology of African Women's Writing.* Oxford: Heinemann; Harare: Baobab Books. 1–5.

———. 2002. *The Stone Virgins.* Harare: Weaver Press.

Vietzen, Sylvia. 1980. *A History of Education for European Girls in Natal 1837–1902.* Pietermaritzburg: University of Natal Press.

Viljoen, Louise. 1996. "Postcolonialism and Recent Women's Writing in Afrikaans." *World Literature Today* 70(1): 63–72.

Vincent, Kerry. 2000. "Translating Culture: Literature, Anthropology and Hilda Kuper's *A Witch in My Heart.*" *Current Writing* 12(2): 113–129.

Visser, N. W. 1976. "South Africa: The Renaissance that Failed." *Journal of Commonwealth Literature* 9(1): 42–59.

von Flotow, Luise. 1998. "Dis-Unity and Diversity: Feminist Approaches to Translation Studies" in Lynne Bowker, ed. *Unity in Diversity: Current Trends in Translation Studies.* Manchester: St Jerome Publishing. 3–13.

Wadley, Lyn, ed. 1997. *Our Gendered Past: Archaeological Studies of Gender in Southern Africa.* Johannesburg: Witwatersrand University Press.

Walker, Cherryl. 1979. *The Woman's Suffrage Movement in South Africa.* Cape Town: Centre for African Studies, University of Cape Town.

———. 1982. *Women and Resistance in South Africa.* London: Onyx.

———. 1990a. "Gender and the Development of the Migrant Labour System c.1850–1930" in Cherryl Walker, ed. *Women and Gender in Southern Africa to 1945.* Cape Town: David Philip; London: James Currey: 168–196.

———. 1990b. "The Women's Suffrage Movement: The Politics of Gender, Race and Class" in Cherryl Walker, ed. *Women and Gender in Southern Africa to 1945.* Cape Town: David Philip; London: James Currey. 313–345.

———. ed. 1990c. *Women and Gender in Southern Africa to 1945.* Cape Town: David Philip; London: James Currey.

———. 1991. *Women and Resistance in South Africa.* 2nd ed. Cape Town and Johannesburg: David Philip; New York: Monthly Review Press.

Wallace, Marion. 1998. "'A Person Is Never Angry for Nothing,' Women, VD and Windhoek" in Patricia Hayes, Jeremy Sylvester, Marion Wallace, Wolfram Hartmann with Ben Fuller, Jr., eds. *Namibia under South African Rule, Mobility and Containment 1915–46.* Oxford: James Currey; Windhoek: Out of Africa; Athens: Ohio University Press. 77–94.

Walton, Marion Nicole. 1997. *Empire, Nation, Gender and Romance: The Novels of Cynthia Stockley (1872–1936) and Gertrude Page (1873–1922).* Unpublished

M.A. Thesis. Dept. of English Language and Literature, University of Cape Town.

Ward, Kerry Ruth and Nigel Worden. 1998. "Commemorating, Suppressing, and Invoking Cape Slavery" in Sarah Nuttall and Carli Coetzee, eds. *Negotiating the Past: The Making of Memory in South Africa*. Cape Town: Oxford University Press. 201–217.

Waterston, Jane Elizabeth. 1983. *The Letters of Jane Elizabeth Waterston, 1866–1905*. Cape Town: Van Riebeeck Society.

WEAVE. 2000. *WEAVE'S INK @ BOILING POINT*. Cape Town: WEAVE.

Wells, Julia C. 1983. "Why Women Rebel: Women's Resistance in Bloemfontein (1913) and Johannesburg (1956)." *Journal of Southern African Studies*, 10(1): 55–70.

———. 1993. *We Now Demand! The History of Women's Resistance to Pass Laws in South Africa*. Johannesburg: Witwatersrand University Press.

———. 1998. "Eva's Men: Gender and Power in the Establishment of the Cape of Good Hope, 1652–74." *Journal of African History* 39: 417–437.

Wicomb, Zoë. 1992. "Nation, Race and Ethnicity: Beyond the Legacy of Victims." *Current Writing* 4: 15–20.

———. 1995. "Reading, Writing and Visual Production in the New South Africa." *Journal of Commonwealth Literature* 30(2): 1–15.

———. 1996. "To Hear the Variety of Discourses" in M. J. Daymond, ed. *South African Feminisms: Writing, Theory and Criticism 1990–1994*. New York and London: Garland 45–56.

———. 1998. "Shame and Identity: The Case of the Coloured in South Africa" in Derek Attridge and Rosemary Jolly, eds. *Writing South Africa: Literature, Apartheid, and Democracy, 1970–1995*. Cambridge: Cambridge University Press. 91–107.

———. 2000. *David's Story*. Cape Town: Kwela Books; reprinted 2001 with "Afterword" by Dorothy Driver. New York: The Feminist Press.

Wildenthal, Lora. 2001. *German Women for Empire, 1884–1945*. Durham and London: Duke University Press.

Wilentz, Gay. 1992. *Binding Cultures: Black Women Writers in Africa and the Diaspora*. Bloomington and Indianapolis: Indiana University Press.

Wilson, Monica and Archie Mafeje. 1963. *Langa: A Study of Social Groups in an African Township*. Cape Town: Oxford University Press.

Wilson, Monica and Leonard Thompson. 1969. *The Oxford History of South Africa*. (2 vols.). Oxford: Clarendon Press.

Whitlock, Gillian. 1996. "A 'White-Souled State': Across the 'South' with Lady Barker" in Kate Darian-Smith, Liz Gunner, and Sarah Nuttall, eds. *Text, Theory, Space: Land, Literature and History in South Africa and Australia*. London and New York: Routledge. 65–80.

Wright, Marcia. 1993. *Strategies of Slaves and Women: Life-Stories from East/Central Africa*. New York: L. Barber Press; London: James Currey.

Young, Robert. 1902. *African Wastes Reclaimed: The Story of the Lovedale Mission*. London: J. M. Dent.

Zenani, Nongenile Masithathu. 1992. *The World and the Word: Tales and Observations from the Xhosa Oral Tradition*. Edited with an introduction and commentary by Harold Scheub. Madison: University of Wisconsin Press.

Zimbabwe Women Writers. 2000. *Women of Resilience: The Voices of Women Ex-Combatants*. Harare: Zimbabwe Women Writers.

NINETEENTH CENTURY

Anonymous, SONG OF THE AFFLICTED

Lesotho 1842   Sesotho

"Song of the Afflicted" is a lament that falls within the nexus of traditional warfare in Lesotho. Departure for battle involved strengthening rituals meant to discourage cowardice and celebrate the brave deeds of warriors. Such rituals, and the songs, poetry, and dances that went with them, focused almost exclusively on men even though some may have been led by such warrior queens as 'Manthatisi of the Batlokoa. The songs and poems go by the generic name of "mokorotlo," which Thomas Mofolo describes in his novel, *Chaka* (1925), as songs of men, songs of war.

Return from battle similarly involved "cleansing" rituals, the purpose of which was, among other things, to mourn the fallen. "Song of the Afflicted" belongs here, although it was performed on other occasions as well. Thomas Arbousset, the collector of this song in 1836, points out that it was "particularly dear to widows," who, when someone had died, gathered outside the village to sing and dance it in chorus to the accompaniment of a goatskin drum.

Oral literature of this kind borrows freely from accessible communal material, and even lone oral artists invent and expand their repertoire in response to the comments, gestures, and exclamations of their audience. Thus they incorporate the group experience into their work. Furthermore, various artists sing sections of such texts differently. For example, Arbousset notes that the line, "Oh! That I might fly thither," is quite elaborate in some renditions:

Why have I not wings to fly to heaven?
Why does there not come down from heaven a twisted rope?
I would cling to it; I would mount on high,
I would go and live there.

In *The Unwritten Song* (1966), Willard A. Trask refers to Henri A. Junod's observation in 1913 that the Thonga people, who live on the border between South Africa and southern Mozambique, perform a similar song, "Oh! How I should love to plait a string, and go to heaven, I would find rest."

"Song of the Afflicted" predates Western influence in Lesotho. The cultural references in it are purely Sesotho, unlike those in the wedding songs from Botswana that contrast the bitterness of marriage and the sweetness of cakes (see the example in the final section of this volume). Arbousset collected this song three years after his arrival in Lesotho as one of the first three missionaries to proselytize there at the invitation of the king of the Basotho.

Leloba Molema

✦

Older widows:
We are left outside!
We are left to grief!

We are left to despair,
Which only makes our woes more bitter!
Would that I had wings to fly up to the sky!
Why does not a strong cord come down from the sky?
I would tie it to me, I would mount,
I would go there to live.

The new widow:
O fool that I am!
When evening comes, I open my window a little,
I listen in the silence, I look:
I imagine that he is coming back!

The dead man's fighting sister:
If women, too, went to war,
I would have gone, I would have thrown darts beside him:
My brother would not be dead:
Rather, my mother's son would have turned back half way,
He would have pretended he had hurt his foot against a stone.

All the women:
Alas! Are they really gone?
Are we abandoned indeed?
But where have they gone
That they cannot come back?
That they cannot come back to see us?
Are they really gone?
Is the underworld insatiable?
Is it never filled?

Transcribed by Thomas Arbousset
Translated by Willard Trask

Kaatje Nieuwveldt, TESTIMONY
South Africa 1858   Dutch

In 1858 a woman of Khoekhoe descent named Kaatje Nieuwveldt appeared before
a commission convened by the Cape parliament to hear land claims at the Kat River
settlement in the Eastern Cape. Against considerable odds, she had come to lodge
a complaint of maladministration against the white magistrate, Louis Meurant.

The 1850s were a time of great turbulence in the Kat River settlement. Indeed,
this settlement had occasioned controversy from the outset. Created in 1829 for people of Khoekhoe descent by the British colonial government on land taken from the

Xhosa leader Maqoma, the Kat River settlement had originally been designed by colonial administrators as a reservoir of troops and a buffer zone between white and Xhosa settlements. Many Khoekhoe settlers, in contrast, saw their settlement as a means of restoring at least some of the land of which they felt they had been dispossessed. They also thought that this particular piece of land was rightfully theirs, because they remembered that their ancestors had lived there before Xhosa conquest. White evangelical sponsors promoted the Kat River settlement as a showpiece of "civilized" black agrarian settlement. The tensions between these visions had become unsustainable by the 1850s in the context of mounting struggles over land.

During two wars between the colony and the Xhosa, in 1834–1835 and 1846–1847, Kat River settlers fought for the colony (of which they were citizens in colonial law). In both wars, much of the Kat River settlement was burned down and settlers lost crops and stock. In 1850, when Xhosa warriors again attacked the colony, many Kat River settlers, like many other colonial Khoisan people similarly pushed to the limits of loyalty, supported the Xhosa rather than the white colony. From 1850 to 1853, people from the Kat River settlement thus fought on both sides in this brutal conflict.

Extensive dispossession of rebels for treason by the colonial state marked the immediate aftermath of the war. Land previously reserved for Khoekhoe settlement (at least in theory, if certainly not in practice) was now opened up for white ownership and allowed to enter the colonial land market. Two Khoekhoe activists, Andries Hatha and Hendrik Heyn, successfully argued that Roman Dutch law did not permit the state to remove land for treason. In consequence a second commission of inquiry was reluctantly convened in 1858 to hear appeals for the return of land and to grant compensation where necessary. Unless individuals had written title, however, the commission dispossessed them if they had not adequately developed their land and house in a "civilized" manner according to the supposed original terms of the land grants. The records of the 1858 commission imply, when read between the lines, that the magistrate of the settlement, Louis Meurant, had long indulged in corrupt practices as he redistributed land to whites and helped define who was a "rebel."

Kaatje Nieuwveldt was the daughter of a rebel, July Rooiberg. She herself spent a week with the rebels (according to her father's testimony), but returned to Eland's Post, where the government had ordered all loyal women, children, and noncombatant men to convene. In common with other rebels, Rooiberg was dispossessed of his *erf* (plot) after the war. He appealed for its return in 1858 but the commission refused on the grounds that he did not have written title and had not adequately developed the land. After his eviction, Rooiberg went to live with his daughter, who had inherited the adjoining erf from her husband, after the latter had been killed by Xhosa troops during the 1846–1847 war.

Nieuwveldt appeared before the 1858 commission. She accused Meurant, whose servant she had been, of having first granted her Rooiberg's erf, but then illegitimately handing it over to a British settler, Daniel Stewart, and arranging to have her crops plowed under. In other testimony not reproduced here, Daniel Stewart (also spelled "Stuart" in the document) and his brother-in-law John Hannah claimed that Stewart had been granted Rooiberg's land in late 1854 by the deputy surveyor general, when Nieuwveldt thought the land was still hers. Stewart said he sowed oats in 1855 but did not reap them as horses destroyed the crop. In 1856, he argued, Nieuwveldt took advantage of his temporary absence to plow and sow her own crops on the land. Whatever the truth, Stewart certainly allowed Nieuwveldt's crop to ripen and then plowed it under. As Stewart approached with his plow, Nieuwveldt asked him, according to Stewart's testimony, "Whether I was a man of peace I said yes, & she then asked me if I was going to Plough up the crops—I said yes—& she replied she would see further about it." In response to Stewart's claim that she had not objected when he first plowed the disputed land himself, Nieuwveldt returned to tell the commissioners, "When Daniel Stewart first ploughed that part of the erf which was open I immediately went to the Magistrate who in my presence told Hannah to tell Stewart not to interfere with what I had done."

In a second case, Nieuwveldt further accused Meurant of failing to do justice in the case of a conflict between herself and a white neighbor, Jan Andries Buekkes, over the ownership of fruit trees. The fight was bitter: Buekkes testified that when he tried to prevent Nieuwveldt's daughter from picking apples, Nieuwveldt "replied I must not come and speak as they did not belong to me, and swore at me, saying the farmers only came in here to rob the Blacks."

At the time, as Nieuwveldt's suit suggests, there was great tension at the settlement. Deep resentment between whites and blacks, rebels and loyalists, and indeed Khoekhoe and loyalist Mfengu settlers predominated, as social worlds were destroyed and power relations reconfigured. Many had lost their families and goods in the rebellion. Many others had been dispossessed of their land. British and Afrikaner settlers were moving into the settlement or hoarding land for speculation. Nieuwveldt's testimony points to ethnic tension in the settlement and the importance of struggles over land. Her deposition also underscores the strength of mind of a particular individual: At a time of much trouble she refused to be intimidated and demanded justice for herself. The final ruling of the commission supported Meurant, and, despite some criticism of Stewart and Buekkes, largely endorsed their respective versions of events.

The two cases also tell us something about the position of widows in the settlement. Nieuwveldt wanted to farm; she indeed turned down a position as a full-time servant to do so. She used a range of survival strategies, depending on men (including white men) to plow for her and perhaps on the cash income from service. She clearly considered herself a good farmer, as she contrasted her impressive crops with Daniel Stewart's miserable yield of a few oats destroyed by drought. She was embedded in family networks and took care of kin. She commanded the labor of her children and the support of some local Khoekhoe men. Nieuwveldt had to fight, however, against men who had the physical means (axes and plows) to invade what she saw as her property, as well as against the local corruption of the magistrate Meurant and the wider colonial state, which was determined to break up Khoekhoe settlement.

Nieuwveldt almost certainly spoke in Dutch (on its way to becoming Afrikaans). Her text has therefore been triply mediated: by the process of recording in writing her oral testimony, by its translation into English by the court, and by the interposition of questions, which are invisible to the current reader. To take just one example, when Nieuwveldt says she was married to her husband, she is almost certainly responding to a direct question about whether her relationship had been sealed in a church ceremony (a question seemingly posed to most female witnesses before this commission). She is therefore responding here to the concern of commissioners that she have legal title in colonial law to her land, and that she fulfill white norms of respectability. Despite these caveats, a sense of Nieuwveldt's strong personality and determination to resist colonial encroachment does emerge, particularly taken in conjunction with the testimony of other witnesses. (Note: Some periods have been inserted in the often run-on text of the handwritten court translation of Nieuwveldt's testimony. Otherwise the punctuation appears here as in the original document.)

Elizabeth Elbourne

✦

I presented a memorial to Govt in which I complained of Mr Meurant the Magistrate.

I was an erf holder in the settlement [at Kat River] at the time Mr Meurant came here—an erf had been allotted to my husband by Mr Hertzog. No. 10 & N. 220 Extent 3 Morgen.

My husband's name was Brander Nieuwveldt. I was married to him, he was murdered by the Kaffirs in the commencement of the war of 1846.

When Mr Meurant came to the Kat River I was engaged to him as servant. I told him that I was an erfholder and that I could only engage myself 'till the Levies were disbanded and my fieldcornet should return to his ward when I would wish to go back to my erf. He asked me whether I could not get some person to work the erf for me, and suggested Jan Fourie who came with me to Mr Meurant but said that he could not do it, and Mr Meurant then said to me "Kaatje then I must take your work upon myself, as a father["]; I then agreed to take service with him; after being some time with Mr M. I told him that I wanted to Plough as it was the season for putting in Indian Corn (Mealies). Mr M then said that he would provide me with seed, Plough & oxen if I would find Leader & Driver; he asked me at the same time whether I was the only child of my father; my father's name is July Rooiberg. He was an erfholder but had forfeited his erf, he is still alive & I know that he has been before this commission to claim it. I told Mr M that I was the only child. This was in the presence of my father at Mr M.'s house. He asked both my father and Jan Paardewagte who was likewise present whether I have spoken the truth & they both confirmed it; Mr M. then said "Kaatje as Magistrate I will give you your father's erf because he has forfeited it for rebellion"; the erf of my father was the one next to mine; the second day after this both the erven were ploughed as far as there was sufficient seed, Mr M. having provided everything he promised. The seed he gave was half a bucket of Mealies. I gathered the Crops. I lived for about 6 months with Mr M. as his servant and then went to reside upon my own erf my father being with me. The second year Mr Scollings ploughed for me and the third year Mr Whittle and it was the crop then standing on the erf which had belonged to my father that Mr M. caused to be ploughed up. There was on it an acre (strip) of land on which two buckets of wheat had been sown; also an acre of Barley being likewise two buckets of seed / an acre on which an acre of Mealies had been sown (a bucket of Mealies) also an acre pumpkins on which 5 quarts of seed had been sown; all these things were sown at the same time but cannot say in what month. When Mr Meurant had it ploughed over the Barley was fit to cut; I had told my son to begin to cut the next day. Within a week after that the wheat also would have been fit to cut; the Mealies were not ripe but fit to eat, and the Pumpkins half grown; & the whole of it was destroyed by being ploughed over; Daniel Stewart ploughed it. Jackalls son of Elias Sauls was the driver; the leader's name I do not know. I knew nothing of Mr Meurant's intentions till my son in law Saul Solomon brought me a message from Daniel Stewart that Mr M had ordered the land to be ploughed over. I then went to Mr M.'s office. Mr Gould accompanied me, and one Flannagin was in the office at the time, there was no one else present; Mr M. asked me what I wanted, & I told him the message I had got from Daniel Stewart and that I had come to enquire whether it was the truth. Mr Meurant replied "yes it is true" and he then asked me from whom have you got the erf of your father. I replied from you Sir. He jumped up & said it is a lie and put me out of the office himself, and I told him that if Daniel Stewart ploughed my land over, I would complain of him. Mr M———. The following day Daniel Stewart came and ploughed over the land and destroyed the whole of the crops. Stewart sowed nothing on it but half a muid of Oats the same day but he never reaped anything because he did not attend to it, & it failed from drought. And since then a Mr J. Hannah sowed one crop of Mealies on the erf which he has just reaped.

I have also in my Memo to Govt. complained that Mr M as Magistrate did not take notice of a complaint which I made before him against Jan Buekkes. On a certain day I cannot say when I sent my daughter Eva to gather some Apples from the trees standing on my own erf not on my father's. Jan Buekkes who was then living on the other side of the river came to me and asked me how I dared send my child into the trees for apples without his permission. I told him they were my trees, which my late husband had planted, and that I did not see that I wanted his permission. He then said that Mr M the Magistrate had given him the trees. I replied the Magistrate could not have been aware that they were mine & Buekkes said to shew me that they were his trees he would get his axe and cut down all of them; he then immediately got his axe and began to cut them down. When I asked Saul Solomon and Jack Andries to go with me and witness what Buekkes was doing I again told Buekkes that they were my trees, and [he] came towards me and held the axe up to my head in a threatening manner at same time using threatening language towards me, said he would cut down all the trees and he did cut down as many trees (apple, peach & fig) as there are notches on the stick I now produce (47) all fruit bearing trees; he was still cutting the trees when I went to Mr Meurant the Magistrate and complained of it; after hearing me, he told me to go home & he would send for me and my Field Cornet. Three weeks had elapsed without my hearing anything of it when I again went to the Magistrate & repeated my complaint. He said he had had so much to do that he could not have attended to it, but I must go home & he would summons me and Buekkes. We were summonsed, and I with my father July Rooiberg and the boer (Buekkes) were before the Magistrate, who asked if I had any witnesses to prove that my husband had planted the trees & I named Jan Skip and William de Klerk. The Magistrate then asked my father who also told him that my late husband had planted those trees; the Magistrate observed that Buekkes said they had been planted by David Prins—my father said that was not the case. Upon this we were dismissed and I had to go home without hearing anything more about it. Buekkes had at the time two erven adjoining each other, formerly Jan Rooi's and Jan de Beer.

I brought this case before the Governor when he was here when he was at Eland's Post (9 February 1855). The trees cut down were all in one row.

My father joined the rebellion, but I remained at home at Eland's Post.

Transcriber and translator unknown

Emma Sandile,
LETTERS AND LAND SUBMISSION
South Africa 1860–1883   English

In 1858 Emma, the daughter of Sandile, senior Xhosa chief in British Kaffraria, was sent to be educated in Cape Town. Her letters stand as the earliest known writing in English by a Xhosa female. As royals, Emma and her two brothers were selected to be "hostages for the peace and prosperity of their country," as defined in a letter from Robert Gray, first Anglican bishop of Cape Town, to the colonial secretary in London (University of Witwatersrand Archives, Gray Collection, vii, 1859–1861). This was the period between the Seventh and Eighth Frontier Wars in the Cape Colony, where the British engaged in battle with the Xhosa for land ownership and political power. As products of the liberal and Christian education provided them, first in the home of Robert and Sophy Gray, and then in the newly established Zonnebloem College in Cape Town, Emma Sandile and particularly her elder brother, Gonya, who was his father's heir, were also expected by the British colonial church and state to have a vast influence over the Xhosa people. As a potential wife and mother, Emma Sandile had special value as the bearer of British culture into the African home.

At sixteen, accompanied by two age-mates as was appropriate for a girl of her status, she entered Zonnebloem College, joining a group of eighteen boys. Besides the religious instruction meted out to both groups, the girls were at first taught only cooking and sewing. They mended the boys' clothing and hemmed towels and sheets. After a year a trained teacher was hired for the girls, and their education somewhat improved. Sandile was baptized about six months thereafter.

As her first letter shows, she begged the governor of the Cape, Sir George Grey, to allow her to go home for a short time. Her request was refused for fear she might marry a non-Christian, and there followed a tussle between the bishop and Emma's father, who indeed wished her to marry a neighboring chief who had offered a generous *lobola* (bride-price). The bishop prevailed, later arranging Sandile's betrothal to Ngangelizwe (called Qeya—his boyhood name—by the government authorities), paramount chief of the neighboring Thembu, the most powerful chiefdom beyond the Xhosa-Cape frontier. Ngangelizwe had shown an interest in Christianity and with Sandile's encouragement might have become a useful and loyal link between the British and the Thembu.

Despite the interventions of Joseph Cox Warner, resident Thembu agent at Glen Gray, the marriage arrangements came to naught, partly because Ngangelizwe's people wished him to have numerous progeny and thus more than one wife, partly because Ngangelizwe wished Sandile to wear not a white wedding dress but a kaross, her skin to be smeared with red ochre, and her arms adorned with brass. Writing to her former schoolmistress, Matilda Smart, who had come to Zonnebloem in 1862, on the occasion of the visit to Glen Grey of the new governor of the Cape, Sir Philip Wodehouse, Sandile suggests also another reason: Ngangelizwe wished to be married by the Wesleyan priest, Rev. Peter Hargreaves, rather than the Anglican bishop, Henry Cotterill of Grahamstown.

Sandile's social position became more and more precarious. After teaching at St. Philip's mission in Grahamstown, she married a minor Mqwathi chief, Stokwe, son of Ndlela, now settled in Indwana in Emigrant Thembuland. She was his second wife (he had probably ten wives in all) but became *nkosikazi* (primary wife) by virtue of her royalty. Now quite cut off from the Christian church, Sandile became alienated from the Thembu as well, who accused her of being an accessory to Stokwe's death at the hands of the British. (Stokwe had led an anti-British revolt.) Sandile's last letter to the magistrate Charles Levey (recently appointed Thembu agent after Warner's departure), followed by her statement to the land commission, shows her petitioning the colonial authorities for the farmland her husband had bequeathed her so that she could do what duty demanded in the way of protecting her children and various cowives. Successful in her claim, and still owning a farm at Cwaru in the Middledrift district in the Ciskei, she managed just before her death in 1892 or 1893 to leave land to her four daughters and one son. But she brought up none of them to be Christians. Following the convention of her time, Emma spells her patronymic as Sandilli rather than Sandile. (Information in this headnote is derived from Janet Hodgson, *Princess Emma* [1987].)

Dorothy Driver

✦

To Sir George Grey, 2 November 1860

My Lord Governor. I want to ask if you please sir to let me go back to see my parents for a short time and I will come back again I will not stop any longer. It is because I do desire to see my own land again I beg you to let me go to see my parents and if you do let me go I shall never for get your kindness. I should be so please to see my Mother's face again. I beg you do let me go my Lord Governor of your kindness I am quite sure that you will, I cannot do as I like now because you are in my fathers place if you do listen to my ask I am sure I do not know what I shall do, because I cannot do any thing for you, and you can do so much for me.

Emma Sandilli.

To Bishop Gray, 3 January 1864

My dear Lord Bishop,

I write to you as a child to her parents and I am sure I need not called you any other way but my father. I have been brought under your care, and was Baptized and Confirmed by your own hands. I am sure I am almost in great hope that although I am not near you still you could do anything for anybody nor matter who they are you show your kindness to them even to us black boys and girls. Really my Lord your kindness to me has been more than my own father would do to me, and when I think that perhaps I shall see you no more in this world, it reminds me of those words which you spoke in the day of our Confirmation and when you turned round to me and said to you my child who are going back to your own country among the heathens.

I could cry now only because I am afraid I should perhaps never see you again both you and Mrs. Gray. She is king hearted, and if you be kind enough to give my love to the young ladies and tell them that I take great pride in them which I hope they will always do the same to everybody. I am not forgotten them yet and I never will.

And also I wish to tell you that I am glad to see my friends again and they come in great numbers almost every day to see me and the Bishop allows them to come. And I am sure he is very kind to me indeed both of them, and I like them very well indeed. But although I am very sorry to be away from you, man and woman you can see them coming up and then they all sit down on the grass, and I must go round and shake hands with them and you can see them put their hands in their mouths saying how fat you are what makes you fat? And to let me sit down no they like to see me stand all the while and when they goes away then they all kiss my hand.

And as for this young gentleman I come to see, I have not seen him yet, and by this time I hope to see my home and see all those that I left behind me which I shall be very glad to see them again here. I am not going to stay with them not more than two weeks and the Bishop is going to take me down to see Mr Owner [Warner]. I think that is his name is it not?

I am your dutiful servant, Emma.

To Bishop Gray, 14 January 1864

My Lord Bishop,

I was very glad to get a kind letter from you because I look upon you as a father and a child. I am not ashamed to write to you or afraid to say anything because I don't see why should I hid it from you, a dear parent to me like you. Never could I forget you as long as God keep my life, and untill death may part us both. I would in pleasure write to you when I have seen Qeya but I have not seen him yet and when ever I see him by God's Mercy I will write to you about him and what I think of him.

Oh! it is a blessing indeed to know the way of salvation and do those things that are pleasing in the side of God who by his great Mercy gave us His only son Jesus Christ to die for the whole world that whosoever believeth in Him shall never die but have everlasting life. I am sorry my Lord to be away from you and I know that you are very much put [out] about me, because I might do as my Countrymen are as you say in your kind letter and do as they do, because they know not the word of God which is the bread of our souls, and what would I asked you more than anything else is your prayer for me and a blessing that the blessing of God Almighty may be upon me, and your blessing also.

I am not in the least afraid to write to you because why? because there is no need of it, was I not brought under your care? Yes I was and I was also Baptized and Confirm by your own hands and what more could I fear, when you are my father. I am not afraid to called you my Father because you allowed me to call you Father. And I hope you will always write to me because it makes me so happy to get letters from you.

And also I must let you know that I am going to Mr Owner [Warner] the gentleman you told me to go to though I don't think I spelt his name right. And please let me know if the ladies are quiet well. I don't mean every lady in the land which could be found but those I knew in your place and in Zonnebloem. And also I wished to ask you one thing if you wont mind me asking you is about my brother being Baptise because I should like him to be because I am.

I have not much to say to you only you dont forget me in your prayers and think about me in the Holy meetings I mean in the Church. And also I should be glad if you where to tell me what you dont think I ought not to write, but I hope I have write nothing to displease you and if you tell me I will try to do better next time when I write to you again if we are all well. I am sorry I cant tell you how do I like Grahams Town because I have not been through it only just round a little way and turn back again. And I am glad to tell you that I am in good health.

And what do you think my friends want me to do, to put a handchief round my head because they say I look better than nothing at all. I told them that I dont want it round my head because I am not used to it now, and I am sure when ever they comes they say the same thing and I don't know what to do!! Oh! but they do make me laugh. And now I must end my long letter,

I am your dutyful servant, Emma.

To Miss Smart (Emma's former schoolmistress), 26 March 1864

My dear Mother,

I was very glad indeed to get a letter from you, and also I was sorry to hear that my cat had been sick, and I hope that when you give it away you will give it to someone who will be kind to it—Mrs Warner's sister (Miss Stanford) is teaching me to play on the Seraphine, and I am sure she tries all she can do for me, and I shall be sorry to part with her now.

And also I must tell you that I have seen the young chief, he is a tall fine young man, and I must let you know that the marriage is going to take place. Oh! how I wish that you could be here and see him take my hand

and kiss it, and I love him to, I am sure you would like him if you were to see him, and you would be quiet amused with him.

I have got so smart since you saw me. I have golden earrings in my ears, crochet lace round my petticoats, high heelboots, a net and ribbons on my head, but I hope I shall never be proud although they like to see me dressed nicely yet they always tell me that dress must not make me vain.

I was very glad to see the Governor and his son at Glen Grey, but very much disappointed that Lady Wode House was not with him. I saw more Kaffirs on that day than I ever seen in my life they all come on horseback to salute the Governor, the young chief Qeya was here also and the Governor was very much pleased with him and the Governor congratulated me on the conquest I had made and kindly promised to fournish our house for us and he told me that whatever I needed he would grant it to me and the Governor also said how much I have grown and how nice I looked.

But one thing I think will disappoint you, we are not going to be married by the Bishop, or a Clergyman [Anglican], because Qeya likes to be married by the Revd Mr Hargreaves, and therefore I cannot do anything but submit as my future happiness depends on my husband. I think it right to try and please him in everything that is not wrong. No one here is anxious to change my Faith, Miss Stanford herself belongs to the Church of England. Mr and Mrs Brownlee, and the Revd Tiyo Soga, are coming to the wedding, and that will be very soon. Then I hope I will let you know all about it.

Please give my best love to Warden and Mrs Glover. Tell them that I will try next time to write a few lines to them, and they must not think that I have forgotten them. I have not. I still love them as my parents, which indeed they have been.

And also I was very glad that you have sent me a copy about your Mountain School. I can remember it very well. And again you asked me if you gave me 'B. Wilson on the Communion'. No dear Mother you have not, and I shall be glad if you sent me one.

To Charles Levey, 27 September 1882
Sir, I am the eldest daughter of the late Chief Sandile, and the great wife of the late Chief Stockwe. At the present time I am living under your care. Though you have been very kind to me and my children, yet you know that we have no fixed place which we can call our home. Please ask the Government Commission for Thembuland to recommend to the Government that I should get a small farm for my children, and the wives of the late Chief Stockwe. We do not wish to make a native location, but simply want a small place we can call our own. We wish to be always under your care and protection.

Submission to the Land Commission, Southeyville, 10 February 1883
I want a place to live on; I have five children of my own, one boy, the others are girls; the boy is about twelve years of age. After my husband's death, the

people of his clan smelt me out, accusing me of being instrumental in causing his death. I went into the bush with my mother and Philip [Stokwe's headman], who were faithful to me. Since the war I have been living close to Southeyville, and living on what I could cultivate.

Petrus Mahongo claims a farm which he says my husband granted to him in his lifetime. It is situated in Seplan, next to the land claimed by the missionaries. I know my husband intended giving him a piece, and came to Mr Levey about it. My husband did not intend giving him the piece that he wanted. My husband spoke to me about the land wanted by Mahongo, and told me that was for me. He also said that he had told this to Mr Levey. He told me that I was to live on that land. I never lived on it, because Mahongo placed a Hottentot on it. There was always a difference between my husband and Mahongo about this land. There were no beacons up, but this was assigned to me by my husband, the chief, at my request, and in accordance with our customs. I could never occupy this land owing to Mahongo's people occupying it. I was waiting for the settlement of the dispute. Mahongo has never occupied this land himself; he let it to a Hottentot on the Nabus, and used to send his stock there from the colony. I do not like the place I am on. I should like the place my husband assigned and gave to me, or sufficient of it to live on and maintain my family, and be secured in my possession. I hear Mahongo has a farm in the colony. I know the people of my husband's tribe were very angry at Mahongo having this piece of land. They remonstrated with him, and that is why he did not like giving him the land.

Urieta (Johanna Maria) Kazahendike, GOD'S PEACE AND BLESSING
Namibia 1861   German

Urieta Kazahendike was born in 1836 in central Namibia to one of the many Herero families impoverished by the conflict between Jan Jonker Afrikaner, leader of the Nama, and Tjimuhua, leader of the ovaHerero. Displaced people, most of whom had lost their livestock, gravitated toward the early missions in search of shelter and employment. Kazahendike was about eight years old when she first joined the missionaries Carl Hugo Hahn and Emma Hahn, who worked in Namibia from 1844 to 1872. She attended and later taught in the school established by the Hahns, while working as a domestic servant in their household. Urieta Kazahendike was the first Christian convert among the Herero. She was baptized by Carl Hahn in 1858 and took the name Johanna Maria.

The missionaries were slow to win over converts, and Carl Hahn was hard-pressed to persuade the Rhenish mission society to allow him to continue his evangelizing efforts. Kazahendike accompanied the Hahns to Germany in 1860 where she was quite literally exhibited at religious meetings in Germany as living proof that Hahn's missionary work in Africa had borne fruit. Hahn wrote without elaboration that Johanna was subjected to "many indecencies" during her visit to Germany.

After Kazahendike's return to Namibia, she married the widowed Samuel Gertze, an employee of Carl Hahn, in 1864, and cared for his eight children in addition to the nine of her own that she bore during her fifteen-year marriage. After her husband's death in 1879 she worked as a midwife and pharmacist until shortly before her own death in 1936. She is remembered and spoken of with great admiration and respect today. In 1998 her portrait was used for a special series of stamps that honored Namibian women of the past.

Kazahendike was a woman of great linguistic ability: She spoke Dutch, German, English, and Nama, in addition to her mother tongue, Herero. In Germany, she continued to be an invaluable but unacknowledged editor and translator for the Herero-German grammar and dictionary that earned Hahn an honorary doctorate. She also worked on the translation of religious material from German into Herero and on a series of nine Herero books that enhanced Hahn's reputation considerably.

Kazahendike's letter to the Hahns, written while she was waiting to sail alone from Amsterdam to Cape Town, reveals both her anxiety and loneliness. She had accompanied the Hahns to Germany for an extended period but left only oblique glimpses of her perceptions of her relationship with the Hahns and her stay in Germany. This letter survives only in Carl Hahn's reports (*Berichte*). The surname Scheudeke that appears in the signature to the letter is a printer's misinterpretation of Kazahendike.

Diane Hubbard

✦

God's Peace and Blessing be with you.

Beloved in God.

Today I went to the home of the blind and was astonished to see their work, because it was more beautiful than the work of people who can see. Stockings and other items which they had made were very neat. When they displayed their happiness, however, my heart was filled with mourning. They can also sing very well and two boys played four-handed on the piano. The girls also sing very well. Now I am staying with Mr Oostmeyer and the tiny bedroom in which I sleep is very similar in size to the one in Gåtersloh; I also have a similar board for the books here, just like over there. God has helped me and consoled my heart and dried my tears, and I thank Him, that He in His mercy has strengthened me.

I want to tell you something. The night after the day I left you, my heart was heavy when I lay down to sleep. I prayed and fell asleep. During the night I screamed loudly in my sleep and woke up; but it was a dream and I was glad that it was only a dream. Then I fell asleep again and I heard a voice which said to me: Don't cry, for behold you have prayed that you want to be comforted.

Well, Jesus has given me strength, and not only today: He will always give it, if I just surrender myself to Him. He is always nearby, He is my leader in death and in life. He satisfies my hunger and thirst. Jesus, make me hunger and thirst for You and for Your word. Jesus, feed me and quench my thirst with Your wounds and Your death. Jesus Christ, in Your great mercy, take me and hold me. You who are the same yesterday and today, in eternity and in splendour. May He hold you and me. Amen.

I thank you very much, dear teacher, for your letter which made me very happy. I received it while I was busy writing to all of you. Yes, I shall always think of you and put myself in the hands of God, and take my refuge, like a child with its mother, in Him in all things.

At the beginning I was very frightened at the thought of the ship; but now I have put myself in the hands of God and I can say: Jesus, do whatever You please, just let me believe and deliver me from evil. Amen.

Farewell, very beloved in God. God bless you in Jesus Christ our Lord, in whom we have salvation, redemption and forgiveness of all our sins.

Give my regards to everyone I know, the widows etc. etc.; also in Barmen in the children's and mission home. The brides send their regards.

I have forgotten to tell you that I received some written words (by the blind people) when I went to the home of the blind. I am sending them to you. Farewell again and stay very, very well.

I am your servant
Johanna Scheudeke

Translated by Mara Miller

Eliza M., ACCOUNT OF CAPE TOWN

South Africa 1863   isiXhosa

St. Matthew's Mission, where Eliza M. attended school, was established in the Eastern Cape in 1854. It was situated at Keiskammahoek in the Ciskei, on the western side of the Kei River, which formed the border between the Cape Colony and the independent African territories to the east, during the first part of the nineteenth century. It was part of a project conceived by two influential figures in the mid–nineteenth century Cape, the governor, Sir George Grey, and the Anglican bishop, Robert Gray (see texts by Emma Sandile earlier in this section). Their intention was to "assimilate" and "civilize" the turbulent border peoples through a program of education, Christianity, and health care. The destruction of African society would also bring laborers to the growing settler community to the west.

Eliza M. was probably one of a group of people known in the nineteenth century as "Fingoes" (Mfengu). These were Xhosa-speaking people whose societies had been destroyed during the turmoil of the early nineteenth century, known sometimes as the "mfecane." While they had found refuge in the Ciskei in the shadow of the Amatola mountains, their right to land and power was insecure. As a result, they formed an alliance with the British. In return for protection and land, they accepted the missionaries and were among the earliest African converts to Christianity in southern Africa. Two of the most prominent African schools in the Cape Colony, Lovedale Institution and St. Matthew's College, were established for them around this time and produced the first modern African political leaders.

The legacy of the missions to the indigenous people of the Eastern Cape was a mixed one. On the one hand their education provided students some access to the world of the white settlers, as clerks, interpreters, or teachers. On the other hand the missionaries, who drew little distinction between Christian teaching and white, middle-class values, imposed a Victorian culture on their students. This was particularly repressive for women who found themselves trained mainly in washing, ironing, sewing, and cooking. The belief of the missionaries that educated men needed educated wives did, however, open some doors to a few mission women, as shown by other texts in this anthology.

The *King William's Town Gazette* was published in a small settler town that had begun life as a military center to protect the frontier. It was one of the many institutions that settlers established as a means of re-creating their former European world. Eliza's article, probably written as a school exercise, would have been published partly because its naivete was amusing to the whites, but also because it was proof of the success of the civilizing policies of the missionaries. It was translated from Xhosa into English by an unknown translator, perhaps one of the missionaries, and first published in the *Gazette*.

Eliza arrived in a Cape Town quite different from the world she had known. Like other visitors to the town, Eliza was intrigued by the exotic dress of the "Malays," often described as the Muslim descendants of the slaves brought to the Cape by the Dutch East India Company in the sixteenth and seventeenth centuries. The name was misleading since none of the slaves came from Malaysia, and Cape Muslim forebears also included the poor of many nationalities who had found homes at the Cape in the preceding two centuries. The term "Slam" (from Islam) was derived from the creole language based on Dutch which had developed in multilingual Cape Town and was later to be formally recognized as Afrikaans.

In multiethnic Cape Town Eliza was confronted with the need to define her own identity. Although Cape Muslims were light-skinned, like many of the Xhosa-speaking peoples, they were clearly not "Kafirs." This term did not have for Eliza the derogatory connotations it later acquired. Although sometimes used for all Africans in South Africa, in the 1850s it often referred specifically to the Xhosa-speaking peoples of the Eastern Cape. On her visit to the South African Museum, Eliza encountered models of much darker-skinned Africans, whose blackness she called "ugly," perhaps out of acquiescence to white missionaries' perception of race. In Cape Town she did, however, encounter some of her own people, including the pupils of Zonnebloem College, a school that had recently been established primarily for the sons of Xhosa chiefs, as part of an assimilationist project, as Emma Sandile's letters show. Some of the chiefs themselves, together with their families, had been brought to Cape Town as political prisoners after their defeat in various frontier wars. This was why the kindly man thought Eliza a prisoner. Even more confusing for Eliza was white usage of the color black. Black as a symbol of mourning was familiar to her but there seems to have been no attempt to explain to her the obscure meaning of May Day festivities or blackface as a form of entertainment.

Eliza's visit coincided with the celebrations on 15 May 1863 to commemorate the Prince of Wales's marriage. As Eliza rightly observed, this was a highly ritualized affair, serving mainly to reinforce the bonds of Britain's growing empire. Such mythic English emblems as Gog and Magog, and Lady Godiva (played by a man), made their appearance. Despite these efforts to inculcate Englishness, the festivities did genuinely incorporate most Capetonians in one way or another, unlike commemorations later in the century when racism was a more powerful force.

Elizabeth van Heyningen

✦

We left East London on the Sunday, while it was raining; the sea was fighting very much, and there were soldiers going to England and their wives. On the Tuesday we arrived at Algoa Bay, and boats came to fetch the people who were going there, and other people came in. The ship went off the same day. A great wind blew, and I thought myself that if it had been another ship, it would not have been able to go on, but in its going, it kept twisting about, it did not go straight, but it went well on the day of our arrival, for the wind was good. We arrived on the Friday. While I was in the ship, I forgot I was on the water, it was like a house inside, but outside it was not like a house. There is everything that is kept at home; there were fowls and sheep and pigs, and slaughtering every day. I kept looking at the thing which makes the ship go. There are two horses inside, made of iron, which make it go; and when I looked inside, it was very frightful. There are many bed-rooms inside. The ship we were in is named the *Norman*, it is a steamer. It was unpleasant when nothing appeared, but when we left the Bay, we saw the mountains till we got to the Cape. One mountain is called the Lion's Head, and another is called Green Point, and I myself saw those mountains. That which is called the Lion's Head, is like a lion asleep. And another mountain above the town is that called Table Mountain; nevertheless it is not like a table, still that name is proper for it.

Before I came into the town, my heart said, "this place is not large," but when I entered it, I wondered, and was afraid. Oh, we slept that day. I have forgotten to relate something I saw the day I arrived. I saw black people, and I thought they were our kind, but they are not; they are Slams, called in English, Malays. Also, I was astonished at their large hats, pointed at the top, and large below. I saw some making baskets of reeds, and I wished I knew how to do it. On the Saturday evening, we went to a shop to buy butter and bread. At night lights were hung up throughout the whole town. I had thought we were going to walk in the darkness. I have not yet seen houses built with grass, like those we live in, they are high beautiful houses. The roads where people walk, are very fine. I have not yet seen a dirty, muddy place in the whole town. On the Sunday, bells sounded; there is one big one, and other small ones; we went to service in the great church.

Early on the Monday, wagons came about to sell things. Really people here get these things for nothing from their owners. A person can get men's trousers for three shilling each, yet in other places a person can never get them for that money. You can get three pairs of stockings for a shilling, a child's cap for a penny; you can get a width of a dress for threepence, if it is five widths, it is a shilling and threepence. There are little wagons, the man who drives the horses sits behind, the proprietor does nothing, he sits so.

Another thing. The shoes of the Malays astonished me. There is a heel, and yonder on before a piece of wood sticks out, and they put it between their toes, and so make a clattering like the Germans. As things are to be got for such little money, how cheap must they be in England!

On Friday I saw a man riding in a wagon, there was a barrel inside and a cross-bar, and the water came out there. I don't know how it came out. It watered the new road, which is being made. And on Tuesday I saw people working at slates, taking off their ends—it was a great heap; the people who were at work were four. On the day of our arrival, a house was burnt, the people escaped, but I don't know whether the goods escaped. There are carts which go every day, carrying earth to throw on the road which is being mended, drawn by one horse.

There is a house where there are all kinds of beasts, and there are figures of black people, as if they were alive; their blackness is very ugly; also the bones of a man when he is dead, and birds and elephants, and lions, and tigers and sea-shells. I was afraid of those people, and the skeleton. There is also an ape holding Indian Corn, and there are monkeys.

In the evening we went out again, we went to the houses of the Malays; we went to see their decorations, for they were rejoicing because their days of fasting were ended. They were very beautiful; they had made flowers of paper, you would never think they were made of paper. We went for the sole purpose of seeing these works. They made a great noise, singing as they walked; you would laugh to see the children dancing outside and clapping their hands.

There are also wagons there for the sale of fish. The proprietors sound a thing like a horn to announce that he who wishes to buy let him buy. There are others for collecting dust-heaps, they ring a bell. There are vehicles to convey two people, he who drives the horses, and he who sits inside. In some there are windows and lights lit at night: those windows are two.

There are not many trees in the town; in some places there are not many at all, but in one place it is like the bush; it is pleasant underneath the trees; there are stools to sit on when a person is tired. That path is very long; I saw two Newfoundland dogs. I did not know that I should ever come to see them when I heard them spoken of. They are dogs with large heads and great long ears; the hair is like sheep's wool, and they have great claws; they are suited to assist people. It seemed as if they could swallow me without chewing; I was very much afraid, but one was not very big, it was about the size of the dogs of black people, when it barks, it says so with a great voice. Also, I saw sheep rather unlike others, in the tail here it was very large, the head was small, and the body was large and fat.

I have forgotten to mention something which I ought to have said before; when I came out of the ship and walked on land the earth seemed to move, and when I entered a house, it seemed to imitate the sailing of a ship, and when I lay down it seemed to move.

I saw an ox-wagon here, but I had not imagined that I should see a wagon.

We go to a very large beautiful Church; I don't forget the people who sing, the English; the prayers are said with thin voices as if it were singing; but the chief thing done is singing frequently, all the while there is continually singing, and then sitting. There is a Kafir school here; I went one day, they were reading; they can read well; there are also carpenters &c.

There is another place besides that which I said is like the bush, and in that place there are trees and flowers, and two fountains; a thing is stuck in, and the water comes out above. I saw the date-tree when it is young; it is one leaf, yet when it is grown, it is a very large tree. In that place there are wild birds, doves are there, and those birds which the English call canaries, and a very beautiful bird, its tail is long, its bill is red.

Yesterday the soldiers had sports, the music-band played, and when they finished playing they fired. They were many, and they fired together. And as we were walking, they fired; I was very much startled and afraid. And to-day they are playing the music. It seems to-day it exceeds in sweetness, I mean its sound.

There came a person here who is a Kafir. I rejoiced very much when I heard that he too was one. He asked me what I had come to do here; I said "I am only travelling." He asked whether I was a prisoner, and I said "No." He said he was very glad, he had thought I was a prisoner. I told him that I was going away again, and he said "May you go in peace, the Lord preserve you well till you arrive whence you came." I never saw a person like him of such kindness; he said he had come here to learn, he came from where I did; but I should not have known him to be a Kafir, and he did not know that I was one.

There are creatures which are eaten; they come from the sea, their name is called crawfish, they are frightful in appearance, yet their flesh is very fine and white.

The person of this house is a dyer of clothes, the white he makes red, and the red green, and the brown he makes black. I saw the wood with which they dye. Soap is cut in pieces, and put in water, and heated and boiled well, and continually stirred. This thing—dyeing clothes, is a great work. Water is even in the house; I don't know where it comes from, a person turns a thing, and fresh water comes out as if it were of a river.

There are also carts for selling meat, and for selling bread. I saw the fire-wagon, I did nothing but wonder. I did not know that it was such a big thing. It is long, with many wheels, they are not so large as those of an ox-wagon; people sit in places inside. The wheels run on metal; I say I could do nothing but wonder very much. I had not thought that it was such a great thing. And when it is about to proceed it says "Sh!" I don't know whether it is the boiling of the water; it hastens exceedingly, a person would be unable to notice it well, yet now some people say that this is a small one which I have seen. If it treads on anything, it must smash it, it is a very great thing. I shall never forget it. Where I saw it, the place was fenced on both sides, and I beheld it from the outside. I entered it another week after I had seen it; we went to Somerset West and slept one night. In the morning we returned by it: when I was inside, the earth seemed to move; it is pleasant to ride inside. I end now although this is not all the news about it. When I was in it, I saw a sugar plant; it is not a large plant, it is short with red flowers. I saw other trees at Somerset West which I had never seen before.

One day I saw people going to a burial, the carriages were black, but that people should wear black clothes is done also among the natives where a person has died; there were stuck up black feathers, and on the graves were placed stones with writing; the name of the person was written, and the years of his age, and the year in which he died.

I have seen to-day another thing which I did not know of, that thing which is said to be always done by white people in this month of May. They make themselves black people, they smear themselves with something black, with red patches on the cheeks; a thing is made with evergreens, and a man is put inside, and two people carry it, and another man carries a pan, and goes begging for money.

Another thing which I saw during the past month, was people going to the Governor's house—little chiefs, and chiefs of the soldiers, some had hats with red and white feathers, and silver coats, and gold swords, and the bishop went too. I heard it said that they were going to hear the things which were about to be spoken by people who had come from Graham's Town, King William's Town, Beaufort, and other places; it was said that these people were going to speak of the state of those towns and the doings of the people who live there. I do not say that those coats were really of gold, I say there was gold on some parts of them, on the arms and the back.

Also I have seen the fruit of the tree which the English call the chestnut; I did not see what the tree is like, the fruit is nice, the outside of it is hard; when you eat it it is sweet and edible like the potato, you can roast it or boil it. There is another fruit called Banana in English, it also is a nice fruit; it is not boiled or roasted, it is eaten like other fruits. There is a great white sweet potato, it is called Sweet Potato; those potatoes are very large, I had never seen them before, they are nearly all long: I do not know whether they are the potatoes named "Medicine" by the Fingoes.

I am puzzled to know how to begin to relate what was done yesterday, but I will try. Yesterday was said to be the wedding-day of the Great Son of Victoria, but it was not really the day of his marriage, for he has been married some time. The thing first done was arranging the children of the schools and I was there too. All walked in threes, going from one street to another. When we left the school-house we took up our station on an open piece of ground, other people climbed on the houses, and others looked on from below. On one house where we were standing there was the figure of a man like a king, a red cloth was put as if it were held by him, it is called in English a flag. Amongst all of us there were flags of different beautiful kinds; we stood there a great while, till we saw a multitude of soldiers and their officers and little chiefs and different sorts of people: one set wore clothes all alike, another had different clothes and ancient hats which were worn by the people of that time. All these now went in front, a very long line, then followed the ranks of another school, and we came after them. When we had finished going through many streets, we went to stand in another open spot of ground. All the time we were walking we were singing the song of Victoria. And there we saw the Governor and his wife; we all saluted. Although it seems that I have written a great deal I have not yet wondered at the things done at night, but let me finish those of the day. We were given food. We saw boats going along with people inside and boys wearing red clothes; there followed one with an old man, his hairs were long and white. There was a woman at his side wearing short clothes. Other boats followed with people in them, all the time they were appearing the drum and trumpets were sounded. I don't know how I shall make myself understood. I never saw such a beautiful thing; some of the men wore short dresses and short coats, and others wore short trousers like those of the French. All these things were red. When we had finished walking we went to stand in an open piece of ground, then we all went home. I do not know if any other things were done.

We went out again in the evening to see the fireworks. First we went into the gardens, where there were what I shall call candles; but nevertheless they are not called so in English. They were lights put inside little red and green glasses—When I was at a distance I thought they were little round things, all these were hung up and fastened in the trees,—there were some large ones and there were others not put in glasses.

We walked and went to a great crowd of people, we could not tell what we should do to see that which we came to see. There we saw a tall man with a high hat, I did not understand how it was made, and another man wearing women's clothes continually playing with that tall man. All these things have their names in English, some were called Punch & Judy, Spectre, Father of the Doomed Arm-chair, or the Maid, the Murderer and the Midnight Avenger, and many other plays besides these. We passed on from that woman and man and went to see white people smeared with soot, they went into a house made of a tent where there were stools, and two came out and spoke to the people saying, "Ladies and gentlemen, come in and see what we have got here inside." Some went in and others did not, afterwards they opened that the people might see; there were black people sitting on chairs and singing. So we left; at the entrance of the garden there was written in letters of fire, "GOD bless Albert and Alexandra." In another place there were other things of fire, that place is called in English the Parade, where there was a thing like a light-house, on all sides there were candles. Some people sent up fire from Table Mountain, others from Green Point, others sent up fire in the midst of the town, it went up and came down again.

Besides these things there was another thing done, an ox was baked whole, the legs were not removed, only the inside and the hoofs. Many tables were set underneath the trees; that ox was intended for the poor people.

I am going to end now; I am very glad that I was brought here to see things which I never thought I should see.

There is another thing which has lately taken place, the birthday of Queen Victoria. Two balloons were made, no one went in them, there were only lights. That sort is called fire-balloons. The first was sent up; it rose very high till it was like a star: I did not see it again where it went. The other reappeared, it did not rise high like the first, it burnt, and fire came down like two stars.

I saw where newspapers are printed; four people were at work. I do not know what I shall say to tell about it. There is a thing which folds the papers and another thing which continually receives them. It made us sleepy.

E. M.

Translator unknown

Anonymous, A MOTHER PRAISES HER BABY

Namibia 1867   KhoeKhoeGowab

This poem was first published in 1867 by the linguist Theophilus Hahn in his report "Die Nama-Hottentotten." The Nama are descended from the Khoekhoe, an autochthonous people of southern Africa, and take their name from the Namib desert in southern Namibia. Many Namas came originally from the southern and southwestern Cape, which they left during the seventeenth and eighteenth centuries to avoid slavery. Others who joined them had lived in southern Namibia for a long time. The two groups shared a cultural and linguistic heritage that enabled their merging into a larger polity known as Nama.

The 1860s were a decade of political upheaval throughout southern and central Namibia. Pressured by British colonialism from the south, the intrusion of German missionaries and traders, and the slow westward movement of the Herero, the Nama polity was also experiencing internal strife. It was changing from being a hunting, gathering, and herding society into a highly militarized one that depended on trading cattle, ivory, and ostrich feathers for guns. Those Nama who traded and had extended contact with European settlers not only came to have knowledge of guns and horses, but also had some mission education, with the result that the leading men were literate. The cultural context of this poem, then, is that of a modernizing elite and a society in transition.

A simmering war between certain Nama clans, particularly those under the so-called lion of the desert, Captain Hendrik Witbooi, and the Herero, led by the great chief Samuel Maharero I, was also a feature of the 1860s. It was a war rich in invective but not very bloody, usually conducted for cattle raiding and less often for land. A man's customary right to a portion of game—and by extension cattle—is taken for granted in the poem.

This praise poem offers insight into women's responsibility for sustaining Nama culture in the face of challenges both internal and external. While the speaker emphasizes male sexuality and reproduction, the male child inherits his clear-sightedness from his mother. Within the extended family and clan, older women were well respected as keepers of knowledge and decision makers. Research suggests that Nama women in the 1890s could hold ownership rights to cattle and usufruct rights to the milk (grazing grounds were not yet privatized). The respect of the son for his mother is foretold here in his bringing her a portion of the cattle he will capture from the Herero.

Yvette Abrahams

You son of a clear-eyed mother,
You far-sighted one,
How you will track game one day,
You, who have strong arms and legs,
You strong-limbed one,
How surely you will shoot, plunder the Herrero,
And bring your mother their fat cattle to eat,
You child of a strong-thighed father,
How you will subdue strong oxen between your thighs one day,
You who have a mighty penis,
How many and what mighty children you will beget!

Transcribed by Theophilus Hahn
Translated by Willard Trask and adapted by Werner Hillebrecht

Lydia Umkasetemba, UNANANA-BOSELE

South Africa 1868   isiZulu

Lydia Umkasetemba (that is, wife of Setemba) performed the story of Nanana for the missionary Henry Callaway in the mid–1850s. Nothing is known about her except that Callaway recorded her name beside ten of the folktales that he published in 1868 under the title *Nursery Tales, Traditions and Histories of the Zulus, in Their Own Words with a Translation into English and Notes*. Most of his other informants were men. Callaway arrived in Natal from London in 1854 and founded the Springvale Mission near the present town of Richmond in KwaZulu-Natal. He later became the incumbent of St. Andrew's Church in Pietermaritz Street, Pietermaritzburg. Setemba, Lydia's husband, was one of his first converts.

In his preface, Callaway explains that when he began learning Zulu in 1856 there was no publication that a student of the language could use, and therefore he taught himself by beginning "to write at the dictation of Zulu natives, as one means of gaining an accurate knowledge of words and idioms." Recognizing that the material he had gathered would be of great use to "the missionary, the philologist, the ethnologist, and antiquarian, as well as to a large portion of the general public," he allowed friends and colleagues to persuade him that it should be published. He also decided that the stories should appear in an English translation, as well as in the original Zulu, so that they could be used to teach "the English Zulu, or the Zulus English." Callaway's nineteenth-century orthography adds the vocative "U" to Lydia's married name of Nanana.

Stories in isiZulu are often derived from proverbs. The originating proverb for "Unanana-bosele" is *"unenkani okweselesele lifun'ukuy'emsamo"* ("a person who is as obstinate as a frog which, when pushed away, keeps returning and hiding in remote areas of the house"). The description of Nanana-Bosele (her name likens her to a frog) as having "willfully built her house in the road trusting to self confidence and superior power" indicates that her stubbornness will prevail in the story. In other Zulu versions of the tale, the monster elephant, rather than the woman, becomes the most important figure. The Zulu versions are concluded so as to reflect a practice known as *ukuxoshisa,* which meant that a heroic deed had to be rewarded. A king would give a particular hero a number of cattle, or even women, as a way of acknowledging a valorous deed. In the various versions, some in other languages of the region, Nanana-Bosele either receives gifts for her heroism in saving the people who had been devoured by the elephant or finds that the people she has saved are willing to serve under her as a way of thanking her. Either way, the storyteller recognizes Nanana-Bosele's bravery.

Because a frog can live both in water and on land, it is a figure of survival in extreme conditions. At a symbolic level this suggests that captivity in the elephant's stomach is a form of death that signals the beginning of a new life cycle. The people imprisoned in the stomach begin to live anew after being redeemed. There is also a moral theme to the story. The elephant is a huge animal compared to Nanana-Bosele—a mere woman-frog—which implies that a small, weak, and seemingly powerless creature should not be underestimated. What is important is intelligence rather than size. Nanana-Bosele proves that determination and persistence can overcome even the most terrifying situations.

N. B. Zondi

✦

There was a woman who had two young children; they were very fine; and there was another child who used to stay with them. But that woman, it is said, had wilfully built her house in the road, trusting to self-confidence and superior power.

On a certain occasion she went to fetch firewood, and left her children alone. A baboon came and said, "Whose are those remarkably beautiful children?" The child replied, "Unanana-bosele's." The baboon said, "She built in the road on purpose, trusting to self-confidence and superior power."

Again an antelope came and asked the same question. The child answered, "They are the children of Unanana-bosele." All animals came and asked the same question, until the child cried for fear.

A very large elephant came and said, "Whose are those remarkably beautiful children?" The child replied, "Unanana-bosele's." The elephant asked the second time, "Whose are those remarkably beautiful children?" The child replied, "Unanana-bosele's." The elephant said, "She built in the road on purpose, trusting to self-confidence and superior power." He swallowed them both, and left the little child. The elephant then went away.

In the afternoon the mother came and said, "Where are the children?" The little girl said, "They have been taken away by an elephant with one tusk." Unanana-bosele said, "Where did he put them?" The little girl replied, "He ate them." Unanana-bosele said, "Are they dead?" The little girl replied, "No. I do not know."

They retired to rest. In the morning she ground much maize, and put it into a large pot with amasi, and set out, carrying a knife in her hand. She came to the place where there was an antelope; she said, "Mother, mother, point out for me the elephant which has eaten my children; she has one tusk." The antelope said, "You will go till you come to a place where the trees are very high, and where the stones are white." She went on.

She came to the place where was the leopard; she said, "Mother, mother, point out for me the elephant which has eaten my children." The leopard replied, "You will go on and on, and come to the place where the trees are high, and where the stones are white."

She went on, passing all animals, all saying the same. When she was still at a great distance she saw some very high trees and white stones below them. She saw the elephant lying under the trees. She went on; when she came to the elephant she stood still and said, "Mother, mother point out for me the elephant which has eaten my children." The elephant replied, "You will go on and on, and come to where the trees are high, and where the stones are white." The woman merely stood still, and asked again, saying, "Mother, mother, point out for me the elephant which has eaten my children." The elephant again told her just to pass onward. But the woman, seeing that it was the very elephant she was seeking, and that she was deceiving her by telling her to go forward, said a third time, "Mother, mother, point out for me the elephant which has eaten my children."

The elephant seized her and swallowed her too. When she reached the elephant's stomach, she saw large forests, and great rivers, and many high lands; on one side there were many rocks; and there were many people who had built their villages there; and many dogs and many cattle; all was there inside the elephant; she saw too her own children sitting there. She gave them amasi, and asked them what they ate before she came. They said, "We have eaten nothing. We merely lay down." She said, "Why did you not roast this flesh?" They said, "If we eat this beast, will it not kill us?" She said, "No; it will itself die; you will not die." She kindled a great fire. She cut the liver, and roasted it and ate with her children. They cut also the flesh, and roasted and ate.

All the people which were there wondered, saying, "O, forsooth, are they eating, whilst we have remained without eating any thing?" The woman said, "Yes, yes. The elephant can be eaten." All the people cut and ate.

And the elephant told the other beasts, saying, "From the time I swallowed the woman I have been ill; there has been pain in my stomach." The other animals said, "It may be, O chief, it arises because there are now so many people in your stomach." And it came to pass after a long time that the elephant died. The woman divided the elephant with a knife, cutting through a rib with an axe. A cow came out and said, "Moo, moo, we at length see the country." A goat came out and said, "Mey, mey, at length we see the country." A dog came out and said, "At length we see the country." And the people came out laughing and saying, "At length we see the country." They made the woman presents; some gave her cattle, some goats, and some sheep. She set out with her children, being very rich. She went home rejoicing because she had come back with her children. On her arrival her little girl was there; she rejoiced, because she was thinking that her mother was dead.

Transcribed and translated by Henry Callaway

Tryn Isaac, AFFIDAVIT

South Africa 1873   Dutch

Tryn Isaac was a well-situated woman in Griqua society. As Adam Kok's niece and a Christian, she belonged to the Griqua elite. She lived on a *werf* (homestead) with her extended family. Everyone on the *werf* recognized Kok's authority; the men formed part of his commando unit assisting on raids and protecting his territory, while the women performed a nurturing and supportive role in this often-violent era. Isaac's affidavit appears to reflect profound family values, since she identifies each of her siblings by name and takes special pride in her brother David's ability to fire accurately, despite his wound.

We presume that Isaac narrated her story in Dutch, and that it was taken down and translated into English by court officials. She tells the story of David's death and indicates where her brother's grave is located. David's grave, known in Afrikaans as *Dawid's graf,* was covered by a few flat stones and a headstone, and was used as a beacon to indicate the division between Kok's and Nicholas Waterboer's territories. The location of this grave was also central to the land disputes between the various Griqua *Kapteins* and the Orange Free State. It was, in addition, widely rumored that the gravestones had been moved a few miles by a Dutch farmer who sought to enhance his land holdings. Disputes over land intensified with the discovery of diamonds in 1868. A commission in 1870 sought to locate *Dawid's graf* and hence to determine who had authority over this diamond-bearing ground. Although the Griqua territories were annexed by the Cape Colony and renamed Griqualand West in 1871, disputes over land ownership continued and Tryn Isaac's affidavit is part of a series of attempts to resolve this matter, as well as the more general issue of authority over the land. Her affidavit was included in a book produced in 1875 by David Arnot (Griqua agent) and Francis H. S. Orpen (the British government's surveyor-general) titled *The Land Question of Griqualand West,* which was intended to help settle claims arising from promises and cessions made before the Griqua territories became British.

Isaac's story may have had a happy ending. James Perkins (the magistrate who heard her affidavit) recommended her in 1873 for a "small pension adequate to [her] daily wants."

Linda Waldman

✦

I am a Christian woman. I was born not far from Cape Town, near Piquetberg, at the farm of one Willem Burgers, where my father, old David Isaac, lived. My mother and the mother of the present chief, Adam Kok, were sisters' children. Our father and all the family emigrated with the first Griqua emigration. He died at Griqua Town. When Adam Kok removed from those parts to Philippolis our family intended following him. We first removed to "Kains," near where Field-cornet du Plooi lives, on the north side of the Riet River, some distance below its junction with the Modder River.

Hostilities broke out between Adam Kok and some Bitterbush Korannas in his district. The men of our "werf" were my husband David, Piet Isaac, Jan Isaac, David Isaac, and Hans Isaac, my four brothers; Cobus Isaac and Paul Isaac, my nephews. My sister Anna, Letta, Lys, and I were also there, as well as the wives of Jan and David Isaac. My brothers, Jan and David Isaac, went to join Adam Kok's commando. After a time one Jan Kok returned from the commando, and brought us news that my brother David Isaac was wounded. The way it happened I heard was this: Adam Kok had beaten the Korannas at Schietmakaar, and David was returning homewards with others when Jan Kok fired a shot at a vulture near to Opperman's farm. Some Korannas in the neighbourhood hearing it, lay in wait for them at a ridge. Setebe, a noted headman among the Korannas, led the party, and was seen and recognized before a shot was fired. He fired, and hit my brother David Isaac below the left knee; my brother staggered, and Setebe cried out, "that hit you," but my brother took aim, fired, and shot him dead; upon which the Korannas carried him off, and our people also carried away my brother David Isaac for some distance, in a "brayed" hide, till he became too weak to carry further, and Jan came on to tell us. On the news arriving, the wagon was prepared, and we started that evening, travelling the whole night. We crossed the Riet River at the drift at the junction, and went up along the road on the south side. It was dawn when we crossed, and about eight o'clock when we reached the place where David Isaac lay, adjacent to the river, and to the left of the road. There were with him Adam Vink, Hendrik Boer, and Jan Isaac. Those who accompanied me in the wagon were Jan Kok, Piet Isaac, Cobus Isaac, Paul Isaac, and my husband David; the women were Anna Isaac, David's wife Fytje, and I. We made a bed for him under the wagon, and put mats round it for shelter. He had been wounded in the left knee as he was kneeling on the other knee to shoot, and the leg bones were split open downwards. About eight o'clock the next morning he died, and he was buried in the afternoon in a grave dug with a spade we had brought. We returned home the next day. The next winter we removed to the little ridge opposite the grave, and close to Jacobsdal, between Jacobsdal and the river. We remained there about a year, and while we were there the small-pox attacked us. It was the same year that Adam Kok had the disease. My eldest sister, Anna, died there, and a Hottentot named Hans, one named Linx, and a Hottentot servant of Piet Isaac. My sister was buried opposite to my brother David's grave, on the other side of the Riet River. During the time we stayed there I often came across to my brother David's grave. We afterwards left, and went with the wagons from that spot down to between the two rivers, near the junction, where we crossed at a drift, and from there we moved to Philippolis. There is now a house there on the north side of the drift, a little above the present Police Camp. Many years afterwards, when Adam Kok went with a commission to Nomansland, before the emigration to that country, I came to visit my brother David's grave with my late brother Jan Isaac and my late husband; we were on our way to visit friends in Namaqualand; the grave was still there, only sunken flat; the stones were there still; they were of round and irregular form; the head-stone was rather long, whilst that at the foot was shorter. I was taken on Saturday last, the fifth of April, to the Police Camp, and from there on Monday the seventh. I showed the Magistrate, Mr. Perkins, and the other gentleman with him the road along which I had travelled to see my brother David die, to the vicinity of his grave, passing by the above-mentioned drift, near and above the Police Camp. I recognized the country, and the particular locality, and got out of the wagon to look for the grave. I could not find it, but mentioned its approximate position as being a little above, say two hundred yards, that which I was afterwards shown by Mr. Maclean as having been pointed out to him by Manel Isaac.

Her
TRYN x ISAAC,
mark.

Transcriber and translator unknown

!Kweiten ta //ken,
WHAT THE MAIDENS DO WITH *ROOI KLIP*

South Africa 1874   /Xam

Little is known of !Kweiten ta //ken beyond the few stories and fragments of ritual information she gave to Lucy Lloyd during the nineteenth century in Cape Town. Lloyd, the sister-in-law of linguist Wilhelm Bleek, transcribed and translated her oral accounts, which were eventually archived in the Bleek and Lloyd Collection at the University of Cape Town Libraries. While Bleek worked primarily on /Xam linguistics, Lloyd recorded the *kukummi*, which, according to J. D. Lewis-Williams, can be approximately translated as "stories, news, talk, information, history and what English speakers call myths and folklore." Lloyd was awarded an honorary D.Litt. by the University of the Cape of Good Hope (now the University of Cape Town) a year before she died in 1914 at age seventy-nine. Dorothea Bleek, the daughter of Wilhelm Bleek, continued the work of her aunt and her father and saw to the publication of the some of the /Xam *kukummi*.

The elements of !Kweiten ta //ken's name, according to Dorothea Bleek's *A Bushman Dictionary*, mean "rainstones and sorcery" in the now-extinct /Xam language. !Kweiten ta //ken came to Cape Town from the Katkop Mountains of

South Africa, north of Calvinia, on 13 June 1874. With her was her husband =Kasin ("Klaas Katkop") and two youngest boys, aged six and two. She joined her brother Dia!kwain at Mowbray, the home of the Bleek family. Dia!kwain had been a prisoner at Cape Town's Breakwater Prison, but was released to act as an informant to the Bleeks. His sister may have come to Cape Town to join him, staying a few months at Mowbray and caring for her children there. Perhaps because of the children, perhaps because of her temperament, and perhaps because Wilhelm Bleek died around that time and may have not been well enough to work, there were months during which !Kweiten ta //ken did no interviews at all. Hence, her contributions to the oral material were few compared with those of other /Xam-speaking people. From her accounts, however, it can be deduced that she had detailed knowledge of hunting and gathering in the Katkop environment and that she lived in a community with a flourishing oral tradition. She was later joined by her two eldest boys, and left Cape Town on 13 January 1875.

In the text reprinted here, the parentheses and endnotes reflect Lucy Lloyd's handwritten original (though she uses asterisks, not superscript numbers). The "R." referred to in the endnotes is an unidentified informant. Throughout the text the abbreviation "acct." stands for the word "account."

Megan Biesele

✦

The maiden, she ornaments the spring with [*rooi klip*][1] when she becomes a maiden; she wishes that the spring may not dry up (lit. go out); because she wishes that the water might remain quietly in the spring. Because she wishes that the water may not dry up; that the water may remain in the spring. Therefore they adorn the spring, when they become maidens. Therefore, they adorn the spring on acct. of it; because they wish that the spring may not dry up, that it (the water) might remain quietly on acct. of it. Therefore, the old women tell them about it; therefore, they (the maidens) adorn the water's springs, on acct. of it. They wish that the spring may not become dry.

Thence it is, that the girls adorn the young men,[2] because they wish that the rain may not lightning kill them (the young men). Therefore, they adorn them, on acct. of it.

The Water's Story.

Therefore, they (the maidens) adorn the young men, on acct. of it; for the rain comes out (in) the young men.[3] Therefore, they (the maidens) adorn them on acct. of it, with [*rooi klip*], that the rain may not come out (upon them). Therefore, they adorn them, on acct. of it.

1. The Bushgirls put it round the springs, & adorn the springs with it, so that the water shall not dry up—R. tells me. The women paint their cheeks with it, & also their *karosses*, R. says. The maidens put it on the men's backs.

2. (with stripes, made by the *rooi klip*, like a zebra).

3. as sores, R. says.

Transcribed and translated by Lucy Lloyd

Noneko (Hannah) Toney,
LETTER TO MISS MACKENZIE

South Africa 1875   English

Noneko Toney came to Zonnebloem College in the Cape about a year after Emma Sandile and her age-mate Hester Ngece (see text by Emma Sandile). She was eleven or twelve years old. According to Matilda Smart, her schoolmistress, Toney was "rescued from almost a state of slavery, and to this day the effect has not passed away." Her abilities, however, were "excellent," Smart noted, "especially in the scriptural knowledge and her reading." Three years later Toney was baptized Harriet Mary but called Hannah Toney.

After the girls' department at Zonnebloem closed in 1869, Toney spent the next four years teaching in the infants' school at St. George's Orphanage, Cape Town. In 1872, she finally returned to her homeland to head the Girls' School at St. Mark's Mission, on the Kei River in the Transkeian territory of Independent Kaffraria. Rev. H. T. Waters, who founded the mission in 1855, was still in charge.

St. Mark's was situated in the midst of a dense African population and by the 1870s was encircled three miles deep by largely Christian villages. A school inspector's report in 1873 notes that the Girls' School was divided into five classes, three "Kafir" and two "Hottentot." In the same "Report on Schools in the Eastern Districts and Transkeian Territory" by Deputy Inspector O. H. Hogarth, Toney was commended for the good discipline and organization in her school. The standard was reportedly high, and the work "for the most part, well done."

The letter reproduced below was written to Miss Anne Mackenzie, editor of *The Net* (the journal of the Society for the Propagation of the Gospel) and the sister of Bishop Charles Mackenzie, who led the ill-fated pioneering expedition of the Universities' Mission to Central Africa. While waiting to join the Zambesi Mission early in 1862, Anne Mackenzie spent a year at Zonnebloem teaching at local mission schools and befriending the Xhosa girls. Following the bishop's death, she returned to England and used *The Net* to maintain much needed support for Zonnebloem through publishing regular reports of the college's work and students' essays and letters.

Janet Hodgson

✦

My dear Madam,—I now take my pen to write a few lines, as I have been thinking of doing so a long time. I often think of you, and I daresay you would like to hear about the school out here. I have sixty girls that attend nice and regularly. I used to have three girls to assist me, but one of them has left for Queenstown, where her father has undertaken the native school. My first class are now able to read in the third reading books, and in compound long division sums. They already know a little geography of this world, and they are more fond of it than I used to be. I teach them the map of Palestine, to make them understand what they are learning. I tell them it all in Kafir [Xhosa], and it makes it quite interesting to them. The Kafir has all come back to me quite natural. The second class read

Peep of Day, and are in addition and subtraction sums. We have a nice large school-room. There is a boarding school for boys. Mr. Waters is thinking of opening one for the girls soon. I daresay you read the account of the Ordination of three native deacons. I will never forget that day; it was as fine as we could wish it to be. There was an early and late celebration of the Communion; the Service commenced at 8 a.m.; it was very hearty, and the chants were beautiful. It was in three languages, English, Kafir, and Dutch. It was so solemn when they were presented to the Bishop by the Archdeacon. Before that, the Archdeacon preached a nice sermon through an interpreter, one of the deacons. I think it will be a day long to be remembered in Kafir land. After they were ordained, each of them read the Gospel, one in Kafir, English, and Dutch.

We have morning and evening prayers, like at St. George's Cathedral [Cape Town]; only here it is chanted the same as Sunday. One of the deacons, the Rev. Jonas Ntsiko, has a station of his own; it is a very large Mission, I believe; the other, Rev. Peter Mesiza, goes about visiting the out-stations; the last, Rev. L. Adonis, is a schoolmaster here; he assists Mr. Waters in the Church; there is also a nice harmonium in it. That is only needed in the English Service, as we do not require it in the native, for we manage better without it. Mr. Waters is so very very kind to everyone; everyone loves him, both Red and Christian Kafirs. I have a very nice little room, fitted up so very comfortable. I live very close to the Kie river; we get our water, also bathe there. It is very large in the rainy seasons; the boys catch eels there, the river fish. Oh it is so very dry out here; we have prayers offered up for rain. I hope we will get some soon, for the cattle and sheep, all that sort of thing, are dying for want of grass. The last prayer meeting we had, the Church was crowded with natives, and the head men on the station were allowed to give a short address in turns. Some of them were very nicely given. We are just at the end of one week's holiday. All the teachers from the out-stations have come for their Quarterly Meeting, to talk about their different work. Two of them are my Zonnebloem old friends. I wonder if I could give you a description of St. Mark's. I think this place is about the driest in Kafirland. We have the mountains all round, and it is built like an English village; it looks so pretty at a distance. There are three shops, a carpenter and shoemaker, blacksmith, tinsmith, and traveller accommodation; so I think we are very well off. I must end. Good night.—Yours respectfully, Hannah Mary Toney.

Anonymous,
THE STORY OF NGANGEZWE AND MNYAMANA

South Africa 1879   isiZulu

Although black women were conventionally responsible for passing on and some-times transforming through their own personal style the traditional narratives that provided much of the educational material in oral communities, white male mis-sionaries generally collected oral material from men. Since early collections and transcriptions involving white and black women are rare, this text—a transcription by Mrs. Hugh Lancaster Carbutt of an unnamed Zulu storyteller—is especially important. Among white women the only other known examples of transcription around this time are by Lucy Lloyd and, later, Dorothea Bleek, working in the Cape (see the text titled "What the Maidens Do with *Rooi Klip*").

Although we cannot assume we have access to the unmediated words of this Zulu storyteller, indications are that Carbutt took care to record them as they were spoken, although her understanding of the language was imperfect. Fortunately she provided the *Folk-Lore Journal* with the Zulu text alongside her own transla-tion and so the text could be retranslated by the well-known contemporary Zulu novelist Lauretta Ngcobo.

Carbutt notes that the story comes from "the daughter of an old soldier of Mpande." Mpande initially led the battle against encroaching Voortrekkers in Natal, but in 1839 became their ally, splitting the Zulu nation by waging war against his half-brother Dingane instead. Mpande ruled his new Zulu kingdom until the mid–1850s, remaining hospitable toward white settlers. He died in 1872. The oral exchange between these two women, then, was made possible in that con-text of relative amity.

The tale describes a struggle for lineage: The chief's *nkosikazi* (great wife) plots against the boy-child who stands in the way of her own son's inheritance of the chieftaincy, but the boy survives, reclaims his rightful place, and forgives his rival. The story's major interest rests on the fragility of genealogical inheritance rights, reflecting ongoing struggles within polygynous families. Each mother has to fight for her own son's share in the family inheritance. Embodied in the story also is a deep philosophical belief, pervasive among Zulus and many other African value systems, concerning the sources of good and evil. The extended family can never be so evil that it is destructive of itself. True evil comes from outside the family. (This is why every Zulu homestead is fenced in, and why a breastfeeding mother will wash her breast on returning home and before feeding her baby.) Family feuds cannot be seen to destroy the family unit; no matter how serious, they cannot con-stitute absolute evil. Therefore, family problems must be resolved. Only those who seek to destroy the family may be cast out.

Dorothy Driver and Lauretta Ngcobo

◆

A long time ago in KwaZulu, there was a King who was rich and famous with a large kingdom. He had many wives, and two of his wives gave him two sons. The older son was called Mnyamana (the Dark One) and the younger was called Ngangezwe (As-Great-as-the-World). The King did not love Mnyamana as much as he loved Ngangezwe. This inspired fear and jealousy in the heart of Mnyamana's mother. She was the senior wife and this should have made her son the heir to the King. But she feared that her husband would influence the people to appoint his favourite son, Ngangezwe, as heir to the throne after his death. And on a personal note, this meant that she would lose her own position of honour and authority as the senior wife. Instead, Ngangezwe's mother would ascend to power as the mother of the King. She herself would be a nobody.

One day, when Mnyamana and Ngangezwe were going out to herd cattle with their respective retinues, Mnyamana's mother called him aside.

"Come here, son," she said as she went into her hut. "My child, you know how much your father dotes on your brother, Ngangezwe. He certainly loves you less. The day he dies your father will make him king even though people know it should be you, his elder son. It seems obvious that Ngangezwe will become king after your father's death. I tell you now, kill him.

"Now take this little stone," she continued. "This is no ordinary stone. I have medicated it. It is covered with a powerful potion. All you need do is follow my instructions.

"When you get to the veld charge your followers with the duty of looking after the cattle. Send them a distance away from you and your brother.

"Then, when you're alone, say to Ngangezwe: 'Let us play a game with small stones, like this.' You gather some stones and while he is not looking, put this little stone among them. Show him how to play the game. Take one stone and place it inside your mouth. Tell him to do the same. You pick this special stone and give it to him. Then you will see."

Mnyamana took the stone and hid it on his person, making certain no one else knew anything about it.

When they reached the cattle, they saw that they were well scattered. Then Mnyamana said to his people, "Go and fetch the cattle. I want to see them."

Once the others were gone, the brothers sat down in the shade. Mnyamana proceeded to gather small stones, occasionally tossing them as if he were playing.

He then called to his brother, Ngangezwe, playfully, "Shall we play while the others are gone?"

"Yes, my brother, shall we? But what shall we play?" asked Ngangezwe, looking around.

"I know a game, a game of stones. You put one in the mouth, like this," said Mnyamana as he put a stone in his mouth. So saying, he picked out the stone his mother had given him and gave it to Ngangezwe.

"And then . . ." continued Mnyamana. But Ngangezwe had popped it in his mouth. He was rolling it in his mouth when suddenly the stone slipped and stuck fast in his windpipe. He coughed and he choked. The stone would not come out. He tried all he could to cough the stone out but it was stuck in his throat. He heaved and spluttered, but nothing happened.

At this point, the first of their followers began to arrive. Ngangezwe was lying on the ground, in a state of distress. They asked anxiously what the matter was and Mnyamana began to explain that a tiny pebble had lodged in Ngangezwe's throat. Confusion ensued. Many of Ngangezwe's followers were hysterical when they saw his eyes popping as though he were dying. But there was no mistaking it, Mnyamana's people were secretly rejoicing for they too knew Ngangezwe was the King's favourite. As things were, they could already surmise that Ngangezwe would die and their own leader would take power.

Mnyamana walked home with a spring in every step he took. It was evident for everyone to see that he and his followers were happy. At some point, Ngangezwe stood up and began to walk home. His retinue followed him dejectedly. They walked slowly with great sadness in their hearts. When they approached the Great Place they went and stood at the gate of the cattle kraal. A person standing next to the King drew his attention to the grave scene at the gate. They observed that Ngangezwe stood solemn and silent while his followers were weeping. The King came out and asked Mnyamana directly, "What's the matter?"

Mnyamana began to explain to his father, "Ngangezwe and I were playing with stones. He put one in his mouth and it slipped into his windpipe. It got stuck there. Now he cannot speak."

The King began to mourn. He could see that Ngangezwe would not recover for he could not even take food. One custom in his kingdom was that once the prospects of recovery had been ruled out, the dying, whoever they were, had to be assisted to die. They would be thrown into a deep hole with a little food and left to die alone, in private. The King knew that his son faced this fate. The hole was deep and dark.

As soon as his condition was ascertained, preparations were made to have Ngangezwe thrown into the deep hole. His followers took his dogs, assegais, mats, pillows, sticks and all his property, and proceeded to the hole. Ngangezwe followed dutifully. Mnyamana and his people went too.

But the King did not go along.

When they came to the hole, they all sat down. Ngangezwe's people handed him snuff and he took it. They too joined him and took snuff as they all wept bitterly. When they had finished taking snuff they began throwing his things, one by one, into the hole. Lastly they threw him in as well. They did it with ceremony, as gently as they could. They then returned home. By this time, of course, Mnyamana was full of great joy.

Ngangezwe was left with his dogs in the hole. As soon as they landed at the bottom, the dogs began to work diligently. They took a pot and began scouting around the hole. Soon they found a fountain of water, good and clear, on one side of the hole. They dipped into it and brought the fresh water to Ngangezwe. They poured it down his throat. This immediately washed off the offending, sticky potion from the stone in his throat. It became unstuck immediately and Ngangezwe was well again.

The dogs then set to work again, digging a passage away from the hole. They worked frantically to get out of the hole, until they reached the surface. Once they had succeeded, they went back and began to carry all his things out. One by one they brought them to the surface. And last of all they brought Ngangezwe out as well. He saw the sun again.

He was safe at last. Where to go from here, he wondered. His heart pounding with the joy of life reclaimed, he stood still, wondering which way to go. One part of his heart said, "Go back home!" and the other part said, "Don't!" In the end he chose to go away and turn his back on all those he loved. He left with his dogs that very day.

He walked for many days. Occasionally, his dogs caught wild animals for him when he was hungry. After about a month of wandering he reached a country ruled by another king. He pleaded with that King to accept him as one of his subjects. And so it was that he became one of the King's servants and he lived in that country for a long time.

The King was impressed with Ngangezwe. He proved to be a clever young man, and his dogs were clever too. He worked hard and could be trusted. The King grew to like Ngangezwe and slowly he gave him cattle and advanced him until he was made a headman in the area. Before long Ngangezwe got married to one of the King's daughters. His cattle increased and he became a rich man. He was able to afford more wives. He soon became a noble man with a large homestead of his own, full of many children. He became well known in military circles as well, and he got a regiment of his own to lead. He was a happy man.

One day, after a long time, he began to think of his father's home. "I want to go to see my father. I want to go and see my country." He went to the King and asked to go home to see his father, but the King would not let him. He feared losing his own daughter, Ngangezwe's wife. Ngangezwe pleaded with the King until he consented.

As soon as the King had agreed, Ngangezwe gathered all his cattle, called up all his soldiers, took his wives and children and bade farewell to the King, and left. Ngangezwe and his people were on the road for a month. Then one day he saw the hills of home and on one of them he set up his new homestead. But he warned his people never to tell anyone who he really was. And they made their way home.

One day, Ngangezwe heard that there was to be a beer-drinking party at his old father's homestead. He took a few of his men and went to the party to drink beer and meet young girls. When they got there they found Mnyamana, his brother, sitting in the cattle kraal where the men often met. He could see some of his old friends who used to serve him when he was a young man. Mnyamana was talking and laughing with his own men, but those who had formerly belonged to Ngangezwe were sitting silently as though they were outsiders. This heartened Ngangezwe because he concluded that his men were still loyal to his memory.

Then he spotted his mother and sister sitting down at the outside gate of the homestead. They looked drab and neglected. After all the years they were still wearing their mourning clothes. As they sat at the gate, the passersby would throw ashes on them, a sign of deep mourning. His mother's hut, too, had been moved from its eminent position belonging to the senior Queen of the King's palace. Her hut was relegated to a spot amongst a cluster of obscure, nameless huts near the gate. He could see the visible humiliation that his mother had suffered at the hands of Mnyamana and his mother.

As the party progressed, girls came and mingled freely with the young men. Everyone joined in, except for Ngangezwe. He ignored the girls, instead he slipped silently away and walked towards the gate. At first his mother and sister did not recognise him. He began talking to them. As he bent over to talk to them he could hear derisive comments from some of the girls. They remarked that such a noble-looking man should stoop to talk to such a debased pair as that mother and daughter. They remarked that his sister was unwashed. But Ngangezwe did not care when they laughed. He just went on talking to his sister until it was nearly sunset. As he was leaving, he persuaded her to be his friend. She agreed. She still did not recognise the fine, noble man as her own brother. He invited both his mother and sister to come and see him at his home. Then he went away.

At the crack of dawn the next day, his mother and sister went down to the river to wash and they oiled their bodies for the first time in years. Their mourning years were over. They set off to his homestead. He was very happy to see them again and he gave them beer and beef and other nice food. When it was evening, they stood up to go and he accompanied them a short way and invited them to visit him again. On the days when they did not go to see him, he used to send them things as presents. Soon his sister began to look round and sleek, and her beauty began to show. The other girls became jealous of her.

As time went on, Ngangezwe went more and more often to his old father's homestead to drink beer and to mix freely with his father's people. Soon the people began to return his visits and they began to like him a lot. But none of them guessed that he was Ngangezwe.

One day he gathered all his people and told them to go along with him to the great place of his father. That day he was resolved to tell everyone who he really was. As he approached the gate he saw a number of his former entourage standing by themselves at the gate of the cattle kraal. He strode up to them and introduced himself: "I am Ngangezwe!" They were startled and they wondered, then they began to rejoice. They laughed and danced and sang. There was a great deal of rejoicing. Then appeared on the scene the King, his father, and Mnyamana, his brother. He faced them, and told them again: "I am Ngangezwe!" The King at first went faint. He could not talk. I cannot even tell you how happy the King was then.

Mnyamana suffered a great shock when he saw that this was indeed Ngangezwe. But Ngangezwe spoke to him gently and told him not to be afraid for he would never hurt him. With time Mnyamana relaxed and inwardly he was happy that he still had his brother alive and well.

Soon after these events, the King declared that as an old man he was ready to step down as king and for Ngangezwe to take his place as the young king. Ngangezwe consented and Mnyamana happily became his great headman. Ngangezwe's mother's hut was returned to its proper place and his sister married a great king of another country.

Transcribed by Mrs. Hugh Lancaster Carbutt
Translated by Lauretta Ngcobo

Anonymous, THE WAR IN ZULULAND

South Africa 1884   English

This essay was written by one of the earliest pupils at Inanda Seminary in the colony of Natal. It is part of a series of essays by pupils that were copied into an exercise book and presented to the principal, Mary Edwards, in 1884. As such, it is the earliest known record of African schoolgirls' writing from the KwaZulu-Natal region. None of the essays has been published before. Sadly, the names of the contributors were not recorded.

Inanda Seminary, South Africa's Mount Holyoke, was established on the thriving mission station of Daniel and Lucy Lindley in 1869. They had been active in southern Africa since the late 1830s, as part of the effort by the American Board of Commissioners for Foreign Missions to establish a presence "in the land of the Zulu kings." In this task the American Board was at first spectacularly unsuccessful, as their missionaries were caught up in the social upheavals, called the *mfecane,* associated with the rise of the Zulu state under King Shaka. When some sort of social peace was brought to the region in the 1840s, the Lindleys again took up mission work in Natal at Inanda, some thirty miles to the northwest of Durban, then named Port Natal. The local chief, Mqhawe, became friendly after he realized the potential material benefits of an association with the missionaries, such as plows, horses, and education. A further reason for there being a cordial relationship was that among the converts at the station were some close relatives of the chief including his grandmother, uncle, and cousin. His uncle, James Dube, was one of the first ordained African ministers in Natal, and his cousin was none other than James's son, John, founding president of the African National Congress (ANC) in 1912.

The missionaries (especially the missionary wives) felt strongly that unless the men being trained as leaders of the new Christian community were able to find suitable marriage partners, only half of the church's future was really ensured. The Lindleys fought hard for the establishment of a women's training center, and realized their dreams with the opening of Inanda Seminary. It was the first school of its kind in southern Africa, catering as it did exclusively to African girls who had already received a primary education. In time, it attracted young women from all over southern and central Africa. For the early pupils at the seminary, life could not have been easy. The redoubtable first head, Mary Kelly Edwards, exercised a severe if kindly authority: All incoming letters were vetted (and confiscated if deemed unsuitable); the girls had to collect water, grow food, keep the campus clean, and do their own laundry; at weekends, they had to assist in mission work; and all in addition to their studies. Yet for those who stayed, the rewards were potentially great: Nearly all the "firsts" for African women in South Africa—first qualified African theater sister (senior nurse in a hospital operating theater), first African sister tutor (senior nurse qualified to instruct trainees), first African woman doctor, and so on—belong to Inanda Seminary girls. Some neither sought nor won fame in their own right, but rather as helpmates to well-known husbands, such as Nokutela Dube, first wife of John Dube. All these women were in the forefront of the creation of an African middle class in South Africa.

The essay reproduced here reminds us that it was not only white settlers who feared the might of the independent Zulu state; so too did the many African refugees who had fled from it. (The "scattering" of refugees continued from the 1820s until well into the 1860s.) It is a vivid account of the onset of a momentous event—the Anglo-Zulu War of 1879 and the conquest of the Zulu kingdom under its king, Cetshwayo—written from the point of view of a young woman whose clan sought to avoid the conflict. It presents an as-yet unheard voice, for nearly all the surviving accounts—whether from the "official mind" of British imperialism, ordinary foot soldiers, or a perspective "through Zulu eyes"—are overwhelmingly male. This account by a young woman is therefore extremely rare, a perfect counterbalance to the story told by Paulina Dlamini from the Zulu side of the war (see "Flight of the Royal Household").

Heather Hughes

◆

A long time ago, when we had not yet come to study in this school, we began to fear that there was going to be a war between the Zulus and the white people. They said that the white people wanted Cetywayo [Zulu king as of 1872] to be caught because he was troubling people very much, and killing many people who wanted to be Christians. At first we could not believe that it was true. We thought that they were deceiving us, but soon we saw people coming away from Zululand. Some came to my home, they were afraid, because they thought there was going to be a war, and we saw some missionaries and their people, and many others who had run away from their houses, and still we could not believe it, but some old people said to us, "Look at the field, and see how much food there is this year, and look too at the birds, and see how many there are." They think these birds go when there is going to be a war.

When I heard them talking I was glad for I thought I should like to see the people scattered, as I had heard my Mother talk about how they were scattered by the war when she was a girl but my Mother said to me, "You would not be glad if you had seen that time, because you would have had no house to sleep in, and no food to eat." A few months after this they told us that the soldiers were coming to Durban to fight with the Zulus, and after a few days we saw some soldiers, and when they came to my house they stopped near there for a little while.

We ran away to stand on a hill, and saw them when they stopped, but we were much afraid to go to the river for water, but my Father told us to go after him, and said "They will not do anything to you, I will go with you," and so we went and came home without any hurt, but while my Father was still at the river, some of the soldiers came to our house and we ran away to Zinkala's house and stood there till my Father came to call us, and told us to go back home.

When we were at home my Father told us to go and light a lamp in the house, for we were in the kitchen, then I was afraid to go alone, but my Father scolded me, and told me to go, so I went running very fast, and looking round me all the way to see what was coming after me.

Just as soon as I was in the house, I was looking for matches. I looked through the window and saw some soldiers coming. I lighted the lamp very quickly. They came to the door, just when I was ready to scream, I saw my Father coming, and I was very glad.

My Father told them to go away. Some of the people asked the soldiers what they were going to Zululand for, and they said "Tina hamba Cetywayo" ["We are going after Cetywayo"] and the people said, "Where is Cetywayo—is he waiting for you in any place" but they only said "Tina hamba Cetywayo." They started to go to Idlilshwani, and then we saw others passing, and we heard that they were crossing the uTugela river [between Natal and the Zulu kingdom], and then I began to believe that they were really going to fight.

After a time, they called for some black people to go with them to Zululand, and all the people around my home were gathered together both young and old men, but the old men were sent home for they had no strength to fight and they were very glad because they were afraid of the Zulu people.

Their friends were very glad too, but we whose friends went were not glad, because we were afraid they would not come back, but we said, "They will not die, if it is not their time to die." The black soldiers were then taught by the white people to march as they do—and guns were given them to shoot with, and some of the young men were very glad, because they thought they would gain a great name among the people. Always at night two of them were sent to stay on the fields, so that they could see when the Zulu people were coming, and if they saw anyone coming, they were taught to say "Who comes here" and if they did not answer right away they were killed.

The Zulus came and fought with the white people. Sometimes they conquered them, and sometimes they did not, but the white people overcame them at last by something which the people called umtubumtulu [word unknown], because they could shew these things a long way, and then they would know where the people [were].

The black people did not help them very much in the war because the white people were not willing for them to go and fight, but used to tell them to stay under the waggons, when the battle was over, then they told the black people to go after them, and kill those who were wounded.

We were very much afraid when we were at home, because we thought the Zulu people would cross the Tugela and kill us, because we heard that they said they were going to cross the Tugela, and were going to eat sweet food in Durban and in Pietermaritzburg, but the white people were wise, they put some soldiers at the place where they were to cross. We heard that they did cross in one place and that they killed a woman and her baby.

Tho' we were afraid we did not go anywhere because we did not know where to go, and we just went to our gardens to weed because it was the time for weeding.

One night as we had just finished our supper we heard a great screaming of "Ingene," "Ingene" ["It has entered," meaning the Zulu army had entered the colony], and so we were very much afraid, we did not know what to do or where to go. My Father went and put a saddle on the horse quickly, and he called Zonakile's brother and said, "Did you hear what they said." Then they took their things and came home to run away with us.

Just then we saw some black people running from the battle, they were our people, but we thought they were Zulus so we ran away quickly.

There were many of us, outside people [traditionalists, outside the church] and station people [missionaries and their converts] and we did not know where my Father was. When we were on the way we saw him coming riding on a horse, he took my brother with him to see if it was true that the Zulus had come, but we went on till we came to the Dhlumbete river, we crossed it, and we stayed there at night, but we could not sleep, for we were afraid. In the morning the boys went back home, and then they came back to tell us, because the Zulus had not come, and so we went home.

A few days after we heard that the Zulus had conquered the white people at Isandlwana [22 January 1879], and had killed many, both white and black people who were at that place, and some of our friends who were at this place were killed and they told us this, and we were very sorry.

While they were still fighting, we came here to school, and after a long time we heard that Cetywayo was taken—but the people of Zululand did not stop fighting with each other. When their king was in England many people from Zululand came to this country to work, and when we asked them how they did in the war they said we were much afraid, but we were not afraid of the guns, we were afraid of something they burned us with. Some of them shewed us the place where the bullets had entered their bodies, and when we asked them if they did not think they would die they said yes, but we did not sit, because we were afraid that the soldiers would come and finish us—they said we overcame in insobane [probably a place name], we killed many white people there, and the white people were much afraid. When they saw one of the Zulu people they said very nice words to him and besought him not to kill them, but the Zulus did not listen to them, they killed them.

They were very glad to hear their king was to come back again to his own land and some who were in Natal went back to see their king.

Kambauruma Kazahendike, Two Lions Who Changed Themselves into People and Married Two Herero Girls

Namibia 1886 otjiHerero

Herero tales are a mixture of fiction, myth, and historical event that carry a strong moral message. They are intended to entertain and teach, thus contributing to the process of creating socially responsible human beings. Older members of society, especially grandmothers who are experts in the parts of the stories that are sung, perform the tales, usually in the evenings around a fire just before bedtime. The fire, the darkness, and the singing add mystery to the tales.

Herero tales usually do not have titles. They are called *Ovimbaharere/Ovipaharere*, which means "things/events that almost happened." Instead of "Once upon a time," they usually begin with *A'pehara, otjipari . . .*, which means "It almost happened, then there was. . . ." The title used here is a translation of the German given by the author or the editor, missionary Heinrich Brincker, to satisfy the expectations of a European readership. Brincker notes in his introduction to his collection of tales that the translations have been "critically reworked," an example of how texts and the cultural experiences they represented were shaped by the interventions of missionaries.

The story below was published in 1886 in an early German-Herero grammar book, but had been collected earlier. In 1862 the Cape philologist Wilhelm Bleek wrote that he received "five legends in oTyi-herero [sic] or Damara language as written down by natives, copied and accompanied by a translation by the Rev. J. Rath." According to Brincker these "natives" were in fact "a Herero girl," most probably Kambauruma (Magdalena) Kazahendike, the sister of Urieta Kazahendike (see text entitled "God's Peace and Blessing"), who also had a few tales published elsewhere. The text below has been translated into English from the otjiHerero included by Brincker.

Cons Uaraisa Karamata and Margie Orford

◆

There were two sisters, the one older than the other. They were left behind when the others moved because the small stock that they were looking after had strayed far. The people moved so fast that the girls could not find them, they went into the field. There they married two lions; these lions had a mother. But the older sister was not very clever, whereas the lions were very cunning as they could turn into people. The lions went and stole small stock and the girls cooked the meat. The girls were shocked at the way the lions ate and the lions asked: "What are you scared of?" They answered: "Oh, it is nothing. Maybe we were just imagining things." Then the lions asked: "Did your father not have hair [*omainja*]?" And the sisters answered that he did. Then the lions asked again: "What are you afraid of?"

The lions then went hunting. While they were in the bush they turned themselves into lions again. In the meantime the mother of the lions said to the girls: "We are actually animals, thus you must flee from here."

The younger girl who was cleverer than the other said to her sister "Please let us go." They left and went into a *omukaru* [a type of tree]. The older girl, who was stupid, said: "I am going back. In my view we live like people who have little worries." And they both returned.

The next day the mother helped the girls escape, and they left. On their way they saw cattle grazing and they went to the homestead. After they had left, the lions came back to their home and asked their mother: "Where are the girls?" The mother answered: "They said that they were going to fetch firewood but I don't know why they are taking so long." The lions went after the girls up to their homestead. Just as they came close to the homestead they turned themselves into humans with musical instruments and entered the homestead.

There was an empty house which was offered to them; they were also offered *omaere* [fermented milk]. The mother and father told the girls to keep the men company for the evening. The girls replied: "Please father, why do you want this? Just see how our cattle will be finished off." The children refused. The father answered: "Just go and face the danger, sleep but do not go into a deep sleep. Wake up in the middle of the night and tie irons to their legs, but make sure not to make any noise. Wait until they are asleep and then sneak out." In the early hours of the morning the lions woke up and turned back into lions and they moved on the livestock. Just when they wanted to catch a cow, it bellowed and the cattle jumped up. The lions then ran to the house and tuned back into humans. The people heard the cattle lowing and the lions' roars and saw how they changed. When the lions were asleep again the girls woke each other up and took their things and returned to their father's house. He came to see whether the lions were asleep and set the side wall of the house on fire. The lions moaned and thrashed about but they could not get out. They were burnt to death.

Translated by Yahmillah Katjirua

Olive Schreiner, LEAVING THE FARM
South Africa 1886–1887   English

Novelist, short-story writer, political essayist, and a central figure in the development of white South African literature, Olive Schreiner was both derided and acclaimed in her lifetime for her pioneering feminism, her rejection of Christian convention, and her anti-imperialism and antiracism. Born on 24 March 1855 in Wittenbergen, on the border between the Cape Colony and Basutoland, at a London Missionary Society station run by her parents, her adolescence and young womanhood were spent largely in the Karoo district of the Cape Colony, first (from the age of twelve) in the house of her brother and his family, helping with the housekeeping, and thereafter on various farms, working as a governess. She received no formal education.

She left for England in 1881, aged twenty-six, with the manuscripts of three novels in her suitcase. *The Story of an African Farm* (1883) brought her immediate success. The other two, *Undine* (1928) and *From Man to Man* (1926), appeared posthumously: The first, written between 1875 and 1877, Schreiner felt should remain unpublished; the second she worked on for long stretches of her life, alternating between despair and exhilaration. During her lifetime Schreiner also published nonfiction, of which *Woman and Labour* (1911) is the most famous, and allegorical fiction, among other works.

Schreiner sent early versions of *From Man to Man* to Havelock Ellis, with whom she had a close and long-standing friendship. The manuscript of the excerpt published here, dated in Schreiner's hand, was written while she was staying in Alassio, Italy, shortly before her return to South Africa in 1889 and her marriage to Samuel Cronwright in 1892. After Schreiner's death in 1920, her husband edited and published the novel. Schreiner's revised version does not differ substantially from the early version printed here, although there are stylistic changes. The original, however, refers more closely to the connection between satisfaction in farm life and the protagonist Rebekah's need for books, and thus points to Schreiner's own voracious Karoo reading: books by Charles Darwin, Herbert Spencer, and J. S. Mill, to name a few. As the novel turns out, Rebekah's sexual hunger is redirected largely into maternal interests, for her husband turns to other women. Although she falls in love with a man of her own intellectual inclinations, she declines to run away with him. Instead she gives him the "crown of her collection" from her premarriage days as an amateur scientist: a fossil of a winged reptile. The winged reptile, a creature made extinct in evolution, symbolized for Schreiner a female potential extinguished in the apparent progress of human existence.

In this extract, Rebekah as yet knows nothing of the psychic enfeeblement that marriage would bring, although there is an inkling of the forthcoming complexities of ethical choice in a world dominated by the inequalities of gender, class, and race. The pacing ox in this excerpt becomes, in later chapters, a restless woman pacing up and down her room, rehearsing to herself arguments and counterarguments about the ethics of historical and contemporary life.

Dorothy Driver

✦

At nine o'clock that night Rebekah sat on the "stoep". It was a dark night; the nightflies buzzed about at intervals. She sat on the step opposite the door with her back to it; a square of light fell from the open door across the "stoep", & dimly onto the stems of the orange trees beyond. She sat with her elbows on her knees looking into the dark. After a while she looked back: through the open door she could see her little mother sitting in the corner of the room in the rocking chair, rocking herself and smiling: Percy Lawrie the new master was at the piano playing, Bertie was standing by him turning over the music for him bending so low her brown hair almost touched his. She could see her lover lying on the sofa with his large arm thrown across his forehead listening to the music; & in the room beyond her father at the bare deal table reading, his black beard pressed against his chest, his black hair falling in a heavy lock over his forehead as he was intent on his book. She looked in for a while & then she looked away again.

What was she leaving it for, that quiet peaceful life?—she folded her arms on her knees. What did she leave it for? The light streamed out from the door, and lay in a square just behind her. To-night, almost too late, she took up the old balances & began to weigh again. What was she leaving it for, this quiet peaceful life?—The blue eyes & yellow hair of her cousin Frank?—she loved him, better than her mother, as well as her father, only a little less than her sister: better than her microscope & collection of insects, as well as her grafting & her experiments, only less than her books. When she was dead she would be buried with these all round her, at her side at her feet, at her head, the books! What was she leaving it for? It was a quiet peaceful life in which the right was the pleasantest & easiest to do, & lay right ahead, in which there was no being torn asunder living between "I would" & "I must"; a life in which there was just so much to be done for others as might yield a grateful sense of selfsatisfaction. A dreamy placid life into which the noisy, babbling, worried worrying world crept only once a week through the post bag of the boy who brought the letters from the town. A peaceful, studious life, in which one might grow wise exceedingly & suck what joy there is from plants & stones; a studious thoughtful life, in which one might read, & creep into the heart of books as can only be when the wheels of the daily life are grinding soft & low. A life in which suffering was small & pleasure was large. What was she leaving it for? She looked back again into the room. The scale looked heavy. On the other side was,—well,—nothing,—only a vague insatiable hunger. Books, black-beetles, well performed duties; she had tried them all, they were chaff! She was dying of hunger. What the far off blue & purple mountains whisper of when they say, "Come! come! come! We have that to give you that you know not of; come! come! come! to us!" That she was hungry for.

When an ox is dying of hunger & thirst & left at the road-side it does not lie down, it walks up & down, up & down, up & down. It does not lie still.

She folded her arms on her knees & decided as before.

Eliza Feilden, PORTRAIT OF LOUISA

South Africa 1887　English

The portrait of Louisa in Eliza Feilden's memoir, *My African Home; or, Bush Life in Natal,* was written in 1852–1853 but not published until 1887. It is one of the earliest portraits of a young African woman in Port Natal (Durban), memorable especially for Feilden's (mis)representation of Louisa's speaking for herself. All that is known of Louisa is what Feilden reports: She and her mother were refugees from the territory of an Mpondo chief, Faku, on the Umzimvubu River in the present border area between KwaZulu-Natal and the Eastern Cape. They probably fled up the coast in the early 1830s after a struggle over land and cattle between the Mpondo and their Zulu neighbors.

Louisa worked for six months for Feilden as a servant in her farmhouse, which was situated a few hours' ride from the new European settlement at the bay. While African men often sought service with settler families, it was unusual for a young woman to do so because marriage, children, and work in the family homestead and fields were expected of them. Louisa seems to have had an independent outlook, which may account for her conversion to Christianity and her interest in the education offered by missionaries.

When Louisa decides to marry, Feilden sees her as "selfish"—a view she rationalizes by noting Louisa's sacrifice of the opportunity to learn more of the language (English) and the skills that would be "useful to her people." Feilden's assumption that Louisa would attain "reasoning" power and would progress through contact with settler culture is typical of the period; what is perhaps less so is Feilden's genuine, though patronizing, interest in her young servant's outlook and her pleasure in recounting what she sees as Louisa's quaint deeds. When Feilden reproaches Louisa for her inadequate sense of duty, she is prompted by her class-biased attitudes as well as her sense of racial superiority. Elsewhere in her memoir she records much harsher criticisms of her white servants.

Leyland Feilden, Eliza's husband, was the youngest son of Sir William Feilden of Feniscowles Hall, Lancashire, England. He first came to Natal under the Byrne (assisted) immigration scheme and returned for the second time almost immediately after his marriage, arriving with Eliza in May 1852. Because he was relatively rich, the Feildens were able to return to England after several floods hit their second farm and sugar mill at Springfield in 1856. This was not an option open to many immigrant settlers.

M. J. Daymond

✦

Our white servants were leaving us; we had had a narrow escape of a well-spoken Scotchwoman from Drummond Castle, so we engaged a fine, strong, tall Caffre girl from the missionaries, called "Louisa." She understands English *pretty* well, and appears to be willing and quick, but I should not like her to put her hands in the bread till I can teach her to be thoroughly clean and nice in her habits, so I must be the bread-maker for a time. She shrugs her shoulders, but does the thing I tell her, but will not obey Gudgeon, who has managed to get taken back. Before we set out from the bay, Louisa came into the parlour in her pink print and squatted herself on the floor, looking very resolved. She "would not go with Gudgeon to the farm," she would "go with missis." I explained that we were riding and would go too fast for her; then she would follow, but not with Gudgeon, to whom she has taken a dislike. How they arranged I know not, but both made their appearance. She "was sorry there would be no school." I undertook to teach her, so as soon as she had washed up she brought her Zulu Genesis, and I heard her read her chapter; I afterwards found she understood my reading of Zulu better than her own, though I only knew what I read by consulting my English Bible. [. . .]

My Durban white servant came to us for a few days, but some heavy rains drove her away, and we were left with only Louisa and Gudgeon. Gudgeon *would cook* and plagued us; Louisa was willing, but knew nothing. I many a time wished I had spent an hour a day in the kitchen in England, for I felt as ignorant of cooking almost as Louisa. She is a nice creature, but wilful, and the difficulty of teaching her to understand in English first what she is to do, then how she is to do it, and lastly, seeing that she does it, is very fatiguing. She comes to me, "What me do now?" Her mind is active, and her body strong. If we can only have patience with her she may turn out a fine creature and learn to be very useful, but you cannot reason with one of another language, who has no ideas upon daily duties. She reads pretty well in Zulu, and opens my English books with a sort of longing look. She opened my little sketch-book, I turned to where some figures were squatted. "Oh, Caffres!" she cried, with a merry laugh. I pointed to herself under the tree, and Gudgeon, but she did not think it like her.

She came to me on Saturday, "You know me want?"

"What do you want, Louisa?"

"Me want go church, all man love God; go church, not work Sunday."

"Quite right, Louisa, you shall go to church. I cannot walk so far, so we have church here to worship God. You must come soon back at night."

"No! me stay all night, me go church, me not work, God rest." So I suppose we must help ourselves on a Sunday in future.

She was back before seven in the morning on Monday, having walked from the station, a distance of six or seven miles. She said the service was part in English and part in Caffre, and they taught her to read. She would like to learn everything, provided I go with her, and do as much as she. I asked if she would like to teach her people. She replied, "Yes, but they not like to learn." When she brings her "Genesis" and seats herself on the floor at my feet, I am reminded of the Eastern saying of the maid sitting at her mistress's feet. It sounds very pretty as a picture, a dark shining skin and eyes, a pink frock, and the Bible in her hand; but in reality she is a great, clumsy, walloping young woman in rags, though she can sew well. But there is something nice about her, and when she can understand us better, we may be able to reason with and teach her many things. She has taken a great fancy to my sketch-book, and is always turning over the leaves. [. . .]

I have drawn a pretty picture of my dark maiden, Louisa, just such an one as the missionaries would seize upon for their reports, which take with the benevolent at home; but it is the sunny side. She is a fine, able-bodied creature, about five feet eight or ten in height, and very stout and thick-set. She looks magnificent as she appears coming up the steep hill out of the wood, with her bucket of water on her head and branches of green standing in it to keep the water steady, her form or bench (for she has been washing) under her arm, and walking erect. But, though active-minded, she is very idle, spares labour on everything, is never anxious to oblige, or to do a single thing she is not ordered to set about. She loves eating as all Caffres do, and stuffs till she is stupid, and then I have to do all, instead of three parts of the work. She talks of love to God, but does not strive to please her mistress, and, so far as I can judge, she does not know that she is a sinner, and yet I suppose she is as good a specimen of a convert to Christianity as most of those—the accounts of whom draw tears—in books or at meetings. She went to church as usual in the afternoon, but I told her she must be back before six in the morning to make breakfast. She arrived when I was washing the breakfast things and putting them away, and expressed no regret. [. . .]

Louisa is a strange, untutored creature; she observed that I look out for my husband when I expect his return of an evening. She came to me one day saying he was visible. I went out to look, but he was hid from sight by bushes. I stood a moment looking. Louisa came behind (she is a sort of giantess), seized me round the ankles, and lifted me into the air, to look over the bushes! I was powerless as a struggling infant in her grasp. At last she set me down with a merry laugh at my discomfiture. She has got a new blue frock now, and did her best to wait at our Christmas party, as well as two Caffres in their best, i.e. they wore a bob of scarlet worsted the size of a pomegranate flower on their foreheads, and brass bracelets; beyond a few strips of rags the size of a philabeg hanging down before and behind, their shining dark skin of nature's bestowing was their only other covering. They drank our healths and seemed to enjoy the fun as much as any of us.

Louisa has gone off to visit her mother for a week. She has only been eight weeks with me, yet she must have as much holiday as she asks.

"Who will do your work, Louisa?" said I.

"I don't know, ma'am."

"Am I to clean the pans, Louisa?"

"Oh no, ma'am!"

"Who then?" She shrugged her shoulders, and suggested "Boy."

"But Boy is busy in the garden; don't you think you could find me a good girl to do your work if I let you go?"

"No, ma'am, no Caffre girl, only one Caffre girl at Mr. B——'s."

"But you could find one, I think?"

"No, ma'am, no girl, they all wife."

So I must manage as I can until Louisa chooses to return. But with all her faults she is truthful and honest. [. . .]

About this time (February, 1853) I observed a smartly-dressed Caffre man came occasionally to pay his respects to Louisa. I guessed what the result must be, so I spoke to her, and she frankly tells me she "tink she like him. Him pray *in* me in church." And soon she told me when I paid her wages, that she must go away, and live at the mission where her lover is; and so she set off, crying when I told her she ought not to leave me unprovided with another, it was ungrateful after all I had taught her. She shrugged her shoulders and was very sorry, but selfishness prevailed, and she set off there and then. Louisa has interested me greatly. She has considerable reasoning powers, and was so desirous to learn to read English, and was beginning to speak and understand it so well, that I wonder she did not see her interest in remaining a little longer. She was very truthful; only once have I known her persist in an untruth. I have known her after a first denial and a little hesitation say, "Yes, ma'am, I did." She took a great fancy to my India-rubber galoshes, telling me they were too large for me, and when I found them split down the front I accused her of trying them on her own great foot. She denied, but I fear she had done it. Louisa is only sixteen years old, but full-grown, and her lover is twenty. Under a missionary she may become useful to her people, though her knowledge is scanty, and her mental education slow. She tells me she is a fugitive Zulu from Faku's country, where her father was killed. Her mother snatched her up on her back, and as she was running off, the child got struck on the back, where she always feels a pain during a cold. She would on no account go back to Faku's land. All in Natal are similar fugitives, and prefer being under English rule, as safer and less tyrannical.

Adèle Mabille, PENELOPA LIENGUANE
Lesotho 1888   English

Adèle Mabille was the daughter of Eugene Casalis, one of the three missionaries invited by Moshoeshoe, founder of the Basotho kingdom, to settle in his territory and teach his people modern learning. The Christian mission that was established thereafter could be regarded as "national in the best sense of the word," to quote Victor Ellenberger in *A Century of Mission Work in Basutoland: 1833–1933* (1936), for the king not only protected it but also held the initiative for change in his hands. Mabille's essay reflects something of the relations that may have existed between the Basotho and the French missionaries. The tone of the document is strikingly free of condescension toward "Natives" and "Kaffirs." In addition, Mabille accepts gifts of money and food from the convert about whom she writes, a reciprocity that has been expunged from most colonial records. In Botswana, Khama III's financial contributions to the appeals of Christian fund-raisers concerned about the English poor have been expunged in a similar manner.

Adèle Mabille's husband, Adolphe Mabille, was the editor of *Leselinyane la Lesuto* when it was first established in 1863, and by the time of the Gun War, hinted at in her piece, he was the head of the French missionaries at Morija. This war was part of a general disarmament war in which the British colonial administration based in Cape Town undertook to disarm black people who had bought guns with the money they had earned as workers in South African mines and industries and on farms. Lesotho's turn to be disarmed came in 1880.

The history of the missions, as officially reported, very often revolves not around missionary wives but their husbands. For this reason it is not generally known that Adèle Mabille translated from and into Sesotho for her husband.

The *Basutoland Evangelist,* in which the piece appeared in 1888, was founded with the dual purpose of informing the European public about mission work and raising funds for the mission.

Leloba Molema

✦

[Penelopa] Lienguane was one of the first to give us a warm welcome when we arrived at Morija 29 years ago. She used to walk once a fortnight from Kolo, a distance of 12 miles, to spend the Sunday on the station. Our little children soon learnt to consider her as their greatest friend. The day before our eldest son left us to go to France for his education she came to bid him good-bye. "You cannot think what a trial it is for me to part with your child," she said to me. "Were you a mosuto woman, I would ask you to give me that child to bring up, as the Lord has made me childless, but it cannot be. This child must be educated so that he may return to teach my people." Then placing 10s. in my hand, she said: "This is to buy food on the road for him." The following year she brought me £1 to help to pay for her boy's schooling. The year after, she brought a larger sum; I expressed my astonishment at her generosity. "I cultivate a small field for that purpose and you shall have every penny that field produces for him." One year when our crops had suffered a great deal through hail, she brought me £2.10 for the same purpose. I begged her to allow me to return the money for that year at least, as I knew her fields had been destroyed by the hail. "No," said she, "the Lord has given it to me for my child and he shall have it."

It will be a satisfaction to our friends to know that the Lord has granted her the wish of her heart, which was that "her boy" should become a missionary to her people, and what is more, he has brought out a bride from Scotland.

"Where there is a will, there is a way," is a proverb that good woman constantly puts into practice. I have often wondered where she manages to get all the money she gives so generously, receiving as she does only a salary of about £7, besides a few extras. Yet her collection towards the church funds is never under £1, besides giving also for the Barotse Mission and other works. When we began the Normal School 20 years ago, it was in war time and after a great famine. We had not much to give the pupils except crushed maize and native bread. A small flock of sheep and goats belonging to Lienguane had escaped when the cattle of Basutoland were captured by the Boers. Every now and then our cook would pretend she sadly wanted a bit of meat to make soup of, and would send for one of her sheep. When once the meat was ready, she would say to me: "Send me those poor boys, don't you see that they are just starving for a bit of meat?" And so the whole of the little flock went. Then when once the first boys left the school to go out as catechists and school masters, when they happened to return to Morija, they were sure to find a nice roasted fowl ready to receive them, or would carry away a little dress for the baby from *nkhono* (grandmother) as she loved to call herself. All these little works of love are supposed to be known by the Lord only, for she never boasts of what she does, and I once got a good scolding for having thoughtlessly spoken of what she did for our son before one of the little ones, who immediately ran to ask her to give her some of the money she gave for her brother. "How could you speak of such a thing," said she, "I thought this was to be between ourselves and the Lord?" I never met with a native woman with such a *large heart* as hers. Her heart seems especially to overflow with love and pity for the heathen, and some years ago her holidays were spent on an evangelizing tour, first in one district, then in another. I believe she has been over all Basutoland in this way. One good woman who usually accompanied her once said to me: "I really do not understand how Lienguane manages, but she has only to enter a house for all the children to come to her, and at once she begins to teach them a text or a verse of a little hymn. She has no trouble to get the women around her, and when she leaves a village she is already the friend of every body."

Some years ago, being in bad health, my husband and I were advised to take a journey through the Transvaal. We were at the same time to look out for a field of labour for the Swiss Mission. Before setting out, Lienguane came and asked as a favour to be allowed to accompany us. "You are my missionary's daughter and I have a right to care for you." I shall never forget her activity, her constant cheerfulness throughout all the fatigues of our five months journey. We had laid in a supply of dried bread and biscuit, such as is always made for a long journey in Africa. Yet we had fresh bread baked regularly all through the journey. This kind soul would knead her dough when we rested at midday, and in the evening baked it in a flat pot; often I would say to her: "We can get on very well with biscuits, for you are really too tired to bake to-day." "No, no," she would say, "I promised when I left Basutoland that I would care for you." Only those who have some experience of African travelling can understand the self-sacrifice it required to bake bread after a hard day's travelling. Some days after our return to Morija, she came to thank us for having taken her with us, and laid down £1 as a thankoffering to the Lord for having brought us all back safely; nor did she seem to realise how greatly we were indebted to her, for she would never receive the least compensation for all the fatigue and work of the five months campaign. This also she did for her Lord. He alone knows what an encouragement, what a comfort this dear woman has always been to us. How often when my husband has been almost crushed by some grievous sin amongst our people has she come *matselisong* (a visit of condolence) to us. "My children," she would say, "do not lose heart, the enemy is strong, but Jesus is stronger than he." What is more, I have never heard a word said against her, nor do I believe she has a single enemy, for she is a friend and a mother to all.

Some time since we were taking a review of the work done during the late years, and she seemed rather down hearted at the thought of the number of young men who had left our Normal School and who were not engaged in the Lord's work. She seemed almost to find that she had spent her strength for nought. My husband, to cheer her, began to count up those of "her boys" who were at work and we found upwards of seventy. Since that the number has increased.

I would fain add that all our Basutoland converts are such bright sterling christians as the one I am writing about; far from it; yet thank God, there are some who are shining lights in the midst of the darkness around us.

Susiwe Bengu, TESTIMONY OF A SCHOOL GIRL
South Africa 1892   English

Susiwe Bengu arrived at Inanda Seminary on 6 August 1892. She had run away from her family home because her father, Dhlokolo, himself a chief, had agreed that one of his daughters should be chosen to be the youngest wife of a much older man, the chief Bulushe, and Susiwe had been selected. Presumably she fled to Inanda Seminary because it was known to offer protection to young women in her predicament (see the headnote to "The War in Zululand"). The seminary probably had to struggle to keep her. The school's records indicate that her father tried several times to get her away from the school, and the local magistrate and the secretary of native affairs in Natal would normally have insisted that "runaways" (especially if they were from families of chiefs) be returned so as not to disturb this aspect of patriarchal power. The record from which her statement is taken does not indicate what eventually happened to Susiwe Bengu. The statement is signed in her own hand but otherwise written down by someone else.

Her flight is an indication of the profound social changes that were beginning in the region: The school is seen as a "haven" by Bengu, but its very existence is also part of the causes of these long-term transformations. Young Zulu women also ran away from the strict regime at the seminary, as Inanda's early register indicates. For their part, the missionaries gave highly propagandistic accounts of their protection of young women. However charged the issues were at this time, it took a great deal of courage for a young Zulu-speaking woman to resist parental authority.

Heather Hughes

About eight years ago, I think it was, when I was a young girl, the chief Bulushe, a very old man, talked with my father about getting one of his daughters. My father was willing, so the chief sent ten of his younger sons to choose one for him. I was the one chosen, but I refused and kept refusing—my father kept trying to make me go but he did not force me to go, and while the matter was still being talked about, Bulushe died. Then his oldest son, Sidada, who had several wives and was old, said that if I had consented to his father, he could not say anything, but now he would take me as he did the other things of his father. I refused, but his messengers came many times—and he came—they said to my father, "We have many things, we will give you anything you choose to ask for, besides the cattle." My father kept pressing me to go till at last I went to that man's kraal, but I did not stay in his hut. There were many people there. I was sent home with twenty cattle, but when they wanted me to go back with the beer, I refused till at last my mother went and took it for me. My father became very angry because I kept refusing to go, and said to me as he was going away for a few days, "If you do not have the beer made when I get back and go with it, you will be taken." After he went I heard that I was really to be taken there when he came home, so I watched for a chance to get away, and came here to you.

Susiwe Bengu

1900 TO 1919

A. M. van den Berg, JOURNAL OF THE WAR

South Africa 1900   Afrikaans/Dutch

Mrs. A. M. van den Berg gave her war journal to an English woman, Emily Hobhouse, in July 1903, while Hobhouse was gathering information about Boer families who had been allowed to return to their farms at the end of the Anglo-Boer War of 1899–1902. Most were destitute since their buildings, crops, and live-stock had been systematically destroyed by the British army during the war. Hobhouse did not manage to translate the many statements she collected until 1924. Thirty of them were published shortly after her death in *War without Glamour*. They provide an early account of the massive civilian suffering that occurs in modern warfare.

Hobhouse, the daughter of a clergyman, was born in Cornwall, England, in 1860. She organized a huge rally in London for women to protest against the Anglo-Boer War. Once in South Africa in December 1900, she witnessed two infamous aspects of General Horatio Kitchener's campaign: the destruction of the farms of all combatants and the internment of their wives and children. Carrying the war to the women was a deliberate strategy to hasten the capitulation of Boer husbands and sons.

Hobhouse's revelations of the dreadful conditions in the camps so angered Alfred Milner's government in Cape Town that, on her second visit in October 1901, she was not allowed to disembark and was forcibly returned to England. Once peace had been signed in May 1902, she again came to South Africa. During this and her next visit, as she collected the testimonies of Boer women, she saw starvation everywhere. Recognizing that their survival would depend on self-help, Hobhouse determined to assist Boer women to develop home industries. After a further three years in South Africa she was compelled by her own worsening health to return to England. In honor of her work, she was invited in 1913 by President M. T. Steyn of the Orange Free State to unveil the Afrikaner women's memorial in Bloemfontein, but, although she traveled to South Africa, she was too ill to attend the ceremony. Her ashes are interred at the monument.

The van den Berg family farm, Witpoort, was in the eastern Transvaal, about thirteen miles south of the small town of Roossenekal to which the women and children fled after their farm was burned. There they were captured by the British and moved to a temporary camp at Middelburg, where van den Berg's daughter-in-law and her newborn child died, along with hundreds of others, because of unsanitary conditions, cold, and starvation. General Louis Botha estimated that twenty thousand women and children died in the camps, in comparison with the four thousand Boer men who were killed fighting. In *Boer War Letters* (1984), Hobhouse describes what she saw on an evening visit to "the largest" of the Middelburg camp graveyards: "rows upon rows of children's graves, most bearing the date of that fatal July written on a bit of paper and put in a glass bottle."

After four months in Middelburg, van den Berg was moved to a camp in Durban where she spent the remaining months of the war. After meeting her, Hobhouse wrote in a letter that van den Berg "talked a great deal about the camps in her mystic Transvaal way, but ended by saying the 'Man Above' had allowed it, so it must have been for the best."

M. J. Daymond

✦

On the 13th [October 1900] before sunrise the enemy came to Witpoort. They remained by our dwelling over six hours in order to carry out their work of destruction. They drove their horses into our lands (viz. cultivated ground) and they carried away over 7,000 sheaves of oats. A large piece of oatland was not yet cut; that they destroyed. Our potatoes, the crop from four sacks of seed, were also destroyed by the enemy. Our stable, wagonhouse and kraals were plundered and ruined. All the pigs and feathered stock they beat to death. A new wagon they took away with them and burnt the other wagon. I asked them why they took one wagon and burnt the other. A man gave me this answer: "The reason is that when the wagons used by the Commandos are worn out, then they come and take fresh wagons with which to fight."

I answered him then: "Our men do not fight with wagons."

Thereupon said he: "You must bring in your husband and sons with their mausers."

Then I made answer: "You will not catch the men, for even with your great power you have not yet gone through the country. The railway is in your possession, but that belongs to a company, not to you."

Then said he: "We have the villages in our possession."

"But our Government has given up the villages to the women and you ought not to go into them at all."

In this way I replied to him.

All that was in my dwelling-house was spared at that time; the reason being that I asked the Commanding Officer for a guard to protect myself and my house, which he granted me. I also asked him that the corn which still stood on the land should not be destroyed which also he willingly granted. So the standing corn was spared.

On the 13th some of our men were again here and on the 14th my husband returned with the cattle.

I had thought that the enemy would not come again but on the 14th November, 1900, they came again from Belfast by the road over the farm Schoonuitzicht, and reached Witpoort in the afternoon at 4 o'clock. After they had first fired a cannonade with maxims over the house and trees, they came up to my house. A man said to me:

"Tante, I give you half an hour's time to take what you want out of your house for I am come to set it on fire."

I asked him: "Why will you burn the house? I am weak, suffering from fever. What will become of me under the naked sky?"

I spoke to the officer asking him to spare the house: he refused to do so. I said to him:

"With God in Heaven there is mercy, have you then no mercy for a poor woman? Because you cannot get the men into your hands will you fight the women?"

The man turned white, gave me no answer and rode away. The others remained sitting upon their horses. One of them said:

"Tante, this is an order and we must carry it out, but bring everything out of the house that you can."

Then they dismounted and began to help me carry out the things, such as the furniture in the sitting and dining rooms, the beds and other goods. Also they brought out for me three sacks of corn and two sacks of meal. They also helped my daughter-in-law to carry out her things. From my storeroom I could save nothing for they refused to allow me to fetch anything from there except my veld-tent which a man carried out and gave me. It speaks for itself that I could do nothing, being but just out of a sick bed where I had lain for three months and my right arm was still powerless. I had spoken gently and had besought; but nothing availed—the house must be burnt. When I went to the pantry to fetch something I found a man there with two packets of fuel. He set fire to it. One packet he threw upon the ceiling of the sitting room the other in a bedroom. The flames rose up instantly in the gable of the house. I stood looking at it— no pen can write what was in my heart. Suddenly flashed into my mind: "Vengeance is mine, I will repay, saith the Lord." When I thought of this I felt steadfast—the dear Lord has more than this to give me—but it was terrible to see everything in flames. As the house stood in flames from gable to gable they took the three sacks of corn and put them in the passage of the house and threw the one sack of meal through the window of the sittingroom.

I asked them why they burnt my food: a man made answer: "Your husband gives you food."

I said then: "The devil thanks you for this: my husband has given me food enough—but you have burnt it."

A Kaffir in the service of the enemy who stood gazing at the house as it burnt said: "It is awful."

I remained silent.

He said for the second time: "It is awful," and added, "it is sin."

Then spoke I and said: "Yes, God will punish you for this."

Then they went back to their camp taking with them my two Kaffirs to carry the goods plundered from me to their camp.

My daughter Bettie then pulled the three sacks of corn out of the house and with the help of my daughter-in-law saved also the sack of meal—all lay outside on the flat. The houses and corn-stacks continued to burn. In the smoke and heat we must get through the night under an oak tree.

When my two Kaffirs came back I got them to put up my tent. We had also two bucksails (which we had made) which must serve for dwelling-room and storeroom. [. . .]

[6 October 1901] It is a pretty district, that of Mooi-rivier right on to Pietermaritzburg, which town is pleasantly situated. There we received corned beef to fortify us and condensed milk to refresh us. A great women's camp was there. We passed on to Durban, arriving at Merebank at 5 o'clock in the afternoon. From all directions the women came to greet us, but were not allowed to speak to us; the Kaffir Police drove them away. Then we got some coffee. Still they would not give us our bedding, so that again we had to get through our night upon the hard benches of the train without blanket or pillow. Believe me it was a hard journey from Middelburg to Merebank, three days in open trucks and two days in third class carriages without bedclothes.

The following morning we had to go and give our names to the Commandant and receive our tent numbers. Thence we went into the camp to be given out tents, some of us remaining behind to keep an eye on our goods. The trucks with our goods arrived and were all off-loaded in a heap in the camp, with a Kaffir constable to guard it. After everything was wet through with rain, came a man with some regard for us, who said each must identify her goods and take them. All the things did not come together, and I did not get mine till the fourth day. As regards the tents some got square tents with sailcloths therein to spread upon the ground which was sandy and soaking wet. Others got round tents. Next we had to go and fetch our rations; doing this my daughter Bettie got wet in the rain, and had to get through those days in her wet clothes and soaked shoes till our goods came. We had each put a change of clothing in a portmanteau to use whenever we should want it, but this was torn out of our hands at Charlestown and thrown upon the goods train. You can understand what an effect the soaking clothes had upon the health of one who had never been used to live in such a way four days and nights. The weather was stormy all the time; and the rain continued incessantly so that we had no opportunity to dry ourselves in the sun. Disheartened, hungry, and weary we dragged through our days in the wet tent. Happily we were able to borrow some bedding and a pot in which to cook from some people, otherwise I do not know what would have become of us. Some suffered much without stretchers on the wet soaked ground.

October 9: We rose up with renewed courage and asked the Lord for strength to bear the lot that had befallen us. After sunrise we had to go again to receive our bread, each person receiving a half loaf a day. The day passed restfully and nothing happened except that we got good meat that day; we felt a little more settled. It had been a long time since we last had got meat. That afternoon we had worship, led by Mr. Luther, who promised us to hold service every day. We sent to the Commandant to ask for passes to go and look at the sea, which he refused us till the following week.

October 10: We celebrated the birthday of President Kruger in a festive way, while silently in the inner chambers of our hearts a voiceless prayer rose to heaven for a blessing on him who is so full of years, that he might be spared to see the end of this terrible war. We also trusted that he as our Head would work on for us. The enemy hunted us round like dogs and then sought to hide their infamy by saying that we were refugees.

The Lord knows they dragged us away from our houses where we were free and where we had plenty of everything and shut us up here in a camp where we are not free and where we suffer want.

To-day at noon there was a great event in the camp; a number of women and children hoisted the "Vierkleur" [the flag of the Transvaal Republic] and a white flag also, and went through the camp carrying the flags. [. . .]

November 1: Bettie's sickness became intermittent, now better, now worse. To-day again two bodies were buried. Our minister's wife went around the camp to-day to visit the sick.

November 2: I was very busy tending Bettie's sickness; three more buried to-day.

November 3: Four bodies placed in the earth to-day. Bettie decidedly better; the doctor came round to visit the sick, he gave Bettie medicine that did her harm. From then she was so much worse that I was obliged to give up the doctor's medicine and to go on with our Boer remedies. Two more bodies were buried.

Nov. 4: Bettie seriously ill, and little Martje not well. Now it was very hard for me; through the night I had to watch by the sick and by day I could get no rest. Then I proved that the Lord sends strength to carry the cross that He lays upon us. Every day help came from loving hands. Camp life claimed so much from us all that it was almost impossible to help one another. For instance the rations must be fetched, then again the wood. It was piteous to see aged women struggling even to the point of falling under the weight of the wood that we had ourselves to bring for our fires. We did not get enough wood from the Commissariat and so we had to go into the bush and cut it for ourselves. This all happened by permission of the Lord for we were being "tried in the fire." "Whoso endures to the end shall be saved." He has promised if the weary and heavy laden come to Him, they shall find rest; that is our trust in our weariness.

November 5: People came again to us, for instance old Mr. Potgieter who helped us much with the sick; the dying trust in him. Again there were burials, two more of our friends had passed away. [. . .]

[1 June 1902] After service Ds. Enslin begged the congregation to wait a little. Commandant Bousefield then came in. He announced to us that Peace was concluded between the government of England and the two Republics. That word "Peace" was a blessed one to hear. It was affecting to see the children how they sprang up clapping their hands and shouting: "It is Peace!"

June 2: The Commandant gave order that we should all assemble at the office at 4 p.m. There he made known to us the fact that our leaders with their staffs had agreed to lay down their arms. It was now peace. He offered us his hand of friendship which Ds. Enslin and a couple of other men pressed in the name of all the women. The great mass of women shook their heads in denial and turned back to their rooms. For the fact of peace we were glad; that was all.

Translated by Emily Hobhouse

Minnie Martin, MOLIEGE'S VENGEANCE
South Africa 1906   English

Despite the fact that it was generally men who first transcribed, translated, and analyzed orature, white South African women writers have been fascinated by the genre and its possibilities for literary exploitation. In "Moliege's Vengeance" Minnie Martin reworks a Zulu oral narrative. Martin arrived in South Africa in 1891 with her husband, a government official, and settled in Basutoland. In the dedication prefacing her book *Basutoland: Its Legends and Customs* (1903), she writes, "We both liked the country from the first, and I soon became interested in the people. To enable myself to understand them better, I began to study the language, which I can now speak fairly well." She also published *Tales of the African Wilds* (1935) and *The Sun Chief (Legends of Basutoland)* (1943), which contains a slightly revised version of "Moliege's Vengeance."

Writing for an adult audience in *The South African Magazine* in the early twentieth century, Martin presents "Moliege's Vengeance" in such a way as to raise questions about white women's reshaping of black women's oral tradition. For one thing, Martin's story stands out as especially meaningful in the context of the developing feminism of white South Africa in the early twentieth century. It is interesting to read "Moliege's Vengeance" as the means whereby a white woman chooses to represent women's rage and revenge through the persona of a black woman. In her novel *From Man to Man,* roughly contemporary with this story, Olive Schreiner used on two occasions the despair, grief, and anger of a black woman in order, it seems, to work out and support the white female character's feelings. Martin's work then, like Schreiner's, reveals a significant and problematic cultural interaction between white and black women.

Dorothy Driver

✦

When the Chief, Manoe, became a man he desired a wife who would be more beautiful than any of the maidens of his own village, so he journeyed from place to place. "For," said he, "if I trust this matter to my Councillors, how shall I know that they have chosen the most beautiful maiden? No, I will see with my own eyes, and so I shall be satisfied."

But Manoe was difficult to please, and as time passed he grew angry and frowned upon his followers because they could not find a maiden beautiful enough to be his wife. After many wanderings they arrived at the village of the old Chief, Letsika, and were told how beautiful and fat was his youngest daughter.

"Will not my father bring forth his daughter that my eyes may behold her?" asked Manoe. Accordingly Moliege was sent for, and her beauty so pleased the young Chief that arrangements were at once made for the marriage, and shortly afterwards Manoe and his followers returned to their own village.

When all the marriage arrangements were completed Moliege was escorted by two old women and many of her young companions to the village of Manoe, where a great feast had been prepared. The people sang and feasted, and for many moons there was rejoicing in the village; but as time passed and there was no child born to Moliege, the Chief began to look with displeasure upon his young wife, and to wish that he could find some way of removing her from his dwelling. His anger and dislike filled with fear the heart of Moliege, so that she went slowly and sadly to and fro in the place.

She became a-weary, heavy of heart, and frightened, for she knew that Manoe intended to kill her. At last she ran away to the mountains and hid herself in a cave, where, for many moons, she lived alone. Her food was the wild roots and berries, and her drink the water from the spring near by. Often she prayed to the spirits of her fathers to take away the curse which had been laid upon her.

One day, as she was making earthen pitchers in which to carry water, she heard a gentle sound behind her, and, looking round, she saw a dove sitting upon a rock close by, and holding in its mouth two large seeds. Again it made the gentle sound which at first had caused her to look at it, and, stretching out its head, it seemed to be asking her to take what was in its mouth.

Wondering greatly at this strange thing, Moliege said to the dove, "What is it that you want?" "I have come," replied the dove, dropping the seeds beside her, "to give you these two seeds. Put one in each of these new pitchers that you are making, and close the opening securely; then wait patiently for that which shall happen."

The bird flew away, and, taking up the seeds, Moliege did as she had been told. She then carried the two pitchers carefully back to the cave where she dwelt, and for nine moons nothing happened. At the end of that time she noticed that both of the pitchers were beginning to crack, as if something big inside were trying to burst forth. At length they broke open altogether, and from out of them rolled two lovely baby girls. How great then was the joy of Moliege! She called them Takane and Takaka, and hid them from the sight of men, for by them when they were fully grown she knew her wrongs would be avenged.

The children grew in strength and beauty, and were to their mother as the sun when he ariseth after the dark night is ended. Never did Moliege allow both her daughters to leave the cave at the same time, nor would she permit them to speak with any person when they went to carry water from the spring.

One day, as Takane went with her pitcher to fetch the water, 'Nkaota, the son of the Chief, Manoe, by another wife, met her on his return from hunting, and wondered greatly where the maiden dwelt; but to his greetings she gave no answer, nor would she even tell him her name. So, telling his followers that he would return home shortly and bidding them hasten back with the wild beasts they had slain, 'Nkaota hid himself behind a rock and waited for the maiden to pass. He then followed her until he came to the cave, but when he reached the doorway he saw only an old woman and two doves, for Moliege had seen him coming, and had changed both her daughters into doves until the stranger should depart.

After greeting the old woman, 'Nkaota asked for water to drink, which she gave him silently. "Ho," quoth 'Nkaota, "this is not the way to find out what I want to know." Aloud he said, "Mother, as I passed the spring below, I saw a beautiful maiden whom, until to-day, my eyes had never beheld. She is not of my father's village, for none of my followers knows her. Can you tell me who she is?"

"My son," replied Moliege, "How should I—a lonely old woman—know aught of such a matter. Trouble not your mind about the maiden and go in peace."

But 'Nkaota knew in his heart that the maiden had entered the cave, so he determined to watch for her another day. But he hid from Moliege the thoughts within him, and returned to his home full of desire for the maiden.

For some days he waited in vain, but upon the sixth day, as he hid by the spring, Takane came again to fill her pitcher with water. As she knelt by the side of the spring, 'Nkaota came from the place where he had hidden himself, and spoke to the maiden, who, when she saw so brave a youth, felt her heart swell with joy. Many times they met thus, and at length Takane confessed to her mother that she loved 'Nkaota, who greatly desired her for his wife. At first, sore indeed was the heart of Moliege, but the tears and prayers of her child overcame her anger, and she consented to allow Takane to become the wife of 'Nkaota if he would promise not to reveal to his father the name of his wife's mother or where she dwelt.

The marriage feast was then prepared, and 'Nkaota returned to his father's village, taking with him his bride; but at sunrise the next day he awoke to find the hut empty save only for a dove, which gazed at him sadly, and flew out into the air beyond his sight.

In great grief he hastened to the cave of Moliege, to whom he told the evil thing which had befallen him.

Moliege promised to restore his wife to him if he would conduct her to his father's hut in the middle of the night.

That night, when all was still in the village, Moliege and 'Nkaota stole into the hut of the sleeping chief. Long and silently did Moliege gaze at the sleeping husband from whom she had so long been parted. Then, taking a horn in her hand, she advanced upon him. At the same time a white dove flew down and alighted upon Manoe. "Mother" came the voice of

Takane, "touch not the father of 'Nkaota, lest I, your child, hate you." The sound of talking awoke Manoe, and, rising up, he saw the woman he had treated so cruelly in the years gone by.

"Moliege, is it indeed you? Can the spirits of my fathers bring back the dead?"

But Moliege answered him not, nor would she remain in the hut. Taking some powder out of the horn she sprinkled it over the dove, which became again the lively Takane. Then, turning to her husband, she said, "May the spirits of your fathers take your strength from you, as you took my youth and gladness from me." Then taking the remaining powder out of the horn, she threw it over Manoe, who became as a little helpless child who cannot walk alone.

Thus was Moliege revenged upon her husband for the wrong he had done her.

Margarethe von Eckenbrecher, OMINOUS WEATHER

Namibia 1907   German

Margarethe Hopfer was born in 1875 in Bernburg, Germany, and trained, unusually for the time, as a secondary school teacher. After teaching in Berlin and England, she married Themistokles von Eckenbrecher and moved with him and their young son to German South West Africa in 1902. Her husband had served in the colonial forces as a participant in the Swartbooi campaign of 1898 and had earned the right to a government farm on special conditions. They took up residence in Okombahe on the Omaruru River in central Namibia where they acquired a farm and traded with the people at nearby Kawab.

In January 1904 rumors of a general uprising against the Germans had reached even this very remote area. A few weeks later, as the uprising gathered momentum, white families were taken to Omaruru. The Herero were very successful in the first few months of the war, but they were eventually outgunned and defeated by the Germans. The von Eckenbrechers lost some of their possessions in this uprising and decided to return to Germany. Six months after their divorce in 1913, Margarethe von Eckenbrecher came back to South West Africa where she remained until her death. For much of this time she worked as a teacher in Windhoek.

In 1907, after her first stay in South West Africa, von Eckenbrecher published an account of her experiences in Okombahe. The book, entitled *Was Africa mir gab und nahm, Erlebnisse einer Deutschen Unsiedlerfrau in Südwest Afrika* (What Africa gave me and took from me: The experiences of a German settler woman in Southwest Africa), was very successful and in 1938 a new edition appeared that provided a more heroic view of the events of the 1904–1907 German-Herero War. This book is typical in many ways of German settler literature in that it offers an insight into how attitudes about race and gender, later viewed as immutable, were constructed in and through the lived experiences of early settler communities. Von Eckenbrecher's writing depicts the ambivalent and often marginalized position that settler women occupied in relation to the colonizing enterprise. Her writing and those of other settler writers like Clara Brockman, Maria Karow, and Helene von Falkenhausen reveal the allure of the social and spatial freedom that suddenly became available to women in the colony when they took up the masculine duties of doctor, farmer, and protector of the homestead.

Rosa Schneider

✦

Peaceful Christmas celebrations were followed by a quiet New Year. The days were hot and sultry, the nights stifling and gloomy. Banks of black clouds massed together above Okombahe Mountain, which gave the village its name. Dark and threatening, they seemed to hang heavily on the desolate giant, ready to send down bad weather at any moment. On the horizon, yellow flashes of lightning shot up like rockets. It was quite unbearable.

The sultriness in nature seemed to communicate itself to the emotions. One felt uneasy. Something was different, but what it was one could not fathom.

The Hereros who lived half an hour away from Okombahe (Okombahe in Herero is, "There where the giraffe . . ." because the mountain, which rises above Okombahe village, has the shape of a reclining giraffe), at Kawab, were very busy. Their local gentry often came to Okombahe to shop in the various stores—more often than usual. If one showed surprise, the answer was, "We are afraid the grazing will deteriorate at Kawab. We want to trek early with the livestock, that's why we are getting everything ready."

They visited us often. We had always been on friendly terms with them and we were surprised that one day they asked my husband with great interest when I would be returning to Germany. Themis was taken aback and replied that I had no such intention. Thereupon Justus Hongera, son of a local dignitary, said, "Mr.v.E., I am telling you that it will be good if your wife goes away. She must go soon and stay away for a long time."

"Whatever gives you that idea?"

"I am telling you that it will be good if she goes. Africa is not for her. It's a country for men who love war. Rough and wild they must be. You can stay. The gun and the saddle are for you. But if you love your wife, then send her away!" Themis was amazed at this talk, and not at all sure what to make of it.

On another occasion we were discussing a journey we had been planning with the deputy chief, Joshua, when he broke in with, "I have a feeling that you will not get far. Stay here."

"What makes you think that?"

"You white people shouldn't think that you are safe here, in the country of the black people. It is written up there in the clouds: Our Lord God will send a terrible war which will devastate the land and kill the whites." We regarded these words as boasts and foolish gossip.

A song by my poetically inclined washerwoman, Emma, made me sit up and listen, "You poor white people. You will die in this country after all. You little child, it's not your fault that you were born here. But you also must die. I am crying and my son is crying, but there is nothing we can do."

"Emma, what are you singing about?"

"Oh nothing, Madam, I am singing what my silly thoughts tell me. You should not listen."

And yet another occasion: "Madam, do you sleep well?"

"Yes, thank you, very well."

"I'm sorry."

"Why?"

"It would be better if you did not sleep well. Put some pebbles between your ribs. You must not sleep deeply."

Samuel, Emma's son, who had accompanied us to Gui-Gams months before, came onto the veranda one day and stared at me. "Why are you looking at me like that?"

"Oh Madam, I am looking at the ones marked by death." I took note of this and discussed it with Ertmann and my husband who were getting ready for a major journey. "Would you not rather stay here?"

"Heaven forbid, no."

"All the same, these things have the ring of hidden warnings. I cannot interpret them."

"Nonsense, the revolt of the Bondelzwarts has shocked people to the core. As soon as the first reports are out, all will be quiet. They're a cowardly bunch."

We watched the revolution in the south in a leisurely fashion. People were used to minor incidents occurring frequently. Even if this thing was of a more serious nature, it did not affect us in Hereroland. The Bondelzwarts, a Hottentot tribe, were on bad terms with the Hereros; the trouble spot was far away; the governor would surely settle the thing with his usual leniency. However, that was an illusion. Chief Christians would not be pacified. He did not want the peace offering of rum and tobacco. Troops were required. When the more northerly district of Omaruru was stripped of its military and when Captain Franke, feared by some people and popular with others, also made his way to the south, then the old, experienced Africans looked concerned.

We were all conscious of the fact that there had been a search for weapons and ammunition at several large Herero settlements the year before and that the efforts had been successful. The Hereros, habitually violent and overbearing, had become even more arrogant. A few behaved in an insubordinate manner towards us whites. At their settlements, where one used to receive a friendly welcome, one now got an ice-cold reception. The possibility of a revolt was in the air. With so few troops in the north, now seemed to be the most opportune moment in time. If the Hereros were considering an uprising at all, it had to be soon. We made all sorts of guesses.

Even the government received warnings. However, it also took a very optimistic viewpoint. It was indeed fortunate that the troops designated to return home had not yet embarked for the voyage when the revolt of the Bondelzwarts broke out.

At Omaruru, four men were left behind. That was a small number indeed. Consequently, the old reserves were asked whether the one or other of them would volunteer in order to serve as reinforcements for the few troops. Several settlers, traders and businessmen, who were not too busy at the time, responded to the call. They had grown old and grey in the battle against the sun and wind. They had worked extremely hard. Now that the fatherland was calling, their bit of personal business could take second place.

The districts of Karibib and Omaruru had been merged into one. First Lieutenant Kuhn had to administer both. It was in the nature of things that very little duty was done at the Omaruru base after the departure of Captain Franke. The horses were with the field company or at Sorris-Sorris, the place of death. As soon as the old reserves had been recruited, a lively, tough tour of duty started which was not easy on them initially.

At the beginning of January, my husband, together with Ertmann, travelled to Swakopmund via Spitzkoppies to buy fresh supplies for us. The old supplies were almost totally used up. I let him go with an easy mind. What will be will be, we cannot fight our destiny.

He had been gone half a day, when a messenger from Omaruru appeared in front of our house, on horseback and dripping with perspiration. He had to deliver draft papers. All the reserves were being called up. Themis received the order to go to the military base at Okombahe immediately and to stay there until further notice. The rider, who was totally exhausted, told me in the strictest confidence that people were beginning to fear the worst on account of the Hereros. The chiefs of the different settlements and many able-bodied men were said to have disappeared. There were rumours of large gatherings, mysterious messages and lively traffic between all the settlements.

I had no choice but to have my husband called back. My most trustworthy messenger reached him and Themis returned by the evening of the second day. He just had enough time to barricade a window in the bedroom and to move some items of furniture, so that I could at least not be shot from the window while I was asleep. He had to stay at the station day and night in order to be able to defend it if the need arose.

I myself, on the other hand, was left to my fate, completely alone in the house with my small child.

I was really upset by the harshness of that order. We, the wives of the settlers, irrespective of our social standing, shared the fate of our husbands in times of peace. We suffered with them, even hunger and thirst. Like our husbands, we put all our strength at the service of the colony. Our children were born under the most difficult conditions. We had to endure more in the colony than would have been conceivable in Germany—and now, in the hour of danger, my husband was taken away from me.

Ten days and ten nights I stayed alone with no one except my nine-year-old servant Isaac, whom I put up in the kitchen so that someone could at least hold the child for me once in a while.

During the day, I had to do all the chores, including my husband's. At night I was left to my own devices. Several times my dogs barked fiercely. I got up thinking that a hyena or some other predator was disturbing the livestock. Because I saw nothing, I turned back. The next morning Isaac showed me fresh footprints in the sand round the house and in the garden. Whether kaffirs or Hereros, they had certainly tried to steal something. The lambs got lost, a calf disappeared mysteriously. I was powerless. And my husband was just twenty minutes away and could not help me.

Nevertheless, things were going to get even worse. At midday on 13 January, two Hereros, whom I knew quite well, arrived with their servants. They wanted to sell a sheep to me. I noticed that the men, six in all, were armed. Two carried guns, the servants had knobkerries. Even in times of peace it happens that one is visited by armed people. But then they lean their weapons on the outside wall of the house as an indication of their peaceful intentions. This time, however, they kept holding them in their hands.

I was not in the mood to buy the sheep. There was no money in the house and we had run out of suitable articles for exchange long ago. They asked for two shirts. In order to get rid of the fellows, I agreed. Since I was completely unsuspecting, I thought no evil when they followed me into the house. We soon came to an agreement and we talked like always after concluding even the smallest business deal. The conversation revolved round the impending revolution.

Geert Afrika, the oldest of the Hereros, asked me, "Do you think it is right that the Hereros want to start a war against the whites?" I answered truthfully that it would be an extremely foolish enterprise in my opinion, because the white man would win under any conditions whatever.

"And what do you think will happen?"

"If you are that imprudent and do start, then a lot of blood will be shed, you will lose land and livestock, and your lives will be in the hands of the white man."

Then another fellow said, "Oh, don't you worry. We are the servants of the white man. The lion who sleeps does not know when danger approaches."

Thereupon they all grinned and, at a casually dropped word from Geert Afrika, two people stood in front of each of the two doors in order to cut off the exit unobtrusively. All at once I became aware of the danger and the seriousness of my position.

Geert Afrika stepped right up close to me, laughing and shouting in my face, "Now we'll have the real talk about the war, you'll see." My heart was beating violently. I forced myself to be calm. There was no help at hand, if I did not help myself. I pulled myself together, "You come to do business with me and you don't know how to behave towards a white woman? Make way, you scoundrel." I pushed past him and went to the door. There I had expected resistance. However, both of the fellows were so surprised that they moved aside without waiting for the push I had intended to give them. In no time the door flew open towards the outside—I was outside.

There I was safe. There they could do nothing to me because the place was crowded with Bergdamaras. They would not have dared to shoot inside either. A blow of the knobkerrie is silent, however. That was what I had expected.

I stopped in front of the store. Geert came out grinning. He lifted his floppy hat, "This time the madam was clever. She was cleverer than we were. It doesn't matter. The time is near when she will hear from me again." Thus spoken he disappeared with his companions.

My young servant Isaac, who had been looking after the child, came running along hurriedly and reported, "I don't even know what the Hereros wanted. They came towards me and the child, asking me whether it was a boy or a girl. When I told them they went away and called to me, laughing, 'You stay here, we'll come back later.'"

I was deeply troubled by the boy's report. They had also wanted to kill my child. Never in my life have I felt so utterly deserted as I did at that moment. And yet, I had to be grateful that I had been alone at the time when the Hereros came. If my husband had been there, they would probably have clubbed him to death mercilessly inside the house. With me, they must have felt uneasy and then had second thoughts about carrying out their plan. Perhaps they also remembered the numerous meals which these two in particular had received from me, the many times they were allowed to grind their corn in my mill, the Sundays when they came to me so often for advice and medication.

I was feeling very ill, but I recovered control of myself for the sake of my child. The responsibility of guarding his life lay in my hands and mine alone.

Translated by Mara Miller

Khami, COURT RECORD

Zimbabwe 1908   Shangaani

The district criminal court records, preserved in the National Archives, Harare, are a significant source for women's experiences in colonial Zimbabwe. Many cases deal directly with laws on marriage and adultery. There are also numerous rape cases. Others, like prosecutions under the Witchcraft Suppression Act, do not necessarily involve women. Nevertheless, women were more often accused of being witches than men. The great majority of prosecutions for assault and murder also turned around sexual relations.

With serious cases the district criminal court carried out a preparatory examination of witnesses. The reports of that hearing were then sent to the solicitor general, who determined whether the case should be brought to the High Court. There were no shorthand writers at district courts and the testimonies translated by a court interpreter were not recorded verbatim. Nevertheless, as in the case that follows, the voice of a woman witness comes clearly through.

Some brief notes are necessary to set the context. Khami's evidence in the 1908 Gwanda assault case is the testimony of a heroic thirteen year old. Like so many cases concerning women, it only came before the court because she was strong enough to make a complaint. Her story involves two long journeys with Segwalagwala, the man she refused to accept as a husband. These journeys were made in order to have the marriage registered before the Gwanda district commissioner. Under colonial legislation, marriages had to be registered, the consent of the woman had to be given, and evidence offered that bride-wealth had been paid. As can be seen from Khami's story, the system did not offer much protection to a girl being forced into marriage, though in the end she managed to get her case brought before the criminal court.

The problem with criminal court records as evidence is that there is no way of telling what happened next. So we do not know whether Khami went on to marry a man of her own choice.

Terence Ranger

✦

Rex versus Segwalagwala, charged with rape
Preliminary Examination held at Gwanda on 29 October 1908 before C. M. Fletcher, with a Shangaan interpreter, the accused being Shangaan. Evidence of Khami, 23 November 1908
I am a Shangaan woman. I live at Segwalagwala's kraal. About nine months ago I remember accused arriving at the kraal. Accused met my father and said he and my father had been called to the Native Commissioner. Accused wanted to marry me and my father agreed but I was unwilling. My father at first refused as the full lobola had not been paid. Accused then assaulted my father, throwing him down. My father agreed to give me up but wanted the lobola. £21 was paid but that was not the full amount. When the assault took place I ran away into the veldt, staying away 4 days. I eventually came back. Then my father told me I was to go to accused. I was then taken to him by my brother. We were all afraid of accused.

I was then left with accused who beat me because I refused to sleep with him. During the night I again ran away and was found by my uncle, Mogwana. I was again taken back to accused who said: "Why do you bring her here? She will only run away again." I again ran away and was sent back. I would not go to accused.

I was then made to sleep with accused by him. He took me into his hut by force, putting his hand over my mouth. I cried out but accused had connection with me against my will, holding me down. I said I was too young. Accused effected his purpose. Penetration was complete. Makolo came when I cried out. He was living at accused's kraal. He did not say anything.

The next day I left for the Native Commissioner's. Accused, Ngatzane and Mvuli came along as well. Along the road accused again had connection with me by force. He threw me down. This happened five times. He effected his purpose each time. We were nine days on the road. Each night I was in accused's scherm. On each occasion he took me to his scherm. I did not cry out but said to accused he had no right. We eventually got to the Native Commissioner's but as he was away we went to the Blanket Mine first. While at the Blanket Mine accused again had connection with me, catching hold of me by the throat. (Nail marks are shown on witness' throat.) I refused to have anything to do with him.

27 November 1908

When I was on my way in to report to the Native Commissioner and have the marriage settled accused threatened me with an assegai he had. He said he wanted to have intercourse with me and also said that unless I married him he would use the assegai. When I came in to the Native Commissioner and was asked whether I would marry accused I refused. Later on I again was questioned and again refused. This was when I had come back from the Blanket Mine. The Native Commissioner then said I was to go back to my kraal and that accused was to have nothing to do with me. Instructions were that I was to go back with my brother and I was handed over to him. I heard the instructions to the accused given by the Native Commissioner and accused replied that he would commit suicide for [me] as [I] was his wife and that he would poison [me].

I have never agreed to become accused's wife. Everything he has done has been by threats. Accused on the way home said he again wanted connection with me. I replied "Have you not heard the Native Commissioner's instructions?" After we left Gwanda accused took me from my brother close to our kraal and took me to his kraal and again had connection with me. I had to stay with him 2 days and then ran away again to my father's kraal but he had left for another kraal as accused had threatened him; he was afraid. Later on I again saw accused and he said we should go to the Native Commissioner's again. My father was asked to come in but said as he had been hurt by accused he could not. My brother and uncle accompanied me and appeared before the Native Commissioner. On the road up accused again forced me to have connection with him on several occasions and threatened me with an assegai.

We appeared before the Native Commissioner a second time and I again refused to marry accused.

My age is about 13 years. The lobola accused paid my father for me was paid about 2 years ago. Since I was handed over to accused by my father I have been living with accused but have never agreed. He has another wife at his kraal.

She made her mark on the record before two witnesses.

Transcriber and translator unknown

Indian Women's Association,
WOMEN'S PETITION:
DOMESTIC UNHAPPINESS

South Africa 1908   English

One of the first known published examples of Indian women's writings in South Africa was a collaborative one, in which women responded to anti-Indian legislation. Act 17 of 1895 required that all indentured Indians who had completed their original contracts with their employers and were not returning to India or being reindentured in Natal, pay three pounds annually for a residence license. The law served either to enforce repatriation or prolong indentured labor, as the tax was beyond the means of the average formerly indentured Indian.

The Indian Opinion, founded by Mohandas Gandhi in 1904 in South Africa, and other Indian newspapers published letters of protest. Formed in 1908 with Gandhi's assistance, the Indian Women's Association added its voice to protests by publishing several petitions in *The African Chronicle.* The act was repealed in 1913 as a direct result of the massive passive resistance campaign that was mounted against it.

The Indian Women's Association, which became known as the Durban Indian Women's Association under the leadership of Kunwarani Lady Maharaj Singh, wife of the agent-general of India in 1927, continues to exist to this day, as the Durban Women's Association. It provided an initial platform for activist Indian women to participate in broader nonracial formations in the decades that followed. In 1952, when Africans and Indians organized the fourth Passive Resistance Campaign, a multiracial Conference of Women was held in Johannesburg. This culminated in the historic march by South African women of all race groups on the Union Buildings in Pretoria, on 9 August 1956.

On 19 September 1908, *The African Chronicle* published the petition of the Indian Women's Association, without the signatories' names.

Devarakshanam Govinden

✦

To the Honourable the Speaker and the Honourable Members of the Legislative Assembly of the Colony of Natal.
This petition of the Indian Women's Association.
Humbly Sheweth:

1. That your petitioners beg leave to make representation on behalf of a class of Indians introduced into this Colony under indenture, and who labour under great disabilities and grievances owing to strict enforcement of Act 17 of 1895. The severity and hardship arising therefrom have impelled your petitioners' Association, to espouse their cause owing to the serious nature of their case.

2. Your petitioners respectfully submit that the Indians affected by the aforesaid Act, irrespective of sex, are subjected to an Annual imposi-

tion of £3, which sum owing to their helpless and indigent state, they are virtually unable to pay.

3. Owing to indiscreet enforcement of the aforesaid Act, great hardship and considerable suffering are inflicted upon them.

4. Your petitioners' Association in their endeavour to ameliorate and elevate the condition of their sex, have been informed of startling revelation of misery and serious annoyance which have resulted from the severe enforcement of this aforesaid Act that your petitioners deemed it their duty to bring the unfortunate and unhappy state of existence to the notice of this Honourable Assembly.

5. In normal times of prosperity, common labourers such as the Indians are, must feel heavily the strain of an imposition of kind of—£3—(for the privilege of living in this Colony) and much keener the bitterness of feeling must be, which no doubt at present exists, owing to chronic depression that prevails in all branches of trade in this Colony, from which the Indians are specially suffering.

6. Whilst the sterner sex—men—keenly feel and resent the severity of this Act, the woman-folk, weak and gentle by nature, who come under the category of the aforesaid Act, must naturally feel the stringency of this measure more acutely.

7. Your petitioners beg to draw the attention of this Honourable House to the tendency of the aforesaid Act, on women and girls, who are liable to pay this £3, which is not calculated to afford protection to the inherent rights of the gentler sex, for it fosters domestic infelicity.

8. Your petitioners regard with great shame and sorrow, that women who are in default of payment are sentenced to imprisonment; and the very dread of being marched up to Court and gaol is enough to numb their intellect and cause terror, to escape from which, the aforesaid Act fosters in them a temptation to barter their female modesty and virtue.

9. The aforesaid Act has been a source of breaking up many a home, alienating the affection of husband and wife, besides separating child from mother.

10. There is no precedent in the legislation of any other country under the British Flag, where women are taxed for the privilege of living with their husbands or under the protection of their nature guardians.

Wherefore your petitioners humbly pray, that this Honourable House will be pleased to repeal the aforesaid Act 17 of 1895 or to grant such other relief as it may deem fit.

For this act of justice, your petitioners will ever pray.

Kandjende's Sister, LETTER FROM KARIBIB

Namibia 1909   otjiHerero

Josephat Kandjende's sister wrote this letter after one of the most brutal suppressions of resistance in Namibia's colonial history. The Herero War began in January 1904 under the leadership of Samuel Maherero. In the first eight months of the war the Herero regained control of much of central Namibia. To counter this the German colonial administration sent reinforcements into battle under the command of General Lothar von Trotha. The Herero were defeated at the disastrous battle of Hamakari, after which von Trotha issued his notorious Extermination Order:

> All Herero must leave the country. If they do not, I will force them with cannons to do so. Within the German borders, every Herero, with or without weapons, with or without cattle, will be shot. I no longer shelter women and children. They must either return to their people or they will be shot at. This is my message to the Herero people.

The policy outlined in the Extermination Order was pursued up until about November 1904. However, evidence suggests that the order, made in early October, merely formalized existing practice. By the time an armistice was signed in December 1905, between 75 and 80 percent of the Herero had perished. Those who survived were subject to repressive conditions in prisoner-of-war camps. Families were split up; men, women, and children were forced to work in conditions of virtual slavery. These camps were not closed until April 1908.

During this period, therefore, travel, and thus communication among surviving members of traumatized families, was very difficult without a pass, which had to be carried by anyone, male or female, over the age of eight. If one were caught without a pass, the penalties were severe. Although the writer of this letter remains anonymous, the author's voice evokes anguish, fear, and strength, despite the hostile mediation of the "translators" of this intercepted letter. The letter survived alongside other letters, translated from otjiHerero into German, in the records of communication between the imperial district commissioner in Swakopmund and the imperial German government. The author's passionate exhortation that her brother destroy his papers provides an insight into the danger faced by an oppressed people when recording their history.

Margie Orford

✦

The Imperial District Commissioner
Swakopmund 23 February 1909
Top Secret
Re: Ordinance of 20 January 1909, no. 1718
In total, about 25 letters of natives have been intercepted, opened, inspected, carefully closed again and despatched to the addressees, so that the latter could not learn about the interception. The interception has not yielded clues about any current movement among the natives. Only the enclosed letter to

the Herero Josaphet Kandjende appeared to be of significance. Even before the letter reached the addressee, his home was searched for suspicious letters, but only completely harmless papers have been found.

Signed, Schenke

To the Imperial Government
Copy. Top Secret
Karibib, to Josephat Kanjende, 1909
My beloved brother! I greet you heartily and let you know, that I am still well. Rudolphine Kanjende intends to come, but her pass has been taken away, because you have not got her a pass from your master and from the police in Swakopmund. Therefore Rudolphine can now do nothing, she is with her relative, and to leave him here is difficult too. Please do make some effort these days to get money for two people. You know I am a weak woman, I cannot transport the people.

From you we have heard, that you have been in jail, it is enough to drive one mad! I tell you this: do not have any papers in your box, if you have any, throw them away, burn them. For a black man there are no papers anymore in our country now. If you have sense, you will take sense from this letter.

Do not write me again that I should take a letter (of dismissal) from my master. And I tell you nothing for certain, you must know for yourself. For the Herero have died, and the enemy kills whoever he finds.

Enough. Keep this first and last letter coming from this place. I posted it with my master, because no black man is going this way.

If you are asleep, open your eyes so they are vigilant, and pray. Greetings to all my relatives. I have no one who judges but God.

Enough. I close with greetings.

(no signature)

Translated by Werner Hillebrecht

Native and Coloured Women of the Province of the Orange Free State, PETITION OF THE NATIVE AND COLOURED WOMEN OF THE PROVINCE OF THE ORANGE FREE STATE

South Africa 1912   English

In 1893, with the passage of Law 8.2 in the Orange Free State (OFS), women were included under influx control regulations that previously and elsewhere had applied only to African men. At this time, only the OFS extended influx control legislation to women. The extension of a pass law to women would mean that those hoping to remain in urban areas would be allowed to do so only if they took up paid domestic labor. Besides this coercion, the police examination of passes put them at risk of being harassed and raped, their homes ransacked, and their families separated. For the local authorities, on the other hand, enforcing and issuing the passes represented a lucrative form of income and a sign of their power.

By 11 March 1912, a petition had been drafted by the newly formed Native and Coloured Women's Association, signed by five thousand women and circulated around the towns and villages of the OFS. On 3 April 1912 the petition—addressed to Prime Minister Louis Botha—was handed to the minister of finance, Henry Burton, in Cape Town by a delegation of ethnically mixed black women across various social classes, a remarkable accomplishment. Their assumption of rights as women and mothers, and their evocation of the principles of justice, lend their petition particular authority.

In 1913 the enforcement of the pass laws became increasingly stringent. On 28 May a women's meeting in Waaihoek resolved to embark on a mass resistance campaign, pledging not to carry passes until the achievement of the goals voiced in this petition. On 29 May, eighty women were arrested for burning their passes and offering themselves up for arrest. The next day, six hundred women appeared at the court house in solidarity with those arrested, shouting, "We have done with the pleading, we now demand." These words spread from Waaihoek to Senekal, Winburg, and Jagersfontein, and launched a spontaneous passive resistance campaign throughout the OFS. Refusing to carry passes, the women offered themselves up for arrest at local police stations; ignoring the fine options, they hoped to fill the jails.

Rirhandzu Mageza

✦

11th March, 1912
To The Right Honourable General Louis Botha, P.C., M.L.A., Prime Minister of the Union of South Africa, CAPE TOWN.
Sir,
    The petition of the undersigned humbly showeth:—

1. That your petitioners are residents of the various towns and villages in the Province of the Orange Free State, and are subjects of His Gracious Majesty King George V.
2. That your petitioners, as inhabitants of the said Province, are under a burden of having to carry Residential Passes in terms of Section 2 of Law 8 of 1893 (Orange Free State Statutes).
3. That this law is a source of grievance to your petitioners in that:—

    (a) It renders them liable to interference by any policeman at any time, and in that way deprives them of that liberty enjoyed by their women-folk in other Provinces.
    (b) It does not afford them that protection which may, peradventure, have been contemplated by the legislators, but on the other hand it subjects them to taxation, notwithstanding the sex to

which they belong—a policy which was unknown in the late South African Republic, and is unknown in the history of British Rule.

    (c) It has a barbarous tendency of ignoring the consequences of marriage in respect of natives, especially the right of parents to control their children, a right which parents ought to exercise without interference from outside; and the effect of its operation upon the minds of our children is that it inculcates upon them the idea that as soon as they become liable to comply with the requirements of this law, their age of majority also commences, and can, therefore, act independently of their parents.

    (d) It is an effective means of enforcing labour, and as such, cannot have any justification whatever on the ground of necessity or expediency.

    (e) It lowers the dignity of women and throws to pieces every element of respect to which they are entitled; and for this reason it has no claim to recognition as a just, progressive and protective law, necessary for their elevation in the scale of civilisation; moreover it does not improve their social status.

    (f) It can only have one ground for its existence in that Statute Book—namely, that it is a most effective weapon the governing powers could resort to to make the natives and coloured women in the Province of the Orange Free State ever feel their inferiority, which is only another way of perpetuating oppression regardless of the feelings of those who are governed; whereas the essence of justice is "Do unto others as you would be done by."

4. That your petitioners are the only women in the whole of the Union who are subjected to such an oppressive law; the women in the other provinces are not subjected to any Pass Laws.

5. That representations were made to the Imperial Government about this matter by the Congress of the Orange Free State Native Association, and the Imperial Government replied that the matter was a local one in which they could not interfere, but expressed a hope that the local authorities would find their way to grant your petitioners relief, and further that your petitioners would be better off under the Union Government of South Africa.

6. That further representations were made to the late Government of the Orange River Colony, the Conference of the Municipal Associations of the Orange River Colony, and to the Town Council of Bloemfontein, and all these bodies have referred the said Congress of the Orange Free State Native Association to the Union Parliament.

    Wherefore your petitioners humbly pray that the Right Honourable the Prime Minister may be pleased:—

    1. To grant them immediate relief from this burdensome law by introducing a Bill in Parliament repealing it.

or   2.   If it be not within the province of the Right Honourable the Prime Minister to do so, then, the Minister responsible be charged with the introduction of this Bill by the Right Honourable the Prime Minister.

or   3.   To grant your petitioners immediate relief from the operation of this law by suspending it, in so far as they are concerned, pending the introduction of this Bill into Parliament by the Minister responsible.

and your petitioners as in duty bound will ever pray.

Adelaide Charles Dube,
AFRICA: MY NATIVE LAND
South Africa 1913   English

Adelaide Dube's "Africa: My Native Land" is the earliest example of a published poem written by a black South African woman. The poem initially appeared and has frequently been anthologized simply under the signature "Mrs. A. C. Dube," without accompanying information given on the author. Adelaide Tantsi was born at Engcobo in the Eastern Cape, the daughter of J. Z. Tantsi, founder of the Ethiopian church in South Africa. She studied first at Inanda Seminary in the late 1890s and then—like Charlotte Maxeke (see her text in this volume)—at Wilberforce Institute in Ohio from 1901 to 1904, graduating with a B.Sc. After her return to South Africa, she founded and taught at an American mission school in Klipspruit, in an area that would later become part of Soweto. She married Charles Dube, the younger son of John Dube (the founder and proprietor of *Ilanga Lase Natali,* the Zulu weekly in which this poem first appeared). She took on the name Charles as her second name, according to custom, and settled with him at Ohlange, where they both taught for many years. She died on 11 August 1933.

The poem reprinted below was published on 31 October 1913, the day the Zulu king Dinizulu was buried and in the year of the Natives' Land Act, which forced thousands of black South African farmers and their families off their land into reserves. The poem celebrates Africa and laments its lost freedom. But like much South African writing at that time, notably that of another Zulu poet writing in English, H. I. E. Dhlomo, it is indebted to an English poetic lexicon and tradition. Nonetheless, the reference to "my troubled bones" marks allegiance to an ancestral religion, alluding to the importance of burial on one's home ground and to the rupture between the ancestors and their offspring through the alienation of the land. The temporal reference—kingdoms rise and fall, and so will the British empire—connects with the temporality of "troubled bones," bones that are not now at peace but will be; indeed, there is a threat in these rattling bones and in the insistence on an unending struggle ("never, never"), a struggle until death and beyond. The sacrificial blood shed in battle has a Christian resonance ("blood was shed to save thee"), but the Christianity preached by nineteenth-century missionaries is questioned from the perspective of the enslaved, who know that what has been taken from them by the colonizers is, according to the gospel of the missionaries, "free-dom—God's great gift."

Interesting, too, is the conflation of masculine and feminine perspectives, and the absorption of a woman's voice and a woman's aspirations and experience into the heroic tradition. Here is a crucial source for the refusal of some black South African women to identify with a European feminist tradition: There is another battle first to be won.

Dorothy Driver and Esther Sbongile Sangweni

◆

How beautiful are thy hills and thy dales!
I love thy very atmosphere so sweet,
Thy trees adorn the landscape rough and steep
No other country in the whole world
    could with thee compare.

It is here where our noble ancestors,
Experienced joy's of dear ones and of home;
Where great and glorious kingdoms rose and fell
Where blood was shed to save thee, thou
    dearest Land ever known;

But, Alas! their efforts, were all in vain,
For to-day others claim thee as their own;
No longer can their off-spring cherish thee
No land to call their own—but outcasts
    in their own country!

Despair of thee I never, never will,
Struggle I must for freedom—God's great gift—
Till every drop of blood within my veins
Shall dry upon my troubled bones, oh
    thou Dearest Native Land!

Louisa Mvemve,
A "LITTLE WOMAN'S" ADVICE TO THE PUBLIC

South Africa 1916   English

Louisa Mvemve worked from 1915 to 1930 as an *ixhwele* (herbalist) in the Eastern Cape and then in Brakpan, east of Johannesburg. The 1916 pamphlet partly repro-duced here is one of several that she herself published, which are all now housed in the Pretoria Central State Archive. Besides its advice, Mvemve's pamphlet contains an autobiographical fragment that recounts her move from her rural, peasant origins to the city where she became a landowner, trader, and herbalist, consulted by white as well as black people.

Mvemve was born near Port Alfred in the Eastern Cape toward the end of the nineteenth century. Born *umntwana wesingxhobo* (with a caul) she was marked as having special powers. She did not have a mission-school education—the usual means of entry into the country's small black elite—nor did she enjoy the patronage of a powerful person, but she was ambitious and enterprising enough to build her own successful business as an herbalist.

In all her work, Mvemve stressed that her powers as midwife, healer, herbalist, and diagnostician came from traditional Xhosa practices, particularly from the nursing skills of her maternal grandmother and the medical knowledge of her maternal grandfather. On the other hand, she was also keen to have Western science confirm the efficacy of her cures so that she could patent them and be licensed to practice. She was, however, up against a growing body of legislation that sought to regulate medical work by those "nonqualified." She was also affected by the increasingly rigid division of towns along racial lines, which eventually forced her to abandon the large herbarium she had established in a part of Brakpan newly zoned for whites. In these ways, Mvemve lived through a peculiarly South African series of tensions between tradition and modernity.

Through all her endeavors and all her trials, Mvemve's humor, tenacity, and confidence remained high. She frequently employed scribes to assist her in her business and legal campaigns, and she is known to us today because she comprehended the power of the written word to present her skills to others and to defend her when these skills were undervalued or resisted.

Catherine Burns

✦

A "Little Woman's" Advice to the Woman Who Has No Family But Wants Children.

Many women cannot get children. Others have them before they are due and lose them from 3 to 8 months old; this is unhealthy for the woman and will eventually kill her unless she follows "The Little Woman's Advice." Take the special herb for this irregularity and the child will not be born before it is the right time (nine months); and the child will be healthy and grow big and strong. The herb is good in all cases of child-bearing. It seems hard to believe what I shall tell you now, but it is quite true:

When my mother got married to my father she had only 2 children; after which she had several miscarriages. She didn't know what to do and tried all sorts of medicines without effect. Then my father said: "If you cannot carry a child until the proper time comes you will have to go back to your father; it is not you that I want but a family." She was then bearing another child. She went back to her father and told him what my father had said; then my grandfather said: "I am sorry that you did not send for me when you first felt the pains; I would have helped you to stop the child coming too soon; come and I will show you something that will prevent the child coming too soon." When they came to the forest he showed her the root and said: "Take this root when you get home, boil it and drink it, then take the bark away from the root, twist it into a rope, make a knot in the middle of the rope, and put it around your hips; that will stop the child from coming too soon, but always drink the water in which you boil the root."

She did as he had told her and the pain went away. Then she said: "What am I to do now, father?" He said: "Go back to your husband and keep on drinking the herb and wear the rope around your hips and the child won't be born until the proper time, and then you will have a fine strong child." She did not have any more miscarriages. The treatment stopped the trouble; the child came duly covered with a skin (caul) so she sent for her father and said I didn't have the child. Then her father said the child was only covered with a skin and prophesised that she would be a wise and strong child and would know all his secrets. Then he said to his daughter: "You will always have children now and no more miscarriages." And his words were true; I am that child and I am strong to-day, alive, well and strong.

These herbs were all my grandfather's secrets. They will cure all manner of diseases.

THE "LITTLE WOMAN'S" ADVICE TO MEN SUFFERING FROM DISEASES CAUSED BY ASSOCIATING WITH BAD WOMEN.

No man need suffer from the bad effects of associating with immoral women, for there is a certain herb which will remove the poison from the blood and will kill the germs. It removes the pimples which form in the water passage, and will cure the ill-effects of strain; it will even cure the worst form of syphilis. "The Little Woman" will cure this disease and make the man well and strong again. Take her medicine and don't drink any other drink; avoid meat and vegetables; live on porridge without milk. You will soon be quite cured and the sores will be healed. Take sour milk with ground bread-crust twice a month; a tablespoon of it cures any blood poison; even if it is poison that has been given to you in food, tea or coffee. Many people lose their lives through blood poisoning.

Don't cut yourself, but paint yourself with the special powder; take the medicine lukewarm. Those people who take this medicine will never suffer. Every night and morning you must paint yourself. Keep away from women (or if a woman—keep away from men).

NERVOUSNESS

Many men and women become restless through having been suddenly frightened by such causes as lightening. This nervous condition can be quite cured by a course of treatment with bread crust and sour milk; and the special herbal mixture for nervousness.

Take no food for a day, and then take a dose of the ground bread crumbs, as recommended for some of the other complaints; after that starve yourself for a week, then take porridge only and the special nerve mixture as hot as you can drink it. The mixture will also remove worms from the stomach. After a short course of the treatment you will become as strong and brave as a lion. It is equally good for men and women.

THE "LITTLE WOMAN'S" ADVICE FOR DELICATE CHILDREN AND THOSE WHO ARE DELICATE AND WEEDY

If your child is delicate give it no food but the juice of a vegetable with which I shall supply you. Boil the vegetable for 3 hours, strain out the juice and feed the child with this before you give it any other food.

There is no need to nurse the child or feed it from the breast. The child will grow strong and quickly and will be free from wind on the stomach and other childish illnesses. Of course, many mothers are not in good health and are often peevish tempered; the milk of such mothers is very harmful to their children and is the cause of many of their disorders.

Sara van Wijk, BASTER AFFIDAVIT
Namibia 1918   Afrikaans

In 1885 an agreement was reached between the Germans, who were then establishing control over Namibia, and the Basters, who lived in the area around Rehoboth. The Germans were to maintain their friendship toward and protection of the Basters, who for their part would offer the Germans no resistance. During the political upheavals of 1893 and 1894 when the invading German troops fought against Hendrik Witbooi, leader of the Oorlams, and during the German-Herero War of 1904–1907, the Basters sided firmly with the Germans.

This alliance continued until August 1914, despite minor differences between the two parties. "Basterkorps" were used for a while by the Germans to assist them during skirmishes with other indigenous Namibian groups, though in general, the agreement held that the Basterskorps were to provide military assistance in the Rehoboth district only. While the Basterkorps used their own weapons, those who possessed none were given German weapons as well as German military uniforms. Some Basters complained to the Germans not only about these matters, but also because members of the Basterkorps were sent to Kraaipoort and Nauchas outside the Rehoboth district to fight. The Basters saw this as a breach of their agreement and, in reprisal, began to rob and kill German families, thus putting an end to friendly relations. The Germans determined to take revenge on the Basters.

The affidavit describes events in 1915, just prior to the invasion of Namibia by South African troops. This affidavit, and others like it, were taken by South African officers after they had established control on 12 May 1915.

Pam Claassen

✦

Katrina Fredrika Sara van Wijk, duly sworn, states:—

I was born in 1861, in the District Amandelboom, Cape Colony. I am daughter of Jan van Wijk, and wife of Cornelius van Wijk, the first witness.

My husband went in March 1915 to Swakopmund. He returned towards the end of April to his farm, Garies. On the return of my husband, there were reports that things were going wrong, and that the Germans were hostile towards our people. After we heard what had taken place at Heuras, my husband sent us away from our home into the mountains. The mountains run almost up to our house. I took my five children with me. The names of the children are:—

1. Anna, 23 years old.
2. Cornelia, 20 years old.
3. Hermanus, 18 years old.
4. Christina, 15 years old.
5. Johannes, 12 years old.

With us also went the wife of Frederick van Wijk and the wife of Stoffel van Wijk with their children. We went with two wagons and camped some little distance from our house. On the 4th May the Germans came upon us. My husband was not then with us; he was at the house. Someone must have told the Germans of our whereabouts in the mountains, otherwise they could not have known of us there. It was still early in the morning when they came. We had no able-bodied man with us, neither a rifle. A few days earlier we had a shotgun with which we shot partridges, but this had been taken back to our house.

The Germans were evidently in the mountains to look for us. When we first became aware of them, two armed soldiers were standing in front of us. We were all lying under a krantz. One of the soldiers then said to us: "I will shoot every one of you dead this morning." On saying this he pointed his rifle at the wife of Stoffel van Wijk. She called out: "Oh! please I am an old woman!" Immediately thereupon he, however, shot her through the breast. She died immediately. She is old and must have been about seventy years. The same soldier thereafter fired on the little boy of Frederick van Wijk, four years and a few months old. This child had part of his skull shot away and also died immediately. The others of us begged for mercy. The same soldier then fired upon the little son of Stoffel van Wijk. He is eleven years old and was wounded in the head. He is well again to-day. The soldiers then ordered us to get up. We got up, and the same soldier then fired two shots at my son Hermanus, but missed him. He then shot dead my other son Johannes. Thereafter they drove us in front of them to the farm. The dead were left unburied there. My daughter Anna then attempted to escape, and then one of another batch of four Germans, who came from another direction, fired at her and killed her. They jeered at us and said: "Where are your English now, that they don't come and help you?" We were kept there at the trees for several hours. The soldiers wished to know where my husband was. They were determined to capture him. I said: "My husband remained behind at the house, but has probably now fled after all this firing." That afternoon they again drove us on in front of them. When we came near the water, Ober Polizei Wachtmeister Dietrichs of Rehoboth, and Sergeant Kuhn, formerly of the police at Bulspoort, Bezirk Rehoboth, came up to us and kept my son Hermanus behind. He only was kept behind. All the others were driven forward. These two soldiers then took my son round a krantz, and a few minutes later I heard what appeared to be a very loud rifle shot. When I heard the shot I knew that it was fired at my son. They did not tell me that they had shot him, and I never saw him alive again. That night they put us on a wagon and took us away. Two days later I asked Dietrichs: "What did you do with my son the day before yesterday? How is it that I do not see him any longer?" His reply was: "I have ordered him to drive on cattle." They took us with them as far as Leutwein Station, not far from Windhuk, where they released us on the 13th May. After they had released us we returned on foot to Garies. On the 19th May I met my husband at Kubis. I told my husband about Hermanus and that I thought that he had been shot. I also told him where the spot was. My daughter Cornelia and I then went with my husband to the place mentioned by me. There we found the unburied body of my son Hermanus. He was lying exactly where I had heard the loud shot fired. A handkerchief was still tied over his eyes. Four cartridge cases were lying close to him. He lay on his back with his head slanting downward. I did not wish to go any nearer and cannot therefore give further details. That same day he was buried.

I do not know the soldier who murdered the wife of Stoffel van Wijk and the others on the mountain. The Wachtmeister Dietrichs and the Sergeant Kuhn I, however, know well.

Sara van Wijk

Transcriber and translator unknown

1920s TO 1950s

Queen Regent Labotsibeni
ADDRESS TO THE RESIDENT COMMISSIONER

Swaziland 1921   siSwati

Queen Regent Labotsibeni, wife of Mbandzeni, was born in 1858. She became the queen regent in 1900 in order to supervise the young King Sobhuza II. During her regency she fought the British over land and established a financial system that still stands in order to buy back the land. To educate her grandson and his advisers, she established the Zombodze National School, the foundation of Swaziland's modern school system.

On 22 December 1921 Queen Regent Labotsibeni transferred all her political power to her grandson, Sobhuza II. He inherited two positions: paramount chief of Swaziland in the context of the British colonial structure and king of the Swazi nation. His was a royal succession, and the transition needed to ensure continuity in the indigenous institutions of governance and the struggle to shape the identity of Swaziland as an African nation.

Queen Regent Labotsibeni had carefully crafted this subtle and complex sociopolitical process. In her eloquent proclamation of the transition, she emphasized human character and ingenuity as critical ingredients in building a nation and its leadership. She pointed out that over a period of thirty-two years, from the death of Sobhuza's grandfather (her husband) in 1889 to the enthronement of her grandson in December 1921, she experienced as "a woman" the "deepest emotions." As "grandmother and Queen," she had brought up Sobhuza as a "Swazi prince" whose spirit was in total "accord with the traditions and the feelings and the aspirations of his countrymen." She emphasized that in carrying out this singular duty, she did so with "clean hands"—without selling a "single right" or land that belongs to the Swazi nation. Few African leaders could say this at the end of the twentieth century.

In singling out her status as a woman, she both reminds Swazi patriarchy of that status and challenges scholars looking for radical female voices. She fought against new forms of domination and social injustice in the form of neocolonialism, structural adjustment programs, and corruption. The speech also testifies to women's contributions despite societies in which gender inequality wastes invaluable resources.

Ackson M. Kanduza

✦

Office of the Swazi Nation, Zombode Royal Kraal, 22nd December, 1921.

His Honour
The Resident Commissioner, for Swaziland.

Honourable Sir,
    This is the day I have always longed for. It has now come at last like a dream which has come true.

King Mband[z]eni died in October 1889, (thirty two years ago). As from that day my life has been one burdened with an awful responsibility and anxiety. It has been a life full of the deepest emotions that a woman has ever had.

The Swazi Nation placed me in charge of the whole affairs of their country as Queen, in the place of their dead King and I have acted as Regent during the minority of two of their minor kings. Bhunu died after only a very short life leaving me with the responsibility of bringing up his infant son and heir. I rejoice that I now present him to Your Honour, in your capacity as head of the Administration of Swaziland. He is yet young as Your Honour can see. He shall constantly require my advice. I and the Nation have every confidence in him. I have brought him up as a Swazi prince should be brought up. His spirit is in entire accord with the traditions and the feelings and the aspirations of his countrymen and what is more I have given him the opportunity to obtain the very best training which any native youth can obtain here in South Africa. I beg to thank Your Honour for all the help which you gave me in opening such facilities for the prince's education. His going away from me always gave me pain, which only stopped when I saw him return having grown greater in stature and in Knowledge. In him I feel that I have done all that as his grand mother and Queen I could possibly do.

I have asked Your Honour to come here and bear me witness before him and the Council of the Nation, to the effect that I have never sold even a single right of the Nation. I have never given away any of their land or people to others. I stand before them with clean hands. All my books are open for his inspection.

Perhaps Your Honour is asking himself as to what my position is now to be and what relationship shall exist between the new Paramount Chief and myself. All this is governed by our ancient customs. I shall reply shortly. He will lead the Nation and deal with the Administration as King of his people and I shall remain greater by the influence which my position holds over him and over the Councils of the Nation. My duties towards him and the Nation will never cease until death. There is no truth in the fiction that the old Swazi Queens are always killed or done away with. Look at our history. They all lived their natural life out except one who was killed through her own open rebellion.

In conclusion I desire to introduce to Your Honour, in your capacity as head of the Swaziland Administration and local chief representative of His Royal Highness the High Commissioner, this my grand son, SOBHUZA II, the Paramount Chief of Swaziland and King of the Swazi Nation. In doing this I commend him to your friendly assistance and help. I cannot give him my experience. During my time I have had the friendly help of five noble High Commissioners and that of three honourable Resident Commissioners of this country. I thank Your Honour and them all for all the assistance which you have always been ready and willing to give me. The

Administration will henceforth address all its communications direct to him. SOBHUZA II gets his name title and position by the right of inheritance from his ancient House whose Princes have ruled over the Swazi Nation from time immemorial. I bid Your Honour farewell.

Most faithfully Yours,
Queen Regent of the Swazi Nation,
Labotsibeni.
Her X Mark

Translated by Josiah Vilakati

Qedabakwabo Moyo, GOING TO SCHOOL
Zimbabwe 1921 English

Qedabakwabo (Qeda) Moyo was a young convert of the Brethren in Christ Church (BICC), one of several Christian mission societies active in Southern Rhodesia. The Brethren in Christ missionaries first came to Zimbabwe (Rhodesia) in 1898, two years after the defeat of the Ndebele state. They were active in the province known as Matabeleland, where siNdebele remains the dominant language. Mission societies arriving after 1896 received large tracts of land from the British South Africa Company (BSAC). Thus the BICC's first mission farm, Matopo Mission, was established in 1898 on land made available by the BSAC. Their second mission farm, purchased from a white settler, opened in 1908 as the Mtshabezi Rescue Home and School for African Girls. Mtshabezi was Qedabakwabo Moyo's chief residence from 1915 to 1921 and perhaps later.

Moyo appears in the Mtshabezi school attendance records. Church marriage records also record her marriage in a Christian ceremony at Mtshabezi to Mtshazo Nkala, a teacher from Matopo, in 1926.

The article written by Moyo appeared in the *Evangelical Visitor* (8 August 1921), a weekly newspaper that circulated among church members in North America and offered a special section devoted to news from the foreign mission stations. The BICC had historical links to the Mennonites of Pennsylvania.

The text featured here is unusual in that it was written by an African convert and not by one of the missionaries. Only rarely, particularly in the decades preceding 1950, did this occur.

It is not clear whether Qeda Moyo's text is a speech that she gave in English on the last day of school, or whether it was translated by the missionary who submitted it, Mary E. Heisey. The slight irregularities in English idiom suggest that Moyo spoke in English. The conversion narrative that Moyo offers follows the BICC teaching (as influenced by Wesleyan doctrines of holiness) that until one receives a permanent indwelling of the Holy Spirit, the Christian will be constantly vulnerable to "sin." It is a stunningly rich first-person account of the family dynamics and social and emotional implications involved for an Ndebele woman converted in the early decades of the twentieth century. We include here Heisey's note that preceded Moyo's testimony.

Wendy Urban-Mead

♦

(This article was written and read on the last day of school at Mtshabezi Mission by Qedabakwabo Moyo. She is the fourth child of her mother and the only one living, three died in infancy. Her mother died while she was yet an infant, leaving her in care of her mother's younger sister. Qedabakwabo does not know just how long she lived with her aunt. She only faintly remembers her as she also died, and Qeda was left motherless the second time. Thus the meaning of her name is Qedabakwabo (the finish of her people). After her aunt's death she was cared for by her grandmother who is still living. She is about 21 years of age, has yielded her life to God, and is doing nicely as a helper in teaching the school.—M. E. H.)

You who are at Mtshabezi today, I will tell you of my life. I am an orphan and have been given a name which denotes misfortune. My name is Qedabakwabo. I have no matter to tell you of my orphanhood only to tell you the beginning of my life.

I want to tell you of my living in sin, my conversion and my learning to know God.

When I was still quite young we did not live at Matyiya (one of the out schools, her present home). Where we lived at that time there was no Gospel, and I lived in sin and according to our heathen customs. After I had grown a little, I desired to go and see my father who lived at Matyamhlope (near Bulawayo). I was only a little child, but I asked my grandmother and she consented. Now my heart was pained, as going to see my father meant leaving my grandmother, and this was hard for me as I loved her very much. It was arranged for me to go. I went, and while there I learned to know what a week is. I also saw people go to meeting on Sunday, but I did not want to go.

My half brother asked me to go, but I refused. He then wanted to teach me from the speller (first book); to this I consented and learned a little while there. When I returned home, I found my people had moved near Matyiya school. I was glad. Before I went to see my father, I did not want to learn; but now I desired to very much.

After a time I went to visit some friends who lived near a school of the London Missionary Society. Here I found that some of my friends had repented. I desired to go with them to meeting, also to school. It was easy for me to learn. It was at this place I learned to pray first.

Now I was sorry because my people had moved to Matyiya. I thought it would have been better had they moved here; and it would be better to learn here, as I did not like the services at Matyiya because they testify and here they do not. When I returned home I found that my people had not yet repented, but were going to the services. I went along to meeting to see how it was. After a time the more I went the more I wanted to go, and was glad when the day came for service. Jesus was beginning to work in my heart, and I did not know it. Now I wanted to stop drinking beer, but I was afraid of the people; I was afraid they would find fault if I stopped drinking.

I went to school and found it was easy to learn; this increased my desire for learning. Now my heart began to fear God. I had confessed all of my sins, but I loved Him and desired very much to leave the world and follow Jesus. I desired very much to know that my sins were forgiven. I stopped drinking beer and was no longer afraid of the people. I loved the Lord and to sing praises to Him gave me much joy. I was tripped by Satan sometimes, as I did not understand then as I do now. I was tempted very much with dancing, as I loved it and knew that my dancing pleased the people; also, I had much trouble with anger. After a time my love began to grow cold and I did not love Jesus as I did before.

I first learned to know what a year is in 1915. In the beginning of this year our teacher said some of we girls should go to the mission and go to school. I desired very much to go, but was afraid to ask the old people. One girl went, this pained my heart. After a while some more girls went and this only increased my desire. I wanted to be angry at the old people; still I was afraid to ask them.

I had not yet learned how many months there are in a year. At threshing time my half brother came to see me and wanted to take me to see my father, who had now moved about seven miles from the mission. I was very glad, but I cried because it meant leaving grandma again. I went and arrived safely. After a few days my brother asked me if I was going to the mission and learn, but I refused. Sunday came and I went along to the mission to services. This was the first I saw Mtshabezi Mission. I saw the girls; now I desired very much to come soon. When we arrived home in the afternoon, I told my brother that now I wanted to go and stay at the mission. He said: Alright, speak to father. I did; he said, Alright, but you must go and tell your grandparents. They sent some one to accompany me, as they did not want me to go alone. My grandmother was very much surprised, but could not refuse, because my way was open to go to school.

I returned to my father soon. My brother said, Now you must stay at the mission twelve months I said, No, I will stay four months. On my arrival, I was told to go and tell the missionary that I had come to stay; this I did. He said, Alright, but the year is so near finished (August) now you will stay next year as well. I had it in my heart to stay four months, but was afraid to say so to the missionary, so I consented.

When I came here I was reading in the first book. I liked to learn, but the love of Jesus was not in my heart. I liked to stay at the mission very much, but at the end of 1916 my people called me and I went home. By this time the light of Jesus was beginning to come into my heart. I desired very much to return to school. I prayed to the Lord and He opened my way. As I yielded to Him, He was near me. After I was baptized it seemed like my strength was finished. I was surprised as I knew my sins were forgiven, and I had no condemnation, but it was hard to overcome. I was like this until in July 1918 when the Holy Spirit came to dwell in my heart. Praise the Lord He is still there, and now I have learned how to over-come by prayer and faith in Jesus. I thank Him for giving me the opportunity of knowing Him also remaining in school a long time. I desire that I may keep near Him and He abide with me and be my guide until I die. I find the way of Jesus precious. I say the joy of the Way cannot be expressed.

Nontsizi Mgqwetho, LISTEN, COMPATRIOTS!

South Africa 1924   isiXhosa

Virtually nothing is known about the life of Nontsizi Mgqwetho, the first and only major female poet to write in Xhosa, apart from what is revealed in her writings, almost all of which appeared in the Johannesburg newspaper *Umteteli wa Bantu* between 1920 and 1929. In a poem published on 2 December 1922 lamenting the death of her mother, she gives her mother's name as Emmah Jane Mgqwetto (the spelling predates the Xhosa orthographic revisions of 1936 and 1955), the daughter of Zingelwa of the Cwerha clan, and associates her with the Hewu district near Queenstown. Nontsizi Mgqwetho may have been educated in the Eastern Cape by the Moravians, probably at Shiloh. The first poem Mgqwetho contributed to *Umteteli,* published on 23 October 1920, is signed with her clan name, Cizama; it was sent from Crown Mines in Johannesburg. Her last contribution to *Umteteli* appeared on 5 January 1929.

Politically, she adopts a position critical of the African National Congress and its leaders, whom she castigates for fragmenting rather than unifying black opposition, and constantly appeals for black unity in the face of white oppression: The title of a poem published on 19 July 1924 is, in English translation, "Strangers strip people selfishly squabbling." She defends Marshall Maxeke, the first editor of *Umteteli,* and celebrates his wife, the civil rights activist Charlotte Maxeke (see the text by her in this volume). She praises members of the rural women's resistance movement known as the *Amafelandawonye* (Die-hards), and in a prose contribution published on 13 December 1924 records her own involvement in a mass demonstration in April 1919 against passes in Johannesburg. She is a firm supporter of the Women's Christian Union, one of the groups known as *manyano,* and was probably herself a member.

Xhosa personal praise poems often employ hyperbole and caricature, and in this poem Mgqwetho depicts herself as ungainly and unattractive, a fearless and outspoken poet whose poetry provokes controversy: "Your poetry puts paid to feminine wiles," she says, rolling up her sleeves. As the first Xhosa woman to publish her poetry in considerable quantity, she sees herself as competing against the dominance of male poets: She celebrates her own outspoken poetry, poetry that benefits the African people and brings her fame, but that is also unpopular among envious poets and those who fault her for invading the traditional male preserve. (Only a male could serve as an *imbongi,* the court praise poet.) She also articulates here concerns that are evident throughout her body of published poetry: black rights, education and morals, especially with respect to young women in the cities, and the erosion of Xhosa custom. A racy, urban tone is achieved in this poem by the incorporation of a number of English and Afrikaans words. The poem is alive with word play.

Fearless, outspoken, committed, pious, contradictory, anguished, and often despairing, Mgqwetho eloquently articulates in her passionate poetry the political and social aspirations of black South Africans in the 1920s and their bitter frustrations. A line that recurs in her poetry reads *Hayi usizi kwizwe lenu, Nontsizi!*, "Oh the sorrow that seizes your country, Nontsizi!" This is a pun on her own name: The Xhosa word for "sorrow" is *usizi*.

Jeff Opland

✦

I sent Christmas, the old year and the new year, packing with praise poems. Now I'm going to sing my own praises, and then I'll move on again to start something new. Mercy, all of you!

Peace, Nontsizi, renowned for your chanting,
Your poems are the nation's bounty.
No elephant finds its own trunk clumsy.
Oh peace, hen of Africa with sheltering wing!

Hen shepherding chicks
Safe from the grasp of birds of prey,
The nation knows you, sky-python,
Poets sneer but discuss you.

Upset Phalo's land, Mgqwetho,
Cast your shadow on nations and sap their strength.
Wild beast too vicious to take from behind,
Those in the know tremble in tackling you.

Peace, dusky woman with the colours of pools,
Your stench reeks like the river snake.
Mercy! Elephant browsing top shoots,
You've made a name for Mgqwetho.

Peace, Nontsizi, African maize tufts
Waving beneath the breeze,
You stubbed your toe and felt the pain,
A slip of the tongue and they stomped on you.

Peace, Nontsizi, African maize tufts,
You strip poetry bare and expose it
And the nation's mountains face one another
As you sway from side to side.

Peace, dusky woman, Drakensberg snow
Like morning dew on Mount Hermon.
I stumbled in walking with whites:
Oh! I felt the cops' cuffs on me.

Peace, woman poet, Vaaibom's flamingo,
Which thrusts its feet forward for take-off,
Which thrusts its feet backward to land:
All the animals come out to bask.

Peace, duck of the African thickets,
Ungainly girl with ill-shaped frame.
Oh, Nontsizi, African maize tufts,
With bow-legs like yours you'll never marry!

Peace, woman poet of Africa with sheltering wing.
Make way! Ugh, I was used.
Peace, starling perched in a fig tree,
Your poetry puts paid to feminine wiles.

Peace, Nontsizi, African maize tufts,
Let spinsters again wear bodices
For no-one knows your ancestors:
Without skin skirts there'll be no marriage.

Where are your daughters? What do you say?
"We roamed the countryside searching for marriage,
We walked away from home and dowry,
Now we're milked though calfless, living with nobodies."

What's education? Where are your sons?
They roamed the land searching for nothing,
Chickens scratching for scraps,
Eager at dawn, at dusk empty-handed.

Peace, Nontsizi, match-stick legs marked
From roaming through thornbrakes prophesying;
Oh, peace, poetic diviner,
Watch out, the wild bird's flapping its wings.

Peace, Chizama, who eats her meat raw;
No-one knows your ancestors.
May the browsing elephants make it home:
If they stay in the open they're lost.

Peace, Nontsizi, Sandile's daughter,
Child of one of the Ngqika chiefs.
You were thrashed on the Ngqika plains
For praising chiefs and not commoners.

Oh peace, Nontsizi, African maize tufts,
Woman, Africa's walls are throbbing
With the sound of your lovely parties:
Oh shame! All the young men wither.

The day of your death will darken, Nontsizi,
The commando's horse will lose its way.
Oh, peace! And to you, Ntsikana,
Who roamed through thornbrakes prophesying.

Mercy, Awesome Saint!
This then is what Ntsikana spoke of:
Little red people down on their knees,
Producing spells when they come to the Mpondo.

Fiery tractors ploughed our fathers' land
And the black had no place to plough.
Mercy, Heavens! Mercy, Earth!
Mercy then, Sun! And mercy, Moon!

You keep our final accounts,
Present the statement to the Highest,
Make a careful case for us,
Where else will we go, Crocodile of the Pool?

Mighty Champion of Africa,
There's the black approaching in tears.
"Agree?" "We agree! By the Cross's Victor!
We agree! Yes, in truth, we agree!"

Oh! So says the enigmatic forest buck:
Toadstools reach up when she's through scratching.

Keep scooping from the cask:
There lies the land of your ancestors,
Harassed by evil spirits.

So says someone disturbed to be spied on
By those bearing arms,
Who watch her even by lightning.
   Mercy!

Translated by Jeff Opland

Baboni Khama, Mmakgama Khama, Milly Khama, and Oratile Sekgoma, LETTER TO THE HIGH COMMISSIONER

Botswana 1926   Setswana

When Sekgoma, chief of the Bangwato after Khama III, died in 1925, his youngest brother, Tshekedi, aged twenty, became regent for the four-year-old heir to the throne, Seretse. Tshekedi had eight older sisters, among them Baboni, Mmakgama, and Milly, who were not eligible for the regency because they were women. Similarly, Oratile, Seretse's eldest sister, did not qualify to be regent because she was a woman. As their letter notes, however, female regency was not entirely unknown. Gagoangwe and her daughter Ntebogang, for example, served as regents for the Bangwaketse chief Bathoen II from 1923 to 1928 (see Ntebogang Ratshosa, "Speech to the Bangwaketse"). Their regencies (Gagoangwe, 1923–1924, and Ntebogang, 1924–1928) were formally recognized by the British, who believed they would protect British interests. Tshekedi's regency was also supported by the British, a fact that contributed to the strength of his position against that of Oratile and his sisters.

In 1925, a situation arose in which the young Tshekedi had to consolidate his power not only over his older sisters, who challenged his regency, but also over his niece, whose inheritance he controlled. As executor of Sekgoma's property, he was in a very strong position. He was able to consolidate his power and defeat the challenges of his sisters and niece in part by maintaining control over their property. When Oratile and her aunts Baboni, Mmakgama, and Milly challenged this control, they were challenging his authority more generally as chief patriarch of the Bangwato and, by implication, the structures of a patriarchy that allowed male junior members of a family to administer the affairs of their female seniors as if those seniors were children.

Interestingly, Baboni, Mmakgama, Milly, and Oratile mention specifically that they are not "claiming the chieftainship or regency," but it is evident that they are involved in political maneuvering, using the languages of both the Sengwato and the British colonialists to alter the situation to their own benefit. (The expression "Pula!" [Rain!] is a common Setswana invocation of blessings and prosperity. See "Speech to the Bangwaketse.")

Leloba Molema, Nobantu Rasebotsa, and Mary Lederer

✦

21st July 1926

To His Excellency The Earl of Athlone
High Commissioner and Governor General of South Africa

May it please Your Excellency—

We the undersigned daughter of the late Chief Sekgoma, and the daughters of the late Chief Khama—Do hereby and solemnly petition to Your Most Excellency that since my father and our brother the late Chief Sekgoma's death, we never had peace with the Regent chief Tshekedi, who is my half uncle and our half brother. This grievious misunderstandings which led to our serious destruction, were caused by ill-natured men who planned fatal intrigues and conspiracies every now and then against us (Khama's family). Men who caused the recent trouble and riot are traitors in the affairs of our tribe, most of them were the ringleaders during the famous Revolt of Sekgoma against his father Khama in 1898 and were responsible for his long exile. These are the men who today, again took advantage of the innocent young blood of Khama (Regent) and themselves led by a man named Phethu, are the dictators.

Can His Excellency expect truthfulness, goodwill and righteousness from such men as described? Never. Proper leaders are lacking in once the tribe of your servant Khama. During the trial a lot was mentioned about ridiculous native laws and customs, which as you know Khama had totally abolished, and now that Khama is dead, they seem to revive them every now and then. Once sacred places of Khama have been turned by traitors, into a witchcraft den. Christianity has been trodden under foot, Chaka's military system of destruction, long abolished, is the system they applaud. Such inhumane and tyrannical practices we have never known before.

It is a big mistake for our Administration to think that we are claiming the chieftainship or regency. Which we could do without fear, had we that intention, surely we have rightful claim, but we never had such wish although we [see] some of our neighbouring tribes as [having] chieftainess, [we claim] nothing but that we upon as daughters with right to our natural position with right to our private affairs. It will surprise Your Excellency that even when instal my uncle and our brother they never discuss the question to us merely to provoke us and to bring us into unnecessary dispute. They entered into the Estate of the two chiefs without anything being mentioned to us, the family of deceased.

Facts known to the tribe made by Khama to members of his family, were in our case stripped from us. Khama's law was equal to both sexes, women had the same right as men. Estate were always proportionally divided to the deceased family, sons and daughters. But in our case they wish it to be different, and in this letter, we appeal to Your Most Excellency that we claim reasonable shares as laid by Khama in the past, and that we ask Your Exellency to give kind consideration to our prayer.

Your Excellency, may recall back,

(a) Sir Charles Warren in 1885 when Khama invites BRITISH PROTECTION.
(b) When he crossed the great ocean waves to meet the Great Mother of orphans and destitutes like ourselves.
(c) With Rhodes he founded Rhodesia, and extend telegraph's line to Salisbury.

(d) Great African chiefs took up arms against Her Majesty's forces, alone
   he laid down his shield before Her Majesty's feet. He alloted vast tracts
   of land to the Crown.

Your Excellency, are these not honourable deeds to squash off guilt and
shame and destruction made against his family by traitors. This is the time
that we should be helped we are wretched and helpless, though we are pro-
voked and rendered homeless by our enemies under cover of the innocent
young regent. And our last request is that we humbly pray that Your
Excellency's visit may God signal it by the discharge of two of our family
who are suffering in gaol through hatred [of] our enemies. Sir, turn Your
Excellency's ear to our cry wretched, ruined, insulted women we are.

   Pula! Pula! Pula!

We have the Acting Resident Commissioner Lieut. Colonel Daniel who
has started his official life with Khama many years ago, who we are sure
knows Khama's good ways better and above all the position and the
intrigues of our tribe.

We are

   Your most obedient servants
   Baboni
   Mmakgama
   Oratile
   Milly

Transcriber and translator unknown

Oratile Sekgoma, INHERITANCE: TWO LETTERS

Botswana 1926, 1929   Setswana

Southern Africans know who Seretse Khama was: the first president of independ-
ent Botswana, a founding member of the Southern African Development
Community (SADC), who married a British woman, Ruth Williams, and angered
the fledgling apartheid state in South Africa under D. F. Malan, the first South
African prime minister after the National Party victory in 1948. The popular press
talked about this "Native Chief" marrying a "white girl." Others know Seretse
Khama as the heir to the Ngwato throne, who as such was meticulously educated at
Tigerkloof (perhaps the foremost college preparatory institution for students from
Botswana), Fort Hare, and Oxford, by his uncle Tshekedi Khama, who was the
regent. He was knighted by the queen of England and is revered for the legacy of
peace and nonracialism in Botswana.

But not many people know that Seretse Khama had a sister Oratile (daughter
of Sekgoma's first wife), easily twenty years older than Seretse. She of course never
went to Oxford, although her meticulous and clear handwriting, almost textbook
perfect, indicates that she received some schooling. She was married to her cousin
Simon Ratshosa, who was banished to Francistown for having made an attempt on

Tshekedi's life. Tshekedi was Sekgoma's youngest brother and the uncle of both Oratile and Simon.

The letters of 1926 and 1929, written by Oratile (as well as the letter of 1926 cowritten with her aunts, Baboni Khama, Mmakgama Khama, and Milly Khama [see "Letter to the High Commissioner"]), demonstrate how royal women appealed to British authorities in an attempt to gain redress in inheritance issues. Thus the struggle between Tshekedi Khama and, on the one hand, his niece Oratile Sekgoma, and, on the other, his sisters Baboni Khama, Mmakgama Khama, and Milly Khama, must be understood in the context of a larger power struggle rooted in succession and social welfare arrangements. Oratile's letters refer to the reforms in inheritance that Khama III had instituted and that Tshekedi was in the process of reversing. After Sekgoma's death, Oratile claimed her inheritance of "5000 head of cattle, 2500 head of small stock, and £15,000 in cash" and sued Tshekedi for withholding it. She lost the case. In addition, she attempted to recover the property that she lost when it was attached and sold to pay debts incurred by her husband, Simon Ratshosa. She lost that case as well.

In its original Setswana—freshly translated here—the 1926 letter has a distinctly oral quality: The cadence, rhythm, imagery, and other emphatic devices allow us to hear her speaking directly to the British, impressing them with her urgency. This letter and others by her demonstrate strong opposition to the patriarchal system in Botswana society which subordinates women to men of the same age or even younger.

The second letter, which we have only in the court's English, is written from Francistown where Oratile Sekgoma joined her husband in exile after withdrawing her appeal to the Privy Council in London, in favor of an administrative settlement. The Privy Council was the highest colonial court of appeal.

Leloba Molema and Nobantu Rasebotsa

◆

Palapye Rd.
26 September 1926
Your Honour,
I am writing to you with great sorrow about my life. I am the eldest daughter of Chief Sekgoma. I have wandered with my father from Lephephe to Nekati in his illness and grief, being his only child for many years and keeping him company. In 1912 my father made his first will. He said that when he died all his wealth would be Oratile Sekgoma's, and the person who would look after it would be Chief Sekgoma, son of Letsholathebe, at Kavimba. A copy of this letter will be found in my father's house; it was there during my father's illness.

I was with my father when he made his second will in 1921. We were in Francistown, on our way to Nekati to prepare for our return to Serowe. The will said, "All the cattle I have are my father's, and my child, Oratile, must be given five of my cattleposts: (1) Baabare, (2) Seisa, (3) Ntloeagae, and two other big cattleposts of mine of her choice. My child must not be hindered in anything that is mine." In 1922 I showed the will to my grandfather, Khama. He did not open it but gave it back to me, sealed with red wax bearing the impression of my father's ring, SK. Khama told me to look after it well. I gave the will to Mr George Smith in 1923 to keep it for me in his safe.

In 1925 my father died and I took the will and went with it to Mafikeng. I asked Mr Minchin to open it. He did so in front of me and Simon [Ratshosa] and Mr Kelly. I took it back with me to Serowe, only to find my houses in flames.

When we moved to Serowe, my father bought me cattle from the white people of Serowe. Other cattle he bought for me from Mrs Blackbeard. These cattle are different from those mentioned in the will. They are cattle that had been mine when my father was still alive. Some of them were brought to me on the hoof, for milking. They are at Mooke.

Tshekedi has confiscated every one of my cattle without saying a word to me. I am shocked that he has burnt down my houses when I have done him no wrong, and that he has gone further and confiscated my cattle that my father gave me. How, Your Honour, am I to support myself when I have been robbed of cattle that are indisputably mine? What shall I remember my father by if all that he left me has been set alight?

Your Honour, I ask you to consider my situation. In 1923 when Khama died my father succeeded him. My father did not take revenge on Semane's household. He confiscated neither the many cattle nor took a small portion of the thousands of pounds that Khama had left them. My father willingly let them have all that was theirs. My father died in 1925 in November, and in December Tshekedi proceeded to single me out as his main target. He ignored the good that my father had done not only for him, but also for his mother and his sister. My father, Sekgoma, gladly handed over to them all their property, not in kgotla [the men's meeting place], as their cattle were not community cattle or even the cattle of servants. It is tribal cattle, for example, the milk of which is distributed to servants, that are controlled by the kgotla. I am surprised, therefore, that the cattle that my father gave me should be a matter for discussion by the kgotla. I am surprised that such discussion should take place at all, as my cattle were given me by my father in the same way as any parent puts aside property for the benefit of his child. Even if my father had not made a will, I would still have the full right to inherit a portion of his property. A third of my father's cattle is due me. My younger brother, Seretse, must receive the largest share of the cattle because he is my chief. My cattle which have been confiscated, together with those mentioned in the will, do not make even half of my father's wealth in cattle.

Your Honour, Tshekedi's desire is that I should get nothing at all of my father's wealth. I wonder, then, why my father bore me. It is the first time I have seen a person robbed of property given her by her father. Listen carefully to me, Your Honour. I do not want to have anything to do with the chieftainship. I have never desired to rule the Bangwato. What I am saying is this: the government must help me to get my property. It is my right. I am Sekgoma's daughter. It is my right to sustain my life. Every man, when he accumulates cattle, accumulates them for his child. No household subsists at the expense of another.

> I stop here, Your Honour, with humility.
> Oratile Sekgoma

Translated by Leloba Molema

Francistown
31st August 1929

The Resident Magistrate, Serowe.

Sir,

Re Oratile Sekgoma vs. Acting Chief Tshekedi Khama.

I have the honour to write you that owing to extreme vagueness and lack of satisfactory arrangements in connection with the above matter, I regret to say I am not satisfied with the Regent's long concealed plans of administering my father's estate.

It is my wish to come to a peaceful arrangement with Chief Tshekedi if possible than to enter into dispute, but he has proved himself to be stubborn and inflexible in his misguided opinion, as if he is not the product of a new environment. He is advised to pursue upon the primitive old customs and laws, which as every one knows had long been abolished by Khama since attaining de facto and de jure sovereign of the Bamangwato. Judging however, from my experience the Regent is still young, and has none of those qualities which had distinguished his great and venerable father; he therefore, needs the closest attention of the Government to teach him to learn to think in the new ways of new things, to perform his duties as Chief.

It is, of course extremely difficult at this stage to make him give up old cherished ideas, and crack the crust of his inflated personal habits, the reason being that from the very beginning of his chieftainship he had been taught to handle the reins of power in an autocratic way; worse still, he fell into the hands of incapable and treacherous advisers of no social standing. It is therefore, impossible for him to be expected to attempt to solve this question in circumstances that constitute the gravest kind of misrepresentations without the guidance or dictatorship of the Government.

Sir, you will no doubt agree that strongly as I feel, and recognise the honesty of the Government, I have been extremely patient as regards my claims to property and birth-right share as one of the two deceased chief's heirs namely Seretse and myself. The Chieftainship I have never wished for—I have been quite satisfied with my position as long as my natural rights were respected.

(a) At Capetown, Sir Herbert Sloley came to say the last goodbye in a railway compartment which my father and myself had occupied. Sir Herbert enquired from me "who would be the Chief?" "My infant brother

Seretse, but Tshekedi would be called to act as Regent," said I.

(b) At Mafeking, Colonel Ellenberger asked me the same question. I still replied in the same way.

(c) At Serowe in the Magistrate's Court before Magistrate Captain Neal, Colonel Ellenberger repeated the question to me. I still replied in the affirmative, recognising Tshekedi as Regent and Executor, adding that my rights and interests as Sekgoma's daughter should be protected.

(d) That Tshekedi has also my assurance in black and white immediately after my father's tragic death.

(e) That at a moment when the infuriated mob had sought to kill Tshekedi's mother (Semane) accusing her of being a witch to have administered a native poison to my deceased parent, in order that Tshekedi, her son, may be the Chief. I was not in favour of that movement. The mob was then unsuccessful in their perfidious action because I did not participate.

(f) In April my cattle posts etc. given to me by my father were all confiscated by the Chief. The drastic action of the Chief still remains a mystery to me.

(g) In July 1926 I addressed a Petition to His Excellency the High Commissioner in connection with these affairs.

(h) In August 1926 His Excellency in person, after attending Kgotla Meeting, commanded Tshekedi, myself and Khama's daughters to attend the magistracy; all representative officials were also present.

His Excellency informed me that he had been made to understand that I refused to recognise Tshekedi as Chief, that I must leave the Bamangwato country as he was determined to put a stop to this internal family strife. Time would be given me, where I desired to go, and that Tshekedi would make arrangements as to my property etc. Not a word was uttered, for the Great One had given his final decision, like a father to his children who punishes and at last forgives. I obeyed His Excellency's stern order and crossed into Tati Territory.

Sir, what is then expected of me? The Chief had at the outset made promises to His Honour the Resident Commissioner that in view of the fact he was interviewing his head men to deal in my share.

In March 1928 I was compelled at last to lay down my claims before the Magistrate; thereupon Tshekedi made a statement before the Magistrate, that he would be quite willing to settle this family matter without going to law. I was advised to withdraw the case to wait and see.

Sir, call to mind that I have been begging for the last three years gnawing the bones without receiving support from Tshekedi in a strange country, and hardly able to get one meal a day. Messrs. Haskins and Sons picked me up lost, and gave me shelter. You will further admit that my claims and share are more than reasonable as compared with enormous value of the estate.

Is it not high time that I should [disclose] my precarious position to the Government, to ask the Government to do me justice, to hasten the time to bestow pity on me, a wretched and simple woman, much too weak to oppose Tshekedi and the whole consistory of Serowe? Their hearts are crammed with arrogance and falsehood, for they have blown the straw between me and Tshekedi, and in truth I trust them not in my case.

Sir, Can you think that any Mongwato dare give me counsel or be a known friend against the Chief's pleasure, 'though he be grown so desperate to be honest? NEVER! Have I not striven to be patient with the Regent 'though I knew he had been ill-advised to hate me, turn me away and let the foulest contempt crown me, and to give me up to the sharpest kind of injustice—unparalleled in the history of any tribe? I am the most degraded and wretched woman, drained of wealth I once possessed, and my energies cramped by a sordid system of misrepresentations to which my interests have been unlawfully sacrificed for the benefit of others. Piles of my hereditary wealth have been accumulated by Tshekedi to his own portion and daily feeding the fortunate favourites with property I had earned with devoted love to my father during those days of painful and heartrending illness and twenty years of his wandering and long exile.

Like the lily that was once mistress of the garden and flourished beautifully, I have been thrown out to hang my head and perish in exile, with nobody to cheer me in pain. Power and honour seem to have vanished, but riches of my father remain to be faithfully apportioned to the heirs.

Sir, I do not intend to wander from the good advice the Government might be aiming at, and if I have used myself unmannerly, pray forgive me, and this time do my service to His Honour the Resident Commissioner to at his pleasure place this pathetic Letter to His Excellency the Great Lion of South Africa at his palatial den.

I have the honour to be,
Sir,
Yours respectfully,
ORATILE SEKGOMA

Translator unknown

Ntebogang Ratshosa, SPEECH TO THE BANGWAKETSE

Botswana 1928   Setswana

Ntebogang was the daughter of Bathoen I of the Bangwaketse and Gagoangwe of the Bakwena. She was the last child of her mother's second marriage; her mother, Gagoangwe, was first married to the chief of the Bakgatla and then to the chief of the Bangwaketse. Ntebogang ruled as regent for her nephew Bathoen II after her brother, Seepapitso III, father of Bathoen II, was murdered by their brother Moeapitso. Gagoangwe is reported to have said, after Moeapitso murdered Seepapitso II, that since one of her breasts had been cut off, let the other one be cut off too; Moeapitso was subsequently executed by the colonial authorities.

Ntebogang delivered the speech printed below on the occasion of Bathoen II's accession to the chieftainship of the Bangwaketse in 1928. It was originally delivered in Setswana (the Setswana version is apparently no longer extant) and translated into English for the official records of the Bechuanaland Protectorate. Ntebogang's speech lists and repeats, a style that is typical of Setswana oratory. In addition to all dignitaries who must be acknowledged and welcomed on formal occasions, Ntebogang recognized all other people present, referring to the commonly held Tswana view that the chief is the chief because of *all* the people.

A Setswana proverb states that the king is a receptacle into which all kinds of rubbish is thrown. Ntebogang is certainly alluding to this proverb when she "welcomes" the thieves and liars, but she also introduces the new chief as "your son," putting him at the service of the family that includes all such members.

Ntebogang uses two expressions that refer to Tswana cultural practices and beliefs. First, "strange" cattle are *matimela*, lost or stray cattle. At regular times, the chief sends a regiment to collect such cattle, and they are brought to the community kraal, where they are claimed by their owners, who must produce evidence of ownership of the brand. Second, the Setswana expression "Pula!" (translated as "Rain!") is a common invocation for blessings, prosperity, and good luck. Because Botswana is mostly desert, rain is extremely important: even the unit of currency is the Pula. "Pula!" can be used either at the end of speech, as Ntebogang has done, or at the beginning. Often when the speaker calls "Pula!" the audience will respond with "Pula!" As this speech closes, the translator has inserted an "etc." to indicate that Ntebogang was concluding her speech according to formulaic patterns.

Mary Lederer, Leloba Molema, and Nobantu Rasebotsa

◆

It is a thanksgiving to-day on the event God has brought for us. We have our Resident Commissioner and Resident Magistrate here and all the Bangwaketse, also the European population. We are collected for the ceremony of one man. I present your son to you to-day. Let him be your Chief in peace. You Bathoen, your own people have presented themselves to you that you may be their Chief. Rich and poor are presented to you. There are wizards in the tribe, they are presented to you, thieves also are presented to you, liars are presented to you, everyman rich and poor is presented to you according to his position. Whatever he be everyone is yours—they are like wives married by one man—wives of one man never love one another, and these wives of yours will belie that. One woman speaks evil of another take no notice—know that the person is yours. Try to know your mind not from hearsay. There are stranger tribes among us to-day, and I also present those to you. There is Chief Letlamoreng of the Barolong here—he is also your subject, you are also his chief. You judge one another. Present are our Resident Commissioner and our Resident Magistrate, they are presented to you also. They have been invited to see the man whom the Bangwaketse will obey. And all the white people are presented to you. You can sometimes assist them as on the other day you collected the strange cattle and each came and claimed his property and took it away and lastly we hand you over to God. You also give yourself to God. As the Bangwaketse are to you so you are to God etc. May God bless his work. Rain!

Transcriber and translator unknown

Florence Nolwandle Jabavu, BANTU HOME LIFE
South Africa 1928   English

Florence Tandiswa Nolwandle Makiwane was born in Tyume village near Alice in 1895. In 1908 she enrolled in Lovedale's College Department; in 1911 she graduated with a certificate in elementary teaching and began teaching at Lovedale. In 1915 and then again in 1922, her parents sent her to Kingsmead College in Birmingham to study music. She married D. D. T. Jabavu, a university professor, writer, preacher, and political activist, thus forging a union between two of the most prominent Christian families in the Eastern Cape at that time. She and her husband had four children, one of whom, Noni Jabavu, is also represented in this anthology (see "Bus Journey to Tsolo"). Fiercely independent, Florence Jabavu was, to quote Phyllis Ntantala's autobiography, "a brave woman who was prepared to fight for those things she believed in."

When she wrote "Bantu Home Life," Jabavu was an important figure in child welfare work in the Cape Province. She launched the *zenzele* (do it yourself) movement in the Eastern Cape in 1927 in order to teach domestic skills to rural women. Her essay was one of several chosen by Rev. James Dexter Taylor for inclusion in *Christianity and the Natives of South Africa: A Yearbook of South African Missions* (1928). Her essay reflects a generally positive attitude toward the missionary influence, as can be expected from a public-spirited Christian activist. (Indeed, her husband referred to her as a nonordained African missionary.) The people she cites were all actively involved in missionary work and in liberal political endeavors in South Africa.

Her own assessment, however, sees the negative impact of colonialism, setting the disintegration of family life against the limited improvement in the lives of rural people. She contradicts the missionary view (held also by her husband) that under polygamy African women were humiliated and exploited chattels, highlighting instead the independence, industriousness, and collective supportiveness of group work, and the absence of these characteristics from the individualized domestic service in which these women have now been employed. While men and boys are trained in industrial skills that broaden their opportunities, women in domestic labor become dependent and passive.

Institutionalizing a view that equates femininity with domesticity, the missionaries and the colonials located African women in the domestic sphere, yet Jabavu's critique of Westernization points to the lowering of the quality of African home life: Aspirations for a complicated, foreign lifestyle led to alcoholism and moral disintegration. Against the missionary view that Westernization would improve life for women, Jabavu held that home life was being destroyed by African women's incorporation into colonial society and, in particular, by the colonial interference in women's central place in the African home in the context of the migratory labor system for men.

On the other hand, Jabavu commends the women's *manyano* movements for their initiative—*manyano* is a Xhosa word that means "union" or "togetherness." These movements (still very active throughout South Africa) were religious formations of solidarity for women, crucial in times of economic and social transition, if insufficiently focused on the training women needed for a fast-changing world.

V. M. Sisi Maqagi

◆

LIFE IN THE KRAALS.

"No people can rise above the standard of its own women" is a saying which is very old, but, nevertheless, full of meaning, especially in the present case when the spiritual development of the great Bantu race is under consideration by a combined organization of missionaries.

It will be best to trace the development of Native Home Life from its earliest stages, that is, life as it was in earliest times, unsophisticated by the presence of Europeans. One writer has depicted it thus: "The exploration of the dark-forested hinterland of South Africa a hundred years ago, was a matter of gravest peril and risk to the body and health of the traveller, missionary and adventurer. The country swarmed with vicious beasts and reptiles whose influence seemed to render human beings equally savage. Even in the [eighteen-]sixties conditions had apparently been little altered; for we read in a Sesuto novel of how two Basuto had to run for dear life somewhere between Grahamstown and Keiskamahoek, being hotly chased by Xosa highway robbers who infested the bush, living on the spoils gotten from the murdered bodies of innocent travellers, and how these men traversed roads strewn with skulls of victims for several weeks until they eventually emerged in the environs of Queenstown. Ours was a land of internecine feuds and unbroken warfare, anarchy and devastation. The Bantu, although they boasted a sound system of communistic tribalism, lived a social life that may be described, from the religious viewpoint, as a haunted nightmare of uncertainty and tyrannical witchcraft. Who of us can forget the terror that must have prevailed in the time of the Zulus of Tshaka and the Ama-Ngwane of Matiwane, or the desolation of superstition brought about by the dictation of the false prophetess Nongqause? The life of a woman, especially, if not even yet an ideal and idyllic one, was one of absolute subjection dominated by polygamous manhood, while man himself lived in constant dread of murderous foes and malicious ambushes. There was no room for hope, no happy anticipation of an afterlife, no spiritual outlook. This was the atmosphere of the social conditions braved by the early missionaries. They must have been animated by a remarkable spiritual zeal. To have changed such a situation within the brief span of a century into what we see to-day, bespeaks energetic work and prayerful devotion." (D. D. T. Jabavu in "What Methodism has done for the Natives.")

To-day what we know as kraal life is no longer what it was a hundred years ago. It has since been affected at many points by the presence of Europeans. The power of the Native chief has been modified. Family discipline has undergone rapid disintegration. But some of the old family restraints are still traceable, such as that of the relation of daughter to mother, and son to father. All home duties are performed at the dictation of parents. Among these one may mention house-errands and helping in daily work. Life is simple and obedience is absolute. Furniture is of the scantiest description. Women are engaged mostly in outdoor work such as cultivation of the fields, fetching water, collecting wood, thatching houses, sewing clothing, selling wares in towns—all this being the occupation of women as well as a training in home management for the girls. The boys, who are under the rule of their fathers, are engaged in herding sheep, goats, calves and cattle, and keeping these away from the fields. They assist their fathers in wagon expeditions and they go out to work in sugar plantations, farms, and in diamond and gold mines for the purpose of raising cash, wherewith to pay the government tax dues, as well as to provide food supplies for their homes.

In connection with traditional customs, we find that the girls partake in certain organised dancing and amusements which mostly occur during the seasons of the first fruits (e.g. Indlame and Ingcube in the Transkeian Territories), and at harvest time. There are also the ceremonies of puberty rites, wedding carnivals and the preparation of Native beer.

The boys engage in hunting, dances, sham stick fighting as well as serious fights often attended with death casualties.

With regard to man, he is father to every boy he meets, possessing the unquestioned right to chastise any boy negligent in his duty. He is absolute head of the family, but is subject to his Chief in his communistic life.

This life is quite ample for its state, but it lacks idealism. It has no motive for morality beyond slavish obedience to custom and law. Its roots are embedded in conservatism, which means doing exactly as what one's predecessors did, on pain of being smelt out as an enemy of society with ostracism as a consequence. The aim is that of maintaining one dreary level of equality of status among all men. He that dares to be ambitious enough to rise above the common level does so at a risk to himself, because any such advance towards fame and wealth is tacitly prohibited. Progressive people are discouraged; while a premium is placed on stagnation.

The saving grace of this life, however, is that there is no subjection in economic life. As contrasted with the common belief that African women are mere chattels to their husbands, one may mention that they enjoy a certain measure of independence in the economic protection of the home inasmuch as they were entirely responsible for such duties as thatching of houses, decoration of homes, the provision of cooking utensils, the weaving of mats and the supply of toilet requisites. The system of polygamy was such that each woman had to be the executive manager of her household, having a definite arable field and live stock allotted to her house, and thus having to husband her resources all the year round with complete self-accountability without having to appeal to her spouse for the provision of multifarious minor needs. Life was also rendered tolerable by the varied character of outdoor occupations that were pursued under the system of group working. While the civilised woman works individually, the kraal women joined in companies in getting together grass for thatching, water and wood for the household. In scuffling the fields, they generally combine and go through the fields in turns. This took away much of the monotony otherwise inevitably experienced by the independent individual worker under civilised conditions.

The present servant system under which a woman is confined to one specific job such as cooking in the kitchen or nursing children year in year out may thus be seen to be in conflict with Bantu tradition and psychology; and it is no wonder that there is much unsettlement and even restlessness in Bantu young women employed in towns under modern conditions; for in such cases they seek employment only for the purpose of raising funds for particular objects and do not enter into the vocation as a permanent life work.

EFFECTS OF WESTERNISM.

The primitive life has to-day been considerably changed by Western modernism, by which we imply the introduction of Christianity, education and Western civilisation.

In outline these are the most apparent effects of the advent of these influences:

Windows have been introduced in the huts, making for some hygienic improvement; there is more furniture, in the shape of chairs, tables, bedsteads, saddles, crockery and linen; there is more bodily apparel in the form of trousers for men (compelled by government laws against nudity), overcoats, ornaments like brass bangles, making for vanity, stimulated by country trading shops. Employment amongst whites has produced new tastes for foods like coffee and sugar and the like, which in turn have resulted in greater living expense. Missions have established country day schools where the arts of reading and writing have been acquired, bringing the people in direct touch with civilisation, with the result that they have been attracted into towns whither they continuously drift to their supposed Eldorado. This exodus is also explained by the fact that these new needs and tastes can no longer be provided by the meagre earnings of rural life. Nevertheless this has given them a widened outlook and an enlarged world of hope and ambition. The mere act of travelling, bringing them into contact with new ideas, has proved to be a vast education inasmuch as they get to unlearn much of what they had been taught at the mission stations when they see the flagrant desecration of the Sabbath by whites in towns. Migration into towns also brings them into the ambit of pass laws with their resultant criminality (see the recent committee report of the Johannesburg Joint Council which enlarges on the subject on "Lawlessness among Johannesburg Natives.")

Government legislation on land questions together with the natural increase of population with its concomitant of congestion has resulted in much landlessness which has in turn resulted in the homelessness of many people and the degradation of the ideals of home life. Westernism, has, however, produced tranquility and order in place of the old unsettlement and tribal friction. The worst forms of superstition have been reduced. Death by smelling out has been eliminated, and life is more secure. In mission stations life is now characterized by a new spiritual life due to the reading of the Bible and the conduct of family prayers, morning and evening—thus bringing about a new form of dignity, greater tenderness, more sympathy, absence of cruelty and new idealism.

The degrading customs of female puberty rites and circumcision ceremonies have been largely destroyed.

The position of man has been greatly altered. His authority is less absolute because under modern conditions he is unable to raise money to meet the increased needs of the family. The young men who are the most able-bodied males in the community are almost continually away working in the industrial centres for the support of their homes, and this has given them a new feeling of independence from the fathers who, being regularly at home awaiting the return of their sons, are placed in the humiliating position of being suppliant to their sons. This condition of things has undone the old fashioned form of discipline. Nowadays a man dare not, as in the kraal, chastise any delinquent boy, on pain of being brought before the magistrate and punished for assault in accordance with European law.

The old Bantu communism is rapidly giving way to Western individualism.

It is encouraging, in face of all these disintegrating factors due to the transition stage, that we have constructive institutions that are destined to prove helpful to the development of the Bantu people in their upward progress in culture. Such are the innumerable elementary schools in the rural and urban areas; the secondary schools especially in the Cape and Natal Provinces, and the Fort Hare College which is the culminating achievement of missionary work. Bantu literature has developed by leaps and bounds under the encouragement of the mission press.

The gratitude of the Bantu goes out to the American Zulu Mission Board for taking the unusual but admirable forward move of setting apart a missionary like the Rev. R. E. Phillips, B.A., for the special duty of developing the recreation of Bantu youth in a town like Johannesburg, and who with Dr. F. B. Bridgman has been instrumental in the establishment of the Bantu Men's Social Centre.

WEAKNESSES.

The advent of Westernism has not, as we have already seen, been an unmixed blessing. Together with the good there has been a number of weaknesses which we may here touch upon. The chief difficulty encountered by the Natives has been that they are striving after a civilisation of which they have very little inside knowledge, practical experience and guidance. Those who see the inside of a European's house are there only as servants and therefore never assimilate anything of the true home life except the externals; whilst there are many who would regard it as derogatory and humiliating to go out as servants. In following what they have seen they find life too costly for their circumstances and fail to make ends meet. Wages are always insufficient for the life they are anxious to lead, and the result is unsettledness and an unhappy home life and also lack of control over children. In one case a certain woman, whose husband was a teacher, finding the economic pinch severe, left her husband, to carry on her profession elsewhere, visiting her home only periodically. In another similar case the young married woman has gone to work at a place too far away for her even to make periodic visits to her husband. In two other cases both the young married women are engaged in work which makes it impossible for them to attend to their family at home during the day. Under the circumstances the children are left either with imperfect supervision or have to fend for themselves. In most cases the environment in which the civilised Native lives is squalid, there being no flowers nor trees to make the home attractive. The congestion of houses, themselves badly built, has made for bad health conditions resulting in appalling death-rate figures, particularly in infants and children. The figures of infantile mortality make sad reading. They range between 100 and 650 deaths per thousand, where under better conditions they would range between 30 and 200; e.g., in Virginia, U.S.A, they range between 32 and 156 according to a recent report.

The evil of drink has aggravated the situation because it has served to deplete the already insufficient income of the bread-winner. It has degraded the moral life of whole communities, so much so that it is quite common for one to find certain portions of Native locations correctly but unfortunately called Sodom and Gomorah. The moral conscience has been so dulled that there is no upright public opinion, and these circumstances of degradation have come to be accepted as the natural order of things.

The women in their daily round of home duties have lost that variety of combined occupations which we have mentioned as being associated with kraal life.

On the one hand, men, owing to their migration to industrial centres, obtain a broadened view of life by coming in contact with a larger world; on the other hand, women, being tied down, tend to become narrow in vision and interest. The training of womanhood has much to do with the situation, because the tendency in training centres has been to lay the most emphasis upon the training of boys and men rather than girls and women. Notwithstanding the existence of such wide movements as the Women's Manyano, which owe their origin to the initiative of the Native women themselves, the missions have neglected to train their womenfolk with the same intensive method as they prepare the menfolk for being exhorters, lay preachers, evangelists, and other forms of leadership.

The woman as manager of the home has not been afforded a proportionate advance in the attitude with which she is viewed and should be respected. Consequently there is a sort of inferiority complex aided and abetted by Europeans to the disadvantage of the Native woman. This is gradually sapping the moral fibre of the race in its endeavours towards culture inasmuch as no race can advance without race pride. Such pride in the analysis depends upon the motherhood of the nation, and upon the self-confidence that can be engendered only by the mother in the home.

Charlotte Manye Maxeke,
SOCIAL CONDITIONS AMONG BANTU WOMEN AND GIRLS

South Africa 1930   English

Two outstanding achievements of Charlotte Manye Maxeke (1874–1939) define her preeminent position in South African intellectual and cultural history in the twentieth century: First, she was arguably the greatest black South African apostle of modernity in that country. Second, as such, she enabled the connections with black culture across the Atlantic that made the construction of South African modernity possible.

Maxeke inherited her profound historical awareness from two brilliant teachers at the Edward Memorial School in Uitenhage in the late nineteenth century, Isaac Wauchope (1845–1930) and Paul Xiniwe (1857–1910). They were part of a group of Xhosa intellectuals who—through their articles and essays in John Tengo Jabavu's newspaper *Imvo Zabantsundu* in the 1880s and in the 1890s—grappled with the historical meaning of modernity's violent entrance from Europe into Africa.

Among the issues with which they concerned themselves were the uprooting of Africans as labor-power from the villages and countryside into exploitative social and economic relations in the new towns; the subversion of African ethos by the new corrupt forces of prostitution and drinking; the complicity of Christianity, as practiced and interpreted by white missionaries, with new forms of domination and oppression; the fundamental importance of education; and the possible historical lessons to be learned from the United States.

Maxeke's presentation reprinted below, "Social Conditions Among Bantu Women and Girls," originally made to the Bantu-European Students' Christian Conference in Fort Hare in 1930 (and published by them), broaches these issues of modernity from nearly fifty years earlier, but makes three unparalleled and revolutionary transformations: First, as a New African Woman, she views the issues from the perspective of the woman question; second, her reading of the positive and negative aspects of modernity inspire and radicalize her to call for political unity across gender and racial barriers and differences; and third, she is historically aware—as had not been the case before—that the end of African alienation is inseparable from the restoration to the African people of lands taken from them by the Europeans.

In 1896, years before this breakthrough essay, Charlotte Manye attended Wilberforce University in Ohio where she studied with W. E. B. DuBois, the New Negro intellectual and great American man of letters. While still a student, she facilitated the link between New Negro modernity and New African modernity by making Bishop Henry M. Turner (1834–1915), of the African Methodist Episcopal Church in the United States, and Bishop Mangane Maake Mokone (1851–1930), the founder of Ethiopianism, aware of each other's historical projects within the international context of black modernity.

On her return to South Africa in 1901 (as the country's first black woman graduate), Charlotte Manye became the foremost articulator of the historical principles and ideology of the New African Woman. Not only may she have been present at the founding of the African National Congress (ANC) in 1912, but—through her Xhosa writings on the "woman question" in *Umteteli wa Bantu* in the 1920s—she also became one of the leading members of the New African Movement, which had been launched by Pixley ka Isaka Seme's 1903 essay, "The Regeneration of Africa." One of the earliest opponents of the system of passes for women, she became the first president of the Bantu Women's League (a forerunner to the ANC Women's League). She also founded with her husband, Marshall Maxeke, the Wilberforce Institute at Kilnerton in the Transvaal and various other schools.

Her greatness was easily apparent to other members of the New African Movement who in various forms expressed admiration and gratitude for her contributions. In 1930, Alfred B. Xuma (1893–1962), who was to become president-general of the ANC in the 1940s, published a booklet tabulating his appreciation of her extraordinary talents, *Charlotte Manye (Maxeke); or, What an Educated African Girl Can Do*. Maxeke belongs in many ways to the intellectual tradition to which the great modern Zulu prose stylist Lydia Umkasetemba (see her text in this volume) contributed in the mid-nineteenth century. For further details about Maxeke's life and career, see James T. Campbell, *Songs of Zion* (1998).

Ntongela Masilela

◆

In speaking of Bantu women in urban areas, the first thing to be considered is the Home, around which and in which the whole activity of family life circulates. First of all, the Home is the residence of the family, and home and family life are successful only where husband and wife live happily together, bringing up their family in a sensible way, sharing the responsibilities naturally involved in a fair and wholehearted spirit. The woman, the wife, is the keystone of the household: she holds a position of supreme importance, for is she not directly and intimately concerned with the nurturing and upbringing of the *children* of the family, the future generation? She is their first counsellor, and teacher; on her rests the responsibility of implanting in the flexible minds of her young, the right principles and teachings of modern civilisation. Indeed, on her rests the failure or success of her children when they go out into life. It is therefore essential that the home atmosphere be right, that the mother be the real "queen" of the home, the inspiration of her family, if her children are to go out into the world equipped for the battles of life.

There are many problems pressing in upon us Bantu, to disturb the peaceful working of our homes. One of the chief is perhaps the stream of

Native life into the towns. Men leave their homes, and go into big towns like Johannesburg, where they get a glimpse of a life such as they had never dreamed existed. At the end of their term of employment they receive the wages for which they have worked hard, and which should be used for the sustenance of their families, but the attractive luxuries of civilisation are in many instances too much for them, they waste their hard earned wages, and seem to forget completely the crying need of their family out in the veld.

The wife finds that her husband has apparently forgotten her existence, and she therefore makes her hard and weary way to the town in search of him. When she gets there, and starts looking round for a house of some sort in which to accommodate herself and her children, she meets with the first rebuff. The Location Superintendent informs her that she cannot rent accommodation unless she has a husband. Thus she is driven to the first step on the downward path, for if she would have a roof to cover her children's heads a husband must be found, and so we get these poor women forced by circumstances to consort with men in order to provide shelter for their families. Thus we see that the authorities in enforcing the restrictions in regard to accommodation are often doing Bantu society a grievous harm, for they are forcing its womanhood, its wedded womanhood, to the first step on the downward path of sin and crime.

Many Bantu women live in the cities at a great price, the price of their children; for these women, even when they live with their husbands, are forced in most cases to go out and work, to bring sufficient into the homes to keep their children alive. The children of these unfortunate people therefore run wild, and as there are not sufficient schools to house them, it is easy for them to live an aimless existence, learning crime of all sorts in their infancy almost.

If these circumstances obtain when husband and wife live together in the towns, imagine the case of the woman, whose husband has gone to town and left her, forgetting apparently all his responsibilities. Here we get young women, the flower of the youth of the Bantu, going up to towns in search of their husbands, and as I have already stated, living as the reputed wives of other men, because of the location requirements, or becoming housekeepers to men in the locations and towns, and eventually their nominal wives.

In Johannesburg, and other large towns, the male Natives are employed to do domestic work, in the majority of instances, and a female domestic servant is a rarity. We thus have a very dangerous environment existing for any woman who goes into any kind of domestic service in these towns, and naturally immorality of various kinds ensues, as the inevitable outcome of this situation. Thus we see that the European is by his treatment of the Native in these ways which I have mentioned, only pushing him further and further down in the social scale, forgetting that it was he and his kind who brought these conditions about in South Africa, forgetting his responsibilities to those who labour for him and to whom he introduced the benefits, and evils, of civilisation. These facts do not sound very pleasant I know, but this Conference is, according to my belief, intended to give us all the opportunity of expressing our views, our problems, and of discussing them in an attitude of friendliness and fairmindedness, so that we may perhaps be enabled to see some way out of them.

Then we come to the *Land Question.* This is very acute in South Africa, especially from the Bantu point of view. South Africa in terms of available land is shrinking daily owing to increased population, and to many other economic and climatic causes. Cattle diseases have crept into the country, ruining many a stock farmer, and thus Bantu wealth is gradually decaying. As a result there are more and more workers making their way to the towns and cities such as Johannesburg to earn a living. And what a living! The majority earn about £3 10s. per month, out of which they must pay 25s. for rent, and 10s. for tram fares, so I leave you to imagine what sort of existence they lead on the remainder.

Here again we come back to the same old problem that I outlined before, that of the woman of the home being obliged to find work in order to supplement her husband's wages, with the children growing up undisciplined and uncared for, and the natural following rapid decay of morality among the people. We find that in this state of affairs, the woman in despair very often decides that she cannot leave her children thus uncared for, and she therefore throws up her employment in order to care for them, but is naturally forced into some form of home industry, which, as there is very little choice for her in this direction, more often than not takes the form of the brewing and selling of Skokiaan. Thus the woman starts on a career of crime for herself and her children, a career which often takes her and her children right down the depths of immorality and misery. The woman, poor unfortunate victim of circumstances, goes to prison, and the children are left even more desolate than when their mother left them to earn her living. Again they are uncared for, undisciplined, no-one's responsibility, the prey of the undesirables with whom their mother has come into contact in her frantic endeavour to provide for them by selling skokiaan. The children thus become decadent, never having had a chance in life. About ten years ago, there was talk of Industrial schools being started for such unfortunate children, but it was only talk, and we are to-day in the same position, aggravated by the increased numbers steadily streaming in from the rural areas, all undergoing very similar experiences to those I have just outlined.

I would suggest that there might be a conference of Native and European women, where we could get to understand each others point of view, each others difficulties and problems, and where, actuated by the real spirit of love, we might find some basis on which we could work for the common good of European and Bantu womanhood.

Many of the Bantu feel and rightly too that the laws of the land are not made for Black and White alike. Take the question of permits for the right to look for work. To look for work, mark you! The poor unfortunate Native, fresh from the country does not know of these rules and regulations, naturally breaks them and is thrown into prison; or if he does happen to know the regulations and obtains a pass for six days, and is obliged to renew it several times, as is of course very often the case, he will find that when he turns up for the third or fourth time for the renewal of his permit, he is put into prison, because he has been unsuccessful in obtaining work. And not only do the Bantu feel that the law for the White and the Black is not similar, but we even find some of them convinced that there are two Gods, one for the White and one for the Black. I had an instance of this in an old Native woman who had suffered much, and could not be convinced that the same God watched over and cared for us all, but felt that the God who gave the Europeans their life of comparative comfort and ease, could not possibly be the same God who allowed his poor Bantu to suffer so. As another instance of the inequalities existing in our social scheme, we have the fact of Natives not being allowed to travel on buses and trams in many towns, except those specially designed for them.

In connection with the difficulty experienced through men being employed almost exclusively in domestic work in the cities, I would mention that this is of course one of the chief reasons for young women, who should rightly be doing that work, going rapidly down in the social life of the community; and it is here that joint service councils of Bantu and White women would be able to do so much for the good of the community. The solution to the problem seems to me to be to get the women into service, and to give them proper accommodation, where they know they are safe. Provide hostels, and club-rooms, and rest rooms for these domestic servants, where they may spend their leisure hours, and I think you will find the problem of the employment of female domestic servants will solve itself, and that a better and happier condition of life will come into being for the Bantu.

If you definitely and earnestly set out to lift women and children up in the social life of the Bantu, you will find the men will benefit, and thus the whole community, both White and Black. Johannesburg is, to my knowledge, a great example of endeavour for the uplift of the Bantu woman, but we must put all our energies into this task if we would succeed. What we want is more co-operation and friendship between the two races, and more definite display of real Christianity to help us in the solving of these riddles. Let us try to make our Christianity practical.

The Native mind in many instances does not understand Christianity, because with the teaching of Christ, and the coming of civilisation, come also so many of the troubles from which the Bantu is to-day suffering, and from which he never suffered before, while he sees the White man apparently happy and comfortable. As an instance of this let me tell you of an old chief, whom I had tried again and again to convert. One day I went to him, and suggested that he was getting old, and that it was high time he was converted, and what do you think he said. He said, "Who is this man who was killed, and why does he cause us so much trouble? We had nothing to do with killing him, why come to me about him? Go to the people who did kill him, and show them what they have done—go to the Jews, and tell them what a lot of trouble they are bringing upon us all." Eventually, he said that he did not want to be converted and to go and live in another heaven to that in which his ancestors were, where he would be lonely. Thus we see the view the old-fashioned Bantu mind takes of Christianity to-day.

In conclusion let me repeat that what we want really, at this stage in our existence, is friendly and Christian co-operation between the Bantu and White women particularly, and also of the whole communities of Bantu and White, to help us solve these problems, which can be solved if they are tackled in the spirit of Christianity and fair-mindedness.

Nosente of the Umgqwashe, THE STORY OF NOSENTE

South Africa c. 1930   isiXhosa

This text is a product of an oral exchange held in the 1930s between a woman identified as Nosente, and Monica Hunter, a white South African social anthropologist widely respected for her research into the social practices of the amaXhosa people of the Eastern Cape. Nosente's story offers a rare and rich first-person account of the processes of courtship and marriage within the context of ancestral religious practices, values, and rituals.

Nosente was born in Nyara in the Transkei, in the Umgqwashe clan of the Gcaleka House of the amaXhosa in the 1860s. Her family was among those resettled by the British in a small reserve in the Ciskei after the Xhosa defeat in the Ngcayecibe War of 1877. This war, like earlier wars, was about land. The Gcaleka paramount chief Sarhili, also known as Kreli, had thrown his full force against the invading colonial army, but with the massive technological superiority of the British, half of his soldiers were killed and the rest resettled across the Kei River.

The story in the text contrasts with the Christianity to which Nosente and her family were later converted. It also powerfully depicts the changes that resulted from the Xhosa people's involvement in the cash-based capitalist economy. Introduced by Europeans, this change affected and framed some of Nosente's experiences of the conflict between her immediate reality and the forces of transition. It is significant that the story is narrated to a white South African women with good credentials in the field of researching amaXhosa social practices. Hunter translates Nosente's Xhosa into colloquial English, and at times uses literal translation in order to retain the original metaphor. She sometimes adds explanatory notes of her own indicated in square brackets, which we have left in this reprinting in order to emphasize the mediated nature of the text.

The text conveys the sense that this is a woman talking to somebody who is out of her cosmology and therefore does not understand the intricacies of the rites of passage contained in Xhosa cultural practices. Nosente explains the process of the exchange of gifts, for example, which is critical to the formation of a relationship with her in-laws. She also gives a detailed account of the values associated with hard work, the notion of respect, processes of punishment rituals, harvesting and food sharing rituals, purification of pregnant women, protection rituals for children, and *hlonipha*, the practice of linguistic avoidance characteristic of Xhosa patriarchy. Virtually all the information offered here is informative to an outside audience in a way that it is not to a local audience. Ritual has a prominence in Nosente's psyche from the perspective of the outsider rather than from her own. Her narrative is full of movement, yet depicts a woman drifting in a sea of change while constrained by values and systems she cannot shake off.

Paradoxically, while envying the recent freedom for the new generation, she simultaneously laments the loss of the "lightness" and security of the past. Perhaps this is a universal paradox: While we anticipate the gains of the future, we also mourn with nostalgia the loss of tradition and the completeness of the family. Yet Nosente's description of the hardship caused by the disintegration of her immediate family is placed alongside the political transition in a way that allows an insight into the very specific suffering that South African social change has caused.

Nomfundo Walaza

◆

When I was at Middledrift [in the Ciskei] I was seen. In those days young men when they wished to marry travelled about the country, looking at the girls. One young man saw me, and he sent messages to my father asking that he might marry me. My father called his brothers, and they talked with the messengers. They talked about the cattle that that man should give to my father. After a time we saw strange cattle in the cattle-fold. We were told that they had been sent to graze in this country, and that my father was looking after them. I had never seen that man. I did not know that I was to be married until one day people said, "You will go to be married today." [This is by no means a universal Xhosa custom. Most frequently the man has spoken to the girl before he approaches her parents.]

I was afraid, but I could not help myself. It was the decision of the elders. I was a very ignorant girl then. All the time since those men had first talked with my father, the old people of the kraal had been getting baskets, and mats, and blankets. They asked for baskets from my mother's brothers. My father sold a goat, and bought other baskets and mats from those who make them, and he bought blankets, and a hoe from the store. But I did not see any of these things. The old people did not tell me that I should be married lest I should run away.

Seven cattle were brought to my father before I was taken to be married. Word was sent to the home of that man to tell them that the bridal party would arrive on a certain day. My sisters from the kraal [father's brothers' daughters] accompanied me, and a sister of my father who was a widow, and another who was divorced, and two men, adherents of my father, to whom he had lent cattle. The other girls and my father's sisters were all carrying baskets, and mats, and new blankets. We went on foot. At dusk we arrived at that kraal. We sat down behind the huts. After we had sat a young man came to ask us for what we had come. The men replied that we were strangers travelling, and that we sought a place to sleep. We were given a hut swept and freshly smeared. When we came to that kraal the people pointed out my husband to me, saying, "That one is your husband." A goat was brought and killed, "to bring us off the mountains" [*i.e.* to welcome them]. Half the goat we cooked, and we ate in our hut. The other half was left to the people of the kraal.

The next day I went early to the river with my father's sisters and the other girls. There we washed, and rubbed ourselves freshly with fat, and with red ochre, and my father's sister put on me the new long skirt which she had brought, and many bead ornaments. The other girls also were dressed in long skirts. [Married women wear skirts to the ankle, unmarried girls, skirts to the knee.] We were given handkerchiefs for our heads, and were warned that none of us should go uncovered, for we must show respect in this kraal as brides.

In the cattle-fold men killed an ox. Meat was brought to us, and I was given to eat first. Many people came to feast. Men and women danced the *umdudo* [wedding dance]. In the afternoon I was taken to "walk in the courtyard." I stood with my sisters before the men of the kraal. My father's sisters took the blankets off our breasts, and we stood that the men might see us. Then I was given a spear, and told to throw it in the kraal. The women of the kraal were running to and fro shouting, "Here people plough, here people weed, here people grind, here people draw water, here people are diligent." After I had thrown the spear, I went with my sisters to draw water and collect firewood. We left the wood and water outside the great hut. At the same time the men from my home were giving presents from the goods they had brought to the parents of my husband and to his sisters.

The next day the people from my home went away. Before they left they exhorted me saying that I should be diligent and humble in this kraal, that I should cook for all the people of the kraal, and behave myself seemly, so that when they came they should hear no evil of me. My husband's people gave me a new name, calling me Nosente, the Mother of Compassion, because they avoided the name by which I was called at home. I do not know why they said Mother of Compassion. They called me what they liked. [. . .]

When I was a bride I had to be very diligent, and respectful to all the people of my husband's home. I got up very early in the morning, and cleared the ashes from the fire, and went to fetch water. Every day I went to gather firewood, and wild green plants for food. I ground meal for porridge and beer, and cooked and swept, and smeared the floors with cowdung. Only I could not sweep or smear the back part of the great hut, for the back part of the hut is the men's part, and it was the hut of my husband's elder brother. In my own hut I could go all over. I could not go near the cattle-fold, or cross the courtyard between it and the huts. Even at night we must not cross the courtyard, and if a wife goes out she must cover her head, for, it is said, the ancestors [*i.e.* ancestral spirits] of her husband are there. When a bride goes from one hut to another she makes a wide circle round the back of the huts, that she may be far from the courtyard and the cattle-fold.

I could not call the names of my husband's elder brothers, or of his father, who was dead. I could not say words like their names. A bride when she first comes does not speak much. She listens to the other women talking and hears what they call things. All the women in the kraal should avoid those words which wives may not use, for if a daughter of the kraal call her brother's name [as she is entitled to do] then a bride may hear, and call what she should not call. When she makes mistakes her husband's mother and sisters reprove her, and tell her what she must say. Sometimes if a bride does not behave nicely, and neglects to do the things which she should do at her husband's home, it is said to her, "You call your husband's father's name," and then she must go back to her own father and get gifts to bring back to her husband's home, to "wash" with. She may bring a goat, and it is killed, and the people of the kraal eat it. But her people tell her that she has done wrong, and that she must not act in such a way again.

I could not eat milk food in my husband's kraal when I was first married. Then one day a beast was killed, that I might eat. My husband's younger brother handed me sour milk, and meat of the beast which had been killed. I ate them together. After that I could eat the thick milk of my husband's cows.

Each wife living at my husband's home had her own field, but we worked together in the fields. People were beginning to use ploughs drawn by oxen then, and the men ploughed the fields. We women weeded with hoes we bought from Europeans. When the weeds were many we took millet, and soaked it in water until it sprouted, then ground it with more millet, and made beer. People saw the smoke when we were cooking the beer, and we told them that we were going to weed such and such a field, with beer, on a certain day. They came with us to the field at sunrise, bringing their hoes, and many people hoed our field. We sang the hoeing song. We carried some beer to the field in baskets, and clay pots, and people drank. Then when the sun was hot they left their work and came to drink at our kraal. We too went to hoe the fields of other people and to drink their beer.

At harvest the grain was brought home, and stored in pits dug in the cattle-pen. The grain was put in, and a stone put over the mouth of the pit, and the mouth was sealed with dung, then the cattle trampled upon it and hid it. Each wife had her own pit. Each in turn cooked food from her field, and all the people of the kraal ate together. I cooked tonight, and my husband's brother's wife cooked tomorrow.

In autumn we repaired our huts, cutting grass, and repairing the thatch, and replastering the walls. When we came to this country after the war we saw people making huts with mud walls and grass roofs. People said, "Look, there are good huts!" and we made them also. The old huts with grass walls were low and caught alight very easily, then people sleeping in them, men, women and children, were burned. When there was much work to do thatching and plastering, we sometimes made a little beer and called our friends, the women who lived near, to help us with the work, then afterwards we drank the beer. The men came to drink also although they had not worked.

Now people make square houses with iron roofs.

After I had been married a short time I became pregnant. I told the wife of my husband's brother. She showed me the plant which I should put in a pot of water. Every day I drank of that water. [A pregnant woman drinks an infusion of a plant as a laxative. Different families use different plants. A woman must always use that of her husband's family.] Every day I still went to draw water and fetch wood, and I worked in the fields. When labour pains began I went to my hut. The women of the kraal came to me. Then when they saw that the child did not come they sent a boy to call Nomanga, whom people said was skilled as a midwife. After she came the child was born. I took it and washed it. Next morning early I put some leaves of the tree *isifuto* on the fire at the back of the hut. After washing the child I swung it in the smoke of the fire, singing as I did so,

> *Hotshi! Hotshi!*
> *Lomtana akule,*
> *Abemdala apike into azaziyo.*

> *[Hotshi! Hotshi!*
> *May this child grow.*
> *When it is old may it deny the thing it knows.]*

This I did every morning and every evening for a month, that the child might grow strong. I called the child uPote, the twisted one, because he was born with heavy labour. [. . .]

All my children went to school. UPote passed Standard VI, and his teachers said that he should go on and become a teacher, but he did not like to do that, and he ran away and went to work in Port Elizabeth. All the others passed Standard V or VI. My daughter died in the influenza epidemic in 1918. My husband also died. UPote, who was working in Port Elizabeth, died there. Another son went to work in Johannesburg and died there. Another went to work in Cape Town and died there. Two are here at home. The elder is not working for Europeans. The younger goes to work in East London for a time, and then comes home.

The elder one living at home is married to a girl from Gqumahashe. When she was brought by her people a goat was killed, "to bring them off the mountain." The next day an ox was killed for the feast, and she was married in church. Before they went away her people gave her advice, saying that she should show respect to her husband's home and conduct herself humbly; that she should cook, that when guests arrived in the kraal she should give them food, and that there should be no one in the kraal to whom she did not give food; that she should no longer go about with young people, but with old people, that she might learn their manners; that when she laughed she should not raise her voice loudly, but that she should laugh softly out of respect. We of the kraal also gave her advice telling her these same things. Then the men of her home presented the gifts they had brought to us, the people of the kraal. They had brought dresses, and shawls, and dishes, and such things.

Now since we are "school people" my daughter-in-law does not avoid parts of the hut, and the courtyard, as I did when I was a bride. She does not call the name of my husband, or of my sons older than her husband, or words like them, but she may write the surname of the family when she writes a letter to her husband. School people do not kill that the bride may eat the milk of the kraal. I gave sour milk to my son's wife, and after that she drank it. She lives in my hut and cooks with me, but she has her own hut to which she goes with her husband at night. She has four children. Now when children are born all the old customs are not followed by school people. Men may enter the hut of the mother of a newborn child before she comes out, but some still do not like to enter. School people do not kill a goat just when the mother comes out of the hut, but the baby is baptized in church, and on that day a baptism dinner is made and a goat is killed for the feast. At the baptism dinner of the eldest child the top tier of the parents' wedding cake which they have kept as their "proof" [i.e. proof of a legal marriage] is eaten.

My daughter-in-law and I work in the fields. I weed much. For a time I worked in the kitchen for Europeans. Now I wash and iron. My daughter-in-law is also hired to sew for Europeans. [. . .]

The difference between life now, and life when I was young, is that now there are poverty, and sorrows. When I was young nothing troubled me. Now the difference is great. Now children do not live with their parents as they used to do. They are scattered. Only two or three children are with their parents. The mother wonders how the others are. She wonders whether they are ill or what. There is heaviness. Children no longer honour their parents as they used to do. Times have changed.

Transcribed and translated by Monica Hunter

Victoria Nombulelo M. Swaartbooi, UMANDISA

South Africa 1934   isiXhosa

Victoria Nombulelo M. Swaartbooi was born in the Ngqamakhwe district in the Eastern Cape in 1907 and died in 1937. Swaartbooi is a common surname among coloured families from the eighteenth century onwards. (*Swart* is Dutch or Afrikaans for black; the etymology of *booi* is highly contested.) Her novel, *UMandisa* (the title is Xhosa for "the bringer of joy"), has autobiographical echoes. Like her protagonist

Mandisa, Swaartbooi studied at Mgwali Training School in 1924, and in 1926 proceeded to Healdtown School near Fort Beaufort for her Junior Teacher's Certificate. Both schools were prestigious missionary institutions. Swaartbooi taught domestic science at the Girls' Practising School at Mgwali in the Eastern Cape from 1929. Her parents were Christians and her father was a principal of the Methodist School at which she was a pupil.

UMandisa, published in 1934 and only fifty pages long, is the second extant novel written by a Xhosa woman. The earliest were Lillith Kakaza's *Intyantyambo Yomzi* (1913) and *UThandiwe wakwaGcaleka* (1914), though the former cannot be traced. Like *UThandiwe wakwaGcaleka*, *UMandisa* focuses on the development of a young girl into womanhood, and targets the adolescent age group in its didactic intention. In a preface Swaartbooi states that she wrote the novel to illustrate the joy of serving people by being educated. Written in simple language, the novel uses songs, poems, word games, and folk tales to project an orderly Xhosa world with a distinctively regional cultural flavor.

Mandisa represents the emergence of a new type of woman: The last chapter closes not with marriage, but with Mandisa's popularity as a teacher, and her success as an independent woman who has become the provider within her home. Moreover, whereas storytellers were usually older women who could give moral guidance to the younger generations, the relatively young Mandisa is positioned as the storyteller, thus usurping the usual position of older women. On the other hand, the theme of Mandisa's first tale affirms the centrality of males and the self-sacrifice of women to bolster that centrality. It also confirms the power of a woman who single-handedly enables her brother to become a man. Overall, however, the novel advocates the independence of young, educated women whose pride is in the uplift of their family, community, and country. Swaartbooi evinces a vaguely liberal feminist consciousness by representing young men and women in a moment of shared nationalism as they sing "Nkosi Sikelel' iAfrika" (God Bless Africa), the hymn that would in 1994 be adopted universally as the South African national anthem. Significantly, she envisions women's equality with men as part of an African tradition, and as necessary if black Africa is to be "brought back."

V. M. Sisi Maqagi

✦

The week after Mandisa heard the news that she had passed, she wrote many letters of application for a teaching post to the ministers in various places. She stated her experience and qualifications.

Two weeks went by but no responses came. Then one day she returned from the shop with many letters which had arrived that morning. On opening them she found that they were replies to the letters she had written. She read the first one and found a rejection, and the second, third and fourth. She opened the fifth and last one from the resident minister at Ngxakaxha. He wanted her to start teaching in a school at Colosa, hoping to interview her on the Thursday of the following week, before schools reopened on the Monday after. It was Thursday when she received the letters, so Mandisa had a whole week in which to prepare herself. She was accompanied by Mbulelo, her brother, to the minister's residence at

Ngxakaxha. The minister and Mandisa reached an agreement, and he told Mandisa which class she was going to teach, after which Mandisa and her brother returned home where they were awaited.

Mandisa was to lodge with a family, since her home Zagwityi was too far from Colosa for her to stay there. Arrangements for her lodgings were made with Bekaphi, the headman of Colosa, who also had children at a seminary school. Bekaphi and his wife agreed to take her in. His letter of acceptance came on Friday, just before her departure on Saturday. It was a very hot Saturday when Mandisa and her father took a train to Ngxakaxha station, and from there they set out to Colosa on horseback. They had borrowed these horses from a friend of Mandisa's father who lived in town in Ngxakaxha. They arrived at Bekaphi's home at dusk and were warmly welcomed. The head of the family knew Nonkululeko, her father, very well. The houses of their fathers had been adjacent when they were young. The old men and women of the home were engaged in conversation deep into the night, and Mandisa kept up a lively conversation with the girls of the house.

It so happened that Bekaphi's eldest daughter was going to teach at the same school as Mandisa. She was going to teach a Sub B class, while Mandisa was going to take the beginners. The name of this girl was Rietta Nomathemba Bekaphi, she had trained in Healdtown. Mandisa and her friend gave themselves time to prepare their lessons.

On Monday morning Mandisa's father left for home as his daughter and Nomathemba prepared themselves for school. This time Mandisa did not cry when parting from her father. They went to school and there was great excitement among the children who admired their new teachers. Nomathemba at least was already known to them; so you can imagine who was the centre of all that gaze. There were fifty children in all who came to be taught by Mandisa, and thirty-nine for Nomathemba.

Within two weeks of the assumption of her work, Mandisa felt quite exhausted from the strain of teaching. Worse was the exhaustion brought about by long hours of standing, and exhausting too were her powers of counselling those many little cases brought to her by the little ones, reports about those who had lost or broken other children's pencils and slates, and those who looked at words which did not belong to them. She had to pacify all who came to report to her, and bring about reconciliation. In about two months she got used to standing.

One day as she and Nomathemba were on their way home after school, Nomathemba remarked, "I feel so tired today, Mandi!" "I sympathise with you, Thembi, my friend. Last week I felt the same." That was Mandisa's reply, to which she added, "What would I have done had I known that teaching was so hard? Truly, I always thought this work was so easy, this teaching, and I looked at the teachers and thought to myself they were having a lot of fun, working in a sheltered environment away from the sun! Now I see how ignorant I must have been."

"My father's child leave that alone. I also had exactly the same thoughts," said Nomathemba.

Thus did Mandisa and Nomathemba continue to think about and discuss the problems they encountered in teaching. They finally got used to the tribulations of a teacher. Actually, the hardships of the teaching profession are likened to the woes of a married woman. These young women went about their duties diligently, doing an excellent job of teaching and training the children, the little boys and girls. Mandisa was quite happy in the headman's house. [. . .]

The little children loved Mandisa very much, because she delighted them.

I shall narrate only two of the many folktales Mandisa used to tell on cold days, when the children at school were few, making them enjoy school. Here is the first one:

USIKHULUM'KATHETHI [HE-WHO-TALKS-BUT-DOES-NOT-TALK]

A certain chief had many children. One day a dumb child was born. This child was greatly loved by his father and mother. If you happened to find them playing with him, you would think he could speak. They gave him the name Usikhulum'kathethi [He-who-talks-but-does-not-talk]. This child grew up and became a big boy. When the time came for the boys to be circumcised, a miracle occurred, for Usikhulum'kathethi started to speak and said to his sister, "I'll go to circumcision, my sister, only when I have a blanket made from the skin of iNwabulele" [a mythical animal of the deep]. Shocked, his sister could not answer at once. When his father and mother heard this, they were very glad. That very day messengers were sent to invite people to a big feast to mark the day when the chief's son was able to speak. But Usikhulum'kathethi's sister thought about what her brother had told her.

The following morning his sister baked many loaves of bread and put them in a basket. She then left carrying these on her head. When she arrived at the first deep pool of the river, she sang the following song: "Nwabulele, Nwabulele, come out and eat me up, come out and eat me up." All was quiet on the surface of the pool. She moved on to the next one and sang the same song, but there was no movement of any kind even there. And so she went from pool to pool until many pools were passed. At last, when she was about to give up, she reached a huge pool, and after her song the water began to stir, and she stood ready to throw one of her loaves of bread as soon as iNwabulele appeared. When it finally came up she threw all her loaves of bread at it. As soon as it ate them it died because she had put poison in them. Then she went to report to the people, and they came and skinned it, and a blanket was made for her brother. So then he went to circumcision.

As a young man he married a chief's daughter and grew up to be a wise man.

[. . .] Readers, let me now conclude the story of this girl. She is still teaching and doing very well, and receives praises from everyone. She succeeded in helping her brother Mbulelo through school, and now he too is a teacher at

Tshembeyi near Queenstown. Now she is seeing Ndyebo through his education and he is doing higher education at Fort Hare. Mbulelo is helping Nosipho through school, and he has sent her to Healdtown. Only last month, Mandisa sent Ndyebo some new black shoes. Ndyebo was at a loss how to thank her and wrote saying, "My sister, eldest daughter of my home, thank you very much, only a witch fights against growth! I am fortunate to be born with such a sensible person. Do what you do today again tomorrow, Dlamini. I thank you for what you have done for me. One day when I am myself an adult, I will show you my gratitude. I am full of appreciation for you."

Nobantu, the last born in Mandisa's home, is soon going to take her first year at the seminary. I hope the young women who happen to read this story will want to behave like the young woman we have read about here. Perhaps they will do even more, will go out into the world and spread the light confirming the last words of our Lord, "Go and make followers of all the nations, teaching them everything about which I gave instruction. I will be with you at all times to the end of this world."

For black Africa to be brought back, the black women of our country will go out together with the black men; then we will begin to say, "Mayibuye iAfrika!" Go on, go on great lady, to make the steps which we are already eager to follow.

"Daughters of Africa, play your role in bringing back and developing Africa, the land of our birth."

After each one of us has played her role and not just folded her hands, we can then say, "Nkosi sikelel' iAfrika, maluphakame uphondo lwayo!" [God bless Africa, let her horn be raised!]

Translated by Abner Nyamende with V. M. Sisi Maqagi

Unangoroa Maherero, Louisa Kambazembi, Edla Maherero, Augusta Kambazembi, Magdalina Katjimune, and Hester Keha, NATION IS GOING TO RUINATION

Namibia 1936   otjiHerero

The Herero expected that their ancestral lands, expropriated by the Germans during the devastating German-Herero War of 1904–1907, would be restored to them after the occupation of Namibia by South African troops in 1915. The South Africans responded by establishing "Native Reserves" in central Namibia, which temporarily met the political and economic aspirations of the Herero but also created a pool of cheap labor for mines and farms. The dissolution of tradition that resulted when the men, and increasing numbers of all young people, were forced to find employment outside of the reserves had severe consequences for the status and prestige of women.

On 17 October 1936 a deputation of about sixty Herero women presented and read two letters to the superintendent of the Waterberg East Native Reserve. Six influential women from prominent families led the group. They spoke on behalf of their community, men and women. These texts—a letter, a speech, and a transcribed interview—mark the confident entry of women into the public discourse of Herero nationalism that emerged during the 1920s and 1930s. The women scandalized the colonial officials who attempted to neutralize and silence them. The officials perceived a potential for general destabilization if women were to continue to appropriate the role of speaking subject.

These forceful texts of protest, which survive only in translation in colonial documents, demand relief from the problems of increasing alcohol abuse, illegitimacy, and promiscuity, as the women felt themselves responsible as custodians of the family for the well-being of the community. These symptoms of social disintegration also eroded women's sources of power and control. The demands indicate a conscious perception that the increasing gender imbalances created in the reserves were a major reason for social conflict. The women make it clear that, "in the earlier days," boys and girls faced equal community sanction for producing illegitimate children.

In a subsequent meeting Louisa Kambazembi, Augusta Kambazembi, and Magdalina Katjimune pressed their demand for "a proper doctor that can locate the poison." The Herero men who were present supported the women who diagnosed what was affecting the "nation" and specified the cure. It is clear from the correspondence surrounding the documents that the colonial officials did not find the women's demands unacceptable in themselves. What caused their response was that the women asserted so uncompromisingly their right to speak, not only for themselves, but also for their "nation"—a realm of discourse colonial administrators perceived as exclusively male.

Margie Orford

✦

MEETING OF HERERO NATIVE WOMEN: W. E. N. RESERVE

On the 17th of October 1936, a deputation of approximately 60 Herero women came to my office headed by native women Unangoroa Maherero, Louise Kambazembi, Edla Maherero, Augusta Kambazembi, Magdalina Katjimune and Hester Keha. They produced and read a letter the following of which is a translation.

The first thing is that we wish to call the "Biggest["] doctor to come and find out the persons who poison us, a doctor that can locate poison.

The second point is, that the men should marry—all men from 30 years of age and who are still single should be forced to get married—single men who have reached that age and refuse to get married should be taxed. A Bachelor Tax of £1 per month should be brought into force to serve as a remembrance for them to marry.

The third point: The men living and cohabiting with women to whom they are not married and refuse to marry, the parents or relatives must take the woman away from the man within three or four days.

The fourth point: The man responsible for a pregnant woman should be forced to marry the woman, if he refuses, he should be made to pay three cows and calves to the woman.

The fifth point: Beer should not be allowed, the man who drinks beer must go to the white peoples country and drink there but not in the reserve.

The sixth: Young boys and girls must not associate with each other—this must stop.

These things that we have written God and the law must help us. Nation is going to ruination.

I am,

Unangoroa Maherero, Louisa Kambazembi, Edla Maherero, Augusta
Kambazembi, Magdalina Katjimune & Hester Keha.

Second Letter
Okakarara,
16 October 1936

We come to tell the Superintendent that the law and habits that God has given to us [and] our grandparents is that each man lived with his brother and family and looked after their children, sons and daughters until they married. There was not one that got illegitimate child, only after marriage did they have children. Out of every hundred women, there are only two that have no children. Young girls who became pregnant before marriage were looked upon with disgust by their parents and family.

The man's parents also looked upon him with disgust. He is also told to marry the girl.

In the earlier days people lived up to 70, 80 or 100 years.

If a person is 2 years old or 60 years old and becomes ill, a witchdoctor is called in to diagnose the case and if he discovers that some person has "bewitched" the patient, that person is caught and given a good thrashing and he is called upon to assist the patient until he recovers.

This old custom of ours is now abolished since the time the Germans captured us up to the present it has been stopped. We have seen many bad deaths.

When a person dies today it takes only a few minutes before the body falls to pieces and this thing which happens so soon after death is a new thing to us and has been introduced by the White people by bringing into this country other native people.

We now wish for a good proper Doctor, so that we can call all the people together and discover what people have poison in their bodies and who "bewitched" the other people.

We wish to have a "Black Doctor" and not a white man Doctor.

Questioned by W.O.
We wish to have a qualified native doctor trained according to the European customs.

Informed that according to my knowledge there are no qualified Herero doctors, but that there are Zulu's and coloured men who are qualified medical practitioners.

Answer: We want any one of these people to investigate the presence of poison amongst our people.

Question: Can you give me the name of any person practicing as a witch-doctor in this reserve.

Answer: There is one Elekem Ganjone who we suspect of witchcraft.

By W. O.:   Do you know that the case in which Elekem was suspected was investigated by the District Surgeon and that a post-mortem examination was held and nothing disclosed.

Answer: We have heard.

Question: Is it your wish that the Government should be requested to expel Elekem Ganjone from this reserve, seeing that you people suspect him of witchcraft.

Answer: No there are no eye-witnesses; we do not wish it.

Question: In the event of an un-married woman who has given birth to an illegitimate child refuses to marry the responsible man—what will be your attitude then?

Answer: The man must pay in any case.

Question: You say a Bachelor Tax of £1 per month must be enforced on all un-married men from 30 years to 60 years. Supposing the party concerned does not earn more than 10/– per month, what do you propose doing then.

Answer: He must pay or leave the Reserve we don't want him here.

Transcriber and translator unknown

Paulina Dlamini,
FLIGHT OF THE ROYAL HOUSEHOLD

South Africa 1939   isiZulu

Paulina Nomguqo Dlamini's lineage is distinguished: On her father's side she was related to the royal Swazi house and, on her mother's, to Mzilikazi, founder of the Ndebele kingdom in present-day Zimbabwe. In 1872, aged about fourteen, Nomguqo was presented to the future Zulu king Cetshwayo to become a member of his *isigodlo*, the women in the king's household whose functions ranged from domestic work to concubinage.

Nomguqo (the Kneeling One) is the name her father gave her; on her conversion to Christianity she chose Paulina. In the first half of her narrative, she witnesses the Zulus' acceptance of Cetshwayo as successor to Mpande; the proclamation of his kingship by Theophilus Shepstone (Somsewu), the secretary for native affairs in the Natal Government; the outbreak of the Anglo-Zulu War of 1879; the *isigodlo* women's flight with the royal wives, children, and cattle after Cetshwayo's army was defeated; and their hiding in caves for almost a year during the civil war that followed.

Dlamini's intimate knowledge of Cetshwayo's domestic life makes her narrative an important and rare document. In recounting how she helped the royal children to safety with Zibhebhu, one of Cetshwayo's senior generals and chiefs, Dlamini indicates her suspicions that she and the other young women would be forced to remain with Zibhebhu. Her distrust of the man seems to have been warranted, for, after Cetshwayo's restoration as king, Zibhebhu, who had been appointed by the British as one of the thirteen ruling chiefs in Zululand, led the faction that rose against Cetshwayo. Dlamini attributes the ensuing civil war, during which Cetshwayo died, to jealousy on the part of his half brother, Hamu, but some historians believe the rivalry was orchestrated by British interests. Its consequences effectively destroyed Zulu sovereignty.

After her conversion to Christianity and when she was working as a missionary in Zululand, Dlamini told her story to a German Lutheran missionary, Rev. Heinrich Filter. In her account of daily life in the royal household, it is evident that, while she wanted to give an honest picture, she found it difficult to admit to her participation in some of their "heathen" practices. Being interviewed by a male missionary colleague might well have increased this tension and produced some of the complex self-censorship evident in her narrative. But at least she was able to tell her story to Filter, whom she addresses as Baba Mhlahlela, in Zulu.

He interviewed Dlamini on different occasions from about 1925 until 1939; she died in 1942. Filter took longhand notes of her recollections in Zulu and then translated them into German, intending to publish the narrative he was putting together as a mission brochure. This seems not to have happened and after his death his papers were given by his widow to S. Bourquin who translated the story into English and edited it for publication in 1986. (The endnotes and bracketed words in the text that follows are his. Words in double brackets have been added by the current editors.) Dlamini's narrative shows the impact of extensive mediation—two European languages and cultures overlay the original—but a distinctive voice remains. It conveys, from a point of view that has not previously been heard, a young Zulu woman's experience of major national events, the complexity of which remains well within her comprehension.

M. J. Daymond

◆

I was still at Ondini when preparations for war were made. The British were kindling a war which Cetshwayo did not want. When he realised that the British were determined to make war, he set about mobilising [*phakela*] his own army. He assembled his regiments and ordered his medicine-men to "doctor" them and treat them with protective and potent medicines. An ox, which had been doctored by the medicine-men, was killed. Without skinning it, it was cut up into strips. These strips of meat were thrown into the air and had to be caught by the soldiers, who sucked at them, spat out without swallowing, and passed the strips to the next men. After this ritual all the warriors had to take an emetic and then they were fortified by being sprinkled with protective medicines.

The war began with the battle of Isandlwana.[1] As soon as Cetshwayo was apprised by his messengers that battle had been joined, he took his seat on the magic coil, the *inkatha*, holding the crescent-shaped *nhlendla* in his hand. He did this to ensure that his warriors would fight with unity of purpose, that they should not waver, and that victory would be theirs. It was generally believed that if the king was sitting on the *inkatha* the influence of his personality would reach out to his people ensuring the unity of the nation. His mothers urged him not to get up from the magic coil to go to the cattle-kraal. They maintained that if he did, the battle could not possibly end in his favour.

Fleet-footed messengers kept coming in with hurried reports about the progress of battle. When the king heard that his regiments were heading towards victory, he began to leave his seat on the *inkatha* every now and then. But the mothers scolded him on that account. In the end it did not help much; the warriors returned from battle carrying the fury of war on their backs. They were covered in blood and had tied up their wounds with grass.

When it became known that a large Zulu force had failed to overwhelm the small British garrison at Rorke's Drift,[2] the mothers reproached Cetshwayo severely. They put the blame on the king for not having occupied the *inkatha* uninterruptedly.

THE KING'S FLIGHT

I was at Ondini when the war drew to an end. It was then that British troops, coming up from the south, were marching on the royal *umuzi* [[homestead]]. The king's older regiments became engaged with the enemy. But then one day, lights began to flash from the Emthonjaneni range.[3] Scouts were sent out and came back with the intelligence that the British had encamped themselves on the Emthonjaneni heights. On that day preparations were made for the king to flee. The *isigodlo* girls were ordered to collect all the king's personal belongings and to take them to a safe hiding place. We left on the very same day accompanied by two of the royal manservants, Lugede Sibiya and Mfezi Thwala. The one went in front of us, the other brought up the rear. We carried all the king's goods and chattels to Hlophekhulu and had to ascend the mountain, which is the home of hyenas and contains deep caves, to just below the white krantzes. With the aid of a rope the king's belongings were lowered into a deep cave.

We returned immediately and on the following day we carried our own possessions into hiding. On that day we consisted of a particularly large group; we were almost an army of our own. On our return we reported to the king that all goods were safely hidden. In reality, however, the king's possessions had been taken to safety for the benefit of those in charge; because when the king was captured and taken away, his possessions were retrieved by the men who had hidden them, and who enriched themselves thereby.

On that very same evening at sunset we left the royal *umuzi*, accompanied by the king, and marched to his late father's *umuzi*, Mlambongwenya. When we got there messages came in, indicating that the enemy had reached Ondini. We immediately continued our flight by moonlight and reached Landandlovu. We had come to the royal *umuzi* of kwaMbonambi late at night; but the intelligence that we were being pursued by British soldiers who were out to capture the king, forced us to flee further. The king went on foot and we walked with him. He hardly spoke a word.

At daybreak Cetshwayo instructed his menservants to take all his wives, children and girls, as also all the cattle to Zibhebhu at Banganomo.[4] The cattle would serve our physical needs and ensure that the mothers and children would not die of starvation.

All that day we kept on walking, without sleep. From then on we no longer slept at any *imizi*, but under the open sky. On this journey it was my task to look after the [eleven-year-old] Crown Prince Dinuzulu. Then, at long last, we reached the place of the king's cousin, Zwide Zulu. It was at Zwide's *umuzi* that we had to part company with the king.

It was here that he selected twenty girls from among us who were to accompany and look after the children. In order that we might not be seen he ordered us to move only at night. I still remember how sore our feet became through walking among the thorns, especially at night when, without even a footpath to guide us, we could not see where we were going. The most gruelling part of our march came when we had to cross the waterless region of Bonjeni. No, my friends, we Zulus are really a tough people!

At long last we arrived at Banganomo, the *umuzi* of Zibhebhu. Great was Zibhebhu's joy when he saw—not us, but the large herd of cattle following us. After our arrival we were split up. The women with children, and I, were taken to Enkalakuthaba. It was a small *umuzi*, but we were received with great kindness and well cared for. The *umuzi* was occupied by two women, who were both handicapped.

On the second day of our stay, Zibhebhu called on us and said: "Now you will stay with me. In due course I shall restore you to your homes and people."

But this he merely said to set our minds at rest, so that we would not run away. In reality, he had no intention of releasing us.

A little later the two royal children, Crown Prince Dinuzulu and Princess Beyisile, who were in our care, were removed by their uncle, Ndabuko, a younger brother of the king. He had his *umuzi* in our neighbourhood, still within the Mandlakazi area. But Zibhebhu refused to part with any of the cattle, which had been intended to provide the children with milk and meat. He made up a lying story to the effect that Cetshwayo had given the cattle to him as a present. He used them all for his own purposes and never made retribution for one single beast. He was a real Judas!

As time went by it became known that King Cetshwayo had been captured in the Ngome forest[5] and that the British had taken him away on board a ship. That meant the final end of the war. This was to Zibhebhu's advantage; because he could now keep the cattle without fear of further challenge. We also heard whispers that Zibhebhu now intended taking all the girls, women and children into his possession. All this persuaded us to flee; a decision which we put into effect three months later.

OUR FLIGHT FROM ZIBHEBHU

In Zibhebhu's eyes we were already his property. He had told his own people: "Take care that they don't run away because I want to return them safely to their homes." But this was a deception intended to allay our fears. Secretly he told his people not to make it known to us, that he would not allow us to leave. However, some of our relatives quietly told us about Zibhebhu's designs; because he was also related by marriage to the Buthelezis. Zibhebhu was one of the Buthelezi sons-in-law. For instance, he was a brother-in-law of Saul Buthelezi, who later lived at the Esibongweni mission station, where he became a church-warden. [. . .]

So the eight of us [[girls]] left the Mandlakazi, never to return. We reached Wele at sunrise and decided to rest and have a good sleep. Our travelling companions went to report our arrival to Ndabuko, a younger brother of the king. He invited us to come to his *umuzi*, where we received kind hospitality. We were regaled with meat, a mash consisting of mealies, sweet potatoes and pumpkin, called *isibhiya* [cf. *isijingi*], and beer. We noticed immediately that Ndabuko had made himself independent and was governing as a ruler. On the following day we took our leave, saying: "Stay well, Ndabezitha. We must press on to reach home; but we shall call again." He replied simply, "Go then, and give my regards to your elders."

We continued our journey and eventually reached our homes where we relaxed and had a good rest. This was a most joyful reunion after a long separation. The festive atmosphere materialised a few days later when a big feast was arranged. Two big oxen and three goats were slaughtered. The first ox was presented as a sacrifice to the ancestors, who were thanked with the words, "Spirits of our ancestors, we thank you for having safely brought back our children." It was a delusion of our people, believing that the spirits of the ancestors would partake of the meat by coming at night to *khotha* [lick] it. What help can ancestors give us? I now wish our people would free themselves from these incomprehensible delusions! [. . .]

We had very many suitors. At times the young men arrived in whole groups; but the young men from our more immediate neighbourhood were not to our liking. Sixhwethu and I were enamoured of two young men of the abaQulusi clan, who lived quite far away. Our own people reproached us for falling in love with men from far away; but we replied: "Our mothers belonged to the Ugudludonga [wall polishers] regiment; but we don't want to be wall polishers like our mothers, that is why our hearts wish to fly over the hills and far away!" This made our people laugh.

We were in love with those two young men, and actually became betrothed to them. They both belonged to the Mazibuko family. Sixhwethu became engaged to Maweni and I to Shikashika. Some time after our betrothal the civil war[6] erupted. Hamu's[7] and Zibhebhu's people fought against the abaQulusi, who remained loyal to Cetshwayo. Our fiancés were both killed in the battle of Emhologo in Hamu's territory.[8]

This civil war was later followed by another one which was fought because Zibhebhu had appropriated the king's cattle. [. . .]

OUR STAY IN THE CAVES

During the armed strife with Zibhebhu we took refuge among the rocks and krantzes and a cave in the mountain called Ngwibi. The whole mountain is called Ingwenya and the pass over the mountain is Isikhala sika Madlungulu. On this, the eastern side of the Ingwenya range is Mount Ngwibi. The cave is not near the summit but in a depression of the mountain.

This cave was discovered by Qina Buthelezi, while he was herding cattle in that area. He is the same man whom you, Baba Mhlahlela, baptised at Lemgo, when he received the name Zakarias. The cave was so big that even cattle could be accommodated inside at the bottom.

On the day on which we moved into the cave a white goat was sacrificed. The ancestral spirits were implored: "Madlozi, you who belong to us, open the doorway, that we may enter, and that we, your children, may be saved. The enemy, who will kill us, if he finds us outside, is close at hand." The goat's gall was sprinkled on the rocks and it was then said that the entrance had thereby been secured. The pouring out of the gall had truly opened the cave.

The men then entered the cave first, to see that everything was in order and safe; then they called out to us, "Come inside! All is well and it is safe." I was one of the last to enter. I was afraid that some of the huge boulders might come tumbling down on us.

By the friction of two sticks, called *uzwathi*, fire was made and all parts of the cave were lit up, enabling us to select nice dwelling-places within that large cave.

Penetrating the cave in the direction of the setting sun, we found deep inside a large pool of water. We turned back in a hurry when someone told us that this was the abode of a huge snake. This dark pool was quite frightening. It was fed by a spring, and its water emerged deep down in the valley. The smoke from the fires was dissipated through fissures in the rocks; they were such that no sunlight ever penetrated.

The cave consisted of a series of large white halls. We found sleeping mats which were alleged to have belonged to Mzilikazi's people. It was said that these mats and the broken earthenware vessels, which we found, had been used by the juveniles from Mzilikazi's clan, who had occupied this cave during their circumcision ceremonies. An old woman who had been one of Mzilikazi's people and was still living in the vicinity, mentioned that it had been a custom, that should one of the circumcised boys die, the clay vessels which he had been using, would be broken where they stood. This woman also related that this mountain was inhabited by the Mzilikazi boys during their circumcision period. They were not permitted to have any contact with the occupants of the *imizi* in the vicinity. Those people who brought food for the circumcised boys never approached closely. They kept at a great distance and merely called out, "Here is your food." When one of the boys had died, their relatives were also advised by shouting: "So-and-So is no longer in existence. He is dead." The mourners were not allowed to cry, as long as there were still some boys whose wounds had not yet healed. Only when all had got well and could return home could the dead be lamented.

One day one of Hamu's and Zibhebhu's *izimpi* took up position at the cave, but did not find us, because we had withdrawn deep into the cave. Our enemies were afraid to enter. They sat on top of the rocks and called to us: "Come out and show us where the cattle are; if you do as you are told, we will not harm you." But we kept very quiet and stayed deep inside the cave, till they moved off again. Those with a little extra courage did venture to peep into the entrance of the cave; but they did not go inside. Our men, who were concealed near the mouth of the cave, would have immediately stabbed any entrant to death. So the enemy moved off again, without having even tried to enter.

They also failed to get hold of the cattle, which were kept inside the cave. The cave was very large indeed. The cattle entered it from the west, and we from the east. The cattle suffered no hardship; there was sufficient grazing and water. The cows were not milked either to stop them lowing for their calves, when they were kept away.

We, however, nearly perished from hunger; because we stayed there for nearly a year and were unable to till any fields or do any planting. We were reduced to searching for and digging up the tubers of a grass-like plant called *inkomfe* or *inongwe*. They resemble the *amadumbe*, but are much hairier. We cooked them, but ate them without salt, because we had none. We also picked *inhlokoshiyane* berries. These berries we cooked and then ground them on stones, as we do with boiled mealie grains. We also searched the forests for edible tubers, such as the *izinongwe*, which are only eaten in time of famine; wild figs; and *izikhwali*, tuberous veld plants, which we dug up. All these could be reached from our cave. I shudder to think of this famine! The Lord preserved us; but our suffering was great.

1. The battle of Isandlwana took place on 22 January 1879. The British camp was annihilated.
2. Following the battle of Isandlwana and during the evening and night of 22–23 January 1879 a portion of the Zulu army launched a heavy attack on the British garrison at Rorke's Drift, but was repulsed with huge losses.
3. The flashing lights emanated from the British heliograph signalling aparatus. Emthonjaneni [loc. at the spring] got its name from the fact that here was situated the spring from which Dingane obtained water for his exclusive personal use, whilst residing at Umgungundlovu.

4. Zibhebhu kaMaphitha was chief of the Mandlakazi. He was a member of the Zulu royal house for his grandfather Sojiyisa and Cetshwayo's grandfather Senzangakhona had been brothers. Zibhebhu was an outstanding military leader, who had served his king well, as *induna* of Gqikazi, and during the Anglo-Zulu war. He was one of the thirteen kinglets appointed by Sir Garnet Wolseley at the conclusion of the war, but on the restoration of Cetshwayo rose in opposition to him.

5. The capture was effected by Major Marter with a squadron of Dragoon Guards on 28 August 1879.

6. The "civil war" following the Anglo-Zulu war, was waged, on the one side, by certain dissident factions led by Zibhebhu, and, on the other, the royalists, loyal to the cause of Cetshwayo and his heirs.

7. Hamu was a half-brother of Cetshwayo, but of uncertain loyalty. At the battle of Ndondakusuka [. . .] he had supported Cetshwayo; during the Anglo-Zulu war he placed himself under the protection of the British; after the war he made common cause with Zibhebhu against the royal house.

8. Revd Filter gives the date of this battle as 2 January 1881; but the editor has failed to identify this battle and to confirm the date.

Transcribed by Heinrich Filter
Translated by Heinrich Filter (isiZulu to German) and S. Bourquin
(German and isiZulu to English)

Katrina Stephanus, Sofia Labau, Magdalena Vries, Katrina Skeier, Emmillie Adams, Sofia Kloete, Katrina de Klerk, and Lissie Kisting, LETTER FROM KEETMANSHOOP

Namibia 1939   Afrikaans

During earlier and unrelated protests in central Namibia, Herero women had identified a "poison" in their "nation" that could only be expurgated by a "prophet-healer" (see text titled "Nation Is Going to Ruination"). The various colonial officials dealing with the women's demands concluded that the "poison" must be venereal disease. By 1939 the administration of South West Africa had "introduced periodic, compulsory examinations of unmarried black women for venereal diseases in urban areas." As customary marriages were not recognized by the administration, virtually all black women, who had managed to evade some of the stringent controls imposed on men, were eligible. Since the administration was concerned with controlling the movements of women in order to extract labor and taxes from them, this new legislation seemed to provide a way of regulating women economically and sexually.

Eight women from the town of Keetmanshoop wrote a collective letter of protest against the threat of forced vaginal examinations of black women by the colonial authorities. Each signatory represented the area in which she resided— Katrina Stephanus, for example, signed on behalf of the women in A Location— which may suggest that similar protests were being made throughout Namibia.

("Location" was the term for a racially segregated urban area where black people lived.) Eventually a Native Affairs official admitted that "We are not enforcing the regulation requiring females to present themselves for examination every six months owing to the first one having been a farce." There were no subsequent examinations in the capital, Windhoek, and very few in other urban areas. After a protest of 250 women in Omaruru, the law was repealed in 1949.

The letter's seemingly diffident style disguises an implicit threat that, if their demand for redress was not met, direct action would follow. The letter was written in Afrikaans, the mother tongue of many southern Namibians, which makes it a very rare unmediated piece from this period.

Margie Orford

◆

Keetmanshoop, 30th June 1939

Your Excellency, Honourable Sir
We have been informed of Government notice No 152 of October 1, 1938, regarding the examination of every female, but this law caught us unawares. Therefore, on the 27th of June, we pleaded in all humility with the local magistrate, in writing and in person, to please repeal or change the law, or leave the matter to us, because we have never experienced something of this nature. Now, according to this notice, all women must be examined on July the third 1939, without knowing why. We all know that we must go to a doctor when we are ill; we have always done that, without fail. It is there-fore very difficult for us to understand that we are forced to do this, and that we shall be prosecuted by the law if we fail to do so. We saw such medical examinations in the time of the German government, but only on the women who needed them, or for whom the law deemed this necessary. One of those women, by the name of Anna Velskoendraer, is still alive and liv-ing in the Keetmanshoop location. She can make a statement, if necessary, about the treatment they had to suffer. All of them stopped getting their periods and they are all infertile, sickly or handicapped. Those who died suffered the most terrible deaths.

Honourable Sir! We trust that Your Excellency will understand how dif-ficult it is for us to be subjected to something we don't understand and have never experienced. We are already afraid, and don't want to offend the doctor at his work or make his work difficult for him on the third of July by someone or other not co-operating. Such action will surely be a viola-tion of the law and will be prosecuted. Because this matter is very urgent, we are turning to Your Excellency in the hope and confidence that Your Excellency will have sympathy and will help us before things go that far. Because we know, where there is a will there is a way.

We would also want to apologise to Your Excellency for any mistake that might be in this letter.

With high regard Your Excellency
  Your humble women
  Katrina Stephanus
    On behalf of all the women in A location
  Sofia Labau of B location
  Magdalena Vries of C and B location
  Katrina Skeier of D Location
  Emmillie Adams of E location
  Sofia Kloete of G Location
  Katrina de Klerk
  Lissie Kisting of F location

Translated by Renee Lotter

Andanette Kararaimbe, Gerhartine Kukuri, Gerhartine Tjituka, Natalia Kaheke, Andeline Kathea, and Sybil Bowker, MEETING OF HERERO WOMEN

Namibia 1939   otjiHerero and English

In 1939 the administration of South West Africa attempted to introduce compulsory examinations of unmarried black women for venereal diseases in urban areas. Since customary marriages were not recognized by the colonial administration, virtually all black women were eligible for these examinations. Despite several attempts by the colonial administration and some male Herero leaders in Windhoek to persuade the women to submit to the examinations, they remained determined in their refusal. A meeting between the women and some male leaders resulted in a riot, requiring several police officers to restore control.

Sybil Bowker, the wife of the location superintendent, intervened, inviting the leaders of the women to meet with her. Fourteen women attended the meeting but only five are recorded as having spoken and are named in the official documents. An interpreter named Fritz Kasuto was present, and the transcipt of the interview represents his translation into English of the words spoken by the Herero participants.

Despite Bowker's attempts to place their discussion within the common ground of their sex, the Herero women remained adamant that they were speaking on behalf of the women of their community and that the gulf between them and Bowker was not to be bridged. They clearly depict invasion of an individual woman's body by a prying colonial doctor as an assault on a woman's cultural and political identity.

Margie Orford

✦

Gerhartine Kukuri: I wish to say a prayer. Holy Jesus Christ, we have appeared here. Keep us together and bind us in love. Amen.

Mrs. Bowker: Before I say anything else I wish to thank Mr. Kasuto for interpreting for me. It is not the custom for the women of my people to discuss these matters in the presence of men, but the matter we have met here to discuss is so important I felt I had to forget my feelings and customs to try and help you. I appreciate the fact that Mr. Kasuto has taken the same point of view.

I thank you for coming to see me. I feel you are angry in your hearts because of the Government's order for medical examination. I thought if a woman told you what she felt about it, it might help you to see the Government's point of view.

This infectious disease is a terrible thing. People can get it through no fault of their own. I know of a person who got this disease through opening a door which an infected person had touched. His hand had an open cut and so made a place of entry for the germ of this disease. The most terrible thing is that children, whose parents and even grand-parents have suffered from this disease, are born with the germ in them. No people, white or black, can hope to live as a strong nation unless this disease can be stamped out from among them. That is what the Government is trying to do to help the people.

Because the Government knew it was hard thing for you to submit to an examination of this kind they first built a modern clinic, it cost £1200 to build and equip. They got fully trained nurses, and only when they had done all this did they order the medical examination, knowing it could be done in such a way that no wom[a]n, european or native, who had the welfare of her family at heart need feel any shame, but could feel proud to do her share to save herself and her people from the consequences of this disease. [. . .] When I am ill and have to see a doctor, I don't think of him as a man, and he does not think of me except as a body that is sick which it is his duty to try and heal. When you see a doctor professionally he is *only* a doctor, everything else is forgotten.

The Government is paying for all those affected by this disease—however little—to be cured. I tell you this as a truth that if the medical examination ordered by the Government is carried out and the people help the Government in the work they are doing, in a few years you will look with wonder at the changed and better health condition of your people, and the number of strong healthy children born to carry on your race. [. . .]

The Government, and the people who work among you, regard the Hereros as a proud race and the most advanced race in S. W. Africa. It was a surprise and sorrow to them to find that resistance to the greatest work for your good that the Government has done came from you, and that the women of this proud race behaved without sense and dignity, and threw stones and screamed at people trying to explain matters to them.

Will you try to think of this order like this:—If you had a child that was sick, and the only thing to cure that child was to make it take a very nasty dose of medicine, you would not sit still and not make the child swallow the medicine to save its life.

The Government is the father of the people and does not order things that are not necessary. I ask you to trust the Government.

Discussion among the women now took place.
Natalia Kaheke: We thank you very much for your good advice and information, which we have heard clearly. We have heard about the help the Government is trying to give us. Please madam, please listen to us with patience. Do not think for one moment it is the hardship of our heads.

The Almighty God has created nations differently. For instance madam sits here without a head-dress but we are wearing it. Another thing madam is wearing a dress and it is shorter than our dresses. If madam even now requested us to take off our head-dresses no one would do it.

Madam, please follow us. We say this bodily examination is a very hard thing for us—very hard. For instance madam, your husband may enter this room and if he so desires he will kiss you in our presence, which is a thing which is not done by our nation. By that is not to say we do not love our husbands—it is the custom of our nation that such customs are regarded by our nation as confidential matters to be kept in secrecy.

Madam we again pray to you to follow and understand us—it is not that our heads are hard—but it is our custom and it makes us unable to submit ourselves freely to the medical examination in that way.

Madam, there is one thing we want to tell you. Many of our people, Hereros, when they feel sickness do on their own account submit themselves to doctors for examination and treatment although it costs them money. That is all I have to say.

Andelena Kathea: At this stage we have no disputes with what we have heard from you. We appreciate what you have said, but there is to be a meeting on Saturday. We wish to be there to hear what is said and thereafter you will hear from us what we have decided to do.

Mrs. Bowker: I had understood that the meeting on Saturday was a final meeting. I also understand that the Government says: The order is law and therefore must be carried out, or the women who will not carry it out must leave Windhoek. If there is an opportunity after Saturday to further discuss the matter I shall be pleased to see you.

Andanette Kararaimbe: I am the woman to whom you addressed the letter yesterday. I thank you very much for the kindness you have done in inviting us in this matter.

I pray to you madam, please be good enough to consider what we are saying to you. We are not for one moment trying to destroy the kindness of the Government. We do realise that the Government is merciful to us.

Madam, see that a matter or custom which never existed in our nation is a very difficult thing for us.

God has created a man and a woman to come together and be together under one blanket, but even our husbands have never seen our private parts.

Now madam, the main thing to us is this: *We have been rushed at in this matter without notification. It came to us like a stroke until it made us shake. We were unable to think what to do at the moment.*

The Rest: We say as has been said.

Mrs. Bowker: I give you the Captain's assurance that the order will not be *enforced* until the end of April, but I must say again the order is law—a big law. To save a people from the consequences of this disease is to give them life—to let the disease go on is Death. Therefore this law is made. Please believe me when I tell you I've understood what you have told me and I know what you feel. I cannot find words to try to help you because I know you feel so deeply. If I speak of smaller things it is to try to express a meaning you must use for bigger things. I am an old woman now and the world I live in today is not the world I lived in as a child, a girl and a young woman. My husband and I were brought up as children by our parents to live according to certain rules and customs, to think of certain things as good and others as bad. Today—in this new world—there are many things we dislike in our hearts. I don't like to see women dressed in men's clothes. If I had worn shorts when I was young my father would have locked me up and punished me. I do not like red paint on girls' mouths. To us who are old-fashioned so many divorces seem wrong.

But what can we do? We cannot put the world back where it was. No-one can live today as they lived 50 years ago. The big air-ships have come, the sea-ships, the motor cars, the wireless. They have changed life for us all.

It may be that the time has come for you to make a sacrifice for your children's sake and conform to an order that is necessary in a new world. We cannot make the world stand still, and it is not for us to say that the new ways are bad or wrong. They are different and we who belong to an old day have to learn to adapt ourselves to the new day.

Gerhardina Kukuri: We thank you very much for your advices. We do hear you clearly. As you have just now stated the world is changing. I myself am an old woman and confirm that the world is changing.

At this stage we have nothing to add. We will go to the meeting, and we wish to see the other women and convey to them the good advices. We wish to talk among ourselves and one day we will inform you and ask you to see us again and to discuss the matter further.

Transcribed and translated by Fritz Kasuto

Doris M. Wisdom (Lessing),
THE CASE OF THE FOOLISH MINISTER

Zimbabwe 1943   English

Doris Lessing is one of the most important novelists of the latter part of the twentieth century. Her first novel, *The Grass Is Singing*, was published in 1950 shortly after her arrival in London. Since then her novels have included *The Golden Notebook* (1962), which has been hailed by feminists and postmodernists, and two major five-volume sequences. In the first, the *Children of Violence* (1952–1969), her protagonist, Martha Quest, moves from Southern Rhodesia to England. In the *Canopus in Argos: Archives* series (1979–1982), Lessing turns away from her earlier realism to create a universe of epic and mythic events. She has also published numerous collections of short stories and three plays. She has been awarded many major European prizes for literature (Italy in 1985 and 1988, Austria in 1981, and Germany in 1982). In England, two novels have been short-listed for the Booker Prize and the 1994 autobiography *Under My Skin* won the James Tait Black Memorial Prize. Lessing's most recent novel, *The Sweetest Song*, is set partly in Africa, in a country she calls Zimlia.

"The Case of the Foolish Minister," republished here for the first time, appeared in 1943 in *Rafters*, one of several periodicals that the British Royal Air Force (RAF) produced in what was then Southern Rhodesia. When she wrote it, Lessing was involved with a small Marxist group established in Salisbury (now Harare) by refugees from Hitler's Germany and members of the RAF. She recalls in *Under My Skin* that other white Rhodesians regarded members of this group as "misfits, eccentrics, traitors, kaffir-lovers." In her fifth novel, *A Ripple from the Storm* (1958), she re-creates with humor the group's theoretically orthodox but utterly impractical Marxist analysis of Rhodesia.

While Lessing wrote "The Case of the Foolish Minister" without the benefit of the hindsight that informs her later books, her witty irony functions in the same fashion, here put to the service of the practical socialist, Adam Green, who naively believes that politicians should get things done. In 1943 Lessing understood that, while capitalist and reformer claim the same populism as authority for their different programs, Rhodesian populism conceived of no place for the vast majority—the black population. Nearly sixty years after this story first appeared, Adam Green might still find Zimbabwe a familiar place.

Anthony Chennells

✦

The case of the Minister for Base Metals and Industries holds a lesson for every aspiring politician; and no young man who hopes to make a name for himself in the political field can afford to ignore it.

Everybody knows that most men, before they have been disillusioned by public life are delightfully naive. We have learnt to take tolerantly those maiden speeches in which they point to all the evils of our State, and promise to cure them; we are familiar with those thundering denunciations of vested interests, corruption and bureaucracy; we have learnt to shrug tolerantly, and say "poor young man."

The hall mark of any experienced politician is that he is able to make speeches for an hour or so, full of phrases like "The time is not yet ripe" and "the natural course of events cannot be hurried." This particular young man, was, I regret to say, an idealist. Everyone knows that one can say no worse of any man. He used to attend debating societies in his youth, and had distressingly practical ideas about equality, freedom, etc. When he first stood for parliament he used to make fiery speeches about the power of money, and big business, and things like that. He held out alluring prospects of an inhabited and developed Rhodesia, when these interests were smashed. He got in on the strength of them, because people could see that he meant very well, and that in due course, when he had settled down, he would become more sound.

Everything happened as usual. As the first session progressed his speeches became quieter and quieter; and before the end of it he had shown his political maturity by making a speech for three hours and a half on the native question. What he said, in effect, was, that the natives are quite happy as they are, and that it would be cruel to educate them, excepting for teaching them things like answering the telephone and how to cook, which would be really practical. People nodded happily. That was the stuff. He would become Minister for Native Affairs, they said; he had a great future. But as things turned out, he didn't. For about ten years he had an uneventful career, progressing from commission to commission. At intervals he would speak to his constituents, and made them sensible, well-balanced speeches—the speeches of a practical business man.

And then the Minister for Base Metals and Industries resigned at the age of ninety-six as a protest because he didn't like all these new socialist ideas, and because he didn't know what the country was coming to. And Adam Green was given the job. Nobody suspected what was going to happen; everyone thought it was an admirable choice. He was just the man, the sound business men thought, because at intervals sections of the people kept clamouring for the nationalisation of this and that, and Green had had a long enough breaking-in to be trusted to tide the whole thing over. But things didn't go the way they were expected to. The first thing he should have done was to make a long speech, pointing out how well everything was going on, and that without private enterprise a country was doomed. Look at Russia, for example. Everyone knew that Russia had done nothing but go to the dogs since things were nationalised there.

But he didn't.

It is difficult to say what had unsettled the sober mind of Adam Green. For years he had been an ornament of the Government. For years he had said nothing that could possibly be construed as unsound or dangerous. Not since the period of his youthful enthusiasm had he had even a thought that might alarm anyone. But at this stage, no one can explain it, he went mad. After ten years of solid and inspiring conformity, he shattered all the hopes for his future, and all the prospects for a career, in a few brief months of thoughtlessness.

Those who were accustomed to read the straws that show which way the political wind was blowing, early became uneasy. For a short while after he became Minister, the country patiently waited for reassuring signs of inactivity. But he made no speeches, he didn't say anything reassuring about necessary stimulus of the profit-motive.

And then, suddenly, while he was speaking to a combined rally of international boy scouts (which was a dubious thing to do, in itself, in 1938), he made a remark that might have meant nothing at all to the uninitiated, but which set the whole business world agog.

There was just one sentence: "The time has now come," he said, "when we must move with the times, and use for our own advantage the experience of other countries." Then he passed on to a more general survey of the position. But that was enough.

A ripple passed through the Chamber of Commerce; the Chamber of Mines stirred restlessly; the Tory Club shook its elderly head over its glass. But they all bided their time.

Then he rashly accepted an invitation to address the Club for studying conditions in New Zealand, and that was his doom. In ten minutes he threw [away] all chance of ever being Prime Minister, and was doomed for all time to be dubbed "that unconstructive visionary," or alternatively, "that utopian critic." He stated unequivocally that this century belonged to the common man; and while this might be forgiven him as a rash figure of speech, when he said that there were things that we might learn from New Zealand, that was the end.

On the strength of this speech a certain section of the population who wanted the salt mines to be nationalised, began to think that there might be some chance for them after all.

But in the meantime the whole business world had gone into action. Within three days the Tory Club had started a whispering campaign that penetrated the country, to the effect that Adam Green was contemplating becoming a Liberal and joining the opposition. Well, people had become so accustomed to this sort of thing that the effects were rather slow. Then three members of the cabinet who held shares in salt, spoke to various influential people, and immediately two opposition papers also went into action. "Green is unsound," was the subject of one leader. "He must be replaced. Can any country as small and backward as ours expect to progress if capital is frightened away?" "There is a rumour," was the tenour of another, "that salt is going to be nationalised, *without compensation*." Shareholders from England, the Union and elsewhere had heard all about it in no time; and soon people were shaking their heads, and saying that there was going to be flight of capital.

But even this was not enough. After all, the country had got so accustomed to this kind of thing, that people were beginning to have the attitude that it was all rather like a kind of parlour game that the influential played amongst themselves.

All this time Adam Green was calmly, poor deluded man, working out how one could nationalise salt mines without hurting anyone's feelings. He sat in his office with a list of influential shareholders and meditated on ways and means of appealing to their better natures. He read various books about New Zealand, and even (when no one was looking) one or two about Russia. But with his long experience he should really have known that his day had come. A new member of Parliament had just made a speech about the necessity of making haste slowly that had set the Government by the ears. But nothing could penetrate that office where he sat, composing a memorandum about the amount of wealth that left the country yearly to shareholders who had long since been recompensed a hundred times over for their original investments; and about how unnecessarily expensive salt was at present. One can only weep for him.

In the meantime the storm outside was reaching its climax. Every paper was full of leaders about wise statesmanship and the conservative British character, and muddling through. This went on for some weeks. And then came the last blow.

A flaming leader appeared in an opposition paper, with banner headlines "Rhodesia for the Rhodesians." "Can we afford," was the opening paragraph, "on the eve of the greatest war in history, to fight Hitler and his perverted ideas with a weapon that is tarnished. Can we afford to let the foreigners in our midst undermine our war effort? Let us rather allow the great empty space of Rhodesia remain empty, than let the solid British character of this country become spoilt. Let us fight Hitler and his Herrenvolk with all our might, but let us be sure that we are fighting for a 100 per cent. British Colony." Somewhere at the bottom of the page there was a remark to the effect that Green's great grandmother on the maternal side *was an Italian Jew*.

That was the end. Even Green knew it. As he walked down the pavement people cut him dead, and when he went into the Tory Club people turned their backs. With a sigh he came down to earth and burnt his memorandum.

There was only one thing for the Prime Minister to do. He re-shuffled his cabinet like a pack of cards, and made the new member who had given that brilliantly non-committal address, Minister for Base Metals and Industries. The very first thing he did was to make another speech, absolutely full of the phrase, "The time is not yet ripe."

The crisis was over; the Chamber of Mines relaxed; all the practical business men went back to their practical occupations.

The Prime Minister, as a reward to Green's long and faithful service in his sane ten years, made him the head of a commission to enquire into the nature and purposes of salt. Within two years the first section of the report came out, distinguished by all Green's old caution and responsibility. To sum up, it stated that salt was a valuable commodity, and was necessary to the life of the community.

There is a rumour that when the time is ripe a committee will be appointed to enquire into the findings of the Commission.

Hamsi (Marie Kathleen Jeffreys), THOUGH I AM BLACK, I AM COMELY

South Africa 1947   English

Marie Kathleen Jeffreys (1893–1968) worked in the Cape Town Archives Repository for twenty-nine years and, using the nom de plume Hamsi, published three volumes of poetry—*Summer Rain: The Songs of Hamsi* (1931), *Sea-Foam* (1934), and *A Little Memorial* (1942)—which, apart from a few contemporary reviews, have received no critical attention. A prolific essayist, her subject matter ranged from the politically topical to the quaintly obscure, with color prejudice, mixed marriages, miscegenation, and the history of slavery at the Cape providing her most abiding themes. Upon her death she bequeathed her substantial private Africana collection to the Cape Town Archives and South African Library, where they constitute an important resource. Indeed, many of the early texts reproduced in this anthology can be found in her library, while a wealth of her own unpublished poetry—housed in archival boxes—awaits further exploration.

Jeffreys made use of her position as archivist to embark on pioneering genealogical studies that deflated the myth of white racial purity and, by extension, supremacy. In August 1959, under the name Miss M. K. Jeffreys, she published the first of six articles on "How White Are the Whites?" in *Drum* magazine. Bravely, given the political climate of the time, her final installment, in February 1960, candidly explores her own mixed ancestry, which she had traced back to Pieter of Malabar and Cecilia of Ceylon. The article concludes somewhat prophetically that "a touch of colour" may "in less heated and touchy times, come to be a point of honour with white South Africans." Jeffreys's best-known poem, twice anthologized in South African collections, is "Colour: A Song of Ancestry." Here she openly celebrates a racial heritage that she still found hard to own with pride in daily life.

In her essays Jeffreys sees early apartheid policy as defeatist. This implicit defeat is also the theme of "Though I Am Black, I Am Comely." As Jeffreys explains in her notes to the poem, "The implication lies in the fact that man himself is so poor and mean that he cannot see beauty in the blackness or darkness of a human epidermis." Deemed "unsuitable for publication" by the *Union Review*, where Jeffreys submitted it in 1947, "Though I Am Black, I Am Comely" is published here for the first time, in a version that appears to have been Jeffreys's favorite. The title of the poem alludes ironically to the biblical Song of Solomon.

The pseudonym Hamsi, Sanskrit for "female swan," was given Jeffreys by V. S. Sankaranarayana Sastri, the Indian government's first agent-general in South Africa from 1927 to 1929. (In their correspondence he is "Hamsa," a male swan.)

Meg Samuelson

Loveliness in me lies! In the dark pall,
Whereon the deep cerulean deeper glows,
Whence the pale lily and blood-hearted rose
        Draw regal splendour!
Flag of the King of trees, emblem of Death am I,
        And man's surrender—

Beneath my sombre cloak, man his first succour drew;
To me at last all men must turn anew.
Unknown the stars would burn but for my mantle:
Man's dreams and fears are mine, his secrets half-divine—
        None can dissemble!
I in the bowels of earth uncover untold worth,
Where subterranean flames quiver and tremble.
I guard the deeps of seas, I keep the crumbling bones
Of the dear dead; even the weak lover's groans
Shield from cold laughter! I close the coward's eyes,
Bear his dull spirit to the Hereafter!
I see the Player throw off his poor disguise,
Assume the master-role! I pitying trace
The fearful murderer's lone hiding-place!
I know the miser's hoard, good done without reward,
The hidden sins of man, small deeds of grace.
The tired beneath my wing find sleep and comforting;
The sick and sorrowing seek my embrace.

Wherefore, then, having eyes, my loveliness despise?
Wherefore my dark delights spurn evermore?
Pluck rather from their place what hath so little grace—
        Servants so poor!

Loveliness in me lies, all wisdom's store!
Without me, ye are nought; I am the greater part—
I am man's inner heart, life's very core!
Complement ye of me; complement I of thee—
        What would ye more?
Though I am black, 'tis I for whom the poets sigh,
        Of whom all heaven knows:
Death, sleep, oblivion, rest and repose!
Deep am I as the sea; high heaven cradled me;
Usher am I of birth; I am the nurse of growth—
        Heart of man's worth.

Comely am I, though black;
Where then in me the lack?
Wherein the dearth?

Nekwaya Loide Shikongo,
SONG OF KING IIPUMBU

Namibia 1953   oshiNdonga

Nekwaya IyaShikongo (c. 1886–1961) was the granddaughter of a former Ndonga king. Although she remained close to the Ndonga royal family, she also became a leading member of the emerging Christian elite around Oniipa, the heartland of Finnish missionary work in Owambo. Following her baptism in adolescence, she was known under the Christian name Loide. Shikongo was the outstanding *omutameki* (lead singer) of the church choir at Oniipa, but apparently never publicly performed Owambo poetry or songs. These were proscribed by the missionaries as "pagan." The "Song of King Iipumbu" was performed in the privacy of the missionary's house for the sake of recording.

Among the Owambo of northern Namibia and southern Angola, an *oshitewo* (poem or recital) is often a commentary on political and social issues. Owambo poetry typically refers to current affairs or revolves around historical persons. In the "Song of King Iipumbu," Shikongo weaves into the praise of her sons a critical appraisal of King Iipumbu yaShilongo of Uukwambi, who ruled between 1908 and 1932.

Iipumbu is one of the most colorful and controversial figures of northern Namibian history both with regard to colonialism and anticolonial resistance. The colonial administration disapproved of his failure to cooperate in the recruitment of migrant labor. But he was also an autocratic ruler who made many of his subjects flee Uukwambi. Iipumbu forced young Christian women to participate in the *ohango* female initiation ritual. His conflict with the mission and the colonial administration came to a head when he directed his intentions toward Neekulu yaShivute, a baptismal candidate, who was his social, and according to some sources possibly his biological, daughter. Neekulu sought refuge with the mission. The king's subsequent failed attempt to recapture her forcefully from the missionaries brought about his military-enforced exile in August 1932.

Decades later numerous praise songs celebrated Iipumbu as a hero of the early anticolonial resistance. Among the older generation of Christian believers, however, he was still regarded as an anti-Christian villain. In 1932, certainly, the Christian community in Uukwambi, and probably the majority of the population there, rejoiced at his departure.

Shikongo criticizes Iipumbu's abuse of power by making use of the new Christian discourse. She also asserts her right to speak out politically, even though she is female. Shikongo reclaims power by using the very same Christian discourse that disallows or threatens female power in the first place. Her position on the deposed king is paradoxical: She repeatedly reminds him that he has brought his fate upon himself by his infamous acts, but at the same time she remains skeptical of the "brick house," a reference to both the mission and the administration. *Etanda*, the circumcision of men, had been discontinued in pre-Christian time, but to the missionaries it was synonymous with all the "horrors" of "paganism." Shikongo adopts this attitude. On the other hand, she remains ambiguous about the *amugulu*, or "big legged": the whites who have settled over the *oshana*, the dry riverbeds, landmarks of Owambo.

Heike Becker

✦

Wait, let me to tell you
Allow me to tell you
You, Iipumbu, Rise!
Rise and witness the initiation of men
Rise and witness the initiation of men
Look at the horrors being done in the sky
Rise and witness the aeroplane
Nelomba, the plane, is moving up in the sky
The big legged ones have settled on the fields
The big legged ones are settling over the oshana
It's you they have been told about
You, it's you they have been told about
You, Iipumbu, Rise
Rise and witness the initiation of men
Look at the horrors of the brick building
Rise and witness the initiation of men
Rise and witness the initiation of men
Are you feeling sorry for yourself?
Are you feeling sorry for yourself?
You, are you feeling sorry for yourself?
You, you brought it on yourself
You brought it on yourself
You brought it on yourself
The big legged are settling over the oshana
You brought it on yourself
Don't you want to see?
Don't you want to see?
Your friends related
Your friends related
how the big legged are settling over the oshana
settling over the oshana
settling over the oshana

You, Iipumbu, Rise!
You, Iipumbu
Rise and witness the horrors

moving up in the sky
moving up in the sky
as the big legged settle on the oshana

You, Iipumbu, Rise!
You are feeling sorry for yourself
You are feeling sorry for yourself
It is obvious the big legged have been told about you
It is you they have been told about
It is you they have been told about
The big legged have been told about you

You, Iipumbu, Rise!
You, Iipumbu, Rise!
You brought it on yourself
You brought it on yourself
The way the big legged are settling in the oshana
Oh! Look and witness the initiation of men
Oh! Look and witness the initiation of men
Oh! Look and witness the plane
Nelomba, moving in the sky
Nelomba, moving in the sky
Nelomba, moving in the sky

Apparently they have been informed about you
It is you they have been told about
when you brought it upon yourself
you brought it upon yourself
It is you the big legged have been told about
I feel sorry for you
I feel sorry for you
I feel sorry for you
What a pity! Iipumbu
Rise! Get out and look at the initiation of men
Witness the horrors being done in the sky
iye, ye ye ya ye
iye ya ye ye ye ya ye ye ye

The brick buildings are standing
the brick buildings are standing
the big legged
the brick buildings are standing
You, you are the one they have been told about
I feel sorry for you

I feel sorry for you
You, you were told
You, you were told

What a pity! Iipumbu, Rise!
What a pity! Iipumbu, Rise!
What a pity! Iipumbu!
Rise and witness the horrors
being carried out up in the sky
being carried out up in the sky
A Royal was made to suffer
A Royal was made to suffer
the big legged, the ones that move in the sky
the ones that move in the sky
when the big legged move in the sky

I am about to tell you
I am about to tell you
I have my own staybehinders
My own restarters
I have my own staybehinders
I have my own staybehinders
Yes, Nangolo the one raised at the brick house
the one raised at this brick house
at a mission, where he is not an offspring
iye ye ye ya ye,
iye ye ye ya ye ye

I feel sorry
No, no. At the place of mercy
No, no. At the place of mercy
Nangolo the one raised at the brick house
at a mission, where he is not an offspring
iye ye ye ye

I have Victor
the one who is over there
he is the one who went to Swakopmund
he went to get the cloth
jersey, underpants and waistcoat
iye, ye, ye, ye
Ask the people
they know nothing about the place
iye ye ye ye
they are on the boundaries

he goes with his friends
iye, ye, ye, ye
at the boundaries
at Ombwala ya Mbwenge
iye, ye, ye, ye
He is reading the people of Omundaungilo and Ombala ya Mbwenge
iye ye ye ya,
iye ye ya ye ye ya,
iye ye ye ya ya ye ye
Why don't you say: "Are you nostalgic?"
Iye, ye, ye, ya, ye

Kambonde, my middle one, you are grown
Iye, ye, ye, ya ye, ye
You are so proud to the point of disrespect
You are so proud to the point of disrespect
with the cockiness of your male peers
iye ye ye ya,
iye ye ya ye ye ya,
iye ye ye ye ye

Nelomba is the one over there
iye ye ye ya ye
Nelomba is the one over there
iye ye ye ya ye ye

I feel sorry
iye ye ye ya ye ye
A Royal was made to suffer
You, Iipumbu, Rise
You, Iipumbu
Rise and witness the horrors
Look at the plane
Look at the big plane
Nelomba is moving up in the sky
is moving up in the sky
is moving up in the sky
The big legged have been told about you
iye ye ye ya,
iye ye ye ye ya ya,
iye ye ya ye ye ye ye ye ya

Transcribed by Ernst Dammann
Translated by Nepeti Nicanor

Federation of South African Women,
WOMEN'S CHARTER

South Africa 1954   English

The inaugural conference of the Federation of South African Women was held in the Trades Hall in Johannesburg in April 1954. The idea for the conference was initiated in Port Elizabeth a year earlier, by a group of trade unionists, members of the banned Communist Party of South Africa (CPSA), and the African National Congress Women's League. The primary aims were to draw women into the broader national struggle for liberation, hear women's voices, and meet women's needs.

Ray Alexander was a prime mover in organizing the conference. As a leading trade unionist and member of the CPSA, she used her extensive network of contacts among women anti-apartheid activists to bring them to the conference. Other planners included Hilda Watts (later Bernstein; see the text titled "Diary of a Detainee"), Ida Mtwana, Josie Palmer, Helen Joseph (Congress of Democrats), and Amina Cachalia (South African Indian Conference). The invitation reflected the particular concerns of women for freedom of movement and settlement, for rights to education and employment, and against racialism and the color bar that restricted occupations to defined racial groups.

The draft of the Women's Charter, drawn up by Hilda Watts, was presented for discussion. It reflected the advanced understanding by South African women political activists of the dual nature of their struggle for equality, in terms of nationalism and patriarchy, harking back to the ideas of early feminists like Olive Schreiner, and presaging the thinking and developments in Western feminism by more than twenty years.

Sheila Meintjes

✦

THE CHARTER
Preamble
We, the women of South Africa, wives and mothers, working women and housewives, Africans, Indians, European and Coloured, hereby declare our aim of striving for the removal of all laws, regulations, conventions and customs that discriminate against us as women and that deprive us in any way of our inherent right to the advantages, responsibilities and opportunities that society offers to any one section of the population.

A Single Society
We women do not form a society separate from the men. There is only one society and it is made up of both women and men. As women we share the problems and anxieties of our men and join hands with them to remove social evils and obstacles to progress.

Within this common society, however, are laws and practices that discriminate against women. Whilst we struggle against the social evils that affect both men and women alike, we are determined to struggle no less purposefully against the things that work to the disadvantage of our sex.

A Test of Freedom

The level of civilisation which any society has reached, can be measured by the degree of freedom that its members enjoy. The status of women is a test of civilisation. Measured by that standard, South Africa must be considered low in the scale of civilised nations.

Women's Lot

We women share with our menfolk the cares and anxieties imposed by poverty and its evils. As wives and mothers, it falls upon us to make small wages stretch a long way. It is we who feel the cries of our children when they are hungry and sick. It is our lot to keep and care for the homes that are too small, broken and dirty to be kept clean. We know the burden of looking after children and land when our husbands are away in the mines, on the farms and in the towns earning our daily bread.

We know what it is to keep family life going in pondokkies and shanties or in overcrowded one-room apartments. We know the bitterness of children taking to lawless ways, of daughters becoming unmarried mothers whilst still at school, of boys and girls growing up without education, training or jobs at a living wage.

Poor and Rich

These are evils that need not exist. They exist because the society in which we live is divided into poor and rich—European and Non-European. They exist because there are privileges for the few, discrimination and harsh treatment for the many.

We women have stood and will stand shoulder to shoulder with our menfolk in a common struggle against poverty, race and class discrimination, and the evils of the colour-bar.

National Liberation

As members of the National Liberatory movements and Trade Unions, in and through our various organisations, we march forward with our men in the struggle for liberation and the defence of the working people. We pledge ourselves to keep high the banner of equality, fraternity and liberty.

As women there rests upon us also the burden of removing from our society all the social differences developed in past times between men and women, and which have the effect of keeping our sex in a position of inferiority and subordination.

Equality for Women

We resolve to struggle for the removal of laws and customs that deny African women the right to own, inherit or alienate property. We resolve to work for a change in the laws of marriage such as are found amongst our African, Malay and Indian people, which have the effect of placing wives in the position of legal subjection to husbands and giving husbands the power to dispose of wives' property and earnings, and dictate to them in all matters affecting them and their children.

We recognise that the women are treated as minors by these marriage and property laws because of ancient and revered traditions and customs which had their origin in the antiquity of the people and no doubt served purposes of great value in bygone times.

There was a time in the African society when every woman reaching a marriageable stage was assured of a husband, home, land and security.

Then husbands and wives with their children belonged to families and clans that supplied most of their own material needs and were largely self-sufficient. Men and women were partners in a compact and closely integrated family unit.

Women Who Labour

Those conditions have gone. The tribal and kinship society to which they belonged has been destroyed as a result of the loss of tribal lands, migration of men away from their tribal home, the growth of towns and industries and the rise of a great body of wage-earners on the farms and in the urban areas, who depend wholly or mainly on wages for a livelihood.

Thousands of African women, like Indian, Coloured and European women, are employed today in factories, homes, shops, offices, on farms and in professions as nurses, teachers and the like. As unmarried women, widows or divorcees they have to fend for themselves, often without the assistance of a male relative. Many of them are responsible not only for their own livelihood but also for that of their children.

Large numbers of women today are in fact the sole breadwinners and heads of their families.

Forever Minors

Nevertheless, the laws and practices derived from an earlier and different state of society are still applied to them. They are responsible for their own person and their children. Yet the law seeks to enforce upon them the status of a minor.

Not only are African, Coloured and Indian women denied political rights but they are also in many parts of the Union denied the same status as men in such matters as the right to enter into contracts, to own and dispose of property, and to exercise guardianship over their children.

Obstacle to Progress

The law has lagged behind the development of women; it no longer corresponds to their actual social and economic position. The law has become an obstacle to progress of the women and therefore a brake on the whole of society.

This intolerable condition would not be allowed to continue were it not for the refusal of a large section of our menfolk to concede to us women the rights and privileges which they demand for themselves.

We shall teach the men that they cannot hope to liberate themselves from the evils of discrimination and prejudice as long as they fail to extend to women complete and unqualified equality in law and in practice.

Educate

We also recognise that large numbers of our women-folk continue to be bound by traditional practices and conventions, and fail to realise that these have become obsolete and a brake on progress. It is our duty and privilege to enlist all women in our struggle for emancipation and bring to them all realisation of the intimate relationship that exists between their status of inferiority as women and the inferior status to which their people are subjected by discriminatory laws and colour prejudices.

It is our intention to carry out a nation-wide programme of education that will bring home to the men and women of all national groups the realisation that freedom cannot be won for any one section or for the people as a whole as long as we women are kept in bondage.

An Appeal

We appeal to all progressive organisations, to the members of the great National liberatory movements, to the trade unions and working class organisations, to the churches, educational and welfare organisations, to all progressive men and women who have the interests of the people at heart, to join with us in this great and noble endeavour.

Our Aims

We declare the following aims:

This organisation is formed for the purpose of uniting women in common action for the removal of all political, legal, economic and social disabilities. We shall strive for women to obtain:

1. The right to vote and to be elected to all State bodies, without restriction or discrimination.
2. The right to full opportunities for employment with equal pay and possibilities of promotion in all spheres of work.
3. Equal rights with men in relation to property, marriage and children, and for the removal of all laws and customs that deny women such equal rights.
4. For the development of every child through free compulsory education for all; for the protection of mother and child through maternity homes, welfare clinics, creches and nursery schools, in countryside and towns; through proper homes for all; and through the provision of water, light, transport, sanitation and other amenities of modern civilisation.
5. For the removal of all laws that restrict free movement, that prevent or hinder the right of free association and activity in democratic organisations, and the right to participate in the work of those organisations.

6. To build and strengthen women's sections in the National liberatory movements, the organisation of women in trade unions, and through the peoples' varied organisations.
7. To co-operate with all other organisations that have similar aims in South Africa as well as throughout the world.
8. To strive for permanent peace throughout the world.

Lilian Ngoyi, PRESIDENTIAL ADDRESS TO THE AFRICAN NATIONAL CONGRESS WOMEN'S LEAGUE, TRANSVAAL

South Africa 1956   English

Lilian Ngoyi was the first woman to be elected to the National Executive of the African National Congress (ANC). A fiery orator, she was also an experienced union organizer and former secretary of the Garment Worker's Union. Masedibe Lilian Ngoyi was born in Pretoria in 1911 and died in Mzimhlope (Soweto) aged seventy. Her life spanned the most tumultuous, politically active, and brutally repressive decades in the history of South Africa. Under her leadership, the ANC Women's League (ANCWL), together with the Federation of South African Women, marched on the Union Buildings in August, just three months prior to this address at the Morris Isaacs Hall in November 1956.

Ngoyi gained recognition both within South Africa and abroad as a radical opponent of apartheid. Together with Dora Tamana, leader of the ANCWL in the Cape, Ngoyi was arrested while trying illegally to board a ship to Lausanne, Switzerland, without a passport. Undeterred by her arrest, she later traveled to Switzerland, China, and the United Kingdom (where she addressed a meeting in Trafalgar Square), to further the aims of the ANC in its fight against apartheid. Ngoyi's contact with women in other liberation movements accounts for her passionate entreaty for solidarity with Algerian and Palestinian women struggling against similar oppression.

Ngoyi's activism involved a strategy of appealing to women as women. She would regularly cite traditional African proverbs—*Mangoana a tsoara thipa ka bohaleng* (the mother grabs the sharp end of the knife to protect the child), for example—to rally women's support in resisting the introduction of passes. Ngoyi supported her family, a mother, daughter, grandchildren, and a brother, on the income she made as a seamstress. She harnessed her skills, both as a seamstress and as a political leader, to the revolutionary movement, and supplemented her meager income by designing and sewing ANC shirts, which were later adopted as a uniform by the Women's League Conference in Germiston in 1953. Worn together with black skirts and gold (or yellow) shawls and scarves, the colors represented those of the ANC: black, green, and gold.

Ngoyi's speech, addressed primarily to women, reverberates with the passionate defiance characterized by women in Vrededorp (a suburb of Johannesburg), where women fought pitched battles with mounted police. It echoes the cries of women in Mangaung, Orange Free State, who, when tricked into obtaining passes by tribal chiefs in 1913, organized themselves and burned their passes in front of the Magistrate's Court. It reveals a passionate determination to organize thousands of women into a phalanx of female defiance that converged on the Union Buildings in spite of a government ban on all gatherings of three or more, just days before the historic march.

Perhaps the most telling testimony to Ngoyi's leadership skills was her audacious request for a thirty-minute silent protest by the twenty thousand women gathered in the amphitheater of the Union Buildings. For thirty minutes, a thunderous silence conveyed the message of defiance the women had come to deliver, to a prime minister who refused to accept their petitions. Ngoyi's cry of "Africa!" and the deafening roar of "Mayibuye!" (return to us what is ours) from the assembled women broke the silence. Prime Minister Johannes Strijdom might have refused to see the women, but he could not silence their voices.

Gail Smith

✦

Mr. Speaker and my dear friends I hereby welcome you to this Annual Conference of the African National Congress Women's League (Transvaal). On your behalf I send your warm greetings to the millions of women of all races throughout the length and breadth of our country and I wish them success in their sacred struggle for justice, peace and freedom.

Although they are not present to take part in person, in the important discussion that will take place at this Conference, we know that they are with us in spirit and that they fully support our struggle against oppression and colour discrimination. To-day we have come together in order that we may take stock of our activities during the last twelve months; in order that we may examine our mistakes and achievements, our defeats and victories; and in order that we discuss our present problems, check and remedy our weaknesses and make fresh plans for the future.

This is an important job and you as representatives of millions of women in our Province and as the most conscious and advanced fighters in our struggle, will be spirited to carry out your duties today with the dignity, seriousness and determination of people [who] fully realise the sacredness of their mission and the heavy responsibility that lies on their shoulders.

The Presidential address delivered at the Annual Conference of the Transvaal Branch of the African National Congress in Pretoria last week as well as the executive Report, discussed several issues of vital importance to the Liberatory Movement. The savage attacks that are being made by the Nationalist Government on the democratic movement, the deportation of leaders, the disastrous effects of the Group Areas Act on the economic and progress of the non-European people, the wholesale removals of vast numbers of Africans all over the Country, the urgent and vital need for a broad united front of the oppressed people [. . .] against the Nationalist

Government, are all matters that are specifically dealt with at that conference and I suggest that you read the conference report most carefully so that you should be fully informed on these matters. In the address I propose to deal very briefly with and to emphasise only those issues which primarily affect the African women.

The principal and most pressing task of the Women's League at the present moment is to mobilise all the women of South Africa to fight against the extension of the passes to African women. Hardly any other South African Law has caused so much suffering and hardship to Africans as the pass laws. Hardly any other measure has created so much suffering and racial friction and hostility between black and white. Any policeman may at any time demand to see your pass and failure to produce it for any reason means imprisonment or a fine. It makes it permissible to violate the sanctity and privacy of our homes. An African, sleeping peacefully in his house, may be woken up at night and asked to produce one and failure to do so may lead to his arrest and imprisonment even though he has committed no crime whatsoever. Before an African is issued with a railway ticket, especially when travelling from one province to another, he must produce his pass to the booking clerk. No trading licence may be given to an African unless his pass shows that he is lawfully resident in the area where he wants to trade. Attempts were made recently by marriage officers to refuse to solemnise African marriages unless a Reference book was produced. All sorts of restrictions are imposed upon Africans under the pass laws. For example, in almost every municipal area Africans are not allowed to be in the streets after 11 p.m. unless they have a special pass from an employer. Under this system thousands of innocent and respectable Africans are arrested, flung into kwela-kwelas, detained in jail and cruelly ill-treated.

The pass law is the basis and cornerstone of the system of oppression and exploitation in this country. It is a device to ensure cheap labour for the mines and the farms. It is a badge of slavery in terms whereof all sorts of insults and humiliation may be committed on Africans by members of the ruling class. It is because of these reasons that the Congress has always regarded the pass laws as the principal target of the struggle for freedom. It is because of these reasons that African leaders, progressives, Liberals and even Government Commissions have repeatedly condemned the system as the source of dangerous, explosive and racial tensions. It is also because of this fact that the Congress has chosen the extension of the pass laws to African women as a major issue of national importance. The issue is perfectly clear. The Government has decided that we shall carry passes. Must we accept this deception? Definitely not! To do so, would be to expose the African Women to all the evils that we have referred to above. We would lose our honour, betray our comrades at Winburg, Lichtenburg and in numerous other towns and villages throughout the country where the daughters of Africa are putting up a glorious struggle in defence of their rights. When the rights of a people are taken away from them and even liberties are being crushed, the only way that is open to them is to mobilise the masses of the people affected to stand up and fight those injustices. *The immediate issue facing us, therefore, is to organise all the various organisations of African women and individuals against this inhuman and wicked decision of the Government. Only direct mass action will deter the Government and stop it from proceeding with its cruel laws.* It is in recognition of these women of South Africa who have launched a National Campaign against the extension of the Pass Laws [that] numerous local and national demonstrations have already been staged with amazing success. In the face of numerous difficulties more than 50,000 women of all races from town and village took part in these demonstrations. The remarkable successes we have gained and victories that we have achieved so far, and the extent in which the women have entered the campaign, reveal that the democratic forces in this country can stop and even defeat the forces of reaction if we work hard enough. We have made an excellent start. The historic Pretoria demonstrations of October last year including 30,000 women constitute an important landmark in our struggle against injustice and will remain the source of tremendous inspiration for many years to come. STRIJDOM, STOP AND THINK FOR YOU HAVE AROUSED THE WRATH OF THE WOMEN OF SOUTH AFRICA and that wrath might put you and your evil deeds out of action sooner than you expect.

In spite of the remarkable victories that we have won, there are still some serious weaknesses in our movement. 50,000 women is still a very small number in a population of 12^1/$_2$ million. More women must be brought into the anti-pass movement in order that the fight should be organised and concerted. The movement against the passes is still primarily centered in the big cities and sufficient work has not been done on the country dorps, on the farms and in the Reserves. In these places the organisation is comparatively weak and the Government has taken advantage of the situation and is busy issuing reference books. The aim is to isolate the stronger areas and thereafter to concentrate all its resources to crush opposition in the cities. We must immediately deal with this situation. I would suggest the appointment in each province of a number of full-time organisers who will visit various areas, talk to women, establish committees and bring out mass opposition to the scheme. We strongly condemn and reject the passes and we shall fight it with all the resources at our disposal to the bitter end, [and] at the same time we must, as far as possible avoid reckless and isolated action. *Action taken in one isolated place and without sufficient work being done and without proper co-ordination may be disastrous to the movement. It may give the Government the opportunity to concentrate all its resources in crushing resistance in that local place, in the victimisation of the active fighters in that area and the crushing of resistance before it begins in others areas. We must learn to place and to co-ordinate beforehand so that we might strike fatal blows at the enemy when the time comes.*

To ensure the defeat of the nationalist Government we must work for greater unity amongst the African people and the broadest possible alliance embracing the Congress movement, the non-Congressites and all those who oppose apartheid. The Manyano women, the National Council of African Women, the Mothers Welfare Organisation, religious, sporting, political and otherwise, should be invited to enter the campaign against the nationalist Government. In this way our movement will become a mighty movement for the defeat of the nationalist Government during our lifetime.

The Minister of Native Affairs has announced that African women will in future be requested to pay poll-tax. This decision has three objectives: firstly it is intended to force the African Women to pay for the cost of Apartheid. Secondly it is intended to answer the attack on Nationalists by the United Party [U.P.] to the effect that the Nationalists are spending more money on Africans than the U.P. ever spent. Thirdly and most important it is an election stunt on the part of the Nationalists. We will fight against this move.

We [live] in momentous times. We [live] at a time when the oppressed people all over the world are rebelling against colonialism and oppression. We are going through a period when some of these people have bravely fought and won their independence. But there are also hours of serious danger. The imperialists, reading that their days are numbered, are becoming more desperate and restless. The unlawful aggression in Egypt by the English, French and Israelite armies is an act of aggression and brings the danger of fear very close to our shores. In such dangerous times it becomes the duty of the women of our country to put the question of peace [forward]. We stand for peace in Africa and the rest of the world. We stand for disarmament and the abolition of atomic weapons; we are against military blocks and pacts. We ask the Executive Committee of the Congress to demand the withdrawal of foreign troops from Egypt, and the end of military operations which seek to end the independence of Egypt. [. . .]

It is fitting that I should close this address by rendering our heartiest congratulations to the brave daughters of Winburg who put up such a united and gallant fight against the passes early this year. It was in Winburg that the passes for women were introduced. It was also in this place that direct mass action was taken for the first time against the passes for women. The whole of South Africa was impressed by the heroism of the women of Winburg. The reverses we suffered there were more than compensated by the historic Pretoria march of 20,000 women on August the 9th this year. Strijdom! Your government now preach and practice colour discrimination. It can pass the most cruel and barbaric laws, it can deport leaders and break homes and families, but it will never stop the women of Africa in their forward march to **FREEDOM DURING OUR LIFETIME**.

To you daughters of Africa I say "MALIBONGWE IGAMA BAKAKOSIKAZI MALI-BONGWE!" [Praise the name of women; praise them.]

Dorothy Masuka, TWO SONGS

Zimbabwe 1956   siNdebele

Dorothy Masuka, affectionately known as Dotty, is one of the most celebrated Afro-jazz musicians of the fifties. She was born in Bulawayo in 1936. She grew up listening to the music of Ella Fitzgerald, Peggy Lee, and Julie London, which her father used to play on the gramophone at home. She started singing when she was twelve. In Johannesburg, while she was attending secondary school, she entertained commuters at the train station. There she was noticed by a talent scout for Trobadour Records. As one of the most celebrated African musicians of the fifties and the number one jazz singer, she recorded more than twenty songs, among them the hits "Nontsokolo" and "Phata Phata." She performed with the Harlem Swingsters, Dolly Rathebe, Miriam Makeba, and the maestro Kippie Moeketsi. According to Miriam Makeba's autobiography, Masuka, who wrote songs for Makeba, was her idol.

In Zimbabwe she sang with almost every musical group, usually to capacity-filled halls. She was well known in Malawi, and she spent fifteen years making recordings in Zambia. In 1980 she returned to Zimbabwe but soon left again for Johannesburg where she had started her career. Clearly Masuka belongs to all of southern Africa. She has recorded a few songs in Shona and Sesotho, but most of her work is in Ndebele, Zulu, and Xhosa, languages that belong or have their origins in South Africa.

"Nolishwa" presents a little drama with two speakers. A very daring young woman for the 1950s, Nolishwa wears trousers and people criticize her both for that and for her going out with more than one man. When they report her behavior to her boyfriend, they hear what they did not expect. In "Hope Does Not Kill," also from the 1950s, we are not told how the young woman has been "sold out" by her boyfriend. Perhaps he has, like so many men of the times, gone to work in South African mines, promising they would marry on his return. Other disappointments might also fit the words of this song, which catches the irony that hope is the agent responsible for extending her suffering.

Joyce Jenje-Makwenda

◆

NOLISHWA

Oh! No, Nolishwa is surprising
Oh! No, she is so proud.
Oh! She stands on her own strong feet and I love her the more for that.

You say you saw her with another boyfriend
But I love her as she is.

Honestly, I saw her with another man yesterday
And she was wearing trousers.

With another man and wearing trousers?
I love her still like that.

HOPE DOES NOT KILL
Hope, they say, hope does not kill.
I say so. Why?
Because I had so much trust in you
And you have sold me out.
Because of what you have done
I would die now if I could die,
But, as they say, hope does not kill.

Hope, they say, hope does not kill.
Hope, they say, hope does not kill.
Why do I say so?
Because I had so much trust in you.
Oh no, they say, hope does not kill.
You have let me down
By what you have done to me,
But hope does not kill.

Hope, they say, hope does not kill.
They say hope does not kill.
I say so because I should be dead now,
But hope does not kill,
Hope, oh hope does not kill.

Translated by Joyce Jenje-Makwenda

Cherry Stephana Mogolo Sibeko, AFRICAN WOMEN DO NOT WANT PASSES

South Africa 1958   English

This letter was written by a member of the executive committee of the Federation of South African Women (FSAW) to the editor of the *Rand Daily Mail*. The letter was part of a broad campaign by the FSAW to rally support for its regional conference, to be held in January 1959. The FSAW had staged a successful demonstration against the pass laws in October 1958, and this letter was a follow-up to that antipass campaign. Cherry Stephana Mogolo Sibeko traveled through the Western Transvaal to advertise the provincial conference. By bus she went from Johannesburg to Potchefstroom and then on to Klerksdorp and several other towns. She relied on contacts in each place for accommodation, but was not always successful. It was a slow and unreliable process. It was difficult to travel without a pass at this time, and women were now targets for arrest. By this time, too, many women had given up resisting and taken out passbooks. The provincial conference was one of the best attended conferences ever held by the FSAW, with more than a thousand delegates.

The letter provides an evocative picture of life under pass laws. Its style is polemical, but written also with some irony. A rhetorical set of questions gives poignancy to the conditions of African women's lives and the threat posed by the pass system to their well-being and integrity. It draws attention to the impact of the pass system, the mechanism used to police the migrant labor system, on family life, and expresses fears about the further fragmentation of the African family. The letter was considerably cut when published, but this version restores its original length.

Philippa Tucker

◆

10709 B ORLANDO II,
Johannesburg.
7th Nov. 1958.

The Editor,

Dear Sir,

The Government of this country is working hard to see that the African has no home of comfort, but must rather be in gaol. The Government knows that in spite of poverty and all kinds of oppression, our menfolk are still happy and consoled by their wives and children as soon as they reach the shelters which are their homes. Indeed their wives will go as far as arguing with the police, who are not contented with asking an African man for his pass in the street, but will knock loudly on the door at dawn when the poor man is resting and wake up everyone.

The pass is the same for a woman. Must an African woman really suffer the same as men? Why? Must an African man really come home to find his wife has been arrested because she had forgotten to hang her pass book around her neck when she went to the shop or to call the doctor? (Or will she be arrested even when she runs after the police van that has picked up her husband for a pass offence?) The government is now working with terrific speed to see that a man will return to his home to find that no fire is burning. The rulers contradict themselves by saying: "You women are not forced to take a pass," for on the other hand the women are being brought with speed by their employers to take the passes, although it is not illegal not to have one. I only wish the government of this country would go forward for peace, not only for the whites, but for all South Africans, and especially the Africans who are the producers of all the wealth and happiness of the white people.

African women do not want passes, not even the identity card, which one African woman suggested in the Rand Daily Mail on November 3rd. The identity card will still be severe and will not solve the misery of the pass. I call upon the government to stop creating unnecessary trouble and to leave the African women alone,

Yours faithfully,

(Mrs.) S. Sibeko.

Phyllis Ntantala,
THE WIDOWS OF THE RESERVES

South Africa 1958   English

Phyllis Ntantala was born at Duff Mission in Idutywa district in the Transkei area of the Eastern Cape in 1920. She came from an educated, relatively well-off family and attended Healdtown College near Fort Beaufort, Lovedale College, and Fort Hare University. She married A. C. Jordan, the renowned author of *The Wrath of the Ancestors* (1940), who taught at Fort Hare, and she herself taught at Lovedale High School. Her autobiography, *A Life's Mosaic,* was published in 1992.

She enrolled for a diploma in native administration at the University of Cape Town in 1957, and subsequently worked for the South African Institute of Race Relations in Cape Town. This organization attempted, among other things, to help African women overcome difficulties caused by the pass laws.

Besides being an editor, journalist, and teacher, Ntantala was also a political activist whose interrogation of the systematic oppression of Africans often focused on women. In 1957 she published "An African Tragedy: The Black Woman under Apartheid" in *Africa South,* launched by Ronald Segal in that year. Her activism was also demonstrated in her involvement in the campaigns against the Bantu Education Act, and in 1960 she published "The Abyss of Bantu Education," also in *Africa South.*

Ntantala describes with sensitivity and power the deliberate impoverishment and the calculated disintegration of African families. She envisions the hardships of women who remain on the land and the perils they must face if they attempt to join their husbands in the cities. Ntantala also highlights the strength, resilience, and mechanisms of survival used by these women, deploying rhetorical repetition to render even more moving their enormous family responsibilities as women made "widows" by the Group Areas Act. "The Widows of the Reserve" appeared in *Africa South* in 1958. Langston Hughes wrote to congratulate her and later included her essay in his publication, *An African Treasury: The Power and the Glory of the Black Experience* (1977).

V. M. Sisi Maqagi

✦

Widowhood—a life of void and loneliness; a period of tension, unbalance and strenuous adjustment. And what can it be to those thousands of African women—those adolescent girls married before they reach womanhood, thrown into a life of responsibility before they have completely passed from childhood to adulthood; those young women in the prime of early womanhood left to face life alone, burdened with the task of building a home and rearing a family; those young women doomed to nurse alone their sick babies, weep alone over their dead babies, dress and bury alone their corpses? What can it mean to those young brides whose purpose has been snatched away, overnight, leaving them bewildered and lost, leaving them with a thirst and hunger that cannot be stilled?

And yet this is the daily lot of tens of thousands of African women whose husbands are torn away from them to go and work in the cities, mines and farms—husbands who because of the migratory labour system cannot take their wives with them and, because of the starvation wages they receive, are forced to remain in the work centres for long periods— strangers in a strange land—but equally strangers at home to their wives and children.

These women remain alone in the Reserves to build the homes, till the land, rear the stock, bring up the children. They watch alone the ravages of drought, when the scraggy cows cease to provide the milk, when the few stock drop one by one because there is no grass on the veld, and all the streams have been lapped dry by the scorching sun. They watch alone the crops in the fields wither in the scorching sun, their labour of months blighted in a few days. They witness alone the hailstorm sweep clean their mealie lands, alone they witness the wind lift bodily their huts as if they were pieces of paper, rendering them and their children homeless. Alone they bury their babies one by one and lastly their unknown lovers—their husbands, whose corpses alone are sent back to the Reserves. For the world of grinding machines has no use for men whose lungs are riddled with T.B. and Miner's Phthisis.

For miles around throughout the country one sees nobody but these women—young and yet stern-faced with lines of care on their faces. This one climbing the slope with a bucket of water on her head and, if lucky, a baby on her back; that one going up the hill with a heavy bundle of wood on her head; another following behind a span of six oxen drawing a sledge with ploughing implements and only a youngster of ten or twelve years as her help; and yet another driving home a scraggy herd of cattle or a flock of sheep numbering twenty at the very most, with yet another small boy by her side.

In the ploughing season they are to be seen behind the span of oxen, holding the plough, leading the team of ploughing oxen. In the cold winter months, alone with young girls and boys they reap the fields, load the waggons and bring in the harvest. A poor harvest! What else could it be? "Bad farming methods of the Native," is the official attitude of South Africa. But how could it be otherwise when the farming is left to women and children, when the whole task of home-building is on the shoulders of these young women and children?

At home in the morning these lonely women see to it that their children get ready for school—those under-fed and scantily-dressed children whose breakfast is a piece of dry bread, mealie-pap without any milk, and for many just cold samp and beans. Their desire to see their children educated is so great that the women themselves go out with the stock in order to keep their children at school—to give them the education that will free them from poverty, the education that has given the other races so much knowledge and power.

At the close of day they light their fires to prepare the evening meal. The fortunate ones milk and shut in the stock, but for most there is no stock to shut in, and their children do not know the milk from the family cow. For some there is a letter of good news from the father and husband far away in the work centre—the long-awaited letter with money has come—part of the debt at the trader's will be paid off. There will be bread, sugar, tea and a few extras to eat for at least a few weeks. For others it is bad news. The loved one far away is ill, has met with an accident, has been thrown into jail because he failed to produce his papers when demanded by some government official. Not that he did not have them, but just that by mistake he forgot them in the pocket of his other jacket. A Black man in South Africa cannot forget! It is a sad day for this one. Her children look up anxiously in her face. They fear to ask her any questions, and she does not know how much to tell them. "Tata sends his greetings," she manages to say at last, "but says we will have to be patient about the money we asked for; he has had some trouble and has used up all the money." The rest of the evening is spent in silence. And when they kneel down to pray, this lonely woman sends to heaven a prayer without an "Amen." Small wonder most of them are old women at the age of thirty, emaciated, tired and worn-out.

Sometimes, in despair, they get caught up in the snares of unscrupulous men of means—the only people in the whole community who can relieve them of their burdens. These men alone are well-fed, full of energy to satisfy their sexual desires; these men alone have the money to satisfy the material needs of these women, clothe them and feed them and their children. Prostitution! Call it what you may. But if they be prostitutes it is not of their own choosing. It is the system that has kept them on starvation wages so that they and their children can perish slowly but surely; a system that has made them barren and their men impotent; a system that has demoralized and dehumanized a whole people—making the ratio of women to men in the Reserves as high as 8:1 and so enabling the man who has the energy and the means to have as many women as he chooses; a system that has kept the men in the towns in a perpetual state of war, in battle-camps where masturbation, homosexuality and rape are the order of the day, turning otherwise decent human beings into beasts which see a woman not as a human being but as a source of sexual satisfaction alone.

Three things break the monotony of their lives. First is the Church where at least they can take a few hours off from their work, where they can sing and unburden themselves in prayer to a God who never seems to hear them; the church which promises them an abundance of life in the next world.

The other is the ceremonial feast—the marriage feast where they can sing and dance and laugh, rejoicing with the young couple. But it is a joy mixed with sorrow, for they know that the joy of the young people can but be short-lived, that they are entering upon a life without a future, a journey's end. And the initiation feast and the beer party—at one time occasions of great pomp and rejoicing—are today poor imitations of the ceremonies of the days gone by. For now the women sing and dance alone, with but the aged men, the blind and the cripples to join in the dance and song, and all miss the rich deep bass chorus of the men.

The third is the funeral—yes, the funeral—where they come together to weep and mourn over their dead, where again alone, except for the Mfundisi, the teacher, the cripple, the blind and the very aged, they accompany their husbands and fathers and brothers on their last journey. The countryside is today so empty of men that it is these women who keep vigil over the dead before burial—a thing once quite unknown in African society.

Tired of their hard life in the Reserves and in despair, they resort to all sorts of ways whereby they can get to the work centres in order to join their husbands. But the pass system which is used to control the movements of the whole African population throughout the country makes it well-nigh impossible for them to do so. Under the influx control regulations, all the railway stations have been instructed not to sell tickets to Africans proceeding to any of the major cities in the Union, unless such Africans produce exit and entry permits from some government official granting right of entry or exit. If it is for the purpose of consulting a specialist in the major cities—the only places where such specialists are to be found—a doctor's certificate to that effect has to be produced. But sometimes even with the doctor's certificate, the official may refuse to grant such right of entry, if he is convinced in his own mind that the woman does not need specialist treatment. If it is for the purpose of tracing a lost husband, brother, or son, or rushing to the sick-bed of a husband in the city, all relevant information—no matter how private and intimate—has to be given, and again it is the official who has to decide whether the matter is urgent.

To by-pass the refusal of tickets at railway stations, these women fall victim to unscrupulous men who offer to carry them in their cars and lorries to the cities where they can join their husbands. Is it the lure of city life that makes them abandon their homes—homes they have struggled hard to build; leave alone the lambs and calves they have brought up by hand; leave their children behind in the care of relatives and friends? Is it the talk of an easy life in town; is it the thought of the cheap jewels they will wear on their ears and round their arms that makes them pay huge sums of money to racketeers, run the risk of landing in jail for entering a proclaimed area without a permit? It is merely the will to live!

In the towns new difficulties arise. The police hound them and, should they catch them without the necessary papers, fine them or lock them up in jail and then truck them back to the Reserves. If they cannot get the papers legalizing their stay in the towns by fair means, then they get them by foul. Would-be helpers are not wanting here too; men who batten on their agony. These are willing to "help" them by selling them the papers at a sum of £15–£25 a piece, though, for a woman with good looks, it may be much less—£5–£10—if she is willing to add herself to the price.

Those of them who are lucky to get jobs on arrival in the city are tied down to their employers under unbearable service conditions. The pass laws, the influx control regulations and the contract system which give their employers the right to cancel their permits and have them endorsed out of the area, give their employers also the power to bully and blackmail, to offer them low wages and the worst of service conditions.

Even at this very moment in the Western Province, those of them who have slipped through are being hounded out and sent back to the Reserves, leaving their husbands behind. And those of them who are in service are required to "sleep in," while their children are sent back to the country whether or not there is some one to look after them after they get there.

In this way many African homes are broken up, families are split up. No wonder the people term the Women's Registration Office in Langa the "Divorce Court." And yet Mr. Rogers, Superintendent at Langa, can say that he and his men will carry out this breaking-up of families as "humanely" as possible. And the Mayor of Cape Town, Colonel Billingham, when the matter was brought to his notice, said he was satisfied that Mr. Rogers and his men would carry out their work "humanely." But how can the splitting-up of families, the separation of wife, children and husband, be carried out "humanely"? How can anybody speak of acting "humanely," when the breaking-up involves so many thousands of women in Cape Town alone? Would these men consider it "humane," no matter how sweet and gentle the officials in charge, if it was their own wives and children who were being torn away from them? It is only in South Africa and when dealing with the Blacks that anybody can speak of carrying out such a breaking-up "humanely"—an action that has brought suffering and misery to so many people—young and old. Back to the Reserves all these must go; back they must be sent to join those hundreds of others to whom each day is like another—one monotonous song of droning flies, sick babies, dying stock, hunger, starvation and death.

Marion Morel (Marion Welsh),
IT'S GOTTA BE CASH FOR A COOKIE

South Africa 1959   English

Drum magazine (established in South Africa in 1951, with East and West African editions) is crucial in South African literary and cultural history. Including monthly features on boxing and jazz, gangsters and beauty queens, as well as short stories and beauty contests, and a plethora of advertisements that lured urban Africans into the apparent "upliftment" provided by a Western-oriented consumer culture, *Drum*'s popularity soared through the 1950s. It was banned in 1962 by a white South African government terrified at the prospect of ever-increasing black power, notably through the African National Congress and the Pan African Congress. Then as now, *Drum* was renowned for its courageous investigative journalism and the liveliness of its writing style. It is also remembered today as the nurturing ground for most of the black male South African writers of the time.

Drum's few women employees were, for most of the 1950s, beauty editors, typists, and clerks. In August 1952, Mavis Kwankwa wrote a short piece called "Birth of a Baby" about the trials of being a midwife, but it was only at the end of the decade that the next women's by-lines appeared. In 1959, Marion Welsh began to write a regular column called "Girl about Town," and M. K. Jeffreys (included in this volume under the penname Hamsi) produced a series of controversial essays on race.

Welsh's feature on a beauty contest in Sea Point, Cape Town, captures the mingled idealization and contempt to which women were subject. Uniquely in current South African reportage, she provides a view of the insults the contestants had to bear. Her writing style is unmistakably *Drum*, with its wordplay and quick rhythms, and there is even a touch of the swaggering nonchalance taken up by male writers. The subtitle, which becomes the title for the excerpt reprinted here—"It's Gotta Be Cash for a Cookie"—could be either a male editorial voice or hers in male guise. Yet beneath all this a certain kind of feminist voice insists, "Full marks for poise."

Drum journalists often subdued political comment under reportage and play rather than using every occasion to protest outright, and Welsh too notes, as if in passing, the differential treatment accorded "non-European" contestants and the poignancy of the dreams of impoverished young working-class women whose career aspirations were given so narrow an outlet at a time of poor education for blacks and "job reservation" for whites. Welsh herself sometimes worked as a model, and in later years—after training in England—established a modeling school in Cape Town, Marion's School of Beauty and Charm, striving (as she herself has put it) to compensate for the lack of lessons in good grooming available to young black women. She also freelanced for local newspapers such as *Die Burger* and the *Sunday Times Extra*.

Dorothy Driver

◆

It was one of those soaking Saturday nights. I was in the queue huddled in the rain, feeling sorry for me and the ten pretty girls who carried well-pressed dresses wrapped in brown paper.

"Who will be Princess 1959? You? You?" a gay fellow darted in and out among them.

The girls giggled good-naturedly. Me, I would have been hopping mad if I were one of them. It was the night of the Non-European Mannequin Competition at Seapoint Town Hall. And although it was scheduled to start at eight we were kept waiting in the rain outside locked doors until almost nine.

Finally we got in, and the crowd began bopping and hopping joyfully to show that all the rain and insults of Cape Town could not dampen their spirits. I went off for a peep behind the screens where the models were changing.

Show was organised by a Cape Town dress firm, but the girls—Coloured, Indian and African—had to provide their own dresses. Factory workers, domestic workers, waitresses by day. Now with a dab of powder, a secret twist of their dresses, they were trying to become the Princess for the Night.

"Gonna, I feel like a baggage of nerves," one girl told me. "I wish I wasn't competing. I wish I was just spectating like you."

Then suddenly one of the organisers asked if I would be a judge. You bet I would. So I sat in front at the big wooden table behind the golden (cardboard) crown.

"Play a march, a march!" shouted an organiser.

The band swung into "Anchors A-weigh," and the girls sailed in. The crowd went mad. They shouted, whistled, bayed and sang. A fellow in an orange shirt posted himself behind No. 19, and every now and then licked her left ear. She didn't blink an eyelash. I gave her ten out of ten for poise.

Another fellow dived flat onto the floor in front of me. He grabbed No. 7 by the legs.

"She wins by the legs alone," he bellowed. And went on holding in case her legs got away. She went on smiling graciously. Full marks for poise.

No. 9 nearly brought the house down when she slunk in wearing a tight, oatmeal-coloured sack-line. No. 18 had the tiniest waist, which quite a few male spectators tried to prove.

All the girls looked beautiful. It was the hardest job of my life to choose the winners. I would have given them all a prize. But finally a prize of £3 went to tall, 22-year old Jane Hoosain, a waitress in a Mowbray hotel.

"Can I put down payment on the Winner Princess?" the fellow with an orange shirt asked.

"Man," someone shouted back, "don't you know you can't get *Cape Town* girls on hire purchase."

Anonymous,
AUNT, STRETCH OUT THE BLANKET

Lesotho 1959   Sesotho

In this song a young woman appeals to her aunt, with whom she lives, to unfold the blankets of the bed fully, because the young woman will not be sleeping alone. This is also a somewhat discreet, less bold manner of asking or informing her aunt about her intention to accommodate a lover. In the same spirit, the next line mentions the young woman's intention to "go out for a smoke," a Sesotho way of saying that she's going elsewhere for a bit of love-making first, so as to spare her aunt the possible embarrassment of having to be present. Basotho women do not customarily smoke tobacco in any form, but rather take it as snuff. Tobacco smoke is associated in Sesotho with the procreative powers given to the living by their ancestors. But immediately she announces that she intends continuing the relationship by accompanying her man in his migration to South Africa (across the Caledon River), and she enjoins her aunt to look after her daughters, and the eldest of these to look after her younger sisters. This request is entirely consistent with the social values enacted through female kinship networks, in which women who migrate either with their men or to work themselves in South Africa can expect their children to be cared for in return for money and goods regularly sent home for everyone's use and benefit.

While the progression of the text expresses the normal, accepted ways in which Basotho women have adapted to the social necessities of labor migration, there is as well a tone of forthright independence and courage—first she is going for a "smoke," then she is going to sleep with her man in front of her aunt, and the next thing she is leaving for South Africa, all in one short song!—that have always been characteristic of Basotho women's social attitudes, and considered suitable to the "poetic license" allowed in village party songs.

David Coplan

♦

Aunt, stretch out the blanket;
There are two of us.
Stretch out the blanket;
I'll be coming. I'm going out to smoke.
When I leave here, going away,
Montsala remain here and look after my children.
Look after Mamotolo and Malerato and Toma.
Toma, look after these children of mine,
Particularly Mamotolo and Malerato.
It looks as if I'll be going away.
I feel I'm going.
I really feel I'll be crossing the River.

Transcribed and translated by David Coplan and Seakhi Santho

1960s AND 1970s

Helena Namases and Emma Narises,
THE GIRL AGA-ABES

Namibia 1960   KhoeKhoeGowab and Afrikaans

The story of Aga-abes, the brave and resourceful heroine, appears in numerous forms in the rich KhoeKhoe oral traditions. This version of the story was told by Helena Namases and the ending was recounted by Emma Narises, both of whom are renowned and prolific storytellers with repertoires ranging from history to myth. Namases, who was born in a German concentration camp on 15 July 1915, has a wide knowledge of veld foods and traditional medicine for both human and animal ailments. Although she is not a professional healer, she sings and dances traditional *Igais* and healing dances.

This particular version was recorded by Siegrid Schmidt, who has published widely on Khoisan orature. In 1994, this story was published in KhoeKhoeGowab as part of a series of illustrated readers. Originally, this and other stories were recorded in KhoeKhoeGowab and a dialect of Afrikaans that is unique to southern Namibia and northwestern South Africa.

Stories about cannibals are fairly widespread. The peculiar speech habits of cannibals cannot be reflected in written versions of these stories, however, since cannibals are reputed to speak through their noses, and are thus characterized by an eerie sound in performance. Another speech pattern difficult to translate into idiomatic English is the extensive use of the passive voice for telling these stories. This translation attempts to stay as close to the original form as smooth reading allows.

Levi Namaseb and Margie Orford

♦

Once upon a time there was a stingy woman. This stingy woman did not want to share anything with anybody else. She had one daughter, but was pregnant again.

Drought came, and the people trekked away but the stingy woman was not taken along when the people moved away. She was left behind because of her stinginess.

The woman said to her daughter Aga-abes: "Oh my child, help me carry so that we can follow the people!" And they followed them.

While they were walking, they arrived in the land of the woman who devoured people. But Aga-abes and her mother did not know that there was such a woman.

When the cannibal woman saw them she asked: "Oh who-o-o are you; walking on the land of my fathers?" Aga-abes replied: "It is me, leading my pregnant mother." The cannibal woman said: "Bring her along here first so

that I can smear her. However in most cases, I just make everything worse."
Aga-abes took her mother to the cannibal woman.

"Oh mercy!" the cannibal woman told the girl. "Go from here and fetch water from the waterhole where the Nama children play." She sent Aga-abes away. And Aga-abes went; she fetched water from a nearby waterhole and returned with the water. By that time her mother had already been killed but not yet slaughtered. The water was thrown away by the cannibal woman who said, "Go again immediately! This water is dirty! Go fetch water at the water pool where the Nama children play!"

So Aga-abes went. And as she left, her mother was quickly butchered, her twin baby boys were taken from their mother's womb and placed in an ostrich egg shell and the meat was put onto the fire to cook.

Aga-abes returned. "Ye-es," said the cannibal woman, "now you have scooped up the right water!"

So now the liver, that of the mother, was cooked and dished up and Aga-abes was told: "Take this food and feed some to your brothers after having chewed it!"

"Oh!!" cried Aga-abes: "Where is my mother?"

The cannibal woman replied: "Ae, your mother accompanied the women who went looking for 'stone-buchu.'"

"My mother is not the type of person who would go looking for 'stone-buchu!'" said the girl.

And then she asked again: "Oh, where is my mother?"

"Ae, your mother went with the people who went looking for 'shoot-buchu,'" said the cannibal woman.

And Aga-abes repeated: "My mother is not the type of person who would go looking for 'shoot-buchu.'"

The girl tasted the liver and called out: "Hnamhnemhnem . . . hnamh-namhnam! Why does the liver taste as if it is my mother's?"

"It's not your mother's!" said the cannibal woman. "Feed the babies! It is not your mother's liver!"

The girl fed the liver to the babies, and once it was finished, she put the babies back. She put them back into the ostrich egg shell and they lay down.

While eating the mother's meat, the boys grew fast—as it goes with people in a story. And once they'd grown up, they made bows and arrows and learnt to shoot at animals such as lizards, agams and mice. After a while of learning how to shoot they could shoot animals like dassies and steenbuck. They took the animals home to cook and eat.

Now the boys were told by the cannibal woman: "That woman Aga-abes had murdered your real mother, and I helped you grow up. Now I am your only mother so never give her the nice soft meat. You must give the tender meat to me!'

The twins then believed that Aga-abes, their older sister, had killed their mother and always gave her the sinewy tendons from the game hunted, while the cannibal woman got the tender meat.

One day after they had grown up, they shot a giraffe and were busy slaughtering it. Aga-abes arrived and climbed into a [tree] without them seeing her. And she sang:

> *You two sons of mother, brothers*
> *Naugub and his brother*
> */Gowarob and his brother*
> *Who protect the one who ate our mother*
> *and treat me badly!*
> *Huhehuuu*

The boys continued slaughtering. They heard nothing. So she sang again:

> *You two sons of mother, brothers*
> *Naugub and his brother*
> */Gowarob and his brother*
> *Who protect the one who ate our mother*
> *and treat me badly!*
> *Huhehuuu*

"Hey brother! A bird is singing!" said the younger brother.
"Agh you lie! Slaughter!" the older brother reprimanded him.
He kept quiet and carried on slaughtering.
So she sang again:

> *You two sons of mother, brothers*
> *Naugub and his brother*
> */Gowarob and his brother*
> *Who protect the one who ate our mother*
> *and treat me badly!*
> *Huhehuuu*

"Hey you! You were telling the truth!" said the older brother.
"Let's have a look first to see who it is!" he said and they went. They arrived at the tree and saw the girl sitting in the tree.
"Oh, no," they said, "it is Aga-abes." They asked her: "Sing again, please, Aga-abes!"
"No," she said, "I am afraid you will tell the cannibal woman and then I shall be eaten. I don't want to sing!"
"No we won't tell her; you can sing again!" they said.
So she sang:

> *You two sons of mother, brothers*
> *Naugub and his brother*

/Gowarob and his brother
Who protect the one who ate our mother
and treat me badly!
Huhehuuu

The oldest brother now cried: "No way, get down!" So she climbed down and as she got down he asked: "What are you saying?"

She told the two: "That woman killed our mother. And I am your older sister."

"Honestly?"

"Yes, honestly!"

"Right, then we must kill her today!" they said and finished slaughtering the giraffe. They hung some meat in the trees, took some pieces along and left. So they arrived at home.

Those days, the cannibal woman treated Aga-abes like a servant. But on that day, when the cannibal woman said: "Aga-abes go fetch water!" she answered: "Indeed, I, Aga-abes, will remain here today!"

The cannibal woman said again: "Aga-abes, bring the wood!" And she replied: "Indeed, I, Aga-abes, will remain sitting today!" So the cannibal woman had only herself to go.

The meat was dished and on that day she, the cannibal woman, got only sinews. While she struggled to chew, she asked: "Oh my child, what is it today? How is the meat today? What did you dish?"

The eldest brother said: "Oh, we only shot an old giraffe today. So just eat!"

"But these are only sinews!" she said. That day Aga-abes was given only the fatty, juicy meat normally given to the cannibal woman.

Right [after], they finished eating and went to lie down. The people went to sleep.

So it was asked: "Grandmother, how do you breathe when you sleep?"

She said: "It is so: when I am still awake, I pass wind 'tfff.' But when I sleep deeply, I go 'bu-u-u-u-u!'"

The children remained sitting and talking next to the fire, but the cannibal woman went to sleep. They heard "tffff!" and said "Yes, she is still awake."

They went outside and placed wood, grass and everything needed to make a fire, near the door. And while they were sitting there, they heard "bu-u-u-u-u!" They whispered: "Yes, now she is asleep, now she is asleep! Let us get out."

They first took some of their things out and then went outside. They stacked grass around the whole hut, packed the doors and set the hut alight. And "beu-beu-beu!" the house burnt. The cannibal woman screamed: "Oh my children, help me. /Gowarob, Naugub! Help me! Huuu! I am dying!"

"Throw out the clean-clean heart of our mother, then we shall help you!" the children said. She threw out her own frothing heart. They looked and said: "Never! This is not our mother's heart!" And they [threw] it back into the fire.

"Throw out the clean-clean heart of our mother!" they said. So she threw the clean heart, the clean-clean heart out. Now they took the heart and left the cannibal woman to burn. She died.

•

They took their mother's heart and placed it in an ostrich egg shell. From there they left for their mother's land, the land Aga-abes and the mother came from. They trekked and trekked and as they arrived in the country, they camped in a place where they found water. There they built a hut in the shade, where they placed the ostrich egg shell and covered it warmly in several skin rugs.

Each morning they went out to hunt and find veld food. One day they came back and saw that the yard was very clean. This was because the mother had already hatched from the egg and, when they left, she had cleaned the yard. But at first she did not show herself.

"Oh, who cleans the yard when we are not here?" they asked each other and so the days went on. And one day as they returned, their mother was sitting there waiting for them. The yard was neat and the fire was lit. As they approached, the daughter told her brothers: "There is our mother, the woman who was swallowed by the cannibal woman! That is our mother!" They greeted their mother, kissed her over and over, jumped with joy and ran around her, and they jumped because they could have their mother back. There they all came together again and lived as a family, until more people joined them and they all lived there together.

Transcribed by Siegrid Schmidt
Translated by Prof. W. Haacke (KhoeKhoegowab to English)
and Renee Lotter (Afrikaans to English)

Hilda Bernstein (Tandi), DIARY OF A DETAINEE
South Africa 1961   English

Hilda Bernstein (née Schwartz) was born in London in 1915. Her father, born in Odessa, emigrated to England around 1900. During the First World War, a time of British revulsion to everything seeming German, he changed his surname from Schwartz to Watts. Hilda Watts moved to Johannesburg in 1932, married Lionel ("Rusty") Bernstein in 1941, and—besides bringing up four children—became active in radical politics. She was elected to the Johannesburg City Council in 1943, the only communist ever elected to public office on a whites-only vote in that city. Campaigning for the rights of black people and women, she was arrested on several occasions—for instance, in 1946 for assisting African mineworkers on strike.

Bernstein was again detained during the State of Emergency declared on 24 March 1960, and it was during this period of detention that she kept the prison diary, closely written in tiny letters, which is excerpted below. On her release from jail, she smuggled the diary out of the country to Ronald Segal, editor of *Africa South in Exile*, who published it the following year illustrated with her own line drawings of prison activities. Along with many others, noncommunists included, Bernstein was banned under the Suppression of Communism Act, and thus prevented from publishing further work under her own name. (She adopted the pseudonym Tandi.) She and her husband went into exile in 1964, where she continued her anti-apartheid activities as a member of the African National Congress and the Anti-Apartheid Movement.

Bernstein has published poetry and essays in significant magazines and news-papers in South Africa, Britain, and the United States, in addition to seven books. Among them, *Death Is Part of the Process*, a political thriller, won the first Sinclair Prize for fiction in 1982.

The diary covers forty-three days, though not each one has its own entry, start-ing on 8 April 1960, and shows Bernstein's astute awareness of the ways in which race and class differences organized prison experience. On May Day, Bernstein and her coprisoners drafted a petition to the minister of justice, Colin Steyn, which they handed to the prison authorities on 3 May. They threatened to engage in a hunger strike unless they received by 12 May "a satisfactory reply to our demand for immediate release." What follows here is the story of that hunger strike.

Mary Simons

✦

The First Day—Friday, 13th May

Five weeks in gaol to-day. The lights went on at six. We are up early. We clean up all the odds and ends, and drink a cup of hot water. It is very cold inside, but wonderful when we go out in the sun. Our food is brought in, but we sim-ply leave it at the door. After 'yard-time' we go upstairs to our cups of hot water, classes, books, knitting. We all feel well, but very hungry by evening.

The Second Day—Saturday, 14th May

We all go to sleep very early. An icy wind blows in the night. We wake to a freezing morning, a bit headachy. M. is keeping a record of every one of us, each day: our pulse, our bowels, our aches and all other symptoms, physical and emotional. We drink hot water, lie on our beds, knit, read, play scrabble, sleep. The day is very long without meals to break it up. We are tired, most of us feel hungry, but we are all cheerful and well. In the evening we each have a lick of salt, and that deadly water. It has turned very cold. We cannot keep awake, and all go to sleep early. One of the women was released today.

The Third Day—Sunday, 15th May

We wake and lie in bed, without much energy. Some have headaches, one or two are not feeling well. This, we find out afterwards, is the worst day of all. Hunger symptoms are still there, and the hot water tastes so horrible, we drink cold water. Our Zulu and Shorthand classes continue, and we have a reading of humorous poetry. This helps to cut up the day. After to-day, the worst is over, and we hope we will not feel so hungry and uncomfortable.

The Fourth Day—Sunday, 16th May

We begin to feel weaker. But hunger symptoms have disappeared. Making beds requires some effort. We have a discussion and decide to send a telegram to the Minister.

In the morning, the Special Branch arrive. We notice them preparing a cell as an office. M. is called out for questioning.

The Colonel comes round, tells us we have made our demonstration, and should now stop. He suggests we will be separated—perhaps some sent to Nylstroom (80 miles away).

In the afternoon we are summoned to stand before the Colonel and Brigadier Steyn, the Deputy-Director of Prisons. He says he has come to tell us that, as we can see, people are now being taken for questioning, that things are moving, that there is no longer any need for us to continue with our refusal to take food. We say we are awaiting a reply from the Minister of Justice, who has not even had the courtesy to acknowledge our petition to him. Steyn tells us we will definitely be separated "for administrative reasons." We inform him that we are continuing with the hunger-strike.

The Fifth Day—Monday, 17th May

Sleeplessness, and a thumping heart. We lie in bed longer than before. That foul taste in the mouth. But on the whole we are remarkably well, if a little slower in our reactions. Two have now been called for questioning, and haven't returned to us. We hold another meeting, and decide on a number of questions for the Colonel. But this morning things start happening fast. More of us are called out for questioning by the Special Branch.

Those who have been questioned fetch their belongings from the big room, and are then locked away in small cells, in pairs.

The routine is the same for all of us. We are taken into a room with several men. We are read that section of the Emergency Regulations which deals with detained people summoned for questioning, and states that they are not entitled to a legal adviser. We are told we are to be asked a number of questions, and that the answers may be used in evidence in any future court action.

All of us, with one or two exceptions, reply that we cannot answer questions unless we know with what offence we are being charged. The questions deal with our political activities in the past, our associations with other individuals, and our views on the present government, apartheid, religion, and so on.

It is a tense, disturbing day. Those questioned spend the night in tiny, dark and very cold and unpleasant cells.

The Sixth Day—Tuesday, 18th May

We are feeling well, but weak. Climbing the stairs is difficult. The questioning proceeds swiftly today. Finally, we are all moved back to our big room again. Only four, who have not been questioned, are kept separate and taken to the small cells.

Some of us cannot go on climbing those stairs twice a day. Better to miss the sun than try it again. We send a telegram to the Minister, and to a Member of Parliament, asking for a reply to our petition. We decide to carry on for a minimum of ten days.

The Seventh Day—Wednesday, 19th May

Every day is a triumph for us. We are a lot weaker, and everything is an effort, but we are surprised that on the whole we have kept well—we expected to feel much worse than we do. Today is visiting day, and we are all determined to see our visitors.

Our classes have stopped, we could not continue with them. We don't read—we find we cannot concentrate. We don't play scrabble. We just talk and talk. What we miss most of all is not so much the actual food, but the whole social ceremony of eating, particularly in the evenings. The day becomes endless without the preparations for a meal, sitting and eating, sitting over our cups of coffee and cigarettes—always the most pleasant time of the day—and cleaning up afterwards. There is no "middle" to the day, it merges into one long, cold, never-ending procession of hours. The late afternoon is the worst time of all, when we used to do exercises together. Now we can't exercise. We come up from the sun to the great, grey and gloomy rooms. We walk slowly, and evening slowly approaches. It gets darker and colder. There is nothing at all between us and bed-time but hours and hours and hours.

We hear from our visitors that the Minister made a speech in the House in which he said the women detainees at Pretoria Gaol are not on hunger-strike; they are refusing prison food, but have their own stocks of food that they are eating. We are nearly crazy with fury at this news. We immediately prepare a telegram to the Minister protesting strongly against his untruth, and giving the facts. We also prepare a statement for the Colonel, who comes to see us later. Challenged, he admits that we are not eating our own stocks of food; but he claims we are existing on glucose. We tell him that we ordered 4 lbs. of glucose to break the fast, and that we rationed out 5 tablespoons to each individual to keep in case we were separated. After the fifth day, we made some of the weaker ones take two teaspoonsful of glucose a day. We challenge him to weigh what is left to see how much we have actually taken.

In the afternoon we have another visit from the Colonel. This time he is accompanied by a Captain Cilliers from the Special Branch, who tells us he has just received a message on the telex from Cape Town. The Minister is considering our petition, investigations will be expedited. Cilliers then says he must send a reply to the Minister by telex this afternoon. He urges us to stop the hunger-strike. We ask for a day to consider our reply, and say we will only discuss it with the four who are separated from us. We then have another argument with the Colonel and Cilliers about the glucose. If the Minister knows we are eating, why is he so anxious for us to stop the hunger-strike?

Back in our quarters, and the four are brought back to us. We have a lively discussion. We decide that the Minister's reply is no reply at all, that we have achieved a great deal already, and that because the House of Assembly rises tomorrow, the Minister simply wants to be able to tell Parliament that we have agreed to start eating. We draft our reply:

"Your communication after 16 days is vague and unsatisfactory, and is in fact no reply to our petition of May 2nd. We are therefore continuing with our hunger-strike. We await more specific information in regard to our release."

The Eighth Day—Thursday, 20th May
We are all getting as thin as sticks. Clothes hang on us, we see bones we did not know we possessed. But we are still all cheerful. We stay in bed much later, move more slowly. Washing a couple of articles and making a bed is exhausting.

Early this morning we are handed a letter from the Department of Justice:

"Madam,
I have been directed by the Honourable the Minister of Justice [sic] to acknowledge the petition signed by yourself and 20 other detainees on the 2nd May 1960, and to inform you that the demand for your immediate release contained therein is under consideration. A further communication in this regard will be addressed to you in due course.
Yours faithfully,
the Secretary for Justice."

This has the air of an 11th-hour drama about it, with Parliament rising today. But there is nothing in it to make us alter our decision.

The six wives are called unexpectedly to see their husbands—ominous, as this is not the day they usually visit. In the afternoon we are brought upstairs from the yard—the Colonel wants to address us. We climb the stairs slowly, resting all the time. We are all gathered in our room, sitting, as we cannot stand for long. The Colonel is here, with a full retinue of staff, and men we do not know.

He says he has two announcements to make. The first is that he has warrants for every one of us, arresting us under a section of the Emergency Regulations, and detaining us until March 28th, 1961, unless lawfully released before. In silence we hear this; our hearts feel as though they have collapsed inside us. We know this is just some sort of formality; but under the circumstances, we feel stunned. As he finishes, the men get busy taking finger-prints from each one of us all over again—a sort of re-arrest within a prison.

The Colonel then reads the second notice. He names eight of us, and says he has an order for those eight to be removed to Nylstroom at 6 o'clock the following morning.

We greet this with bitter indignation. And find after eight days without food that we cry very easily. This is a blow; three of the women have husbands here, and six of them have children they had hoped to see. Now they will be in a prison that can only be visited by their relatives if they have the whole day to spend driving there and back.

We ask to see the Director of Prisons, and are informed he is in Cape Town; we ask for the Deputy-Director, and after some discussion, the Colonel agrees to call him. While this is going on, the formal arrests and finger-printing continue. And at the same time, some of the women are called down for an examination by a doctor who has come at the request of some of our relatives.

When Brigadier Steyn (the Deputy-Director) arrives, we request that the women should not be moved, particularly in view of their weakened condition; and that permission be granted for us to apply to Court for an urgent interdict to restrain the authorities from moving them. Steyn argues with us; he will not let us apply to Court for an interdict that night, after which it will, of course, be too late. He refuses to postpone the removals, even for a day.

We get disastrous news from the doctor. He tells one of the women: "You must cease your hunger-strike immediately. Your heart condition is serious, and if you continue you will endanger your life." He says it is not a permanent defect, but due to a lack of potassium to the heart. He warns two other women that they are developing the same condition.

There follows another of our vocal meetings, with more impassioned views expressed, but ultimately we agree to end the hunger strike on medical grounds. We then prepare the following statement:

> "*To Colonel Snyman:*
>
> *Tonight, several women were examined by Dr. De Villiers, who informed two that their condition was serious, and if they did not stop fasting immediately, they would harm themselves irreparably. One other woman has already been similarly warned. These women do not wish to stop fasting whilst the rest of the women are not eating.*
>
> *On these medical grounds, and as responsible people, we have therefore decided to call off our hunger-strike tonight. We wish to make it absolutely clear that this is our only reason for doing so.*
>
> *8.30 p.m., May 20th, 1960."*

We ring the bell, and tell the wardress to call Matron.

Lassie Ndondo, PAST AND PRESENT

Zimbabwe 1962   siNdebele

Lassie Nombembe was born in 1934 in Bulawayo of Fengu (or Fingo) parents. She proved to be a very capable student and was sent to Goromonzi School, the first government-sponsored secondary school for Africans in the country. Afterward, she attended Waddilove Teacher Training College and became a qualified primary school teacher. In 1957 she started teaching at Mzinyathi Mission where she met her colleague Lionel Ndondo, whom she married the following year. They had four children, three of whom have also joined the teaching profession. Lassie Ndondo, who has been teaching in primary schools for over forty years, is presently head of Sigombe Primary School in Bulawayo.

Take Care of Your Children (*Qaphela Ingane*) is her only published work. She wrote it in 1960 when the Southern Rhodesia African Literature Bureau, which had been established in 1953 to encourage and publish authors in Shona and Ndebele, launched a competition in novel-writing in these two languages. Ndondo who "had been good at writing stories" since her schooldays, decided "to take up the challenge and write in siNdebele" despite the fact that her mother tongue was Xhosa and Zulu was her second language. At the time she entered the competition, she did not know her book would be, by virtue of its having won second prize, the first published novel by a black woman in Rhodesia.

The plot of *Take Care of Your Children* centers on two boys, Sikhumbuzo and Themba, one brought up by a weak father and a despicable mother who spoil him, the other by a Christian and upright family. They become friends, and inevitably the one corrupts the other. Because they fail to obey the words of the Lord, they are punished, as are their parents who did not teach their children properly—hence the title of the novel.

While the novel does not differ in its plot and moral from much literature written in the same period, Ndondo comments on issues that were considered extremely sensitive at the time. She offers a positive assessment of traditional beliefs and customs, describes the brutality of the police, and openly criticizes the government for having introduced the so-called destocking program, that is, the program to control the number of cattle the Ndebele could keep.

Cristiana Pugliese

✦

If one looks back to the time when Mzilikazi first entered the country that was later known as Southern Rhodesia, it will be seen that the people had a very different way of life to what they have today. In those days people knew only how to fight, seizing cattle and grain and young men, something that today we find unacceptable. A man would go off with his regiment to fight, knowing that he might never return but remain dead and unburied in the bush to be eaten by vultures and wild animals. Or if he was lucky he would come back from battle chanting songs of victory.

But in those days too the earth yielded abundantly. They knew that whatever they planted would flourish, so no one went hungry, and they drank beer lavishly. Every family had had sufficient grain and meat, and there was so much milk from the cows that a great deal of it was simply thrown away.

Today all that is no more. The white man came with his way of life, his law and taxes and changed the nation, introducing new customs and new beliefs, all kinds of things that were wholly unknown in traditional society before we were defeated. He came carrying a small flat piece of metal like a button without holes and it was said that this was the means by which people would live. To get these pieces of metal men had to abandon their homes and families and go to the towns and mines to work and sweat for them. They lived on what they could in these places where there were no cattle or crops and where a new breed of people called *uTsotsi* or criminals came into existence whom no one had ever seen before.

Can we even count the number of new things that appeared in this new world? On a cloudless day one would hear the sound of thunder and ask, What is that? And that was a radio. And at night when you went outside you found lights up in the air so bright that your eyes could not stand their sharp dazzle that was like lightning in its brilliance. Nothing like that was ever seen in the past, nor did the people of those olden days peer up into the sky and speak of the sputnik. And today's music, when you listen to it you feel your whole ear filled up with the sound and your whole body vibrating to the noise. People's speech too is so different from what it was.

The old order of all things has changed and today no one abides by traditional customs and no one knows how to behave properly. And change is still going on, rapidly transforming us at such an alarming rate that those who behave today as they did yesterday are called old-fashioned. Is it any wonder that our children don't know the difference between right and wrong? For a child depends upon his parents for guidance, parents who commit themselves to moulding the child's behaviour, and where shall we find such parents now? If the child strays into a life of wrongdoing we must put the first blame on the parents and hope that they themselves will be haunted by a sense of having failed the child. As our people say, *You can only shape the hide when it is wet and soft, but not when it is dry.* The white man says, *It's no use crying over spilt milk,* but one cannot help crying. This is the kind of confusion and crisis that our society has fallen into while everyone, young and old, men and women, rush to the towns. If we do not advise our children properly and teach them that the love of money is the root of all evil—hatred, robbery, banditry, murder—then we have failed. Because all evil things come as result of the love of money which was brought by the whites. The great wise man named Ntsikana from Macicheni, beyond Nciba among the Xhosa people, prophesied: "The white man will come with two things; in his right hand he will hold a Bible, and in his left he will hold a metal button without holes. You must take the Bible and leave the metal button." However, we were an ignorant and unheeding people, we took both, and that is why today our world is in such a quandary.

Translated by Samukele Hadebe

Noni Jabavu, BUS JOURNEY TO TSOLO

South Africa 1963   English

Noni Jabavu was born in 1920 in Middledrift in the Eastern Cape. She was the daughter of Nolwandle and D. D. T. Jabavu, who were members of a family of political figures, journalists, and educators (see text by Florence Nolwandle Jabavu). At thirteen she went to London to study music at the Royal Academy, and later became a film technician. After marrying the English cinematographer Michael Cadbury Crossfield, she returned to South Africa only occasionally. In 1960 she published *Drawn in Colour,* and in 1963 *The Ochre People,* both memoirs. In 1976 and 1977 she spent time in South Africa collecting archival material for a projected book on her father. During this time she published a weekly column in *The Daily Dispatch,* a newspaper in East London. She now lives in Zimbabwe.

This excerpt from *The Ochre People* describes part of Jabavu's bus journey to Tsolo in the Transkei (Eastern Cape) to visit her maternal uncle. The Great Kei River separates the Ciskei from the Transkei. Jabavu is highly conscious of the ambiguities of her position as an outsider/insider and of the class differences between herself and her fellow travelers. Yet they share much knowledge: Xhosa history and culture, the separatist social and economic structures of the apartheid system, and the Native Laws Amendment Act (1952) restricting Africans' stay in the urban areas and spawning the seasonal migration between city centers and the reserves. History becomes alive for the bus travelers as the scenery raises issues of land dispossession, harking back to the decision made by Sir George Grey (governor of the Cape Colony, 1854–1861) to populate the land with German military settlers. Also recalled are the Xhosa First Frontier Wars of 1779–1781, when one of the Khoi kingdoms fell to the Xhosa, so that the Khoi were assimilated as Sukwini. The sight of the cycling "pagans" recalls the historical conflicts over succession and political power that split the Xhosa nation into Ndhlambe and Gcaleka followers. The denunciation of Ndhlambe's ambition raises a similar criticism of Dr. Hendrik Verwoed, the architect of the apartheid system, who introduced the Bantu Education Act in 1953.

V. M. Sisi Maqagi

✦

Although my father had studied railway time-tables and mapped out my journey, I felt intimidated by the connections, the tedious waits at junctions, and decided to take the long-distance Native Bus instead from East London to Umtata, the Transkei capital; and from there a local bus to Xhokonxa, the infinitesimally small town nearest my uncle's place in the depths of the country. He asked if I had not forgotten what such a journey could mean. It would be rough, physically trying: I would be squeezed tight among yokels anointed with fat and surrounded by mountains of household goods; would have to pick my way through knobkerries and fighting sticks held upright in the bus by pagan braves; probably sit between squealing piglets and hens strung up and contained in pillowcases—the sort of journey he had made hundreds of times into parts of the country far more primitive than ours on The Border where we were, so to speak, comparatively refined. I could avoid the inconvenience by travelling "incapsulated" in a second-class compartment all the way, rubbing shoulders only with those of my own kind. When he had pointed out the hazards and found I did not shrink (actually because I was shrinking from the train journey), my father was delighted.

"Well, you will not be comfortable, Jili. But there is no better way of improving your Xhosa than by taking such a trip. You will be among people who truly speak the language. To keep your ears open will be an education and a pleasure."

The bus did not carry only Africans, but it was they who mainly used it. It was part of the service run by South African Railways into inaccessible rural districts; cheap fares, spartan accommodation, wooden benches only, no unnecessary luxury of leg room.

The bus had, however, a special compartment sealed off by a glass partition at the front that was different—upholstered, roomier, which cost more. There was a curtain inside it which could be drawn across the partition, but was not always so drawn. That section, however, was labelled "Europeans Only." The few whites who travelled in such buses were generally bound for European estates within the Reserve or hamlets where they ran trading stores, the little gold-mines like the one in Alice that sell "Kaffir Goods."

At the terminus near East London's railway station, I found a great crowd and thought they must be seeing off friends in the usual gregarious fashion. But I soon realized that practically everyone in sight was clambering on to the bus. Women with babies tied on to their backs with thick woollen shawls, and leading toddlers by the hand; men of all ages, some carrying newly bought portable gramophones, satchels of mechanical tools, knobkerries, fighting sticks, tin trunks, pillow-cases filled like Christmas stockings with personal belongings. The pillow-cases were hand-embroidered with legends in English such as: "Beloved," "Persevere," "The Time is Nigh."

Some of the girls and women balanced Singer sewing-machines on their heads, or new cooking utensils that gleamed in the morning sunshine. In the bus they piled them on the floor or on their laps. Every kind of "sophisticated" or "backward, primitive" seemed to be represented, with the gradations in between. There was the usual uproar, laughter, shouts, outbreaks into song.

The white driver and conductor stood apart with two or three fellow whites who were coming, looking on at us with the familiar expression on their faces which reminded me of how Africans say, "They have a philosophy of joylessness those people, meet life with clenched jaws, are grim." None of the Africans paid them much attention and, watching the contrast, I was struck as often before by the ebullience of the blacks which seemed to mesmerize the whites as they stared, chewing, clenching jaws at the scene of irrepressible gaiety, the yells of delight despite the discomfort.

I soon heard (because they yelled it), that many boarding the bus were going home to the Reserves after spells of working in town as house "girls" or garden or messenger "boys." They were going back to the country to attend to their responsibilities, since they were, of course, grown men and women. Their thoughts turned to these home affairs for the shouted conversations were about them as people exchanged greetings; asked after one another's health; into reasons for travelling; and for news of births, marriages, deaths.

The scene seemed exotic even to me because although most of the men were dressed soberly enough in Western clothes (ancient tweeds and flannels, Prince of Wales checks faded by many suns), there were those who draped the ubiquitous toga over their shoulder, on top of shirt and trousers. One such man, wearing a new and wide-brimmed jet-black Stetson hat looked like a Spanish grandee. And his two companions wore earrings and spotted kerchiefs round their heads. They reminded me of storybook pirates. The women wore variegated coloured cotton dresses under home-knitted cardigans or sober-coloured heavy store-bought woollen shawls. I thought how when women have to watch every penny, and skimp and make things do, their clothes look haphazard and sad, not gay despite the bright colours. The more matronly wore black turbans drawn to a knot at the back and thrust through in front with old-fashioned hatpins. The younger ones wore white or coloured berets set at rakish angles, and crocheted cloches—favourite style enduring since the twenties. And as I climbed up the steps in my uncrushable suit of man-made fibre and laden only with a lightweight case because of travelling by air, I realized that other people were examining my get-up as much as I was examining theirs, for they made comments.

I walked down the corridor of the bus between the stark wooden seats, and remembered the remark the passer-by had made to our housemaid about pounding his behind on third-class railway seats to Queenstown, how he had exclaimed, "But it was travel, nevertheless!"

We set off through the seaside town along metalled roads bordered by European bungalow-houses washed white or cream. Convolvulus, morning glory cascaded over porches; and roofs were painted or tiled red or green. The dwellings looked inviting, cared-for. Soft lawns lay in front of them and black gardeners held hoses, watering before the sun should rise in the sky. In the hedges as we sped by, there were flashes of colour: poinsettia, hibiscus, flamboyants. East London, *eMonti*, is a clean, orderly, bustling port and residential town with a long frontage on to the Indian Ocean, almost all of whose pleasant sandy part beach-line is reserved for "Europeans Only." It was not long before the bus was heading out of the town and inland.

We climbed up, then down and round the spreading hills of now rather bare countryside, sometimes dotted with huge granite boulders and stumpy succulents, or with thorn trees short, bent and twisted; or it stretched out smooth and featureless, with isolated houses in the distance protected by windbreaks of tall trees. There were occasional windmills whose shining metal wheels were immobile because the day was windless, although fresh as yet and bathed in that clear light which is a feature of the Eastern Cape; mornings when, after the vivid colours of sunrise, the day settles into tones of silver, and afternoon becomes flat, almost harsh.

We started the journey in the transient, luminous phase which makes one so wish that South Africa had its Vermeer, its Corot—some such miracle painter of light. I noticed my companions on board looking out at the land-scape. They sat back when they had loosened shawls and togas, and settled down to what comfort was possible in the restricted space, and prepared to enjoy the spectacle. Their faces, the usual varieties of browns, looked happy and expansive as the sun's rays filtered in through the windows. They grad-ually assumed the expressions of people "sitting-in-the-warmth (of sun)." There is a verb for it, not to be confused with the other that refers to enjoy-ment of a different source of warmth—fire. Neither of them have English equivalents. Nor do we have an equivalent in our language for "sun-bathing" because southern Africans never engage in it. You see them sitting in the shade, only watching Noel Coward's "noon-day sun." I had been astonished when "abroad" on the same continent to find not only English-men sitting smack in it but blacks too. My fellow southerners in the bus would have been equally taken aback. We were enjoying the sun now in the customary way, *ukugcakamela*, warming you benignly right through your body, not "broiling your outside like a piece of bacon," as we say.

I had a corner seat. Beside me was a woman who looked in her middle thirties. She had boarded the bus carrying a baby on her back. To sit down, she had unstrapped the shawl tied across her chest, swung it round her body with the child cradled in it still asleep but automatically adjusting its little legs from their clasping position round the mother's hips; and she laid it across her lap.

She wore a neat, spotted knee-high frock, crumpled at the saddle of the back because of the baby. A red scarf was tied round her head, perfuncto-rily, for it did not quite cover the thick plaits in which she had arranged her hair. She smelt very clean, of carbolic soap; and glanced round, her eyes bright, expectant. She craned her neck to see into the far corners of the bus as if hoping to espy a friend. For a time she fidgeted so much, sizing up all the occupants, that I wondered the child did not wake. But it lay in her arms and breathed deeply, its chubby cherub's cheeks framed by the shawl softly draped about its face. The baby seemed as peaceful as the mother was restless. She lost no time in striking up conversations with those near—with me, then with people in the seats before us; then to her right, to those before them; to say nothing of those in the seats behind us. She found nobody she knew, but those present would do. We were transfixed by quan-tities of bags and baggage, baskets of provisions to eat on the long journey. In between them inquisitive infant girls attempted perilous steps, clutching some treasured tattered doll made of rags; or mealie-husk doing duty for one and wrapped in cotton scraps; or little boys a battered toy motor car. But mothers would drag them back, straighten out miniature frocks or trousers, and ruthlessly wipe running noses. All of us bobbed up and down as the bus bumped and swayed, and it was difficult to control one's voice. We shouted, answering shouted personal questions about one another.

After a while, personalities began to assert themselves and one of these was a man sitting behind me. He gained the attention of the entire bus-load by launching on a discourse about the locality we were passing through. An authoritative-looking man, in his fifties; obviously a labourer, but dressed as one long accustomed to town life. He wore a blue scarf like a cravat at the neck, a respectable felt hat and underneath the heavy overcoat which he unbuttoned, an exceedingly old suit in clerical grey, chalk-striped. When the bus was outside Potsdam, he called out, "*Heyi!* Do you people *see* the good country those Germans received here when they were brought to settle? These rolling plains, my friends—land *made* for cattle. *Bafondini!* It is said that of old, this grass was so nutritious, cattle grazed themselves to a standstill, were bewildered by repletion. Then these Germans were allotted the land, dislodging people who already herded here. And, of course, they wanted to remind themselves of their country. Hence 'Potsdam' here, 'Berlin' there. Little Germany! Yet the Hottentots, *amaLawu*, had already named these places, having been here even before *we* arrived. Or rather, *ama*Xhosa arrived." It was already clear from some of his phrases that he was not a Xhosa man.

"Now *um*Xhosa lived alongside *i*Lawu, on crossing the Kei River. Hear the *Lawu* names of these local rivers: *Q*welra, *Nx*aruni, which the whites pronounce '*K*welega, *Nah*oon' like infants because defeated by the virile Hottentot sounds. But when *um*Xhosa arrived, *he* pronounced them all right; had already taken over those Hottentot click embellishments into his own language. Why? Because Hottentots were people of our ilk: reared cattle. Did not *um*Xhosa give Hottentots a praise-name, salutation, 'Sukwini,' referring to the skill of that tribe in tanning hides? Those people lived all right with Xhosa, 'side-by-side'; both lived proper *masihlalisane.*" Everybody burst out laughing for he used the word in its new "town" sense in which it refers to a sociological phenomenon; "improper temporary sexual partnerships" of men and women working in the urban areas, one spouse absent, looking after the home in the country, relationships for which the pagans use a harsher name. His speech was an elaborate joke. We all knew for instance that Hottentot and Xhosa had recognized each other's societies, had intermarried legally, accepting each other as neighbours. He was playing with words and we joined in his merry mood of comparing the past with modern town life—now that the bus was taking us away from it all. His comments made us all look at the countryside anew. People fired questions at him about it, or contributed from their own knowledge.

Climbing up a gentle incline, one of whose slopes was covered with rows of pineapples, we met a group of pagans cycling. Their robes billowed in the air behind them, like red sails. They free-wheeled, laughing and shouting, teeth flashing in the sunlight. The speaker half rose as they drew level, and called out to them through the window, all our heads turning to watch him and them. Then he said to us, but still—of course—shouting, "Behold the people of Ndhlambe! Daubed in their special shade of ochre, the dark red that reminds of dried blood." It was different from the one preferred in my Middledrift and Alice districts. "These ochred ones are getting civilized—eh? Their Europeans grow these pineapples, wax fat on the exports. Some of that fat drips on to us and these cyclists. Now I approve of that. Why should a pagan bother to *eat* those things that rot the teeth? *He* has more sense, spends the money earned from working on them on buying things he wants. In East London some pagans own cars. Chaps who can't read, would go cross-eyed if you spelled 'a*a*, *ebe*, *nci*' on a blackboard for them!" Roars of laughter, interruptions. "Why trouble himself? Is he not doing all right? I tell you people-of-this-bus, you Xhosa-of-Gcaleka from across-the-Kei, these Xhosa-of-Ndhlambe-on-*this*-side of the river are overtaking you. Progress! They aim *to privately own land!* To be themselves exporters, not for ever 'work like small boys' for the European." You had to smile. My father had been right about the idioms. In addition was I not listening to the things people dreamed about? I was suspicious for example of the cajolery about motor-owning pagans. Was it a reflection of the man's own secret wishes? Everyone knew that pagans were not interested in the Westernized life. They pursued their own alongside ours (whom they call almost pejoratively "school" people); and restrict themselves—when forced by circumstances into towns for temporary work—to the acquisition of only such habits or possessions (bicycles, sewing-machines, ploughs) as did not conflict with membership of their society. Therefore did the lofty amusement over the Red people reflect a secret admiration for their serenity, positiveness, the "lack of *doubts*" that my father's friend had talked about? In any case the chatter was different from some I had heard on country buses in England, my other homeland. Here people were not avoiding personal matters or universal human themes; certainly not steering clear of religion, sex. They discussed history, politics, land reform, property, sociology—analphabetic though most of the speakers were. These seemed to be the topics they considered important, which superseded "small talk" about the weather, wages, or whites. Not that those three were not pressing. One saw that they were, but did not seem to occupy the whole of the bus-load's frontal lobes. The travellers probably did not consciously classify any of these subjects. Conversation hinged on them because as individuals they were preoccupied by the history of "the migrations" of tribes and the encounters that these had brought; and, naturally, by the structure of society, since that had been the root cause of those movements of populations. The bus was now crossing country that had been migrated into and settled by Chief Ndhlambe; and it was his descendants and followers whose huts we were passing and whom we saw walking and bicycling. Their territory stretched from East London to Idutywa, on the far bank of the historical river that lay ahead of us, *i*Nciba—the Great Kei.

The migrations had been, of course, the only way in which a polygynous nation could solve the political problems that accompanied royal succession; the whole thing an expression of the patriarchal family system, based inflexibly on primogeniture which every one of us clung to; so that history was not dead but alive. It was drilled into us subtly or overtly from the moment we learnt to talk. The authoritative labourer was dealing with subjects close to our hearts in talking about who peopled the land; the particular successions that had brought them; about heirs; about the "*idiocy*, nay backwardness, savagery, of nations such as Boers whose custom allowed *all* of a man's sons to inherit in equal proportions!"

How then was that succession arranged, whose consequences filled our conversation as the bus rolled on? That was what we talked about, and the complex relationships that it involved. People delved into those archives that they carry in their heads. We discussed events like the recurring activities of Regents who tried to usurp the patrimony; a perpetual historical hazard, because the patriarchal system had meant that when the Chief died, the heir was invariably an infant since the "Great Wife"—the "national" wife and mother of the successor—was never the first woman he had married; under polygamy Chiefs were supposed to get into practice, so to speak, in their earlier, "personal choice" marriages, and only "marry for the nation" (with cattle contributed by it) in middle life when they were proven sires. This very Ndhlambe had "usurped," and at the great Battle of Amalinde not far from Middledrift had tried to displace his young nephew Ngqika ("Gaika"), the true Right Hand heir who had removed to what is now called the Ciskei; and whose "following" my own family belonged to by descent. My male relations came under a further sub-division for the purposes of war. Each was a subject of the subsidiary ruler in whose territory he happened to have been born: my brother's liege lord was Maqoma, as the old man had said when my uncles and I called on him. My grandfather's had been Ntinde, in the King William's Town area; and my father's yet another, in the Peddie district; yet all "people of Ngqika." Thoughts of Ndhlambe and his type stirred one woman passenger to shout in a clear treble, "Usurpers—true examples of the intransigence of human nature, of individuals who do not *regulate* those emotions that are inimical to the public interest!" Upon which lively rhetoric broke out:

"What medicine ever cures covetousness?"

"Or sinister deeds."

"Or power madness—*ukukhukhumala!*" (I relished that lovely word.)

"Will society *ever* perfect the devices by which it tries, *tries* to eradicate man's anti-social tendencies?" The bus bumped along while a latter-day aspect of the theme was given an exhaustive airing: "the enigma of *today's* 'Paramount Chief of the Bantu.'" For that was how Dr. Verwoerd had recently styled himself, and the bus resounded with jokes, "Cuckoo in the nest"; "Anti-social"; "Wrecker of established order"; "Usurper, worse, gate-crasher; and *okhukhumeleyo* at that, puffing that chest like a pouter pigeon, in a nest where he had no rights whatsoever, either by blood or cattle." I could only reflect how differently the countryside must appear, wonder what thoughts it inspired, if like some of the Europeans hygienically sealed off from us by the glass partition you perhaps did not know the language and could not understand what was being said. You would note the scenery to be sure, with its roadside advertisements for "South African Beers," or "Cigarettes." You would note the characteristic hamlets at which the bus stopped at petrol pumps labelled in English, "Pegasus Oil," or in Afrikaans, "*Ry met die Rooi Perd*"; and see the white-owned stores standing in dust and rubble; the indigent natives, the sunburnt whites; all features that created an effect of spiritual barrenness because not apparently integrated. However, I had not much time for these private thoughts. Indeed, the attitude of society, as exemplified even by my fellow passengers, towards individual privacy was one of the undeniable drawbacks in the life at home. Privacy was "antisocial, contrary to the public interest" so that inwardly, chasms yawned before you if your personal inclinations and habits tended against the principle. Marvellous, I thought, that people like my father managed to write and think, always exposed to the public gaze, to sociability.

The woman beside me asked my clan name, where I was going, and why. The man behind us heard, having for the time being finished his speeches, and promptly exclaimed, "*O?* So we have a Jili in this bus? Do you people *know* Jili?" sweeping the question right round. Three admitted not knowing, upon which he cried, "'*Kwek!*' Ignorant people are abroad these days," and proceeded to repair their knowledge. Meanwhile the culprits gazed at me good-naturedly. Two of them were the young men who had put me in mind of pirates when I spotted their ear-rings and the kerchiefs round their heads, the third wearing the Stetson hat. "Country bumpkins," the man now called them in Xhosa slang. Immobile and silent, they put me in mind of yet another imaginary type—my idea of American Indian braves, for each held between his knees like a tomahawk a nearly six-foot polished knobkerrie. One of them had an aquiline profile, the nose almost hooked. And all three looked at me with bland, dark eyes. I stared back thinking how handsome they were. They smiled faintly now that the older man twitted them:

"*Kaloku* these are *ama*Mpondo, as you see," he explained. "That is the reason they know nothing. For what is the main preoccupation among them and the *ama*Mpondomise, over on that other bank of the *um*Bashe? Beer Feasts and Stock-theft. Is it not so, young men?"

But while they glanced at one another uncertainly, he continued, "Of course it is. *I know.* I am one of you. My clan name is Jola. I am *m*Mbo. No Xhosa, I, although having lived years on end in Ndhlambe's territory, in East London working for these whites. So handsome ones, I may tell the truth about ourselves, eh?"

They acknowledged his privilege with abashed smiles, not speaking. So he went on, talked about himself in order to "explain about *ama*Mpondo." As usual the impression was not of an inordinate egocentricity but that he was using a personal experience to illustrate the variety of life's circumstances. He was "representing" others like him to show how their ideas were tempered by the changing times.

"Now look at me: *I* am one of those who weaned himself *early* from that life of tranquillity-in-sterility in the Arcadia of Pondoland," and he used a metaphor that made us all laugh, one of those that people loved. When the laughter died down, he went on, "I left *thirty-five years ago* to work in town —understand?" The warriors gazed at him obediently, since he wished it, had taken charge, and they had no choice because of his seniority, "You see, our chiefs had long ago sent word to '*abefundisi*, teachers' (missionaries) to *come* to us. It was they who taught me to read and write. Wesleyans. Presbyterians. Church of England. Men of *beautiful* works. Their wives ran little hospitals, and sewing classes and such things. Ah, it was beauty, beauty! Then I wished to go forth, see the world, and work; and did myself a good turn. For as you now see me, I know things that I would never have known— through *work*. Therefore," he harangued, "pay attention while I tell you who this person is." Not only the Pondo braves, the whole bus-load turned to look at me, craning necks to do so. However, before he could launch on my family history, a woman of about his age intervened. She could not see from where she sat exactly what he did as he stretched a hand towards my shoulder, and she cried out, "*Yo!* Is he *pointing* at her?" But everyone hastened to reassure her, and Jola shouted, "No indeed, mother, I declare I am only tapping her shoulder, certainly not being so savage as to *point*."

The elderly lady laughed good-naturedly, then *she* now launched on a dissertation; about pagan beliefs in the evils of pointing at people. It turned out that she too was a Pondo, a "converted," of Christian family. Now that the talk was about the life of her tribe she was moved to contribute, for Pondoland was a reservoir of ancient lore.

Presently it was Jola's turn to take up his interrupted tale about my family. The mood was expansive for we had all day in the bus. The woman interjected pieces of her own knowledge about Makiwanes, for it transpired that she came from Umtata where my younger uncle lived and where I was to spend the night in order to catch an early local bus the next day to my uncle at Tsolo.

The bus came to the Great Kei. The river lies in the folds of a breathtaking valley, between hills covered with bush and brown boulders. The road twists back on itself down steep inclines until level with the bridge. From above, the water looked like a great serpent and always reminded me of folk-stories our nursemaids used to tell us surreptitiously—about "water snakes, people of the river," creatures employed by sorcerers; denizens of dark holes in the reeds who had the power to mesmerize and "draw you into the deep."

Excitement mounted, for we were approaching a landmark indeed and the olden migrations rose again in our minds. As we reached the bridge and drove slowly along it, we looked from side to side at the waters spreading on to the dunes on either side. A hush fell on us all. We had now left the territory of *kwa*Ngqika, were now "in The Great House of Xhosaland —*kwa*Gcaleka."

My neighbour was moved to cry out, "O, thus-we-arrive, *komKhulu!*" She became so excited that the infant woke at last, stirred, then struggled out of its nest of the heavy shawl. Its mother now took the stage, started to speak about her life and experiences. The opening sentences marked her out immediately as a species of "New Woman," partly broken away from the society that bred her; independent, fierce, unabashed. She fumbled quickly—clearly a highly strung person—in a small bundle tied round with a handkerchief, brought out a sandwich, began to stuff pieces of it in the child's mouth. It started to eat contentedly, though still sleepy and dazed. She addressed the passengers.

"This is a child that I have 'picked up,' an illegitimate treasure. Treasure because this was my *third*, and thank God that I conceived a second girl. And I am bringing her *home*, to Gcaleka-land."

We were very startled. Everyone looked at her expressionlessly, following the custom of "hearing the speaker out." For a moment she was silent, assembling her "speech." While we waited only the older, maternal, converted woman made a sound. She moaned, then clucked her tongue in distress. When she did it a second time, the speaker cried, "*Mama*, you would not be shocked if you knew the obstacles that I have overcome in this Vale of Tears." She must have sensed that the scriptural overtone would not fail to stay the old lady. Then she addressed everyone on board, "Here is how it all began. I was a young girl; proper; virginal. I was courted. But the suitor 'changed his mind—*wandala*.'"

There was an outbreak of clucks expressing everybody's shock. Encouraged by the response, she repeated herself for emphasis, raising her voice; a crescendo of pain, "Rejected me, I say. Even renounced the cattle he had already produced in part towards the contract. *That* was how utterly I was rejected. Found he did not want me after all. Saw another. Oh, the matter was discussed at home and intermediaries hurried to and fro; his father, ashamed, mine insulted. '*Kwakubi*—Things became hideous.' But he no longer wanted this MaFaku, this MaNyawuza whose story you are hearing today."

Again she played on our sympathies by drawing on the clan names for they established her as someone who "belonged to *people*"—who prized her. The salutations gave the family an identity and at once we felt for them; no need to know who they were.

"From that moment, how could I trust a man? My heart was not broken—it was *rent*. I had loved that suitor. I lay in my hut and sickened. When at last I emerged, *thin, thin*, I 'betook myself to the River'; washed; scrubbed; anointed my body. Then made it known to my father that I had "'gathered myself together' and must go forth. For me, the land of my birth, this beautiful Gcaleka had *gone black*. I went."

"Went? Where?"

"'*Ndaziyel' edolophini*—Took myself to town. Worked.' I tried many jobs. First I became a nurse-girl; kept my eyes on the cook as she did her work. And how she helped me to learn, improve myself, that *mama* who cooked for those Europeans. She was a widow, *u*MaNtande by salutation, from Tembuland. Never will I forget her. I got a job as a cook. My Europeans ate well, liked my work for I assure you I have skill for that job. When I cook, I 'hit that stove,' man, until Europeans lie on their sides replete. And they *pay* their staff, those Europeans of mine, unlike some who squeeze your essence but reckon your body must manufacture it unstoked-up by *them*. Years passed. The heart mended. At last I stopped thinking of that suitor. But also came to *entertain thoughts of no others*. My next step was to provide for my old age, for I had decided to be a *Nongendi*—(a 'not-marry'—the term for a nun). I conceived a baby as provision for that future. Yes, just 'picked it up.' No marriage, cattle, nothing. A little nameless thing. My Europeans let me continue working until almost the birth. And to my joy it was a girl. While I suckled of course I could not work, Europeans not liking the smell of nursing mothers. Yet had to live, had I not? I could not go home, not having told them of the path I had chosen, and fearing their wrath and distress. So I set up with a *masihlalisane*. Yes, took up with *that* life of no life. For more than a year, I was a *kephita*—(kept woman). But guess what happened next. Having weaned, I was about to return to my Europeans. But one-two-three, I had conceived again. Yet no longer wanting to *kephita* with that man because he had begun to want to make a permanency of that no-life arrangement. Huh! A man with wife and children in the country—what would I ever be to him? Did he not merely want a permanent 'wife' but without cattle, contract, licence, one denied a place in society? Such was his cheek. Yet my Europeans wanted me back and I too wanted work."

The elderly woman murmured as if involuntarily, "Ah, when one gets good employers and *good* work, what else to do but cling to it? *Clutch* such a job, '*dig the digits into it till fingernails sink to the very quicks.*'"

That drew groans of assent and the younger woman turned to her, saying, "That is what I have learnt to do. Yet this fix of another pregnancy was preventing me. Finally I could only send word to my flesh and blood and take my girl-child home to the Transkei, deposit her with my mother to raise up. Painful, but a grandchild is precious. Do not even shameful, nameless ones bring their own load of love and consolation? I am on my way to visit that child.

"But that unwanted pregnancy resulted in a *boy* and, as you can imagine, the father wished to have it because it was a man-child. Produced the necessary cattle to my people for the fine for spoiling me, and therefore took his son."

"*Kwek!*" cried Jola at last, dejected by every aspect of the case. But she cried sharply, "No, Jola, *I* did not feel deprived. What use are boys to such as me? It is *girl*-children who support their mother when she grows old and useless. Boys of nowadays have other fish to fry. Now here is my life's plan: *Every time*

I conceive a boy, I will let the father produce the fine in cattle to my people—which will entitle him to take the child into his lineage group! But I will conceal each girl, whisk her away to the home of my birth. These are my gold," she cried, suddenly lifting the infant on high. "My heart is rent no more when I contemplate them." She sat back, cuddled her baby and was silent.

But her words describing that life's plan left us dazed. Yet had she not shown that she felt no self-pity? Need we feel it for her? But the cynicism, the anti-social aspect, the amorality of it affected everybody; not so much the personal case but its wide implications. Jola took over. We had to strain our ears to hear him. His voice was low and solemn.

"People-of-ours, a painful thing is taking place in our life." He paused. The silence was marked only by noises from the baby who seemed to have catarrh, breathing stertorously while munching the bits of sandwich. Jola expressed himself, and I am almost "defeated," as he would have said, by trying now to put it in English.

"Kaloku tina esiNtwini sasuka sa PUMA *enkonzweni yokuhlonipa intombi;* this painful thing of which I speak is that 'we-of-our-culture *Bade Farewell* to our former reverence for virginity.'" He heightened the key words by adding those catalysts that have no equivalent in English: *Kaloku, ukusuka*—the "Deficients," technically so-called, that give what the grammarian W. G. Bennie has described as "a snap to the action," and in prose can shift meanings and thought patterns to the level of intensity that a poet can achieve in English verse. Jola's remark forced you to contemplate the disaster on many levels; to consider the setting we lived in; the vicissitudes that involved all the people; and to ask yourself what could be the outcome of the changes being wrought in the nation. Many of us now looked to him as one whose experience might offer an answer, or at least some consolation. But having thrown the idea among us like a man broadcasting seed he said no more. It was the matron who spoke, her voice as sad as his.

"We mourn the passing of the days when girls behaved nobly because the *community* so behaved," she said. "Society was strict with itself, therefore strict with them for they were its symbol of honour. At intervals girls had to be examined lest they had been deflowered despite the vigilance of the chaperone. Present generations feel that this was crude. But we *were* a rough people. Nobility does not presuppose queasy petty sensitivities. *That* attitude belongs to *isiLungu*—Europeanness. It is not related to *the sensibility* which belonged to *isiNtu*—Africanness; which was what we strove after, even if indelicate, crude. The ideal of *nobility-in-living-with-people* was served by, among other things, society's demand that a man who transgressed the code about virgins be disgraced, disgraced! The matter had to do with the symbols of our self-respect. Where now that striving, and what use a community that abandons even the outward *symbols* of its thought?" The Pondo braves shifted their knobkerries uneasily as if the reference to transgressions struck near the bone. I would have liked to say what I thought but didn't. It would have been out of place for me to comment. People began gathering up parcels and belongings. We reached the sleepy-looking town, built on the site of the kraal, or "Great Place" of the Gcaleka Paramount Chief Hintsa, who had reigned when Europeans first penetrated into Xhosaland. The bus stopped and many disembarked. Those of us who were going on said good-bye and watched the new-comers about to join us. I stepped out with other passengers to stretch my legs. When it was time to climb back into the bus, old Jola followed behind me. As he went to his seat he scrutinized faces; exchanged a word with those who had been with us from the beginning; hailed new-comers. He had to halt when I reached my seat because my neighbour had risen and stepped aside into the corridor, child in arms, in order to let me pass through to my corner. But when she sat down, he still stood looking down at her as if worried about something. I hoped he would not start all over again on the subjects she had raised. When he spoke, it was in stentorian tones, throwing his voice dramatically as everybody did, and demanded:

"*K'awutsho, MaNyawuza: le bus imile nje kodwa umchamisile umntana, wazithuma?* – Kindly say, I beg, MaNyawuza: this bus having stopped and afforded the opportunity, did you *piss* that child and make sure her bowels moved?'" His labourer's face wore a look of real concern, of a parent, probably grandfather, putting the question to a frank and far from queasy or prettily sensitive audience. They judged it entirely proper, echoed it vigorously, and looked at the mother for assurance.

I was delighted not to have missed that exchange. It seemed to strike a note appropriate to my coming interlude in yet another setting within the society we had talked about throughout the ride. Rough the journey had been in all conscience: bucolic, uncouth, odoriferous, inconvenient; but also lacking none of the elements my father had promised: reciprocity, tough-mindedness, imagination, the irrepressible sense of fun.

"Segametsi Molefe," "Banabotlhe Kwena," and "Matshediso Moeng," THREE COURT STATEMENTS

Botswana 1964   Setswana

Under British rule, the *kgotla* came to be known as the "Native Tribunal." Women could attend *kgotla* only as witnesses or litigants in cases such as divorce, adultery, infanticide, and abortion. One could, however, appeal to the Magistrate's Court against the findings of this tribunal. The three statements selected here give direct voice in a public record to ordinary women presenting their cases within the limitations of male-run colonial and tribal administrations. In the interests of privacy, none of the parties' real names are used here.

Segametsi Molefe acknowledges that she was drunk at the time the defendant "came under [her] blankets," but she nevertheless understands that she was raped. Hence, she fetched the headman (chief's representative) as the first step to bringing the case to court. Her statement was made in Setswana and translated in court; the original is unfortunately not available.

The next two statements concern cases of infanticide. Banabotlhe Kwena reminds the court that she did not become pregnant by herself and that she is thus not solely responsible for the death of the infant. Her repeated—and veiled—accusations against Phologotswana Ramasedi stand in contrast to Matshediso Moeng's apology at the end of her statement, in which she expresses both remorse and fear of her father. In Botswana society, children are expected to express reverence for their parents. About Moeng's case, the prosecutor writes, "Am not pressing for heavy punishment particularly but consider it my duty to point out that offences of this nature, and abortions, are becoming prevalent amongst young women. Would like to see some salutory sentence imposed but do not ask for anything excessive."

Mary Lederer

✦

SEGAMETSI MOLEFE (27 JULY 1964)

I am Segametsi Molefe. I live in Molepolole. I remember July 21st. I woke up during the night and found accused sleeping with me. I found that he had taken off my clothes, and that the petticoat I was wearing was wet. When I woke up, I found he was holding my neck. He was fully dressed, as he is now. I know the accused. I used to see him. He had carnal intercourse with me without my consent. When I went to sleep, I was alone. He came later and came under my blankets. I did not wake up when he came into the house. I was drunk. I did not know what happened.

When I woke up, I went to call Balekanye to come and see the accused. He is a Headman. I told him the accused had raped me.

BANABOTLHE KWENA (7 OCTOBER 1964)

I wish to say that I was impregnated by PHOLOGOTSWANA RAMASEDI. Phologotswana gave me some pills to swallow which I did. Phologotswana had told me that if I took the pills the unborn child would die and I agreed to take the pills so that the child should die.

I took the pills on a Friday and the following day—Saturday—the child was still-born. I buried the dead child at my mother's court-yard and I was alone.

MATSHEDISO MOENG (16 NOVEMBER 1964)

I have nothing to say really except to ask for forgiveness. (In answer to Court.) I am sorry it happened. I was frightened because of my father's anger. If I had given birth to that baby he would have turned me out of the house. I have a child three years old whose father is in Rhodesia. I do not expect to see him again. When this baby was born my father was very angry. He had often said he would throw me out if I had another child. The father of the child I have now killed is in Johannesburg.

Transcriber and translator unknown

Jane Chifamba,
THE WIDOW AND THE BABOONS

Zimbabwe 1964   chiShona

Jane Chifamba was in 1964 the first woman to be published in chiShona. A dedicated teacher who was aware of the need to preserve traditional tales for future generations, she found herself the victim of male discouragement and ridicule when she wrote her collection of folktales, *Ngano Dzepasi Chigare* (*Stories of Olden Days*). "Why do you waste so much paper—writing on so much paper? . . . We can put it to better use in rolling our cigarettes!" said the men, according to Chifamba in a 1990 interview with Fiona Lloyd at a women artists' conference held in Harare. Her collection of folktales reflects little modification of the traditional tales. They have a characteristic opening "*Kare kare, kwaiva . . .*" (Long ago / Once upon a time there was . . .). The end of each story is signaled by the statement, "*Ndipo pakagumira sarungano*" (the story ends here). Direct speech reinforces the individuality of each character in the story, and a song ensures the participation of the audiences in each tale. The black-and-white drawings that accompany each story are lively, add a touch of humor, and match the text closely. Perhaps Chifamba wanted the children to be read to and shown pictures by an adult.

"The Widow and the Baboons" draws our attention to the plight of widows who were, and sometimes still are, deprived of inheritances and victimized on the deaths of their husbands. Besides being entertaining, teaching the art of language, and deepening experience, folktales were valued for developing a strong moral sense in the young. "The Widow and the Baboons" has all these qualities.

Chifamba had not published anything else when she died in 1996.

Chiedza Musengezi

✦

Once upon a time when the world was young there lived a man and his wife who unfortunately had no children, and when the man died his relatives came and took everything that her husband had left her. They left her suffering. She had neither clothes nor food, so she started to beg for a living. Those who were generous gave her food and clothes. One day she came to the home of a blacksmith who pitied her and decided to give her something that would help her for a long time. He gave her a hoe and told her to use it to get food. He wanted to find out whether it was laziness that had made the woman a beggar.

The widow thanked the blacksmith and went to the village headman to ask for a piece of land. She was given a field in a *vlei* where no other crops would grow except *tsenza* and rice, so she went home and looked for seeds in the bag where she put all the things that she had received from people. She found a few *tsenza* seeds, cultivated her field in the *vlei*, and planted them.

Now her field was next to a hill which was the home of some baboons. These baboons were a menace to people with fields near the hill, but now the widow's field became a shield to all the other fields. The baboons tormented her, for they came to dig up her *tsenza* and she had to spend most of her time guarding her crops.

When the *tsenza* were ready to be harvested she dug them up bit by bit and took them home where she exchanged them for maize and *rapoko*. While she was harvesting she didn't take her hoe home every day but would hide it because she couldn't carry both the hoe and the *tsenza*. When the baboons saw that her field was no longer guarded they came down from the hill to look for any left over *tsenza*, and while they were there a big baboon discovered the hidden hoe. He took it and used it to dig up the *tsenza*. He also made sure that he hid it in a place where he alone could find it, and every day when the baboons came to dig up the *tsenza* with their hands, the big one would use the hoe.

When the widow next came to her field to dig up more of her crop she couldn't find her hoe. She realized that the baboons had taken it. And at the same time the baboons decided that since there was not much food left here they had better look for another field to rob. They set off along the road that the woman used when going to her field. Very soon they met her and of course she asked them about her hoe. She asked each one of them as they passed her, for they walked in single file with the youngest in front and the oldest at the back. And as she asked them she sang a song to which each of the baboons replied, and their voices ran together like this:

> You are guilty—liar. You are guilty.
> Yawiri yawiri[1]—you are guilty—liar
> Yawiri yawiri—you are guilty—liar
> Have you not seen—you are guilty—liar
> The hoe I borrowed—you are guilty—liar
>
> I wouldn't take—you are guilty—liar
> A hoe that you borrowed—you are guilty—liar
> I swear—you are guilty—liar
> By my child Zimbabwe—you are guilty—liar
> Whom I left in Chitsunge—you are guilty—liar
> Where we used to eat *tsungwe*—you are guilty—liar
> *Kabwa kabwa kuchu uku gwande*
> *Koromoka chiromo chafunda*
> *Mhuno dzangu dzina murindira.*[2]

As each baboon said *kabwa kabwa kuchu uku gwande* it would shake itself and roll on the ground to show that it was not hiding anything. When it was the big baboon's turn he tried to do what the others had done, but the blade of the hoe, which he had removed from the handle and hidden in his armpit, fell to the ground with a clattering sound, and he ran away in shame.

The widow picked up her hoe and went back home. She later married the blacksmith who had seen how clever and industrious she was, and they lived happily ever after.

The story ends here.

1. Nonsense onomatopoeic words.
2. These last three lines are for onomatopoeic effect only, although the associations of meaning lend to the sense of confusion.

Translated by James Mahlaule and M. Furusa

Princess Magogo kaDinuzulu,
BALLAD OF NOMAGUNDWANE

South Africa 1964   isiZulu

The version of this song printed here was sung by Princess Magogo and recorded by David Rycroft in 1964; she had also sung it for him on three other occasions. It was performed as a solo with the singer accompanying herself on the *ugubhu* (musical bow) and follows a well-established tradition of solitary love songs sung by girls and young women. Often they are songs of longing because of separation, but this one has its own special characteristics. It has a long ballad-narrative quality that is not found in other typically far shorter love songs, and its great age makes it particularly interesting. Princess Magogo, as a daughter of the royal Zulu household, spent much time as a young girl in the company of the wives of her father Dinuzulu and her grandfather Cetshwayo kaMpande; she heard the ballad from one of Cetshwayo's wives. It may have been composed in the mid-nineteenth century in the long period of stability when Mpande was king. Certainly it gives no hint of great social disturbance and focuses completely on the settled domestic domain and affairs of courtship, love, and lost love.

The narrative sets a story within a story, as the singer tells her tale of rejection to her younger sister, Nomagundwane (Miss Rats). What shines through the text is the intensity of the teller's emotion, her desire to be part of her chosen one's family, her tension as she arrives and is greeted by her lover's mother—who will not kiss her as "her mouth is sore." She is then greeted by her rather enigmatic lover, feels final bitter disappointment, and makes an abrupt departure when she realizes that against all her expectations she has been sidelined for someone else, the second arrival, the girl who is, unlike her, kissed in greeting by the mother of the homestead. The theatrical nature of the ballad's telling is also interesting. The narrative is carried forward largely through dialogue and slowly, almost like a film going into slow motion as the entrances, gestures, and greetings are highlighted in sequence. The contrast between the singer's reception and that of "Miss Favourite" makes clear the feelings of the mother of the homestead. And finally the ballad focuses on the far more opaque feelings of the son, the beloved.

David Rycroft notes that the artistry of the performer is brought into play with each presentation, and that points of diction and phrasing, and techniques such as the extent to which Miss Rats is addressed, varied with each performance he heard. Thus the ballad's textuality is not finally rendered by the version we have here.

Liz Gunner and Mary Lederer

Alas! Woe is me!¹
Oh, what sorrow, Nomagundwane!
Bring me my ugubhu musical bow in the hut there, O my younger sister!
I have been travelling, O sister;
Eventually I reached the homestead;
I found the young men's hut closed;
I opened it and entered;
I drew out a sitting-mat and sat down, O sister.
Then some people entered;
And they greeted me;
And I reciprocated, O sister.
Then in came my boy-friend;
He said to me: "Greetings, child of ours!"
And I reciprocated, O sister;
He said: "Is it still going well at home?"
I replied: "Yes, they have sent greetings";
And we sat with the people.
Then [his] mother came in;
She said to me: "Good day, my child!"
And then I reciprocated, O sister;
She said to me: "I shall not kiss you, my child";
She said: "My mouth is sore."
Having said that, the mother went out.
Then in came Miss "Favourite girl";
And she knelt further up than me;
They drew out a sitting-mat for you and you sat down, O Miss Favourite!
You were greeted by your boy-friend;
And you reciprocated, O Miss Favourite;
And then the people greeted you;
And you reciprocated, O Miss Favourite;
And then I greeted you, O Miss Favourite;
And you reciprocated, Miss Favourite.
Then in came the mother;
She entered with a well-kept spare blanket;
She was now wearing a shawl;
She greeted you, O Miss Favourite;
And you reciprocated, Miss Favourite;
She said: "Let me kiss you, my child!"
And you were kissed, O Miss Favourite.
Then her son asked a question;
He said: "Why do you kiss only this one?"
And she said: "I no longer know her, my child."
Once again her son asked;

Saying: "Oh, but do you know this one?"
And she said: "She is someone from nearby, my child."
Then darkness fell, as is inevitable;
Alas, O mountains! Night fell, as is inevitable;
Alas, O my father! Darkness fell, as it inevitably does!
Then we lay down to sleep, O Miss Favourite.
Then dawn broke, as is inevitable;
It dawned, it dawned, inevitably;
Alas, then came the dawn, as it inevitably comes.
Then we said: "We are leaving."
And then some people came in;
And we came out and went on our way;
Then my boy-friend came after;
And he said: "Bring that girl back with you, little sister!"
As for me, I said: "I am just seeing off someone else."
Then we returned with his sister;
We arrived at the young men's hut.
His sister drew out a calabash container, and left;
Saying to me: "Let us go and wash!"
We went to wash, and came back;
We entered the young men's hut.
His sister came, bringing water;
And she went out again.
She came in with some food, it was brought covered up;
I started to uncover it;
And I cried out: "Oh, but it is thick milk!"
I said: "Please call my 'child' for me!"
I kissed my "child"
And then I removed my bead necklace and put it on her;
I said: "Goodbye, my child!"
I took off my girdle, and threw it over her shoulders;
I took my personal belongings and placed them on her shoulders;
I came out, crying: "Now he has spurned me!"
I cried: "Woe, O my father. Today he has spurned me!"
I cried out: "Woe, O mountains! Now he has spurned me indeed!"
Alas, O people! As for me, he has now spurned me!

1. This line is repeated by the singer before each subsequent line, thereby creating a series of couplets throughout the song.

Transcribed and translated by David Rycroft

Bessie Head, FOR "NAPOLEON BONAPARTE," JENNY, AND KATE

Botswana 1965   English

Bessie Head's pathbreaking writing acquired the accolades it deserves mainly after her death in 1986. A South African by birth, Head wrote her best-known works in Botswana, where she lived from the age of twenty-seven. She was the child of a black father and white mother who, separated from her daughter shortly after giving birth, died in a mental institution. The traumatic effects of the law that made interracial sexual unions illegal in South Africa, and that led to Head's painful experiences of homelessness, are extensively explored in her fiction and prolific correspondence.

Head's posthumously published *The Cardinals* is the only novel she set in South Africa and offers an explanation of why the author found her birthplace so creatively debilitating. Three of her novels set in Botswana explicitly draw on autobiographical experiences: *When Rain Clouds Gather* is based on her stay on a Botswanan development farm; *Maru,* focusing on a woman schoolteacher deemed racially inferior by the Batswana, reconfigures Head's sense of her own subordination and exclusion; and in *A Question of Power,* a novel that has prompted lively critical interest, Head explores unconscious processes from the perspective of a character's experience of acute psychological distress. In later works, *Serowe: Village of the Rainwind, A Bewitched Crossroad,* and many of the short stories in *The Collector of Treasures,* Head deals mainly with the history and cultural ethos of Botswana and especially Serowe, the village in which she settled.

The piece offered here was written before 1965, when it was submitted to *The New African.* It was, however, published in the *Southern African Review of Books* only in 1990. Fusing essay and short story conventions in ways that often characterize Head's eclectic writing, it anticipates her intricate explorations of interpersonal relationships in later works. Avoiding categorical interpretations of individual subjectivity and social relationships, she dwells on the spiritual, psychological, and individual complexities that shape human experiences. She often stresses, for example, the ambiguities of characters in positions of authority. Like her character Napoleon Bonaparte, the figures of great men that recur in her short writings and in novels like *Maru* and *A Question of Power* embody a baffling combination of malevolence toward others, emotional vulnerability, and visionary insight. Head is also concerned with the undercurrents of encounters and personal feelings that are seemingly ordinary and straightforward. Her compelling visions of freedom emanate from a determined imaginative invention of "new worlds."

Desireé Lewis

✦

The last night I spent in that little village in Bechuanaland was perhaps the most bitter and the most lonely hour of my life. There was a central part of the village with four shops, a post office and a garage. The sun was just setting. I sat on the steps of the post office and my feet were buried in the thick loose dust of the road. I thought perhaps that the red-streaked sunset might shout an answer at last so I concentrated my mind silently and steadfastly on it for a long time. But the twilight puffed itself away and the peaked roofs of the mud huts became sharp black silhouettes against the sky. A goat stepped jauntily down the road. It eyed some orange peels lying about my feet and thinking that I must be a part of the stone on which I sat, it nuzzled roughly about my legs to get at the peels.

I stood up and sauntered slowly back to my mud hut that had been home for nearly a year. Everything that had meant Africa to me had been contained in a small semi-desert village in the wild thorn bush country of Bechuanaland. It seemed I had been born anew that year. Then I lost that centre of gravity. There is no continuity in the life of a refugee. You are here today and gone tomorrow. It may be just that I am not really a refugee. I cannot bear it. I only know that I had a little money and an unbearable pain; that I could not get a passport; that I am not anybody's stooge or spy or agent. Still I was entangled in the snarls and hazards of refugeeism. Entangled to the point that now I do not know where I am or what I am doing. I am alive but it may be that I sit in someone's lunatic asylum. I mean, I could not have a normal mind now because everything is strange and unknown. Nothing leads on to something else. Only the past is vividly alive and I traverse it over and over again.

The police constable, Peto, brought me the letter. In a way he was my friend as I had stayed at his house when I first arrived in the village. I later learnt that he was much distrusted. He really loved British authority. It made sense to him. He was very tall and fat with huge popping eyes that rolled and slided away from a direct glance. He always waited three seconds before laughing at a joke perhaps mentally checking up if the authorities would approve. He had an odd tone when speaking English. He rolled words around on his tongue the way people do who come from America.

"Hullo, Mr Peto," I said. "How are you?"

He laughed "Har, har" and rolled his eyes away.

"A'm all right," he drawled. "Ah have some bad noos for you."

He handed me the letter. It read:

> *Dear Madam,*
> *We regret to inform you that your application for a resident permit has been unsuccessful.*
> *Your obedient servant . . .*

I looked at Peto carefully. Maybe he would help me with a bit of sympathy. But he kept his face blank; only his big eyes rolled round and round.

"What does this mean?" I asked.

"It means you cannot stay here," and he shrugged his whole body.

"But how do I get away from here? I have no travel papers. I'm a non-political refugee. It's a relay system. Political refugees in Dar-Es-Salaam vouch for those coming on behind. Then you get an identity paper that lets you through Zambia. It's very top level like a V.I.P. I'm just an ordinary person."

He clucked sympathetically.

"We can give you a travel paper," he said.

I laughed: "You folks of Bechuanaland are behaving as though Bechuanaland's in the Mediterranean Sea. You don't know anything about Africa. It changes every day. Besides, its always looking for spies of the South African government. Since you folks here are so buddy-buddy with those folks down there do you think Tanzania would look at a Bechuanaland travel document?"

"Har, har," he laughed. "You chased your troubles this way. We didn't ask for it."

He only spoke like that because the British made him feel safe. There weren't any newspapers circulating in Bechuanaland that would have shown him quite clearly that some dreadful calamity could make the British and their little island disappear overnight. There were too many agents of destiny around with their intense private causes and they were dealing blows left and right. No one was safe; not even an anonymous individual in an anonymous village in the wilderness of Africa.

"Well, well, that's that," I said.

"Governments want everyone to get going these days; so, I'll get going."

Peto adopted a confidential tone.

"You could have got a resident permit easy. Just like that! Only because you were friendly with that Jenny woman. She was poison to the authorities."

I looked at him indignantly yet half wanting to laugh at the same time. I raised my voice to a shout.

"Well if they aren't giving me a resident permit because of my friendship with Jenny then the rotten buggers can keep their bribery and corruption."

"Shush! Shush!" Peto said anxiously.

I waved my hands: "The Republic of South Africa where I come from is a pretty rotten country but no white man there ever succeeded in making a black man an enemy of a black man! We made up our own minds about that! The Motswana of Bechuanaland is captivated by British treachery!"

Peto got up and fled. It wasn't the kind of talk a good, obedient civil servant should listen to. I had a good laugh on Peto but then I could have cried too. At least he'd have a good chance of staying in Africa. Bechuanaland was his home. I had no home. On the wall of my mud hut I had pasted a piece of paper in big bold capitals:

AFRICA

Underneath I had written:

"Africa does not need me but I need Africa."

It had seemed then that I could not live without Africa. I was right. I don't live now.

The trouble with the political and non-political refugees from the Republic of South Africa is that we cannot really be tolerated in the independent African states. We're so outdated. Information about what is going on just does not get through via sea and air routes and through magazines, newspapers and books. It travels overland by word of mouth and sort of gets into the air. Thus the interpretations are often confused and erroneous. Previous to 1958 no one had heard of Padmore and Pan-Africanism and yet it had been going on all the time in London. Previous to 1958 everyone was a Marxist- Leninist or Stalinist or Trotskyite. Then after 1958 a few of us became Pan-Africanists though there is much doubt as to whether the latter would ever take hold there. I can mention an experience. After reading George Padmore's book my whole manner of speaking and thinking and walking changed. It totally unsuited me for living in such a climate and environment as South Africa. It gave me a new skin and a new life that was totally unacceptable to conditions down there. To survive with this new life I had to remove myself. Doctrines such as Marxist-Leninism seem peculiarly suited to suit an environment like that. They stress the universal man; at least, the Marxist-Leninists and co. are very hostile to Pan-Africanism which is an attempt to establish a strong type of African personality. Anyway Marxist-Leninism has survived for almost a century in South Africa. I do not know much about it except that I have gained the impression that it is formidably intellectual, exact, scientific with all the answers worked out beforehand. It's a kind of quick method to over-coming the inferiority complex whereas Pan-Africanism reveals how dreadfully over-inflicted with inferior-complex and insecure an African of Africa can be. Pan-Africanism is certainly the more difficult road of the two. It's a kind of something leading on to something else along an unknown path. It would have been deeply satisfying to me had I been allowed to live in Africa. Everything of Africa would have been a guide, a tip, a hint, a clue. There wasn't anything in that little village that a historian would care to write about. The whole way of life seemed rather like some dark age in time moving dreamily within itself. Yet aspects of its life began to grow on me like patches of cloth—instead of a cup, the carved-out husk of a calabash would be used for scooping water out of a pail. Outside stoves and ovens were built of mud; porches and houses of mud. The fierce November thunderstorm would wash all the mud away but women with patient hands would again build up all their mud necessities. And because I was poor I too became a part of this mud life and a part of the hungry goats that lived off the windswept papers scattered about.

I had been living in the village for five months before I met Jenny. She was the only other refugee than myself who drifted inland. Others hung about in towns and villages near the main railway line for lifts out of the territory. As we were both from South Africa it was inevitable that we should drift together. I had never heard about her in the newspapers or anything but in Bechuanaland she had made a notorious reputation for herself. She was on a big top-secret organising project that was a supreme mystery. She was in the centre of some well-informed inner circle and I do believe she had divided the whole of Bechuanaland into her inner and outer circles; because, apart from organising her own top-secret project she also flung herself into the subtle and extremely treacherous maze of Bechuanaland politics. The only comparison to the complexity of Bechuanaland politics is Nigerian politics. They have all the evils of human society—poverty, illiteracy and disease; corruption and bribery, etc., but they do not want to bow down to the one party government or the Marxist-Leninist solution. This infuriates people who have dedicated their lives to the elimination of poverty, illiteracy, disease, bribery and corruption. Jenny could not understand how the illiterate peasants had gone and voted for the chiefs who were hand in glove with the British oppressor when she had organised the whole opposition into doing hut to hut campaigns. All around it was a very strange election. The chiefs never made an appearance. They had a kind of Napoleon Bonaparte with a sullen, intense, magnetic personality and a spell-binding effect on a crowd. This Napoleon Bonaparte was convinced unshakeably about three things: that Communism and Pan-Africanism are no damn good; that change is unnecessary but if it is to come it should come along the right channels—through the chiefs; that refugees should all be put in jail or thrown to the hungry lions roaming about the outskirts of the village.

Napoleon Bonaparte frightened everybody. It was just their luck that the British and the chiefs had him on their side. If he had been on the side of the Communists and Pan-Africanists he would have swayed the vote their way. He could do as he pleased with a crowd of simple villagers. He also spoke with a power and authority all his own. He could be dramatic, tragic, emotional, persuasive, aloof, endearingly charming—turning on each mood as he pleased; just doing as he pleased with vigorous masculine abandon. The women were crazy about him. Women rushed to register for the party of the chiefs. Women, just by temperament and instinct love power and masculinity in a man. It was very shrewdly done. They kept Napoleon Bonaparte working on the inland villages and they swept all these villages with a stunning majority. They lost the towns near the railway line where poverty, illiteracy and disease are discussed in a sophisticated manner. The strange thing about Napoleon Bonaparte was that he declined a high government post. People said it was because he was really treated like a dog by the chiefs. He did all the dirty work but they kept him out of their inner circle. People said it was because he was not "upper-class." He had a bad habit of drinking heavily and then falling down stiff like a board. He was also over-fond of the company of prostitutes and he also made white people uncomfortable— there was something too violent, brutal, earthy and direct about him that shattered their delicately-bred demeanours. The chief's party worked in close collaboration with the most delicately-bred British demeanours.

Anyway Napoleon Bonaparte was poison to Jenny. It was inevitable. He was about campaigning and so was she—both on the wrong side of the fence according to the other. It was Jenny who inspired in Napoleon Bonaparte an undying hatred for refugees. He wasn't the kind of man who could hate a woman but he hated Jenny and then he hated all refugees irrespective of sex. They were out to upset the status quo and he was a firm supporter of the status quo. He could be anything he liked but he wanted the status quo to stay the status quo. Any real change from the top would have created chaos and disorder in his view. It is undoubted that Napoleon Bonaparte wanted power himself. He wanted to get control of something as a release; an outlet for the intense drives within him but the great cause that would channel his feverish energy, had not, until the time I left made its appearance. Napoleon Bonaparte smouldered. One day he would burst into flame. He would. There was a tremendous power drive in him and a ruthless and unswerving concentration.

There is a wild frustration in me when I think of him. He wanted something from me or wanted to tell me something but he never approached. He never once spoke to me. He had a way of catching hold of my eye so that I could distinctly feel the penetration and the look boring down into some unknown depths. And I could never release my eyes until he would turn away abruptly and walk off. He would always catch me off-guard. I'd turn around a hedge and there he'd be walking towards me and he'd just lock my eyes up and I'd never have the power to pull them away. Then he'd just brush past and the atmosphere would almost shout aloud with violence. Once I greeted him and his reply was a sharp, fierce sound that caused my heart to palpitate in extreme alarm. I never tried greeting him again. In fact I always looked around cautiously wherever I went so that I might dash in the opposite direction should I see him approaching. I was plain stark terrified of the man. Once I awoke during the night for a drink of water. The water-pail was under the window. It was moonlight. I parted the curtains on an impulse and looked out. There he stood, the moonlight glistening on his ferocious face—the sharp straight line of the brow and the harsh, deep lines of the mouth unsoftened by the beautiful pale light. He had been looking with fixed concentration at the door of my hut and then he turned his head with a slow, appealing; yet aloof and god-like gesture and looked at the window. I dropped the curtain. It seemed as though I had lost control of my limbs. They trembled violently. I could have cried out with the intense pain—either my heart had stopped beating or had twisted up into a tight constricted ball.

Perhaps, a mouse sat near the wall of a newly-built dam. They opened the floodgates above and the water came crashing down on him in huge shining billows.

"This is the end," he thought before blacking out. And yet; when he had regained consciousness it was rather that he found he could live in a new element. He was a water-rat. All other elements were shut out and only the dazzling roar of the water was about, within and around him all the while. He could not get out; escape. He even had to drink water for nourishment. He was forever trapped by water till maybe he even became water and could no longer care to maintain a separate identity.

I would not even care to question whether I love or loved Napoleon Bonaparte or whether he loves or loved me. I only know that like the mouse I accidently, unknowingly approach a dam; not knowing there was water up above or a terrible unfathomable mystery that would go its own way; a power outside myself controlling and yet uncontrolled by me. That is why I prefer to believe I am insane. I do not control my own life. I am living and breathing. There are crowds of people all about me; yet I am contained in a wall of silence. All attention, alertness is concentrated within as though at some day, some time I should hear a call that would end this strange and painful exile. It isn't that I do not resent this helpless condition. I resent it bitterly. At times I am overcome by a deep wave of despair. I want my life to myself. I feel this way because I am alone now. It wasn't so bad while I still lived in the village. I came to accept the fact that a powerful and subterranean current had been established between my life and that of another human life because I was able to establish a pattern in the sudden agitations and distress that took possession of me.

One afternoon I sat in my hut absorbed in a book. For no reason I could fathom I flung the book aside, and paced about the hut in extreme distress exclaiming over and over again: "Don't worry! It does not matter! Don't worry about that!"

I later learnt that a political meeting had taken place in the village and that Napoleon Bonaparte had got himself into a mess by attacking the Communists and Pan-Africanists. They in turn had struck a blow below the belt by calling his mother a prostitute of the village; which was in fact true. My friend Kate told me that tears just dashed into his eyes and he walked abruptly away from the meeting amid much ribald laughter from the enemy.

"I do not like the style of those politicians," my friend Kate said indignantly. "A secret of the village is a secret. They are bringing strange ways into the nation. I'm not going to vote for them!"

My friend Kate was, so to speak a typical, die-hard, tribalistic Motswana of Bechuanaland. We lived next door to each other. I longed to tell her about Napoleon Bonaparte and yet; I feared the whole matter would become confused in her mind with fanatical tribal loyalty.

She was always saying: "I shall tell you a secret of the village but if you spread it about I'll call you a liar and never speak to you again."

The tribal structure was in itself a tight closed circle, and, within this circle were born many fierce and violent individualists who caused extreme distress with their wild and wilful ways. There was a blind attitude toward these disturbers of the peace. They were punished severely by the scribes and elders who dictated tribal justice. It was a system that contained and suppressed the misfit by ignoring him for as long as possible until his misdeeds became of such a nature as to really threaten the sameness and flow of life. Then the whole village would rise up in a turmoil and then the miscreant would be dragged through the mud for a string of crimes committed perhaps ten, twenty years ago. An awful lot of pretending and ignoring was done about the strange behaviour of Napoleon. Really he was intensely feared and detested. There was no precedent for him. Even the heroic chief Tshekedi, who had had a somewhat eccentric behaviour pattern was quite a normal man and had been perfectly comprehended. The stress today is only on the political revolution taking place in Africa. No attention is fixed on the individuals within that revolution. There is an insane belief that Africans of Africa are somehow a different species of mankind. Politicians with an Oxford, Harvard education are hell-bent on fixing us up with five-year plans as though we are mass-produced humanity with a rubber stamp and a number and a box in which we are made for export— a politician's export. Some of our writers too with university degrees are writing glib nonsense about the dancing girls as though we are a great, happy band of child-like savages dancing our lives away in an empty, erotic frenzy. Everything is being made for export in Africa and we are not really supposed to care. We are not really supposed to be men and women; individualists with a behaviour pattern all our own. We are not supposed to be like ordinary mankind the world over, human beings of feeling, sense, intuition, reasoning, evolving within ourselves in the smoke and fire and struggle and suffering that is a part of the lot of all mankind. We are vulnerable and exposed victims of the overnight ideologies of vain, conceited, dangerous cranks who would hammer our lives into a false pattern of their own choosing. We seem to lack the mental alertness to resist these trends; the battery of propaganda that flows in from all directions because we are within the victims of suppressive tribal institutions and foolhardy prejudice.

It is assumed that a man begins and ends his life from the point of birth to the point of death. How false. The point stretches infinitely backward into the dim reaches of time and infinitely forward into unending worlds and unending lives. One life is an hour; a stitch in the many coloured tapestry of the universe; or, like a pebble dropped in a pool that ruffles the water and causes ever-widening circles of movement, till maybe at some far away point in time the movement reaches its limit and there is a stillness. I have heard that the mathematicians are making exact calculations along these lines. It is a comforting thought. It may be possible that one day soon we use those mathematical calculations in Africa to rid ourselves of the soul-crippling doctrines and ideologies that harass us so. It may be that one day, through sheer necessity we become a continent of exact, precise calculating mathematicians and so forever rid ourselves of oppressors and foreign domination. In some such way I am hoping that Napoleon Bonaparte will liberate himself. If not he will destroy himself and I should be destroyed too.

I know I should not go on and on like this about Napoleon Bonaparte and Africa. It may bore everybody. It's just that I have a desperate need to communicate and it may be that a stranger somewhere would comprehend my suffering and help me. That is why I am putting down everything. Even if I am insane, at least someone could help me to accept it and I should at least have peace of mind.

Once I got to telling Jenny about it I plagued her almost every day. I am surprised she tolerated me. She wasn't the kind of woman to get involved in "nonsense."

"What nonsense!" was one of her favourite phrases.

The friends in her inner circle always said good-bye to each other with the words: "Keep up the struggle against the imperialist, capitalist oppressors." At first I did not even hold out a hope that I would ever be a friend of Jenny. She reserved all warmth and frankness for her inner circle. They were people with remarkable characteristics.

Just as there are some people who never become stock brokers or financiers because they are temperamentally unable to sustain the shock of the rise and fall of the stock market; just so do political circles inspire a nightmarish terror in me.

"Did you hear? T. is a spy! Did you hear? J. is a spy!" and so on and so on. They eat each other with hate.

So I say: "To hell with you all—good, bad and sympathisers. If there isn't a benevolent overshadowing presence in the universe taking care of the destinies of all men—then who am I to think I can take care of Africa?" And because my life is one of uncertainty, pain and a strange inner humility I wish to believe that there is a protective, all knowing force at work among the affairs of men.

Therefore Jenny and I had some flaming rows at the beginning of our friendship. Maybe she thought I had not got the message—that every black man and woman was committed to the liberatory struggle hands, feet, legs and heart. That was what it meant to her. The fact is I had got the message but had taken off in a direction all my own.

There is a sure-fire method of getting a convert. Deal death blows to the ego. I got phrases like this flung at me: "You're full of contrived confusion! You're an escapist! You're an exhibitionist!"

I'd sort of catch on to a word here and there to save myself.

"I couldn't possibly be an exhibitionist. I am lonely and loneliness does not boost the ego," I'd say.

She gave me a book to read. It was called *The Third World*. It really dealt a blow to my self esteem. I thought I could read any book in English but I got through a couple of pages and had to go right back to page one again because words, meaning, sentences were not connecting in my mind. In the end I had to give up. It obviously was understood by Jenny because large sections were heavily underlined and the word AMEN!! printed in bold capitals in the margin throughout the book.

I returned the book feeling very mortified and embarrassed. It was the first time a book had defeated me.

"It's very difficult to read," I said.

She laughed: "Yes it's rather technical. I could lend you something simpler."

"No thanks," I said politely. "I have something to read at home."

Funny thing. I had a similar experience some months later. Someone in the village gave me a pamphlet entitled: "Consciencism—The Philosophy for the Decolonization of Africa."

Though I re-read it several times words, sentences, meaning could not connect in my mind. I felt extreme alarm. Perhaps, a form of English was evolving that I would never comprehend. I took the pamphlet to Jenny.

"What's Consciencism?" I asked.

She laughed: "Oh, that's just one of the latest ideologies of Kwame Nkrumah."

I was relieved that it could be dismissed so lightly but there was a nagging thought.

"Is there perhaps a connection between The Third World and Consciencism?" I asked.

She gave me a hostile stare.

"You really have an inferior mind," she said. "You never listen to Africa. You just hear your own noise all the time."

"What do you mean?" I asked anxiously. "Is The Third World Africa or is Consciencism Africa?"

She shrugged impatiently.

"All this contrived confusion," she said. "Our friendship could progress beyond this point but you never listen. You haven't a clue about what's happening in Africa."

"I don't like the way you keep trying to make out that I'm not an African of Africa," I shouted in a sudden fury.

"Oh, for God's sake stick on a badge—I'm AN AFRICAN OF AFRICA," she shouted back.

Conversations always ended like this. And they were wildly illogical. I was being pressed to accept some faith but I was dominated by a feeling of acute distress. I wanted to talk to another woman about Napoleon and I could not talk about him to Kate. Jenny was my only other woman friend in the village. But I dare not even mention his name to her. One night he had been roaring drunk and had walked past her hut and bawled out that she was a Communist revolutionary and that all Communists should go to hell and all refugees should go to hell.

"He's a nasty brute," she remarked when telling me of the incident. "I'm not a Communist and could never be."

"He doesn't understand a thing about politics. Besides he's too emotional," I said.

"Don't be fooled," she said. "That emotionalism is just a cover-up. He's been deliberately placed to create contrived confusion."

"Apart from politics," I said warily. "As a man he is an extraordinary and dynamic personality. He's a damn good public speaker. He is intensely aware of people. You know, even if he dislikes you he looks you straight in the eye. I find everybody here, except the very poor and lowly, looking over everybody's head and adopting false mannerisms."

"He is a great humanitarian," she said gently. "I like him and always will."

"You mean that?" I asked unbelievingly.

"Yes. And I do not think he will stick around with that political party of so-and-so's because of his humanity."

"I wonder. There isn't anything around here except so-and-so's. And goats and cattle. Egypt's land, I call it. I've been invaded by swarms of flies, then swarms of scorpions and when I had killed them all there were swarms of moths the size of birds. Tell me, what is a normal relationship between a man and a woman?"

"I'm sorry I haven't time for lady talk," she said primly.

The last time we ever had a flaming row was over George Padmore and Pan-Africanism. We were not on speaking terms for a month and it was during that time that I found out how much I loved that puzzling, contradictory woman. Perhaps the cause of the rows was that I really would have liked to oblige by accepting her faith—just as I had let many other people down because I must be free mentally to take off in any direction I choose. To choose freedom is also to choose loneliness.

George Padmore is a prophet to me. Over and above that he was the initiator, the liberator of Africa; he was too a kind of John the Baptist crying in the wilderness—make ready the way. And we who come on behind keep preparing the way with our ideas. And then, long after we are gone our Jesus Christs and Abraham Lincolns are born who give shape, define sharply, unmistakeably, the part we are to play in the destiny of mankind. What else does the liberation of Africa mean to me but this inner awakening and alertness—as though from some direction I may be given a hint, a clue and eagerly pass on this small grain of truth to some other seeker to question, examine and add his grain. Could it not be that within the turmoil and struggle to end poverty and oppression that writers may live too without fear of banishment or playing footsy to some impossible, dictatorial ideology? I do not want my mind controlled therefore I have no home on this earth. I have sealed myself within a wall of silence. Except that which I wish, should enter.

I have forgotten the details of my quarrel with Jenny; except that at the time it was painful. After a month I went creeping back again.

"Look here Jenny, I'm sorry I had a row with you. We need not ever discuss Pan-Africanism or any other controversial matter. I really don't know what Pan-Africanism is except that it seems personal and not political."

"All right. Get off the lectern," she said. "I was wondering when this absurd game would drag itself to an end. I must say you have a colossal vanity. You had to nurse it for a whole month. Of course, mine needs a little watering down from time to time."

"I'm really worried about my sanity, you know," I said.

"Oh don't worry about that," she said expansively. "We're all of us quite insane in our own ways."

"Really, I'm in a god-awful mess. I've battled against the thing the whole time and tried to appear normal but I'm just falling to pieces. I want to tell you something but it's so difficult."

There was a wide-open mocking laughter in her eyes.

"Go ahead," she said. "I know who you want to talk about."

"How on earth did you know?" I asked, surprised, embarrassed.

She gave me a superior smile: "It's just that some people are born secret agents and others, as soon as they have a secret, talk about it with their facial muscles and eyes. You're a give-away, chum."

"Have you ever seen such a beautiful-ugly man in your life before?"

"You see him. I don't," she said. "I've got a man and another one saved up for hard times."

"The only thing that bothers me," I said, "is the terror. I'm terrified of the man. It would seem that after a year I've become terror itself. They say the nervous system can adapt itself to all states but I find that it's an unpleasant state and I don't think I'm really adapted because I'm beginning to fall to pieces."

"There's quite a simple explanation for terror," she said. "He's just as terrified of you as you are of him. He's afraid you'll reject him and you're afraid he'll reject you. To simplify matters further, you love him and he loves you."

"Good God! I never even thought about that! You mean he loves me? I'm not the kind of woman men love."

"You dearly love to think of yourself as an exceptional species," she said scornfully.

"It isn't so, really. I haven't that kind of arrogance and it seems to need an assertive arrogance to believe one is loved."

"You'll have to grab a man one day in spite of yourself. Women do that, you know. Look, why don't you help the man? He's been living in hell all his life. That man's living in hell. The expression is one of permanent, excruciating suffering. Get up and *do* something. He's not Africa about which you sit and moan all day. He's a real man with pants!"

I wrung my hands in agony.

"I don't believe the man loves me. It rather seems as though some terrible and sinister accident has happened between us and he's furious about it. I know I am. I have all these overwhelming problems of refugeeism and on top of that the most extraordinary, unfathomable phenomena has been taking place in my life this whole year. Please, for God's sake, Jenny, believe me. I'm a strong-minded woman in the sense that I don't see ghosts and I'm not susceptible or faint or anything like that. It's just like somebody has been living inside me all this time. The terrible thing is that it's involuntary—involuntary conversations, involuntary agitation and involuntary physical reactions. You know, I used to be somewhat of an alcoholic when I lived in South Africa but now I'm a complete teetotaller. The sensation of retching when you have drunk too much is the most abysmally miserable in the world. I'm often getting that feeling and being as sick as a dog. The involuntary conversations—they happen just out of the blue. I'm always having to advise, counsel and I talk out quite loud. I do not know the cause and only at a later time do I get a hint from Kate that he's involved in some mess in the village. It's quite true what you say about hell. I'm very familiar with it. Oh Jenny, I can't get him out because it is involuntary. One of these days I'll be fired out of here because they really cannot tolerate refugees—then what will I do?"

"Cross that bridge when you come to it. In the meantime try to establish some physical communication."

"I can't do that. The atmosphere is too violent. Besides, Kate tells me he says the most terrible things about refugees."

"There's only two of us here. That's meant for me. I've had word that I'm going to have transport provided for a forced removal. They've done everything to move me out by normal channels. Now they got to use handcuffs and chains, it seems. Anyway for a while I'm going to get me on the diplomatic junketing roundabout and eat on the inches I've lost in this abominable country."

"Why should one live if one is welcome nowhere on earth? Why? Why?"

"You wouldn't be half as pessimistic if you got off your seat and flung yourself into the battle. Anyway we're both southern women. Temperamentally, we fit in with the way things are down here. I'm getting back here after I've driven the oppressors of mankind to hell and I'd advise you to do the same. We fit in here. We belong here no matter what the so-and-so's have to say."

"Shall I ever resolve this unfathomable mystery, Jenny?"

"I don't know. Some men would rather cut off their tongues than tell a woman they love her. Or it may be that he has to pass through a fire of his own and cannot share his life with a woman. But I don't really know."

I wonder where Jenny is now. She left a month before I received that letter. I wonder if we shall ever meet again and when? And for how long will Napoleon Bonaparte gaze with ferocious eyes into the smoke and fire and struggle of his life? For how long shall I wait and wait and listen and listen? And Kate? If there were inventions and machines and the hammer and din of progress in her village she would so easily be beguiled away from the small fanatical world of tribal secrets. For I too have my small inner circle of strange fancy, wonder and conjectural things and they were among the elect few I had invited in; they were a beginning of love.

Maureen Kim Sing, WHAT OF THE FUTURE?

South Africa 1965   English

For the Chinese, life in South Africa in the 1960s was fraught with insecurity. Apartheid laws became ever more threatening as families faced the loss of their shops and homes with the enforcement of the Group Areas Act. This community of fewer than five thousand people countrywide was shrinking with the steady emigration of its educated young professionals. Press reports frequently highlighted anomalies in the treatment meted out to this minority group, which had long straddled the dividing line between black and white.

Within the community there was an increasing level of introspection, evident from the appearance of many new, though short-lived, publications. These included *The Voice of SA Chinese, The Eastern Province Chinese Review, New Youth, South Wind, Weekend Review,* and the *SA Chinese Student,* produced in either English or Chinese. One that flourished in the 1960s was the *Student Spectrum,* a newsletter directed at the Chinese students at the University of Cape Town (UCT). Published irregularly between two and five times a year, its twenty to thirty pages of essays, interviews, cartoons, letters, jokes, and campus news were sometimes controversial.

One of its contributors was Maureen Kim Sing, daughter of a Port Elizabeth community leader who spent decades opposing discriminatory legislation. She majored in English literature at UCT before leaving South Africa in 1966 to study for her master's degree at the University of California at Berkeley. She married a history lecturer, Keith Haight, and became increasingly involved in anti-Vietnam, antiracist, environmental, and community movements. After moving to Ireland she and her husband were at the forefront of the Cork branch of the Irish Anti-Apartheid Movement and helped launch the antinuclear environmental movement that produced the Irish Green party. She worked as a freelance journalist and with her husband (her anonymity was often necessary to protect her family in South Africa) published anti-apartheid articles and letters in the *Irish Times* and elsewhere. She has also lectured extensively on nutrition. Kim Sing has lived in France for the past fifteen years, writing, teaching, and working as a professional translator under her own name. She is currently working with her husband on a book on Ireland's hidden history, and edits the monthly bilingual newsletter of her local branch of the Women's International Club.

Analyzing the concerns of the young Chinese in "What of the Future?" she offers a down-to-earth examination of the attitudes prevailing within her community. Written in 1965 during her final year at UCT, her arguments reflect the intensity of the debates that took place among her peers and encapsulated both the fears and the fatalism of a minority that survived the apartheid years by living up to the stereotype of a quiet, law-abiding community.

Melanie Yap

✦

WHAT WILL HAPPEN:

Recent events, as mirrored by the local papers seem to indicate that the Chinese will soon be placed on the "wrong" side of the colour bar. However, the issue is not quite so clear-cut: there is the question of degree. Events seem to favour a separate classification . . . i.e. Chinese will be classed as Chinese, not white or non-white. Nationalist Government policy is separate development; so while they will not grant us white rights, neither will they force us to integrate with any other group. There are obvious reasons for not granting us white status; Dr. Verwoerd's speech at Heidelburg recently outlined the reasoning, viz:— "Grant that . . . they are not inferior to the Japanese, but by the same token, are the Indians culturally any less refined than the Chinese? And then are the Coloureds inferior to the Indians." Etc. (Quoted from Sunday Chronicle, 26th September).

WHAT CAN WE DO ABOUT IT?

There are three courses of action open to us. One is quite unpracticable to our communities' nature and circumstances, but the other two solutions have interesting possibilities. These solutions are: resist, escape or adjust.

1) RESIST:

This is the course followed by some of the English-speaking people in South Africa. Active resistance has always been their method of survival until quite recently. Ours was and is passive. We have got where we are by being inconspicuous and this is still our best course of action. In any case, to have effective resistance, leaders are needed, plus backing; whilst the nature of the Chinese people is essentially passive—apathetic, in fact. Furthermore, we have no bargaining powers—economical or political. So that takes care of *that* solution.

2) ESCAPE:

Emigration seems to be becoming the "done" thing. However, there are a number of drawbacks. Firstly, not all of us are lucky enough to be able to "get away from it all"—because of financial difficulties, business and family ties, etc. Secondly, where can we go? The majority of the Chinese are small businessmen. Some countries have restricted immigration—professional people have the best opportunities. Thirdly, conditions will be different and competition will be much tougher. Fourthly, there is no guarantee that pickings will be better elsewhere. Racial discrimination exists elsewhere too, and while there will be no official legal colour bar, social conventions could prove much tougher to crack. Here, we are sure of what we have and have not: another country will be an unknown quantity. Lastly, climatic differences may seem trivial, because we in S.A. have always taken these things for granted: Hong Kong has its typhoons and drought, England its snowbound winter, America its annual hurricanes and floods, certain parts of America are so humid that one cannot walk in the streets for more than 10 minutes without fainting! (People go from air-conditioned houses via air-conditioned transport to air-conditioned shops, cinemas etc.)

3) ADJUST:

The majority of the Chinese will stay—because they have no other choice, and because things will not be so bad. Now, judging in abstract, the future seems bleak, but there are a number of consoling factors:

The Nationalist governmental policy is separate development. The Chinese have never been particularly keen to mix with other groups in any case. Had apartheid not existed, pressure from within would have enforced it in any case—possibly even more strictly than outside pressure alone would have made it. The fear of most minority groups is of losing their identity—apartheid will preserve ours.

The government has promised that our livelihood will not be threatened. However, they have their policy, which they intend to carry out so that they cannot make exceptions. The Group Areas Act permits Chinese to retain businesses in other areas until the death of the present owner. Theoretically this allows time for us to seek other means of existence. However, certain other factors are accelerating this process. Many businesses have been expropriated for reasons of street-widening, civic amenity improvements, etc.

However, this may not be a bad thing. Once upon a time, the Chinese communities were homogenous—socially, economically, etc. However, better education and higher standards of living have led to increased diversity. There has been an increasing amount of widening out but the process has been very slow. The discrepancy between the homogeneity of occupation despite increasing diversity of interests, particularly among the new generation, has led to frustration, and unhappiness. Many of our elders complain that the young people no longer want to "work in the shop." There is no reason why they should. In one way, recent events will benefit the Chinese by forcing them into other spheres of business, the trades and professions.

Furthermore, as mentioned above—by staying here, one is certain of what one has. The structure of S.A. economy (Job reservations) has its advantages, in a way. Open competition, e.g. in U.S.A. and U.K. is very fierce—which is why S.A. is attracting so many immigrants despite her drawbacks. Here, most Chinese have their own homes, cars, and a large measure of security. We may not be so fortunate as to have this elsewhere, although theoretically there may be more opportunity, in other words, second-class citizenship in S.A. may be a lot better than first class citizenship elsewhere. Furthermore, class distinction based on money and education is very strong overseas (in S.A. it is superseded by racial distinction) and the majority of Chinese would find it tough going to comply with the requirements for the standard of living they already enjoy in S.A.

Socially we are in a rather ambiguous position. There are two possibilities: this state will continue, or it will be clarified. If it is clarified, it will be to our disadvantage. For years now, there has been this disparity between legislation on the Chinese position, and the actual lack of enforcement. This is an indication of the benevolent attitude of the government toward the Chinese. Unfortunately, although the officials turn a blind eye to conditions, when it is pointed out to them, they are forced to apply the official ruling. The recent tightening up on the rulings for the Chinese in sport, entertainment and other matters, is a direct result of the barrage of the press publicity from the English press.

The function of an opposition newspaper is to make the government look ridiculous whenever possible: they are not interested in us, except as another means of showing up a weak point in the government. However, this continual underlining of our ambiguous position can have only one outcome: the ambiguity will be removed, and we will suffer. As far as we are concerned, no news is good news. Any publicity is bad because it focuses attention on us, so it is rather stupid to feel flattered because the Sunday Times runs a full-page feature on the Chinese: "Poor Chinese—they're such nice people and look how horrible the government is to them." We can do without such sympathy, as this only serves to irritate the government.

Possibly only when the entire machinery of apartheid is in full swing, will they begin granting concessions again. However, at the moment they cannot do so at the risk of antagonising the other race groups. In the meantime, it could take them anything up to 50 years to complete the process. It is [likely] that this ambiguity could continue. As we have seen, the government is prepared to turn a blind eye to our "trespassing," but continual hammering at them to clarify our position will achieve nothing . . . or the wrong result. The sport question is very important. It appears that the government is still prepared to turn this "blind eye" to things. However, when for example, the W.P. [Western Province] Association *asks* for a decision, they will be forced to give one. They would have done better to select Chinese players indiscriminately—it would probably have been ignored. But the Argus headlines about the "dilemma" has done us great harm.

We cannot oppose the government, but neither can we actually agree with them either—taking into consideration other groups and overseas opinion. So where does that leave us? All we can do is what we have done in the past: sit tight and wait. Don't talk, and do try to suppress publicity of any kind wherever possible.

Ingrid Jonker, I DRIFT IN THE WIND
South Africa 1966   Afrikaans

Ingrid Jonker walked into the sea at Three Anchor Bay, Cape Town, on 19 July 1965. Early the next morning newspaper headlines proclaimed, "Beauty Queen of Afrikaans Poetry Commits Suicide." Nearly thirty years later, in the parliament where once her father had denounced her politics and writing, she walked back into the limelight when Nelson Mandela quoted her poem, "The Child Who Was Shot Dead by Soldiers at Nyanga," in his inaugural speech on 23 May 1994.

Born in 1933 to parents whose marriage ended when she was three, Jonker's upbringing was characterized by poverty. Under her grandmother's guidance, she started to write poems for use during church services that included coloured people in the Cape Flats area. From the age of twelve, after both her mother and grandmother had died, she lived with her father, a well-known Afrikaans writer and, later, a National party politician. At the age of sixteen her first poems were rejected for publication but gave her contact with poet D. J. Opperman who encouraged and advised her. She published her first collection of poems, *Ontvlugting* (Escape), at the age of twenty-two. When she submitted *Rook en Oker* (Smoke and Ochre), the publishers wanted to remove two poems, including "The Child Who Was Shot Dead by Soldiers at Nyanga." She refused. Publication brought her the Afrikaanse Pers-Boekhandel Prize, but cut her off from the "Afrikaner king poets," even Opperman.

The volume *Kantelson* (1966), published after her death, contains some of her most beautiful work. "I Drift in the Wind" was written six months before her death and probably shortly after she returned from a period in Europe. The poem captures a crucial dilemma. If her writing is about the body and lovers, the (male) literary world treats the poet as a "beauty queen," as one with more sex and emotion than talent. If a female poet writes about politics, the male discomfort is audible in the paternalistic tone of words such as naive, innocent, angry, or decadent.

The voice in the poem feels misunderstood and deserted by friends, family, and *volk*—only black Africa accompanies her lonely fingers into death. In the new translation offered here, the word "*los*" is translated not as "free" (as the standard translation has it) but as "loose": cut off, deserted, forgotten, uprooted. The poet has no one and nothing, no mother, father, hearth, friend—only a bitter landscape. In the second verse she makes a distinction between her "rotted *volk*" and Africa. (The earlier translation has "*volk*" as "nation," but the word refers specifically to Afrikaners, who saw themselves as an exclusive cultural entity with a specific destiny.) She knows that these people have rotted away from her, like her own father and mother. She warns them that a hand, like the loose hand of her father against the sky, needs another hand to pray. In the last verse she sees death covering her, her sister, her nation, and perhaps also Africa.

Antjie Krog

✦

(for Anna)

Loose I have my own independence
from graves from treacherous friends
the hearth I have comforted glares at me
my parents have broken themselves off from my death
the worms stir against my mother, my father
is clasping his hand which feathers loose against the sky
loose I believe my old friend has forsaken me
loose I believe you had mountains toppled in me
loose my landscape reeks of bitter sun and blood
What will become of me

the cornerstones of my heart bring about nothing
my landscape is mine hardened
fierce embittered but open
My *volk*
follow my lonely fingers,
people, wrap yourself in sincerity
veiled by the sun of the future
My black Africa
follow my lonely fingers
follow my absent image
lonely as an owl
and the fingers of the world becoming lonelier
lonely as my sister
My *volk* rotted off away from me
what will become of this rotted *volk*
a hand cannot pray alone

The sun shall cover us
the sun in our eyes for ever covered
with black crows.

Translated by Antjie Krog

Anonymous, I AM A WAILING FOOL

Lesotho 1967   Sesotho

This song is an example of an old woman's genre that, like the old Sesotho marriage songs and some other forms, has been replaced by Christian hymns of mourning at Basotho funerals. Unlike hymns, *koli-ea-malla* (laments) were sung only by women upon the death of a husband or close male relative. In this song, which is sung in the characteristically African leader-chorus "call and response" format, the soloist immediately establishes the theme of desolation and ruin of the household that follows the death of her husband. The chorus reinforces this theme in their reference to rain, expanding the particular loss of the soloist to a general statement about the loss sustained by the community when "real men," fathers who led and sustained families, die off, leaving behind only the shiftless and unreliable.

Perhaps the most moving passage is the soloist's final verse, in which she evokes the image of herself tiptoeing to the door at sunset to see if her husband is returning, although she knows too well he will never again return. The final three lines illustrate the Basotho performance practice that enables, even encourages, a supporting social group or individual to express the emotions felt by someone else. Hence in this song, this last chorus virtually repeats lines three and four of the soloist's opening verse, giving the composition as a whole balance and closure.

David Coplan

✦

Solo:
I am a wailing fool who remains among ruins.
I am a wailing fool who remains in a bare, open field.
Where do I remain,
By my father, with whom do I remain?

Chorus:
Men died; with whom do we remain?
Men departed; only the worthless remain.
Real men departed; with whom do we remain?

Solo:
I am a wailing fool who remains among ruins.
When the sun has sunk low,
To the door I go,
On tip-toe advancing slowly,
Supposing him coming alone,
Supposing him returning from the hunt.

Chorus:
Men died; with whom do we remain?
Men died; we remained in ruins.
Men died; we remained in a bare, open field.

Transcribed by David Copland and Seakhi Santho
Translated by David Coplan

Fatima Meer, MURMURS IN THE KUTUM

South Africa 1969   English

Fatima Meer, a sociologist and writer born in 1929, has been an important politi-cal activist in South Africa. Her writings cover a variety of genres—biography, local history, essays, travelogue, short stories, speeches, polemics, and letters. Meer's father worked for *The Indian Opinion*, a newspaper founded by Mohandas Gandhi in 1904. Influenced by Gandhi, Meer's involvement in political activity began with the Passive Resistance Campaign of 1946. She was banned from 1954 to 1956, and in 1976, in the wake of the Soweto uprising, she spent a little more than four months in detention with women such as Winnie Mandela. She was not brought to trial.

To counter the disabling effects of apartheid on potential black writers, Meer set up the Madiba Press in 1989. Through it and the Institute of Black Research at the University of Natal, she has been instrumental in getting many works published.

She has written two biographies about key South African political figures, *Apprenticeship of the Mahatma* and *Higher than Hope: The Official Biography of Nelson Mandela.*

The *Portrait of Indian South Africans*, from which "Murmurs in the Kutum" is taken, is one of her earliest works. While she resists the racist, ghettoizing politics of the apartheid regime, she undertakes to restore knowledge and appreciation of one of the many racial and cultural groups in South Africa. In this cameo, Meer uses a fictional mode to present the Indian *kutum*, or extended family, and the precarious ethnicities of mid–twentieth century South Africa. The Indian shop is at once the place of border crossings and transactions that expose racial othering. In the gendered spaces of the *kutum*, women's opportunities are limited compared to those of the men in their families.

Devarakshanam Govinden

✦

Hlatikulu, the Great Forest, is an African Reserve. The landscape is bush and scattered trees and rounded huts that look like some browning vegetation sprouting from the earth. Near the mountain, it is really a hill, there is a store which belonged to Amod who died five years ago, and before Amod, to Amod's father Ebrahim, and before Ebrahim to Dawood. Now Amod's widow and his eldest son Unus run the shop. There are other children— Yakub in London studying to be a lawyer and Suliman in Dublin who will be a doctor, and there is Farida who helps her mother with household chores and in the evenings, keeps a firm eye on neatly tabulated notes from the Correspondence College. She learns History and Geography, English and Afrikaans and Botany in preparation for the Matriculation exam.

In the shop, large curling sacks of beans and mealies, hlubus and flour lean against the wooden counter; brightly coloured scarves, square cotton dresses and men's checked shirts hang from the ceiling. Tins of food and rolls of material line the shelves; bunches of billy cans dangle from king-size nails and an old gramophone beats out a rhythm to which picannins dance. The customers come when there is money—women big-bosomed and big-bottomed with wired ankles and beaded necks, and sometimes men with rippling muscles and shiny flesh.

Next to the shop is a verandah, cool with fern and cacti, and behind it, dwelling rooms. Except for the verandah and the sitting room which leads off from it and the new bathroom and toilet with a flushing system, this has been the home of the family ever since the days of Dawood.

To this homestead, there comes on a sultry December noon, a happy contingent of three cars; one from Durban, one from Pietermaritzburg and the third from Dundee. An excited concert of hooters herald their arrival. The various members of the Amod family hurriedly leave what they are doing, and quickly assemble on the verandah to welcome the relatives who have travelled such distances to emphasize the warmth of their blood bonds. Some of these bonds are remote. There are present in the party, not only a brother and his family, but also the brothers-in-law and cousins whose great grandfathers had been first cousins to the original Dawood, and *their* families.

Voices pour out of the cars: important authoritarian voices, diffident subordinate voices, restrained, educated voices. Absent are the voices of children for these have become suddenly withdrawn and silent. The owners of the voices shake themselves out like so many fowls, the old women in wide smocks and wide trousers, the young girls in tight shifts and tight trousers, little boys in stylish (just like Dad's) suits, the little girls in fancy stretched out skirts.

Voices and bodies pour exuberantly into the doorway and there is much laughing and greeting and slapping of backs and sharing of giggles. The children, awed by the sudden revelry of the grown-ups, cling tightly to their mothers and look around in wide-eyed wonder until they are noticed and admired by the hosts and playfully chastised by their mothers for being unsociable and not playing with each other.

"Is that your little Iqbal?" one cousin kindly asks of another. *"My, how he has grown. How like his father,"* and she sinks into sighs of how quickly time flies, how old they are getting, how they will soon be mothers-in-law (they are barely twenty-five); and little Iqbal shrinks in size and nibbles the elaborately embroidered end of his mother's head drape, *awdnie,* only to be scolded for doing so: then he plunges all the deeper into her skirt. *"Your Shamima is grown up now,"* an ageing sixth cousin with three sons to be married, notes meaningly as she eyes a helplessly blushing dark-eyed, dark-haired girl who has newly entered her teens. Her mother retorts sharply, protectively, *"She is still at school,"* and walks away to complain to another relative of *Budie Bai's* strange notions. *"Some people cast their evil looks even on children, Chi."*

Soon the group separates. The men crowd into the little sitting room, the married women into Mrs Amod's room, the young unmarried girls into another bedroom; the children, at first reticent, are soon raucously running through the passage and into the garden, followed by helpless female pleas to be careful of the dangers. The fifth group, of growing men, hang around the window where the young girls are gathered, hopeful of a little prank, a tiny flirtation, but quite without courage to stimulate any. So they hang around, and after a while forget what they are hanging around for, and become mercifully absorbed in each other and drift away into the yard.

The two Amod women and Annie, their domestic help, grow boisterous with work, but helpless in the confusion of hilarious voices demanding their attention. There is a tussle—a resistance. The Amod women snatch away plates and kitchen cloths and remonstrate in feigned horror. *"Oh, no, no. We can't allow you to work. You hardly ever visit us. Sit and relax and talk."* The visitors complain about being treated like *visitors;* and not like people of the house. *"We are one,"* they affirm. *"How can we come again if you make divisions like that."* Helpless against such rebuke, the Amod women surrender with the dignity of martyrs: knives are picked up, radishes and onions cut, papads fried, pickles and plates taken to the table and finally the men are called in to lunch.

"Finish up the children too," a visiting mother suggests. *"Put them on the floor. Haven't you some chatais (grass mats) and some newspaper?" "Are, are"* Mrs. Amod protests, *"How can you put them on the floor. We'll put them on the table when the men are finished." "They're just children"* is the carefree reply. *"When will we finish if everybody eats on the table?"*

"Ah, yes, that's true," Mrs Amod agrees as if it is some sagacious revelation, *"and the children must be hungry after the journey,"* and with feigned reluctance, but obvious relief, accepts the suggestion.

Grass mats are spread out on the verandah. Newspapers are laid in the middle, the children are seated on either side, and the food brought in amid the excited chatter of juvenile voices. First vermicelli, fried brown in sugar and butter and flavoured with cinnamon and cardemon, then rice, generous bowls of chicken curry; papads, bubbly and golden brown, heaped high on plates, and salads and pickles made of mangoes, lemons and vegetables.

The men are served in the dining room. Three tables are joined to make one. Unus offers them soap and towels, and pours the warm water over their hands, from an imposing looking silver urn. They eat happily, hungrily, chaffing those whose helpings are thought to be too large, warning others whose manners are considered too good.

The table is cleared, table-cloths dusted, the table relaid; the women sit down to eat. The meal over, appetites quietened and bellies heavy, the various groups withdraw to their chosen quarters to relax with the ease and the informal familiarity of persons who know each other intimately.

Male conversation soon plunges into a discussion of affairs of business. The lawyer is much in demand and protests that he is not in his office and that he has made it a rule not to discuss legal business on holiday. Unus is particularly disturbed by an ejection order from the Community Development Board. Everybody agrees that it is evil, pernicious, inhuman. They do not have strong enough words to describe it. *"After 70 years of business! Seventy years of blood and sweat! Evil, evil."* They shake their heads. *"It is a sign of kayamuth"* (end of the world) an ageing uncle prophesises with the special kind of authority which comes to people given to much telling of beads. *"They will suffer, the Nasaras* (Christians). *They will burn in the fire of hell." "The pigs of lecherous brothers-in-law,"* a younger uncle contributes hotly. The politically conscious member of the family remarks, *"You can refuse to submit. You can refuse to move out." "And then what?"* another challenges.

"Go to gaol—satyagraha, passive resistance," the Congressite continues, with increasing excitement. *"Gandhi did it. Nehru did it. Dadoo and Naicker did it. Who are we to think the gaols too good for us? Nana Sita is doing it. That's it—gaol!"*

"Not easy," the same voice stubbornly persists. *"What do you get out of gaol?"*

"It is not what you get. It's what remains. Your dignity, your integrity as a

people." He waxes eloquently. The others are abashed and listen with respect. "*Do you know what Helen Suzman said to some conservatives who sought her advice? Give me a hundred Nana Sitas! One hundred Nana Sitas and there will be no Group Areas Act! We have only one Nana Sita,*" he sighs dejectedly.

The women have arranged themselves on the large four poster and the three single beds in Mrs Amod's bedroom. Some sit cross-legged, some recline and the younger sit on the edges. Budie Khala (big aunty) has spread out the various components of her *paan dabba* (betel leaf box) on her generous lap and is preparing *paans* to meet the voluminous demand. A child watches with fixed interest. Leisurely, Budie Khala stretches out a firm green leaf on silk clad knee, smears it white, with lime, sprinkles it, ochre with *katho*, scatters it finely with betelnut, garnishes it with cardemon and caraway seeds; then, expertly folds it into a triangular packet, nails it in place with a clove and ostentatiously directs the watching child to give it to his Gorie Ma-mie (fair aunty). One favour bequeathed, she goes on to serve the next and the careful ritual begins again and all the while she draws attention to herself and complains that she is valued for her paan alone and nobody cares for her for reasons other than that.

A four year old approaches her with outstretched chubby palm and a mumble "*For me too.*" "*Aw haw,*" Budie Khala laughs with pleasure. "*So you also want paan, he? Tell your father to open me a paan shop.*" And that provides a cue for a new diversion on the topic of paan and paan shops and the money to be made from such a venture. The popularity of Budie Khala's paan is finally confirmed beyond doubt, when Mohamed, the new Dublin returned Doctor, pushes his head through the doorway and joins the queue. A very special paan is made for him and Budie Khala chaffs, "*I thought that doctors were against paan—cancer, he cancer? Cancer my Anus! I never heard of cancer, until I came to South Africa—the old people never had cancer and they all eat paan!*"

"*Ask him now, ask him now,*" a frail little creature urges the plump old thing stretched out on the bed, with naked white feet and naked white ankles peeping out of her trouser. "*Yes, yes,*" she responds urgently, and heavily draws herself up. "*Ha Bhai, I have been troubled with this rash for months now,*" and her voice fills with the memory of pain, and tears gather in her eyes. "*Nothing seems to help. Bhai you see, and tell me what the trouble is. Tell me of some medicine I can use.*" The young man's smile is patronising. He expects such consultations and has already learnt that they do not pay him special tribute. He is a minor accident in the string of general practitioners and specialists already consulted. "*Itchy? hu?*" he asks expertly. "*What are you using?*" "*The last doctor gave me some pills and some lotion.*" She lifts her dress and extracts a phial and a tube from the pocket of her petticoat. "*But they don't help,*" she whines. Mohamed examines these elaborately. "*And what did he say?*" he asks. "*When do they say anything, these doctors? It is only a doctor of your own house who will examine and explain carefully. The others just look and give.*" Mohamed is almost flattered, almost tempted, but he withholds himself in time. *"This medicine is good. Keep on with it, and if the itching doesn't disappear, I'll send you a lotion I have at the hospital."*

Somebody quips that it is time he married. His return quip is not very funny, but everybody laughs. He leaves the women, his mouth, a bulge, his saliva, red. His mother usually quiet, now feels called upon to say something. She sighs: *"You know the children of today. You can take a horse to the river—you can't force it to drink."* She relaxes happily as all nod in vigorous agreement.

Somebody comes up with a consolation. *"Well at least he didn't yoke a White female and bring her along." "That is God's mercy,"* his mother sighs once again. *"You should have been in Bhanjee Bais' house that day,"* the new contributor continues, *"When they received news that her son in Dublin had married a White girl. It was like a funeral,"* and urged by the rest who don't know the details, she recounts with feelings of propriety how Bhanjee Bai had fainted with justifiable provocation and how with equally justifiable provocation, cursed her son and his children to be—and, with even greater provocation, had decreed that they were dead in her eyes. They click their tongues in sympathy with Bhanjee Bai, and wag them in malice against the son and the prostitute of a White woman who has misled him. *"She must have bewitched him,"* offers one. *"Ba—it is too risky to send children out to study,"* says another.

The children discover the well. Somebody removes the lid. Little bodies crowd round and lean over, mesmerized by the threatening emptiness which separates the water that appears to continue for miles. They throw out their voices, first one, then two, then three, then a chorus, and thrill as the voices come back to them—one, two, three, then a chorus. They take stones and drop them in, one by one, and wait in great awe for the sounds as they strike the water, and are relieved when they do. And all the while, each child feels himself falling down, down, down to the bottom of the well. *"Hey, you stupid rascals. Do you want to die?"* a shrill adult voice shatters their taut nerves. A child screams, another is plunged into tears. The spell is broken.

The young unmarried girls giggle and talk. Those engaged to be married are shy with importance. Others tease. They talk about clothes and films and marriage and about bad girls who talk to boys, and some that even have dates. *"Dates?"* they exclaim in horror. They then talk about schools, and studies, and ambitions.

And so the afternoon is spent, and the sky grows red with the setting of the sun and the evening is on them. The time has come for leave taking. Who knows when next they will meet, and of those gathered, how many.

Aw-Jaws (come agains) are exchanged. *"It is so nice here,"* the visitors compliment. *"It is jungle here,"* the hosts reply with suitable modesty. *"Next time don't pay us such a niggardly visit." "And you, when will you be coming?"* Promises are forced. Promises are made. Children are enticed to stay, children are scolded and secretly pinched, for taking such enticements seriously.

The doors are closed. Hands wave. The headlights burst open the dusty road. The parties leave, and the Amods close the door of their homestead, light the hurricane lamp, and suddenly feel empty, alone and exhausted.

!Unn/obe Morethlwa,
TOBACCO, SUGAR, ALCOHOL, AND COFFEE:
THESE THINGS HAVE TURNED US
INTO SLAVES

Botswana 1971   Ju/'hoansi

This account comes from a woman named !Unn/obe Morethlwa, who spoke on tape to me in 1971 in Kauri, Botswana, in that country's Northwest district. She had lived much of her earlier life in Ghanzi district to the south, first as part of a traditional hunting and gathering band, and later as a serf doing barely recompensed labor for Afrikaner farmers. From her perspective at outdoor kitchens and laundry lines behind the settlers' houses, she described these early ranchers and how they settled Ghanzi. She had lived for a while on a mission station as well, but rejected the religious teaching in favor of her own healing religion.

In 1971 !Unn/obe was living in a grass hut in the bush again, in the sixth decade of her life. She sustained herself as part of a socially traditional community by gathering wild foods and selling ostrich-eggshell beadwork to occasional tourists, who in those years and in that place numbered few more than two or three per year. Her people's isolation and hunting and gathering heritage were at that time increasingly under pressure, not only from white ranchers, but also from black Tswana and Herero pastoralists who wished to expand their cattle herds into the former San foraging areas.

!Unn/obe's perspective on changing times was informed by a great deal of experience on the boundaries between her own and the incoming societies, both black and white. She had all the ingredients for trenchant political analysis. She explained without rancor but with great clarity the process by which contact with the Ghanzi settlers gradually circumscribed her people's freedom. She said that what had "ruined" them were four things brought into her remote area by outsiders: tobacco, sugar, alcohol, and coffee. "These things have turned us into slaves," she said.

Megan Biesele

✦

When the white people had filled up Ghanzi, we then saw for the first time the things which came with them. We saw for the first time engines to draw up the water, and all the things that we had never seen until the white people came. The white people certainly have a lot of things!

But when the first whites came, they had to pound up and eat what the black people ate. They used digging sticks like ours at the beginning. They collected food and ate it. In fact, I came to know zan roots [used to sour milk distinctively for churning butter] through the Boers. They spoke, and we dug zan roots for them and pounded them and laid them out to dry. Then we'd churn and churn and churn with them, receiving only black coffee to drink for doing this. Then we'd churn and churn some more, and the butter would come, and they'd put it in bowls, put it in bowls, put it in bowls, and then they'd sit and drink the buttermilk and distribute some to us also.

Another portion of the milk they would refuse that we churn, because they wanted us to put it into their coffee for them to drink. When the empty tins were full, the Boers were finished with this work. The milk spent the night here, and the butter spent the night there. The water engine would stop and make a sound like "ko-ko-ko" but the cattle still drank. We Ju/'hoansi drew and drew and drew water by hand. We cranked and cranked until the trough was full and the cattle could come and drink. If there was no engine—uh-uh! A Bushman would do the work! Bushman worked hard! We, the red Bushmen, are the ones who did the work at that place, Ghanzi.

Women did the work of drawing the water. Women took care of the cattle. Women took care of the calves. Women took care of the sheep. Women took care for the horses. Women took care of the donkeys.

The men worked cutting the trees for poles and lumber and all kinds of wood uses. Men did this, and they milked the cows. The women were slower about getting up in the mornings, because they had no warm clothes. The Boers for whom we worked at that time are no longer in Ghanzi, as we sit here now. Then the word came to us, the word of Seretse [Seretse Khama, first president of Botswana]. The word was Ipelegeng [self-reliance]. Seretse said to the Boers, "White people, treat your employees nicely and with respect." When that word came down, they ran off. They are no longer over there in Ghanzi. There are only different Boers there now.

Transcribed and translated by Megan Biesele

Nongenile Masithathu Zenani,
A MAN HIDES FOOD FROM HIS FAMILY

South Africa 1972   isiXhosa

Nongenile Masithathu Zenani has achieved a considerable reputation as a prolific and consummate performer of *iintsomi* (*intsomi* is the Xhosa word for oral narrative; the plural is *iintsomi*), in which she interweaves and expands on the core stories handed down through oral tradition. Including in her repertoire the genealogical and epic accounts generally believed to have been typically performed by men (one of her performances has extended over seventeen days), she transgresses the conventional associations between gender and genre.

In this *intsomi*, performed and recorded in 1972 at her home in Nkanga in the Gatyana district of the Transkei, three story strands are drawn together. The tale focuses on the transition of a wife from her house of birth to her house of marriage, and on her establishment as a force for normalcy in her new homestead. When she discussed the story, Zenani argued that the husband is damaged by his irresponsibility. He becomes powerless in the same way that his family does. In the logic of the narrative, the husband is the drought; the wife is the instrument for change. Through offerings of food, the wife will move the husband toward plenty, toward normalcy. She takes over his functions.

With the help of her biological family, she establishes its influence in her husband's homestead. The food is, in this respect, an extension of the in-laws, a chain connecting the wife to her house of birth. The husband is seen as an adversary, a negative force to be brought into the framework of the house of birth. The move to the house of marriage is a move into a drought-stricken area where she and her children are at the mercy of her husband. Only when the presence of the house of birth is felt in the house of marriage is harmony achieved. The ties with the wife's house of birth are purposely broken by the husband: The food chain connecting the two houses is severed when he moves the food into the cave, sending the in-laws' representatives back to their homes. The kinship system will not allow this deception to prevail. The food represents the channel with the in-laws, and this channel must be kept open, or drought will destroy everything. The force of the wife must be formally and firmly established in the homestead of the husband.

The second and third parts of the story underscore these themes metaphorically, with fantasy characters coming to represent symbolically the husband's actions in the real world. They become poetic commentaries on the destructive activities of the husband who, in his selfishness and greed, breaks the marriage bond. This is a narrative of transition, a drama of conflicting powers; the final argument centers not so much on drought and plenty, or even responsibility and irresponsibility, though these are obviously involved. Rather, the narrative focuses primarily on the establishment of the presence of the in-laws in the house of marriage, for the protection of the woman and the children, and for the protection of the in-laws themselves. In the process, the role of the wife is emphasized.

Zenani was born in 1906. Her autobiography, recorded on 3 August 1976, may be found under the title "And So I Grew Up," in Patricia W. Romero, ed., *Life Histories of African Women* (1988).

Harold Scheub

✦

There were a woman and a man. It happened that this woman gave birth; she bore some children, including a boy. The children were of various ages, the boy a little older than the others.

Time passed then. Time passed at this home of theirs.

After some time had lapsed, the people ate the crops that they had cultivated. They harvested the crops. Then winter came—and these activities were all repeated.

During all these times, that woman lived happily with her husband.

Time passed, years followed years, and eventually there came a season of drought. Everything was parched. The trees lost their leaves; rivers dried up. And as the rivers dried up, it became obvious that there was nothing to eat. People resorted to eating old food: pit corn was dug out of the corn pits; sour food was now being eaten. Some of the pit corn had maggots in it, it was so old. And the people were not fond of it. They would sometimes develop stomachaches, caused by the corn that was three or four years old—it had finally rotted in the pits. Yo! What will be done with this corn?

The man of this homestead had some livestock—some milk cows, a few milk goats. There were corresponding calabashes for the stock, a separate calabash for the goat milk, called "the calabash for children." And the calabash for cows' milk was called "the calabash for the older people," the mother and father. Milk would be poured on the pit corn. Or the pit corn, having been ground up, would be cooked, then milk would be added. On another day, to give their stomachs a break from the pit corn that was so old and rotten, they would shift to milk.

Time passed in that way, and the family continued to eat these rotten mealies. Time passed, time passed, and this man regularly went out to herd his livestock. But whenever he saw some people, he would go to them, leaving the cattle behind. He would go to them, greet them, and they would converse, discussing the drought.

"This is awful for us, too."

"We've stopped eating those bitter mealies."

"The food has rotted. It's developed maggots."

"Now we're eating roots."

The man asked, "What are these roots?"

They told him about the root: "Well, it's something that's dug up in the pasture."

"Then it's roasted and put into the hearth. But you can eat it when it's raw too."

"But it really should be roasted, so that it settles well in the stomach. A fire should be kindled, and it should be roasted to remove the rawness."

"When it's cooked, its quality as a plant comes to an end."

The man asked them to point out the roots to him, because over there at his home starvation was imminent. All they had was milk. Milk was the only thing they had in their stomachs. It was as if one drank milk and nothing else: "No matter what one pours the milk over, it's as if one has eaten only milk. He tastes nothing else."

When the conversation was at an end, the people helped the man to find some roots.

One of them said, "There's one!"

They showed him where it was, so that he might dig it up himself.

One of them said, "Dig it up."

Then they told him to taste it, to see what it was like, so that he would be able to identify it.

All day he dug these roots, and at last he was able to identify them properly. And he began to dig for other roots. He put them into a bag. He had a goatskin bag that he had tanned and provided with some pockets. In the pockets of the goatskin bag were places for putting things, one could force them into the pockets. That is what he did.

At length, these roots were a bundle, and he put them down. Then, when it was time to go home, he turned the cattle around. He went home, and, when he got there, he put the cattle into the kraal.

His child, this boy, said, "Mama! Mama, look! What's Father carrying?"

His mother said, "What is he carrying, my child?"

"He's carrying something. But I don't know what it is. He's carrying something on his shoulder. Maybe he's bringing some corn."

His mother said, "Mhm! I wonder where he got them from, my child?"

They sat in hope, constantly looking out at him. He put the cattle into the kraal, and, when he emerged from the kraal, he went into the house.

He dropped the load.

"Nobani, kindle the fire."

"Mhm?"

"Please kindle the fire so that the children can have something to eat. How have things gone today?"

His wife said, "We've been hungry all day. Even my breasts are dry. Nothing comes out of them because I'm so hungry."

"Kindle, kindle the fire, Wife. You'll be satisfied today."

The wife got up and got some firewood, and she built the fire. Then the man uncovered his load, he poured the contents out on the ground. He divided these things, he divided them, saying, "These on this side are yours. They're for you and the children," and he snuggled the roots into the hearth. He showed his wife and son how they were to be roasted. They continued to push the roots into the hearth. When they had been properly put into the hearth, the roots would whistle. Then they would burst. The members of the family would take them out, allow them to cool, then they would eat them.

This went on, day after day. Soon, the threat of starvation had been alleviated. When they drank milk, they drank it when it had been poured over these roots.

Whenever this man left home, he would dig for these roots. Whenever he herded cattle, he would dig for roots. Every day, he dug up these roots.

So it went. A month came to an end; a second month appeared. The family was beginning to feel that "Really, these roots aren't corn."

"This is a plant."

The root began to be felt in the stomach. It began to show evidence that "I am not really corn. Even though I'm eaten, I'm just a plant." And that plant became tiresome. But there was nothing that could be done about it because it did remove the feeling of giddiness that the hunger caused.

The wife said, "Sobani, please go to the home of my birth." She said, "There's never been this kind of starvation at my home. Many crops are cultivated there—corn and pumpkins, beans are grown there, millet is grown. And because so many things are cultivated, it's unlikely that there's nothing left over there. I'm a nursing mother, so I cannot go. Please go for me, my husband. Go to my home."

The husband said, "But Nobani, with whom will I leave the cattle?"

His wife said, "I'll just put my child on my back. I'll find time to go and herd while you're gone. I can't herd the cattle for the entire day, but I'll do it part of the time. This boy and I will help each other. Now please go! I have a little baby here. I can't go. We'll all die because of this hunger."

The man journeyed then. He got up the following morning and did what his wife had asked. He went to his in-laws' place. He traveled; he walked and arrived at his in-laws' place. When he got there, he knocked at the door and greeted them.

They responded, asking where he had come from.

He said that he had come from his home, that he had been sent here "by my wife. She said, Father-in-law, that I should come here to her home. My wife has given birth to a child, and the starvation is about to kill her—it's especially difficult for her because she has just given birth. Her child is also in danger of starving. In that entire land of ours, no one visits anyone else anymore. All we do is eat roots that are dug up on the veld. They're put into the hearth and roasted. We've been eating roots for two months now. And we've come to realize that this root is only a plant; it's not corn."

The mother-in-law and her companions were concerned. "Yo! How could she give birth while she was starving? Well, you'll return to your home in the morning."

His sisters-in-law were there, and there were some young men there too, and boys; his father-in-law was there and his mother-in-law.

"You can go back tomorrow. The young women will accompany you."

Before the husband went to sleep, a beast was slaughtered for him there at his in-laws' place. He gorged himself. He kept one side of the beast, from the foreleg to the hindleg. He kept that. He would take it home with him. He would take it to his own homestead.

At dawn the next day, the man was ready to go home. Various things were prepared for his journey: he was given corn, beans, and millet, all in equal quantities. And there was also the whole side of meat.

When everything was ready, when the food had been prepared, the husband said, "Mother," speaking to his mother-in-law, the mother of his wife.

His mother-in-law responded.

He said, "We're also lacking a pot over there at my home. The one we used to have is broken. My wife asked if you would lend her one. And, because of the problem of starvation, there isn't even any salt. We use salt on nothing now. Please give her some salt, too."

All this was done for the husband. He was given some salt; he was given a large quantity of salt that would last a long time. And he was given a small pot. These things were tied into three bundles so that he would be able to carry them more easily.

He was accompanied by the young women. They helped him to carry his load. They were told to accompany him right to his home.

He traveled with those young women, walking to his home. There was a river that had to be crossed. When they got to the river, the husband said, "Well, my in-laws . . ."

The young women answered, "Brother-in-law?"

"Please stop here, my in-laws. Stop. Really, it's all right now. Just turn around and return to your home. I'm fairly close to my own home now. You don't have to accompany me further. Just take these loads to the other side of the river and deposit them over there. Then you can turn back. I saw the amount of work that has to be done over there at your own house, work that you're needed for. Now I've left the land of my in-laws. The country on the other side of the river is mine. I'll tie the bundles together and carry all three of them myself. I won't be laughed at for carrying such a big load, not on that side of the river—because, really, I was born in that country. Turn around, my in-laws."

These young women said, "How can you go home carrying such a big load? What will our sister say? She'll wonder why we left you, why we didn't help you to carry such a burden."

The man said, "No, my in-laws, really, I cannot accept further help. I have already been assisted greatly by you. And because of that, no one can say anything negative about my in-laws. Turn around, go back."

The young women turned around then, and he remained there. When the women had disappeared in the distance, this fellow took the three bundles, one at a time. He began by taking the corn. He ran with the bundle. He hurried with the corn and went into a forest—there was a forest not far from his homestead. He got to the forest; there was a little cliff there. He looked around for a cave. He found one, then put the load down in it. When he had put the load of corn into the cave, he returned; he went to pick up the load of beans. Again he ran, and he put the beans into the cave also. Then he returned once more. The load of meat and the load of millet were still there at the side of the river. He ran and put these into the cave as well.

When he had satisfied himself that all was well, he thought, "I'll just go back and pick up the pot and the salt."

He returned to the river. Then he ran and put those things in the cave.

When he got back to the cave, he began his first task. He took the millet, then looked for a stone. He ground the millet thoroughly. He ground it, he ground it. Then he moistened it with water and molded it into little loaves—the loaves were the same size as roots, the roots that are dug up in the pasture. He took eight of these loaves, and put them into the fire. Then he cut the meat and roasted it in the fire. He roasted it, he roasted it, and he ate quite a lot of it—until he was sated. Then he took the little pot. He went to the river and dipped water. He returned. He drank this water. When he was finished, he departed.

The sun was setting now. There he is, going toward his home—and he was not carrying even one of those things that he had been given by his in-laws. He had left all that food behind in the cave.

When he was fairly close to his home, he looked about for roots. He dug them up. He dug, he dug these roots. Then he took them to his home, and he threw them down near his wife.

He said, "Yo! You made such a fool of me! Sending me so far! And for nothing. They're really starving over there. Yo, they're starving. They're really starving! They have nothing to eat at all. They eat roots. There's nothing, nothing at your home! You sent me there for nothing. I looked like a fool! So I just went about, scavenging along the road." So saying, he threw the roots down, then brought the cattle into the kraal.

His wife said, "Didn't you even get some millet at my home?"

He said, "No."

"Weren't there even some grains of corn?"

"No, there was nothing."

"Not even a few beans?"

"No."

"Didn't you even get a pot at my home?"

"No."

"This is a sad affair." The wife sat down. "My hopes have been foiled. I did not think that you would return home with nothing. I hoped there would be some relief."

Time passed. She kindled a fire. These roots sizzled. They were snuggled into the hearth and roasted.

As for the husband, he put his "roots" [millet loaves] on his own side of the hearth. But his wife caught their scent.

"What kind of roots are those? They have a peculiar smell. And why don't your roots whistle? What's the matter with them, Sobani?"

Her husband was evasive. "Well, really, your roots are of the variety that belongs to women. Mine are the kind that belongs to men. The two kinds are not the same. Yours—well, you know that you tend to char them badly. That's the reason for the difference. You women overheat them. They get burned on the outside and aren't cooked on the inside. We men put ours under the ashes."

His wife was quiet. This fellow ate his roots, eight of them.

Again, his wife said, "Ee, Sobani! Why is it that your roots don't crunch when you chew them? Yours are quiet; ours crunch!"

"What's the matter with this woman? I tell you, you must remember that you women overheat the roots, then take them off the fire while they're still raw. Mine get well-cooked. I put them in the hearth, then pile on the coals so that the roots become nice and soft."

His wife was quiet.

The next morning, the fellow took his cattle out to the veld, leaving his family behind, hungry. They had to resort to drinking milk. This fellow went off, and when he was a distance away, the wife said to the boy, "My child!"

The child: "Hmm?"

"Have you noticed that your father hasn't roasted as many roots for himself since his return from my home? Since the day he got back, there's been a change in the amount of roasting that he does. He just roasts two roots. What does he eat? Sometimes he doesn't even drink milk. And milk is plentiful at home now. What is your father eating?"

The child said, "I don't know."

She said, "Your father is eating something. Now you stay here for a while with the baby." So she said to the boy, who took the child and remained there at home with it.

The woman traveled. She walked and walked, keeping to the shadows. She went over there to the mountains, far in the distance. She looked carefully, going to the places where the man usually herded the cattle.

Then she saw him—and she noted that he was looking around. He was looking around furtively. He ran then and disappeared in a cave.

The woman came away from the mountains, then went back another way. She arrived, and when she got there she saw smoke coming from inside the cave. She stood at the outside and heard someone saying, "Be on the lookout, my penis cover! Is anyone coming? Is anyone coming?" Then she heard the sounds of grinding. And she knew that he was grinding.

The woman looked around for a rock, a big round rock that would stay in a track, that would be certain to hit him, to smash him over there. She aimed the rock—the woman knew that meat was being roasted inside the cave, she could tell by the smell. So she rolled the rock, she kept it straight in its course. She rolled it, and the stone flew over there to the place where the man was roasting the meat.

Suddenly the man heard something in front of him—*nqhoooooooo!* He was startled. He ran, leaving his clothes behind. He fled—naked! And whenever he looked back—Yo! This rock! Here was this rock, "coming straight at me!" He ran; he ran and ran. He looked back each time he crossed a river, and— "Yo! This rock! Here's this rock, coming straight at me!" The man ran, and the sun went down, and he was still being pursued by the rock.

In the meantime, this woman went into the cave, and when she got there: "Oh, here's meat! And here is corn! And beans! Millet! And here's the pot!"

The woman took these things. She made several trips. She traveled with those foods, a bundle at a time—walking with them, going to her home with them. She arrived, put the bundle down, then went back to get another. And she put that one down, then went back to get yet another. And she put that one down too.

She sat. And when she saw that the sun was going to set, the woman took some corn and cooked it. When it was cooked, she took it off the fire. She ground it, then poured milk over it for her children.

And they ate.

Then she put the pot over there, in the house. The woman did not hide these things—she carefully put them in the upper part of the house, in full view, so that her husband would see them when he came in.

The woman cut the meat into pieces, put the pieces into a pot, and cooked them. The meat was cooked.

And they ate it.

She and her children finished the meat, and she took the bones and put them in the upper part of the house. She did not hide them. She wanted them to be seen.

The great man arrived after the sun had set. He was driving his cattle. He closed them up in the kraal, then returned to the house. He returned, bruised —he had lacerations on his feet, his legs, everywhere, even on the thighs. He had been scratched by trees, pricked by things as he fled from that rock, as he ran and stumbled. His feet were in pain, and he was limping.

His wife said, "What's the matter? Why are you limping? What has happened?"

"No, no, I was looking for the cattle and couldn't find them, that's all."

"What happened to the cattle?"

"They just wandered off. They went to graze far off. I was looking for them."

"Oh, and you got all scratched up like that just because you were looking for the cattle?"

"Yes."

"Oh."

She took a dish and dipped out some corn for the children; they ate the corn, and so did the woman. This fellow poured out his roots, and his wife said, "Just eat those roots of the kind that belongs to you, to men! My children and I will just eat the kind that belongs to women. As I was going about seeking food, hungry, I found some roots of the kind that belongs to women. You eat yours. You eat the kind that belongs to men!"

The man had a problem. What could he do about this? Here in the house, he could see all the things that he had hidden away in the cave. But he could not understand how his wife could have found them. And he was afraid: he feared that his father-in-law and others of his in-laws would hear about this. What would they say? After all, he had come to them with a special plea for food for his wife. Then he had not given her any.

This fellow was silent.

After a long time, in the morning, he was hungry, and he said, "Oh, Nobani, won't you give me just a spoonful, to satisfy my heart?"

She said, "Never! Not until you bring back to me the thing I sent you for, the thing you were to have brought from my home! Not until you learn to give me a full account of what happened, and say things were like this and like that. Then I'll give you something to eat. Then I'll share those things with you. But until then—never!"

So he sat there, suffering, unable to eat anything at all.

Time passed.

Time passed in that way for this fellow, and he was very hungry. The others in the house went on eating His wife and children continued to eat this fine food, without ever once giving him any. He was hungry. He lost weight: hungry, drinking only milk, eating roots and nothing more, eating resin from mimosa trees and nothing else, fighting with the monkeys over that resin—that is all he had.

After a while, a long while, it became clear that the supply of food at home was diminishing.

Then it was gone.

One day, this man was walking, herding his cattle in the usual way, eating this resin, and he found that the mimosa trees had been cleaned out. He had been constantly rifling through the trees, combing through them for resin. The day before, he had gone through these trees, and some days before that, and now today as well. The resin had no chance to grow, to ooze out. And the man was getting hungrier and hungrier, a little hungrier each time he looked for the food. He walked a great distance, seeking resin, finding none. He traveled all day.

Finally, he came upon a tree that contained an abundance of resin. But there was something that was clinging to it, something that was clinging to the mimosa tree.

He said to it, "Get down! Who are you, clinging to this resin? Get down. Let me get some of it!"

The thing said, "I'll never come down! Who are you?"

Again this fellow tried because he could see that the resin was plentiful here. He knew that he would be satisfied, if only he could get to the resin. He went to some other trees in the area. He went to other trees, but then he returned.

He looked closely at this thing.

He said, "Say, Friend! I told you to get down from there, so that I can get some of this resin."

The thing said, "No one has ever made me get down."

Again, he said, "Come down from that tree. If you do, I'll let you suckle on this cow of my home. Look, that one with the big teats. If you'll come down, I'll carry you on my back."

The thing said, "Nobody carries me! I'm The-Clinger-I'll-Cling-to-You! That is my name, and I can cling to you too!"

The man said, "No, my friend, please come down."

It was getting late. The sun was about to set. It was time for him to return to his home with his cattle. But the man was vexed by hunger pangs, and he was afraid to go home. He was hungry. He wondered how he would be able to go to sleep in such a state.

So he again begged, "Yo, Friend! Please come down. I'll let you suckle on this cow—you'll be satisfied; the cow is in milk." This fellow said that. Then he went and brought a cow from among the cattle. He brought the beast close, holding the cow, saying, "Look! Look, this cow is in milk! Come down!"

The thing said, "I told you that I've never been made to come down."

"Come down, Friend! I'll carry you! Please come to me. I'll carry you— just let me get some of that resin. Please, it's getting late."

"I'm The-Clinger-I'll-Cling-to-You! And I can cling to you too! All right, I'll come down."

The man turned his back. He turned his back to this thing. He moved toward it backwards, moving with his back toward the thing. Then he removed his garment. The thing detached itself from the tree, and it clung to the man's back; it clung to his back. It held on tightly with its claws. It had long claws; it held on with its claws. It had four legs, and its claws sank into the man's flesh. They sank into his flesh. The thing clung to this man.

The man said, "Get down. Get off my back! Get down, get down! Get down! Get down! Yo yo yo! I'm dying! Get down!"

The thing said, "I told you that I should not be carried! I am The-Clinger-I'll-Cling-to-You! You told me to get down from that tree!"

The man traveled then, a crumpled figure—powerless. This thing was trying to destroy him; its claws had disappeared into his flesh. Its claws seemed to be reaching to his very liver and lungs, reaching inside him. He was doubled up as he walked. He was scarcely able to walk at all as he drove his cattle. He moved slowly, and he had not even eaten any resin. The thing had come down from the tree. It had detached itself from the tree and then with its claws attached itself to the man—so that he was unable to eat the resin. This thing was causing him intense pain.

The man drove his cattle. He went home with them.

As he was coming along, his wife said, "What's the matter with this man today? Why is he walking so slowly, doubled up like that?"

The boy appeared, and he said, "I don't know what's the matter with him. He's so doubled up! I don't know what's the matter with him."

"Yo!" said the wife. "He really has peculiar habits. Knotted up like that. What's the matter with him?"

In time, the man entered; he came into the house, bent over in pain. He sat in the room, but he did not come close to the others that day—he sat at a distance.

His wife said, "What's the matter? Why are you sitting so far away from us? What's the matter now?"

"No, no, nothing's the matter."

"Are you cold?"

"No, I'm not cold."

"Oh! How can you not be cold? It's not hot, yet you're not cold!"

"No, I'm not cold."

The man continued to sit over there, and the others ate their corn.

Then the wife said, "Why don't you roast your roots? Here's the fire."

"No, really, I'm not hungry."

"Oh, what have you eaten?"

"I ate some resin from the trees."

His wife said, "Oh, is it your practice to fill yourself with nothing but resin? Without roasting roots?"

"No, no, I'm full."

His wife did not bother him further. But when they went to sleep that night, it was clear that something was on this man.

While he slept, he kept saying, "Mmmh! Mmh! Mmmmmh! Mmmmmh!"

His wife said, "Sobani! Sobani!"

"Mm?"

"What's the matter?"

"What are you talking about? I'm only dreaming."

"What is the matter? Why are you making such a noise? Why this groaning? What's the problem? Where are you aching?"

"No, I'm not aching at all! I'm just stretching."

"Mh!"

"Nothing's wrong."

"Oh."

Time passed for them, and when it was morning he got up and departed. It was difficult for him to get up. He was doubled up. He walked off slowly to let the cattle out of the kraal. And his wife and child stared at him. He walked away, going to herd the cattle. So time passed for him.

His wife said to the little boy, "My child, please follow your father. Observe him. Find out what is wrong with him. He has become such a stiff thing! Watch him. See if you can discover what it is he's hiding. But don't let him know why you're following him. Just go."

The child went. He walked over there with his father.

"Go home! Go home, Child. Go home."

"No, Father. I'll turn the cattle and keep them from straying."

"Go! Go, my child. Go home. You must be hungry."

"No, Father, I'm not hungry."

The man left him alone. The boy went about repeatedly, herding the cattle. Whenever his father disappeared somewhere, the boy would watch him. The child observed him when the man disappeared to one side. He watched as his father let his garment fall, as he exposed his shoulders.

He said, "Please come down, Friend! Please come down! Come, let me suckle you. Here's some milk! Yo! You're killing me!"

The thing said, "I told you that I'm The-Clinger-I'll-Cling-to-You! I'm not to be carried on the back!"

As soon as he saw the thing that was on his father, the child ran. He headed for home. He arrived there and went to his mother.

"Mama! I've seen the thing that's on Father! He's got something that's monstrous! It's on his back! He keeps saying, 'Come down, Friend! I'm dying! Get down! It's painful!' And that thing says to my father, 'I told you! I said that I'm not to be carried on the back! I'm The-Clinger-I'll-Cling-to-You!' Father's all swollen! The thing that is clinging to Father is causing him pain!"

The mother of the child said, "Be quiet, my child. Don't speak of this again."

The child sat then, and the man herded his cattle the whole day, not realizing that his secret had been discovered. Because of the pain, he was no longer even digging up roots. He was bent over. He went home. He took the cattle home. When he arrived, he shut the cattle in the kraal, then went to the house. He sat down.

His wife dipped out some corn and ate. When she had eaten her corn, she gave some to her children. And they ate.

"Why don't you roast the roots?" she asked. "Why don't you eat over there on your side of the hearth?"

The man said, "No, I'm full."

"What are you full of?"

"Resin."

"Oh, what kind of resin is this, that you're full day after day? You don't eat here at all."

"No, there's nothing."

"Why are you so doubled up? You can't walk properly! You even have difficulty wrapping yourself in your cape! You can't make your bed! What's gripping you? What part of your body is aching?"

"No, there's nothing wrong with me! There's nothing wrong with me!"

"Mm?"

"There's nothing wrong with me!"

The woman closed the door and said, "You're going to tell me what's wrong with you! What is the matter with you?"

The man lacked strength because of what this thing was doing to him, so he gave in at last, and said, "Well, Nobani, just sit down here. I'll tell you."

His wife sat.

"I was eating resin, Nobani. And while I was eating it, I suddenly saw something that was clinging to me. This thing had attached itself to me. It clawed me. It refused to get down. It tortured me. Now I'm swollen. This thing is painful—it's painful!"

"When did this happen?"

"Yo! On some day or other."

"Why didn't you tell me about it? What's this all about? How can it be that you took such a creature from a tree? You worthless thing! You low person! I send this miserable thing to my home, and it proceeds to eat the food in a secret cave! And now, you go about getting these things from trees and putting them on your body! What kind of brain is that? Now uncover yourself. Let's see this thing."

The wife uncovered him and found that her husband was badly swollen —with this weird thing clinging to him, sinking its claws into him. This thing was alive.

The woman said to the thing, "Get down! Get out of here!"

The thing said, "I will not come down! I have said that I'm The-Clinger-I'll-Cling-to-You!"

"Yo!"

The woman wondered what she should do. Her husband would die at the hands of this thing. She boiled some oil, she boiled some oil. She heated it. She heated the oil, and it was very very hot.

Then she said, "Get down!"

The man uncovered himself, and the woman quickly poured the oil. She poured hot oil on this thing.

Yo! The thing now began to peel off. It peeled off along with the man's flesh. Then it fell to the ground. The woman killed it and threw it outside. Then she began to heal her husband, and he became well again.

When the man was healed, the wife repeatedly assailed him for the things he had done, those despicable things.

This man went out and again herded his cattle as he had in the past—herding the cattle, digging roots.

One day, something said to him, "Please give me a root."

It turned out to be a person who had only one arm.

The man looked at this person, and said, "What's happened to this person, a person with only one arm who goes about saying that he should be given a root? What kind of person is this? He has only one side!"

The thing said, "You too could come to have only one side! Just give me some roots. I am unable to dig for roots."

This fellow refused. He said, "Go on! I don't have time for that!"

He said, "Come and sit by me. You'll see better that I have no arm."

The man approached, and when he came near to this creature: "Oh, this person does resemble a human being, except that he has only one arm, there's only one eye! One leg! And the thing doesn't move from this place! He has only one finger on his hand, one finger with a long nail!"

The man squatted then and dug for roots. And this thing suddenly moved its nail, and ripped off the man's rectum, throwing it over there.

It threw the man's rectum over there.

This fellow said, "Yo! Dear friends, what is this that I've come to now? What will my wife think of me?"

Then he ran. He headed over there—and his rectum was making a noise: "Hooooooo! Hoooooooooo!" Each time he took a step: "Hooooooo!" When he ran, his rectum moaned: "Wo wo wo wo wo!" And when he stood still: "Wooooooooo!" And when he ran: "Wo wo wo wo!"

He said, "What am I to do now? And my wife! Today I am bringing yet another problem to her. She just finished with that other thing that was on me!"

This fellow took his garment then. He took his cape and tore one side of it. He stuffed it into his rectum. He stuffed it—stuffing it, molding it into the shape of a rectum. And he put it where his rectum should have been. He made it firm, so that it would stop making this noise. Then he went on his way.

Again, as he neared home, he heard the sound: "Wooooooo!" So he again stuffed a part of his garment into his rectum. "Wo wo wo wo wo!" He tore the garment once more, the cape gradually diminishing in size because he had been tearing and stuffing it. That thing was heard making the noise, and again he tore the garment and stuffed it into his rectum.

"Well, my cape is getting smaller."

The garment was indeed getting smaller, and finally there was only enough material left for settling on his shoulders, then the neck—it was as if it were a mere scarf now. The fellow went on his way and arrived at his home. He put the livestock into the kraal.

His child said, "Mama! Mama! Just look at Father! He has no clothes! He's naked!"

His mother said, "What's the matter with him now?"

"Just look at him!"

His mother appeared in the doorway.

"Well, what's the matter with this man? Why is he naked?"

The man secured the livestock in the kraal, but he was afraid to go to the house—afraid of his wife. So he tarried, moving about here and there on the outside. He did that until it was dark, then he went into the house. As he was entering, his wife said, "What's the matter with you? Why are you naked? What has happened to your clothes?"

"Well, this is how it happened. While I was rounding up the cattle, I got caught on a tree stump. My clothes were torn and were left behind there. Then, when I was chasing the cattle at another place, my cape tore and remained in a thicket over there, among thorny trees. I was pricked by those thorns. The shrubs clung to the garment. My clothes were ruined!"

The woman said, "Heeee! I'll find out about this! I'll find out what kind of man we have here! This is a strange man that we've got here in this house. I can't understand him."

Time passed for this woman, and the man went to sleep. The woman loaned him a garment, and he went to sleep.

In the morning, she took the garment back, and said, "Go, go with that rag of yours!"

When the husband had taken the livestock out and he was going down the hill below the kraal: "Wooooooooooooo!"

His wife said, "What's making that noise?" She and the child listened.

The cattle were very troublesome that day, straying this way and that. The man frequently had to run to turn them around, to bring them back. As he rounded up the cattle on this side, as he pursued them, this thing would make that noise: "Wo wo wo wo!" with each step that he took.

She said, "Heeee! Something's moaning, it's coming from this man! This is a mystery!"

The man went on. He gradually brought the livestock together. He herded the cattle; he herded and herded. Then he went to that thing.

He went over there and found that thing sitting—that person with one arm, with one eye, one leg, the person with one finger on his hand—and one long nail.

"Hello there, sir."

"Yes?"

"Please give me back my rectum. My clothing is finished."

The thing said, "Come here so that you can see me better, so that you can see that I'm a human being. Because when you're standing over there, you can't see so well. Please come here."

The man said, "When I came close to you before, you tore off my rectum. And now my clothes are gone. I ask you to give me back my rectum."

The thing said, "I said, please come here."

But this fellow refused to approach. He was in great pain because of this thing.

He went and herded his cattle. In time, he turned them around and went home. All the while, his rectum kept making that noise. And he stuffed it with cloth, again tearing off a piece of what remained of his garment. He stuffed it into his rectum; he stuffed it, he stuffed it.

Finally, he came to his home. He closed the cattle in the kraal, then went to the house. The woman closed the door behind him. He stood there in the doorway.

She said, "Now tell me, what's making that noise? You're going to tell me about it today!"

Her husband said, "Mhmm! This is what happened to me, Nobani. While I was digging roots the other day, I encountered someone. Now this person told me to give him some roots. I said that I had none, but he kept begging me. I asked him who he was. And he told me to approach so that I could see that he was really a person. I went to him, and while I was digging, he suddenly ripped off my rectum! But this person wasn't a proper human being! He had only one arm, one leg. He had one hand, one finger—with one long nail. Now, when I left that place, my rectum began to make a noise. So I tore off a piece of this garment, and that's how it came to be finished."

"Oh!"

"Yes."

"All right then, this is what you must do. Give me your garment," said his wife, "and I'll take the cattle out tomorrow morning. You remain behind. And if you should happen to go out of the house, pretend to be some other person. Loan me your garments, and your knitted hat, and that bag of yours, the stick for digging roots."

"Oh!"

Well then, the next day, in the morning, the wife went about the business very purposefully, taking a stick, taking an axe, the digging stick, the man's clothing, his knitted hat, the bag into which the roots would be put. And the woman went on her way, taking the cattle out to the pasture.

The woman traveled, going out with the oxen in the customary way. When she had gone off with the cattle, she herded them out there on the veld.

She had said to her husband, "Don't come along." He was to keep his distance, and he did indeed stay far behind.

She traveled. The woman went ahead. She walked a long way, herding these cattle, walking, digging for the roots, until she finally came within sight of this thing. When she saw it, she continued walking, digging, getting closer and closer to it, approaching it little by little.

This thing said, "Just give me a root."

The woman said, "Oh, who are you to say that I should give you a root?"

The thing said, "Please come here. Come to me, and see for yourself. You'll see that I'm a person, and you'll know me and give me some roots."

The woman said, "Well, I know that you're a person. I can see that. As for the roots that I've been digging up—I've got responsibilities. I need them for my family at home. I didn't dig them up for you. But I'll give them to you on one condition—that you not insist upon them, that you not demand them forcefully."

This thing said, "All right, I won't demand them forcefully. I say to you, please give me those roots."

The woman said, "I'll give them to you if you follow my custom. You must turn around and ask for them with your back toward me. And I too, I'll respond to you with my back toward you. We'll approach each other in that way. Then, when I get to you, I'll turn around and face you."

So this thing turned around. Its back was toward her. The woman watched carefully.

The thing said, "I say, give me those roots."

The woman walked slowly, and she said, "Yes, I'll give you the roots when you ask me for them, when you beg me. I'm digging them up for the people of my home who are in dire need of food."

The thing said, "I'm in dire need, too. I'm very hungry. But I don't have a digging stick."

The woman said, "I have a digging stick. If you follow my custom, I'll give you roots."

This thing said, "I'll follow your custom."

Little by little, she was getting nearer.

"I'll follow your custom, yes."

The woman said, "When I hit against you with my back, I'll go around to the front of you. Only then can you have the roots."

The thing said, "All right, fine. Hit against me; let it happen. Hit against me, behind me, then I'll see you finally when you come around to the front."

The woman came to the thing in that way—it still had its back to her. But she came straight to it. She did not turn her back to it. She did not move backward as she had said she would. But it had its back to her, not looking at her, not seeing her.

When she got to this thing, she cut off its head. With a cutter, with the axe that she was carrying.

And she found her husband's rectum, just sitting there. The thing was not being especially careful to guard the rectum, so desperate was it to get the roots.

She took the rectum, then called her husband.

The thing was dead.

She said, "Sobani! Sobani!"

The man responded.

She said, "Come and see where you left your rectum."

The man came, running hard. He arrived and found that the thing was dead. His wife was now carrying this rectum in her hand. She pulled the rags from her husband's buttocks and replaced his rectum. It fit tightly. Then she threw the rags away, and they left that creature there. They returned to their home. They went, going home with the cattle, going together now, looking for roots.

The man said, "Yo! My wife, you've really helped me! It's not the first time either. You've been helping me for a long time! But today, I've learned my lesson. I'll never go near such a thing again. All day, I've been remembering the time I was pursued by that stone that you threw at me when I returned from my in-laws'. I returned deceitfully, hiding the food that had been prepared for you. I also recall the day when I was almost dead of hunger because of what I had done. Then I peeled off The-Clinger-I'll-Cling-to-You from the resin, and it settled on my back. I groaned with it for a whole year. I was in great pain! Then, today, I was called by a thing that was lying on the ground, a thing that I did not recognize, a thing that demanded that I give it roots. In that situation, too, I was helped by you. I shall never go against your commands again, my wife."

Time passed, and they came to their home. When they got home, they closed up the cattle and went into the house. They roasted the roots; they drank milk.

The man was ingratiating himself with his wife now. He did not want these things to be mentioned—the things that he had done, the things that had happened to him. In particular, he did not want his in-laws to learn of his actions, of the contemptible things that he had been doing.

Again and again, he said, "My wife, don't mention that, please!"

His wife said, "I'm really disgusted with you. I loathe you because—"

"No! No, don't talk about that!"

So they were happy. The man began to have confidence in her because the woman had more brains than he had.

Transcribed and translated by Harold Scheub

Gladys Thomas, FALL TOMORROW

South Africa 1972   English

Poet, dramatist, and short-story writer, Gladys Thomas was born to Dorothy Adams (née Claythorne) and John Adams in 1935 in Salt River, Cape Town. Upon completion of primary school she worked in a factory until she married. As the child of an interracial union, Thomas's identity as a "Coloured" was to become significant for her passage as a writer in South Africa. Also important would be her marriage to a man whose political and literary activity would intensify her experience of apartheid. (Albert Thomas was detained under the Terrorism Act for his involvement in an underground movement, the Coloured People's Congress.)

Thomas's sensitivity to the pain and suffering around her, however, made her an activist in her own right. She regularly participated in protest marches, was detained for chaining herself to the gates of parliament, and shared the stage with now-prominent political figures like Trevor Manuel of the African National Congress.

The poem reprinted here is, among other things, an inspired condemnation of the Group Areas Act of 1950 and its numerous amendments, which removed people from their homes and displaced nonwhites to barren and isolated areas. Thomas said in a recent interview that the poem was written in a single train ride: "I didn't know I could write but when the Group Areas Act forced our family out of Simonstown . . . I wrote 'Fall Tomorrow' in retaliation." Simonstown—the seaside town in which Thomas and her family lived, and in which Albert Thomas had been born—was declared a white group area, and all nonwhites had to leave. Those classified as "Coloured" were moved to an area called Ocean View, which, despite its name, offered only a view of endless "seas of sand." The term "yellow monsters" refers to the bulldozers that were used to overrule any refusal to leave; local children tried to defy them by destroying houses before they could be bulldozed. These same children, Thomas says today, are among those "living lost lives."

"Fall Tomorrow" originally appeared in 1972 in a volume called *Cry Rage!* along with several of her other poems and a larger number by James Matthews. As Thomas said, "Poems were real weapons." The government's perception of the threat they represented resulted in the banning of *Cry Rage!* in 1973. It was the first book of poetry to be banned in South Africa.

Through the 1970s and 1980s Thomas continued to write poetry, fiction, and reportage, winning literary awards. In 1978 she was included on the Kwanzaa list of black women writers noted for opposing apartheid in their writing, and in 1983 she received a fellowship at Iowa University's International Writers' Program. She is one of the founding members of the Congress of South African Writers.

Candice Petersen

✦

Don't sow a seed,
don't paint a wall,
tomorrow it will have to fall.

Let the dog howl and bark,
tomorrow he will
sleep in the dark.
Let the cock crow,
let the hen lay,
tomorrow will be their last day.

Let the children chop trees,
let them break,
let the destructive little devils
ruin and take;
for tomorrow they know not their fate.

Don't sow a seed,
don't paint a wall,
tomorrow the yellow monster will take all.

Let our sons dazed in eye
rape and steal
for they are not allowed to feel.
Let our men drink,
let them fight,
let what is said about them
then be right,
for they are not allowed to think.

So bark, howl, crow,
chop, break, ruin,
steal, drink, fight.
Let what's made of us be right.

Tomorrow we gaze at a new view,
seas of sand given by you.
And we say:
sow the seed,
paint the wall,
be at home in our desert for all.
You that remade us
your mould will break
and tomorrow you are going to fall!

//Ukxa N!a'an,
THE OLD PEOPLE GIVE YOU LIFE

Botswana 1972   Ju/'hoansi

This version of a widespread Ju/'hoan San folktale was told by //Ukxa N!a'an (Old //Ukxa) in Dobe, Botswana, in 1972. The tale gives a dramatic indication of the importance of old people in the lives of these formerly hunting-gathering people. Although the Ju/'hoan people do not keep count of their own ages in an absolute sense, they show great concern with relative age in their relationships. Reflected in respectful terms of address, seniority in any relationship between two people is accorded small but real prerogatives. The older one becomes, the greater the number of relationships in which one is the elder, and the more respect one is accorded. An "old" stage of life is distinguished linguistically by the suffix "!a'an," which is applied to those who are no longer bearing or begetting children, but who may still be active and vigorous.

Many old people among the Ju/'hoansi are vigorous and independent. Even when they begin to grow frail, their society does not condone the ageism found in some other parts of the world today. They are cared for by those in whom they have invested a lifetime of gifts and services, their children and other young relatives. This tale reflects the mystical connectedness between the grandparental generation and the youngest Ju/'hoansi, a connectedness honored by their tradition of name-sakes. In a very real sense, the oldest Ju/'hoan people "become" the youngest, giving their very identities to the children of their offspring. In this story, the metaphor of the girl who grew in secret, tended by her grandmother, is the tenderest of tropes for intergenerational caring. The old make for themselves a kind of immortality through investing in younger individuals; literally, they "give you life."

Megan Biesele

◆

. . . Now the elephant girl had already warned her grandmother that something might happen to her. She said, ". . . Watch well: a little wind will come to you. The little wind will come to you with something in it. It will bring you some droplets of blood. The blood will come to lodge inside your groin. Take that bit of blood and put it into a container. Don't let on what you're doing—just take it and put it into something. Something like a little dish or a little bottle." . . . It happened just as the girl had said. A little wind came back to her grandmother. The little bit of blood came to lodge in her groin. The grandmother saw it and said, "Didn't the child tell me something like this would happen?" She didn't speak aloud, she just said this in her heart. She took the drops of blood and put them in a bottle. . . . Then she sat and thought, and asked herself, "Should I go to see what has happened to my granddaughter? No, it has already happened just as she said it would, so he must have killed her already and there's no help for it." Meanwhile the bit of blood was growing. It grew and grew until it was too big for the bottle. Then the grandmother took it out and put it in a skin bag. It grew again and burst the bag, so the grandmother put it into something bigger. Then it grew some more and broke that. Only the grandmother knew about it. No one else knew that she had the elephant girl and was restoring her to life. She kept it a secret. She had the bit of blood and it grew and she fixed it, and it grew some more and she fixed it. When it had grown completely it was a woman again! She looked just like she had before.

One morning when the camp awoke, the women decided to go gathering berries. They got up and went picking berries. The elephant girl's little daughter went with them, saying, "Today I'll accompany my aunts and eat berries." The old grandmother said, "Go ahead, go with them." So the elephant girl's mother and all the other women went gathering. The old woman stayed home alone. She spent the day quietly. In the afternoon she took a skin and spread it in the shade, spread it in the late afternoon shadows. Then she took out the elephant girl and sat her upon the skin. She ground ochre and spread it on the young woman's face. She replaced her old rags with soft, new skin clothing and hung her all over with ornaments. Then the old woman tied copper rings in her granddaughter's hair the way people used to tie them long ago. She fixed her up so that she was the beautiful elephant girl again.

Later the women came back from gathering. Towards sunset they returned. The old woman was telling funny stories and the elephant girl was laughing. As they came near the village, her little daughter said to the others, "Who's that laughing just like my mother in the village?"

Her aunt said, "How can you be so crazy? My older sister died a long time ago. Don't go saying you hear her laughing someplace."

Another woman said, "My aunt is certainly dead: this child is crazy."

So they came closer, listening. The elephant girl laughed again. This time they said, "Can it be? Whose laughter is this? When we left there was nobody but the old woman in the camp; we had all gone gathering. What young girl can that be whose laughter sounds just like our sister's?" When they came into the camp they saw the elephant girl sitting there with her grandmother. Her daughter cried, "Mother, mother, mother!" and ran to her, flopped down, and began to nurse. The others cried out and said, "Yo! Who has accomplished this?"

The young woman answered softly, "Granny, of course. Granny lifted me up. Granny spoke the word and I sat up and was alive. If it had been up to you others alone, I wouldn't be here. Long ago Granny took me and sheltered me in a skin pouch and now I am alive again. That's how it was. The old people give you life."

Transcribed and translated by Megan Biesele

Nehambo Magdalena Shamena, EMERGENCY CALL FROM THE WOMEN OF NAMIBIA

Namibia 1973   Afrikaans

Nehambo Magdalena Iihuhua, born into the royal family of Ondonga, was educated in Lutheran mission schools and graduated from the Okahao Women Teachers Training College in 1956. She thus belonged to the tiny number of Owambo women who obtained a professional qualification at that time.

She and her husband, Ndeulimane Erastus Shamena, joined the South West Africa People's Organization (SWAPO) shortly after it was founded in 1960. Their activism led to increasing conflict with the South African colonial authorities. Erastus Shamena was arrested in 1967 and spent a year in prison in Pretoria. In 1973 he was arrested again. Magdalena Shamena and her husband wrote of these traumatic events in an autobiography, *We Children of Namibia*.

In the early 1970s, Owambo chiefs aligned with the colonial authorities subjected Namibian women and men indiscriminately to floggings while the South

African authorities subjected Namibians to torture in detention. In 1973 Magdalena Shamena, then secretary to the Women's League of Namibia, wrote to the secretary general of the United Nations. This letter, smuggled out of the country by a Finnish missionary, became known as the "Emergency Call from the Women of Namibia." She signed the letter, the first known piece of writing by a Namibian woman involved in the national liberation struggle, to foreground the experience of women. She signed with her full name, an exceptionally brave act in the repressive climate of that time.

Her resistance was not tolerated by the South African administration and the increasing threats eventually caused the Shamenas' flight into exile. Along with thousands of other Namibians, Magdalena and Erastus Shamena departed their country in 1974, leaving their six young children behind in the care of their mother's brother. Magdalena Shamena became one of the first SWAPO women to undergo military training in Zambia.

Heike Becker

✦

Hear our cry in need. We are being tortured here in Namibia in secret, but because we live in isolation we have not the possibility to make our need known and if we succeed to do so we are tortured by the South African government.

We, the women of Namibia, have hard times.

Many of our children are now in jail. Many of them are burned with electricity and many of them have been killed.

Now, from August 15, 1973, nearly all freedom-fighters are put in jails which burn them like hot grillpans. These jails are built with corrugated iron only and are standing in the burning sun. Those inside turned pale because of the heat and we fear what can happen to them.

The women of Namibia are beaten and tortured very much, e.g. Anneli Dama, and others. The women are ordered to lie on their stomach and then they are beaten shamelessly. Some of them are still in jail and suffer a lot.

The freedom-fighters are being beaten up by the Chiefs. When the South African government could not bring in any charges against these men they were sent to the Chiefs who had beaten them with palm sticks, 15–20 strokes, e.g. Andreas Nuukwawo, J. Nangutwala, and others received as many strokes.

Heavy laws are being put into practice against the teachers to prevent them from active political involvement. Many of them lose their work without knowing the reasons why—Jonathan Shoombe, Valde Nampunya, John Otto, Shikondjeleni Vatuva, Engobe and many others.

Translator unknown

Joyce Simango, WOMEN ARE WEALTH

Zimbabwe 1974   chiShona

The first woman Shona novelist, Joyce Simango was not aware that she was breaking new ground when she wrote her novel *Zviuya Zviri Mberi* (For a Better Tomorrow) in 1974. Cut off from village life at Honde Mission School in the Eastern districts where her husband taught, Simango found herself with little to do except housework. She was a voracious reader and got her supply of books from the mission bookshop. Listening to a radio program, "Mabhuku naVanyori," run by the Rhodesia Literature Bureau and the Rhodesian Broadcasting Corporation, where authors read from their own published works and listeners were encouraged to send in manuscripts to be considered for publication, she developed a desire to write. She wrote in an environment of educated and supportive people. Her husband helped with hand-printing the manuscript as required by the publishers.

Simango wrote about a rebellious wife, Munhamo (No Freedom from Trouble), who runs away with her nine-year-old daughter, Tambudzai (The Troubled One), in order to save her from marriage to an old man. Her father, Munhamo's husband, wants to exchange his daughter for the bride-wealth he needs to buy his sixth wife. Tambudzai, brought up as a Christian, is enrolled in school; after successfully completing her studies, she trains as a nurse, then marries an educated, professional Christian. When asked what influenced her to choose the theme of this novel, Simango named her family background and her belief in Christianity. In its portrayal of patriarchal social relations, her novel may be seen as an antecedent to *Nervous Conditions* by Tsitsi Dangarembga.

Born in 1948, the eldest child in the family, Simango has confessed to an unhappy childhood. Her father had eight wives and her mother had been pledged to him at a very early age. Her mother had been the eldest of the cowives, but when she was divorced, she left Simango in the care of one of the other wives. At fifteen, after completing her primary education, Simango married a man who came from Mozambique and taught in the school she attended. The extract from *Zviuya Zviri Mberi* that has been translated here is from the beginning of the novel.

Chiedza Musengezi

✦

On a very cold winter's dawn, a Tuesday, Munhamo and her two children, Tambudzai and Chemwandoita, sat shivering in their hut. Munhamo, who was weeping, was wrapped in a shawl which she used as a blanket as well.

On the other side of the hut Tambudzai and Chemwandoita sat by the fireplace. Tambudzai had a shawl covering just the lower part of her body while her chest was completely bare. Chemwandoita had only a piece of cloth tied around his waist and this was all they had in the way of clothes.

Munhamo was of light complexion and medium height and one could easily see the resemblance between her and her daughter. She was still youthful even though Tambudzai, her first-born, was now nine years old, for she had married young. Her son, Chemwandoita, was six. Munhamo was the fourth wife of Nhamoinesu, and though other children had been born to her, none had survived except these two.

They lived in Nyamhinda in the Portuguese country in the east. Nhamoinesu's wives earned their living through tilling the land and they had to provide their own clothing by bartering the maize they grew. Nhamoinesu was quite different from other married men who bought clothes for their families. In all he had five wives, the fifth he had only recently married. And he had already pledged Tambudzai in marriage so as to raise the money to pay the bride-wealth of his youngest wife.

The day was approaching when Tambudzai would leave for the home of the new husband to whom she had been pledged, and therefore Munhamo was weeping. But Tambudzai was quite happy, unaware of what was about to take place.

While Munhamo was so full of distress she heard a voice.

"May we come in, please!" It was a man's voice accompanied by hand clapping.

"Come in!" Munhamo replied, wiping away her tears. The man entered carrying a small hare in his hands.

"Receive it, Tambudzai," said her mother. Tambudzai simply accepted it and placed it against the wall of the hut.

"No," said the man, "to be sure there's nothing here to be very grateful for. It's just a small hare caught in one of my stone-traps which I've just been checking, and I thought of coming to give it to Amainini Tambudzai."

"Thank you," said Munhamo, clapping her hands. "By the way, did I ask how you are this morning?"

"No, we have slept well. How about you?" the man replied.

"It's just these coughs. How are the others at home?"

"They have just gone out. How are you, Tambudzai?" the man asked, looking at her.

"I'm well and how are you?" Tambudzai replied, her head tilted sideways. The man was so very old that Tambudzai appeared like his granddaughter beside him. His name was Mundogara and he also had five wives, being the same age as Nhamoinesu. He had provided Nhamoinesu with the money to pay the bride-wealth for his fifth wife, and in return Nhamoinesu had promised to give him Tambudzai as a wife. Mundogara had replied with the proverb, "Accept whatever is offered to you as a gift," and so he intended to take Tambudzai and bring her up in his household.

"Is father awake?" Mundogara asked.

"I don't know! Let me send a child to check for you." Munhamo looked at Chemwandoita who quickly ran off and returned in a flash.

"Did you find him?" mother asked.

"Amainini said he has gone fishing."

"It's all right. I'll go and see him there at the river," said Mundogara, getting up from his seat. After Mundogara had left, Munhamo started weeping again.

"Mother, why are you crying so much?" Tambudzai asked, she and her brother looking into her mother's face. Munhamo continued to sob, but in a little while she said, "Tambudzai my child, on Saturday that man who has just left this hut will come to take you to live with him forever as his wife."

"Why?" Tambudzai asked.

"My child, your father pledged you because he wanted money to pay the bride-wealth of his youngest wife, your junior aunt."

Tambudzai surprisingly didn't ask any more questions and remained silent, looking into the fire. No one could tell from her expression what was going on in her mind. Munhamo roused her from her reverie by sending her to fetch water from the well, which was some distance away. She walked very slowly, thinking about what her mother had said, and tears ran down her cheeks at the thought of having to leave her mother.

Her mother meanwhile was busy thinking of what to do. She was determined that she was not going to let her daughter go. This family, she said to herself, doesn't like me. I bear children whom they kill through witchcraft and my husband seldom comes into my hut. And now they want to take my child, the one who is so dear to me and so young. Over my dead body, I swear by my mother of the Shava totem! Let them take Shoorai, the daughter of Mwandionesa. I won't let mine go. As for that old man and his small hare, does he think I can get excited about that? Well, at least he has done one good thing, provided me with something to eat on the road I intend to take. While she talked to herself like that she heard her husband speaking to Tambudzai, who had just returned from the well.

"Is your mother in her hut?"

"I don't know. But I left her there when I went to the well. She said she had a headache," Tambudzai replied.

"May we enter, please," said Nhamoinesu.

"Come in, please," replied Munhamo, almost choking with her suppressed anger mixed with her sobs.

"How have you slept? Tambudzai tells me that you have a headache."

Tambudzai had actually lied. She was afraid that her father, finding her mother with red eyes, would guess what she was weeping for and in his anger beat her. Among other things he was an accomplished wife-beater and would batter her hard even for a slight offense.

"My eyes are paining me," she said with her head lowered.

"I will go and look for some herbs to ease the pain shortly, but the matter that brought me here is this: I was planning that tomorrow you will pound maize and rice which we'll eat on Saturday together with Tambudzai's husband, and you should prepare a pot of beer as well for the same occasion. But if you have a headache, your senior co-wives can do that and I'll slaughter that small black goat. Do you understand?"

"You are the father," his wife replied, lowering her head to look at the ground his feet stood on. Lowering one's head was a custom practised by women: it showed that they were in agreement with what their men-folk said.

Nhamoinesu then went off towards his youngest wife's hut. His homestead was very large, built in a circle consisting of many huts for his daughters-in-law and his sons. The huts were built of poles and dagga and had thatched roofs. In this home meat was eaten only by elders. The young boys, when they caught just a small mouse in their stone-traps, would eat it at night under the cover of darkness, afraid that the leaders might snatch it from them. Nhamoinesu did not possess much livestock, only ten head of cattle and eight goats. His real wealth was the women. When he intended to marry another wife, he would first of all pledge one of his daughters so that he could raise the money to pay the bride-wealth.

Sometimes he would even marry using the mutengano custom, whereby he would exchange one of his daughters for a girl from another family who would become his wife. He had fathered ten daughters and thirteen sons, many of whom were already married. The land where this family lived was part of a very wide plain, so flat that if you looked around in all directions you would not see even the smallest hill.

There was no school or grinding mill nearby and only one small store. Nhamoinesu's wives had to pound maize to produce mealie-meal, while rapoko they had to grind. Although Tambudzai was only nine years old, she was already an expert in pounding and grinding grain.

When Nhamoinesu had gone, Munhamo called Tambudzai and asked her to pound some rice, and when that was done they cooked some sadza for lunch, but nobody enjoyed eating it. What was left was put together with the rice in a reed basket. The hare they prepared nicely roasted so that the meat turned reddish brown in a way that made one's mouth water, it was so appetizing. They caught two of their chickens and slaughtered and cooked them and put these together with the rice and the roasted meat in the basket. All this was done without attracting the attention of others in the homestead, and while the two children saw everything, they were not aware of the purpose behind it all.

The night was clear and starlit when Munhamo went outside to check whether the homestead was asleep. There wasn't a sound except for the faint rustle of the grass in a light breeze blowing from the east.

She stood for a while going over the details of the plan she had made. She had determined to flee to a place in the west called Rusitu on the border between the British and Portuguese territories. Her uncle, her mother's brother, lived there, and although she did not know the way, she argued that she could not get wholly lost when there were people to ask about her route. Having finally made up her mind she went back into her hut and quietly woke her children. "Tambudzai! Chemwandoita! Wake up!"

"What is it, mother?" Tambudzai asked.

"Wake up and let's go."

Translated by Chiedza Musengezi

Jennifer Davids, POEM FOR MY MOTHER

South Africa 1974   English

Born in Cape Town in 1945 to an insurance agent father and a working mother, Jennifer Davids attended Harold Cressy High School and trained as a teacher at Hewat Training College, specializing in art. She later taught in Langa, a black township in Cape Town. Now living in England where she still teaches, she is currently working on a project she hopes to publish in South Africa.

"When something's on the page, it doesn't belong to you any more," she said in a December 2000 interview, responding to critics' reactions to her work. Davids's politics were often called into question during the height of the Black Consciousness Movement, and more recently, too. As Grant Farred comments, she has been hard to "locate on the map of disenfranchised writers" because of her "inability, or refusal, to declare her colouredness."

The poem reprinted here was published in 1974 in *Searching for Words* but written much earlier during her teens. Although she now sees her parents as supportive and proud of her, the poem presents a dismissive mother, which Davids has explained as a crystalization of "teenage *angst*" and petulance. While Davids's other poetry—written during the period when she attended politicized poetry readings and Black Consciousness meetings—often refers to contemporary politics of apartheid, she maintains a preference for expressing political awareness "in a quiet way."

Candice Petersen

✦

That isn't everything, you said
on the afternoon I brought a poem
to you hunched over the washtub
with your hands
the shrivelled
burnt granadilla
skin of your hands
covered by foam.

And my words
slid like a ball
of hard blue soap
into the tub
to be grabbed and used by you
to rub the clothes.

A poem isn't all
there is to life, you said

with your blue-ringed gaze
scanning the page
once looking over my shoulder
and back at the immediate
dirty water

and my words
being clenched
smaller and
smaller.

Winnie Madikizela Mandela,
DETENTION ALONE IS A TRIAL IN ITSELF

South Africa 1975   English

Winnie Madikizela Mandela's involvement in South African resistance politics began with her marriage to Nelson Mandela, imprisoned for life in 1963 and released in 1990. For the twenty-seven years that her husband was in prison, Winnie Mandela was persecuted by the state. She was banned, imprisoned, and banished. Her suffering became a living symbol of apartheid oppression, and her courageous spirit made her an icon for struggle. She became an independent political leader in her own right.

In 1969 she and twenty-one others suffered detention under the draconian Terrorism Act. This permitted 180 days of detention for interrogation under conditions of solitary confinement. She was held in this condition for seventeen months. She and the others were eventually charged under the Suppression of Communism Act for furthering the aims of a banned organization. Although acquitted, she was banned and placed under house arrest, which meant reporting to the police daily and being at home from six in the evening until six in the morning.

During the brief two-week period between the acquittal and the imposition of the banning order, she took the opportunity to speak publicly at a meeting held to protest the detention system. She spoke about the system of detention and about her personal experience. She knew that the risks of rearrest and further banning were great.

Mandela's speech is a moving testament of detention. In later years, Mandela said that her own detention "changed her as a person." But she spoke very little of either her feelings or her private life. What she hints at in her talk is that the combination of solitary confinement and interrogation was a process that few could resist without some experience of personal disintegration. It appears to have been the stark choice of collaboration or the cause of liberation that kept Mandela focused and sane.

Sheila Meintjes

◆

Detention means that midnight knock when all about you is quiet. It means those blinding torches shone simultaneously through every window of your house before the door is kicked open. It means the exclusive right the Security Branch have to read each and every letter in the house, no matter how personal it might be. It means paging through each and every book on your shelves, lifting carpets, looking under beds, lifting sleeping children from mattresses and looking under the sheets. It means tasting your sugar, your mealie-meal and every spice you have on your kitchen shelf. Unpacking all your clothing on your shelves and in your suitcases, and going through each pocket. It means you no longer have a right to answer your telephone should a call come through, no right to speak to anyone who might come to find out if you need help. It means interrogating your employer to find out why you are employed, questioning fellow workers to find out what you discuss privately, planting informers at work, around your neighbourhood, amongst your friends, in church, in school, etc.

Ultimately it means your seizure at dawn, dragged away from little children screaming and clinging to your skirt, imploring the white man dragging mummy to leave her alone. It means leaving the comfort of your home with the bare essentials of life that hardly make life bearable in your cell. It means the haunting memories of those screams of the loved ones, the beginning of that horror story told many a time and that has become common knowledge, yet the actual experience remains petrifying.

To review but the minimum bare facts: it means, as it was for me, being held in a single cell with the light burning twenty-four hours so that I lost track of time and was unable to tell whether it was day or night. Every single moment of your life is strictly regulated and supervised. Complete isolation from the outside world, no privacy, no visitor, lawyer or minister. It means no-one to talk to each 24 hours, no knowledge of how long you will be imprisoned and why you are imprisoned, getting medical attention from the doctor only when you are seriously ill. It means a visit from one magistrate and a retinue of the prison officials against whom you may wish to lodge a complaint and at whose mercy you are held. The very manner in which you are asked for complaints in fact means "How dare you complain."

The frightful emptiness of those hours of solitude is unbearable. Your company is your solitude, your blanket, your mat, your sanitary bucket, your mug and yourself. You have no choice of what you are given to eat even though you have not been charged. You have only one hour exercise per day depending on whether there is enough staff to spare. To you, your very existence in prison seems to be a privilege. All this is in preparation for the inevitable HELL—interrogation. It is meant to crush your individuality completely, to change you into a docile being from whom no resistance can arise, to terrorise you, to intimidate you into silence. After you have suffered the first initial shock of imprisonment for those who are inexperienced, this initial shock followed by the detainee's adaptation to prison has an effect of changing the detainee's personality and outlook in life.

In some cases it means severe moods from fervent hope to deep despair. Each day of nothingness is a struggle to survive. What sustains you is the spontaneous defence mechanism, that granite desire to defend and protect at all cost [against] disintegration of personality. You ask yourself questions without answers day after day, week after week, month after month, and then you keep telling yourself—I am sane and I will remain sane.

You're subjected to countless stripping of all your clothes. You must be quite naked for the white prison wardress to search your body thoroughly, to run fingers through your hair, to look in your mouth and under your tongue. There have been alleged suicides in detention; you keep asking yourself whether you will leave the cell alive for you do not know what drove those who died to their deaths. Sometimes it is a serious effort to remember what happened, the mind becomes completely blank. Then suddenly when you have gone through all this you are whisked away from your cell to the interrogation room.

Here now you have to enter a debate within yourself. There are only two divisions, you decide whether you will emerge a collaborator with the system or continue your identification with whatever your cause is. [. . .]

MaMhlalise Mkhwanazi, THE BASKING LIZARD
South Africa 1976   isiZulu

The *izibongo* (praise poems) of MaMhlalise Mkhwanazi are in a sense far more modern than the "Ballad of Nomagundwane" sung by Princess Magogo (see the text, recorded in 1964, in this volume). Yet the very confidence of the poems, their sure handling of the rhetoric of praising and of recurrent praise names, which all composers can make use of and call their own, show that the line of aesthetic production of dynamic and vigorous praise poems is a cultural skill to which women have had access for many, many generations. I recorded these *izibongo* of MaMhlalise on 22 January 1976 at Mtshiva Gorge near KwaDlangezwa, which is not far from Empangeni in northern KwaZulu-Natal. MaMhlalise, then well into middle age, lived until 1998, and her passing was much mourned by her fellow women members of *Ibandla lamaNazaretha* of the Wozawoza temple at KwaDlangezwa.

The praise poem included here is a vehicle through which MaMhlalise speaks to her own vigorous and strong personality and in which she sketches, in a highly compressed and abstract way, some of the contours of her own life. She brings into her *izibongo* a sense of married life, and before that, her careless youth. She plays with words and wit, using a well-worn and still expressive praise name that puns on her own family name. Her family name is MaMbambo (Miss Rib), and Mkhwanazi is her married name, so she takes MaMbambo and hitches to it the popular "I am Ribs-Pressed-Me-In / I would have been a well-built girl" and makes it a mark of her youth in her brief life-poem. She plunders and reuses other well-known praise names as well, taking "The Mimosa Bush with thorns" (also a praise name of Isaiah Shembe, to whose church she belonged) and expertly turning it to her own use as she cryptically captures some of the tensions of polygamous married life and the competition among wives. Her humor is earthy and unabashed and her audience of women at the time of recording enjoyed her rendering of the praises. She hints at her role as senior wife—"The Beater of those who use corrugated iron for doors"—and then again with great gusto turns her attention to the sexuality not of her cowives but of a "Bull," whose real identity her praise poem does not reveal but whom her listeners would surely know. Boldly, she mocks him for his infidelities, which absorb him so much that he is sexually "useless at home"—and no good to any of his wives.

MaMhlalise was a widow of the late Chief Nikiza Mkhwanazi and had, after his death, become the wife of one of his brothers, Japhane Mkhwanazi.

Liz Gunner

✦

The Basking Lizard lying in wayward abandon at her sister's,
   Nomchitheka's.
I am Ribs-Pressed-Me-In
I would have been a well-built girl.
(I am) Doves-that-woke-and-pecked at the roof.
The High Greenish Grass tufts
that will one day be jumped by the clever ones.
The Mimosa Bush with thorns for keeping out
those wretched vaginas of their mothers! [a burst of laughter from the
   women]
I am Squish on something and they say, "She's crapped!"
But she hasn't crapped, it's her co-wife that's crapped!
The Beater of those who stand, legs apart, lazy and stiff-legged like
   cooking pots.
I am The Beater of those who use corrugated iron for doors. [she pauses
   and continues]
I am what kind of Bull is it
that mounts outside its own kraal
but is useless at home.
Hah! What do you say to that you old Khandempemvu [grey-headed]
   fellow!

Transcribed by Liz Gunner
Translated by Liz Gunner and Mafika Gwala

Joyce Sikhakhane, WORKING ON THE *MAIL*

South Africa 1977   English

Joyce Sikhakhane was one of the first black women journalists in South Africa, and a political activist detained and finally charged under the notorious Terrorism Act. Prevented from continuing her career as a journalist after her acquittal, she left the country in 1973 to join the liberation movement in exile. In 1977, through the International Defence and Aid Fund in London, she published *A Window on Soweto*, skillfully interweaving personal narrative (including family history) with historical and sociological accounts.

Sikhakhane was born in 1943 and brought up in the Orlando district of Soweto, at that time a conglomerate of twenty-six locations covering thirty-two square miles, where more and more black South Africans were being resettled after having been forced to leave Sophiatown. Her grandfather was one of the first African ministers of the Lutheran church and an early African National Congress activist who gave to his granddaughter the Zulu name Nomafa, meaning "inheritance"; in later life she took this to signal her destiny as a political activist. She became a journalist with the *Rand Daily Mail* in Johannesburg in 1966.

A Window on Soweto is, among other things, an important account of the systemic dangers and insults faced by black professional women: the meager earnings, high taxation, and minimal benefits (despite white newspapers' dependence on black journalists for stories to which white journalists had no access); the police harassment; and the constant threat of imprisonment, torture, and death, as well as of "repatriation" to areas deemed ethnic "homelands."

Arrested in 1969 at much the same time as Winnie Mandela, Rita Ndzanga, Martha Dhlamini, Thokozile Mngoma, Nomwe Mamkhala, and Santhie Naidoo under Section 10 of the Terrorism Act, Sikhakhane was detained without trial, and kept often in solitary confinement, for seventeen months (see Mandela's text in this volume). Interrogated in Pretoria Central Prison, transferred for a time to Nylstroom Prison (after she had refused to become a state witness), and returned once again and released in September 1970, she was served with a banning order that prohibited her from all social and political gatherings and from entering newspaper offices, educational institutions, and factories. After she left South Africa for Zambia, now with a second child, her daughter Nomzamo, she married the Scots doctor referred to in the excerpt; worked in Mozambique and Zimbabwe as a journalist, scriptwriter, and researcher; obtained a degree in England; and returned to South Africa in 1994. Until February 2001 she worked as an editor at the South African Broadcasting Corporation. She is currently writing a historical narrative on Albertina Sisulu as well as the authorized biography of Albertina and Walter Sisulu.

Dorothy Driver

✦

Nkosinathi was only three weeks old when I returned to work because I had withdrawn all the meagre maternity allowance. My mother was still working as a dressmaker and she agreed to look after my baby, thus Nkosinathi was saved the agony of being shunted from house to house in search of grannies. By 1966, I earned more than R10 a week, thus liable to the Pay-as-you-earn [PAYE] Tax Scheme and Maternity Benefit Fund. I must point out that strictly speaking this form of taxation in South Africa was specifically designed for the white privileged class whose wages are never less than R10 a week. In addition to this tax, the Bantustan levy was deducted from my salary. Only a fraction of the African professional or skilled labourers earn money that qualifies them for the PAYE Scheme. The majority of African women hardly earn R6 a week.

After working for a few weeks back with the *World*, I walked out because I could no longer tolerate reporting sensational crime stories. I had, after all, gained typing experience and learnt how to present news.

I walked to the *Rand Daily Mail* offices and asked if I could get a job as a reporter. I remember the "Township" News Editor of the *Mail* saying to me that the *Mail* had never employed a black woman before. I argued and persuaded him. He gave in by saying I could give it a try as a freelancer. The *Mail* had a big African readership. It was a liberal newspaper which had recently published a series of stories exposing the horrifying conditions of South African prisons.

I started as a freelance reporter but at the same time I was pressing to be employed on a full-time basis, the reasons being, first, all African part-time journalists were refused registration as full-time workers by the labour office. This meant they were employed on a daily labourer's permit, whose fee was R1.50 a month and renewable at the end of each month. This meant that each reporter had to make the usual nerve-racking call at the pass office once a month. Secondly, working as a freelancer meant hard work in order to earn a living wage. Payment was according to the number of stories published by the newspapers you freelanced for. In order to keep good reporters for itself, the *Mail* offered a basic retainer's fee which was not adequate by any standards and a part-timer lost should he not be productive enough. To overcome the labour registration hazard, I did not take a discharge from the *World*, I now and again popped in there with sensational crime stories.

To the *Mail* I brought in the right type of stories—like the mass removal of Africans from their own areas, because of the Group Areas Act. Stories of political trials, of strikes by African workers and so on. By this time the *Mail* needed African reporters because white journalists need special permits to enter African areas. Although an African needed a permit to enter other African areas it was invariably easier to sneak in if you were African. I enjoyed the art of sneaking in and was able to get good stories for the *Mail*. This was the time of the notorious "resettlement" areas—Limehill, Stinkwater, and other removal areas. I remember in Limehill about five babies died in my arms—at different times—because of exposure or malnutrition, because their parents had been forcibly dumped in the open veld without any food and shelter. Together with Father Cosmas Desmond and others, we laid a tombstone in one such grave to commemorate such an agonising death.

The tears of those bereaved mothers still haunt my mind today. After making my name, the *Rand Daily Mail* had no choice but to think of employing me on a full-time basis. They were reluctant at first because the whole South African Associated Newspapers Group (SAAN) had never employed an African woman before. The Group had to consider what salary to pay me. Not forgetting the toilet facilities in a country where people of different racial groups cannot even share a toilet. I remember that one day I was so pressed I had to go to the loo. At this stage SAAN had not yet allocated a toilet for me, so I went to the Ladies. While I was sitting there a group of angry white women came and pulled me out of the seat. SAAN had no way of defending itself because the law required that there should be separate toilets for each racial group. Subsequently I was given a whole block of toilets on the ground floor. It was a bonanza!

Another physical assault on me as a black person happened hundreds of miles from Johannesburg. It was at a restaurant in Lichtenburg, in the Northern Transvaal. I had been travelling in a car with a group of African women who had been to a three-day annual meeting of the National Council of African Women. I was at the conference for press coverage. As we were driving on this hot Sunday afternoon, we all became thirsty and decided to stop the car after spotting a restaurant.

I then walked over to buy cold drinks for the whole group. On approaching the restaurant, the outside of the door did not display the customary segregated entrance sign. I went in straight to the counter and ordered five bottles of Coke and Fanta. There were no customers standing at the counter at the time. From the face of the woman shop attendant I read an expression of mute consternation. It puzzled me. Without saying a word, the man in attendance with her picked up an empty bottle of coca-cola and came out from the counter towards the huge freezer standing next to me. I thought he was going to take out the drinks I had ordered. The next thing I felt was a thud on my head. I fell on the ground and fainted. I regained consciousness later, as cold water was being poured on me. I was lying on the pavement. In my stupor, I could hear women's voices saying "She is alright now." They picked me up and helped me to my feet heading to the car. I gradually recalled what had happened. I got very angry. In the car the women explained to me that as they were sitting in the car, they saw two men coming out of the restaurant carrying what looked like a woman's body by its legs and arms. The men dumped the body on the pavement outside the shop and returned inside. Recognising the colour of the body's dress, they were sure it was me. In panic they all ran out of the car to find out what had happened. A "deranged" white man came out of the restaurant, shouting that "no kaffir had ever entered his shop through the front door." Local Africans, who had by now gathered around, had pointed to a side window through which blacks purchased food from that restaurant. But then we Jo'burg Africans were used to using the same doors in certain City restaurants which do not display segregated entrance signs.

I, in turn, related the attack to the group, and we decided to drive to the local police station. As we approached it a car overtook us at full speed, stopped, and a white man brandishing a gun got out and threatened to shoot us if we drove to the police station.

We decided that reporting to the police was not worth risking our lives. I would instead report the assault in Johannesburg. That rascal's car followed us a few miles out of Lichtenburg.

We arrived in Johannesburg after midnight. We were all tired and I decided I would discuss the attack first at the *Mail* before going to the police. On the following day, the *Mail* News Editor advised me to go straight to John Vorster Square and lay a charge of assault. He explained that should the *Mail* publish the case, the police, government and its supporters would accuse it of being sensational and harming race relations. The *Mail* would instead give full coverage of the case once it was in court. The News Editor asked a crime reporter to accompany me to John Vorster Square. In the SAAN car, driven by an African, I sat in front, the other reporter at the back.

On arrival at John Vorster Square the crime reporter and I used separate entrances leading to the "Nie-Blankes"—"Non-White"—charge office. Inside a mid-high wall partition separated whites from blacks. So my colleague spoke to the man of his colour, while I told the African one that I was accompanied by a colleague who was explaining my case at the other side. The "colleague" reference puzzled the African police who asked if "that white man" was not my boss.

Then the policeman from the other side came and instructed the African one to take my statement. He stood by as I described the attack. Before I started my colleague asked to be excused. Calling each other's first names we said bye bye to each other. It was all foreign to both policemen. After dictating the details to the African police, the white one asked for the name of the restaurant. I did not know it, but said I could point it out on the spot. He then asked for the description of my attacker. I told him, adding that it would not be difficult to identify him since at the time of the attack there was only the woman and the man in the shop. The man had also said he was the owner of the restaurant. I gave the names of my witnesses. They were all respectable women, teachers and nurses. One of them had actually grown up in Lichtenburg and was now wife of a lawyer. She was also the national president of the National Council of African Women. The white police took the statement and said I would be contacted when the investigation was finished.

After a long lapse, I went back to John Vorster Square to inquire about what had happened to the investigation. A few days after my inquiry I received a note from the investigating officer stating that after a thorough investigation, it was decided there was not enough evidence to institute prosecution. That was the end of the case. By this time the *Mail* had no legal power to publish the attack. It had been through the hands of the police.

Being on the road collecting good stories which exposed the brutality of the apartheid system had its dangers. One day, photographer Peter Magubane and I were stopped by the Security Police as we were driving around in Limehill. We were thoroughly searched on the spot. The police demanded our press cards which we did not possess anyway. In South Africa it is the police who issue press cards! We produced the passbooks which they demanded. Peter's film spool and my notebook were confiscated. The police then led us out of Limehill and warned us we would be arrested on return.

Because the *Mail* was taking a long time in deciding on my job prospects I staged a demonstration by walking out and taking a full-time job with *Post* and *Drum*.

I went back to the *World* to get a discharge. The white accountant wanted to backdate the discharge to the day I walked out of the newspaper. I defended myself by saying "But really I've been still working for you." It was true. For the two years of freelance work I did send crime stories for the *World* publication. I got an updated discharge, thus escaping the question "What have you been doing in the past two years" from the labour office. In South Africa's white cities, Africans get "repatriated" to the homelands if it is deemed they had been idling for a period.

As I was now in great demand, I wanted to prove a point to the *Mail* that as an intelligent black woman journalist I was a force to be reckoned with. After only three months with *Post* and *Drum*, the *Rand Daily Mail* wrote a letter offering me a permanent job. I went back. I rejoined the *Mail* because the *Post* newspaper, which was a weekly, was not as outspoken as the *Mail*. It also depended a lot on crime sensation stories and pin-up girls pictures. During its heyday, *Drum* was popular for its coverage of feature stories which involved political organisations. I had been unfortunate in that I had entered the journalistic trade at a time when outstanding black and white journalists were either in gaol or in exile, banned or underground.

The publishing houses were being seriously threatened by tougher legislation of press censorship. The remnants of press freedom were in the process of being further curtailed. Given the prevailing conditions I was relieved to have been called back by the *Mail*. It was a good personal achievement. If I remember correctly this happened towards the beginning of 1968. My work on the *Mail* was however destined to be short-lived.

Not long after I returned I experienced one of the happiest moments of my life. I became secretly engaged to Kenneth Rankin, a Scottish doctor, whom I had met during one of my "daring" assignments. Because our respective complexions are similar to the advertisement for the Scotch whisky "Black and White" we could not get engaged in public in that sorry country. Ours was an illegal affair.

Our courting was a risky business. I recall an attack on us as we were driving down Jan Smuts Avenue one night. I had made the mistake of sitting in the front seat as Kenneth was driving. The car behind us suddenly pulled next to ours on my side as we stopped at the red lights. We heard voices screaming and we looked. There were six bully-like white fellows in the other car, gesticulating with their fists and shouting at us, pointing at me in particular. The lights changed, and Kenneth drove off at full speed. The other car followed suit. It was a chase. Thrice it drove ahead of us and tried to block us but Kenneth managed to steer clear. He made a mistake leaving the motorway and turning into a smaller road. All the six men jumped out of the car, one held a gun and was threatening to use it. We had locked our doors. The men surrounded the car attempting to open the doors. I braved it, and unlocked mine, the next moment I was dragged out and shaken by the men as if they were loosening dust stuck in a blanket. They hurled me back into the car, but in the back seat. All insults which belong to the gutter were flung at me. I was warned by the men that "in future I should know where my place is." They got back into their car and drove off. We followed at slow speed and made a detour at the first chance we got. We did not drive to our planned destination, but Kenneth dropped me off at a taxi rank instead.

A few days later, Kenneth left the country, after we had planned that I would follow him with Nkosinathi by whatever means. A few weeks later I was, instead, an inmate of a solitary confinement cell held under the South African Terrorism Act. Suddenly my life was in complete ruins, with the shadow of death lurking in the surrounds of Pretoria Central Prison.

1980s

.

Lauretta Ngcobo, THE RENDING OF THE VEIL

South Africa 1981   English

Lauretta Ngcobo (née Gwina) was born in South Africa in 1931, of Zulu and Xhosa parents. She completed much of her school education at American Board missionary institutions such as Inanda Seminary, and gained a B.A. degree and teaching qualification at the University of Fort Hare in the Eastern Cape. After teaching in various South African schools, she married A. B. Ngcobo, who was active in the Pan African Congress. She went into exile in 1963 to escape arrest by the South African security police, living in Swaziland and Zimbabwe before moving to Britain in 1969 where she remained until her return to South Africa in 1993. She remains active in politics in KwaZulu-Natal.

Ngcobo is the author of two novels, *Cross of Gold* (1981)—from which the excerpt below is taken—and *And They Didn't Die* (1990). She is also the editor of an anthology entitled *Let It Be Told: Black Women Writers in Britain* (1987). Her short prose pieces have been included in various anthologies, and she has written introductions to other southern African women writers' work. She is the mother of three daughters.

Cross of Gold (1981) appeared during a period of literary production marked by the influence of Black Consciousness, and forms part of the genre of "protest fiction." "For many years it lay in a drawer, until I met a person . . . who wanted to read it," Ngcobo said in an interview. Written in the 1970s and published outside South Africa, it was one of the first novels in English by a black South African woman. While the novel refers to the mining revolt of 1946 and the impact of the Sharpeville massacre of 1960, it may also be read as a response to the Soweto student uprisings of 1976. As such the novel attempts to address and inscribe black responses to the oppressive South African system of institutionalized racism.

The excerpt from Chapter One focuses on Sindisiwe Zikode's flight into exile across the South Africa–Botswana border; the chapter ends in her death from a wound received from the South African border patrol officers. She dies under the gaze of her sons, whose story the novel then tells. Ngcobo noted in a 1989 interview that, while she tried to write a woman's story, she was unable to imagine the woman surviving beyond the initial pages.

In diagnosing the position of women in post-apartheid South Africa, Ngcobo has argued that "Black women should soon grow confident and find room enough to speak for themselves, so that others will no longer find it possible or necessary to speak on their behalf." She has responded to her own injunction in her second novel, *And They Didn't Die,* where she brings the full focus of her art as a writer to bear on the experiences of rural South African women.

A. C. Fick

✦

Sindisiwe Zikode lay behind the huge boulder in the silence of the night among the straggly bushes of the barren land. She listened and strained for any sound that would make her feel she had some company; that she was not so utterly alone; but all she could hear was the loud thud of her heart—a heart that reminded her of all her fears, her grievances, the treacherous hopes and the clotted emotions that filled it. In that darkness without breeze or insects or crickets that cheer the night with their hum and song in South Africa, she prayed for one thing only, and she told God that it was the last great request she would ever make to him. She gave promises and turned that sheltering rock into an altar for her penitence. She thought of the past and the future in wide sweeping circles that whirled in her mind till they were spirals that lifted her in supplication to God.

But this great prayer, unlike all her former prayers before her doubts had arisen about God, kept running aground upon her sorrow and wishes. She was waiting there for her sons, Mandla and Temba. They were just beyond the border, a few hours away from her. Those few strands of barbed wire fence stood between her and her children, her home, her husband and her country. Her thoughts about all these dear things raced and chased each other in a circle that came to no end. If only she could be stronger to bear the disappointment, if it came. Would they come that night? Would they be safe? Could they cross silently, undetected, alone, without being accompanied? Would they be able to spot the exact place of "the big boulder," would the driver see the boulder at night, would the guards go away to their sleep after midnight? Of late they were more alert than usual, they took turns to guard the fence—but the fence was long. God's hand would guide the Boer police away from her children.

Sindisiwe had suffered much in the past few months, and told herself she could still suffer more if called upon to do so. But again, almost shamefully, she admitted to herself that the courage and defiance that her political training had given her were wearing thin; how else could she account for her frequent relapses into prayer in those last few months? In that formless mute darkness she tried again to merge her belief in God and her belief in herself. She drilled her conscience again into believing that violence is morally better than passive submission; and that acquiescence is evil. She told herself over and over again that it was right that her children should join her in this monastery of her refuge and learn all its disciplines.

The hours crawled by, and her thoughts outpaced the hours. This no longer frustrated her. It was one discipline she had acquired in this lonely exile, where she feared to confide even in those nearest to her. She could now contain most of her restless thoughts. But tonight her thoughts were sterile, they gave her no emotional stability. She was restless, with clammy hands and a head that swirled. They were woolly thoughts that turned and lashed like a multitude of snakes.

At first, soon after midnight, she thought it was the extension of her cowardly heart that fluttered and thudded, so that the whole place filled with a soft hum. Another moment told her it was the car. It must be the car, the car that was bringing her children. Almost beside herself she moved and stood up to peer through the dark. She tried to listen if there was anyone else around, but the sound of her heart, even more than that of the car, drowned any other sound. She heard the car stop at a distance. She at last had come to the endless end. She knew he had stopped a long way away, but she admitted to herself that the driver could not drive any further without risking being found out. She debated whether to go over the fence and meet them or to wait. Her eyes, accustomed to the darkness, could see the little ribbon of a footpath that local people used without fear of consequence during the day. She would not follow that path. It was a day path for guiltless people whose lives harboured no conspiracies. Her whole body was flushed in a flood of warm mother-love that she had denied herself for so long. The very thought that her two children were a matter of yards from her stirred her into hot tears.

She sniffed and crouched under the fence and crossed to meet them. She could not let them face the danger of that border alone; besides, something seemed to have taken complete possession of all her physical body; she could not hold back her feet, even if she had tried. Soon the formless darkness shaped itself into a moving shape. She could not hear any sounds, not even of her own fleeting steps. A few whispers of gratitude and the man turned on his way back, happy in the knowledge that one more "mission" had been accomplished.

Sindisiwe gathered her sons into the warmth of her arms and love in that speechless darkness. She felt their rigid bodies melt in fearlessness. She smeared them with the tears of her joy but the children were dry in their bewilderment. The last few days had tossed them through strange situations, alone, without the certainty of life as they had known it with their grandparents. Avoiding the path again, she softly tripped through the grass. . . .

Then, right there before them, next to the fence rose a form. She whispered dryly "*Cushani!* (crawl through!)" and her sons scattered to cross like lonesome sheep. The boys were accustomed to fast movements across fences in the freedom of their life in the country, but Sindisiwe was not; she carried their suitcase, she knew the danger and her knees wobbled when she heard the first shot. The darkness screamed with the sound of the gun; she heard another one and thought she felt something on her thigh, but she told herself it was the wire that had scratched her. Once on the other side of the fence she felt the heaviness of her leg and could no longer doubt that she had been wounded. "Yet I can walk; maybe I'm not wounded."

Her concern in any case was not for her leg but for her children. She knew they must have crossed and, because they were faster, must be ahead of her. A quarter of a mile down, with the suitcase on her head, she felt the hot pain and some faintness. She decided to sit down and call her sons. Mandla was near but they could not find Temba; he had run even further. Sindisiwe, not wishing to alarm her son did not disclose her injury, but told him to go and look for Temba. Naturally, Mandla was reluctant, but his mother assured him that they were safe where they were; they were in Botswana and nothing could harm them any more. More out of concern for his beloved brother than from lack of fear, Mandla went on stepping silently.

He dared not shout, but Temba, who was straining for any sounds of his mother and brother, gave a slight cough. Sindisiwe persuaded her children to spend the night with her outside on that cold autumn dark night. Unseen, she tied a stocking on the wound that was bleeding freely and would make her very weak. "It can't be a serious injury or how can I walk?" They sat there, unable to sleep for they were cold and heavy with the misfortunes of the dark night. And for Sindisiwe there was the added burden of a hidden, unknown injury. The weight of it, the fear of its possibilities, lay there and stiffened her thoughts. "It is best to reveal wounds in the light of day—daylight takes away their mystery."

Just before the darkness broke, she heard the rhythmic breathing of her sons—they were asleep at last; they were tired. She got another chance to relax her steeled nerves, she melted into another hot flood of tears. But soon she told herself she had to be strong; for their sake she could not afford the luxury of self-pity. She had to bear even the pain with a serene face. She began to worry whether her leg would allow her to walk the next ten miles back to Gaborone. She was apprehensive, and again she turned to God. This time she almost laughed at the game she played with her God. He no longer seemed God the creator, but the God that she had created herself for her manifold needs. A few hours earlier she had entreated him for her last request, but now she had yet another; her trust in his infinite goodness waxed stronger. She prayed now, not for one specific request, but simply laid her life at his feet for his use in his infinite wisdom. She did not know what to pray for because she truly did not know what to do, though she knew she desperately needed some assistance. Who would take an injured woman with children? Up to now she had shared one hut with six other women, four of them with babies and three of them with husbands who lived and slept in another hut two miles away; refugees like her. She had saved her last bit of money in the hope that when her children came she could persuade one of the other villagers around to accept the money in exchange for the use of one of their huts. But she had put off finding the hut until her children came. How could she have told people that she was expecting her children, even before they came? People's movements had become such very personal matters. Whom could she have trusted with such a secret? The South African spies were everywhere; nobody was close enough to be trusted. And now she was wounded—how would she explain her injury to the villagers, any villagers? Besides, they had all been warned against South Africans "who crossed the borders to cause trouble in their own land."

When the boys woke up they realised with horror their mother's helplessness. They were perplexed—it all seemed a nightmare. She sent them for their breakfast supplies from a little store further down along the border.

They moved in fear, whispering to each other all the way, even though the brilliant sun shone on the dry land that opened its arms in welcome. They could not reconcile the violence of the night with the peace of day. As the sun rose in that treeless stretch they saw the pain in their mother's eyes and the helplessness she could not hide. She could not walk, for the whole leg was swollen as it lay on the dry clotted blood. Mandla thought of medical supplies, but the inside of the store had shown him it could offer nothing in that line. Finally he asked hesitatingly where they could find a hospital or clinic. There wasn't one for ten miles.

Towards sunset Sindisiwe was beginning to feel very feverish and she began to fear that the simple wound could turn septic. So she sent her sons to look for assistance. She dared ask for assistance, though she knew all the people around feared for their own safety. The villages were not very far away, but the boys received no more than a cold stare as they tried to explain their trouble. They encountered a new unexpected problem. These people spoke Tswana and because they had spent most of their time in Natal, they spoke only Zulu. Beyond the language gulf they saw fear in the cold stares.

After passing through several huts, when the sun was red on the distant mountains, the boys came at last to the home of one woman who broke into a flood of Zulu. In spite of their sorrow they smiled and explained their plight. The language barrier had been breached, and by the time they broke the tragic news of their mother, the woman could no longer recoil completely. She was a Motswana who had lived in Johannesburg for some years and had learned not only Zulu but suffering, and fearlessness of strangers. Her name was Makeletso and she had kept the secret of a husband on Robben Island very successfully. So she told the boys of the dangers surrounding their request; though a political activist herself, she wished to shy away from any further involvement now that she was back home. The neighbours would know she was harbouring a wounded strange woman and sons; obviously these would be South African trouble-makers. The news would reach the chief before the following sunset and from there who knew what might happen. Indeed, nobody knew what could happen; but if the Botswana Government did not act, then the South Africans at the border in their own right would be very unkind to the villagers who wanted to cross over to the other side. There were bigger shops across the border and besides, many of their own friends and relatives lived just across the border. These borders were Whitemen's borders. They cut through tribes and divided villages and relatives. She would bring sorrow to the whole village.

Nevertheless Makeletso consented to return with the boys when it was dark, with food, hot porridge and some medicines. She had learned to live here in this "wilderness" as she called it, with some supplies of her own, her Dettol, bandages, ointment and aspirins. The boys were tired, but this gave them hope. They began to hope again, as though she had promised them her whole life. After all what do boys of twelve and fourteen, who have grown up in the country, know about the complications of bullet wounds?

To them it was the wound; they had hardly given a thought to the bullet that nestled deep in the muscle, close to the bone.

With the hot porridge warming their blood, they walked back with Makeletso through darkness, stealthily, to the spot where their mother lay groaning. She could no longer hide her agony. She was cold and very feverish. Sindisiwe felt her spirits rise, just to know somebody cared enough to risk her own safety. But it was only her spirits. The treatment left her pain unchanged. Makeletso had to rush back before anybody found out about her absence, but she carried a heavy heart, for she knew the gravity of Sindisiwe's condition, and she was powerless to help. But how could she leave a woman to die in the cold autumn night, with no one but her young sons to tend her? "Tomorrow, tomorrow I'll work it out. I'll go there, and pretend I found her by accident." She worked it all out through the long sleepless hours.

The next morning, it was clear to Sindisiwe that she could not live. She thought about her children and wondered why they had to come, only to see her die. What punishment was this; what for; and which God visited parents' punishment on children—had she really sinned to suffer this? She did not fear death as such; she had toyed so often with the idea of dying that she had often pictured herself actually welcoming death. But she had thought of only one kind of death—dying while resisting the tyranny of oppression of her people; certainly not so defencelessly while running away from the Boers who had made her whole life, and those of others, such a misery. She had dreamt of heroic death, not this.

Her wandering gaze stared unseeingly at the vast burial ground of her hopes, the freezing snowland of her strongest desires. Then her mind switched to her two sons who sat abjectly on either side of her, shielding her from the hot sun with an improvised shade of a shirt on a stick. She thought too of Sipho, her husband. She had made the good habit of thinking as rarely of him as she could possibly afford; it was an exercise that had taken her many unbearably long months to master. How does one outgrow the habit of living with a loving husband, from whom one has been separated by a long prison sentence? She had ached and ached and ached for him and had fumbled a lot at first, learning many new things in his absence in the belief that he would have wanted her to take the stand she had taken. Once more she regretted that they had never shared, and now would never share, this new life she had learned in his absence; it had been basically for him she had done it all. She had taught the heart that yearned after him day and night, and every minute of her waking life, to drown its desires in hard work, work and more work. Perhaps he would never know her devoted contribution to the cause that he loved so well. And would he know she was dead? Those prison walls—did anything ever penetrate them? Could news of her death cross borders and waters to the fortress of Robben Island? With a deep sigh she whispered audibly, "*Ngangiyoze ngiyizeke*! (If I were to live, I would tell a long strange story!)"

This gave Mandla the courage to ask what it was that had brought her there where she had called for them so insistently and pathetically that their grandfather had had to release them so reluctantly to face the hazardous trip on their own with only strangers for companions. She was sweating profusely from the fever, not from the sun, and in spite of her heavy breathing she answered, "I cannot now tell you the long story, but I have some of my life stored away for you in my case. It is a strange story, my child. But from here, when all is over, you will go to Sharpeville, Number 20, Tema Street, where you will find a good friend of mine. She is the one who sent the message to you people about my escape to this place. She is Mrs Zethu Zungu. She knows the whole story. I left all my things with her, my clothes, your father's clothes and some of my furniture. She will tell you everything—"

Sindisiwe looked down at her leg, lying there, so impotent and so vibrant with pain. She lapsed into silence. Thinking about her sons—their present and their future—was futile; besides, it was unbearable. Instead, she fell into a reverie, slipping back into her past. Her childhood, so free of pain and threats; in those early years she had never known what a cloud hung over all life; she had not even known what was lacking in her life, until that unforgettable day. After that time, that day, no one could hide it from her: the pain of separation, the lack of love and the need for money. A memory rose before her eyes, a memory as alive as the land in front of her. She saw her father in her mind's eye, hobbling before her, and knew that if she were to live through this, she too would hobble for the rest of her days. She admitted to herself, in the throes of her pain, that such an end was inevitable—she was her father's daughter. Somehow there was a connection between that distant year and the present; something had inexorably drawn her to this fate, even without her knowledge. She had spent so little time with her father before "that year," that even now, she could not remember how he had looked before the instant grey hair of that year; before he came back from the mines to live out his days on the Reserve with them; before he had that hobble in his walk.

Miriam Tlali,
THE HAUNTING MELANCHOLY
OF KLIPVOORDAM
South Africa 1981   English

In 1980 "The Haunting Melancholy of Klipvoordam" was awarded third place in a short story competition run by *Drum* magazine. Although *Drum*'s November issue declared that the story would appear the following month, this was not to be. It was instead published in the literary magazine *Staffrider* in 1981, and later incorporated into Miriam Tlali's collected stories and essays, *Mihloti* (1984).

Tlali's association with *Staffrider* started with its first issue in March 1978, which contained her story "Soweto Hijack." The first issue was banned: *Staffrider* had introduced itself as "a skelm [rascal] of sorts" willing to confront the apartheid censorship board. Tlali later became a regular contributor, publishing several short stories and acting as an interviewer for the "Soweto Speaking" column. She had previously made history as the first black woman inside South Africa to publish a novel written in English. *Muriel at Metropolitan*, published in 1975, was banned in the same year, as was her second novel, *Amandla* (1980). Tlali was to cross swords again with the censorship board, and she developed ways to circumvent it. When, for example, her story "Just the Two of Us" was banned (she had only read it at a conference in Ohio), she published it as "Devil at a Dead End" in her volume *Footprints in the Quag* (1989). (This volume appeared in the same year in the United States under the title *Soweto Stories*.)

"The Haunting Melancholy of Klipvoordam" is unusual for *Staffrider* because it places the racist prescription of apartheid as subtext. Like other Black Consciousness writing, however, Tlali's story presents the reader with black humanity despite the oppression of apartheid. Whereas Black Consciousness writing in the main concentrates on black male characters, Tlali's writing here and elsewhere decenters the male. Moreover, the characters in this story are not defined solely by apartheid: Her writing motions toward a vivid world that unsettles expectations and defies pigeonholing, not least through the way two families—interacting in a contradictory space—discover possibilities of leisure not previously considered. In her creative texts as well as her essays and interviews, Tlali refuses to provide the hard and fast answers often produced by Black Consciousness writing.

Pumla Dineo Gqola

✦

It will take me a long long time to forget that New Year's eve—the last day of the year 1979. On that morning, we left Soweto bound for what was to all of us a unique experience. By "us" I mean Donald, his wife Pauline, their two nieces (Mpho and Mmaphuthi), my daughter Moleboheng and myself. We were a happy lot, all the six of us, packed and cramped into the Volkswagen Combi with provisions, blankets, mats, tents, umbrellas etc., the typical camping equipment the devoted couple had accumulated over the years. Peeping into the vehicle, I gasped with astonishment at the sight of all the paraphernalia when our hostess opened the door to us. She had earlier in the week invited us saying: "Come. You'll be our guests." And, needless to say, their hospitality throughout was something one can only marvel at.

I take the liberty of calling them "Don" and "Paul"—the way *they* so fondly refer to each other. The like of them in a place like Soweto should be protected from extinction; they should be honoured and revered. They are like a rare and endangered species of God's creation. They are among the few who still strive to bring about order where there is only chaos and despair. In the jumbled shattered existence of the Soweto Ghetto, they hanker after the sustaining force of mother nature. For does nature's eternal seasonal cycle not offer the propagation of new life in place of the withering and dying and hence hope for the future?

•

It was early in the morning, and the cheerful crowds of people determined to make the most of the holidays were not yet roaming the streets when we left. There was little traffic all along the Soweto Highway right up to Booysens where we joined the M1 Pretoria Highway. Soon, we were traversing the tree-lined affluent "white" northern suburbs of Johannesburg. The scantily-populated vast countryside on the way towards Pretoria district looked green and peaceful. We detoured into the Hammanskraal main road and followed the signs pointing to the small "dorpie" of Brits where we stopped to refuel and buy refreshments. Then we set out eagerly on the road again.

One would have expected that we would arrive at some border post, some line; a river or a bridge, at the end of which would be stationed a pair of stern-looking uniformed guards. That these honourable gentlemen would be wearing labelled epaulettes over their proud shoulders, or even medals on their lapels. I had looked around expecting to see sign-posts along the road reading: "Welcome To The Sovereign State of Bophuthatswana."

Yet we knew that by leaving Brits behind and taking a turn away from the smoothly-tarred road, onto the gravel one, we had in fact departed from the so-called "white" South Africa. We had left behind all the comfort that goes with that part of this land. We were now part of the so-called Bophuthatswana self-governing black state, having automatically relinquished all that was of merit. The whole transition had been as easy as taking candy from a child. Just like that. No lines of demarcation had been drawn, no signs, nothing.

It would have been redundant. We knew it; our bodies *felt* it. We were all aware that the one world had come to an end and a new one had begun. The dry dust, the thorny scrub on either side of the uneven road had warned us. Our driver—"Ntate Dono" as little thumb-sucking Mpho called him—had to dodge and meander around heaps and heaps of sand. It lay all over as if it had been transported in truckloads straight from the Sahara Desert. And no one had bothered to scrape it off. The Volkswagen bumped and joggled; it twisted this way and that, all the way kept under control by the driver's able dexterity. I wiped the sweat from my brow with a piece of tissue paper. It was a sweltering hot day. In fact, it was later reported to have been the hottest day that summer. Looking around at my co-travellers, I wondered whether their clammy foreheads were due to the weather or to the taxing drive.

I decided to stop reflecting on the rather sudden transformation; to indulge in no thoughts of the past or the future, but rather to try to enjoy what the present brought before me, and be thankful for it. We all sighed with relief when we realised that we were nearing the end of the hazardous journey. Our combi entered the bushy settlement and went on for a short while along the dusty road. Further on, there was a sharp bend where we came to an abrupt halt. The few scattered brick and corrugated iron structures were the offices of the holiday resort. Mpho, Mmaphuthi and Moleboheng (who had cuddled together right at the rear of the vehicle) jumped happily out, enjoying the cool shadows of the trees. They scampered around the place laughing and frolicking in anticipation. The beautiful unfamiliar trees nearby attracted our attention. Their patulous yellow flowers broadened out in full bloom and sparkled in the piercing sunshine. The kind smiling officials at the offices welcomed us happily. One of them came over to us and greeted us while "Ntate Dono" went on to the "stately" building to announce the arrival of our party and receive formal permission to enter and camp there. Paul and I decided to go for a short exploratory walk in the vicinity. It was the first time I had the honour of visiting a "black" recreational area in a so-called independent state in my own country and naturally I was curious. The official who accompanied us during our brief walk was willing to answer the numerous questions we asked, but he frankly admitted that he could not enlighten us on many of them. What were the names of the lovely trees with the yellow flowers dotted all around? Could we grow them in Soweto? Were there many different kinds of wild birds and animals, and what varieties were there? And the fish . . . would we be fortunate enough to catch many of them? The whole prospect of what lay ahead for us on the eve of the new year seemed fascinating and exciting. There was ever so much to learn. He informed us that we were amongst the few earliest holiday makers who had come, and the choice of where we would pitch our tent and settle down for the duration of our stay would be all ours. There were also rooms to hire for those who did not have their own camping equipment and many were still vacant, our guide said, but these were nearer the offices and far from the beautiful dam.

And what about all the rolls of steel wires, the poles and the enormous heavy concrete cylinders lying around . . . What was about to be constructed, I asked expectantly. "Nothing," the man explained, "there's no money. The Bophuthatswana authorities must still get the money to develop the new improvement projects. So much was still to be achieved. The place is there waiting. The land with all its potential resources. But there is no money. The whites were going to develop this place into a really fine holiday resort, but they stopped when Bophuthatswana was handed over to the blacks. They left everything as it was and took away the money!" "And what about the big imposing iron casements standing upright with the thick wiring?" we asked, and he replied: "Those were to be parts of a huge plant; an electricity generating machine which was to supply power to the entire concourse but that too has come to an untimely stop." No money. The poor skeletal left-overs. We looked at them, quietly reflecting. It dampened our spirits. The whole business of the poverty—the ever-present legacy always so readily bequeathed to the "honourable" inheritors of the so-called free black states. Who bothers about freedom in a deprived desert anyway, I wondered. I was happy to say goodbye to the kind guide with the parched lips and the worn uniform. And I wondered just how far "our" contribution of fifty cents for our stay there would go towards "improving the quality of life" in Klipvoordam Holiday Resort.

•

Little eight-year-old Mpho and her "Ntate Dono" immediately started to work. She momentarily abandoned her favourite pastime of thumb-sucking and demonstrated to all of us her expert knowledge of the camping and angling "trade." She had accompanied Ntate Dono on many previous occasions ever since she was a mere four-year-old. After the two had chosen what they considered to be the best spot to plant the three pairs of steel pegs to support the fishing rods in position, Mmaphuthi and Moleboheng joined them in digging, in anchoring posts and pitching the rectangular tent. Everything seemed perfect. We would all cast glances now and again at the vertically-suspended red and white spherical plastic balls (which Mpho and Don referred to as the "policemen") and which would show any slight movement, suggesting the presence of a "catch" at the immersed end of the line. I assisted Paul with the preparation of our lunch and the kids stripped and garbed themselves in the swim-suits they had brought along with them. Moleboheng, being of the same height and stature as Mmaphuthi, easily fitted into the extra pair the latter had had the presence of mind to provide. They wasted no time in plunging into the cool beckoning waters and we could hear their deafening hilarious cries as they swam and threw sandballs into the air. I envied them. I had never possessed a swim-suit. All my life I had yearned to go for a holiday at the coast; anywhere away from the hustle and bustle of the city, but I could never afford it. How many of us are so fortunate in Soweto anyway? It struck me that it would be quite preposterous and shocking for me to do what I learnt was the common alternative to having no swim-suit to wear—like the majority of those of my fellow Sowetans and other blacks who managed to find themselves at the Klipvoordam—to strip to the underwear and just have a good swim anyway! Finally, tired of "ho lebella ngoale ha e khiba" (of watching the initiation girl do her dance) as we say in our vernacular, Paul and I decided to indulge in the more "acceptable" alternative we could manage—that of sitting on the edge of the dam and only immersing our legs and thighs into the inviting cool water—shame.

The tall trees behind us were throwing their shadows further and further into the middle of the dam. We watched the images as they grew longer and longer, bringing with them the mind-refreshing air of late afternoon.

About the possibility of catching any fish, our angling expert had not been optimistic. Paul had earlier intimated to me: "You know, Don said to me last night at home that because there was a full moon, for some reason or other, the fishes would not be easy to catch. That made me feel disappointed because I would have liked you to enjoy with us the excitement of pulling out a fish from the water." Don had been right after all. So far, ever since our arrival before lunch-time, the "policemen" had only quavered slightly, indicating that the fish had merely got near the bait to gnaw at them and then withdraw to their "hiding places." It struck me that these aquatic creatures must be very very intelligent indeed, after all. The slowly rising full moon was rosy and majestic. I wondered why the fish would want to shy away from it at all. For hours since we first sat there, not one of them had even leapt over the surface of the water, whose gentle waves the moon kept touching slightly with her crimson glow.

The arrival of one more group of holiday-makers in a convoy of one big American car and a packed panel van, made me believe what Paul had said soon after we had settled down near the "deserted" resort. She had observed: "It's so quiet and lonely now; but by midday tomorrow—New Year's Day—this place will be so congested that there'll not even be enough space to move." I had not taken her seriously then because to me the likelihood of such an occurrence seemed quite remote. We watched them from time to time as they pitched tent a good distance away from us, and observed that their huge vanload consisted of many cases of beer, wine, and all types of intoxicating spirits. To them, the arrival of the expected multitudes would mean a good share of their holiday pay. In the scorching heat of the Klipvoordam, with its vegetation of spiky-leafed scattered trees with hardly any shade at all, the visitors would drink more and more to try and quench their thirsts. It would be business and more business!

Two more flickering lights on the far-off bank diagonally opposite to where we were announced the arrival of two more camping companions.

We had left Soweto behind. There were no loud sounds of exhilaration and shouting. No cheap screechy turn-tables incessantly and noisily blaring away the latest Bob Marley or Jimmy Cliff reggae hits to echo and accommodate the eager throbbing souls of Soweto's jolling, body-wiggling young and old. Here was peace and quiet; something we had come a long way to enjoy. There were only the sounds of the birds and the mysterious low moaning and subdued grunting and snarling of what our expert angler said were the wild animals in the vicinity. Don, being the devout naturalist he is, was the only one who could distinguish the various calls of the wild. Had it not been for our complete reliance on his very excellent knowledge of the behaviour of the beasts and the fluttering yellow flames of our neighbours' lamps, the somewhat disturbing low cries in our immediate proximity would have driven me crazy with fright. It required real courage on my part to ignore the recurring wailings.

I had remembered to bring my tape-recorder with me. The soothing, reassuring voice of Brook Benton—one of our favourite Gospel and Ballad singers—seemed to me to be the best way of easing my nerves. I turned the volume knob on more to drown the sounds emerging from the dark forest all around . . .

> If you think God is dead, just look around.
> I look at the sea and realise no man can drain it.
> We've all got to die one day but no one can time it.

*Who else could make the moon and the sun shine over every
city and every town?
If you think God is dead, then you haven't looked around . . .*

As if aware of our peculiar setting and environment, the singer's solemn hushed tone insisted, inspiring us and providing a firm background to our feelings. We chatted on softly, listening, assimilating and enjoying the free endowments of nature. The cool breeze fanning the waves; the moon, the stars, the stillness. And all the time, the music . . .

*Look at the sea
Look at the trees
I guess you can hear the breeze
Look at each other.*

*So you see, God is not dead
If you don't want to see Him,
You won't see Him
But if you want to see Him,
You look around . . .*

We spoke of death. Each one of us remembered our dear departed ones. I thought of my mother's passing, and the hollow emptiness, the loneliness I experienced at the time, came back vividly and I held back the tears which came flooding into my eyes.

We spoke of happiness . . . of Zimbabwe and the prospect of the end to long-raging war and the imminent "uhuru" for that country so close to "ours." "Just think what it will mean!" we kept remarking. To the Zimbabweans it was certain that the new year would bring freedom, peace and prosperity for all. It would bring hope. Was there any hope for us, we wondered.

We looked around. There was a narrow winding path leading from the hedges at the back of us to the edge of the dam. Pieces of rock were lined at regular intervals along the edge of the water. The fast-approaching midnight brought with it isolated human calls of "Happy! Happy!" from somewhere behind the trees. They seemed to come from far away. An eerie, sombre undertone lurked and echoed after every cry. It was evident that enthusiastic late night arrivals had shown up and they had hired rooms in the resort. Dark figures kept emerging from the bushes one by one, walking slowly along the worn footpath. On reaching the end of the road near the rocks, each figure would straddle over a rock or just stand there and look into the dark far-off end of the still water and the distant horizon. Without saying a word, the lone viewer would saunter slowly back into the spiky grove. This rather strik-ing behaviour of these holiday-makers did not disturb nor surprise us. Except for the progressively-waning lonesome screams of "Happy! Happy!" the soli-tude was complete. There is something haunting and mysterious about the sight of wide expanses of the moving waters, the gentle ebb and flow of the waves, which never fails to make the mind wander away into deep thought and marvel at the miracle of creation.

We talked about the approaching midnight and the end of the year, every year, and the birth of another one in "our" Soweto. How different it *was* then. There was, we knew, all the euphoria and exaltation; the singing, ululating and dancing; the beating of drums and chiming of bells; the crackling and bursting of crackers and explosives. And, as the bustling finally wears itself out, the great excursion would begin in earnest. Busloads, truckloads, hooting cars adorned with colourful ribbons, carrying hundreds of eager men and women (mostly teenagers) dancing to the rhythm of thunderous portable radios, stereos and tape-recorders. These would be speeding through the grey townships to anywhere—all corners, nooks and crevices; to any "available," "permitted" or "open" picnic spots— where blacks may be "allowed" to relax for the day. These would be somewhere well out of the way of the "whites only" reserved luxury spots of course: something like "our" Klipvoordam . . . out of *their* line of vision.

Minutes before the decisive hour struck, Don announced, smiling and looking at us: "I have a surprise for you two."

We watched him curiously and were puzzled as he looked at his wristwatch.

He explained: "I have a bottle of wine for all of us to drink a toast to the New Year of 1980."

He then went over to the portable cooler and brought a bottle of wine and three glasses. All three of us pronounced the toast simultaneously, raising our glasses and letting them touch lightly in the cool air as we declared: "To the New Year . . . May it bring hope, peace and prosperity to all mankind . . . And to the liberation of Azania!"

"Tsogang tlheng bathong! Tlayang tlheng le tlo bonang!" (Oh wake up, people, please! Oh please do come and see!)

The first to respond to the urgent call was Mphonyana (little Mpho). Ntate Dono had been calling; he had been trying to rouse us. He had never slept. The patient wakefulness he had developed over many years as an angler, had come as second nature to him. He once quoted James Rennie who in 1823 had said: "Angling is a sport that requires as much enthusiasm as poetry, as much patience as mathematics and as much caution as house-breaking."

He had failed to lure the fish to his hook—an eventuality he had predicted even before we started on our trip. He had therefore not been disheartened by the extent to which a novice would have been.

When the sun's first rays touched the clouds over the horizon, his keen fisherman's eye spotted them. He had not been able to resist the overwhelming magic of it all, and the desire to share the experience had overpowered him. He called to us all to come and witness the fascinating spectacle.

"Mafube . . . " I deliberately choose to make use of this word in our African vernacular because to my mind, in the English medium in which I am writing, no word that I can think of describes adequately the whole mesmerising excellence of the break of dawn than "mafube," especially when seen in the clear open emptiness of unspoilt nature. The word—pronounced with the middle syllable rather drawn out—captures, expresses and implies the presence of the varying hues and their related spectral shades; the reds, yellows, pinks and so on.

It must have been in the hypnotising spell of those magical moments that little Mpho reiterated Ntate Dono's pleadings. It was not easy to be persuaded to leave our comfortable floor beds. We were not as quick and alert as Mpho, the aspirant angler. The urgency in her voice was what made me shake off my inertia. She was peeping in at the tent-door calling us to join them outside. Determined to make the most of my stay there, I snatched the pocket camera next to my pillow and stormed out.

I shall not try to describe the whole tantalising scenery but will leave it to the imagination of the reader because I know that I shall fail in my attempt. The three of us stood there amazed. Through the corner of my eye, I could see Mpho sucking more vigorously at her thumb. We just stared and said nothing. "Even attempting to describe all this would be destructive—it would spoil it." Don sighed.

Our attention was distracted by the appearance from the thicket of a tall dark figure. He came walking slowly along the footpath. He had his hands tucked into his trouser pockets and plodded his way towards the end of the path. He seemed not to be aware of our presence, but only of the glow over the horizon, which was casting a golden aura all around. He crouched on the piece of rock near him, all the time staring ahead. Perhaps, like most of us, he was in pursuit of deliverance from boredom; to understand the mysteries of "truth," of "being," which the ancient scholars like Pythagoras and Socrates had tried to fathom and unravel. Two raven-like birds with long wings fluttered above his head and headed towards the sun's rays. The man lowered his head (probably from exhaustion) and sank it into the angle between his forearm and the biceps and remained in that position like a weeping child. It was almost tear-provoking. So moved by the spectacle was Mpho that she remarked: "Look, he looks like someone removed his head!" To me the whole spectacle suggested the perfect illustration of loneliness. The man was very likely trying to escape from the helplessness of a lifetime of unfulfilled aspirations—an existence where hopes and dreams remain forever a receding mirage. The opportunity had availed itself and he had come to the dam, even if like so many of us he could not afford a swimsuit. The melancholy of the entire episode of going and never arriving; of ever approaching and desiring seemed to be embodied and finalised in those moments. I looked away and focussed my eyes on another area far from the man. I remembered the lines in one of the songs we played over and over again:

> *Heaven help the child who never had a home.*
> *Heaven help us all.*

Heaven help the black man
If he struggles one more day
Heaven help the white man
If he turns his back away
Heaven help the man
who kicks a man and makes him crawl
Heaven help us all
who won't reach twenty-one
Heaven help the people
with their backs against the wall . . .

Brook Benton's voice kept haunting me. I turned my head and looked at the dejected "headless" outline of the man. Even the intrusion of another figure, a woman, who must have decided to interrupt the sad-looking crouching form by walking fully-clad right into the still calm water did not seem to shake him into any response. Soon after the sun had shown its tip above the surface of the water, he raised his head slowly, listening and looking into the waves which were drifting in bigger and bigger circles away from the woman's legs. I had only taken a picture of the stooping frame, but I knew then that I would have been happier if I had possessed the skills of an expert artist.

The three of us watched the man as he stood up and turned back into the narrow path by which he had come, still looking as unaware of our presence as when he first appeared. He trudged on and vanished into the shades, leaving us wondering. Who knows, it could be that he had come to catch a glimpse of, and draw strength from the magic of the gathering "mafube."

And the words of the ballad singer's song kept on lingering in my mind:

Keep hatred from the mighty
And the mighty from the strong . . .
Heaven help us all.

Lily Changfoot, RETURN JOURNEY
South Africa 1982   English

Lily Changfoot's account of running the racial gauntlet offers a vivid insight into aspects of growing up as a Chinese girl in South Africa in the 1940s and 1950s. Born in Prospect township, on the outskirts of Johannesburg, she lived on a farm near Krugersdorp, attending the Krugersdorp Indian School for four years and later St. Angela's Convent in Kensington, Johannesburg, the private white convent referred to in her account.

Catholic and Anglican schools were the first white educational institutions to admit pupils of color, and those Chinese parents who could afford the fees took advantage of this rare opportunity to give their children a private education. Because only a handful of Chinese were accepted annually, such a privilege was highly prized and both children and parents made sacrifices to secure it.

Public transport was one part of daily life in South Africa in which Chinese children encountered the "real world." Apart from trains, there were as many incidents on trams, buses, and planes. Because of the community's ill-defined position between black and white, their place in the apartheid scheme became the subject of much controversy in later years when newspapers used it to ridicule the government's segregation policies.

Changfoot's recollections were published decades after she emigrated from South Africa to settle permanently in Canada. There she wrote a successful Chinese cookbook as well as an inspirational work entitled *The Wealth of Jesus's Love*, the companion volume to her autobiographical *A Many-Coloured South Africa: The Diary of a Non-Person* from which this chapter is taken. Her experiences are recalled with all the sharp simplicity of childhood.

Melanie Yap

✦

It rained that first afternoon after school. Not knowing if I were permitted inside the tram-stop shelter as it had "Whites Only"— *"Alleen vir Blankes"* painted across the front, I stood outside, while the other girls were within, sheltering from the rain. Growing up in a society in which I had been constantly hurt—both emotionally and physically—I preferred to get wet, rather than be embarrassed by being told to leave the shelter, especially in front of the girls, because a policeman was standing nearby. But having learned more about Johannesburg in due course, I did not hesitate to use the shelter afterwards.

Standing on the "non-White" section of the wet, grimy, concrete platform, at Jeppe Station, I was nervous, afraid and distraught. I moved from one spot to another, trying to evade the water seeping through the steel and concrete roof, which was actually Main Street, potholed from the timeless pounding of streetcars.

It was the end of my first day at St. Angela's Convent, and the second time I would be boarding a train, the first having been the ride into Johannesburg of that morning from Krugersdorp. The cloudy skies matched the dimly lit, dismal station.

I, a Chinese, not accepted in a White society and distrusted by the African, stood motionless, desperately awaiting the arrival of the 3:30 p.m. train. From the corner of my eye, I could see the groups of Africans milling about. My school hat was snatched from my head. Turning around, I saw a Coloured youth about twenty years old, threatening to molest me.

"Ha, here's a pretty China girl," he said.

Overcome with fear and weakness, I could not cry out, but burst into tears.

The train arrived: it was a "Godsend." I rushed into the carriage, hoping the youth would not pursue me. My relief was brief, for when I looked up, he was seated beside me, gloating with victory. He attempted to put his arms around me, and tried to kiss me. Petrified, I prayed and hoped the conductor would appear, but in the meantime wrestled and struggled.

The first-class "non-White" compartment consisted of an enclosed four-seat cubicle which could accommodate about ten passengers. No one could know of my grim struggle, unless the conductor came through. No working African was in a financial position to travel first class. This compartment was used by non-White "professionals" such as Indian and Coloured school teachers and the odd "outsider" like me.

I was used to being insulted, cheated and sneered at, the price of being born with a yellow-skin. But I had never experienced the terrible situation of a helpless girl being attacked in a lonely train compartment.

Up to then I had become resigned to the fact that I was a "second-class" citizen, and had become immune to taunts, ridicule and profanity at its worst, hurled at me. To return hate for hate would only degrade and lessen my human dignity. But at this moment, seated in the compartment, I was overcome with hate at this half-breed, forgetting my own afflictions and colour. I detested him, not because of his birth, but that he should choose an innocent girl not responsible for his circumstances, to let off steam. I screamed, shouted, and pounded on the door separating us from the conductor's compartment. I was in a fit of rage, and determined to cause him such annoyance that he would refrain from touching me.

About ten minutes later, which seemed an eternity, the conductor came through the second-class door, evidently working his way down from the third-class carriages occupied entirely by Africans. They were usually so overcrowded that it has happened that a passenger got trampled to death. I recall a dear old servant who remarked, "It is not that there are no trains, but they are so overfull that they cannot fit in another person."

My distress was obvious to the White conductor. As far as he was concerned, the youth could molest me, but since he was on duty on this train he wanted to avoid trouble. He reprimanded the youth, and with a shake of his fist expelled him from the train at the next station. That ordeal left me more determined than ever to continue my schooling.

Through the years of high school, I encountered and crossed three social, racial and economic barriers each day, tasting the sweetness and the bitterness of each. The bitterness was greater.

Occasionally during school hours I would be told that I was looking tired. "Just a little worn-out," I'd reply. I did not bother to enumerate the harassing conditions and situations that I was subjected to daily—being "caught in the middle"—neither Black nor White.

As a South African Chinese, I was sandwiched between Black and White. Despite their rationalizations against me, I do not hate them, nor am I vengeful: only grieved that South Africa, such a beautiful country, is made ugly by its policies. I'm saddened by my student memories, but prize the education I gained.

"Thandiwe Mhlanga," Angela Kotler, and Hazel Hall,
ARRESTED FOR BEING WOMEN

Zimbabwe 1983　English

On 28 October 1983 the Zimbabwe government launched a campaign against prostitution that resulted in the arrest and imprisonment of 6,316 women throughout Zimbabwe. Hundreds of women were kept in local prisons and several thousand were sent to an old military camp in the Zambezi Valley. The Vagrancy Law, under which the arrests were made, was amended retrospectively to enable the police to hold them for longer than the forty-eight hours allowed under the law. The campaign was called "Operation Clean-Up," and women were arrested indiscriminately—grandmothers, schoolgirls, nurses coming off duty. Simply to be a woman was to risk arrest. As a result of this attack a handful of ordinary black and white women came together and mounted a nationwide protest, in the face of which the government, after a few weeks, abandoned the operation. But the group of protesters remained together, determined that such an outrage should never again be perpetrated against women. The group recorded the testimonies of some of the arrested women, two of which appear here—that of "Thandiwe Mhlanga" from Harare, and that of Angela Kotler and Hazel Hall from Gweru. (A pseudonym has been used to protect the identity of the woman from Harare; the women from Gweru have since left Zimbabwe.) The protesters remained together as a pressure group and in 1987 were registered as the Women's Action Group (WAG). They are still active today, protecting and furthering the legal, educational, economic, and human rights of women. Their story is told in *Determined to Act*, published by WAG in 1998.

Peggy Watson

✦

"THANDIWE MHLANGA," HARARE

On 29 October I was walking home alone down Fourth Street, at about 8 p.m., after visiting my sister and her husband. I was approached by a group of about seven men, two in the blue uniform of the Police Reserve, the others in plain clothes, and was told I was under arrest. They asked me where I was going, where I lived, and where I had been, but ignored my answers. They told me I had to go with them to Central Police Station.

There was a large group of women in the street at the time, all under arrest. There was another group of men who had been with the women. They were not under arrest, just trailing behind.

I ran away from the police to my flat but they followed me and banged on my door. I was forced to open it. I showed them the flat. They asked me who paid for it. I told them I was working at the Ministry of Education as a registry clerk and paid for it myself. They insisted a man must be paying for it.

They took me to the police station. There were a lot of women there. We were asked our names and addresses. They wrote "Prostitution" after all our names. At least one woman was handcuffed. They took us to Chikurubi. There were men, women, everybody altogether. They gave us each a blanket. This was on Saturday night. On Monday we were interviewed by Social Welfare and again "Prostitution" was written after our names. When we asked why they were doing this we were told that they had been told to do it.

During this time we were given some food but it was inedible. You couldn't feed it to dogs. While I was there there was a riot by some people who were detained. Tear gas was used to break up the riot. The police had threatened us and treated us very badly. They threatened to hit us and were very rough. I was with some nurses. The police said to the nurses, "So you earn your own money. We want to see how you are going to spend it in Chikurubi."

On Monday afternoon my sister came with evidence of my job and I was released.

I now feel uncomfortable at work. People are joking about it, implying that I am a prostitute. My supervisor is deliberately picking on me. I intend to apply for a transfer from my department.

ANGELA KOTLER AND HAZEL HALL, GWERU

On Friday 11 November, 1983, we had been to see a film, *Wild Geese*, at the Gweru theatre. We were leaving at about 9.30 P.M. when some armed soldiers came into the foyer and grabbed hold of us. When we tried to resist they became extremely agitated and started pushing and shoving and threatening. They were just grabbing women, mainly black women. We were dragged away from our friends. Outside the theatre it was chaos, a huge crowd, people protesting, shouting, crying and all the women being put into land cruisers. In the one we were in there were two girls who were only 14. We were taken to Gweru prison and told to sit on the ground in the rain. There we waited until more truckloads arrived. Then we were herded into cells. We two held hands and went into the same cell. It was about 3m x 5m and there were 17 of us in there and also a tiny baby. It was stiflingly hot. No attempt was made to take our names or identify us and at no time did anyone explain to us what we were being arrested for or what was to happen to us. We were not allowed to contact friends or relatives and a lawyer who tried to see us was refused access. The lights were turned on and off about an hour at a time. For several hours we could hear more women being brought in, then someone shouted that we must be quiet and gradually the shouting and the crying stopped.

Angela Kotler
Hazel Hall

Regina Ntongana, CROSSROADS

South Africa 1984   English

In 1986, in Crossroads, a squatter camp near Cape Town, one of the most brutal forced removals in the history of South Africa took place. This was in response to the increasing threat of the powerful political activity in the area, as residents resisted the "offer" of new houses in New Crossroads, where rents would be high and resettlement would fracture the political solidarity and support of the existing community. Regina Ntongana, who had lived in Crossroads since 1975 and who was elected chairperson of the Crossroads Women's Committee in 1976, had been crucially involved in building up this sense of community in the fight against apartheid.

In this interview, given at least two years before the final massive forced removal and at a time of relative optimism about their resistance to it, Ntongana casts back to the personal circumstances that led her to live in Crossroads. She speaks of the deaths from starvation of her children in the Transkei, where she had been forced to live, and the urgency of her need to live with her husband in a community that could offer schools, clinics, and the possibility of work. She describes the birth of a local women's movement. She speaks in English, not her mother tongue.

On one occasion in 1983 (not referred to in this interview) when Ntongana was being terrorized, she made a statement, published on 31 December 1983 in the *Cape Times*: "We, the women, are the foundations of Crossroads. Since the men took over [in 1979], things have never been the same. The men are only concerned with their own benefits."

That her husband Jeffrey had been secretary of the Crossroads Executive Committee (though he resigned in April 1983) added to Ntongana's difficulty in working with the Crossroads Women's Committee. In the interview published below, she briefly refers to the domestic awkwardness that ensued, and speaks of it slightly more fully in an earlier interview with Josette Cole in 1983 (published in Cole's book *Crossroads* [1987]), conceptualizing the difficulty as a conflict between her commitment to women and to her husband: "There were days [when we] weren't speaking. And the women were also looking at me to see which way I would blow. I can say it was almost divorce."

Dorothy Driver

✦

I first came to Cape Town in 1959 because the granny I was staying with passed away. When I got here there was a big fight because the women didn't want to carry passes—I was very young and didn't know nothing about strikes—back there we doesn't know about strikes. My mother was one of the Federation women, when I came I found they was always having meetings and talk about this. It was difficult to me because I didn't know about it. . . . I mean I just listened to them and sometimes I went to meetings or I asked my mother, "What's going on, why are you trying to be against the government?": then she was sitting down and trying to explain to me.

I always saw my father just as strong as her, they were both strong, but he believed that a woman is stronger than a man. He always said, "If a woman say a thing she's not going to change, she's going to do it." At that time, too, it did seem to me that the women were stronger, because there was this big raid by the administration board in Nyanga—the men were beaten up but the women were shouting and swearing at the police: the inspectors did nothing to them; they were marching and singing songs, freedom songs.

When I got married in 1964 I was staying at Nyanga with my husband's family and there was a rule, a sort of law that if you stayed with people you must be registered that you are a lodger. So we went to the office and they tell me my husband is not qualified to stay because he hasn't worked ten years in one place—he was a labourer at Park Gate, Strand Street, but only for four years. So that means that I have to leave, although I have been born in Cape Town.

I went to Transkei, to my husband's family; it was so sad and bitter to me that sometimes I just have to cry. But he couldn't do nothing. I couldn't do nothing. He say to me, "If you going to come up they're going to arrest you every time." But later on, when two of the children were dead, I just decide I must come up. I come with two, two were already dead, died in Transkei . . . we were starving in Transkei, I must say it. There wasn't doctors there, they were miles away. When I came to the doctor the child was already passed away. It was really and truly starving, all we had was stamp mealies, no fat, a piece of meat if a cattle die. Sometimes we have to drink dirty water; you just take a white cloth and then have to strain it because it's dirty, the cattle are drinking the same water, there's no other place. My baby was seven months when it died, the other one was two years and four months.

I decided they can do what they like to me, but I am not prepared to stay any more in Transkei, so I came up with the train. My husband was living in the single men's barracks at Langa, so he took me to his auntie and we lodged there, but it was really very difficult, they arrest us every time. We live like that for three years, and then decide we must go to the bushes, for the people there would help us find a place to stay—a few coloureds were staying there, and they say we can stay with them. That was not Crossroads, but an earlier camp: we built a shack for the family. There were water, but no lavatories, just a hole in the ground, and for rubbish collection we dig another hole. Then after a time it was the administration board that said we must go to the emergency camp at Crossroads, because we was in a coloured area . . . they show us Crossroads, and we came here in February '75. It was called a "site and service" camp—at first they didn't try to make us leave.

Between '75 and '77 we came to be strong, because we had all these meetings every day; we share our views and our thoughts on each and everything, even before the removals. When we first came we decide to make a meeting of women community members, we must elect a few because when the board came during the day the men are at work, only we women are there. It was up to us to find out who is arrest and who is not arrest; then we decided to go and see the lawyers and that's really how we came to be a community, a women's community at Crossroads.

It was an elected committee after our outside meetings; we decided we must have some in front to lead, we must know who is going to work—so we elected thirty women . . . at first the men didn't like it, they say we do things too fast for them. Later they decide also they must have a men's committee, to come behind us and see what's going on. But the problem for the men was that they were working, and during the day we was going to all the offices to find out what was going on! So we know more than the men . . . sometimes when we put the agenda to them they start to be jealous and they say why does we always know the things; how does we always know the things? Some of them were really jealous, they stop us to have a meeting . . . later on, when we thought, as women, we must sit down and show how things are happening, really they did accept us.

I suppose we did win that fight, to stay here in Cape Town, and to stay in Crossroads. But now we don't want to go to the New Crossroads they building, now that the demolition of our camp is no longer in front of us. Even though they are brick houses, with running water, and lavatories and bathrooms—the rents are too high. Some of them doesn't work, some are widows, so they are really afraid of it . . . they wouldn't mind if the government can leave the squatters' camp. It's my feeling too, although I know I did spoke with the government and tried to say we want better conditions. Crossroads is all right except when it's raining and it gets muddy; but we have got clinics here, we have each other. We're like the township and we wouldn't mind to stay here.

We really developed a good system as a community. If there's something wrong, we make an agenda—and first the committee decide what it can do, but it doesn't just finish there: we take it as it is and share it with the general residents. And when we've had a meeting to negotiate we also take it back to all the residents. We call meetings: we've got loudhailers, both men and women using loudhailers. We as women reporting some of the matters, although not for a time because there was a misunderstanding between the men and the women, but now things are coming right. It was funny, really, because it was the women who started the struggle—but for a time it was decided that we should have only one committee, and that it should be men. But now things are all right again because they want the women's group again—they say things doesn't go right like they did when we was doing it.

My husband—sometimes he likes my actions, I must say it. But then suddenly he change and it makes it look as though I like to be boss. Then we sit down and we talk each one and it helps . . . sometimes he say to me, "You were really good then, that really helped us." He does give support.

We know that black people in other parts of the country look to us—I'm proud when they do it. What made us to be so strong is the struggle and the hard feeling, we are really struggling hard, and so we thought we must stay together: if only they can stay together they can be strong like us. And our women, if we see something wrong we discuss it, never mind it takes the whole night, we don't care. If we doesn't understand it, we doesn't close that meeting, we sit down and discuss—and we wake up tomorrow morning with better thoughts. We sit together every day if necessary, so it's not to say I'm going to put my views alone, but the other one, and the other one—that makes a community really to be together and strong.

But it was not only meetings—when we decided and had a vote we would take fast action: going to an office here, telling this one we will not be dumped, saying things to the newspapers. We were planning everything, we went to the lawyers. Then the minister had to make a plan, they could not just pick us up and arrest us because the whole community would be standing there. They would strike at night, and in the morning it would be there in the newspaper. We were fast as anything—we didn't have telephones, but we were fast to call our friends and neighbours, to call help where we need help. Now we would like to help these new people being dumped near us.

Transcribed by Beata Lipman

Nehambo Magdalena Shamena, KANDISHIWO—I DON'T KNOW

Namibia 1984   oshiNdonga

Nehambo Magdalena Iihuhua and her husband, Ndeulimane Erastus Shamena, joined the South West Africa People's Organization (SWAPO) shortly after its founding in 1960. Along with thousands of other Namibians, Magdalena and Erastus Shamena left for exile in 1974, leaving their six young children behind in the care of Magdalena's brother. Shamena became one of the first SWAPO women to undergo military training in Zambia. Her letter to the United Nations in 1973 (see the text titled "Emergency Call from the Women of Namibia") marked another first, as she placed the suffering and resilience of Namibian women in a global context. Writing her autobiography was also a pioneering act.

Autobiographies of SWAPO freedom fighters form a significant genre of Namibian struggle literature from the 1960s to the 1980s. With the exception of *We Children of Namibia* by Magdalena and Erastus Shamena—who wrote alternate chapters—these were all written by men. This book, based on original accounts in oshiNdonga, has been published only in Finnish and German.

Magdalena Shamena's writing is unique as she describes her husband's arrest and detention in Pretoria, South Africa, in 1967. She depicts the warm and close relationship she shares with her husband and the difficulty of coping with her anxiety, advanced pregnancy, and four small, frightened children as she tries to manage her work as a teacher and find her husband.

In exile in the 1980s the Shamenas opposed the SWAPO leadership when its security department detained and tortured hundreds of the organization's members in Angola as alleged "spies," a scandal that is still unresolved but one in which the Shamenas remained closely involved. Erastus Shamena was a founder of the "Breaking the Wall of Silence Movement," a group that works for opening up the debate about illegal detentions by SWAPO and rehabilitating former detainees. After returning to Namibia, Magdalena Shamena put much of her energy into the movement for gender equality until her death.

Heike Becker

✦

When Erastus returned from Windhoek in the evening he was very tired and did not even want to eat. The next morning, I tried to convince him to have at least a cup of tea before leaving for school but he said: "I'm not hungry right now. I'll come at ten during break time to have some ontaku. Right now I'm fine."

"Please, don't go without having had anything. At least have some tea and bread."

My eyes followed him when he left. Standing at the fence, I watched him. I was seven months pregnant with our fifth child. Erastus's back disappeared behind the trees.

Then I also left for school. After the morning prayer one of my colleagues said jokingly: "Meme Shamena, did your husband go for a ride with the Boers?"

"With the Boers?"

"I saw him and Shoombe in the car."

To me, this was where the joke ended. I began to ask questions; some other people had seen them as well. So it had indeed happened. They had been detained. I did not remain at school; instead I went to see the principal of the training seminar. He reported briefly that the police had come and had taken Erastus in for interrogation. He had been picked up from the classroom.

That day it was raining. I asked Kalle whether he could take me to Oshakati but he said he could only do this after three o'clock. Therefore, I went home. In the afternoon we drove to Oshakati and went straight to see the chief of the police. There things were very busy. All the time soldiers came and left. They carried heavy boxes. Kalle said the boxes contained ammunition. More and more soldiers arrived. Then we were received by the chief of the police. Kalle said: "We've come here to look for one of our teachers. He is a teacher at the training college. He was brought here earlier today and those who arrested him said he would be released before two o'clock. But now it's well past two and he still isn't back."

"Whom are you talking about?"

"Erastus Shamena. This is his wife. She wants to know where her husband is."

"I see—so this is Mrs. Shamena."

"I've heard of people being tortured and being burnt with electricity."

"Who's been telling you this? There is no electricity where Erastus is. He's fine. He is as well as he was this morning when he left home. Don't worry."

And yet—this very moment Erastus was being tortured with electrical shocks.

The chief of the police told me to leave. I thought he did not want to let me sit so long inside; after all I was seven months pregnant. I waited in the car. Kalle came soon enough. When we were on the way back to Ongwediva he stopped and said: "Please don't get a shock, Magdalena. I know you believe in God and that he guides everything. I have to tell you something heavy. The police officer said that Erastus's case has not been cleared up. He will be sent to Pretoria."

"Why? What has he done?"

"He didn't give any reason. He only said that the case has not been cleared up yet."

What could I do? I went home. The children were already waiting. Immediately they said: "Meme, Tate is still not back from school."— "Where is Tate?"

What was I supposed to tell them? Softly I said: "The police has arrested Tate and taken him to Oshakati. He won't come back now."

The children started crying, and I cried with them.

"Tate, Tate, where are you?"

"We don't know where he is. We can't see him. But there is the one who sees him and knows where he is. Crying doesn't change anything. Let us pray."

One after another the children said a small prayer. From then on we did this every night.

"Jesus, our lord, you know where Tate is. You know what he eats. You know when he sleeps. Guard him and protect him. Grace his food. Give him strength."

We also sang in the evening. I was especially fond of the hymn that goes: "I don't understand everything. Please, do guide us." I was pregnant and sometimes not in control of my nerves. My mother and my grandmother feared that all this crying might have dire consequences. In order to hear whether the baby was okay I went to the hospital for a check-up. Everything was fine. No police officers harassed us while I was pregnant. I was allowed a peaceful time with the children. When my time came I went to Onandjokwe hospital to give birth.

While I was there in the maternity ward one of the Finnish midwives asked me: "Meme Magdalena, do you know where Erastus is?"

"Kandishiwo—I don't know."

When the baby came she was very weak. She could not even breathe on her own. She did not cry either. The midwife nicknamed the baby Kandishiwo. This name stuck with her for a long time.

The delivery was not complicated or painful. In me there was a much bigger pain than the pains of labour. I thought of Erastus. All along I wondered where he might be.

I even considered that he might be dead already. There were rumours around that prisoners were thrown out of a helicopter when it flew over the desert.

Next to me in the ward was a lady from a royal family. Her relatives came to visit often and brought all kinds of different food. I just turned to the wall, crying. I had no idea where Erastus was, but still I did not want anybody to see my grief. Very often my prayer was just a sigh: "Lord, you do know Erastus."

I returned home with my little Kandishiwo. Friends came to greet me. They brought food, flowers and other gifts. Among them were Namibian nurses but also some missionaries.

I decided to wait with Kandishiwo's christening until Erastus would be home. I was absolutely sure that he had not done anything for which he could be jailed for life. I firmly believed that he would come back. I consulted some pastors. All of them agreed that I was right. Should the baby fall seriously ill we could baptize her quickly. Otherwise we would wait for her father to return. God made sure little Kandishiwo stayed in good health. [. . .]

I won't allow them to hold me up.

Erastus was said to be in prison but for months I had not had any news from him. He could as well have been dead. Everywhere in the world there are prisoners but their relatives know of their whereabouts and can even visit them in jail.

One of Erastus's colleagues, Hosea Namupala, went to South Africa and brought back the news that those that had been arrested would be put on trial within the coming months. This is when I got the idea to travel to Pretoria to listen to the court proceedings. Immediately I went to see Johanna Shoombe. We decided that together we would go to see Shakomba, a black policeman, to ask him whether he had any news. All we heard from him, however, was that our husbands were not dead. Time passed. The trial was about to start. We could even read about it in the newspapers.

"Listen, Johanna, I'm planning to go and see Dr. Olivier. He is the highest-ranking white official here. I'm going to ask him whether I can go to Pretoria to listen to the proceedings. Everywhere on this earth wives are allowed to attend their husbands' cases. Why shouldn't I be allowed to do it?"

We discussed practical things, such as money. All would work out if only we got permission to travel. Johanna seemed to be excited, too. But then she mentioned our plans to some pastors and teachers at the training college. These men tried to talk us out of it: "These days the Boers don't even shy back from beating women. Let's not do this thing, please."

I would not even listen. I thanked them for the assistance offered, which I valued, but continued: "I want to go myself. If I'll be arrested or beaten because I inquire about my husband, so be it. I have to know how he is. I know very well what Erastus has done. If ever he had committed a crime and wouldn't tell me about it, I had to go and ask him myself."

The men thought I was stubborn but didn't put any more pressure on me.

"Well, you can see it this way, too. Do what you like."

My brother Frans was working as an interpreter in Olivier's office at the time. I went to see him and told him that I needed an appointment with Olivier. Johanna would come as well. Frans did not say much. He just moaned: "Well, the Boers may give you trouble."

"I'm already having difficulties. I won't find peace of mind as long as I don't know where Erastus is."

When school was over on Wednesday we went to Oshakati. Olivier greeted us in his office: "What can I do for you, ladies?"

"Our husbands have been arrested. They are in Pretoria. We hear that there'll be a trial. We want to know whether our husbands are among those to be put on trial. We intend to travel to Pretoria to be present during the verdict and sentencing."

The man was clearly taken by surprise. He obviously had had no idea of our concern.

"What are your husbands' names?"

"Jonathan Shoombe and Erastus Shamena."

"All right. I'll ask Ondangwa quickly."

After speaking on the phone for a while he came back to us.

"Your husbands are not on the list of the accused. They are not even in jail anymore. They are living peacefully in the location in Pretoria. No need to worry, ladies. They are having a good time there. They go to the movies in the evening, and there are gorgeous women in South Africa."

Johanna got angry. She hit with her fist on the table: "I have no parents. All I have is my husband. You are going to speak the truth now! You tell me, now, now, where he is, the only person I have. If he is not in prison, then where is he? Why can't I see him?"

Olivier had to realize that we had not come in a joking mood.

I said: "I have five kids with this man Erastus. I need him to look after them. One of the kids is a small baby. I can't cope on my own. Erastus is having a good time in Pretoria while I'm struggling with the kids? What's the real story now?"

"Listen. It's exactly as I said: They won't be put on trial. And you can't go there. They will come back soon. You can write a letter, all right, and also send pictures. We'll pass these on."

"We'll do this. But if they don't come back soon we'll be back here. It's impossible that they stay there out of their own free will."

We wrote the letters. In September I received a reply from Erastus. He had written in English although he knew that I did not read this language. Frans translated the letter for me. Some of it had been blackened. Frans could not read these parts but when Mikko Ihamäki returned from his home leave, he and his wife came to see me. He held the letter up against the light and read the blackened parts. He said Erastus had written about his time in prison. Later Erastus confirmed this. He never got the second letter I wrote.

Translated from German by Heike Becker

Kristina Rungano, THE WOMAN

Zimbabwe 1984   English

Kristina Rungano Masuwa (in her nom de plume, she dropped the family name) was born in Zimbabwe on 28 February 1963. Her father was a small businessman. After her schooling she went to the United Kingdom to train as a computer scientist, returning to Zimbabwe in 1982 to work for a couple of years in her profession. At the end of this interval, she left again for the United Kingdom, where she has since been living and writing poetry.

In 1984, Rungano published *A Storm Is Brewing*, a collection of about seventy poems, most of which she wrote as an eighteen-year-old schoolgirl. At the time of its publication, the whole volume aroused much attention through its freshness of voice and uninhibited search for self-knowledge. In "The Woman" the female persona addresses a man for whose pleasure the world turns. Her longing for gentleness and beauty contrasts sharply with the pain of her permanent subservience. The poem is an outspoken and bold statement by a young girl in Zimbabwe of the 1980s.

Flora Veit-Wild

✦

A minute ago I came from the well
Where young women drew water like myself
My body was weary and my heart tired.
For a moment I watched the stream that rushed before me;
And thought how fresh the smell of flowers,
How young the grass around it.
And yet again I heard the sound of duty
Which ground on me—made me feel aged
As I bore the great big mud container on my head
Like a great big painful umbrella.
Then I got home and cooked your meal
For you had been out drinking the pleasures of the flesh
While I toiled in the fields.
Under the angry vigilance of the sun
A labour shared only by the bearings of my womb.
I washed the dishes; yours

And swept the room we shared
Before I set forth to prepare your bedding
In the finest corner of the hut
Which was bathed by the sweet smell of dung
I had this morning applied to the floors
Then you came in,
In your drunken lust
And you made your demands
When I explained how I was tired
And how I feared for the child—yours; I carried
You beat me and had your way
At that moment
You left me unhappy and bitter
And I hated you;
Yet tomorrow I shall again wake up to you
Milk the cow, plough the land and cook your food,
You shall again be my Lord
For isn't it right that woman should obey,
Love, serve and honour her man?
For are you not fruit of the land?

Athaliah Molokomme, Leloba Molema, Opha Dube, Motsei Madisa, Ruth Motsete, and Onalenna Selolwane, CITIZENSHIP: AN OPEN LETTER TO THE ATTORNEY-GENERAL

Botswana 1985   English

Until the mid–1980s, the women's organizations that existed in Botswana tended to fall into one of three categories: those directed at home improvement; those, like the Young Women's Christian Association, directed toward improving the quality of life for young women; or professional bodies with worldwide branches, such as the Professional and Business Women's Association. Then in 1982, the Citizenship Act was amended to deny citizenship to children of married parents whose mothers were Batswana but whose fathers were foreigners; in other words, citizenship was defined through the "legitimate" male line. Several newspapers carried letters from women challenging this narrow definition of citizenship, pointing out the unfairness to children whose parents were married and therefore lived according to socially accepted standards. To protest this amendment, a different kind of women's group was founded called *Emang Basadi* (a phrase that comes from the national anthem, meaning literally "Stand up, women!"). *Emang Basadi* successfully enlisted the support of women's and human rights organizations overseas for its first project: to raise funds for a test case brought by Unity Dow, a woman with Botswana citizenship married to a U.S.

citizen whose children, therefore, were excluded from Botswana citizenship. Dow challenged the constitutionality of the amendment, and with the help of *Emang Basadi*, won her case. The hope was that all Botswana's laws would be tested for sexism and brought in line with the equality guaranteed by the constitution, but the Attorney General's Chambers has limited itself to dealing with cases as they come up.

The writing in this piece is lucid, fluent, cheeky, and polemical, and captures the mood of a time when women in Botswana began to involve themselves in shaping the issues that concerned them.

Leloba Molema and Mary Lederer

✦

YOUR HONOUR—This letter is prompted by the comments attributed to you by the Botswana GUARDIAN of October 11th, 1985, headlined "Don't marry a stranger if you don't want his citizenship."

According to The GUARDIAN you made three main points:

(1) You ask why a woman would marry a man whose citizenship she does not want for herself and her children.

(2) You are quoted as having said that general international practice holds that citizenship by descent is through the male parent except in cases where the mother is unwed.

(3) You apparently argue that most Batswana women would be against their children acquiring citizenship through them because they themselves believe in being dominated by men. This you say is in "the nature of our society."

We wish to respond to these three points in the order in which they were made.

First, Your Honour is misleading the public by implying that women are (morally or legally?) bound to assume the citizenship of their husbands— even under Botswana law! Moreover, it seems to us that the kind of women you have in mind are more a figment of your imagination than *real* women in *real* life. The latter, for your information, Your Honour, marry not the various citizenships but the men in and for themselves.

What is more, they do not look for protection from them principally but for partnership, and partnership is guaranteed when both man and woman contribute to their relationship from positions of mutual strength. Your argument encourages dependence rather than partnership.

We are indeed aware that in traditional Setswana logic, women were objects of male protection. At the same time, we are also more than aware that in practical terms, this same logic did not exclude women from participating in decisions affecting them and their families. But unfortunately traditional Setswana logic and practice is being distorted by modern males (led in this instance by Your Honour).

Traditional Setswana society had no alternative but to recognise the positive economic contribution of women because its insistence on collectivity left nearly all of arable agriculture and the distribution of its fruits in the hands of women. This means in effect that the Tswana State was, and is still being, led by its women. This is why avenues existed for regular consultation in decision-making.

Another area calling for corporate decision-making on a regular basis included the status of children as they went through the rites of passage (e.g. questions of marriage in which maternal uncles and paternal aunts played a leading role, to mention but one instance). It is thus surprising, Your Honour, that you use the same Setswana culture to deny women a say in the citizenship of their children.

In response to your second point, we wish that you clarify precisely what you mean by "international practice" since according to you (as reported by The GUARDIAN) dual citizenship became unpopular after the 1960s. By that date we take it that by "international practice" you mean in reality post-independence Africa.

But we know, Your Honour, that Africa of the post-independence era has not always been a model of democracy and justice, and we suggest that the further afield one looks in this matter the better—to the aphorism of a Swiss called Max Frisch for example, who said, "Democracy is there not so much to be defended as to be established." All of Africa, including our "Shining" democratic Republic of Botswana, would do well to keep this aphorism squarely in mind.

In addition, we would also like to point out that because the Citizenship Act denies Batswana women the right to marry whoever they love and to live with them wherever they see fit, we are already thinking of how to circumvent its provisions. Your Honour, we shall "live in sin" with the men we love so that our children may retain Botswana citizenship.

In response to your third point we confidently challenge your conclusion that only a small proportion of Batswana women would support an appeal for citizenship to be acquired through the female parent because of the "nature of our society." May we know the following about the statistics you base your views upon:—

• Who, in terms of sex, were the people you interviewed?
• Where are they normally resident?
• Which of them have never been to school?
• Have they been to school up to standard three? Up to standard seven? Up to J.C.? Up to matric? Up to university?
• What was the size of the sample you interviewed?

According to the report of the Law Reform Committee (of which you are an Honourable member) a total of twenty-seven people were orally interviewed in Mochudi, Kanye and Good Hope and a number of unspecified written submissions received. Are we to understand that this is the "majority" you are referring to?

What do you actually mean by the "nature of our society"? Haven't we all, women as well as men, been colonised? And haven't we all, since then, even had to restructure ourselves and our institutions in order to keep abreast of the change by bending with the wind, thereby accommodating forces which we were in no position to halt?

Is it "in the nature of our society" for example that chiefs rule not in their own right, but are now answerable to Parliament?

Is it "in the nature of our society" that thousands of people leave Botswana each year to work in South Africa? Is it "in the nature of our society" that there is a preponderance of female-headed households? That there are all manner of non-Batswana people working in Botswana, and that we ourselves go to places outside Botswana for conferences, protracted studies, seeing friends, relatives or simply to have a holiday?

Since our whole society has had to undergo a drastic re-organisation ever since we were colonised, and the momentum seems to have increased since independence, what makes you think, Your Honour, that male/female relationships have themselves remained static? In any case what criteria do you (and others we have charged with making responsible decisions on our behalf) use to retain some aspects of "our culture" and abandon others?

We are not arguing for blanket dual citizenship, but rather that children born to a Botswana parent (irrespective of sex and marital status) have sufficient descent links with this country to be given an option to acquire its citizenship. The apparent tendency to view this issue as being purely a question to women's rights causes hostility. The hostility is in turn justified by allegations that only elite or "radical" women, who are a small minority, feel strongly about this issue. The reality however is that for historical reasons, men and women continue to marry one another across borders which in any event are of relatively recent creation.

In our case, intermarriage between Batswana and people who live in the countries bordering ours is a fact of life: e.g. South Africa, Zimbabwe and Namibia. These are not always members of the elite but mostly "ordinary" people living their lives with those they wish to share it with. It is abundantly clear that those living within our north eastern and north western borders were not consulted in this case. Why was this so? Why only consult 27 people in three southern villages?

It is in the light of the above that we wish Your Honour and the Law Reform Committee to reconsider your grounds for having recommended the unjust abolition of dual citizenship as it relates to children of Batswana mothers and non-Batswana fathers. We intend to make further recommendations for the abolition of this part of the law and other laws and practices that are unjust.

Athaliah Molokomme, Leloba Molema, Opha Dube, Motsei
Madisa, Ruth Motsete, Onalenna Selolwane, GABORONE.

Nise Malange, I, THE UNEMPLOYED

South Africa 1985   English

Nise Malange, a celebrated performance poet particularly concerned with the position of women, was born near Cape Town in 1960 and grew up in a one-room shelter. Because her mother was classified "coloured" and her father "African," she was doubly penalized by the apartheid laws. When her family moved to Guguletu in 1966, she was sent away to a "coloured" school in Elsies River. In 1975 her family sent her to school in the Transkei. About this move she said, "When I was leaving Cape Town, the only thing in my heart was that I'm going to have very fresh food and live a life where I won't see a policeman, no thugs, no harassments." She was sent back to Cape Town during the 1976–1977 uprising. Then her parents sent her to Ciskei; this is where Malange witnessed extreme deprivation and poverty. After rioting broke out at her school, she was expelled and sent home again. In 1982 Malange migrated to Howick in Natal, to live with another branch of her family.

While still at school, she and her brother started a small student players' group which performed in the streets and community centers, usually putting on sketches about topical issues such as the 1976 rebellion and the granting of "independence" to the Transkei. When Malange arrived in Durban to work for the Transport and General Workers' Union, her interest in theater led her to join in making the *Dunlop Workers' Play*, which demonstrated the forces controlling the striking factory workers' lives. Then she played a key role in the workshop creation of *Why Lord?* a play about the experiences of migrant job-seekers: "I suggested that if we wanted to have a play let's make it from our own life experiences; we must all contribute writing. We decided to do something on migration; to show people how it came about and the problems of migrant workers."

This subject matter is one that Malange has again chosen for her poem "I, the Unemployed," which she first performed on May Day (Labor Day) in 1985 at the founding of the Congress of South African Trade Unions at Curries Fountain in Durban. Malange characteristically takes this opportunity to remind her fellow unionists of the thousands of desperate, unemployed people whom she embodies as female, who could not even hope for a union to represent them.

Malange's poems are usually written in English; she has been an active member of the Congress of South African Writers and set up the women's branch in Natal. She continues to run writing groups for workers at the Trade Unions' Bolton Hall in Durban.

M. J. Daymond

✦

I'm here
Living under a Black cloud
Here, living in thinning light
Here

Freedom is nailed to a tree
To die.
Here I am living: in a match box

I am here dying of hunger
And my country is also dying
My children are dying too
Look at them:
How dull their eyes
How slow their walk and the turning
Of their heads
Nothing for them to eat
Can you hear?
They are crying.

I spit at the sun
Shining on me
Blazing everyday
I am waiting for the rain to come
And I cannot plough this beautiful piece of earth.
Here I am: unemployed
I
the unemployed
I am here but invisible.
Preacher man pray for the rain to come

White collars
In your chrome and brown arm-chairs
Please brighten up this thinning light
I am appealing to you oppressors
To free
Freedom from the tree.

My face
Buried with anger and sorrow
My stomach
Filled with hatred and pain
I behave like a lunatic
My kids are dying—
Malnutrition, Kwashiokor
There is nothing growing here
And the animals have died.

All I hear now
Is the wind at night

It whirls around
Spelling the agony of a death
I'm dying.

Tsitsi Dangarembga, THE LETTER
Zimbabwe 1985   English

Tsitsi Dangarembga was born on 14 February 1959 in Mutoko, Eastern Zimbabwe, to parents belonging to the country's emergent educated elite. She spent her early years in England with her parents while they pursued graduate studies. There she began her schooling, and English became her predominant language. When the family returned to Zimbabwe in 1969, Dangarembga began to relearn Shona, as she attended Marymount Mission School in the Mutare area and the private Arundal School in Salisbury (today Harare). In 1977, she returned to England to study medicine at Cambridge University, only to return after three years to the newly independent Zimbabwe. There she studied psychology at the University of Zimbabwe in Harare, while working as a copywriter for an advertising agency. She also began to write and produce plays with the university's drama club and the theater group Zambuko. She wrote and produced three plays in a short period.

Similar experiments with prose writing led to the publication of "The Letter" in Sweden in 1985. In 1989, after receiving the Commonwealth Prize for *Nervous Conditions*, she entered the Deutsche Film und Fernseh Akademie to study filmmaking. Three years later, *Neria*, a story about the impact of the clashing forces of tradition and modernity on women's inheritance rights, was made into a feature film that won twelve international awards. With the release of *Everyone's Child* in 1995, Dangarembga became the first black Zimbabwean woman to direct a feature film. Focusing attention on the quiet desperation and unacknowledged heroism of two adolescent siblings newly orphaned by HIV-AIDS, the film won several prizes, including the 1997 award for Best Film by a Black Filmmaker at the Black International Cinema festival in Berlin.

Set in South Africa's apartheid era, "The Letter" is a cross-border text. Yet it connects on fundamental levels with the author's later work, establishing early on the recurrent themes of alienation and its pervasiveness in women's lives, the liberating quality of education, and the oppressive nature of ideological systems.

Tuzyline Jita Allan

✦

This morning I received a letter from my husband, the first in twelve years. Can you imagine such a thing? As has been my custom during all this time that I have been waiting, I opened my eyes at four o'clock when the first cock crowed, and lay remembering the day that he left, without bitterness and without anger or sorrow, simply remembering what it was like to be with him one day and without him the next.

At five o'clock I slipped out from under the blankets, softly so as not to disturb my children. There is Busi who is thirteen and ought to be sleeping in a bed of her own now that she is so old and grown into quite a woman. And there is Thandi who is only five whose father is not my husband, but a man who comforted me during a few hours of solitude. Busi and Thandi. They look quite different from each other since neither has inherited anything of my looks. Busi resembles her father who is tall and large and black. Thandi also resembles her father who was of medium complexion and slight build, so you can see that it is impossible to pass them off as children of the same father. Sometimes, when we meet uncompromising strangers, this is a cause of concern to me. But on the whole it is good. Otherwise I might have deceived myself into believing that I am a more virtuous woman than I actually am.

As I have said, this morning began in the way that has become usual since I came back to my village in the homeland, three years after my husband left us in Sebokeng. I drew water from the tap outside, waiting for fifteen minutes until the trickle of water that escapes when the tap is turned on full had filled the drum. (There is a drought this year and the water pressure is low.) Having filled my drum, I poured a little of the water into the enamel washing basin and washed myself. Then I heated more water on the paraffin stove for my mother and daughters. Yes, we are quite a colony of women here but we are self-sufficient. My work, teaching in the village school, pays enough to provide us with food and clothes and the children are very active, always planting this and that in the vegetable garden, keeping the house clean and always ready to run errands when I ask them. Where there is a serious problem, as when Busi was ill and needed to have her tonsils removed, my brother who is still in Sebokeng, sends us money to see us through. But such things do not happen often, so really, my only worry has been the absence of my husband and the anxiety caused by not knowing where he is or even whether he is alive or dead. This is why I visit the Post Office everyday.

Every day of the week, except Sunday, when the Post Office is closed, I go there to see whether my husband has written. On school days I inquire briefly, sometimes not even taking time to go inside, but on Saturdays, since I go shopping afterwards, I make an occasion of it. I dress myself up and even wear some make-up, a little lipstick, but not more since anything heavier is out of place in the village and apt to make people stare and whisper behind my back about my morals. Although I never speak more than a few pleasantries to the postmaster, he is kind and sympathetic. He understands my preoccupation with the mail because I am not unique—there are many families here in the village who have a father, a son, an uncle or a nephew who has not been heard of for many years, who has been imprisoned, or who has been reported missing or dead. So you see, although I inquired about the mail daily, I did not in fact expect to hear from my husband. It was a ritual I performed in order to maintain my bond with the past and to let me not forget the necessity of my circumstances.

Do not misunderstand me. I am not resigning myself to my lot. No, indeed, I am glorifying in it. You see, it was painful for me when I lived in the Township to see my mother wipe the faeces hourly from the plump buttocks of an overfed Boer baby while her children scavenged dustbins in the shanty town and had no need of the toilet for a week. Nor could I tolerate watching my father abused for daring to walk over the land of his heritage without the *baas*'s permission. I felt my young brother's adolescent frustration and bitterness when I saw them mutilate each other in gang fights and I despaired with my uncles and sisters when they were shot down at random by Boer policemen for so much as whispering that there is life after Botha. Yet we are forced to work for them, in their houses, in their factories, their streets and their farms, without self, without soul and without recourse to justice! My husband and I observed these things together in Sebokeng. Together we saw the tension that dissects South Africa quite clearly disclose to us our only course of action—we became political people. But in my country political black people, which is to say black people, are threatened with genocide. Therefore it was not long before my husband was considered a major security risk. Ha! Those Boers! Deploying squadrons of men, fleets of police cars and rounds of ammunition to capture a single black man in one little street of decaying ghetto! During the last few days that my husband was in Sebokeng, we did not live as man and wife because our house was watched day and night. But my husband escaped by sleeping in this house one night and that house the next night and so on until arrangements were finalised for his flight across one of our borders, which one I am not sure. I have been completely ignorant of his whereabouts since that day except for the usual rumours that begin with those of us who occasionally travel into Zimbabwe, Lesotho, Moçambique and Botswana, but which are impossible to confirm.

So imagine my surprise when I saw the postmaster waiting for me at the post office door this morning with a letter in his hand. Feel how my heart stopped when he gave me the letter and I recognised the writing immediately. Consider how my hand shook and the sweat trickled from my armpits in a dark patch down the sides of my dress as I took the letter from him. Do not think me rude when I tell you that I did not respond to his greeting or smile at him or thank him for his concern. To tell you the truth I did not see him or the Post Office or even the letter. All I saw was the writing, the familiar style with the "t"s crossed so heavily, and occupying my field of vision, dominating all else.

A few minutes later I returned to a more normal state of consciousness to find myself wandering through the stores (which really are no more than tuck-shops and kiosks), the letter still in my hand begging attention. In my happiness I wanted no considerate acquaintances inquiring whether my news was good news or bad. But my joy would express itself in spite of my caution and I laughed out loud as I walked alone. But there were only a few people about, intent on their own business with no time to spare to take

394 ♦ 1980s

any notice of me. I wanted to hug my mother, to kiss Busi and throw Thandi into the air and catch her as I used to do when she was a baby. Instead I forced myself to walk even more slowly than usual and as I walked, I recited to myself the names of each pupil in my class in order to restore some balance to my mind.

By the time I arrived home I was sober once more. All I wanted now was to slip into the bedroom to read my letter not only once or twice but several hundred times, over and over again without stopping. Only when I saw my mother taking the sun in front of the house did I remember that I was still holding the letter for all to see. "You have a letter," she observed in a tone that told me that she knew my letter was from Themba. My first selfish instinct was to lie, but my mother had accepted my pain over these twelve years as her own and in this way had helped me to bear it with courage, even when it was at its worst. Therefore I went and sat beside her and, glowing as though I had performed some wonderful feat, told her that finally Themba had written. For the first time I examined the letter.

"Look, Mother," I said, "it has a South African stamp! He must have given it to someone to post inside the country. And look at the postmark. It is dated Monday. It arrived here really quickly!"

Mother was silent while I chattered on and on. When I eventually ran out of details and description she said, "After all these years. Perhaps it is good, but I find it strange." I paid no attention to her words, concerned as I was only with what Themba had to say. At last in my bedroom I opened the letter, and then, holding it in my hand, a single page closely written with hardly any space between the words or lines, I found I could not read it. Perhaps he had returned to South Africa and had been captured and imprisoned and they had forced him to write this letter, dictating every word, as a final insult. Or it was possible (no, probable!) that he had settled down with some other woman and was happy and secure in a new family. I glanced at the first few lines. "My dear wife" I read. (Wife! Wife! I am still his wife!) "I am in Botswana at present." (Botswana! Botswana! Near enough to visit!) My suspicions allayed, I read on. He asked me why I had not replied to his other letters and I wept with the injustice of it—if I had only known where he was I would have written him a thousand letters! He told me that I should go to him in Botswana if it were at all possible, but that I would have to arrange the journey myself since he could not communicate freely with me. I should bring Busi. I should regard it as a permanent move. I sank into depression. What would I do with Thandi? I could not leave her. As I re-read the letter I began to wonder if our reunion was truly possible. Would my husband allow me to take Thandi into our new home? Or perhaps with the knowledge that I had had a child with another man he would no longer want me. Worried by such thoughts I sat down immediately to write to Themba explaining my apprehension. Of course I wanted to post the letter as soon as I had finished writing it, but by the time I was ready it was late afternoon with the Post Office closed until Monday.

I would have liked to have remained there in my dim bedroom a while longer, recreating for myself the contentment and satisfaction of my marriage in defiance of the loneliness I had contained through the years. What a luxury it would have been to allow myself the comfort of such memories. I could not afford it. Instead I turned my mind to practical matters—what would we eat for the evening meal? Hiding the letter under the mattress, I went into the kitchen. "Now that you have read your letter you should destroy it," my mother said as soon as she saw me. Of course she was right, but I was not yet capable of such an action. Perhaps tomorrow when I had read the letter a few more times and could remember every word of it, I would be able to do so. But now the thought of it lying there under my mattress gave me back the hope that I had clung to and renewed my faith in the future.

"It is a personal letter," I told her, not looking at her because I did not believe myself. "There can be no danger."

After the evening meal the last traces of my excitement left me too energetic to rest. I began to clean the house, the kitchen, the living room and the two small bedrooms, scrubbing and polishing recesses that previously I had hardly noticed, cleaning windows and tidying cupboards. Busi and Thandi helped me for a while, but soon grew sleepy and went to bed. Although my mother usually retires early, this evening she would not leave me. Consequently we were both in the living room, I working, my mother watching me and dozing from time to time, when the army jeep crawled up our narrow driveway and stopped outside the front door, lights suddenly blazing into the room through the open window. Ha! Those Boers! An armed vehicle and six camouflaged soldiers to arrest one small woman in a remote homeland village! Searching the house, it did not take them long to find my letters and decide that they were subversive. I was bundled into the jeep and brought here to the police station.

I will not tell you how they threatened to shoot my children to make me confess to my terrorist activities, nor will I tell you how they beat my mother when she pleaded for me. As for myself, well, I have already told you that I became a political person twelve years ago in the township. Therefore I have had ample time to get used to the aberrations of people in the grip of totalitarian fervour. I do not know what is going to happen to me. I may be charged with an act of treason plotted in Pretoria, or they may hold me here to abuse me physically and mentally for a while before conceding that my desire to be with my husband is not grounds for indictment. Whatever happens I know that they will make sure that we cannot reach Themba, but this is not my concern since I have told you my story, not to arouse your pity, but only so that you may know that these things are happening to us in our country.

Ingrid de Kok, OUR SHARPEVILLE

South Africa 1987   English

Ingrid de Kok spent her childhood in the mining town of Stilfontein, near Johannesburg. In her three published collections of poems, *Familiar Ground* (1988), *Transfer* (1997), and *Terrestrial Things* (2002), she writes often about children scarred by emotional and physical violence in a society riven by inequality. "Our Sharpeville," like other poems of De Kok's about her Stilfontein years, probes the sensitivity of a child who is made complicit in the injustices perpetrated by her adult protectors in the name of her own safety, even while she feels drawn toward the forbidden world her own community excludes.

The massacre of sixty-nine black people by white policemen at Sharpeville (a township in the mining belt around Johannesburg) on 21 March 1960 was one of the defining moments of the South African liberation struggle. The people who were shot at Sharpeville on that day were taking part in a series of national protests against the pass laws. The political significance of the events at Sharpeville was not something that the young child at the center of Ingrid de Kok's poem could have recognized. The child in the poem, like so many of the children of apartheid's beneficiaries, lives inside a cocoon of protective adult strategies designed to keep the brutal political actions of their leaders, and the human misery they produce, far out of sight and consciousness. "Our Sharpeville" is less a poem about this one historical event than a depiction of the entrapment of a child by the adult values that govern her life, the dreadful bargain with the devil of adult love that every child makes in order to honor her parents and their vision of who she is, what she ought to be.

Karen Press

◆

I was playing hopscotch on the slate
when the miners roared past in lorries,
their arms raised, signals at a crossing,
their chanting foreign and familiar,
like the call and answer of road gangs
across the veld, building hot arteries
from the heart of the Transvaal mine.

I ran to the gate to watch them pass.
And it seemed like a great caravan
moving across the desert to an oasis
I remembered from my Sunday-school book:
olive trees, a deep jade pool,
men resting in clusters after a long journey,
the danger of the mission still around them,

and night falling, its silver stars just like the ones
you got for remembering your Bible texts.

Then my grandmother called from behind the front door,
her voice a stiff broom over the steps:
"Come inside; they do things to little girls."

For it was noon, and there was no jade pool.
Instead, a pool of blood that already had a living name
and grew like a shadow as the day lengthened.
The dead, buried in voices that reached even my gate,
the chanting men on the ambushed trucks,
these were not heroes in my town,
but maulers of children,
doing things that had to remain nameless.
And our Sharpeville was this fearful thing
that might tempt us across the well-swept streets.

If I had turned I would have seen
brocade curtains drawn tightly across sheer net ones,
known there were eyes behind both,
heard the dogs pacing in the locked yard next door.
But, walking backwards, all I felt was shame,
at being a girl, at having been found at the gate,
at having heard my grandmother lie
and at the fear her lie might be true.
Walking backwards, called back,
I returned to the closed rooms, home.

Di//xao =Oma,
OUR GOVERNMENT IS A GLOWING EMBER

Namibia 1988   Ju/'hoansi

This piece of political oratory was spoken by a Ju/'hoan San woman in the Nyae
Nyae area of northeastern Namibia in 1988. Di//xao =Oma is a community representative of the Nyae Nyae Farmers' Cooperative (NNFC), a people's self-help group
that, through its ceaseless and effective activism, has come to be recognized as the
"traditional authority" of the area under the independent government of Namibia.
Di//xao is the sister of the first chairperson of the NNFC, Tsamkxao =Oma, and also
the sister of the cooperative's present manager, Kxao Moses =Oma. She is one of two
representatives from her community, /Aotcha, and has traveled to a large number of
local, national, and international meetings in that capacity.

In 1988, however, news of the implementation of United Nations Resolution 435 for free elections and independence in Namibia startled her and other Ju/'hoan leaders into a quick realization of the magnitude of possible changes. Apartheid practices of the South West African Administration, under the internationally illegal mandate of South Africa, had long held the Ju/'hoansi and other Namibians of color in political paralysis. When the United Nations finally acted, members of the NNFC went on the road throughout their extensive, remote area, bringing the news of the international peace talks respecting Namibia, held in Brazzaville, to far-flung communities, none of which at that time had a radio.

Di//xao spoke at the southernmost Nyae Nyae community, N=ama, inside a grass hut while a sandstorm raged outside. Perhaps twenty people crowded into the small space with eyes tightly shut against the blowing sand. As with speeches by other representatives, Di//xao's speech hinged on making bridges between traditional understandings and the newer challenges brought by the rapidly changing political ground rules in pre-independence Namibia.

Di//xao's speech reflects the inventiveness sparked by that era among Namibian San, a kind of verbal creativity that helped make the future seem lively and possible to these people. Yet in her speech we hear that the old technology of relatedness to land and long-tenured lifeways was still the basic model. It is clear that the treasured *n!ore* system of land stewardship, part of the social and environmental technology that stood the Ju/'hoansi in good stead for so many years, was still alive in their hearts and minds.

Megan Biesele

✦

When they say, "You people have no government," we say our old, old people gave us our government, and it was a glowing ember to start a new fire. I know this place where my fathers and mothers gave birth to me and nourished me and I grew up to be like I am. But we don't know where these Afrikaaners were born or who their fathers were: where are their fathers' and mothers' *n!ores*? What do these people know about carrying embers to start a new fire? Have they ever picked up an ember and gone forward with it? We say, "Don't hold us back: we want to lift ourselves up." We have our own talk: it isn't other people's talk. Long ago when we went to our new camps, we brought embers from our old camps. When has this government ever come to us with an ember?

Transcribed and translated by Megan Biesele

Mavis Smallberg, FOR WILLY NYATHELE

South Africa 1988   English

Born in Cape Town, Mavis Smallberg grew up and lived on the Cape Flats. After training as a teacher, she taught physical education, creative dance, and English in both primary and secondary schools in Cape Town. In 1996 she left teaching to pursue her interests in historical and cultural research, and—after being appointed artist-in-residence on Robben Island—began working full time in Robben Island Museum's Heritage Department. She was a testimony summary writer for the Truth and Reconciliation Commission. She is also a founding member of a recently established women's creative initiative called Women's Education and Artistic Voice Expression (WEAVE), based in Cape Town.

As a charter member of the Cultural Organization of South African Women (COSAW), Smallberg participated in numerous creative writing workshops for youth, worker, and women's organizations and during the 1980s performed her poetry at community events.

In "For Willy Nyathele," originally published in *Women Speak*, Smallberg re-creates in poetic form a news report from the *Weekend Argus* of 25 August 1986 about a twelve-year-old boy whose political activism was inspired by racial discrimination, repeated arrests by the state security forces, and the poverty of township life in Tumahole Location, Parys, Orange Free State. Willy is a child of the 1980s, a time of continual clashes between the police and the United Democratic Front, of mass rent boycotts, boycotts of white-owned shops and shopping centers, "necklace" murders, and police murders of political activists inside and outside prison.

Children witnessed and sometimes participated in this violence, and were both politicized and traumatized by it. Disillusioned by what they read as adult ineffectualness, gangs of youths regarded themselves as the eyes and the ears of the community. The news report to which Smallberg is responding notes that these youths saw themselves protecting the township residents against vigilantes working with white Administration Board officials, but it also makes a simpler point: The boy wanted "from the bottom of his heart 'To eat and eat and eat!' He was tired of being hungry."

V. M. Sisi Maqagi

✦

First the face, and then
the caption caught my eye:
Small Boy Seen As
Threat To State Security

The face is oval
the cheekbones high
the mouth a generous curve

and then,
those eyes
The eyes are almond-shaped
with wrinkles underneath:
the eyes show largely white:
the expression in those
serious sullen eyes
is a danger to the state!

A small boy should not have such eyes
eyes which glower, two black coals
smouldering on the page:
eyes which cannot seem to smile
eyes unfathomable
filled with hate, or tinged
with fear?
eyes which look as if they've
never known a tear
a small boy should not have
such eyes

A small boy should not be
detained
A small boy should not be
in jail
Not once,
not thrice,
not four times in a row!
A small boy should not be shut
into a cell
so that he can break
a small boy should not be
a danger to the state!

And yet
the small boy knows the slogans
knows he has to fight
a system which pays his mother
R60.00 per month
The small boy fights against grown men who
pose as "vigilantes"
The small boy
frowns when comrades drink
getting drunk inside shebeens
The small boy

with a hundred others who call
themselves "the fourteens"
run the place—Tumahole,
a township in the Free State
This small boy
just released from
Heilbron prison in Parys

But right now
the small boy only wants
"to eat and eat and eat"
he fidgets in his chair and says:
"white children sit in chairs
like these."
The small boy talks about
democracy
and says his brushes with the state
have only made him "stubborn"
This small boy
this Willy Nyathele
who with his brothers three
live on salt and porridge
and who, together with his sister,
often hungry goes to sleep,
this small boy knows his fate
and wants his country
free

Ah, woe betide our fate
that such
a small boy
is a danger to the state!

Agnes Sam, JESUS IS INDIAN
South Africa 1989   English

Agnes Sam is best known for her collection of short stories *Jesus Is Indian*, and is one
of a small but growing number of South African women writers of Indian descent.
Sam claims that she became a writer out of a deep sense of frustration as an exile living in the United Kingdom. Born in Port Elizabeth in 1942, Sam left South Africa
to attend university in neighboring Lesotho, then moved to Zimbabwe and Zambia
where she taught science. She arrived in the United Kingdom in 1973; here her
experiences of attempting to take a further degree while supporting her three chil-

dren, and at the same time struggling to publish her writing, convinced her that this was an inhospitable climate for black women writers like herself.

Sam has since returned to South Africa, but her written works all date from her time in the United Kingdom. These include two radio plays, poems, and short stories published in *Kunapipi* between 1982 and 1988. *Jesus Is Indian* was published in the United Kingdom in 1989. The humor and subtlety of Sam's depiction of a child's cultural negotiations, with both the power invested in English and the authority of her community's customs, indicate why the story included here continues to be important in post-apartheid South Africa.

Miki Flockemann

✦

(Who invented school? Who said little children must sit still in a desk pretending they wide awake when they dreaming of comics and swings and stealing fruit from Mrs Mumble?)

(Me, I'm not a good girl, but I'm even praying for the bell to ring, frighten even to look at Sonnyboy standing behind Sister, moving every way Sister moves and making monkey faces behind her back. You know me, once I start to laugh, I won't never stop.)

(You can't blame Sonnyboy. It's Sister's veil and skirt and things. It makes so Sister can't see what's going on right behind her. Jesus, Mary and Joseph, every time Sister look like she's turning round, I think I'm going to faint. Won't we all be in big trouble if Sister catch him? Of course yes. Even when we sitting still!)

(Here's Sister turning around—and easy as you like. Sonnyboy make like he's picking up his pencil. Poor Sister's puffed out. And she's not finished cleaning the board. Anyone can see Sister's new. Our old teacher make each one have a turn cleaning the board.)

(Now Sister's saying, No copying from the blackboard. I got to ask her why.)

"Sister, why lately Sister keep saying, No copying from the blackboard today?"

(Sister says she wants we must write from up here—she's tapping her head.)

"Then why Sister keep on changing every word we write?"

(Sister says she wants we must write like she writes.)

"But why?"

(Sister don't want me must ask so many questions.)

(The way Sister wipe the board you think she's waving to a train to stop and there's someone lying on the train lines! Now look at us! We all look like we got dandruff. And just hear how Cissie's coughing! But you know it's Cissie's own fault. Why she want to sit right under Sister's nose? Like she never talk in class and make jokes. Goody-gum-drops!)

(Before Sister turn round again I better make like I'm working hard. Maybe she'll go worry someone else. I know a good trick from last year. You fall over your desk like you sleeping and put your head on your arm so no-one can see your page, like when you doing a test and no-one must copy off you, then the teacher thinks you working hard. I just got to hide my one line of story or Sister will know I been playing. From up here in my head is coming a story about Honey.)

Me an Honey fight like tigers . . .

(Here's Sister like a ghost by my elbow. She says she wants to read my story so far. She got her red pen out.)

"Honey and I, Angelina! . . ."

"Yes, Sister."

(Hama always say you got to respect the nuns. Because they don't get married. But Hama don't say why they don't get married. Sister's standing by Edie now. She's a good girl. She don't swear. And she don't talk back to Sister.)

Honey and I fight like tigers. Scratching. Biting. Spitting. Kicking. Pinching. Pulling hair. Hama tie . . .

(Sister's back!)

"Mother tied, Angelina! . . ."

"Yes, Sister."

. . . Hama tied Honey and I's arms together . . .

"Mother tied our arms, Angelina! . . ."

"Yes, Sister."

. . . Hama tied our arms together. Me an Honey pinch with the other hand . . .

"We pinch each other with our free hands, Angelina!"

"Yes, Sister."

We pinch each other with our free hands. We scream. Like tokoloshe bite us . . .

"Tokloshe?"

"Don't Sister even know what's a tokoloshe? It's like a . . . like a little . . . something people can't see . . . It comes in the night . . . like a spook . . . to bite little children."

"As if a vampire bat bit us, Angelina! . . ."

"Yes, Sister."

. . . as if a . . .

"Vampire . . . Angelina . . . v-a-m-p-i-r-e."

. . . bit us. Then Hama tie . . .

"Then mother tied, Angelina! . . ."

"Yes, Sister."

. . . Hama tied me an Honey's arms to the table leg . . .

"Then mother tied our arms, Angelina! . . ."

"Yes, Sister."

. . . Hama tied our arms to the table leg, arms touching . . .

". . . with our arms touching . . ."

"Yes, Sister."

. . . with our arms touching. Hama say . . .

"Mother says, Angelina! . . ."

"Yes, Sister."

. . . Hama says it's a sin for sisters to fight! What Hama know? Hama think Honey's so sweet . . .

"What does mother know? Mother thinks Honey is so sweet. You are a very stubborn child, Angelina . . ."

(Sister's floating away like a ghost. You can only hear the beads. I wait till she's at the far end of the class.)

"Sister, are people vampires when we drink the body and blood on Sunday?"

(I got to hold my mouth with my two hands so I don't burst out laughing the way Sister shouting me for being cheeky.)

(This Sister Bonaventura! She make me so sick and tired I ever hear this word school! I never say I want to come to school. Why I'm wasting my time? . . . Sitting here? . . . Writing a story? . . . When my poor Hama can't even read English? And everytime I do a clean page—with neat handwriting—and no crossing out—this Sister come and spoil it with red marks! All over my clean page! Mother says this—and mother says that!)

(Edie's whispering behind her hand to me, Sh! Sister got powerful ears.)

(I'm looking at Sister's back like I can shoot poison arrows into her. Lucky for me Sister's looking somewhere else.)

Hama forget Honey and me under the table. Me an Honey fall asleep. We wake up good friends. Hapa say, no wind can blow between too-good-to-be-true friends like me and Honey.

Even when we fight in the week, Honey and me become best of friends every Saturday. Saturday's the day we go to town alone.

Alone? The busybodies put their hands to their mouths—open their eyes wide—talking behind their hands. Me and Honey don't take notice. We got no money. But we come home an tell Hama what dresses we see. Hama cut. And Hama sew. Then Hama fit. Hama put pins in us. But me and Honey don't even say, "Ouch!" Just in case Hama stop sewing. We say, It don't hurt, Hama. So we get ragamuffin sleeves. Sweetheart necklines. Peter Pan collars. Then we showing off. Swaying our hips with new dresses not bought from town.

One Saturday me and Honey coming from town, we see a boy standing outside his father's shop. Just a ordinary boy. Short hair cut. No moustache. All the Indian boys we know wear moustaches. So this one looks handsome. Honey and me know him. Only we never talk to him. On Sundays he bring his Hama to visit our Hama. Only he has to sit in the car and we must stay in the house. I say to this boy, "Hello! You look busy." Honey say I'm forward. The boy get shy because Honey standing far away like he got yellow fever. Then Honey start to walk away and I must run after her or the busybodies think he's my boyfriend.

Honey say she will tell Hama. Even Hapa. I say, what you will tell, Honey? I never stand and kiss the boy! Ooh! Honey's so shocked! She make like I commit mortal sin just to say this word "kiss." I say why you don't come in the shop? She say she will come in next time, if he's not my boyfriend. But he is my boyfriend, Honey. He can't be a girlfriend. Honey say I don't know what's a boyfriend.

Next Saturday Honey says she'll bring a book for the boy to read. But first we got a haircut.

From the day me and Honey can talk we begging Hama to cut our hair. I don't know why Hama must ask the big people what to do. They say Indian girls must keep hair long. Me and Honey ask, Why? Why Indian girls must keep hair long like a monkey's tail? First the big people say little girls must listen to their elders. Then when Honey and me say we getting to be big girls they say, "It's got to do with religion!" What religion Hama? We not Hindu girls. Why we must keep our hair long? Hama say electric light children ask too many questions! Long hair take too long to dry, Hama! Say there's no sun, me and Honey can't wash our hair. Hama can see we right, but Hama say the big people will say we got no respect. Lucky for us Honey get headaches. When Hama take her to the doctor, guess what he say? He say Honey's hair is too heavy for her head! He tell Hama to cut Honey's hair. I don't get headaches, but I cry like someone in the family just died the whole time Hama cut Honey's hair till Hama say I bring bad luck. So Hama cut my hair too.

Every busybody's shocked! Shame! Such beautiful hair! Behind Hama's back they saying, "These Christian girls! They got no shame!" But Honey and me, we showing off. In front of all those one-plait Indian girls. Swinging our heads. Page boy hair style. Like Veronica Lake.

"Angie! Here Sister's coming again," Edie's warning me.

(Sister's standing a long time behind my desk reading my story.)

(Sister says to leave out words that are not English.)

"Why Sister?"

"Because I don't know them, Angelina."

"I can teach you Sister. Is easy."

(Sister's whispering to me just like we do when we're not supposed to talk in class. Then there she goes gliding away.)

"What she say?" Edie asks.

"Sister say she never come to learn. She come to teach!"

(This Sister Bonaventura! Walking with her nose in the air! One day the rain will fall in.)

Now every Saturday Honey and me come from town, we go to the boy's shop. His shop's not busy. Me and Honey just stand and chat to him about what's showing at the bioscope. He gives us free Coca-Cola.

One night we looking in the long mirror and Honey say she's taller than me. I say, "It's your hair Honey. Standing like a bush on top. And don't stand on your toes." But Honey turn sideways and pull her stomach in and stick her chest out. "You look like them pigeons in the park, Honey. Why you stand like that?" Honey say I'm jealous. "Jealous of what, Honey?" She say I don't even know!

And then guess what? Hama say not to stand on the stoep at night. Not to play in the street any more. Why Hama? A drunk man coming pass? Hama say electric light children got no respect for their elders.

Hama say we mustn't talk to boys. And Hama say I must tell her if Honey get a boyfriend. We got no boyfriends, Hama. What we want to do with boyfriends? Hama must learn to trust us. We only want to go to parties. Do the Charleston! The Jitterbug! Foxtrot with Victor Sylvester. Hama says, "No!" Honey and me can't go to no parties. Only if Hama is there. We only can go to weddings, engagements and christening parties. But why Hama? Hama want to dance too? Hama swing round and slap Honey's face. I got under the table in time. Honey's crying and asking why Hama always hit the one near to her. Honey, why you never learn to do like I do? I always move slowly away before I answer Hama back.

From under the table I ask Hama how Honey and me will meet a husband? Honey and me won't meet a husband in church. "You can't talk in church, Hama!" Hama want us to be nuns? Like Sister Bonaventura? "We can't eat curry and rice in the convent, Hama! What's the use you teach us cooking? Hey, Hama?" Hama say Hama will choose a husband for us. Like Hapa.

But Hapa drink too much. And Hapa waste all the money for food on drink. Now Hama's trying to hit me under the table with the feather duster. Hama say, "Who tell you such lies?" "Hama you say so when you fight with Hapa." Hama say she'll take some chilli powder and wash my mouth out! Hama say electric light children know too much.

I got another question to ask Sister.

"Sister? Why Sister don't just sit down and read the paper like a real teacher?"

(I can't say all the things Sister is saying now. Only remember, Sister don't like you must ask questions.)

"Sorry Sister."

(I'm standing in front of the class smiling at my pals and making like I'm the teacher, while Sister's going down the rows. Everybody's scared even to look at me! Now I won't finish my story about Honey. Why this Sister can't leave me alone to do my writing? Why she must get cross when a person ask a simple question? Good job the bell's ringing. Everyone's running round the class putting things away.)

(Sister wants me must finish my story for homework.)

"Yes Sister."

(Writing at home is better. There's no stopping every five minutes for Sister's red pen. And you can listen to the wireless same time.)

Suddenly Honey's putting on high heel shoes. I run to tell Hama. Hama say it's all right. But no talking to boys! "Can I put high heel shoes on, Hama?" "Why not? What about lipstick then, Hama?" Hama just favour Honey. Hama want Honey must get a husband and I must stay at home till I'm a old maid.

Now Honey don't want me to come in the bathroom with her. Even when she's not having a bath. Why Honey? We always bath together. Why you special, suddenly? Honey say she's a young girl. "I'm also a young girl, Honey. How can I be a old lady?" Honey's laughing at me.

On Sunday when Hama's washing the rice and I'm stamping garlic and ginger I ask Hama, "Why we didn't stay in India, Hama? Why Hama want us to speak our language, but Sister Bonaventura want I must leave out Indian words?" Now Hama say she don't want us to go to school anymore. Hama thought Sister Bonaventura is teaching us our language.

(I don't like this Sister Bonaventura, but I rather go to school than stay at home and do cooking and housework with Hama. Now I'm sorry I told Hama about Sister teaching us English in school.)

"You want no-one must understand us when we want to make friends, Hama? Hama! Ouch Hama!" Hama still want to beat us? But we growing big now! I leave the stamper and stand by the kitchen door, ready to run into the yard. Hama will beat us when we are big married women? Hama says, "Yes." And if we don't get married? Hama says she will beat us harder! But Hapa never beat Honey and me! "I'll run away from home, Hama." Hama say she will catch me when I come in for supper.

Now guess what? Honey say I mustn't come with her to the boy's shop any more. "Why Honey? He's my boyfriend too. He's not only your boyfriend!"

Honey say I don't know what's a boyfriend! "What then? What's a boyfriend? What a boyfriend do? Don't laugh Honey, don't laugh! Sister say my English better than yours. What a boyfriend do? Kiss? He kiss you? When? Why I never see?"

Never mind. I won't go with Honey if she don't want me. If Hama and Hapa find out, Honey don't blame me! I got no friends now. Hama's not worried about me, only Honey. Honey don't like me. And the boy don't like me too. Maybe I'll run away.

Honey got a nerve! She say I must wait for her outside the shop. Keep a look out. In case the busybodies come pass. What she doing in the shop? Just talking to the boy over the counter. Big romance! He was my boyfriend first. I don't like Honey any more.

(I never have time to finish my story at home because I have to help Hama in the kitchen. Sister's checking our homework. It's my turn. I close my eyes and say my prayers. All of a sudden Sister shut my book and throw it into a corner of the room.)

(Sister say, "This is a very bad story about a very bad girl.")

"Sister?"

(Sister say I heard her.)

"I was praying Sister, I never heard you."

(Sister ask why I never tell Hama Honey was meeting a boyfriend.)

"He's not Honey's boyfriend, Sister. He's my boyfriend. I saw him first."

"Angelina!"

"Sister?"

(Sister's banging her flat hand on the table. She look really mad. I look at my friends in the class. Then I go to stand outside the classroom. Sister comes out. There's Sister marching away to the office. And I'm trying to catch her.)

(Sister want to write a note to Hama. She ask what's my mother's name.)

I say, "Kamatchee."

Sister ask, "What's your mother's Christian name?"

"Hama got no other name Sister. Only Kamatchee, Sister."

Sister make like she don't hear me. She ask again, "What's your mother's Christian name?"

"Kamatchee, Sister."

Sister's laughing. She say, "Little Cabbage? Little Cabbage? Your mother's name is Little Cabbage?"

"No, Sister. Hama's name is Kamatchee."

(Sister say she will write a note to Little Cabbage if I don't tell her Hama's Christian name.)

"Sister Bonaventura, why you can't learn to say Hama's name? Why you say 'Little Cabbage,' 'Little Cabbage,' 'Little Cabbage'? Hama's name is Kamatchee. Say Kamatchee. Go on, Sister. Say 'Ka-ma-chee.'"

(Ooh! The way Sister's going on. Like the Sermon on the Mount.)

"Sorry Sister. Hama never told me is a sin for a Christian to have a Hindu name."

(Jesus, Mary and Joseph, rather send me a book for Christmas with all the Christian names so I don't give my children a Hindu name by mistake. I don't want my poor children must die and go to hell for damn nation.)

(If I tell Hama Sister chased me away from school, Hama will be glad because she don't want me to learn English. Anyway, now I got time to lie in bed and I can finish my story and not worry about that Sister Bonaventura and her red pen.)

I knew it! Honey's been found out. She think she can go alone into the shop every Saturday afternoon and talk to the boy and the busybodies won't talk? Now she's going to get a hiding. The boy's in the front room. With his Hama and Hapa. Their car is parked outside. All the children in the street climbing all over the car. And Honey's hiding in the kitchen.

I told you, Honey. It's okay to speak to a boyfriend when you a good girl like me but not when Hama say you can't stand on the stoep at night.

Honey says I told Hama. I didn't! How can I do such a thing? Didn't I visit the boy too before Honey got big ideas about him? I thought Honey want to hit me, but she's standing there shivering. "Honey I never told Hama. True as God. Must be the busybodies."

Hama's in the kitchen with us. Hama want us to make tea. Honey don't want to take the tray inside. But I'm not frightened of the big people.

The boy's there. All dressed up. He never come in before. Always drops his mother and comes to pick her up. His Hama and Hapa are there too. All dressed up in Sunday clothes. One auntie and one uncle are smiling, smiling, smiling, all the time I pass the tea around. But Hama and Hapa look very suspicious.

Just when I want to put a cup on the side table my eyes catch a small gold tray. Looks like a nutmeg, turmeric sticks and some leaves on the tray. I look at Hama and Hapa. They don't look comfortable.

I go back to the kitchen to tell Honey what they doing. Hama comes in. Hama goes up to Honey and begins pinching Honey's cheek, like she's playing, but also like she's cross. "What you been up to, hey?" Honey says, "Nothing Hama, nothing." Now I'm getting scared. I say, "It wasn't Honey's fault, Hama. It's my fault. Don't hit Honey." I pull Honey away from Hama and try to get Honey under the table. But Honey's like she's stuck. And Hama don't stop. She keep asking Honey the same question, "What you been up to, hey?"—till Honey burst into tears. Then I burst into tears.

Then Hama laugh. Just in time. Hama say they come to ask for Honey to marry the boy. Lucky I never tell Hama about going to the boy's shop on Saturdays.

(Jesus, Mary and Joseph, forgive me for being so selfish. Thinking about my children going to heaven and forgetting about my poor Hama. Rather don't give me that book for Christmas. Rather tell me how my poor Hama will go to heaven if she got a Hindu name? Must I give up chocolates for Lent? Or boyfriends?)

"Hama, why you didn't get a Christian name when Father baptised you?"

(Hama say if she's a Christian and her name is Kamatchee then Kamatchee is a Christian name.)

(Honestly! This Hama got a answer for everything. Maybe she should go to Sister's school. She will learn better than me.)

"But Hama, Sister say you won't go to heaven. Because you got a Hindu name."

Hama laugh. Hama holds her head up high and makes it wobble about. She say, "*What* that sister know? Hey? Don't Jesus wear a dhoti like Gandhi? Don't Hama talk to Jesus in our language? Don't Jesus answer all Hama's prayers? Don't Honey get a rich husband? You so clever, what you think that means? Hey? You electric light children and you don't know? Jesus is Indian. You go to school and tell that Sister."

(Jesus, Mary and Joseph, never mind what I said before about the book with Christian names. First I want to go to town to do window shopping before I tell you what to get me for Christmas.)

(Hama never get the letter from Sister, so I go to school to say I'm sorry. For three days Sister don't want me to come in the class. So I stand by the door all day. On the third day Sister say I can come inside.)

(Now Sister's come to mark my story to see if I take out the boyfriend. But I left it in. Because the boyfriend is going to marry Honey. Then Sister ask me in front of the whole class what's this Indian word doing in my English story? Every page got this Indian word two or three times even. Sister say I'm stubborn like a mule.)

(So I stand up in front of the whole class and I tell Sister I never going to call Hama "mother." Even when I'm writing English in my book. Sister can say mother for Sister's mother. I say Hama for my Hama. Because Hama say Jesus is Indian because Jesus wear a dhoti and Jesus can understand our language.)

(I know the busybodies going to hear about this and say I got no respect for a holy servant of God. And I'm waiting for Sister to send me home again. And then Sister say, "All right Angelina." And everyone is turning to look at me. And now I'm swinging my page boy haircut, and pulling in my stomach and pushing out my chest when I walk home from school.)

Mekulu Mukwahongo Ester Kamati,
CHILDREN OF NAMIBIA

Namibia 1989   uuKwanyama

Mekulu Ester Kamati has played with words since she was about ten years old. She weaves her poetry around traditional forms, her own independent thoughts, and what she observes in the world. As she comments on her own art, "To create a poem has no specific time. Writing a poem is like a game wherever you are, you always feel like playing that game." She started by elaborating on and reciting the traditional names of great chiefs and kings. Her musical style captivates her audience. While she has had very little formal education, she is gifted with an inquiring mind. Her work has remained firmly in the realm of orature for, as she says, "My mind is my book." She wishes to see her poetry passed on in a printed form for future generations.

Kamati lives in a village in northern Namibia and is renowned as an oral poet. Her talent is highly valued and she is frequently invited to perform at weddings or birthday parties. She commemorates days of national importance with her ceremonial poems, composing and performing "Children of Namibia" for instance to celebrate the return of Namibia's exiles in 1989 when the many thousands who had fled the war were finally reunited with their families and congregations.

Kamati's child, like so many others, went into exile. As a mother, she experienced the agony of not knowing where her child was, whether she was dead or alive. In 1989, approximately 45,000 Namibians were repatriated, most of them returning to their rural homes in northern Namibia. Even though not all returned, the overwhelming joy of witnessing the children of Namibia return is perfectly expressed in Kamati's words of praise and welcome.

Kaleni Hiyalwa and Fredricka Ndeshi Immanuel

✦

Children of Namibia
you returned
calves with no horns
left in the kraal
howling like hyenas
faces and mouths pointed northwards
welcome friends
you returned gracefully

Children of Namibia
like a joke we see you
like a dream we look at you
your faces were not visible in this land
your shadows were seen in death.

Children of Namibia
your mothers mourned
mourned for you with hot tears

Though true they died
those of them
who came home
to fight for their land
hunted like antelopes
and summer springboks
with broken legs
though true they died

Children of Namibia
your mothers mourned you
mourned you with hot tears
no bed was without drops of tears
no pillow was without mucus

Welcome, you've returned
gracefully, we have waited for you
we welcome you
we rejoice for your return

Let us shake hands
in strong friendship
and love from God
in the lord's scars
that have united us

Parents of Namibia
we have blown off tears
and wiped off mucus
but now our tears
have turned into happiness
our cries as parents
have resulted in jubilation
though not all returned
we say thank God
for bringing along a nation.

Translated by Kaleni Hiyalwa and Fredricka Ndeshi Immanuel

Gcina Mhlophe, PRAISE TO OUR MOTHERS

South Africa 1989   English

This praise poem was performed in 1989 when Gcina Mhlophe first met Nokukhanya Luthuli, wife of Chief Albert Luthuli. He was president-general of the African National Congress (ANC) during the 1950s and Nobel Peace Prize winner in 1961.

Nokukhanya was born into the Bhengu family in 1904 at the Umngeni American Board Mission near Inanda, outside Durban. Both her parents valued the book-education that the missionaries offered and named their daughter Nokukhanya (Mother of Light) in the hope that she would share their values. Nokukhanya went to school at the Ohlange Institute, founded by Rev. John Dube, and later to the Inanda Seminary. There, because her father had remarried and was no longer willing to support her, she had to do domestic chores in the school in order to pay her fees. She studied further at Adams College, and in her last year there she met Albert Luthuli, who taught her in Zulu and in school organization classes. They were married four years later. The regulations against married women teachers compelled Nokukhanya to become a wife and mother who remained at home, but she did not allow herself to be confined or inactive. Besides caring for their seven children, she supplemented her husband's meager salary by growing and selling vegetables, and later her profits enabled her to begin farming sugar on their land at Groutville, on the coast north of Durban. As she acquired cattle and extended her crops, her neighbors expressed their admiration by saying, "She's not a woman, she's a man!"

Nokukhanya's support of her husband's ideals demanded great fortitude in coping with political intimidation. From 1961 to 1966 she had to spend six months of the year alone in Swaziland looking after the farms that had been purchased with some of the Nobel Peace Prize money. These farms served as a shelter for ANC members escaping from South Africa. After her husband's death in 1967, Nokukhanya continued her modest, active life; at her eightieth birthday celebrations, her speech focused on women's part in the struggle for liberation. At the age of eighty-five, she joined a freedom march in the nearby town of Stanger and the following year (1990) she attended the huge rally in Durban to welcome Nelson Mandela on his release from jail. He introduced her to the crowd as "Nokukhanya Luthuli . . . the mother of the nation."

Nokukhanya's national maternal role is the focus that Gcina Mhlophe chooses for her poem. She says that performing it on the afternoon in 1989 when she met her icon "was my most important performance ever." Mhlophe was born in 1960 in Hammarsdale, KwaZulu-Natal. Her name [Noku]Gcina means "the last" child in a large family. She was sent to school in the Eastern Cape and began writing in Xhosa, turning to English much later. In 1986 her play *Have You Seen Zandile?* was performed at the Market Theatre, Johannesburg, where, in the early 1990s, she was the first black resident director. Mhlophe has also published short stories, poems, and stories for children. In recent years she has worked on television but her chief focus is the performance of traditional folktales for children in order to teach them about their cultural heritage.

M. J. Daymond

If the moon were to shine tonight
To light up my face and show off my proud form
With beads around my neck and shells in my hair
And a soft easy flowing dress with the colours of Africa

If I were to stand on top of a hill
And raise my voice in praise
Of the women of my country
Who have worked throughout their lives
Not for themselves, but for the very life of all Africans
Who would I sing my praises to?
I could quote all the names
Yes, but where do I begin?!

Do I begin with the ones
Who gave their lives
So that we others may live a better life
The Lilian Ngoyis, the Victoria Mxenges
The Ruth Firsts
Or the ones who have lost their men
To Robben Island and their children to exile
But carried on fighting
The MaMotsoaledis, the MaSisulus
The Winnie Mandelas?

Or maybe I would sing praises to
The ones who have had the resilience
And cunning of a desert cobra
Priscilla Jana, Fatima Meer, Beauty Mkhize
Or the ones who turned deserts into green vegetable gardens
From which our people can eat
Mamphela Ramphele, Ellen Khuzwayo

Or would the names of the women
Who marched, suffered solitary confinement
and house arrests
Helen Joseph, Amina Cachalia, Sonya Bunting, Dorothy Nyembe,
Thoko Mngoma, Florence Matomela, Bertha Mkhize,
How many more names come to mind
As I remember the Defiance Campaign
The fights against Beer Halls that suck the strength of our men
Building of alternative schools away from Bantu Education
And the fight against pass laws

Maybe, maybe, I would choose a name
Just one special name that spells out light
That of Mama Nokukhanya Luthuli
Maybe if I were to call out her name
From the top of the hill
While the moon is shining bright;
No—Ku—Kha—nya!
NO—KU—KHA—NYA!!!
Maybe my voice would be carried by the wind
To reach all the other women
Whose names are not often mentioned
The ones who sell oranges and potatoes
So their children can eat and learn
The ones who scrub floors and polish executive desktops
In towering office blocks
While the city sleeps
The ones who work in overcrowded hospitals
Saving lives, cleaning bullet wounds and delivering new babies
And the ones who have given up
Their places of comfort and the protection of their skin colour
Marian Sparg, Sheena Duncan,
Barbara Hogan, Jenny Schreiner.
And what of the women who are stranded in the homelands
With a baby in the belly and a baby on the back
While their men are sweating in the bowels of the earth?

May the lives of all these women
Be celebrated and made to shine
When I cry out Mama Nokukhanya's name
NO—KU—KHA—NYA!!!
And we who are young, salute our mothers
Who have given us
The heritage of their Queendom!!!

Joan Hambidge, T.M.T. ♡ T.B.M.G.

South Africa 1989   Afrikaans

Joan Hambidge, born in 1956 in South Africa, is currently an associate professor in the Department of Southern African Languages and Linguistics at the University of Cape Town. To date, she has published sixteen collections of poetry, the first of which appeared in 1985. She has also published an academic text on postmodernism, three satirical works featuring the gay heroine, Sonja Verbeek, and one semiautobiographical novel—the first in Afrikaans to explore in some detail the development of a homosexual Afrikaans girl. Her latest collections of poetry are *Lykdigte* (2000), which contains poems in both English and Afrikaans, and a collection of poems translated into English entitled *Wheel of Fire* (2002). The poem reprinted here, "T.M.T. ♡ T.B.M.G.," was first published in Hambidge's seventh collection, *Kriptonomie* (1989).

Hambidge's poetry is typically personal and self-reflexive, with critiques of South African society and male domination occurring surreptitiously and additionally to contemplation of the nature of poetry itself. "T.M.T. ♡ T.B.M.G." is an example of the way in which Hambidge's consideration of a love affair comes to incorporate the nature of poetry and writing. Writing becomes a means of coping with a relationship while simultaneously writing it into being.

Chandré Carstens

✦

T.M.T. ♡ T.B.M.G.*
There is more to life
than patterns: boy meets girl,
buying a Sterns ring, et cetera.
There is more to love
than a beginning, middle or end.
Because you (and I) refuse to accept.

Oh the first encounter (shall we say: exposition)
runs over ever swiftly into the high point
(that is to say: the climax or consummation,
the cumbersomeless cum). Both: entrapped.

Who wants to guess the rest?
For that which goes *up*, must come down.
Ecstasies last only as long as the flowersending
or Romance's sweet forgery lasts.
Dénouement: informs the glossary, an "unknotting
of complications." A discovery that passion
—for one? Perhaps both?—is running out.
With us the dénouement: the discovery of your treachery.

There is more to love
than patterns: girl meets girl,
invests in love, togetherness, understanding.
There is more to love
than a beginning, middle or end.
Because you (and I) become caught up in symbols.

*There is more to love than boy meets girl

Translated by Chandré Carstens

1990S AND 2000S

Zoë Wicomb, ANOTHER STORY

South Africa 1990   English

According to the received ideas of apartheid, Zoë Wicomb would have been called a coloured writer. Usually inserted between quotation marks or qualified by "so-called," the term is sometimes seen to indicate an uncertain or "in-between" identity, but is also sometimes claimed to define a distinctive cultural group. The term remains an uncomfortable one in post-apartheid society, and its complexity is the topic of much of Wicomb's writing, including her short stories in *You Can't Get Lost in Cape Town* and her novel *David's Story*, as well as numerous essays in literary and cultural criticism.

"Another Story" is, in part, a response to Sarah Gertrude Millin's novel *God's Stepchildren* (1924), which speaks of colouredness as "nothing but an untidiness on God's earth—a mixture of degenerate brown peoples, rotten with sickness, an affront against Nature." Well-received in its time in both South Africa and especially the United States, *God's Stepchildren* tells of four generations descended from a white missionary and a Khoi woman. The characters aspire to whiteness, but the "flaw" of their blood is passed on with each generation until Barry Lindsell realizes that he belongs with the "brown people" and abandons his chance to be integrated into white society. In "Another Story," Wicomb offers a conscious alternative to Millin's conclusions.

While Wicomb currently lives in Scotland, her fictional interests are South African even after thirty years of self-imposed exile. She left for England in 1970, returning for brief family visits and a longer period in the early 1990s to teach at the University of the Western Cape (where she had been an undergraduate). Born in 1948, she grew up in a small Afrikaans-speaking Griqua settlement in Namaqualand, Northern Cape. She now teaches at the University of Strathclyde in Glasgow.

Mary Watson

✦

Approaching D. F. Malan airport. The view from the window on the right, that is, as you enter the aircraft: it falls out of the blue, suddenly, even with your eyes fixed on the ground rising towards you—a perfect miniature plane, a razor-edged shadow in the last of the sunlight, earthborne, yet flying alongside where before there had been nothing. And then it grows. Because the sun is low and because nothing, no nothing will remain a little toy-thing. (A darling little toy-thing, but that sort of word has no place here and must be excised.) Yes, flying across the earth, it gradually grows larger. Still wonderful while its outline remains sharp, until an ungainly leap in size when overblown, with edges grown soft and arrowed wings blunted, the once-lovely little thing spreads and is swallowed. A simple multiplication and division sum, a working out of velocity, height, angle of the sun etc. could have foreseen that moment. But she didn't. Or perhaps couldn't. So that was that. And the plane landed with the usual bump and the ping of the pilot's intercom.

To tell the truth, Miss Kleinhans was scared. And Dollie's voice as she leaned over the wild with morning-glory fence rang in her ears.

"If you asking my advice Deborah Kleinhans, I say stay right here where you belong. You not young, man, and there's no need to go gallivanting after family you don't know from Adam. I mean, family is now family, but the whole point is that family is family because you know them. It's not a stranger who gets to know you through ink and how-do-you-do on paper. And remember Cape Town is full of troubles with people throwing stones and getting shot. And what with you being a stranger in Town. Have you listened to the wireless today?"

Deborah's head spun in an attempt to work out how knowing or not knowing blood relations affected the claims that such people could legitimately make on her, for she had come to see the visit as a duty. Also, the morning-glory trumpets had started yawning and she watched the first fold up neatly, spiralling into a tight spear that betrayed nothing of its fulsome blue.

"Dollie, this thing will take some thinking about. But it's too cold out here for me." She had not asked for Dollie's advice; she had merely spoken of her indecision. But if only she had listened to Doll who was after all a sensible person, a neighbour she could rely on, even if that husband of hers was a good-for-nothing dronklap. I should have been a spinster like you, hey, Dollie sometimes said in exasperation, but Deborah could tell how the word spinster cut into her heart, for Doll would swirl the remains of her coffee and gulp down the lot as she rose with just that hint of hoarseness in her voice, I'll have to go and get ready the old man's bredie. Or his socks, or boots, or ironing, and even she, the spinster, knew that that was not the worst a woman had to do. She who had worked for years in white households knew more about things than people thought.

There had been two letters. The first simply a matter of introduction. A certain Miss Sarah Lindse from a wayward branch had traced her, a great-aunt, wishing to check the family connection and with Old Testament precision had untangled the lines of begetting into a neat tree which Deborah found hard to follow. Coloured people didn't have much schooling in her day but she knew her Bible and there was no better education in the world than knowing the Bible from cover to cover. Still, enough names on those heavy branches looked familiar, although so many children, dear Lord, why ever did her people have so many children. Family tree! It was a thicket, a blooming forest in which the grandest of persons would get lost. And she pursed her mouth fastidiously; she had a lot to be thankful for.

There were times when you had to face the truth; times like this when you'd made a wrong decision and the good Lord allowed you the opportunity to say, I have been guided by vanity. And in the same breath she found her vindication: for a woman who had worked as a respectable housekeeper all her life, but in service all the same, the connection with this grand young woman was only what she deserved. A history teacher at the university in Cape Town. The drop of white blood, no doubt, and she sighed as she thought of that blood, pink and thin and pure trouble. Ag, that was a long time ago and now she had a niece, a lovely girl who was educated and rich and who wrote in the second letter, I'll send you a plane ticket. Come and have a holiday in Cape Town. To her, an old woman whom the child had never even met. And Deborah, who had been timid all her life, who had kept her feet firmly on the ground and kept her eyes modestly fixed on those feet, for once looked up to see the serpent of adventure wink through the foliage of the family tree. And she was undone. And at her age too, but she replied, keeping to the lines of her Croxley pad with a steady hand, although these modern pens behaved as if light upward strokes and bold downward strokes were the last thing they hoped to achieve: I have always wanted to fly and would like to look around Cape Town. But I don't need a holiday so you can save up the darning and mending and of course I could do the cooking while you get on with bookwork. Thank you for the offer.

It was also that nonsense of Dollie's. She had managed to think it through and it simply did not make sense. Family is family and the whole point of such an unnecessary statement was that you didn't have to know the person. Vanity again: she had proven her ability to reason things out for herself and in showing off to Dollie had brought upon herself this business—this anxiety.

If only she had someone to talk to on the flight. Silence was something still when you were on your own but here with a flesh and blood person sitting right by your side, the silence fidgets between you, monitors your breathing, stiffens the body and makes you fearful of moving. So many new things cannot become part of you unless you could say to the person sitting right there, My what a business this is, without of course letting on that you've never flown before. But the red-faced woman next to her had swung round to the aisle as if she, Deborah Kleinhans, freshly bathed and in her best crimplene two-piece, as if she had b.o. Ag, it's the way of the world, she consoled herself, these whites don't know how to work things out, can't even run their own blooming homes. If she were in charge she'd have Apartheid to serve the decent and god-fearing—that was a more sensible basis for separating the sheep from the goats, but she sighed, for how would one know, how could one tell the virtuous from the hypocrites, the pharisees. These days people grew more and more like jackals and the education business only helped to cover up sorcery and fornication.

And here Miss Kleinhans felt once more a twinge of regret, a tugging at her intestines which happily could be diverted from the new niece to the wonderful South African Airways lunch. All nicely separated in little compartments that Dollie could well be alerted to, her with the eternal bredies, day after day everything mixed together, meat, potatoes, tinned peas and veg and then, on the plate, that man of hers would stir in the rice, pounding, as if it were mortar to be shovelled into the cracks of his soul. But it would've been nice just to say to the red-faced woman, Isn't it oulik these little brown dishes like housie-housie things. Last time I flew they were orange you know. Just in case. And she lifted her head high; no one could accuse her of being ignorant, green and verskrik as a young farm-girl. The Goodlord she felt sure would forgive her. Especially after the temptation, the terrible desire to put one in her bag, only the little SAA pudding dish of cream and brown plastic and with the white woman's back virtually turned to her, nothing could be easier. But she didn't. And she praised Dearjesus who resisted forty days in the Wilderness and felt sure that He would not expect her to fast just because He had, not on this her first flight with food so prettily packed.

That was before she thought of the order of eating. She knew that one did not just start any old where you liked. Her de Villiers household always had fish or soup to begin with but how was she to determine the order of things that in fact were the same. A test that would have made the woman, if her back had not mercifully been turned, giggle at her ignorance, for there in the little compartments was tomato and lettuce alone and again tomato and lettuce with meat, and how was she to decide which came first. More than likely the two halves of the same tomato turned into different names on different plates, which only went to show how silly all this blinking business was, but she was grateful all the same for the disdain of the woman who had swung round into the aisle. At what point was she to eat the round bread? Only poor people, her father had always said, ate bread with their dinner, so she would look upon it as a test, like in the fairy tale of a round red apple or something to tempt and catch the heroine out. Why else would the two large black berries have been hidden under the lettuce? She would have arranged it on top to set off the green and red; she had always paid attention to presenting food attractively and Mrs de Villiers never had anything but praise for her dishes.

The pip of the foul-tasting berry proved yet another trap. How was she to get the damned thing out of her mouth and back on to the plate? Would she have to pretend that she was not hungry, that she could only just pick at her food? What nonsense, she admonished herself. This was no boiled sweet destined to dissolve; she could not very well keep a pip hidden in her cheek until god knows when, so she spat it into a paper napkin under cover of wiping her mouth, and niftily tucked it into her sleeve. There was no one watching her; she would tuck in and not waste the poor girl's money; this food—never mind if it didn't live up to the cute containers—was expensive and, what's more, paid for. How could she, a grown person, be so silly and she chuckled audibly so that the red-faced woman took the opportunity to adjust her discomfort, to straighten her spine and allow herself ten degrees that would bring Miss Kleinhans's fork just within her line of vision.

The girl must have been relying on a family resemblance; why else had she not suggested ways of identifying herself. Perhaps she should wave a white handkerchief or something. That was what people did in *Rooi Rose*, which only went to show that *Rooi Rose* then was not for people like her. She could never do such a thing, make a spectacle of herself. It must have been the flight through high air that made her think such unusual thoughts. As if she had taken a feather duster to her head so that those stories, she now clearly saw, were for white people. Which did not mean that she couldn't read them: she was used to wearing white people's clothes and eating their leftovers, so what difference did it make reading their stories. As long as she knew and did not expect to behave like a *Rooi Rose* woman. It was difficult enough just sitting there, waiting, with so many idle eyes roving about. She lifted her head to concentrate on the lights flashing their instructions about smoking and seat-belts until they finally clicked off, the messages exhausted, and felt herself adrift midst empty seats and the purposeful shuffling of people anxious to go.

Deborah looked about and caught sight of the red-faced woman who flashed her a warm smile. What on earth could the person mean? She was not to be lured by a smile of falsehood, here where there was no danger of striking up a conversation. As far as she was concerned it just was too bladdy late. Haai, what a cheek, but then, not keeping track of things, a smile leaked from her lips all the same and she had no choice but to incline her head to nod a greeting.

The usual Cape Town wind awaited her, just as Dollie had said, and Deborah smoothed her skirt and patted her head to check that the doekie was still in place. Crossing that space was not simply a question of putting one foot before another. The tarmac felt sticky underfoot; the wind snapped like a mongrel; and her ankles wobbled unreliably above the Sunday shoes. Ahead, through the glass, a tinted crowd waited, waved, and what would she do if the girl was not there? That she could not allow herself to think about. The Goodlord would provide. Although the Goodlord so often got His messages mixed up, like telephone party-lines, so that good fortune would rain into the unsuspecting lap of that heathenish husband of Dollie's, when it was she, Deborah Kleinhans, who had spent the holy hours on arthritic knees, praying. If red-face walking purposefully just ahead of her was expect-ing no one, you could be sure that some thoughtful niece on the spur of the moment had decided to meet her after all, while she, a stranger in this town . . . But this time, and Deborah was careful to smile inwardly, this time, He got it just right.

Sarah was confident that she would recognise her great-aunt by the family resemblance and indeed the woman walking unsteadily across the tarmac could be no other than Deborah Kleinhans. Who, incidentally, was the only elderly Coloured woman on the flight. Sarah corrected herself: so-called Coloured, for she did not think that the qualifier should be reserved for speech. It grieved her that she so often had to haul up the "so-called" from some distant recess where it slunk around with foul terms like half-caste and half-breed and she stamped her foot (which had gone to sleep in the long wait) as if to shake down the unsummoned words. Lexical vigilance was a matter of mental hygiene: a regular rethinking of words in common use, like cleaning out rotten food from the back of a refrigerator where no one expects food to rot and poison the rest.

The old woman was stronger, sturdier than she imagined, with the posture of someone much younger. But she was tugging at the navy-blue suit which had got nipped, or so it seemed, by her roll-on, so that her hem-line dipped severely to the right. Also, threatening to slip off, was the doekie which had to be hauled back over the grey head as she struggled with a carrier-bag in the wind. But they met without difficulty.

"So we found each other. Something to be grateful for these days when you lose and search for things that disappear under your very nose . . ."

"And people going missing by the dozens," Sarah interjected. Deborah looked alarmed. Whatever was the child talking about; not her, she had to get back home; Dollie would be expecting her in precisely one week.

"Ag, they say big cities swallow you up but we're old enough to look after ourselves. Dollie's people," she added, "even in Kimberley, you know, after the riots. Clean disappeared. But one never knows with these children. Dollie is now Mrs Lategan who's been my neighbour for twenty years." Then she chuckled, "But what if we are not the people we think we are, or no, that's not what I mean. Let's sit down child, I get so deurmekaar and I need to take a good look at you." They sat down and looked at each other surrounded by squeals and hugs and arm-waving reunions. In the two pairs of eyes, the flecked hazel eyes derived from the same sockets of a long dead European missionary, there was nothing to report. The improbable eyes, set generations ago into brown faces, betrayed nothing, as eyes rarely do, but both claimed to read in the other signs and traces so that they held each other as firmly as the rough and wrinkled hand gripped the young and smooth. Deborah wondered for the first time why the girl had brought her all that way. Sarah thought of her father who in his last years had kept a miscellany of rare physical complaints. A man who knew his viscera like the back of his hand and could identify a feeling of discomfort with self-claimed accuracy—his liver, or pancreas, or lower section of the colon—an unnecessary refinement since the remedy of Buchu Essence served them all. She hoped that her great-aunt would not get ill; those were surely the eyes of a hypochondriac.

The girl was rather disappointing: untidily dressed in denim without a dash of lipstick to brighten her up. There was something impenetrable about her face, a density of the flesh that thwarted Deborah who prided herself on looking right into the souls of strangers. Also, her car was not at all what Deborah had expected but then she did not think any car smart except for a black one. The house that they pulled up at was very nice, but modest, she thought, for a learned person. With so much rain here in Cape Town it seemed a pity not to have a proper garden. Just a little patch of untrimmed grass and a line of flowers sagging against the wall. Yellow and orange marigolds, their heads like torches, so that she turned to look back at the dark mountain and saw the last light gathered in the flaming peak of a cloud.

The medicinal scent of marigolds followed them into the house. Through the passage lined with old photographs. So many people with nothing better to do than stand around and wait for the click of a camera. And right into the kitchen until the marigolds submitted to the smell of coffee. From a blue enamel pot like her very own the girl poured large cupfuls and her heart leapt, for city people, she thought, only drank instant coffee, didn't have time, Dollie said, for Koffiehuis. Washed in a caffeine-induced well-being she felt her feet throb all the more painfully so that she eased off her shoes to find two risen loaves straining under the nylon stockings. Why feeling good should have reminded her of feeling bad she did not know, but oh, she felt like a queen being led to her room with a bowl of hot water in which to soak those feet. But queens get their heads chopped off, so it was not too surprising that in that dream-wake state as she rested before dinner, Deborah orbited wildly in a marigold-round, her eyes chasing the pinpoints of light where orange turned to fire, and her head threatening to fly off. She rose clutching her throat.

At table Sarah talked too much. Deborah, used to turning her own thoughts slowly round, this way and that, and then putting them away safely for another inspection day, found the girl's insistent ways too exhausting. Like Mr de Villiers's office with rows and rows of narrow drawers packed with papers—the girl's head was like that. And she spoke fast, whirring like a treadle-machine that made her own head, still delicate from dreaming, spin once again. And all these things from the past, the bad old days that Sarah wanted to talk about. Stories folded and packed in mothballs right at the bottom of Deborah's head. To disturb those was just plain foolish, just asking for things to come toppling down.

"Perhaps later this year I'll come to Kimberley. To look around all those places. The old farm, Brakvlei, all those places where the Kleinhanse lived," Sarah said.

But the old woman would not be roused. "Nothing there to see. Not a Coloured person left in those parts. You won't find a riempie or a rusty nail. No, it's years since I left and soon after that the others trekked. The drought, you know. Girlie, this is a lovely bobotie. I haven't had any for so long; being on your own you can't really make such elaborate food."

The girl was not a bad cook. And the bobotie was good although Deborah liked it just a little bit sweeter. Just a spoonful of apricot jam to set off the sharpness of the dried apricots. That's what she liked about bobotie—the layers, different things packed on top of each other. She always did it in a pyrex dish so that you could see the separate layers of curried mince, apricots and then the thick custard just trying to trickle down to the dried fruit. Almost a pity to eat it.

"No really," she said through slipping dentures, "there's nothing like a good bobotie. Bananas are also good you know, but to contrast with the custard, apricot is best."

In the tall, frosted glass of Fanta, the orange bubbles broke merrily at the brim, almost too pretty to drink. On the same principle Deborah's good clothes remained unworn at the back of the cupboard, but today, in her Sunday wear, eating and drinking the beauty of it all, her old heart was content and this Sarah was a girl to be proud of. She would bring Dollie along next time; my, what a time they would have.

Then Sarah said in a preacher's voice, ". . . nothing but an untidiness on God's earth—a mixture of degenerate brown peoples, rotten with sickness, an affront against Nature . . . So that was the farm."

They had slipped into comfortable Afrikaans, a relief to Deborah whose English pinched like the Lycra roll-on that Dollie insisted had to be worn for the visit. And now the girl had switched to English once again so that she groped and grunted, for syllables from the two languages flew to each other to make wild words; because she did not understand about the sickness and death and because she felt a great weariness, a cloud settling around her head. The girl was surely mad. Everybody gets sick and dies, but Brakvlei was never rotten. Oh no, theirs was the cleanest of farmyards, the stony veld swept for hundreds of yards and even the fowls knew not to shit near the house. In that swept yard a young man rested his brown arms on the latched lower door, leant well into the dark but spotless kitchen with the sun behind him lighting the outline of his tightly curled hair. And Deborah, sick with shyness, packed more wood into the full stove and felt her hem a hot hoop below her knees, for she had outgrown that dress, and she had never been looked at in that way. Even when he offered to cleave a log that refused to go into the stove, his eyes burned and then her Pa came, to see his favourite daughter, his miracle late-lamb, younger than the grandchild, tug at her skirt and he ordered Andries away. That day she tore the dress into rags and braved a beating for she knew that a strip of plain cotton could simply have been sewn on to lengthen the skirt. But a beating has never done anyone any harm and she could thank her Pa now for sitting here where the girl's strong hands came to rest on her shoulders.

"Auntie feeling alright? Perhaps a drop of Buchu Essence?" she inquired, once again in Afrikaans.

"No, I'm alright. Just put a little bit of bobotie on my plate." Then Deborah remembered the libel. "Cleanliness is next to godliness. That's what my mother always said. And it was my job every morning to sweep all around the house. Really, it was just re-arranging the veld, making our own patterns of earth and stone with the grass broom, but Ma said, The veld will swallow us up if we don't sweep. No, you can ask anyone; Brakvlei was the tidiest little place you've ever seen. If your people thought otherwise, well, then they just don't know what tidy means. All my life I have kept that motto: Tidiness is next to godliness." And then her anger subsided: her mother would not have quoted the adage in English as she just had, not at home. What had she in fact said? How unreliable words were, lodging themselves comfortably in the memory where they pretended to have a rightful place. Deborah did not hold her memory responsible.

"No, no," Sarah soothed, "I'm sure you're right. I have no doubt that Brakvlei was well kept. But I wasn't really talking of Brakvlei; it was just something I remembered. From a story." But the young woman's eyes burned so brightly, so busy-bodily, oh Deborah just knew that passion for probing deep into other people's affairs. Who did this child think she was, wanting to pry into her life and she who had never said a word to anyone about Andries, the tall young man whom she saw just once more before her father waving the old shotgun told him not to set foot in that swept yard again.

"People come and go and in the end it's no bad thing. No point in brooding over things that happened a long time ago. I haven't got time for those old stories," she said firmly.

"A pity really; it's an interesting story that needs to be told by . . ."

"And what would you know about it?" Deborah interrupted, "It's never been interesting. Dreary as dung it was, sitting day after day waiting for something to happen; listening for hooves or the roll of cartwheels." But she checked herself. Hearing only the wind howl through the bushes and the ewes bleat, she had made up stories. Of driving through streets lined with white-washed houses; of friends, girls in frilled print frocks who whispered secrets under the breath of the wind; and of Andries on horse-back galloping across the swept yard right up to the kitchen door. But she said, "You know I have my books—*Rooi Rose* every fortnight, I haven't missed a book since I started working for the de Villiers and when I retired I kept it up. Every fortnight. Good stories that seem to be about real life, but well, when you think about it, you won't recognise anyone you know. They'll give you no useful tips. They're no better than the nonsense I used to make up in my own head to kill the time. My advice child is to stick to your business and forget about stories of old times."

"It depends surely on who tells the story. Auntie Deborah, that's what I must ask you about. Do you know if someone has written the story of our family, from the beginning, right from the European missionary? Do you by any chance remember a woman, a white woman speaking to your mother or brothers or yourself about those days? A woman who then wrote a book? Have you ever heard of the book, of . . ."

"No, I don't believe it. What nonsense, of course there was no such woman. A book for all to read with our dirty washing spread out on snow white pages! Ag, man, don't worry; it wouldn't be our story; it's everyone's story. All Coloured people have the same old story." And then Deborah slumped in her chair.

Sarah knew it, just her luck, the old woman travelling all this way to put down her head and die at her table. She held a bottle of brandy to the life-less lips. The eyelids fluttered and Deborah sat up with remarkable agility as if the laying of her head on the table had been a deliberate gesture of exasperation.

"Just tired child. Don't worry I'm not going to die here; I'll die respectably in my own house and that not for some time yet."

Sarah helped her to bed. "Tomorrow evening," she said, as she tucked her in, "I have to go to a meeting. But in the morning we'll go out. Somewhere exciting but let's talk about that tomorrow."

"To the Gardens girlie; that's where one should go first. I've heard so much about the Gardens in Cape Town. Where the fine ladies parade." And she giggled for she knew it could not be as her mother had described so many years ago. And even then it was a second-hand account, told by her grown-up sister Elmira whom she had never known.

Deborah was not surprised by the knock. Her heart had swollen, filling her chest with a thunderous beat and rocking her entire body as she heard the footsteps steal past her window, round to the back of the house. Skollies with armfuls of stones, just as Dollie had warned her. Then a low, barking voice—Quick. Here. Slowly, she twisted her head to look at the clock. Then Deborah leapt out of bed. She would not await death lying prone in her bed. Oh no, if skollies planned to kill her, well, they would meet her standing up straight, ready to meet her Maker. Her hands groped for the dressing gown but the old arms shook too violently to guide them through the sleeves. She crept out to the hall; she could at least telephone the police. But they were already at the door. What kind of cheeky skollies were these who thought she would open the door to her own death? Why did the girl not wake up? She pulled on the dressing gown. The knock grew louder and someone shouted, "Open up; it's the police." They had come for Sarah.

•

Deborah waited for Dollie in the Lategans' kitchen. Mr Lategan put the kettle on for coffee, making an elaborate display of not knowing where to find things, so that she suggested that he put on his shoes while she made the coffee. That the man should be told to make himself decent, as if she would divulge a word to someone sitting in his socks. And she thought of the folly of having expectations, of how she had imagined sitting at that table with Dollie, telling her story.

But there they sat drinking the coffee she made and Mr Lategan knew exactly where to find Dollie's buttermilk rusks which they dunked. And so she told him, for she could not expect the man to ask again. About the police who came for Sarah at five-thirty in the morning, pointing their guns as if they were in a play on the TV. And how they turned the house upside down and even looked in her suitcase. But they were very polite, especially the big one in command who apologised nicely and said to her, "You should have kept an eye on the girl," so that she turned to him triumphantly and said, "So you don't know everything like you said you did. I've known this girl for less than a day." Mr Lategan interrupted to say that if they didn't know that, they could so easily have got the whole thing wrong, the wrong house, the wrong woman, everything. Which was exactly what Deborah was about to say, but it was so nice to be back and because she could have added, also the wrong Deborah Kleinhans, for she felt as if the story had been playing on the TV, she allowed him to be the author of the observation.

There was also Cape Town to tell about even though she knew that he had been twice. But the city was so big that he could not possibly have been to the same places and he certainly listened with great interest. Sarah had written a letter to her neighbours, the Arendses, and even then Deborah marvelled at the girl's skill, how she wrote like lightning, her hand flying across the paper in such straight lines, even though the big policeman leant over her, checking every word. Busybodies, that's what they were, going through people's things and reading their letters. Mrs Arendse took her to the Gardens but her heart was not in it. Someone else, a young woman whose name she could not recall, took her to a museum to see what the girl called her ancestors. Hottentots in a big glass box, squatting around an unlit fire of all things, so that she left in disgust. But she said nothing to him of the large protruding buttocks and the shameful loincloths of animal skin. No, her heart was not in it and Mrs Arendse arranged an early return flight for there was no point in waiting to see Sarah again. They telephoned many times but there was no point, everyone said.

When Dollie came she told it all again and she did not mind Mr Lategan sitting there until he tried to correct her. If things were slightly different the second time round, well she was telling it to someone different and he should have had the decency to keep quiet. So she went, taking her bag, for she had not yet been home and Dollie shouted after her, "I'll come with," just as she unlocked her door.

Dollie lay across her bed while she unpacked. The frock for parading in the Gardens, a bold print of yellow daisies on white, she folded away into a bottom drawer for the nights were drawing in and really it was perhaps too bright for someone of her age. And then she told Dollie. Of how she had offered to make a nice pot of coffee because it was so early and that's just what you needed in order to think clearly. If the policemen burst rudely into the house, well, she was brought up decently. Sarah shouted at her but she knew how a civilised person should behave. And she paused in an attempt to trace the moment when things became muddled but all she recalled was an unmistakable smell of marigold, a weariness and the precise timbre of the sergeant's voice as she finished pouring the coffee: "Milk and sugar for the other two but just black and bitter for me." Then without thinking, without anticipating the violence of the act, Deborah Kleinhans took each cup in turn and before his very eyes poured the coffee into the sink. Together they watched the liquid splash, a curiously transparent brown against the stainless steel.

Cheche Maseko and Loice Mushore,
WAR FROM WITHIN
Zimbabwe 1990   siNdebele and chiShona

During Zimbabwe's liberation war, when the two guerrilla armies, the Zimbabwe African National Liberation Army (ZANLA) and the Zimbabwe People's Revolutionary Army (ZIPRA), fought the Rhodesians for the liberation of their country, rural women endured their own pain with enormous resilience and quiet but determined strength of purpose. *Mothers of the Revolution* includes the stories of thirty rural women, each in her own way representative of the complex, life-threatening problems experienced during the long guerrilla war. The two voices below focus on being a "sell-out," a terrifying concept used by all three armies. This accusation was the most frightening and intimidating threat of all, because it was very difficult if not impossible to refute, and because it was potentially pervasive: Your neighbor with a personal grudge could accuse you of being a "sell-out."

Cheche Maseko's daughter was accused of supporting the guerrillas. Her punishment and death were intended to be exemplary. The community, including her mother, was required to watch her die. Loice Mushore's husband was accused of supporting the Rhodesian forces, and she watched her husband being killed by a contingent of ZANLA guerrillas.

These stories are by no means unique but the memories they contain make palpable the misery and brutality of a war as savage for the civilian population as for the armed forces. Maseko told her story in siNdebele, and Mushore in chiShona.

Irene Staunton

◆

CHECHE MASEKO

My early life was very good. I was a very strong, beautiful and proud girl. I had a big body—someone who could be called fat. I did not have any friends outside my family. I played with either my sister or my cousin and I liked doing what I did alone. [. . .]

But when my father-in-law wrote and told me that my third and youngest son also wanted to join the struggle, I went to Tsholotsho to see him. I pleaded with him not to go. I promised to buy him a pair of shoes that he wanted very much, and promised him that I would do everything I could for him, if he did not go. In the end he stayed. He really wanted to go, but he was only about ten years old, and as his two bothers had left, I did not want him to go.

The eldest son was fourteen when he left: his brother was twelve. I did not think they would survive but I prayed to God and I also put snuff on the ground to appease our ancestral spirits so that they would keep our children safe. A lot of children died but fortunately mine survived.

It was my daughter who died during the war and that was a very painful experience. She died here at home in Siphaziphazi. She was beaten by a big stick. She was hit hard with a big, big stick as if they were pounding millet. She was hit hard, and at first she was crying and then she was silent but they continued hitting her. She was not the only one who was killed that day. The soldiers came at dawn and took people from different homes and killed them at the same time in one place. We were ordered not to cry or say anything as they were being killed. We just sat there, with the old man Mkandla, singing political songs very low and quietly. They were killed by the soldiers who said they were collaborating with the freedom fighters. They wanted to use them as examples to frighten others. Many people were killed but some managed to run away. Some were badly injured, but survived, after receiving treatment. After the killings, the villagers were ordered to bury the dead within a short time and the elders buried them. I was so pained and so weak that I could not walk to the burial place. Because there was no transport, I had no means of telling her father, and he only heard about the death of our daughter some time later.

After her death, my grandmother wanted to commit suicide but my uncle stopped her, saying that she was not the only person in the country who had lost a child in the war. He told her that she should accept it as it was: what had happened, had happened. He advised her to pray and throw snuff on the ground. But my grandmother was very, very distressed and she could not eat for many days and we had to plead with her to do so. My uncle also grieved, although he knew he had to be strong. He told us that the children had died for us, had died to free Zimbabwe. We salute those that died. They are heroes.

LOICE MUSHORE

It was, I think, the following year that the comrades came to Chief Ruzane's area and only the year after that, in 1977, that they came into our area. All the adults in the village were summoned to the headman's house and we were told that the comrades had come. We could not see them clearly at all. Their faces were shadowed by their hats. After that we did not see them again for some time. But they used to pass through our district about once every two months.

However, the night after they finally came to stay in this area, they arrived at my house at around ten p.m. We heard sharp knocks at the door. My husband and I opened it and they told us to get up and follow them. We carried a lamp into the kitchen hut. The comrades ordered us to go and wake the children and then they were ordered to stand outside the kitchen. My husband and I sat in the kitchen with the comrades. I offered to cook for them but they refused. I asked if I could light the lamp, and I did. The comrades then ordered me to go outside. They started to interrogate my husband. Unfortunately he had always had a stammer and the comrades interpreted this as an attempt to lie. They accused my husband of being a sell-out. They alleged that he had spent the day at Chisasike with the soldiers. I heard everything outside and so I stood in the doorway and demanded to know what they wanted. They refused me entry into the kitchen. I told the comrades that they were being unreasonable and I reminded them of what they had promised when they first arrived—that they would thoroughly investigate each accusation before punishing anyone.

At that, one of them opened fire on my husband who was seated cross-legged by the fireplace. The comrade was standing at the doorway. The comrade fired four shots but they all missed my husband who asked, "Why do you want to kill me? What have I done?" The comrade did not answer but aimed his fifth shot. This time the bullet pierced my husband's neck. My husband collapsed and I saw blood begin to flow. I could not believe what was happening.

The children were then told to move out of the yard and the comrades set all our rooms alight, including the two granaries and the storeroom, although they took our wireless and my husband's special pair of shoes out of our house first. I just stood there, in the courtyard, with my baby on my back. I had nothing with which to cover it. The comrades had removed the baby from the house before they set fire to it, but they did not bring anything like a blanket with them.

The comrades then said they wanted to kill our cattle. So I explained that the cattle were my mother's. In fact they were *mombe dzemai*.[1] So, in darkness, we went to the kraal. When we got there, one of the comrades said that, no, he didn't think it was right to shoot the cattle, but others disagreed with him and they argued amongst themselves. Then they told me to go and tell the soldiers what had happened. I told them simply that I would not go, I did not know any boers and I did not understand their reason for killing my husband. So they went off in one direction and I went in the other.

I did not go back to my home, although the fire was dying down. I collected my children and I went to a friend's house. I only had on my dress without a petticoat, headcloth or shoes. I felt terribly confused. The next day I was treated at the hospital and I stayed there for two weeks. I felt I was losing my mind. Our neighbours were very kind: they looked after the children during that time. At the hospital I was given some clothing. After I was discharged I went back home and I was told by the comrades to go elsewhere.

1. Special cow given to a mother as *roora* [bride-wealth; here a portion given to the bride's mother].

Transcribed and translated by Margaret Zingani Zingani

Karen Press, KROTOA'S STORY

South Africa 1990   English

Karen Press has published five volumes of poetry, the most recent being *Home* (2000). "Krotoa's Story" first appeared in *Bird Heart Stoning the Sea / Krotoa's Story / Lines of Force* (1990). Short excerpts have appeared in a number of school history textbooks since 1994.

The poem had its origins in a children's story called *Krotoa* (1990), which Press published while working as a teacher and materials developer at the South African Council for Higher Education. The story was part of a broader educational initiative whose origins lay in the 1976 Soweto uprising, to excavate suppressed histories that would tell schoolchildren about colonization and resistance from the perspective of indigenous South Africans.

According to Dutch records, a Khoikhoi woman named Krotoa served as an intermediary and translator between the Dutch East India Company and the Khoikhoi people, later becoming the wife of a European official. After her husband's death, however, the records note that she was accused of drunkenness, her children were taken away from her, and she was kept a prisoner on Robben Island. After her death, it was said that she had, "like a dog to its own vomit, returned to the ways of her people."

Press draws on the available documentary evidence, but develops from the bare outline a lyrical version of Krotoa's life and death and a speculative psychological drama. She imagines the strengths and vulnerabilities produced by Krotoa's ambiguous position: a young woman inserted by powerful men into a situation of political maneuvering in which she had no choice. The poem speculates on the ways in which someone located between conflicting desires and requirements lives—as both a vulnerable and proactive figure, trapped within and between worlds. The poem reclaims the complexity of Krotoa's history from the simplifying footnote she became in the official records. The epilogue of the poem memorializes Krotoa by returning her name to her. The version here, for reasons of space, has been cut.

Ingrid de Kok

✦

I

I am Krotoa.

I am the daughter of Maqona.
My sister is the wife of the great Cochoqua chief, Oedasoa,
and in his kraal I, Krotoa,
spend my time with the women of his household.

When I am older I shall marry one of the sons of the rich men
amongst us. I have already chosen from them

two whose looks and actions I shall watch
as they grow older. Then the chief Oedasoa, my brother,
will arrange the wedding with the one who is bravest
and most handsome.

Now I learn the skills
of basket weaving, shaping pots and finding plants that heal.
My sister teaches me to plait my hair
and to make ornaments for my body from copper wire.

Walking alone through the bushes
I feel the sun turning my skin to gold
and the hot wind playing against my legs:
at such times I know how beautiful I am.

There are two kinds of people:
the ones who huddle over the ground
afraid that their fingers will drop off before the work is done,
and those who climb trees and cry out
to see how many birds they can put to flight.

I know I will not be satisfied
until I have frightened the black-winged hawk
off his perch in the high mountains.
Heitsi-Eibib will bless me, and keep me from danger.

.

It was Oedasoa himself who came to call me,
my sister plaiting my hair in the sun
next to the old tree, and his shadow fell
over us suddenly so that we both jumped up
stood heads bowed before him
my sister spoke, "what is it, my lord?
what can I do?" and he, "nothing, nGai,
it is Krotoa I have come to find"
my face hot as fire, he has not done this before
pain dived into my sister's eyes and disappeared
Oedasoa took my hand, "come, Krotoa,
I must explain something to you, something we want
you to do to help protect your people from the strangers"

I went with him
I sat beside him on a stone
and he instructed me

afterwards I went out to the edge of the camp
and sat where a bush owl slept on a tree
but the sounds of the earth seemed to move away from me
like birds drawing back from a fresh kill
after a while there was silence
and though I fixed my eyes on the owl's claws
it was Oedasoa's voice that beat on my ears
until I couldn't see anything
couldn't hear anything

like a dry twig
fallen off a tree
I sat silently in the long grass

•

who is this person Oedasoa has commanded
I have not met her before

who is this person who will go
and live among strangers
to learn their meaning?

her name is Krotoa, but I do not know her

•

riding on a shining ox
high above the shoulders of the men
the long grass touching my feet
I am the chief's sister
everyone knows my mission
I am the young one, the clever one
sent to meet the strangers
I am the pointed spear
flung into the heart of the enemy
I will return over these grasses
trailing their secrets like the entrails
of the captured impala
I have been blessed by Heitsi-Eibib
I have been covered in the perfumed fat of the chief's pot
sitting in the sun I ride
into the heart of the enemy
[. . .]

III

In the night of that first day, I did not know what I was.
Prisoner?
Guest?
No-one spoke to me. They showed me to a room. Dark, cold,
like skins soaked in rain and forgotten. I stayed there until
so long had passed that I seemed to have gone far away.

Then I thought, I must see whether I am free, went out of the
room, walked, following the smell of air until I came out under
the sky.

It was warm, but there was no-one anywhere.

Standing outside the walls I looked at the stars, neck bent back
I imagined round me the fire where they were all sitting now,
on the other side of the mountain, the stories, songs, nGai next
to me, I cried, but silently in case this was not allowed. I did not
know what to do except to go back inside and wait to be called. I
could not find my room, so I stayed in the open place between
the walls where they keep their animals. In the morning I woke
up, two men were standing laughing at me, I felt afraid. I stood
up and waited in front of them looking at the ground. When
they had stopped laughing they went to let out the animals, I
followed the cattle and sheep outside, no-one stopping me.
There was one I recognised, a cow from Oedasoa's kraal, I used
to milk her. I could not stop myself from crying.

I could keep walking, would they stop me?
I could go back across the veld and over the mountain,
no-one has talked to me, I could just blow away like a leaf
going back to its tree—then Autshomoa's eyes found me,
and tied me down to this place.

.

I learn Dutch

I say "Good morning," "Thank you," "My name is Eva"

I say "Commander Jan van Riebeeck says"

these are the words I learn:

ox sheep dress table mevrouw hottentot mountain ship dutch
sea pearls because soon gold milk far exchange danger skins
man sick wine copper meat holland slave bed shoes bring god
one many bible elephant onions boundary promise

I say "My name is Eva"

Commander Jan van Riebeeck taught me

Eva dress shoes
Eva room dark
Eva eyes
Eva mouth

Eva is the dutch word for Krotoa
[. . .]

IV
after many seasons I went home
in the spring, back to my people, I said goodbye
to the Commander, to the dutch Council,
they gave me presents for my services,
I promised them I would remember their interests
at home, and I left them

but in the autumn I returned

(my home, my path over the mountains,
and this chair of dark wood in the office
where I have sat watching the Commander,
soft hair bending over me, gentle hands
in this dark cave, my flowers, my yellow birds
calling me, I am coming to you!)
[. . .]

V
no word came for me from Oedasoa, ever

and so I stayed among those people
became a dutch wife, learned
to speak in long dutch sentences,
became a widow, standing like a wild buck
in the yard of the foreigners

they would not take me in, hottentot woman
nor would they let me run away, they broke my legs

mine are the crippled footprints
worn into the rocks along the harbour wall

the beginning was an exploding sun
I ran dancing into the fire
the end unravelled like an old root,
dry with sorrow, lasting forever

•

EPILOGUE
I am looking for one bird—
a bird from the flock of tall lagoon-dwellers
that I watched quietly digging for fish
in the waters of my childhood—
one who will listen to me
and then tell my story to one other
who in turn will pass it on
along the edges of the lagoon
up and down the coast these ships follow
forever, let it lodge between the stones of every beach
where my own tears have carried on the waves
to moor themselves:

Krotoa became Eva
and then became again
Krotoa

died at the Cape, 29th July 1674
and is remembered

•

Sindiwe Magona, STELLA
South Africa 1991   English

Sindiwe Magona was born in the rural Transkei in 1943 and moved to Cape Town
at the age of five, living first in Blaauvlei and later, as dictated by the apartheid
forced removals, in the sprawling township of Guguletu. She trained as a teacher,
but when she unexpectedly found herself pregnant, had to resign. Magona ascribes

her inadequate sex education to the breakdown of family and other authority structures in her community. Her husband absconded when she was in her third pregnancy and, faced with the urgent demands of survival and few other available options, she became a domestic worker. In her autobiography, she describes this as "the kind of work . . . that breaks the body and crushes the spirit."

Magona was able to leave domestic service and return to teaching in 1967, continuing her own formal schooling through correspondence. During these years she became active in such community organizations as Church Women Concerned, the Women's Movement for Peace, and the National Council of African Women. In 1976, she represented South Africa at the Brussels meeting of the International Women's Tribunal of Crimes Against Women. In 1981 she was granted a scholarship to Columbia University in New York, where she completed an M.A. in social work before taking up a post at the New York office of the United Nations. She continues to live and work in New York, but plans to return permanently to South Africa upon her retirement.

She has published a two-part autobiography, *To My Children's Children* (1991) and *Forced to Grow* (1992), and two collections of short stories, *Living, Loving and Lying Awake at Night* (1991), from which the story below is taken, and *Push, Push and Other Stories* (1996). Her first novel, *Mother to Mother*, was published in 1998 and imagines the chain of events that led to the fatal stabbing of American Fulbright scholar Amy Biehl in August 1993 in Guguletu.

Drawing on her own experiences, Magona has written vividly about the difficult and complex lives of domestic workers. "Stella" is a prime example of the neat vignettes of Magona's early writing.

Meg Samuelson

✦

"Saw your medem's car drive off. Guess she's off to her Self Defence class? Thought I'd pop over. Put the kettle on, girl. You know my Goat Food Woman, the fridge is full of leaves, seeds, growing things, and smelly rotting things. The milk is from beans, she tells me. Beans. I wasn't raised by people who milk beans. Beans have teats? Hey, if we're not careful, one of these days these strange women we work for will feed us snakes and frogs I tell you.

"There, the kettle is boiling. We have no tea or coffee in that house: 'Those are drugs, Stella,' my medem tells me. But my head tells me something else.

"Thank you, sure smells good. Thank you. If I had the money, I'd buy myself at least coffee and put it in my room.

"I don't know why I go on working for such a sour *suurlemoen* of a woman, you know? Believe me, I know we say a lot of bad things about stork legs, your medem, but at least with her, you know where you stand. Not that change-face so-and-so I work for.

"I'm sure you've seen her with her always-mouth-open-face: she could win a Mrs Sunshine Sweetest Smile Competition; couldn't she? Always cheerful she looks, hey? Don't be fooled. I could tell you things about that woman—things you would never believe.

"Gets me downright mad to think of the way she has used me over the years. But, I get even. I pay her back; and then some more.

"She wipes her sunshine smile away when she talks to me and she wants to tell me something she knows is not nice.

"'Stella,' she will say Thursday lunchtime, 'can you please be back for dinner? I'm having visitors tonight.'

"Now, tell me that is not cruel. Here's a woman who has seven days a week like everybody else. When does she choose to entertain? On the one evening a week she knows her maid is off. And her smile is there for everyone to see how kind she is.

"From the word go, I knew there was something not nice about this woman I work for. First day here, what do I find? There's her bath tub full of water. The same water she's just had a bath in. Her dirty water. Dirty from her own body. It is too dirty for her to put her hand in and pull the plug out. Can you believe that? This woman would leave her bath water for me to let it out?

"I'm not saying she should wash the tub. Hey, she's paying me to do that —O.K. But, you mean she can't let out her own, own water?

"And, if you think that's all I found in that tub you're wrong. There, swimming, afloat in that water of hers, was her panty . . . she'd left it in there for me to wash.

"What! Me? I taught her a lesson, that very first day. I took something, a peg, I think, and lifted that panty of hers and put it dripping wet, to the side of the bath which I then cleaned until it was shiny-shiny.

"You think she got my message? Wrong. Doesn't she leave me a note: 'Stella, wash the panty when you wash the bath.'

"What do you mean what did I do? I did not go to school for nothing. I found a pen in her bookshelf and found a piece of paper and wrote her a note too:

"'Medem,' I said in the note, 'please excuse me but I did not think anyone can ask another person to wash their panty. I was taught that a panty is the most intimate thing . . . my mother told me no one else should even see my panty. I really don't see how I can be asked to wash someone else's panty.'

"That was the end of that panty nonsense. You see, she leaves the house very early. And at that time I worked sleep-out for her so we used to write a lot of messages for each other.

"And then every Sunday she's off to Church. Hypocrites, these white people are. Real hypocrites. Never practise what they preach.

"She goes to Church every Sunday, but when Master isn't here, you should see what goes on in this place. Then, she comes home early from work: 'Stella, you can take the rest of the day off.'

"What am I supposed to do with a half day off I didn't know I was getting? You think I have money to be running up and down for nothing? But, that doesn't worry Sunshine Smile. All she wants is that there's no maid to see her business. Hypocrite and *skelm* on top of it too.

"But me, I take the cheek out of her. I take the half day off she gives me. But I stay right here in my room and give myself a rest.

"And she doesn't know I need to rest. She thinks I am a donkey that can go on and on working. When I'm off, do you know she can think nothing of giving me a whole suitcase full of clothes. Don't think she's like other medems who give their girls their old clothes. Not this one, my friend. She wants me to sell those clothes for her.

"'Here Stella,' the smile is bigger than the whole sky, 'I'm sure your friends in Langa would like these clothes. Almost new.'

"That's the woman I work for. It is not enough I work for her six to six, six days a week. On my half day off I must be working for her. Selling her second-hand clothes. She even pins the price on each one.

"Now don't think these almost new clothes have been dry-cleaned. You think she'd spend her money like that? There, I must carry clothes smelling her smell, carry them home and sell them to my friends. Of course, the one's the donkey can wash, those she sees to it that they *are* washed and ironed. She's not stingy with my strength, oh no!

"Then she'll take one of these clothes, look at it like it was a child going away, and say—'Take this one for yourself.' That is how she pays me for carry-ing a heavy suitcase, making my friends laugh at me selling her silly clothes. You know, sometimes I just save myself the trouble, take the clothes and pay her the money—bit by bit—until I've paid all of it. Then, when I find someone going back to the village, I send the clothes to my relatives there.

"You don't think you would be sick working for someone like this—making you work like a donkey and feeding you goat food? She really gets on my nerves. But I must be careful. If there's one thing that makes her out and out mad at me—it's when I'm sick.

"My sickness she never understands. She thinks I'm made of stone. She, can be sick and when she's sick I must run all over the place making her feel good: 'Turn the TV on. Turn the TV off. Make me black tea. Warm me some milk. I want dry toast. Give the margarine. Go get me the news-paper. I forgot, *Cosmopolitan* is out. Take all calls and write down the messages. Is that Joan? I'll take the call.'

"But I must never get sick. 'You think I run a clinic here, my girl?' That's what she says first day I'm sick. Day number two: 'Maybe you should go home and send one of your daughters to help.'

"You know this woman has children the same ages as mine. I must send my children here to help her and her children while I'm sick. My children must miss school to come and make sure their goat food is made, the beds are made, their shoes are polished, their clothes are washed.

"I also discovered she doesn't like me to be sick and stay here. I think she believes my sickness will jump onto them and kill them all. It's all right for me to catch their germs when they are sick. But my germs—that's a different story.

"Ho! White people! You slave for them. Slave for their children. Slave for their friends. Even slave for their cats and dogs. And they thank you with a kick in the back.

"Anyway, I must go. I'm making yoghurt bread over there, the dough must be ready by now. Hey, thanks for the coffee—now, I'm really awake."

Beh N!a'an, GIRAFFE SONG

Namibia 1991   Ju/'hoansi

This story recounts a moment of creative inspiration that took place in the early decades of the last century, probably sometime during the 1930s. It was told to me in 1991 by Beh N!a'an, a Ju/'hoan San woman living then at N=aqmtjoha, Namibia, in what is now Otjozondjupa district in the northeast part of the country. Beh had told her story during the 1950s to ethnographer Lorna Marshall, who included it in an article in the journal *Africa* and more recently in her book *Nyae Nyae !Kung Beliefs and Rites*. Although the versions told to Marshall and myself differed in some details, they were clearly variations of the same story.

There are several other versions of Beh's story that other Ju/'hoan people have told as well. Each one has slightly different details. Oral storytellers in the Ju/'hoan tradition like Beh say that they are faithfully "repeating" a tale when what they are actually doing is telling it in their own words. These words reflect the performance situation of the moment and cannot be extricated from it. Concentration on words and details per se is a phenomenon of alphabetic literacy that has long distorted outsiders' understanding of communication in oral societies.

In Ju/'hoan society, there is a high degree of tolerance for individual contributions to both religious life and oral tradition. This high tolerance may be related to the egalitarian nature of the society, whose norms are enforced not by dogma but by a creative participation of all members. Where spoken communication is the model for information exchange, two messages may be regarded as "the same" even though they are rarely verbatim equivalents.

One of the ways others told Beh's story was this: A woman named Beh was alone one day in the bush. She saw a herd of giraffes running before an approaching thunderstorm. The rolling beat of their hooves grew louder and mingled in her head with the sound of sudden rain. Suddenly, a song she had never heard before came to her, and she began to sing. G//aoan (the great god) told her it was a medicine song.

Beh went home and taught the song to her husband, /Ai!ae. They sang it and danced together. It was indeed a song for trancing, a medicine song. /Ai!ae taught it to others who also passed it on. Old men can name the people who learned the song in turn as it spread eastward from Namibia into Botswana. The giraffe medicine song tradition, stemming from a single inspired individual, has virtually replaced the earlier gemsbok singing and dancing over vast areas of the Kalahari.

The version printed here is one that Beh told when she was a very old woman; it contains a lively welter of details. The excerpt ends on a note of sadness, with Beh saying that she has outlived her husband and all her old playmates. Beh N!a'an ("Old Beh") died in 1992, in an accidental hut fire, shortly after her middle-aged son /Ui, who had learned the giraffe song as a very young child, died of tuberculosis. This 1991 version was videotaped by Thomas Dowson and I, and is available from the Witwatersrand University Film Unit.

◆

I am going to start with where the giraffe ran toward me. We were walking along up to the death place of the meat, we went to the place where the eland had died. When I saw the giraffes I began to sway in rhythm with them, it seemed as if I easily began to do that. I did it, and did it, and continued to do it.

My husband said to me, "What are you doing?"

"What am I doing?" I asked.

"You are swaying like a giraffe."

The death place was as close as this *appelblaar*. The giraffes were coming from this direction. They came past us. My son's younger sister was not born yet, at that time. In fact the giraffe spirits had long ago entered me. I kept doing, doing, doing it, and that was the Great Giraffe Song . . .

The Great Song has never ended. My voice is gone and my eyes are split, and I don't know . . . I am going deaf. I can't hear; my ears can't hear. That is what disturbs me.

If I did not feel like death, I would be singing a song for what is happening in the sky now [rain is coming as we speak]. I would sing and sing. If I had eyes I would sing and look around . . .

We ate the meat and I was swaying and trembling. Swaying like a giraffe, I helped pack up the meat and bring it home. And we just stayed well in the village and ate the meat. I almost died but instead lived.

We sat quietly and ate the meat. But in fact these people—the giraffe spirits—had climbed inside me. I ate meat and it tasted good. I had been hungry for a long time but then I had meat. That is where I got the giraffe song. My husband, who has a soft diaphragm [meaning he goes into trance easily], got *n/om* [spiritual medicine] then. And those were the songs of it, what one that people go around dancing. Those songs came out of my mouth. Those who came from the west, the giraffe people, brought them home. They came to me but my diaphragm was hard [this kept me from trancing]. My husband's diaphragm is soft. That is where he was able to enter it.

[Later my son began to dance too.] He danced and I watched him. He danced and danced beautifully and moved forward like a snake. And I watched him.

Sometimes my husband would speak to the rain and it would not listen, but I would sing and it would listen [and the thunder would grow soft]. You say to the rain, "Wait, slow down. Bring us water. Make the earth healthy, cool under the children's feet."

A woman can run out of her house and speak thus to the rain. Or if I go out gathering, I might find an animal that has been killed, or the chest of

GIRAFFE SONG ◆ 443

something [that the carnivores have left]. But if it was a man, it would also be good for him to find the track of something like that in the bush and bring it home for us to eat. You say this: "That is how it is, that is how it is."

You say, "Let the *sha* look good and ripe." Then you dig, dig, dig it, and spend the day, the two of us, eating it. A woman can run out and say that. That is what you say. And your husband will enter and agree with you, saying "Why are we two trancing?" "Yes," you say, "but the two of us have this song and it is a great thing. They have brought us this thing and we can dance it and be alive." My husband said, "They have brought it to you and both of us will dance and sing it."

So I hung beads all around my head. The young women of our village all hung dangling beads around their heads. The young men also tied leg bangles on their legs. You go visiting to the north and the people from there watch you. "People, let's watch this beautiful thing they are doing here." People gave gifts of ostrich beads, and people danced and watched and watched. We were very beautiful. We combed our hair with oil, and combed the men's hair with oil. That is what we did. I danced and sang until I lost my voice—my "tongue was cut." But the young girls who were singing then have all died. They did not eat correctly [did not observe food avoidances] and they died. I am the only one left. Nobody is left, even my friend /Asa has died. All that is left are the trees standing in that place.

People are finished, and I am finished. Those people have all died. I have grown old and stopped dancing, and today just sit. I am old and have no strength. The tall camel thorn that was the Giraffe, the Giraffe Dance has broken. It died with my husband's death; it has grown small. The young girls have all died, and I am the only one left. That is how things are.

Transcribed and translated by Megan Biesele

Maria Munsaka, NHAMIWA'S MAGIC STICK

Zimbabwe 1991   Tonga

"Nhamiwa's Magic Stick" was told to me in 1991 by Maria Munsaka. Photographer Margaret Waller and I went to Binga, on the shores of Lake Kariba, to interview Tonga women about their rich traditions, and to collect material for publication.

The Tonga are justly famous for their verbal dexterity, their love of stories and riddles: "Who is the handsome man sleeping in the dust?" "A sweet potato!" Tonga oral tradition is also dynamic, in touch with changing times and needs. Women are considered "the stone houses of Tonga culture," as explained by Joseph Mudimba of the Binga Craft Centre, "especially when it comes to storytelling, song and dance. Without their knowledge we would have no identity as a people."

Waller and I had a special reason for visiting this remote part of Zimbabwe. The Tonga are a minority group in Zimbabwe who were displaced in the 1960s to make way for the construction of the Kariba Dam, which created one of the largest artificial lakes in the world. Although the government made an effort to save wildlife, no assistance was given to the Tonga to save their ancestral shrines. In the 1980s the Tonga did not benefit much from the developmental programs that were introduced after independence.

Maria Munsaka, we learned, came from an older generation of storytellers. Celebrated for her lively style and wry humor, she had acquired a large repertoire of tales from her grandmother. She began entertaining village audiences in Binga district when she was nine years old. Because Munsaka is married to a polygamist, her favorite story is about Nhamiwa, an unloved second wife.

Fiona Lloyd

✦

Once there was a polygamist who had two wives. He loved the first very much but treated the second wife cruelly. Her name was Nhamiwa and she had spiritual powers. With her magic stick she could separate the waters of the Zambezi. Every day she accompanied the polygamist to the river bank. She beat the water with her stick and immediately the river parted, leaving a dry pathway in the centre. Her husband could walk across without even getting wet. As soon as he reached the other side the waters closed. He made this daily journey to steal cattle. At sunset he would call across to Nhamiwa:

"Nhamiwa, Nhamiwa,
Beat and part the water!
I have three fat cattle
And the middle one is yours!"

Nhamiwa would beat the water so he could cross. But when the succulent meat had been cooked and was ready to eat, she was always given bones.

One day the polygamist went down to the river as usual. Nhamiwa went with him and beat the water with her stick, just as he requested. He made the crossing and, at sunset, Nhamiwa heard him calling from the opposite shore:

"Nhamiwa, Nhamiwa,
Whose strength can part the water
Use your stick to let me cross
And you'll eat meat tonight!"

But Nhamiwa's ears were deaf. The polygamist called again. And again. Eventually Nhamiwa sang to him across the river:

"I will not beat the water
I will not let you cross
Today you'll be fixed!"

Suddenly there was a great commotion. The owners of the beasts had discovered who was stealing their cattle. Brandishing spears, they surrounded the polygamist. He called to Nhamiwa yet again. This time his tone was desperate:

"Nhamiwa, Nhamiwa
They've come with sharp spears!

Beat the water with your stick
So I may safely cross!"
Nhamiwa did nothing. The owners of the cattle set upon the polygamist
and killed him. His body was thrown into the river.

Transcribed and translated by Fiona Lloyd

Gasethata Segaise, Mmatsheko Pilane, and Motshabi Molefhe, "LEND ME A DRESS": TESTIMONIES ON EDUCATION

Botswana 1991, 1999   Setswana

For many Botswana women of the early twentieth century, going to school was secondary to family responsibility. Nevertheless, some indomitable women managed to go to school, and some became teachers, though, sadly, we could find no documents by or about them. Instead, we interviewed women in their seventies and eighties who had taught in the 1930s and 1940s. Three excerpts appear here.

Gasethata Segaise was born in 1921 and started school at the age of twelve. In 1940, aged nineteen, she entered the newly established Teacher Training College in Serowe. She then taught in a number of primary schools, and even after her marriage in 1968 continued teaching.

Mmatsheko Pilane and her sisters went to school as a matter of course because, as she says, they were "fortunate" that they were all girls. She was born in 1915 and started school at Linchwe School in Mochudi, about twenty-five miles from Gaborone. She became a domestic science teacher at the same school, but then left for Johannesburg in search of better cash opportunities in white people's kitchens and nurseries. She returned after a year to work as a teacher once more. After her marriage in 1939 she gave up teaching.

Motshabi Molefhe, born in 1910, attended school for six years before becoming a teacher. She also worked in Johannesburg for ten years until her mother took ill, forcing her to return to Botswana to look after her until her mother's death.

None of these women kept a private archive of their letters, journals, or other material, even though they could. Two of them, Pilane and Molefhe, said that they burnt their letters.

Lily Mafela and Leloba Molema

✦

GASETHATA SEGAISE, INTERVIEWED JANUARY 1991
Women were constrained from attending school because in Setswana tradition girls had to grind corn, cook and draw water. Also, one could be lent to one's relatives to help them out if they did not have younger girls to per-

form these household duties. In our times, it used to be that when one's aunt had a baby, one would be sent to mind the baby. Then maybe when one returned home one might find that another aunt had also had a baby, and one would be sent there. One could be exchanged around like that, so that in the end one would not get a chance to go to school. In my case the situation was especially bad because I was the only girl in our household for quite some time, and I eventually had to force matters to go to school, because my parents used to say, "You cannot go to school, you have to mind the children. . . ." I actually took myself to school, nobody sent me there.

This is how it happened: it was during harvest time and we were at the lands at the time, when I decided to borrow a dress from one of my age-mates and she lent it to me. Then I ran away from the lands and came back here to the village to register myself at the school. It was at the moment when I was [in the] registration process, that my father came riding his horse looking for me. . . . He went over to the principal and told him, "I have tracked down and followed my child here because she ran away with the others yesterday." I was called out by name, and I tried to hide but there was nowhere to hide, so I had to stand up. And then my father said out loud, "Yes, that is her, she is the one I am looking for. . . ." Mr. Sebina was the principal at the time, and he was adamant and told my father, "We have already registered this child and there is nothing we can do. We cannot erase her name, and right now we actually require her to pay the three shillings school levy." My father was very upset, but there was nothing he could do except to pay the required fee, and so I stayed in school.

MMATSHEKO PILANE, INTERVIEWED FEBRUARY 1999
When I left teaching I was very hurt because I did not have my own money anymore. In my marriage I was happy except for the fact that I was controlled. In those days when you married you did what your husband told you to do. Even if you wanted to be a schoolteacher you gave it up. Cattle-rearing was my husband's choice and decision. Cattle supported me when he died. I am now too old to help manage them.

One day when the Chief, Chief Isang, came to talk to my husband about his need for teachers in the school, my husband replied, "This woman is my wife, not our wife. This woman has helped you so far. Now it is my turn."

Yes, I did get my inheritance from my father because [i.e., even though] we were girls. In those days when you were born a girl, inheritance would be passed to your brothers. We were fortunate because we did not have a brother.

MOTSHABI MOLEFHE, INTERVIEWED FEBRUARY 1999
I don't have lesson plans or any form of writing. Not even letters. You can never keep letters. You have to throw them away because sometimes they will land you in trouble, so you have to get rid of them. At times someone

might find you throwing a letter into a blazing fire and ask, "Why are you burning that letter?" and you respond, "It's not a letter. It's just a piece of paper." You fear to be in trouble.

Translated by Lily Mafela (Segaise) and Alpheons Moroke (Pilane and Molefhe)

Nokwanda Sithole, A BROKEN FAMILY
South Africa 1991   English

Nokwanda Sithole was one of the first young black women students to complete a journalism diploma at the (until then) exclusively white Natal Technikon. She gained wide experience in the press before becoming editor of the magazine *Tribute*. A fearless and promising investigative journalist, she died young in a car accident in the early 1990s.

The African township of Chesterville is one of the oldest in Durban, having been built in the 1930s when there was still extreme municipal resistance to the idea of "family housing" for African workers in the city. The preferred option was to rely on male migrants, who would leave their families in their countryside homesteads. Chesterville became a hub of social life for Africans in Durban, cater-ing to both workers who enjoyed the music and drink of the shebeens and the more refined middle class, who organized dramatic and debating societies.

In the 1980s, however, Chesterville, like other African settlements in the KwaZulu-Natal region, turned into a battleground for the warring political organ-izations, the United Democratic Front (UDF) and Inkatha. The UDF, formed out of over six hundred community-based organizations in 1983, was the first mass national political movement to emerge internally since the banning of political activity in the early 1960s. (The two organizations referred to in Sithole's account, the Congress of South African Students and the Council of Unions of South Africa—later the Congress of South African Trade Unions—were both UDF affil-iates.) The UDF, while not affiliated with the African National Congress (ANC), was widely identified with the general ethos of the ANC, with the difference that its leadership was dedicated to a peaceful resolution of the political impasse. In certain regions of South Africa, however, the UDF found itself embroiled in intensely violent conflict with other movements also claiming to be the "legiti-mate" internal expression of resistance to apartheid.

The premier example was Inkatha in KwaZulu-Natal. This movement, built specifically around a Zulu ethnic identity, claimed mass support in the region and in mines and certain parts of the Johannesburg area (now Gauteng) where there were significant numbers of Zulu-speaking workers. Inkatha was in direct ideological confrontation with the UDF, resulting in years of terrible bloodshed in hundreds of communities. Chesterville was one of these, and one where the combatants on both sides were Zulu speakers. Murder and "necklacing" (the killing of opponents by plac-ing burning tires around their necks) continued into the early 1990s, even as the var-ious political parties were finally negotiating an end to apartheid. Sithole's evocative piece captures the pain of such intense division within a single family.

Heather Hughes

◆

Somewhere in Chesterville, a township outside Durban, there is a broken family—broken not in the sense of being physically separated, but rather torn apart by the different, seemingly irreconcilable political ideologies that have caused endless bloodshed in the province of Natal.

At the head of the family is Absalom Dumakude, fifty-three, a burly member of the KwaZulu Police Force. He has been an ardent supporter of the KwaZulu homeland chief minister and Inkatha leader, Mangosuthu Gatsha Buthelezi, since the early 1970s. He transferred from the South African Police to the KwaZulu Police Force when it was formed in 1985. "Joining became a natural choice," he says.

Esther, his wife, is a frail, harassed-looking person. She has no political affiliations of her own, and says, "Where my husband is, I'll be." She says she "accepted Christ" in 1984, and believes that if humankind would dedicate itself to seeking solutions to its problems in Christ, this would be a better world.

Siphiwe, their eldest child, lives with them in their four-room house. He is not Mrs. Dumakude's natural son, having been born out of wedlock to Mr. Dumakude and a Johannesburg woman thirty-one years ago. In 1976 Siphiwe was a student activist in Soweto. He was there on June 16, when students took to the streets to protest the use of Afrikaans as a teaching medium and the police answered with a brutality that shook the whole country.

Twelve years later, Siphiwe is a "won't work" whose face is battered by years of heavy drinking. He says he doesn't want to discuss politics: "You must not tell me about politics. You do not know politics. I know. . . . I was in the frontline in 1976.

"Where did it get me? When the police started chasing me, I had to run. I came to Durban to live with my father. In 1977 my father said he did not have the money to send rebels to school. If I had been man enough to rise against authority in Soweto, he said, then I could run my own life."

Schooling for Siphiwe thus stopped in June 1976. He has had two jobs since—at a petrol station, and as a cleaner in an office building. He is bitter because some of his peers got chances to leave the country after the 1976–77 uprising and have studied abroad, making him feel left behind.

His two sisters, Thembelihle and Khanyisile, rent two rooms in Lamontville, another Durban township. Both are staunch United Democratic Front supporters. Thembelihle, twenty-nine, works in a Pinetown factory and earns R100 a week; from this she pays her sister's school fees. Khanyisile, twenty-two, is a student at a local school and was a member of the Congress of South African Students (COSAS). She is doing fairly well at school and plans to attend a university next year.

They did not want to leave home, but had no choice. In Chesterville, they were trapped between, on the one hand, a helpless mother and brother with whom they could not share their aspirations and, on the other, a father who was hostile to those aspirations.

In addition to the divisions within their family, Thembelihle and Khanyisile had problems with their political associates.

"I could sense that at meetings, people were being careful about what they said in front of us," says Thembelihle. "It was terrible. . . . At the same time, what choice did our comrades have? Our father has been an Inkatha man for a long time. And he is our father. If I were your enemy, would you be able to eat and drink freely with Khanyisile? No, because Khanyisile and I are relatives . . . you are the outsider."

Thembelihle and Khanyisile left home in 1984, at the height of the violent confrontation between the UDF and Inkatha over the incorporation of Chesterville township into KwaZulu. Shortly after they had gone, an incident took place that left strong feelings of suspicion in the family and widened the gulf between the father and his daughters.

Mr. Dumakude was away visiting relatives and only Siphiwe and Mrs. Dumakude were home. Around midnight, Esther was awakened by the crash of breaking glass: "There was no doubt in my mind what it was. There was a war going on in Chesterville between Inkatha and UDF, and since my husband was associated with Inkatha and the police, we had been expecting it. A petrol bomb landed right next to my bed, and I thought it was all over. By the grace of God, it did not go off, but another landed outside and started a fire.

"Siphiwe had also been woken up by the shattering glass, and together we managed to extinguish the fire on the grass outside.

"When my husband came home the following weekend, he found us a bundle of nerves. It was worse because Siphiwe thinks he can drown his sorrows in liquor whether there is an immediate problem or not. We could not really sit down and talk about what to do, because the only man in the house just wasn't interested."

The day after Mr. Dumakude arrived, three men were dispatched to guard the house. He refuses to say where these men came from, whether they were from the police or Inkatha or were vigilantes.

Mr. Dumakude blames his daughters for the bombing, which he still talks about with emotion four years later. They were responsible, he says, for the "attempted destruction of my family."

What if the bomb had detonated? What if his wife had been killed? Would he see his daughters punished—even killed—for the deed he attributes to them? Mr. Dumakude does not answer. He merely mumbles a barely audible, "Where did it all go wrong?"

If he met his daughters in the line of duty, when he had orders to shoot to kill, would he carry out those orders?

Mr. Dumakude still does not answer. He only says: "You do not know, you will never know how it feels to bring up children the proper way. You think that you have instilled in them your values, that you are winning, and then suddenly they turn against you and effectively tell you that you wasted your time bringing them into this world.

"Thembelihle and Khanyisile do not live in this house today. My own daughters were taken up by what foreign people, people who are strangers to them, taught them. If ever their chosen path becomes too rough for them, they must not come back here."

Mr. Dumakude is an angry man. He feels hatred for the people he calls "foreign," people who came and encouraged his daughters to choose a different way from the traditional one that he hoped they would follow and respect.

Thembelihle says she and her sister grew up in an "apolitical" home: "I would say that if anybody had any political beliefs when we grew up, he or she never expressed them. My father started showing admiration for Chief Buthelezi in the early 1970s. My father is the kind of man who does not allow any democracy in the house. He had to be the sole policy maker. He would sing the praises of Buthelezi and we would listen. We were not exposed to any other political opinions then, and I have vivid memories of actually developing a great admiration for this man who was being presented to me as a liberator—the great leader of the Zulu nation."

In 1975 Thembelihle went to a new school where she mixed with students from all over South Africa, some of whom had a much broader political awareness. Those were black consciousness days. Thembelihle and her new friends would hold discussions on the political situation in the country, and she began to form her own ideas on strategies and solutions.

"Although Khanyisile was still a child, she was the only person at home with whom I could discuss my ideas. I would bore her for hours with my stories. . . . That was the beginning of a strong bond between us."

Thembelihle says she could have kept her political feelings to herself for the sake of family unity. She admits that she had seriously considered that option, but in the early 1980s she found herself in a situation where she had to make a difficult choice. The turning point came when she worked in a factory where the workers had been organized by the Council of Unions of South Africa (CUSA).

"Some workers who were not as politically conscious as I was refused to join factory-floor organizations," she recalls. "My situation was different. I understood every word that the CUSA representatives were saying when they were organizing the workers. I knew that workers were the vanguard of the struggle, and that without us the struggle was doomed."

Thembelihle became an active labor leader and later participated in community organizations. Khanyisile, in turn, joined COSAS [the Congress of South African Students] in her teens, a fact that had to be kept secret from the family at all costs. Meanwhile, Mr. Dumakude's police and KwaZulu connections had become a great embarrassment for the two sisters in their political lives.

"We could no longer follow my father's wishes blindly," says Khanyisile. "The final straw came in 1984, when my father was told, apparently by a teacher, of my COSAS involvement. He never asked me if I was actually a member or tried to find out why I had joined or tried to discourage me from the organization. The *sjambok* (lash) was the only language he seemed to think I could understand."

Thembelihle says that she and her sister do not hate their father, and they wish he would understand that they had nothing to do with the attempted bombing of their home.

"There was a war going on at that time," says Khanyisile, "and there were two sides to it. It is possible that our home was hit by the 'comrades.' But my father seems to forget that there is a criminal element which has crept into the whole situation. And he also knows the kind of people my brother mixes with. He is always owing people money and provoking them. So it is also possible that the bombers were my brother's 'friends,' trying to take advantage of the situation."

"Our father is one of those in Natal who have mud over their eyes, who have not seen the real truth of the situation," says Thembelihle. "One day he may realize and appreciate what we stand for. One day he may realize that we are incapable of trying to kill our own family. I just hope it is not too late."

Thembelihle feels sorry for their mother: "It seems she will go to her grave not having known what it is to formulate an idea of her own."

She says that she and her sister talk about their mother a lot, wishing she could shed her submissiveness and take hold of her own life.

Esther, for her part, says she misses her daughters: "They are my children. My children left home for the wilderness because of politics. I stayed with my husband because I do not know why my children refuse to listen to us."

How does this family see its future?

Mr. Dumakude: "Thembelihle and Khanyisile will soon see the foolishness of going against their family. But when they decide to come back here, there may be no place for them."

Thembelihle: "Our family is but a tiny fragment of what is going on around the country. If we work toward a better future for the whole country, our family will automatically fall into place."

Khanyisile: "It is hard to forgive and forget, and I never really try to picture our family together again, but I hope we do not stay enemies forever."

Siphiwe: "Thembelihle and Khanyisile left our home. I told them they will not get anywhere. I told them to look at me. They were lucky because I am here, they can see what happened to me. This family will never have children it can be proud of."

Mrs. Dumakude: "I pray every day that my family may become one again."

Cinikile Mazibuko and Makhosazane Nyadi,
TWO DREAM-MIRACLE STORIES
South Africa 1992   English

The two women who related these dream and miracle stories are sisters and followers of the prophet Isiah Shembe, who founded *ibandla lamaNazaretha* (Church
of the Nazarites) around 1911 in Inanda, near Durban. Shembe died in 1935.
Today his church is spread throughout southern Africa but its members are located
chiefly in KwaZulu-Natal and Gauteng; they are thought to number between
250,000 and 1,000,000 people. The Nazarite ideals are founded in traditional
Nguni principles of respect and public male authority; collective participation in
ritualized performances of prayer, sacred song, and dance; and the exchange of
dream-miracle narratives called "sermons." Sermons enable women to speak in
public spaces where Zulu women would traditionally keep silent, and, in giving
evidence of the power of their God, Shembe (his prophet takes the same name),
the women's words become part of a collective store of Nazarite truth.

In as much as these narratives relate individual women's lives and experiences,
and contain their critical understanding of state and traditional patriarchal power,
they indicate a way in which Nazarite women may claim their identity and place
in history. Common to all their stories are the pain and hardship of life under a
racist government and within traditional patriarchy, followed by a triumph over
suffering brought about through miraculous or dream encounters with Shembe.

On two nights of each month, called *amaforteenies* after the date, the married
women of the Nazarite church meet and exchange stories about their personal
encounter with, or witnessing of, the power of Shembe to provide healing for the
sick, fertility for the barren, economic resources for the destitute, and, through his
mediation with the ancestors, reunion of family members lost through warfare,
migrant labor, and other misfortunes.

The significance of the date, 1937, in the second story is that the events
described took place two years after the death of Isiah Shembe, by which time he
would have been firmly associated with the ancestral domain. His miraculous
bringing of children represents a reintegration of the ancestors into mission-taught
Christianity, an anticolonial realignment of traditional Nguni epistemology with
the teachings that underwrote colonial power.

The first story by Cinikile Mazibuko, from Dube in Soweto, recounts the experiences of another woman in her group. It illustrates the effects of extreme economic deprivation on a woman's life, indicates how she managed her anxiety, and
then recounts the sudden and miraculous appearance of money. The second story,
about Shembe's healing their mother's infertility, was begun by Cinikile Mazibuko
and completed by her sister, Makhosazane Nyadi. The *dokoda* to which Cinikile
refers is a temporary shelter representing the Old Testament tabernacle and used
during the January and July gatherings of the church.

M. J. Daymond

Cinikile Mazibuko: First Story

After standing up, she told us that one day she had no money. No money to give her children to carry to school. Even her husband hasn't got money. She had only a ticket to go to work. Her husband used to collect her from work to home. That day, her husband came late to collect her.

During the day she failed to get money because even when she went to the bank, they didn't give her money. . . . On their way home, they were not talking to each other because they haven't got money. You know, she said, on the highway next to Diepkloof, the traffic cop passed them. He was running at high speed. He passed them.

Then she saw something like papers coming away from the scooter. Then this lady said, "What is this?" She tried to pick out of the—look at . . . What was it? What was falling out from the traffic cop? The traffic cop didn't wait. He just passed.

Then she asked her husband to stop the car. The husband stopped the car, and they got out. Those that were coming out of the scooter was the money. It was in *fifties*! Fifty papers! They picked those—she didn't say how much. But, she said, it just went away from the scooter like papers. They, they picked it. The husband was picking, she also was picking.

That's how Shembe helped them, because she said that if it was not because of Shembe, she was not going to get that money. But, because of Shembe. . . . She asked him, "Shembe, can you help me? Because I have got no money." Then Shembe put the money to this traffic cop, then blew it away. So they got the money.

Cinikile Mazabuko: Second Story

My mother said when she was *umkhoti*, or newly-wed, she used to get children and the children used to die. Maybe when the child is six months, less than a year, the child dies. Now, here were six children dying.

They came in *Nhlangakaze* [the Nazarite holy mountain], the very same *Nhlangakaze* that it was in 1937 when my mother came here to this *Nhlangakaze*. When [s]he came here, [s]he says there were them [*izimbongi*], as you always hear shouting—people must do this and this—you see. So she said, they were here. Then somebody came and said, "Shembe says that all those who are here, who want children, must come up to him on the mountain."

So my mother went up with the other women who didn't have children. Up to where Shembe was going to pray for them. They all went up. My mother said then Shembe came and said, "People must be ready." They must pray, you see. You see, as we pray, we close our eyes. My mother says as [s]he was closing her eyes, [s]he heard Shembe coming.

In her vision, my mother [s]he saw that Shembe had a basket. In the basket there was something like stars. [S]he said Shembe was taking the stars like this, he was throwing the stars like that. [S]he said some other stars too, were coming to my mother. [S]he said she just took them out [like] this, and do like this to hold the stars. The stars were just flying too. But the stars were jumping from one woman to the other women. Not everybody was getting these stars. But, to my mother, those stars came.

She said that she just put out the dress to hold the stars. The stars came. Then [he] was just praying for them, that "God, I am just praying for them, I am just asking that you please help this person, this poor woman to please get children." Like that [he] was praying, praying that side [in heaven]. "Amen." When Shembe said, "Amen," my mother was holding like this, because she saw that vision of the stars in the basket that Shembe was giving the people.

When my mother came down from the mountain, here to the *dokoda*, she was here with, she came with her mother. She said, "Mother, you know, I saw this vision up there. I saw Shembe had a basket full of stars, and he was throwing stars to everybody. The stars were jumping, going from [one] to [the] others, and the other stars came to me, and I just held them like this." Then my mother said, "My child, you are really going to get children. When Shembe has prayed for you, and you've seen that, you really are going to get children."

Makhosazane Nyadi completed the story:
When my mother is sleeping, she had a feeling at the back, a pain. She asked the other women, "Just look at the back. What's going on with my back? There is something." You know when you get burnt, maybe it was hot water—it was something like that. My mother was crying, and the other followers—women of Shembe—said, "No, you must not cry. It is the way Shembe is healing you." My mother said, "Whooo, how can that be?"

Then my mother went home. When she was at home, she got pregnant. One day she was sleeping and she heard somebody telling her, "I am Shembe. I am bringing you children. Your first-born will be a girl. Her name will be Makhosazane [Princess]." I am Makhosazane now.

Transcribed by Carol Muller

Elizabeth Ncube, PRAISE TO MBUYA NEHANDA
Zimbabwe 1993 siNdebele

Until her death at the age of thirty-six in 1996, Elizabeth Ncube was generally considered one of Zimbabwe's finest praise poets. She began by performing praise poetry in the Bulawayo township beer-halls. Her program originally included established praises about Shaka Zulu and the amaNdebele kings, but later she began writing her own poems about political leaders and the liberation struggle. Her performances, which dealt with contemporary political issues, became popular and she was invited to perform at state functions and traveled abroad to

Holland, Canada, and the United States.

Ncube was herself a traditional healer and spirit medium. She was inspired to create her praises of Nehanda partly to celebrate women in the liberation struggle and also because of men's hostility to her performing praises—traditionally a male activity. At the neShamwari Festival in 1992, when Ncube entered a competitive section for amaNdebele praise poetry, her performing angered a group of older men from Bulawayo. One of them came on stage reciting one of her own praise poems in opposition to her. They engaged in a shield and stick fight. Ncube was able to drive him off the stage using her superior fighting skills. Although pleased by the victory and sure that it had proved that the ancestors authorized her performing praises, she was hurt by the men's opposition to her work.

When performing traditional praises, Ncube wore the dress of a male warrior because she was undertaking a male activity and wanted to honor her male ancestors. When performing her praise to Nehanda, Ncube dressed in the black cloth worn by women spirit mediums. In doing so she was calling forward the ancestral grandmothers—not a metaphoric act, since invoking the gods when you know they are present can be a dangerous undertaking—and transforming her performance from a male to a female activity. Her poem, recorded on videotape in 1993 by Martin Rohmer, engages national issues as well as gender politics. In praising a Shona ancestral spirit in siNdebele, Ncube's choice of language acknowledges that Nehanda is a national spirit, an ancestral spirit of Zimbabwe.

The Nehanda spirit is a *mhondoro* spirit. In Shona culture *mhondoro* spirits give rain and are the most senior ancestral spirits. Nehanda has two official mediums, one in the Mazoe area, near Harare, and the other in the Dande area, in the Zambezi Valley. In 1896, the Nehanda medium in Mazoe, a woman named Charwe, was a major leader of the rebellion, or First Chimurenga, against the colonial state. She was captured, sentenced to death, and hanged. While on trial, she remained defiant, refused to convert to Christianity, and (according to legend) prophesied that her bones would rise to win back freedom from the Europeans. Many Zimbabweans believe that during the Zimbabwe War of Independence in the 1960s, the Second Chimurenga, the Nehanda medium in Dande sanctioned the fighting when she moved to Mozambique to support the liberation struggle. Nehanda became both a spiritual symbol for and an embodiment of the long-awaited victory over the European colonial oppressors, and a major figure in the songs and writings of the liberation struggle.

At traditional ceremonies, the grandmother spirits are usually the first to possess the mediums so as to "open the way" for the rest of the spirits. In this case, Mbuya Nehanda opened the way for Zimbabwe's independence and now, in this poem—like a prayer and close to a curse—for the liberation of women.

Christopher Hurst

✦

Heroine, Mbuya Nehanda
You finder of the nation, being a woman
You stand for the nation, being a woman
Open the way for us, we are your orphans.
You left us while fighting the enemy.

The suckers of our wealth sucked the wealth of the nation
Being proud and giving themselves power.
Mbuya Nehanda, you prophesied saying
Your Bones would rise from the dead.
The spear of the nation changed
To hold fire and became a rifle
Dub! dub! dub! dub! [noise of gun]
Which brought freedom to our country.
The wealth suckers are the ones who know
Who sucked the wealth of our country
Sucking the blood of our nation
Giving themselves power.
Mbuya Nehanda, you prophet
Sleep and rest, rest, you heroine
We praise your brave death for the nation
Mbuya Nehanda
Sleep and rest, heroine
Sleep and rest.

Transcribed and translated by Musa Ndlovu

Thoko Remigia Makhanya,
A NOBLE WOMAN OF AFRICA
South Africa 1993   isiZulu

Thoko Remigia Makhanya first met the subject of her praises in 1984 when Nokukhanya Luthuli celebrated her eightieth birthday. The idea of a book about Nokukhanya was born at that party, and Makhanya learned the family's history as she participated in the research for the book. Then, and after reading the book in draft, she felt equipped to write her poem to Nokukhanya. She performed it in isiZulu at the party given upon the book's publication in 1993. She translated her poem into English herself and says that it is impossible for English to capture the deep poetry of the Zulu language.

Beginning as it does with lineage matters, Thoko Makhanya's poem conforms more to the traditional pattern of praises than does Gcina Mhlophe's "In Praise of Our Mothers" (see text in this volume). Makhanya also focuses on Nokukhanya's political achievements, as she pictures her "silently . . . shout[ing]" to the world that women build and sustain a nation. The phrase, "Mrs Edward's Place," is a characteristic way for praise poetry to refer to a location—Inanda Seminary is the place of its first principal. The poem draws on the comparatively little studied Zulu practice of women's composing their own praises and of women's performing clan and other praises. Unlike much men's praise poetry focused on violence and courage, this poem, like most praise poetry by women, celebrates the braveries of "perception" and "building and sustenance of the nation."

Makhanya was born in Hlokozi near the town of Highflats on the KwaZulu-Natal south coast. She attended a mission school in her area before going to St. Francis's College, Marianhill. She then trained as a nurse at St. Mary's Hospital, Marianhill, before specializing in midwifery at McCord's Zulu Hospital in Durban. She worked chiefly in rural areas before returning to study as a nurse educator at the University of Natal. After twenty-three years in this profession she took early retirement and since 1998 has been running HIV-AIDS workshops in the rural areas for the Women's Leadership and Training Program. Although she has some writing tucked away at home, this poem was her first publication.

M. J. Daymond

◆

The seed that came down from Swaziland
And got planted among the aloes of Ntunjambili
Got washed down with the Umngeni floods
And took root in Umngeni valleys.

In the midst of the Ngcolosi valleys
We saw a light flicker and then shine bright;
Still marvelling at this apparition
We heard that Nozincwadi of Ngidi
Had blessed the house of Maphitha of Ndlokolo
Of Bhengu of Ngcolosi
With another daughter—Nokukhanya.

Maphitha of Ndlokolo of Bhengu
Saw that this light was temporal in this area;
He deployed his work party by moonlight to the fields
So that this light might complement the moon
And shine beyond the Ngcolosi valley in time to come
And warm the Madlanduna (Luthuli) offspring.

The ancestor in education has shown the way;
John Langalibalele Dube
Took this flickering lamp out of the mist
And planted it in the well of education
In Ohlanga school

When Nozincwadi was called to her ancestors
This little lamp was left blown about by the winds
Till those from Mrs Edward's Place took over;
When they saw enthusiasm and thirst for knowledge
They took her under their wing
And only demanded sweat from her brow.

A star that arose from Umngeni
When others appear in the sky,
A fire that was lighted at Ohlanga
Stoked at Inanda and Amanzimtoti
And burned all the way to the hills of Mpushini
Manzimtoti, you have played a great role
By keeping this fire warmly lit
Till it settled on the plains of Groutville
To warm the Madlanduna Clan.

Little did Maphitha know
That he had donated a light to the nation;
He let it move across the valley and hills acquiring knowledge
To fulfil Nozincwadi's wishes.

You have been cooked in a hot one
And have come out as pure as gold
Praising Maphitha's iron hand.
Your perception is amazing
You see a silver lining in every cloud.

We've seen you carry your load
With a steady head and a straight back.
With zeal you've contributed
To the building and sustenance of the nation
Silently you shouted to the deaf world
That it is women who sustain the struggle for liberation.

Who has not seen you in Swaziland
Toiling away to achieve Mandlanduna's aims;
You were his hands and feet
Reaching where he couldn't because of his chains;
With all this you still kept the nest warm and adequate.

Who has not heard of you in Groutville?
At dawn you are already in the fields
Keeping company with your new-found friend the soil
Together solving problems that failed abler minds.

This is the mole of the Nkungu Clan
That toiled by night leaving mounds of soil
As the only evidence of its presence.

Mountains and valleys your silence bothers me;
Echo my shouts across and beyond

As I wonder at this unseen work
And praise these achievements
That have been kept in darkness.

Receive you valleys and steeps
This song of praise for the great farmer
Who challenged the tradition
And achieved feats beyond her given status.

I praise the many-roled woman
Mother, father, wife, teacher, nurse,
Farmer, environmentalist and theologian;
You've played all these without shortcomings.

I applaud the broad back
That carried the struggle up the steep hills;
Surely, Luthuli, you were paired with a leader.
The field you've covered together is praiseworthy.

Home hills and mountains
Even though you are silent
The worlds across the seas have heard;
Waves, I praise you for carrying my voice across the oceans
To the shores of Norway and America;
I am now consoled that the corners of the world have heard.

Nokukhanya of Maphitha of Nozincwadi
You have made your contribution;
The Bhengu and Luthuli ancestors
Have blessed you with many years;
We too thank you for the nine decades of life
Shared with us and your children's children
Teaching us the way to go;
We shall struggle to make your dream come true.

Woman of Women! Mother of the Nation!
We praise the Name of Woman!

Translated by Thoko Remigia Makhanya

Communal, SWAZI WEDDING SONGS

Swaziland 1993   siSwati

These Swazi wedding songs, recorded in the early 1990s, describe the traditional culture of the wedding itself and also the construction of marriage, often seen as hurtful to, or at least difficult for, women. On the morning of the wedding, for example, Song One describes the way in which the bride's hair is dressed into a beehive hairstyle. During the main day of the wedding, the bride remains hidden behind the front row of dancers. Relatives and friends strain to see her while they listen to songs about her beauty. She appears only to dance the main song, the request to her mother-in-law for a place in the new home. Similarly, Song Two alludes to the bride-price sent by the groom's family, usually in the form of cows, an act that precedes preparations by the bride's family for the wedding. Song Three describes what actually will happen: The bride will leave her family's home "justly"—with her father's permission and blessing—to become forever part of the groom's family.

Songs Five, Six, Seven, and Eight, on the other hand, describe in an ascending scale the tribulations of marriage for women. Song Six concentrates on personal selfhood: "To get married is like throwing away your own bones." Song Seven tells the story of a woman "defeated" by marriage, for she has lost her youth, strength, and energy. Song Eight reminds the bride that she has to care for her mother-in-law regardless of her own feelings. Finally, Song Nine dramatically poses the repeated refrain "Beat her, man," with the lines describing the husband's violence and the wife's protestations of innocence.

Sarah Dupont-Mkhonza

✦

SONG ONE
Oh what a beautiful hairstyle, young bride.
You must be joking you of the King,
I travelled until I was too tired.

SONG TWO
Subject of the King is playing.
I walked till noon.
I struggled, I suffered.
My sister's cattle.
Oh you were beautiful, my sister.

SONG THREE
I left home justly,
Oh yes.
If I were you I would not be deserting my people.

Come, my father's pride.
I have completely left my people.
I left with my father's approval.
My father's wish should be fulfilled.

Song Four
I have been contaminated.
Hey you, Ngwane people, we are in trouble.
I have touched a spear.

Song Five
Pick me up, my darling.
Put me on your shoulders.
Now I can see the heavens.

Song Six
I told my father, you subject of the King.
Oh my mother, I told my father
That to get married is like abandoning oneself.
To get married is like throwing away your own bones.
I even told my mother, you of the King,
That to get married is like throwing yourself away.

Song Seven
I got married young.
I do not have any energy left.
All my energy got wasted in marriage.
All my energy, all my strength is gone, oh my Lord.
I got married young.
All my strength is gone.
Marriage has defeated me.
All my energy is gone.
Marriage has defeated me.

Song Eight
Go well, my mother's child.
Oh it is hard in marriage.
Please, you must go well, my sister.
You must take care of your mother-in-law.
Oh it is hot in marriage.
You must behave yourself.
Oh it is where people grow weary.
Oh it is so difficult; it is where one grows weary.
You must greet your in-laws for me.
Oh we are tired, we are tired.

SONG NINE

Here is the man killing me!
(Beat her, man.)
Here is a man stunning me.
He has been misinformed.
(Beat her, man.)

Here is a man killing!
He has been informed.
(Beat her, man.)
I have tried to plead and beg.
Here is a man stunning me.
He has been misinformed.
(Beat her, man.)
Help! help! women.
The man is beating me.
He is killing me.
(Beat her, man.)
He has been misinformed.
He was told in bed.
He is fed with stories in bed, on a pillow.
He is killing me.
(Beat her, man.)

Every day, I shield myself from big canes.
Here is a man beating me.
(Beat her, man.)
I shield myself from big canes.
The man beats me every day.
(Beat her, man.)

Translated by Thulisile Motsa-Dladla

Communal,
IZISHO ZOKUSEBENZA—WORK SONGS

South Africa 1993–1994   isiZulu and isiXhosa

These work songs were performed by women laborers in the timber and sugar plantations on the KwaZulu-Natal coast north of Durban and were collected by me between September 1993 and August 1994. I taped and/or filmed the women singing and made notes describing their actions. The songs have been translated from isiZulu and, in the case of the third item, from isiXhosa, with the help of Lillian Sambo, Jabuliswe Masinga, Robert Sambo, and Elliot Zondi.

Their singing helped the women carry out their manual labor. It was often heavy: stripping bark off felled gum trees ("Separate These People" and "My Child Is Crying"); removing refuse; hoeing and fertilizing the ground ready for planting ("I've Been Abandoned," "My Brother-in-Law," and "It Is This Man"); hoeing between the rows of cane to remove weeds ("Mother Is Not Here" and "What Can You Do?"); and cutting the cane—the latter usually men's work.

A strong rhythmic repetition provides the melody and shapes the interactions between lead singer and chorus—all of which serve to sustain the women in their arduous, monotonous work. For example, the singing of "I've Been Abandoned" was almost drowned by the sound of hoes thudding into the ground, whereas "Mother Is Not Here" is based on a lullaby that would usually be sung while the baby is rocked in the singer's arms. Only in some of the cane-cutting songs did their labor seem to leave the women too breathless to sing a whole song with sustained vigor.

While singing "My Brother-in-Law," all the women flung down their hoes to dance and clap in delight while in other songs, one or more of the women interrupted her work to dance alone. On one occasion the dance was that of the traditional *ukwemula* ceremony during which a girl's readiness for marriage is announced.

The subject matter and the mood of the women's songs vary. During its performance, "Separate These People" developed into a mournful dirge with strong clapping and ululating, and one woman at a time left the line of dancers to dance what was reminiscent of a Zulu male dance. When asked about its reference, the performers indicated the conflict between (male) African National Congress and Inkatha factions in their community (see also "A Broken Family" in this volume). The origins of "My Horn" are ancient for the horns of cattle carry rich symbolic meaning in Zulu culture. The performer of this song explained that she was taught it by her grandmother and said that the horn referred to was a musical instrument.

While these songs accompany work in modern farming conditions, several of them draw on much older communal work songs, such as corn-threshing songs. The lead singer and chorus provide traditional balance between personal and communal concerns. Even if "I've Been Abandoned" began as a particular woman's complaint, its chorus shares the experience. Masking of direct confrontation also occurs in "It Is This Man," when the other singers join the lament and so cover a possibly dangerous accusation against a particular man.

A blend of gender and politics suggested by "It Is This Man" appears also in "My Brother-in-Law" and "Separate These People." Although rural Zulu women have customarily been confined to a domestic sphere, their songs allow them a spirited interaction with the larger world.

Dianne Stewart

✦

SONG ONE: WHAT CAN YOU DO?
What can you do to please someone?
What can you do on this earth?
What can you do to please someone?
What can you do on this earth?

If you do something good, you are killed
If you do something bad, you are called a fool
Don't forget that here on earth we do everything through the power
of God.
Even if you kill me, you won't achieve anything
But in the end, you too will die.

SONG TWO: MOTHER IS NOT HERE
Solo: Woo! child

Everyone:
Mother's not here
She has gone to buy bread
And she hits me with it
Saying I have eaten the maas [sour milk]
But I haven't eaten it
It's been eaten by the dog
Granny's dog
The spotted one   (sounds of baby crying)
The spotted one
The spotted one

SONG THREE: MY CHILD IS CRYING
Woman A: Wo! My child
Woman B: Is crying

A: Wo! My child
B: Eyee! . . . (crying sound)

A: Wo! My child
B: Owoo . . .
   (repeated with variations)

A: (spoken) Be quiet child, your mother is coming soon. You've been
crying for a long time.

A: Wo! My child
B: Is crying
   (repeated)

A: (spoken) Where is his mother? Did you give birth to this baby?
Where is his mother? Be quiet, child! (crying sound)
B: Keep quiet, child (crying sound)
Woman C: (gruff, impatient tone of voice) Hit him! Hit him; the child
is crying; hit him!

A: Wo! My child
B: Is crying
   (repeated)

A: (spoken) Don't make my brother's child cry. Where is his mother? We'll look for her at home.

SONG FOUR: I'VE BEEN ABANDONED
Woman A: I've been abandoned by my boyfriend
Woman B: I've been abandoned by my boyfriend

A: A lover, fit to be abandoned
   I've been abandoned by my boyfriend
B: I've been abandoned by my boyfriend
A: No one is sympathetic to me, abandoned by my boyfriend
B: I've been deserted by my boyfriend

A: No one loves me
   I've been abandoned by my boyfriend

(Spoken, while chorus continues song)
It's not a sin to be abandoned, dear. He's not the only one in the world. There are others more worthy than he. Go young girl and look for them.

SONG FIVE: MY BROTHER-IN-LAW
Woman A: My brother-in-law was handsome and he dressed well
Woman B: My brother-in-law.
A: He had only one fault, he wouldn't pay lobola
B: My brother-in-law.
   (repeated)

(Spoken by one woman at end of song)
I will never pay lobola for you because you waste your time drinking beer. I want someone better than you. I don't like seeing all my money going to your home. I work hard but you come home late and drunk, having wasted time drinking, just to sleep and I'm made fun of by you, a loafer.

SONG SIX: IT IS THIS MAN
Woman A: There were times when we were drinking
Woman B: There were times when we were very drunk
   (Chorus repeated five times by two singers; song follows.)

A: It is this man

B: It is this man
A: My neighbour
B: It is this man
A: Who killed my child
   That's why I'm experiencing hardship
   (repeated)

A: It is this man
B: It is this man
A: My neighbour
   He killed my child
   He who practices witchcraft
B: It is this man
A: I'm afraid, I'm afraid
B: It is this man
   Who killed my child
   (repeated)

SONG SEVEN: SEPARATE THESE PEOPLE
Woman A: Separate these people or else they will kill one another
Woman B: Separate them
   (repeated twenty-four times)

SONG EIGHT: MY HORN
Woman A: Yes, my horn
Woman B: My horn was left on the tree.

A: Oh! my horn
B: My horn was left on the tree.
   (repeated at increasing speed)

Transcribed and translated by Dianne Stewart

Nadine Gordimer, APRIL 27: THE FIRST TIME
South Africa 1994   English

As the first South African to win the Nobel Prize for literature, Nadine Gordimer is South Africa's most famous writer. Her career predates, spans, and outlives apartheid. She published her first short story in 1937 and her first collection of stories in 1949, and had by the year 2001 written thirteen novels and over two hundred short stories. The Nobel Prize, awarded in 1991, confirmed her international reputation, already established by a number of other prestigious awards, including the James Tait Black Memorial Prize (1971), the Booker McConnell

Prize (joint winner in 1974), the Grand Aigle d'Or Prize (1975), and the South African Central News Agency (CNA) Literary Award (1975 and 1991).

Gordimer has continually used her writing, and the public voice it has afforded her, to draw attention to the atrocities of apartheid. A founding member of the Congress of South African Writers in 1987, she has regularly championed South African writing, using her Nobel acceptance speech to draw attention to South African writers who were banned or imprisoned. Three of her own novels were banned: *A World of Strangers*, *The Late Bourgeois World*, and *Burger's Daughter*.

Gordimer was born in 1923 in Springs, a small, mostly Afrikaans-speaking, racially segregated mining town near Johannesburg. Her parents were immigrants: her Jewish father was from Lithuania, her mother from London. Although she has traveled extensively, Johannesburg has always remained Gordimer's home.

In "April 27: The First Time," Gordimer captures the sense of urgency that characterized the democratic process. Given apartheid's legacy of a high rate of illiteracy, it is significant that Gordimer marks the crucial moment of transition through the conflation of two critical acts: voting and writing. Characteristically aware of her politically and socially privileged position as a white South African—her ability to speak when others have been silenced—Gordimer thus metaphorically hands over the act of writing to the historically disenfranchised people of South Africa.

Colette Guldimann

✦

Is there any South African for whom this day will be remembered by any event, even the most personal, above its glowing significance as the day on which we voted? Even for whites, all of whom have had the vote since they were eighteen, this was the *first time*. This was my own overwhelming sense of the day: the other elections, with their farcical show of a democratic procedure restricted to whites (and, later, to everyone *but* the black majority), had no meaning for any of us *as South Africans*; only as a hegemony of the skin.

Standing in the queue this morning, I was aware of a sense of silent bonding. Businessmen in their jogging outfits, nurses in uniform (two, near me, still wearing the plastic mob-caps that cover their hair in the cloistered asepsis of the operating theatre), women in their Zionist Church outfits, white women and black women who shared the mothering of white and black children winding about their legs, people who had brought folding stools to support their patient old bones, night-watchmen just off duty, girl students tossing long hair the way horses switch their tails—here we all were as we have never been. We have stood in line in banks and post offices together, yes, since the desegregation of public places; but until this day there was always the unseen difference between us, far more decisive than the different colours of our skins: some of us had the right that is the basis of all rights, the symbolic X, the sign of a touch on the controls of polity, the mark of citizenship, and others did not. But today we stood on new ground.

The abstract term "equality" took on materiality as we moved towards the church hall polling station and the simple act, the drawing of an X, that ended over three centuries of privilege for some, deprivation of human dignity for others.

The first signature of the illiterate is the X. Before that there was only the thumb-print, the skin-impression of the powerless. I realized this with something like awe when, assigned by my local branch of the African National Congress to monitor procedures at a polling booth, I encountered black people who could not read or write. A member of the Independent Electoral Commission would guide them through what took on the solemnity of a ritual: tattered identity document presented, hands outstretched under the ultraviolet light, hands sprayed with invisible ink, and meticulously folded ballot paper—a missive ready to be despatched for the future—placed in those hands. Then an uncertain few steps towards a booth, accompanied by the IEC person and one of the party agents to make sure that when the voter said which party he or she wished to vote for the X would be placed in the appropriate square. Several times I was that party agent and witnessed a man or woman giving this signature to citizenship. A strange moment: the first time man scratched the mark of his identity, the conscious proof of his existence, on a stone must have been rather like this.

Of course nearby in city streets there were still destitute black children sniffing glue as the only substitute for nourishment and care; there were homeless families existing in rigged-up shelters in the crannies of the city. The law places the ground of equality underfoot; it did not feed the hungry or put up a roof over the head of the homeless, today, but it changed the base on which South African society was for so long built. The poor are still there, round the corner. But they are not The Outcast. They no longer can be decreed to be forcibly removed, deprived of land, and of the opportunity to change their lives. They *count*. The meaning of the counting of the vote, whoever wins the majority, is this, and not just the calculation of the contents of ballot boxes.

If to be alive on this day was not Wordsworth's "very heaven" for those who have been crushed to the level of wretchedness by the decades of apartheid and the other structures of racism that preceded it, if they could not experience the euphoria I shared, standing in line, to be living at this hour has been extraordinary. The day has been captured for me by the men and women who couldn't read or write, but underwrote it, at last, with their kind of signature. May it be the seal on the end of illiteracy, of the pain of imposed ignorance, of the deprivation of the fullness of life.

Mpho 'M'atsepo Nthunya,
BEFORE THE BEGINNING

Lesotho 1996   English

Mpho 'M'atsepo Nthunya's father, like so many Basotho men, was forced to leave Lesotho to find employment. He was in Johannesburg working in a factory when she was born. His infrequent visits ceased when she was a very small child, and by the time she was seven, she and her mother were wearing sacks and eating grass and insects. Her devout Roman Catholic mother told her to "sing the hunger away." Then in 1938, when she was eight, her father sent for his family. In a township outside Johannesburg, Nthunya attended a mission school, progressed through eight years as a star student, learned seven languages, and began writing. After her marriage, she returned to Lesotho and lived in the mountains, where she found "the education of books was useless." In her long life she bore nine children, ran a large and successful farm, and took domestic work after her husband died.

She developed as a storyteller, a keeper of oral traditions, and an elder in a large family that embraces people of all classes. In 1992 she began telling her life stories to me when I was visiting as a Fulbright scholar from the United States; I transcribed and typed them for her and served as copy editor. Those stories were published in South Africa, the United States, and the United Kingdom as *Singing away the Hunger*.

Kathryn Limakatso Kendall

✦

I was married with a good Mosotho man, and we left Benoni and lived in the Maluti Mountains where we had many children, raised sheep, grew maize, and listened to the quiet. At the beginning we were hungry and our children were hungry; but after many years of working hard we were no longer poor. We had many animals and fields. Then my husband died, and I had to come back to my mother's home, in the Roma Valley, to find work. I lost or sold the animals and left the fields and my houses in the mountains. Now I live in Mafikeng, the village at the gates of the National University of Lesotho. I have worked at the University cleaning houses since 1968. It is at the University that I meet Limakatso, I call her *motsoalle oa ka*, my very good friend. I tell her my stories and she writes them down in a computer to make them a book. *Mohlolo!* [Miracle!]

Talking to Limakatso, I remember many things which I forgot for a long time. This is a good thing for me. I'm looking back, and it's like looking at an album of photos from my whole life. If other people can look at it too, that's fine. But it's my album, and it pleases me to look at it. I'm telling stories for children and grown people in other places, because I want people who know how to read and have time to read, to know something about the

Basotho—how we used to live and how we live now, how poor we are, and how we are living together in this place called Lesotho. I'm also telling stories for Basotho like my grandchildren, who read books but don't know the old ways of their own people. If they can read these stories, maybe it will teach them where they come from. And maybe it can help them to learn English, so they can find work.

I tell these stories in English to my *motsoalle* so she can write them in the computer. I can tell these stories better in Sesotho. When I tell stories in Sesotho, the words roll like a music I am singing with my heart. When I speak *Sekhooa*, the white people's language, I start and stop. I stare at my *motsoalle*, at the ceiling, looking, looking. I say, "What can I say? What is the word for this?"

I am like a car trying to start on a cold morning, coughing and stopping. Limakatso says people who read *Sekhooa* never get to hear the stories from women like me, and I think it must be true. When would we write them? I have only a Standard Five education, went to Standard Six for a little while but didn't finish it. I don't know the people who publish books, don't know where to send a book if I could write it. Limakatso says people are hungry for these stories. They want to know. So I say, "*Ho lokile*. Fine. It's OK with me. We can write them." Maybe I make a little bit of money to buy maize meal for the children.

I try to imagine what I can do with a book written by me. I think of my mother. I imagine that I can give this book of English words to her, and because of the wisdom of Heaven she can read it. I say to her, "Take this book and see your story: when you were married, and what happened to your daughter, who always loves you. Here are the stories of your daughter's children, and their children. None of this would be, without you. And now others can know your story." So I say this book is my album for my mother, Valeria 'M'amahlaku Sekobi Lillane, who passed away. Others can look at it if they like.

Transcribed by Kathryn Limakatso Kendall

Ellen Ndeshi Namhila, THE PRICE OF FREEDOM

Namibia 1997   English

Ellen Ndeshi Namhila left Namibia in 1976 at the age of twelve and returned nineteen years later to vote in the first independent elections. She fled the intensifying war waged by the South African Defence Force in northern Namibia against the South West African People's Organization. Namhila's experience was typical of the many thousands of Namibians who went into exile during the liberation struggle that culminated in Namibia's independence in March 1990.

Namhila's long years of exile, during which she lived in Angola, Zambia, the Gambia, and Finland, were marked by the corrosive insecurity of being a refugee, denied the power of making decisions about the course of her life. Her autobiography, published in 1997, is the first book about exile and return written by a Namibian woman. Her experiences also reflect the experiences of female refugees from South Africa and Zimbabwe. Much heartache and many small personal triumphs have been lost in the euphoric focus on the future that followed liberation and independence. In many cases women were expected to revert to subordinate social roles, something unacceptable to most after their experience either as combatants or as independent equals during the struggle. *The Price of Freedom* describes the events of exile, but it also explores the difficulties faced by women when they return to the longed-for utopia. Reconciling the complex relationships among gender, nationalism, and memory prompted Namhila to write her book:

> When we were in exile, in the struggle, in the refugee camps and in foreign countries, I did not question my national identity. I felt strongly Namibian. I wanted to return home to Namibia, so that I could reclaim my identity, and my rightful place in society, having lost all my childhood during the long, long years of the apartheid war. While I was in exile I remembered home through things I had known. Now that I am in Namibia all that I knew of Namibia, of home, has changed. I am finding myself lost in my own country. . . . If I am lost, if my past is lost amongst historical events over which I have no control, who then shall make or remake my history?

> *Margie Orford*

✦

It was an early Sunday morning in April 1976, my heart was heavy, but in my head I could hear sounds of early morning birds wishing me a safe journey. I was determined to leave Namibia. I silently slipped out of the homestead, walked across the military camp to the pastor's homestead, where my friend lived. We quickly joined the others in the nearby forest at Eenhana, where we were briefed by two unknown men about how to get to the heavily guarded and fenced border between Namibia and Angola. They told us where we would spend the night, get food and what to tell those who might ask where we were heading.

It took us a whole day and a half to get to a South West Africa People's Organization (SWAPO) transit homestead near the Angolan border where we spent a week. Here we were joined by other people. My friend, Maria, and I were the youngest in the group. One evening, our host told us that it would be better for us to go back home. He said we were too young to face the journey especially as there was war in Angola. He also told us if we were to go on that when we would get there we would have no role to play except to act as wives to the soldiers in the bush. This prospect so terrified us that we even considered taking his advice. I was twelve years old.

Our lives in the village had been turned upside down since the arrival of the South African Defence Force (SADF) military camp at the village at the end of 1975. Many young people had fled the country in order to organize themselves for the liberation struggle. Even though it was not publicly discussed, it was known that these young people would one day come back to liberate the country. It was believed that those who left the country would eventually come back. But no-one was certain about this.

I did not discuss my plans to go into exile with my parents or any of my relatives. I kept my plans a tight secret between me and Maria, who informed me about her brothers' plans to leave the country and asked whether I was interested to join them. I had always wanted to escape from the repression, so I thought this was my opportunity to do so.

The reasons for keeping these plans away from my family were several. I was very young, and I doubted whether my family would have allowed me to leave. This journey was a risk to the whole family. Families of those who went into exile were always targeted for arrest and interrogation whenever the SADF fancied they were getting threats from the local people. For example, tate Haimbala ya Shixungileni was arrested on several occasions and forced to reveal information on the whereabouts of his brother Kambo ka Shixungileni who went into exile in the 1960s. By leaving the country I knew I might be leaving trouble for my family. But, as will be told later, I had been shot at, had seen my teachers being violated, and had witnessed my uncle being beaten half to death and many other atrocities committed against people who had done nothing wrong. The memory of violence committed against innocent people at my village was still so fresh in my mind that I decided anything, marriage to soldiers included, was better than what we might go through if we returned to Eenhana. We were worried that the information about our escape had already leaked out of the village to the SADF base. And what they might do to us, knowing that we were escaping from their repressive system, and the example they might make of us so terrified us that we decided to continue our journey into the unknown.

We were woken at three o'clock the next morning and led by five huge men to the Angolan border. We walked and walked through the Angolan villages and forests for three days and when we got really tired, the soldiers asked us to rest. For part of this journey I was carried on the shoulders of the soldiers and older men from our group. In some areas it was possible to walk only during the evening and early mornings.

We were advised to always walk two metres apart following in the footsteps of the person in front. This we were told was important for two reasons: if the enemy troops were following us, they would have a hard time estimating how many people we were if we all walked in single file. Secondly, there were lots of unexploded anti-personnel land mines planted by National Union for the Total Independence of Angola (UNITA) and the SADF before they left Angola in 1975. By walking in single file we were minimizing the risk of detonating the land mines, we were told. We were also told to speak softly and never to raise our voices when we were laughing.

I noticed that in most of the Angolan villages we walked through, the homesteads were burned down and what remained were ashes and charred poles. The danger was obvious. In some areas the soldiers told us to strictly follow their orders, which were: to keep two metres' distance, and keep silent; while in some areas where the enemy's activities were unlikely they just kept quiet.

During the journey, we survived on drinking water from the soldiers which they carried in small green bags around the waist. The soldiers advised us not to drink from any open water or at least to first make sure that there were living insects inside the water before drinking it or washing ourselves with it. Among the open water we came across there was a dam which had thousands of dead insects washed ashore. The soldiers told us that this dam had been poisoned by the enemy and any humans who drank its water would die just like the insects.

As soon as we arrived at a resting place, we all dropped to the ground and rested. While we were resting, three of the soldiers would disappear and after a while return with food and water. Sometimes they would ask some of us to assist in carrying the food from the Angolan homes to the bush. These meals mainly consisted of oshifima, a thick porridge made of millet flour, which was served with evanda (dried spinach). In some places we were served oshikundu (a drink made from millet). This food must have been collected from several homesteads and brought to us in the bush because it was too much for one household to prepare at short notice. The two soldiers who remained with us did not rest but walked up and down in a circle around us. They did not talk much to each other either and when they did, they kind of whispered.

When night fell, the soldiers took us to a homestead where we spent the night. They advised us to avoid making unnecessary noise or being seen outside the homestead. This, they said, was important for our own security. Then they disappeared.

In homesteads where we arrived during the day, the Angolans obliterated the traces of our footsteps by herding the cattle or goats over them or by sweeping the way we had come with sticks.

We walked for three days through Angola before we reached a place where we spent our first three months. It was a SWAPO military camp, from which People's Liberation Army of Namibia (PLAN) fighters were given missions into Namibia. This was the first time we saw our soldiers, black soldiers with guns and in military uniforms. As darkness approached I wondered where we would spend the night. The man who spoke to us on arrival told us that we had committed ourselves to a very difficult struggle, that of liberating Namibia. Some of the difficulties he mentioned were hunger, thirst, and sacrifice and dedicating of our lives to the bitter but just struggle which would cost lives. This struggle needed unity and comradeship, as a slogan said:

SWAPO
Will Win
Namibia
Will Be Free
Everything for the Struggle
All for Victory

Slogans like this were not just slogans; they were a meaningful social and political force that mobilized the people and their dedication to the struggle. As soon as the commander uttered the last word of Everything for the Struggle, every soldier responded vigorously All for Victory giving a power salute and breaking into a revolutionary song. The atmosphere at the parade got electrified. I was inspired by their style of singing and acting like free and liberated minds. At that point, I carefully watched the soldiers, thinking this was probably the time for them to disappear or magically turn into objects, as I had heard in stories told back home. But to my disappointment the parade ended and no-one turned into an object.

Later on, some combatants spoke to us briefly but they did not shoot at us or beat us up like the South West Africa Territory Force (SWATF) did to people in villages back home. The combatants were busy all day long and we only met them sometimes during meals. Maria and I were afraid to enter into any discussions with them because we had been warned that our role as girls would only be to act as wives to them. Time went on and none of the soldiers spoke to us about marriage, so the fear of becoming a wife to someone began to fade away from my head. The atmosphere was also very reassuring.

I noticed that all the soldiers wore broad belts, and wondered why. I concluded that they were probably meant to reduce their stomachs so that they could stay for long periods without food or drink. I was surprised that the camp gave us three square meals a day and yet I never saw where the food was prepared. There were no pots and no kitchen, but there was always something to eat. When we left the camp we still did not know where the soldiers got their food from. Later on I found out that food was [carried] in by the Angolan civilians. There was a point where the soldiers fetched it and brought it to us.

One morning we were told to pack up and get ready to leave for another camp far away from the Angolan border. In this camp we found girls among the male soldiers who were also dressed in military uniform and carrying guns. They made a very big impression on me. I thought it was fascinating and I wished I could be one of them. They looked so brave, beautiful and healthy. They spoke different languages.

I had until then not been aware that there were other language groups in Namibia besides Oshiwambo to which I belonged. This was the first time that I had left Ovambo. I was born and raised in Ovambo where everyone spoke Oshiwambo and I never had the opportunity to live with non-Oshiwambo speakers.

This is how my nineteen years in exile started.

Colette Mutangadura, NGONYA'S BRIDE-PRICE

Zimbabwe 1997   English

Colette Mutangadura was born in 1945, is married, and has five children. She is a primary school teacher and a member of Zimbabwe Women Writers. Mutangadura is actively involved in promoting reading and writing among women in Goromonzi district where she teaches. She wrote her only published novel in Shona, *Rinonyenga Rinohwarara* (The Duplicity of Desire), in 1983. The novel's central character divorces her husband and successfully raises her children.

Mutangadura's grandmother, Ngonya, was born in 1900 in what later became the Murewa Communal Lands. Mutangadura's mother, Ndati Christina, remembers her mother as a very beautiful woman. This story of grandmother Ngonya was told to Mutangadura by her mother and her great-aunt Ndakatukwa.

"Ngonya's Bride-Price" is unusual in that it was kept alive for three generations and will survive for longer in print. Thus Mutangadura has successfully bridged the gap between oral and written stories as she preserves some of her family history.

Chiedza Musengezi

✦

Ngonya was my maternal grandmother, born in 1900 in what later became the Murehwa Communal Lands. My mother, Ndati Christina, remembers her as a very beautiful woman, and I can well believe that, for my mother was herself one of those who could make men turn their heads as she passed, and one can still see her beauty, though she is now 76 years old. This story of my grandmother's short life was told to me by my mother and by Ndakatukwa, my great aunt.

When Ngonya was sixteen a white farmer called Jan settled on land that her family had farmed, making them move their home some considerable distance away to the south near a hill that was known as Matungamhara. This white farmer would send his foreman to their new home and to all the surrounding villages to recruit labour when there was a lot of work to be done on the land. In the beginning only the men went, while their womenfolk carried on with the endless daily tasks of collecting firewood, fetching water, gathering fruits, weeding crops, and looking after their children. But in the summer of 1917 the white farmer had a bumper harvest and so he compelled all those who could work to come to the farm to help bring in his crop, leaving only the old women and the young children at home.

Ngonya was rather pleased by this demand for her labour, for her elder brother Gadzai had for some time been working there and bringing home cloth and sugar and other goods for his wages, and so Ngonya thought that she too would get some of these things that she so much desired, especially cloth. She wanted to replace her wrap-over skin skirt with one of cloth. Like all the girls she wanted a change because she believed that she would look much prettier in such a skirt.

The work was hard and the farmer, Jan, though young, was a harsh master. He used to give out the wages himself. The usual wage for 30 days work was two yards of material, a sixpence, and a cupful of sugar which was poured into the worker's piece of cloth. When it was Ngonya's turn to receive her wages he winked at her, put out his tongue, and said, "*Yah, iri mushe here*" (Are you all right?). She was afraid and would rather not have been noticed. Still, she continued working for him, through the harvest and then into the following season of sowing and weeding, and during that time she brought home more wages than the other workers. Jan would pat her on the shoulder and give her names she didn't understand, and altogether make her feel puzzled and fearful by such attentions.

One Friday afternoon he came to the fields, collected three of the girls including Ngonya, and said in Chilapalapa that he wanted them to help the houseboy. When they arrived at the house two of the girls were given jobs to do outside, but he took Ngonya inside. Jan was married but his wife was not there, and Ngonya learnt afterwards that she was in the maternity hospital in Salisbury. He stood close to her and touched her, gently caressing her back, her neck and breasts. She wanted to scream, but at the same time felt so weak, as though her whole body were melting under his fingers. He lifted and carried her to a room and laid her on a big brass bed, and there, pressing his lips against hers, thrusting his tongue into her mouth, he made love to her while the setting sun streamed through the window. She had many things to take home that day, but she looked so unhappy that when her mother commented on it she had to pretend to be feeling sick.

She didn't go to work the next day. Jan sent a messenger to say that she was needed on Monday, and Ngonya, remembering stories her father had told her of the savagery of the whites in the Chimurenga of 1896, was so fearful that the white man would act violently against her family that she agreed to go. But now she no longer worked in the fields. While Jan's wife was still away, he made love to her on Madam's bed, and when the Missis, as they called her, returned with her baby he continued his affair with Ngonya in the barn, the milk shed, or even in the bush. He was a gentle lover, never rough in either word or action, and sometimes he would bring her a cool sweet drink. And so things went on for four months until the fact of Ngonya's pregnancy could no longer be concealed.

She told her aunt and mother that the white man was the father of the child she was carrying, and they of course were greatly shocked to learn that a thing which they thought of as taboo had occurred. Her mother attempted to commit suicide but was prevented by women who told her that times were changing, and it was not only her daughter who would soon be holding a white man's baby on her lap. Many more would fall prey to them. Her father was furious and said she deserved to die. So it was secretly arranged by the family that Ngonya should go to an aunt in Chikore in Manicaland province with the message that the child, when born, had to be killed, for they feared the appearance of a child with a white skin among them.

When a whole week had gone by and Ngonya had not reported for work at the farm house, the white man sent his foreman to tell her that she must come, and when there was no response to this summons, Jan himself came one morning riding on a black horse. He fired his gun into the air and demanded to see Ngonya. People slid into their huts and peered out fearfully through the cracks. Ngonya's father, Munbenga, came out and talked with the white man, promising him that she would return in a short while. But she didn't, and so one chilly morning a very angry Jan came again calling for Ngonya. He had brought men with him, and when she didn't appear, he ordered his men to open the cattle kraals and drive the cattle to his farm. He shouted that if Ngonya did not come back to him, then their cattle would be forfeited.

Everyone was angered by the white man's behaviour, and at a loss to explain it too, since by rights he should have come with a gift of cattle, a bride-price, to the father for the girl he had taken and made pregnant, yet here he was insulting everyone and taking not only his girlfriend's father's cattle but those of others in the family too. Ngonya's grandmother ran into the cloud of dust raised by the cattle and Jan's horse, so that men had to chase after her to bring her back out of danger, promising to recover the beasts by some means or other. She cried aloud to her ancestors, lamenting her granddaughter's conduct.

My ancestors! You have brought doom to my son through his feather-brained daughter. How could she have opened her legs to that frightening creature? Oh, how could she have looked into those fearful eyes? Was it sugar that made you let that beast lie on your breast Ngonya? Ngonya, my granddaughter, you are a disgrace to all the family. You have brought disgrace on all the women of our clan, Ngonya, my granddaughter, Ngonya. Now that the cattle for spiritual sacrifices are taken away, with what shall I appease the spirits of my ancestors, Ngonya?

The old woman spent the whole day lamenting and blaming the white man, calling him all sorts of names, boer, oppressor, thief, racist, and so on. And Ngonya's mother cried too until she could cry no more. People had to guard her because she was still thinking of committing suicide.

And people also gossiped—at the well, in the bush, even enemies spoke together of this thing that had happened. Ngonya was the talk of that day, and that day stretched into weeks.

Her father, who was the headman of the village, called a meeting of the elders. These men met together under a big *muhacha* tree, the usual place for taking counsel on the affairs of the village. They talked and talked but they couldn't find a solution to the problem of retrieving their cattle from the boer, as he was now called by nearly all. They finally decided to report their case to the Native Commissioner. This they did, but nothing happened. They waited for weeks, and then months, but there was still no response. So they consulted their spirit medium who advised them to take their cattle from Jan's farm and move away from the district, and this is what they decided to do. The men went off for several months to build a new village some thirty miles away, beyond the mountains near the Munyuki river. There they erected new huts and then the women and children moved in to plaster the walls and beat the floors. They liked the new place because of its nearness to water, and agreed that their ancestors had guided them well.

Two weeks went by, and then, by night and in collaboration with some of Jan's farm workers, the men drove all their own cattle out of the farm together with twenty from the boer's herd which they declared was the *lobola*, the bride-price, for Ngonya. As they began the long journey to their new home the rains poured behind them obliterating their tracks, and after four days, crossing several flooded rivers, they reached their new village where they gave thanks to the ancestors for protecting them from pursuit. Days went by, then weeks, months, and finally a whole year. The boer did not show up.

One autumn afternoon the aunt from Chikore arrived with Ngonya and her baby son. Many of the men of the village were away hunting, and some of the women too were out seeking fruits and vegetables along the river valley. But Ngonya's mother was at home. She had been feeling tired and had told friends that she thought she might have a visitor arriving or be about to hear some bad news. As it turned out her visitor was her only daughter carrying her first coloured grandson and she was overcome with joy at seeing the two. This made things somewhat easier for Aunt Nyatahwa who explained how she had not killed the child as the family had asked because she was beginning to go to church.

What was really surprising was how Ngonya's father took to the baby. He was very proud of his grandson. There was of course gossip. Some said the child's name should have been Sugar instead of Andris because Ngonya had thrown herself on the boer for it. For her part Ngonya had been heard to say that Jan might come by one day, and with that in mind she washed little Andris twice a day instead of the customary once a week, for she said he would want to find his boy clean. Andris was a great joy to her, and neither he nor the children he grew up with took any notice of his difference in colour.

Ngonya eventually maried Mudzingi, my grandfather, in 1922 and gave birth to my mother, Ndati, that same year. In 1925 she bore a son who died and she herself died shortly afterwards. Jan had never re-appeared. Her father, my great-grandfather, was said to boast of her that she had enriched him with a bride-price of ten head of cattle from Mudzingi but with twenty from Jan.

Sheila Masote, TESTIMONY: TRUTH AND RECONCILIATION COMMISSION

South Africa 1997   English

The excerpt below is from testimony given by Sheila Masote at a human rights violations hearing of the South African Truth and Reconciliation Commission. The commission was an important component in South Africa's democratic transition.

Established in law and offering a form of justice frequently described as "restorative," its tasks were fourfold. It was to compile a report that documented the nature, cause, and extent of gross violations of human rights committed between 1960 and 1994; to offer a limited amnesty; to identify the fate and whereabouts of victims; and to make recommendations on reparations and rehabilitation. In terms of the Act that brought the commission into being, victims were entitled "to relate their own accounts of the violations of which they are victims," that is, to tell their own stories of harm.

Approximately ten percent of the deponents who gave statements concerning killing, torture, abduction, and severe ill-treatment were invited to testify in seventy-six public hearings held across the country in 1996 and 1997. Simultaneously translated into the main languages in each area where hearings were held, the hearings were also widely broadcast in South Africa and beyond.

Public hearings were emotional events. Testifiers—victims, their families, and friends—described the full range of violations that the commission's operational definitions admitted, including terrible torture, injuries, and death. They also evoked the everyday humiliations of apartheid and a diversity of harms that the commission did not consider gross violations of human rights. Early in the hearings process, marked patterns emerged, most pronounced of which was the tendency for women to testify mainly about the experiences of men, usually their sons or husbands. Concerned about the absence of women's own experiences of gross violations and bodily harm, the commission instituted special hearings on women that were held in Cape Town, Johannesburg, and Durban.

Sheila Masote was the first witness to testify before the Women's Hearings held in Johannesburg in July 1997. Describing her life as a well-educated child in a cultured family, her fractured testimony suggests the range and consequences of apartheid's harm and the effects of the struggle against it on individuals and families. Like many other women who testified, she lamented diverse losses: opportunities; status and community trust; extended family networks and the support they offered. Her testimony describes the narrowed scope of sociality in the face of state violence and political engagement, while her description of family life affords a glimpse of the devastating effects of surveillance and brutality: families stretched to the breaking point; violence that feeds inward and endures. Unlike other women who gave accounts, Masote explicitly rejected the role of representing her family. Her account details her own experiences, including the effects of patriarchal relations, and speaks to the difficulties of maintaining both family relations and a coherent personal identity in conditions she characterizes as "my crumbled world."

Her strength in overcoming such conditions is evidenced in both her testimony and her current activities. She is now the director of the African Cultural Organization of South Africa, an organization that uses music and cultural activities to inspire youth from disadvantaged communities. She is also director of the Orchestra Company in Johannesburg. In 2000, she was a nominee for the Shoprite-Checkers South African Woman of the Year Award.

Fiona Ross

✦

On the programme it says I'm here to speak about—on behalf of—the family. No, that is not what I am here about. My mother has put in a submission as an individual and representing the family.

I then felt, yes, I'm part of the family, but I refuse to be family and have no identity as Sheila. The problem that I have always suffered and I have always said to myself is that I don't seem to be having an identity like belonging to me. I'm always either Zeph's daughter, Mothopeng's daughter or Mike Masote's wife. Or Neo Masote's mother and Zeph Masote's mother. But no, I feel I am me. And this is why I am here.

As a little girl, as a teenager, as a woman, as a mother and as a builder and as somebody who has really contributed to the struggle, I may not have been seen in the forefront, but sometimes I believe they also serve who only stand and wait.

Therefore I—it's such a big story that I have. It's a long life. I am 52 years old and most of it I have been born in a family that's been through the struggle. And I should be presenting a statement, maybe this big. I know others are as big as this room, but mine has also formed a part.

But I tried to summarise here in picture form, because so that I keep in focus. I have here some of what I was stripped of. And I have a ball, representing my crumbled world. [She shows an illustration of a ball; a nd then another of it crumbled; and a third, in the shape of a heart, of repairing.]

I was born in a very, very up family; my father and my mother both teachers of those days, the Royal Readers, the best and they stayed in the best place. When so it had started, it was not so. It was Orlando-East and then into Orlando-West. And this is the elite. This is where you find the Mandelas, the Sisulus, the Mathews, etc. [. . .]

I start with the late Zeph Mothopeng. My father was a cultural man. He was the first president of the TATA—the then Transvaal African Teachers' Associ-ation, which later became TUATA (Transvaal Union of African Teachers Association). He was the first chairperson of the then Johannesburg Bantu Music Festival, that has brought forth all this Eisteddfod, all the culture that you see, the coming up of Dorkay House.

During those days, it happened right in Orlando West, musicals and all that. I'm trying to show, my mother herself has been a teacher, a conduc-tor, a singer with the coloratura soprano voice type. You may wonder why I—where I get these tales from. I'm highly cultured and I need no apolo-gies; I am—I am married to a highly cultured man. The only man, the only black in Africa who holds a licenciate in violin teaching. [. . .]

Now, I want to tell you; my mother still runs a choir of children, young girls. They're called the Nightingales. They started way back in the fifties, 1952 she says. It's a community programme. All of us, the Barbaras, the Sisi Ntombis, they have come through this choir and have passed. [. . .]

Now, I am saying to you, my crumbling world was—I had a family that was a home and togetherness. My school work suffered a lot, because I had a lot to carry on me. I couldn't study, I couldn't be worried about my dreams. I needed to be a lawyer, at one time to be a social worker. Yes, a teacher, because you would look up to your mother or your father.

I had no trust at that stage. It went. The church, I couldn't trust, because I didn't belong. Why all this happening to my family? Why all this happening to Orlando West? My friends and my neighbours, they got away from me, because the Special Branch always came to my home. They harassed my family. They went to the family, to the neighbours, to the children I played with and they threatened their parents. [. . .]

I come to my family's breaking. The main thing was society. I would also say this communal living—I could go to granny next door, I could go to Memama. And I knew I would find help. If there was no milk at home, it was easy for us to go and ask for it. Or just to visit and play next door. I knew I'd come back healthy and well and well fed.

My mother would go work and she knows her children are safe. Our keys, door key, would stay at the third house from your house. Next time the next house. Nobody would come and steal. Everybody would look after it.

But all that crumbled, because the Special Branch had to come in and tell people, these are terrorists. You dare be seen associated. And then my family, that is my whole family. Then my father got dismissed. When they did the introduction of Bantu Education, joblessness came and my mother had to follow suit, lose her teaching post, because she can't go and work for the system when her husband has been unfairly dismissed.

My extended family, they started fearing us. My brother went into exile. There was loneliness. There was non-stop harassment by the Special Branch. There was a series of imprisonment. . . .

My mother was very frustrated, unsupported and lonely. In all this, all this torture, I have the world and my family and down there is a big load. And there was me as a girl child.

I won't read through my story. I have it on paper, but I would like to say with all that, I used to go for ballet, I used to sing, I was a little girl in tutus, ribbons, pretty little thing; the only daughter of a well-off family. [. . .]

And it all went, because when ballet was stopped for black little kids. [. . .] I resorted to ballroom dancing. Then that's where my conflict with my mother started—I love my mother and I would like to say to you people what I'm mainly saying and that even my daughter there is worried. And I've come along with my mother and she has suffered and I'm not trying to be—we're just trying to show the suffering we went through together.

I have seen my mother break down. I have seen my mother when she did least expect it that I know, crying, sobbing. I had questions as a daughter. Mom, what's happening?

Then PAC's [Pan African Congress's] policy was that women should stay at home, should not participate. [. . .] It was all by way of trying to say when we [men] go out to jail, when we go out and be killed, you look after the children.

So my mother was always there for myself and brothers. So I would always say, Mama, what is happening? And they were not told. The husbands wouldn't share much. And therefore this started to make me angry, because I didn't understand then; have an attitude towards my mother. Why, why doesn't she share with me? Why doesn't she understand me? Why does she beat me up so much? Why?

Because she was frustrated. And I was the only one close to home. My brothers turned to, like boys would have it easier maybe, they would go to bands, play, they started the All-Rounders, an all blind band that started in the sixties, seventies and later on they formed Batsumi (a jazz band). They have been outward-going. I was always at home, looking after my mother.

She started to be sick. She would be going to hospital in sessions. I would be the sole person in the house, exposed to, if people wanted to rape me. Fortunately it hasn't happened to me. It almost nearly happened, but never happened.

There were other things, traumas that I had. My home was now very cold, very needy, very—no friends. Except a few friends, later on, that did come onto the scene. I went to school with her, among other things. And she was supportive to me in many ways. I'm not saying everybody moved out, but I'm saying the world crumbled.

I would like to say, my adult life—all this time there was—the police, I think, have always thought I'm the strong one of the family. Yes, I look weak outside, but yes, I am very strong. I have carried a lot. I've carried even things for my mother. Even when she wasn't aware, I was carrying for her.

Sometimes I wasn't even in her way. I remember even when my father was very sick, terminally ill, when he was released from prison. To my mother I looked like I don't know my role. I am forward.

But she was very sickly, because of her hip transplant. But because she's also a firm and strong woman, we had to be hitting against one another. And I had to put my foot down now and again. She had to be swearing at me. It was very clumsy and some scars are deep. [. . .] When my mother wanted to bash somebody, it was me. I must say I have been very much abused; by stick, by mouth, by just non-performance, maybe by denials of my rights as a child, which I may not go deep, because maybe people may think I'm ungrateful.

But because I'm sitting here with her, I see this as a chance that out there, like I am here to represent other children that want to speak, but maybe think it improper as we are socialised as girls and women we must be quiet. . . . She was breaking the very family she was trying to keep together.

And this I carried along even into my married life. I also bashed my son. I almost killed my son. Today he's in Switzerland. He is the finest cellist and the Lord dear hold the man in school. I'm trying to show you how cultured we are.

But the sister at the age of about eight, saw him go up; he was about six, trying to hang himself in a tree when we were staying in Phefeni. Because I used to bash my son for no reason and often. . . . That is what used to happened to me, my friends, I would beat him. I would beat him. I don't know what for. I would beat him until my neighbours jump over the fence: "Sheila, you'll kill the boy, Sheila."

That is what my son went through. I went through the same. I did it. I don't know what it is I haven't done. I have done lots to my daughter. Today she is a lawyer. I'm trying to—I'm not boasting, I'm showing when you have the will to live you can beat the worst of forces. . . .

Grannies, where are you? Little girls, where are you? Who tells about mysteries? And who tells you about what's happening? Do we still tell stories to our children? That's what has happened. My children can tell.

Keamogetswe Kwere and Lesie Kwere, WE WILL BE LEASING FOR OURSELVES

Botswana 1997–1998   Setswana

There is no universally accepted term for the historically marginalized people of mainly Khoesan-speaking origins. The people of Khwai refer to themselves variously as Bugakhwe or Basarwa. The Khwai people moved to what the Kwere sisters refer to as "old Khwai" in the 1920s and 1930s. At that time, they occupied a territory much larger than that to which they are now confined. In recent times, they have been displaced again and their way of life substantially interfered with by conservation policies, which, for example, limit hunting to particular species and particular times of the year.

The Khwai people find their traditional way of life undermined both by tourism and wildlife interests and by other (non-Basarwa) groups in the region. The wildlife industry tends to disregard them altogether, but even when indigenous land rights are acknowledged, permanency of settlement has assumed greater rhetorical significance than antiquity of occupation. Here the Basarwa suffer from the widespread (though academically contested) perception that they were historically "nomadic" and so never really settled anywhere. Additionally, non-Basarwa local communities are sometimes in conflict for resources; however, they usually recognize the primacy of Basarwa occupancy and the history of social and economic ties.

Clearly, the Basarwa's existence as a community has always been under threat, but the new strategies open to them are few and limited in scope. Their main source of income is restricted to collecting and selling grass and reed for thatching roofs. Basketry now forms part of their economic activity, and women have mobilized themselves to build a curio shop to sell their baskets and other crafts. They spend this money on food, clothes, and the maintenance of their children. Most of these women are heads of families, such as the Kwere sisters, without whose active involvement in village affairs, according to many people in Khwai, nothing would happen.

The interviews published here are part of ongoing research on the "River Bushmen" of eastern Ngamiland in Botswana, whose history and culture are poorly understood. The interviews are remarkable for their forthright quality. The sisters demonstrate a strong sense of social identity, not only asserting a positive sense of community but also identifying their ties to other communities. They are very clear about the process that has robbed them of their way of life: They recognize the components of enforced alienation and identify them specifically as part of a pattern of displacement and oppression. For additional information, see A. Barnard's *Hunters and Herders of Southern Africa: A Comparative Ethnography of the Khoisan People* (1992).

Maitseo Bolaane

✦

KEAMOGETSWE KWERE, INTERVIEWED 4 JULY 1997

We are called River Bushmen because the river is important to us. We drink water from the river; we catch fish from the river, and we get various vegetables such as *tswii.* There are also reeds which we get from the river to make mats. Even shoes we had. They were made from buffalo hide. We are all Basarwa, but we differ in our languages [dialects]. We understand the others when they speak, just as they do when we speak. But their language is theirs, and ours is ours. Even today it is clear that we share common cultures. They depend on hunting as we do.

The first time my uncle Kwere was moved, there were two camps, the Fauna and Game Camps. Fauna Camp was the first area to be conserved by the Batawana. But the Batawana, due to lack of resources and sound management, sought help from the Department of Wildlife to assist them in running the area. That is how Wildlife took over. My uncle Kwere agreed to leave his first area [Xhuko] without conflict with Wildlife because they told him that they would like to have the park without people in it. That is how he came to stay at Segagama. We ploughed at Segagama in the second year, and the following—third—year, Wildlife came to us again and told us that they had expanded the conservation area from Xhuko to Segagama, so they were going to move us again. Since we were used to being moved, we did not argue with them, but we did not want to be moved. We were afraid of the law. We did not think that we could argue with them, because we thought the law had decided. We didn't know that we had the right to refuse, as we know now.

Wildlife cheated my uncle Kwere Seriri because at that time he had no one who could write or read. What I mean by cheating is that when the Wildlife people came, they advised him to have a permanent home, but what transpired later was that where they told him would be his land is the same land which now the government has given to the white people, and so they want to evacuate us again.

They say this land belongs to the whites, whereas these lodges came after we moved here. When the lodges were built, we as owners of the land were not consulted. However, during the official opening of the Khwai Lodge by the late Sir Seretse Khama [Botswana's first president], he refused to conduct the opening until we were called to be part of the ceremony. When Tsaro Lodge was opened we were reluctant to participate in the official opening; however, because they sent us a Botswana Defense Force truck, we went because we were afraid of the soldiers. I think the fake good relationship which is posed by the lodges is due to the fact that they heard that the Basarwa of Khwai are petitioning to be given their land. So they are trying to be nice to us because they are afraid that once we are in control, we will oppress them.

LESIE KWERE, INTERVIEWED 3 JULY 1997

The places we used to know have been changed. Our parents cultivated crops there. They also hunted and collected honey. The Bayei people were always with us. They were after the meat which we hunted. We used ropes to trap birds such as francolins and guineafowls and small animals such as duiker, antelopes, kudu, and bushbucks. We had no dogs at that time, so we used traps. Animals such as giraffe our grandfathers chased until it was tired, and then they killed it with a spear. After the kill, the Bayei would come and eat with us. They also would bring sorghum and give it to friends. This is how we became friends. There was no superiority or inferiority involved.

Those who passed by our areas were Bakgalagadi. They would come along with their Basarwa servants carrying loads of items. They sold things such as ochre at Sankuyo. During their traveling they had nothing to carry except a rifle and fly-whisk. All the items were carried by their Basarwa servants. The Bakgalagadi behaved as if we were their donkeys, but the Bayei saw us as fully human beings.

I think our great grandfathers were once servants to the Bakgalagadi, but our fathers could not tolerate this because they challenged anybody who had that attitude. So we also grew up rejecting any kind of oppressive attitude. We came to know and see this attitude from one Mokgalagadi man who came with his Basarwa servants and spent a couple of nights at my uncle Kwere's home. This man told my uncle that he would like to have fresh Basarwa children from my uncle's family to carry his goods because the ones he came with were tired and could not reach Sankuyo. My uncle asked him to repeat what he said, and then told him to leave his home immediately. My uncle housed this man thinking that he was also a human being, but if he had these attitudes, then he should leave.

At that time, the Batawana chieftainship was dominant. The Batawana people were responsible for making other people their slaves. The Bakgalagadi picked up this attitude from the Batawana. The Batawana even took our relatives away on the pretext that they were in love with them. Some of our relatives still live there in Maun. They have their own homes and children; they are no longer owned as slaves. Their children still call themselves Babugakhwe because their parents were Babugakhwe. When we have social crises such as death, they come here for funerals and to console the bereaved.

We farmed for two years in Xhuko. During the second year, Wildlife found us living there. In the third year they came again and told us that they would like to establish a conservation area because they were afraid that if they did not, they would lose all the animals to the white people who were hunting them.

When the park was established, there was no consultation because in a consultation process, we expect things to be done patiently and slowly. When Wildlife came to us the second time, they told us that they were going to move us. They said we should pack because they had a safari vehicle. They burnt our houses as well as things that we forgot to take. We did not like to see our houses burnt because what they were doing showed that we meant nothing to them. They took us to a place called Segagama. We spent a year there. In the second year they told us again to move out because they expanded the park. We told them that we had property which needed to be transported. They told us that they did not have a vehicle. So we took our belongings and went to the other side of the river.

What is most painful is that presently the [Wildlife] people again claim that we are in the wildlife area. They want us to move to Mababe or Sankuyo.

These people, the present government, the councillors, are the people who came and told us that we are disturbing the animals in their area and we should move. Then we asked them, "Between you Batswana and us, the despised Basarwa group, who has the knowledge of conservation?" They said it was us Basarwa. Then we said, "Since we have lived with these animals for a long time, while you finish yours, is it then your desire that we should move out of here so that you can come and finish what we have conserved?" We then told them that we would not move to Mababe nor to Sankuyo. In our final words, we told them that if it was their wish to kill us, they could do so, but we are not going to move out because we are not used to life far away from the river.

At the moment, we are in our original area. We told the government that we would like to have a school. Their response was that if it was our wish to have a school, we should move to a different area, then we would be given a school. Then we told them that we will send our children to the schools in Maun.

We were here four years before the arrival of the first lodge. In the fifth year, Safari South built Khwai River Lodge. Then later came Tsaro Lodge. They employed the Babugakhwe during the construction of Tsaro Lodge, but not as many as at Khwai Lodge. The owners of Safari South, which was Khwai, did not discriminate against people on the basis of their ethnicity. However, at present our children are not working there, because the lodge now is no longer Safari South but Game Trackers. There is only one Mosarwa employee there. We approached the lodge owners and told them in a *kgotla* meeting that we do not like their system of discrimination against us.

LESIE KWERE, INTERVIEWED 1998

The government asked us about this tourism activity: What do we want to do? Some of our local people (from Khwai) responded by saying that they want to consume the wildlife like they used to in the past. But others responded by saying that it is not wise to do so. Instead they wanted to conduct a tourism activity like the government is doing so that we can benefit from the wildlife through the profits we will be making. Then our children will find this process going on and take over from us. And so we agreed upon this proposition.

Then the government stated that after it gives us this land, we will have to invite a white businessman who will conduct the tourism activity. We the people of Khwai disagreed because if we invite a white man, he is going to control everything. By this I mean that if there is a photographic area and hunting area with a quota [regulating the number of animals that may be killed per year in any area], he is only going to pay us for the quota, but the money from photography is his. That is why we stated that we want to conduct our own business, so that tourists can come and buy wild animals from us, and then we can see whether we won't progress.

For the people in Sankuyo, I do not see any benefits except for the quota. The white man controls the people. If he says no hunting is to be carried out, the people of Sankuyo will not hunt. He closes their dirt roads. He even made an empty promise that he would employ all the people of Sankuyo; right now some are suffering because they cannot find jobs. We see that Sankuyo does not benefit. The procedure of inviting a white man is useless.

Those in Chobe work by choosing a white man. When he does not treat them well, in the coming year they choose a different one. I have realized that changing people every year is caused by the discomfort brought by these white men. If a white man stays in the joint venture with the community for three or four years, then that means he is working well with the community, and the community will renew his contract. But if you see a white man working with the community for one year and then he is removed and a new one chosen, that means he is cheating the community. In Chobe I heard that one white man disappeared with the community's money. Then they chose another white man. Through the years, they have been changing white businessmen. I have realized that there is something that causes these frequent changes.

We will be leasing for ourselves, the people of Khwai.

Transcribed and translated by Tselanngwefela Komerese,
Beauty Malope, and Enamile Tlhobolo

Yvonne Vera, WRITING NEAR THE BONE
Zimbabwe 1997   English

Born in Bulawayo, Zimbabwe, in 1964, Yvonne Vera was reared by her mother and grandmother. Her mother, a schoolteacher, encouraged Vera's early fascination with the written word, while her storytelling grandmother imbued in her a deep appreciation for the oral tradition that continues to inform her writing. After completing her initial schooling in Zimbabwe, Vera went on to study film and literature at York University, Canada. She earned a doctorate in 1995 and returned to Zimbabwe, where she was appointed director of the National Art Gallery in Bulawayo, a post she continues to hold.

Vera has consistently won awards for her fiction. Her collection of short stories, *Why Don't You Carve Other Animals* (1992), explores the contradictions of the Zimbabwe War of Liberation and asks probing questions about the possibilities of art in such a world. *Nehanda* (1993), her first novel, re-creates the life of the spirit medium who led the First Chimurenga, or anticolonial resistance, of 1896–1897. (For a poetic representation of Nehanda, see Elizabeth Ncube's text in this volume.) *Without a Name* (1994) is set in 1977, at the height of the War of Liberation, or Second Chimurenga, while her third novel, *Under the Tongue* (1996), which won the Commonwealth Writer's Prize for the Africa Region, ends with the cease-fire of 1980. *Butterfly Burning* (1998), her most recent novel, is set in 1950s Bulawayo. In 1999 she edited a collection entitled *Opening Spaces: An Anthology of African Women's Writing*.

The essay below seeks to bring the body and the earth into the act of writing, thereby remembering the physicality of the oral word and rooting the written word in the African soil. The emphasis, though, is on the importance of writing. As Vera states in her preface to *Opening Spaces*, "If speaking is still difficult to negotiate, then writing has created a free space for most women—much freer than speech. There is less interruption, less immediate and shocked reaction. . . . The book is bound, circulated, read. It retains its autonomy much more than a woman is allowed in the oral situation. Writing offers a moment of intervention."

Meg Samuelson

✦

There is no essential truth about being a female writer. The best writing comes from the boundaries, the ungendered spaces between male and female. I am talking of writing itself, not the story or theme. Knowing a story is one thing, writing it quite another.

I like to think of writing in limitless terms, with no particular contract with the reader, especially that of gender. When I have discovered that unmarked and fearless territory then I am free to write, even more free to be a woman writing. Sometimes the light coming through my window has been much more important than the fact that I am a woman writing.

There must be a serious purpose to my work, that is all. I must be in touch with the earth. I can never mistake that source of inspiration and energy to be gender, it is something we all share. It is true, however, that one writes best on themes, feelings, actions and sentiments one is more closely connected with. In this regard I like to think that I am writing. I am a woman. I am writing.

The woman I am is inside the writing, embraced and freed by it. For me writing is light, a radiance that captures everything in a fine profile. This light searches and illuminates, it is a safe place from which to uncover the emotional havoc of our experience. Light is a bright warmth which heals. Writing can be this kind of light. Within it I do not hide. I travel bravely beyond that light, into the shadows that this light creates, and in that darkness it is also possible to be free, to write, to be a woman.

I like the peasant shoes which van Gogh painted for example, their lack of light. They are a lot darker than the reprints suggest, no light at all except an almost clear patch of ground behind them and that is hardly light, really. You feel the absence of light in these pictures and that really draws your head closer and your emotion and you really want to look and you feel heavy with a new delight. You look at these shoes and wonder where they have been and who has been and what has been and did these shoes ever grow anything that held some life in it, that breathed perhaps, that threw some kind of light into the world. When I went to the gallery shop in Amsterdam I looked for a postcard with the shoes: the reproduction was so bright, I said this is terrible I will not buy this card even though I want so much to do so. I went back into the gallery and looked at the shoes again and found a large evocative canvas, thrilling in its sadness. I knew this had been written not without light but beyond light.

I found the same immaculate transcription of image and emotion with "The Potato Eaters." It was a lot darker than the "Peasant Shoes." There were four or five little cups and something properly muddy was being poured into them. The cups were white but free of light. And figures in the foreground, possibly a child, had her back to the viewer. It was difficult standing and watching the back of this child who somehow was a potato eater and was about to drink something so muddy from a cup that was nearly white. There was a lantern of some kind hanging above the group but its presence created shadows, not warmth or recognition. The picture was very imposing in its emotion, but beautiful, harmful.

I learnt to write when I was almost six and at the same time also discovered the magic of my own body as a writing surface, I lived with my grandmother for some years while my mother was pursuing her studies. Many other children lived with my grandmother. The house was very small and most afternoons we were kept outside where we woke with some cousins and sat on large metal garbage cans, our legs hardly long enough to touch the ground.

The skin over my legs would be dry, taut, even heavy. It carried the cold of our winter. Using the edges of my fingernails or pieces of dry grass broken from my grandmother's broom I would start to write on my legs. I would write on my small thighs but this surface was soft and the words would vanish and not stay for long, but it felt different to write there, a sharp and ticklish sensation which made us laugh and feel as though we had placed the words in a hidden place.

Our hope increased we travelled downward to the legs where the skin broke like black clay, and we wrote our names to all eternity. Here we wrote near the bone and spread the words all the way to the ankles. We wrote deep into the skin and under skin where the words could not escape. Here, the skin was thirsty, it seemed, and we liked it. The words formed light grey intermingling paths that meant something to our imagination and freed us and made us forget the missing laughters of our mothers. We felt the words in gradual bursts of pain, the first words we had written would become less felt, the pain of that scratching now faded, and the last words where we had dug too deep would be pulsating still, unable to be quiet.

We looked up and laughed and drew figures of our bodies there, and the bodies of our grandmothers which we squeezed among the letters. It was possible, when you had used a small piece of dry bark for your pen, to be bleeding in small dots. Such words could never depart or be forgotten. This was bleeding, not writing. It was important to write. Then, before running indoors to my grandmother who would have been distressed at the changed shades of our bodies, we would use handfuls of saliva to wipe our bodies clean. This saliva spread a warm and calming feeling over us.

I learnt to write if not on the body then on the ground. We would spread the loamy soil into a smooth surface with the palm of our hands using loving and careful motions, then we would write with the tips of our fingers. Bending over that earth, touching it with our noses, we would learn to write large words which led us into another realm of feeling and of understanding our place in the world. Proud of our accomplishment we would then stand back to see what we had written. We had burrowed the earth like certain kinds of beetles and we were immensely satisfied. We left these letters there, on the ground, and ran off to do our chores. I always liked writing after the rains when the soil held to our naked feet and claimed us entirely. Then we drew shapes on the ground which could be seen for distances. Our bodies and our earth, the smell of rain, beetles and our noses, this was writing.

Ellen K. Kuzwayo, AFRICAN WISDOM
South Africa 1998   English

Ellen Kate Kuzwayo was born in Thaba Patchoa, in the Thaba 'Nchu district of the Orange Free State. Her parents divorced when she was two years old and she spent her childhood on her maternal grandfather's farm, Tshiamelo (Place of Goodness). On the farm she was also called Motlalepola, a name suggesting she was born on a rainy day. Her family lost the farm in 1974 when it was declared a white area under the Group Areas Act.

After attending St. Francis College and Adams College in Natal, and Lovedale in the Eastern Cape, she had a short career as a teacher. In 1941 she married and had two sons, but in 1947 left her family after refusing to submit any longer to her husband's abuse. Seeking refuge with her father in Johannesburg, Kuzwayo had a new lease on life. She married Godfrey Kuzwayo in 1950, thereafter living with him and their child in Kliptown, Johannesburg. Later, her two sons joined her. In 1955 she qualified as a social worker and in her new career achieved recognition as a relentless fighter for human rights, women's rights, and a better life for the young, earning a people's title as "Mother of Soweto." In 1976 she was also appointed a member of the Committee of Ten, an activist committee based in Soweto. She left the Christian youth organizations with which she had been largely involved and took up a post in the School of Social Work at the University of the Witwatersrand. She was detained without trial for five months in 1977 under the Terrorism Act; in 1979, she was named Woman of the Year by the Johannesburg *Star*, and in 1987 was awarded an honorary doctorate of law by the University of the Witwatersrand. She was, until recently, a member of Parliament.

Besides the book from which this excerpt is taken, Kuzwayo has published an autobiography, *Call Me Woman* (1985), and a collection of short stories and fables, *Sit Down and Listen* (1990). Her first book made her, in 1985, the first black South African to win the prestigious CNA (Central News Agency) Prize.

Kuzwayo's Setswana proverbs function as a window on African life, providing cultural values in a condensed form. Noting that violence and abuse continue to increase daily, including senseless rapes and killings of young and old women, she suggests that proverbs may serve to reconnect Africans with *ubuntu* (respect for human dignity). In this spirit, she offers proverbs she learned in childhood as one possible instrument of change.

Abner Nyamende

✦

Looking back on my life, it suddenly dawned on me that, possibly from my birth, and certainly from the age of five years, I was exposed to two distinct systems of education. While I consciously embraced one of these systems, I was hardly aware of the other.

From the age of six or seven, I attended school at Thabapatchoa Primary in the district of Thaba-Nchu in the Free State. This school was on the farm of my maternal grandfather, Jeremiah Gopolang Makgothi. At the turn of the century, he himself had built the school with the assistance of his immediate family and the community of other families living on the farm.

This was the only farm in the area which provided a school for Africans. The few coloured children living on his farm and on the surrounding white-owned farms also attended Thabapatchoa Primary. [. . .]

The school was run and administered by one teacher. In those years, beginners attending school were provided with small reading books known as *Sepelete sa Setswana*, which meant Setswana spelling books for Setswana-speaking pupils. Indeed, inside of a year those young pupils became proficient in reading, writing and spelling. [. . .]

In addition to formal learning, our schooling also provided us with the opportunity to make friends, to play, to socialise and to develop in all directions. The long hours at school compelled us to bring something to eat at break. Pupils from the village of farm workers generally brought lovely sour porridge, known as "motogo-wa-seqhaqhabola," in silvery containers with handles. These containers were clean and shining. We, on the other hand, brought butter-and-jam sandwiches to school. Soon, we were exchanging our lunch of sandwiches for motogo-wa-seqhaqhabola, which we greatly enjoyed, whilst our friends loved the sandwiches. [. . .]

These memories of my formal schooling still give me great joy. To this day, I value and treasure it as part of the foundation of who I am today.

It was thus with great sadness that I watched as "Bantu Education" was introduced. The legacy of Bantu Education saw many students leaving school and drifting into the streets or becoming unemployable. In the seventies, as most people know, Bantu Education led to an eruption of violence as school children rebelled against an inferior and oppressive education system.

As a consequence, violence and lawlessness increased dramatically in the past two decades. Although I am fully convinced that the blame for today's violence and crime should rest squarely on the shoulders of the old Nationalist government, the violence in my community has given me many sleepless nights. As I turned these problems over and over in my mind, my thoughts suddenly drifted back to the time when I was young. And this was when a second, less formalised system of education came back to me.

•

I recall my mother's voice which called me to order, and often ended with some strong proverb to express the gravity of the wrong done. In those years, parents' reprimands were taken seriously and with respect. It was common practice for my mother to send me off soul-searching with a proverb. That proverb said it all.

As I write this now, I can hear her voice: "Tsholofelo"—her favourite name for me, meaning "hope"—"ngwana yo o sa reetseng molao wa bagolo, o tla thanya lomapo lo le tsebeng."

This is one of the commonest proverbs used by adults when they reprimand youth. The literal meaning is that a child who does not heed the elders' warning and advice will suffer the rupture of his or her eardrum: Children who are disobedient will meet tragedy.

Of the many interactions I had with my mother, those many years ago, one stands out with clarity. I remember the occasion when Mother sent me to the main road, about twenty yards away from the homestead, to invite a passing group of seasonal work-seekers home for a meal. She instructed me to take a container along and collect dry cow-dung for making a fire. I was then to prepare the meal for the group of work-seekers.

The thought of making an open fire outside at midday, cooking in a large three-legged pot in that intense heat, was sufficient to upset even an angel. I did not manage to conceal my feelings from my mother, and after serving the group, she called me to the veranda, where she usually sat to attend to her sewing and knitting.

Looking straight into my eyes, she said, "Tsholofelo, why did you sulk when I requested you to prepare a meal for those poor destitute people?"

Despite my attempt to deny her allegation, and using the heat of the fire and the sun as an excuse for my alleged behaviour, Mother, giving me a firm look, said, "Lonao ga lo na nko"—"A foot has no nose." It means: You cannot detect what trouble may lie ahead for you. Had I denied this group of people a meal, it may have happened that in my travels some time in the future, I found myself at the mercy of some of those very individuals.

As if that was not enough to shame me, Mother continued, "Motho ke motho ka motho yo mongwe." The literal meaning: A person is a person because of another person. Its closest English equivalent is probably: "No man is an island."

This particular proverb is found among all ethnic groups in South Africa. I believe it is similar to the concept of "Ubuntu" in the Nguni languages, isiZulu and isiXhosa, and "Botho" in the Sotho languages, Setswana, Sesotho and Sepedi.

This one proverb lays down the principles and values of "human" interaction for all African inhabitants of southern Africa. I would not be surprised if it is also found in the rest of the continent.

In African culture, "Botho" expresses the interdependence of all people regardless of age, sex or social standing. When we in South Africa discuss the violence of the present day, we often end up saying: "What has become of Botho?"

I am haunted by the prevailing violence; the abuse of young girls, the rape of young and old women, the car-theft, the senseless killings of people . . . I sometimes wake up in the middle of the night and ask myself: "What has happened to Botho? How can it be restored?"

As I grappled with the frightening violence and racked my mind for remedies, I had to conclude that any effective remedy would have to combine a variety of solutions. And the language of proverbs struck me as one of the instruments, which could help.

Marevasei Kachere, WAR MEMOIR
Zimbabwe 1998   chiShona

The Liberation War, one of the most significant events in the history of Zimbabwe, was a civil war in which black people overthrew the minority white government through an armed struggle. At first a trickle of black militants secretly left the country to train as guerrillas in Zambia and later Mozambique, and to come back and fight for national independence. The trickle turned into a flood in the 1970s as thousands of men, women, and children joined the struggle. The story told by Marevasei Kachere in a series of interviews is one of the few accounts by women that speak of their involvement in the heroic task of establishing an independent Zimbabwe.

Although the desire to achieve independence was the main cause of the war, more immediate ones provided people with reasons to join in. These included unemployment, the violence of the Rhodesian regime, and the love of adventure and excitement. In the military camps in exile, men and women trained together. They were informed about the history of the grievances of the black people and their leaders promised them that, in the new Zimbabwe, these grievances would be redressed and land, jobs, and a better life would be within everyone's reach. The active involvement of women in the war heralded a new era in which traditional women would be accorded equal status with men, since they had fought as men. Women cared for the sick and wounded, but they also carried supplies to the front lines and fought when needed with the guns they had been trained to use.

Kachere's story throws light on all this and on the suffering in the camps from hunger, sickness, and enemy attacks. But it is silent on how women were still abused and exploited by their male counterparts during the war. The film *Flame*, produced in 1995, generated controversy for, among other reasons, screening a scene that exposed a senior officer in the liberation army raping a woman fighter. The public was not yet ready to acknowledge the additional hardships that women suffered in the military camps. Eighteen years after independence, Kachere's high hopes and expectations of the 1970s remained unfulfilled. The small lump sum paid out to each ex-combatant in 1997 and the small monthly pension fall far short of what she and others had expected.

Chiedza Musengezi

✦

My name is Marevasei Kachere and I was born at Uzumba in Murewa District in 1961, the last in a family of eight children. I went to school at Chidodo when I was eight years old and stayed there up to grade seven. All the children in our family went to school but none of us progressed beyond grade seven, the top class of the primary school. My parents were unusual, as, unlike most parents in our village, they chose to send their daughters to school. This may have been due to the fact that my father had been an only child and so had not experienced discrimination against girls in his family. My education was brought to an end by the Liberation War. I didn't even see the results of my grade seven examinations since we had to leave our home before the results were available. When I eventually came back after the war, I was told that all the school records had been burnt.

Each day, after school, I had to look after the cattle and work in the fields, sometimes helping my father and one of my brothers to plough. I would lead the plough oxen so that they kept on the right course. As with schooling, there was no discrimination in our family between boys and girls as far as work was concerned. Any of us could do anything that had to be done. For instance, my brothers often used to fetch water from the well, something that is considered to be a girl's job. We lived very simply. It was only on special occasions that I was able to eat the food that I loved best—bread and eggs—and that, of course, disappeared along with our hens when we were forced by the Rhodesian soldiers to move into the keep or protected village.

In the early 1970s I used to hear the old people talking about a war and about terrorists, but at first I didn't understand what this meant. Then, round about 1972, when the war was getting hot in the Mount Darwin area, we heard stories that told of terrorists who were invisible. If the Rhodesian soldiers came anywhere near them, they would see only their hats but not the actual people.

We just heard these stories without, as I say, understanding them. Understanding what war was came to us when the soldiers arrived in our district. When they first came they questioned people about the presence of terrorists, and I think that at that period only a few people had been in contact with them, bringing them food and other necessities. But then we were told that on such and such a date we were going to be moved into a keep, although we had no idea what a keep was. So on the appointed day in 1975 the soldiers came and, going from house to house in our village, forced the people at gunpoint to leave with everything they could carry. Anyone who refused to move was shot. And then the soldiers burnt all our houses.

There were no houses in the keep and, at first, people made simple grass shelters to stay in—with no roofs—until they managed to build huts. A whole family was crowded into each of these shelters, but in my case, I was lucky since my brothers and sister had married and I was the only one staying with my parents.

The keep was a large area surrounded by a very high barbed-wire fence. It was so high that one couldn't possibly climb over it and the wires were placed so close together that no one was able to squeeze through it. There were no two ways about it—when the soldiers said that we had to stay inside we had no choice. They were afraid that if we were allowed to go freely in and out we would carry food to the "terrorists" as they called them. Of course people had to be allowed to go out at set times to fetch water and to tend the vegetable gardens, and on these occasions everyone who went out was searched to see if the container he or she carried held food. And on coming back, if you were carrying a bucket of water the guards would stir it with a stick to see if there were any explosives in it. You had to make quite sure that you had brought in enough food and water for the family for if the gate was kept closed, as it sometimes was, then there was nothing you could do but go hungry. And if you came back late, after being outside, you would be shot.

Our school was also inside the fence, and every morning we had to go to school. The soldiers used to come to check the register to make sure that every child was present. If anyone was absent the rest of us were beaten with a length of hosepipe—every one of us—by the soldiers who were trying to get us to say where such and such a child had gone. We never did say for we believed that if they found out where the child had gone that child would be killed.

I was not invited by anyone to join the Liberation Struggle, but I was forced into going by the intolerable circumstances in which we lived. The soldiers used to come and take us to a place called Mashambanhaka where they put us in drums full of water and beat us almost to death. This painful routine went on for some time. Even old people suffered in the same way.

Indeed, anybody who was suspected of having fed the guerrillas was taken out and beaten and then locked in the keep again. I was tired of being beaten and so I decided I would go out to join the Liberation Struggle. Doing that, I thought, might lead to my death, but as far as that was concerned I was under a constant threat of death in the keep, so it was all one whether I stayed or went. On balance I thought it better to go.

While I was still in the keep some guerrillas arrived at a base called Birimhiri and a message came that we should prepare sadza and take it to the comrades. We cooked the sadza, and on that day we were lucky for the soldiers had gone off to read their newspapers, and the DA's were holed up in a strong point fortified with sandbags which was called *zvimudhuri*, so we slipped out carrying the food, and I never came back. I was with a friend called Kiretti and we just walked saying nothing to each other for there was nothing to say; I mean we had no idea what to expect when we arrived at where we were going. This was all done in a moment, completely unplanned. I had not even told my mother that I was going.

That was my first day to meet the comrades. They were just ordinary people, quite visible, wearing uniforms some of which were plain khaki and some camouflage, and carrying their guns which, I noticed, they never let go of since they might have to fight at any moment. We were a bit afraid at first but soon got used to them. There were ten of them altogether. When they had eaten and were about to leave we told them we were going with them; that we wanted to go to Mozambique because we were tired of being beaten. At first they refused to take us and said they were taking boys only, and that though they had taken girls before, they did not encourage those who were very young to go. But we insisted that we were not going back to the keep to be beaten to death or to be injured, as my hearing had been impaired through the punishment I had received. And eventually they agreed.

When we left there were four girls and quite a number of boys from our keep in the group. We did not know what to expect but I did not regret what I had done. We started our journey at night, around eight o'clock, and travelled to Karimimbika which is still in the Uzumba District. Another group of comrades joined us there and we went on, travelling always by night, going via Mudzi and Area 6, and then straight to the border between Rhodesia and Mozambique. My tennis shoes were soon worn out, and I had to make do with the one dress I had been wearing when I left the keep.

After we had crossed into Mozambique we camped at a base called Mubhanana where we stayed for some time, carrying supplies of arms for the comrades who came from Chambere. Then we moved to Zhangara Camp where there were about seven hundred people, including two hundred who were my age. At one stage there were more women than men in this camp, but in my age group there were more boys than girls, and there were no old people. At Zhangara, as in other camps, we were taught politics. Our instructors told us about the war and its origins and said that we should not think of returning home since we had chosen to come and fight for our country's independence.

For my part I never wanted to go back while things were as they were. Yes, I missed my parents, but I was in a large group of young people, all of whom were in the same boat, and that made it easier to forget about your own problems. Most of the time I was happy because I had friends— Ebamore, Tarisai, Mabhunu and Shingirai. We sang together in the choir; in times of hardship we comforted each other; we plaited our hair and mended our clothes. If we were lucky enough to have needles we made small bags in which to keep personal things out of our old dresses. Discipline was fairly strict in the camp. Girls were separated from boys and we never had boyfriends. If a girl did leave camp to meet a boy and was caught she was punished. It wasn't easy to get out of the camp because the exits were guarded. Pregnancies were rare, but girls fell pregnant when they left camp to perform military duties like carrying arms and ammunition. The most common offence for which one was beaten or made to carry ammunition was escaping from the camp to barter clothes for food in the surrounding villages. Beatings were not carried out in the open and we only saw people being called to report for a beating. In all the time I stayed at this camp I never broke the rules, except on one occasion: my friends and I missed a meal because we had stayed too long at the river where we were getting rid of the lice in our hair. Luckily we were not punished for that. [. . .]

We also did some training with "arms," wooden guns that we ourselves had made. Being educated was a big advantage in the camp, and it was the educated ones who were usually the first to be selected to become trainers. I wasn't considered to be educated but I was good at physical activities so I was asked to help with military training. After we had finished the initial training we were allowed to handle real guns, and were given lessons on the different parts of a gun and on how to dismantle and load them. All this time boys and girls were taught together, and we had both male and female instructors. These lessons gave us confidence and a sense of power, so different from how we felt when we were untrained and unarmed.

The most distressing episode in this part of my life was when Tembwe was bombed on November 25, 1977. On that day people were carrying out their duties as usual but another girl and I hadn't gone to work because we were sick. I had an extensive burn on my leg as a result of an accident in the kitchen. Shingi and I had been to the clinic and on our way back we spotted a plane. We were heading for the kitchen, an area of shelters and large drums on fires in which to cook sadza, but before we got there this plane dropped a bomb right in the middle of it. All those on duty in the kitchen were killed—some by the explosion and others by the porridge from the drums. We ran to the river and hid among the reeds but then soldiers appeared and began shooting towards us and I thought I was going to die. I was hit, and the bullet wounds on my leg were deep, but I survived, though it was three months before my injuries healed.

I had never thought of the possibility of dying in a battle before. During my training I had imagined an exchange of gunfire, but nothing more. I had never seen a dead person, but now I saw so many. As we ran to the river I had stepped on the bodies of those who had died, and the thought of that experience horrified me. People die in war and I knew it then all too fearfully.

Soon after the attack on Tembwe I was sent with other survivors to Maroro where I completed my military training. I was then chosen, together with five girls and nine boys, to carry arms—what we called caches—to the comrades who were in the field. These arms—grenades for instance—were packed into sealed bags, and with these we crossed the border into Rhodesia, protected by an armed guard who knew the way. We entered the Mutoko area in July 1978 and went straight to the traditional healer in that area who gave us the go-ahead to operate there. We had been instructed not to seek confrontation with the Rhodesian security forces, and to hide if we came across any. My one experience of action in the field was in Area G. We were having a meal of sadza when we were attacked. We ran away. But four of our comrades were killed by the enemy in this engagement.

In December 1979 a cease-fire was declared. [. . .] We celebrated Zimbabwean Independence on April 18, 1980. We talked about the fact that we had liberated our country and that now no one would be a beggar in his or her own land. We believed that every person in the country would get enough food and a place to stay, and yes, I expected to get a job that matched my education and training. We had great expectations. At that time our leaders told us that what we expected would come true.

As it worked out, some of us were sent to schools, but then the schools were closed. The leaders came and asked for those who wanted jobs, but only the highly educated were taken and given jobs in, for instance, the police force. I stayed behind in that camp while others went off to work, and on top of that they said I was too short to join the police.

Meanwhile, a cousin of mine had come looking for me, as relatives did in those days when family members who had long been lost were returning to these assembly points. As a result I went to see my parents and we wept on one another's necks when we met. They were poor. They had lost everything in the war, and they couldn't help me, nor I them at that time. After staying with them for a short time I went back to Manyene. My hope lay in the promise of jobs that had been made, and I was anxious to get back because I did not want to miss out. [. . .]

Eighteen years after Independence most of the promises made to us remain unfulfilled. We were all promised houses and jobs and a good life, regardless of one's standard of education, but this has not happened.

The hard conditions in the camps in Mozambique have affected my health badly. I think I picked up diseases there from which I have never fully recovered. I would never recommend my daughter to follow my example if such a situation arose again.

The major change of the last couple of years has been the $50 000 payout and the $2 000 monthly pension. I managed to buy a plough, a cart and two oxen, and I was given land to use. I don't have to dig my field with a hoe anymore. But I think the money is too little. I suffered for too long and the money came too late.

Transcribed by Grace Dube
Translated by Chiedza Musengezi

Antjie Krog,
THE BIRTH OF THIS COUNTRY'S LANGUAGE

South Africa 1998   English

Antjie Krog, an acclaimed Afrikaans poet, was born in Kroonstad, Orange Free State, South Africa, in 1952. An outspoken opponent of the apartheid state, she participated in the historic 1989 Victoria Falls meeting between Afrikaans intellectuals and writers and the then-exiled African National Congress.

For two years, under her married name Antjie Samuel, she reported on the Truth and Reconciliation Commission (TRC) for the South African Broadcasting Corporation and, with her team, received the prestigious local Pringle Award for excellence in media coverage. It is out of this experience that Krog wrote *Country of My Skull*, from which the following excerpts are drawn.

Country of My Skull engages with the TRC on an intensely personal level, providing both a record of and a response to what many see as the crucial event in the formation of the new South Africa. Krog uses a multigeneric tapestry of styles and voices in order to arrive at her own truth, a truth "quilted together from hundreds of stories." Her own testimony revolves around a search for a new way of belonging in South Africa. Shocked by the exposure of farms as the base of hit squads and the site of torture, she revisits the farm of her childhood, once a source of poetic inspiration. She searches for a rebirth of language and draws attention to the TRC as a national moment that will allow storytelling, and healing, to begin again.

Krog has won numerous awards, local and international, for her eight volumes of poetry, beginning with *Dogter van Jafta* (Daughter of Jafta) (1970), published when she was eighteen. More recently, she has added to her repertoire children's poetry and prose, two coeditions of Afrikaans verse, a prose murder narrative, and a play, *Why Is It That Those Who Toyi-Toyi in Front Are Always So Fat?*, which brings black and white women into dialogue with one another. In 2000 she published her ninth volume of poetry in Afrikaans as well as her first English volume, *Down to My Last Skin*. *Country of My Skull* shared first prize in the 1999 Sunday Times Alan Paton Award for nonfiction and saw Krog awarded the prestigious Hiroshima Prize.

Meg Samuelson

Tension is plain to see in the faces and body language of all the Commissioners. Archbishop Tutu is continually rubbing his right hand, several pairs of shoulders are tensely set, their faces look tired and drawn beneath two big South African flags and Truth Commission banners. The city hall of East London is packed from wall to wall. Even in the galleries people are sitting on the steps.

Last night, the Archbishop says, he had butterflies in his stomach: "We were aware from the beginning that the Commission could go terribly and horribly wrong. But this first victims' hearing is the making or breaking of the Commission."

"So what are your worst fears?"

He laughs nervously. "Silly things, like the microphones not working, security problems . . . or terrible things like victims not showing up or violence breaking out."

Commissioner Bongani Finca starts with the well-known Xhosa hymn: *Lizalise idinga lakho.* "The forgiveness of sins makes a person whole." As the song carries, the victims file into the hall and take their seats at the front. Through ritual they are physically separated from the rest of the audience.

Archbishop Tutu prays. But untypically he sounds as if he is praying from a piece of paper: "We long to put behind us the pain and division of Apartheid, together with all the violence which ravaged our communities in its name. And so we ask you to bless this Truth and Reconciliation Commission with your wisdom and guidance as a body which seeks to redress the wounds in the minds and the bodies of those who suffered."

Everyone stands with their heads bowed while the names of the deceased and disappeared who will come under the spotlight today are read out. A big white candle emblazoned with a red cross is lit. Then all the Commissioners go over to the row of victims to greet and welcome them, while the audience stays standing.

But the journalists in the media room are hardly aware of this consecration of space. Frantic shouting accompanies the attempts to tune in TV monitors, establish clear sound reception and set up laptop computers. Radio has its own small room. We have a whole newly appointed team, which has to cover the event in all eleven official languages. Today's hearings will be broadcast live, after an hour-long programme on the meaning of the legislation, the origin of amnesty, the workings of the Commission and an interview with the Minister of Justice, who sanctioned the legislation. Somewhere in a corner, foreign journalists are being briefed on the history of the Eastern Cape, how to pronounce "Qaqawuli" and "Mxenge," who the Cradock Four and the Pebco Three were. Like people possessed they take down notes. The locals watch them from a distance.

.

To seize the surge of language by its soft, bare skull

Beloved, do not die. Do not dare die! I, the survivor, I wrap you in words so that the future inherits you. I snatch you from the death of forgetfulness. I tell your story, complete your ending—you who once whispered beside me in the dark.

"When I opened the door . . . there was my closest friend and comrade . . . She was standing on the doorstep and she screamed: 'My child, my little Nomzamo is still in the house!' . . . I stared at her . . . my most beautiful friend . . . her hair flaming and her chest like a furnace . . . she died a day later. I pulled out her baby from the burning house . . . I put her on the grass . . . only to find that her skin stayed behind on my hands. She is with me here today."
"I was trying to see my child. Just when he was about to open the police van at the back, I heard a voice shouting, saying: 'No, don't show her anything—*hou die meid daar weg!*' ['Keep the kaffir girl away from there!'] But I managed. I pulled a green curtain . . . I saw . . . my . . . child . . . sleeping among tyres . . . and he was foaming in the mouth and he was . . . already dead . . . Then they pulled him out and threw him on the ground . . . And I looked at him . . . And he was dying . . . and they won't allow me to hold him . . . and my key fell on the ground . . . And they asked, quickly: 'What's that? What was that?' . . . And I said: . . . 'It's the key of my house.'"

"This inside me . . . fights my tongue. It is . . . unshareable. It destroys . . . words. Before he was blown up, they cut off his hands so he could not be fingerprinted . . . So how do I say this?—this terrible . . . I want his hands back."

"It was Sunday. And cold. He came into the kitchen. 'Make me some bean soup.'
"'It's Sunday, *jong,* I want to cook special food.'
"But he wanted bean soup.
"While dressing for church we heard the noise. The youths were coming down the road. We were standing in our bedroom. We were not talking. We were not moving. They surrounded the house and they shouted: 'Let the spy *die,* let the spy *die!*' They threw stones through the window. When they left, he said to me: 'Don't cry Nontuthuzelo. A person dies only once, not many times. I know now where these things are leading to. Come, let's make soup.' We went to the kitchen and put the beans in a pot.
"Then someone we knew knocked at the door. 'The comrades are burning your shop, Uncle Mick!'
"'I'll be back for lunch,' he said to me.
"They told me afterwards. He walked up to the door of his shop, he didn't look back . . . someone in the crowd shot him in the back . . . They told me afterwards Craig Kotze had said my husband was the one who betrayed Steve Biko."

502 ✦ 1990S AND 2000S

"Two policemen got on either chair and they dragged me to the window, and then they said I can now jump . . . I refused . . . they grabbed me by my shoulders and lifted me physically up and pushed me out of the window . . . and they were holding me by my ankles . . . each policeman holding one ankle. All I could see was the concrete floor at the bottom—we were three floors up, and all of a sudden one would let go of one foot—as he's about to catch my foot, the one he had released, the other chap lets go—and they played like that . . . and you know you thought: God, this is the end."

"They held me . . . they said, 'Please don't go in there . . .' I just skipped through their legs and went in . . . I found Bheki . . . he was in pieces . . . he was hanging on pieces . . . He was all over . . . pieces of him and brain was scattered all around . . . that was the end of Bheki."

"At Caledon Square I heard a loud sound. Policemen were celebrating. They said: 'We've got Looksmart!' I was in my cell when I saw Looksmart being dragged up a flight of stairs by two policemen. They were beating him as he went up the stairs. I noticed that his beard had been pulled out . . . one by one . . . on one side of his face. He was bleeding heavily from the mouth. Two days later they took him again—his hands handcuffed behind his back. That was the last time I saw Looksmart Ngudle."

"And the man there sitting next to the ambulance driver—he stood there with my son's intestines in his hands and he was actually holding it and carried it into the ambulance."

"In the mortuary—after the Queenstown massacre, I had to identify my son. We waited in front of the mortuary . . . a thick black stream of blood was running from under the door . . . blocking the outside drain . . . inside, the stench was unbearable . . . bodies were stacked upon each other . . . the blood from my child's body was already green."

"This white man with the red scarf, he shot into the outside bathroom where Sonnyboy was hiding . . . I was standing in the kitchen . . . I saw him dragging my child. Sonnyboy was already dead. He was holding him by his legs like a dog. I saw him digging a hole, scraping Sonnyboy's brains into that hole and closing it with his boot. The sun was bright . . . but it went dark when I saw him lying there. It's an everlasting pain. It will stop never in my heart. It always comes back. It eats me apart. Sonnyboy, rest well, my child. I've translated you from the dead."

"I asked them, 'Show me the mark on his chin, then I will know it's my son.' They showed me the mark on his chin, and I said: 'It's not my son.'"

"When Fuzile didn't come home that night I went to look for him. Now this makes me mad really. My son was shot and nobody told me. I looked everywhere and nobody told me my son was in the mortuary . . . they later gave me his clothes. His T-shirt looked as if it had been eaten by rats."

"As she had a baby, the police said that the corpse could breastfeed the baby."

"Barnard was a frightful man—the cop we couldn't kill. He always drove this red Valiant and wore this red *doek*. Rambo of the Western Cape, he called himself. Whenever his car appeared on the shimmering horizon leading the yellow Casspirs, we knew: someone dies today. We will remember the man with the red scarf who shot dead our sons."
"This was the last thing I saw: Barnard standing next to his car. He spoke Xhosa like a Xhosa. He pointed his firearm at me. I felt something hitting my cheek. I felt my eyes itching. I was scratching my eyes and yelling for help. Since then I've been blind . . . and unemployed . . . and alone and homeless. But today . . . today it feels as if I can nearly see . . . "

"I heard shots . . . I ran . . . slipped and fell . . . I crawled out at the front door . . . On the steps my son sat . . . with his father's face in his hands . . . He was covered in blood . . . He cried over and over: 'Daddy, talk to me . . . ' Today he is 21 years old. I am still woken at night by his cries: 'Wipe the blood . . . wipe the blood from my father's face.'"

"That morning I did something I had never done before. My husband was still at his desk busy with the accounts of our business. I went up to him and stood behind his chair. I put my hands under his arms and tickled him . . . he looked surprised and unexpectedly happy.
"'And now?' he asked.
"'I am going to make tea,'" I said.
"While I poured water on the tea bags, I heard this devastating noise. Six men stormed into our study and blew his head off. My five-year-old daughter was present . . . That Christmas I found a letter on his desk: 'Dear Father Christmas, please bring me a soft teddy bear with friendly eyes . . . My daddy is dead. If he was here I would not have bothered you.' I put her in a boarding school. The morning we drove there we had a flat tyre. 'You see,' she said, 'Daddy does not want me to go there . . . He wants me to stay with you . . . I have watched him die, I must be there when you die . . . ' She is now a teenager and has tried twice to commit suicide."

•

In the beginning it was seeing. Seeing for ages, filling the head with ash. No air. No tendril. Now to seeing, speaking is added and the eye plunges into the mouth. Present at the birth of this country's language itself. [. . .]

In a wild arch of air I rock with the Commissioners in the boat back to the mainland. I am filled with an indescribable tenderness towards this Commission. With all its mistakes, its arrogance, its racism, its sanctimony, its incompetence, the lying, the failure to get an interim reparation policy off the ground after two years, the showing off—with all of this—it has been so brave, so naively brave in the winds of deceit, rancour and hate. Against a flood crashing with the weight of a brutalizing past on to new usurping politics, the Commission has kept alive the idea of a common humanity. Painstakingly it has chiselled a way beyond racism and made space for all of our voices. For all its failures, it carries a flame of hope that makes me proud to be from here, of here.

But I want to put it more simply. I want this hand of mine to write it. For us all; all voices, all victims:

> because of you
> this country no longer lies
> between us but within
>
> it breathes becalmed
> after being wounded
> in its wondrous throat
>
> in the cradle of my skull
> it sings, it ignites
> my tongue, my inner ear, the cavity of heart
> shudders towards the outline
>   new in soft intimate clicks and gutturals
>
> of my soul the retina learns to expand
> daily because by a thousand stories
> I was scorched
>
> a new skin.
>
> I am changed for ever. I want to say:
>   forgive me
>   forgive me
>   forgive me
>
> You whom I have wronged, please
> take me
>
> with you.

Communal,
BOJALE—SETSWANA INITIATION SONGS
Botswana 1998　Setswana

Initiation songs are normally sung by the initiates at either *Bojale* or *Bogwera* (initiation schools for girls and boys, respectively). Before the advent of Christianity many ethnic groups in Botswana regarded these schools highly. But soon after most Batswana embraced the Christian religion, these customs were abandoned as unchristian. In fact Chief Khama III of the Bangwato abolished these initiation practices while the Batawana, Bangwaketse, Bakwena, and Barolong abandoned them, and the Bakgatla simply suspended them. At present, those who have continued the practices include the Bakgatla, Balete, and Batlokwa, who occasionally serve some willing initiates from other ethnic groups.

Bojale, designed to usher girls or young women into womanhood and adulthood, are run privately and exclusively for young initiates, who are subjected to a complex web of rules and taboos including a dress code: "bare breasts, bare head, bare feet [or cheap tackies], and ordinary wrapper around the waist." The greatest taboo is sharing *Bojale* experiences with those who have never undergone the initiation rites.

The main objective is to educate the young women on their rights and responsibilities as full citizens of their communities. This, for example, is done by teaching the girls the value of avoiding premarital sex, the benefits of airing grievances in a nonconfrontational manner, the importance of treating older people with reverence, the virtues of being productive and dependable members of the society, and the merits of endurance and perseverance during hardships.

The teachers' lessons and the initiates' responses to the instructions are sung conversationally so as to create a sense of dialogue. Taken together, the songs offer a commentary on the harsh realities of womanhood and life in general. The songs are short, often five to six lines, yet they convey complete and meaningful ideas. The singing itself is long because lines or even whole stanzas are repeated. Metaphor, mockery, parallelism, and rhetorical questions are also characteristic.

These songs were collected and published by Ntikwe Motlotle in 1998. Some, which she had sung at her own initiation in Mochudi, she first recorded in 1984 for a radio program at the National Museum, Gaborone. Some were recorded and transcribed by Elizabeth Nelbach Wood in 1975.

Nobantu Rasebotsa

✦

COMPLAINTS BY THE INITIATES
Song One
I dig hard clay
Womanhood is a hardship
Yes, yes, womanhood is a hardship
Yes, yes, womanhood is a hardship

Please help me dig this clay
Womanhood is a hardship.

Song Two
Escaping, I try to hide outside the wall
Trying to hide outside the wall
The ears heard of it, the ears heard of it
As I try to hide outside the wall
The ears heard it
It got back to the ears.

Song Three
I am not going anywhere
I am not going anywhere
My mother chases guests away
It's a month since I visited
My mother chases guests away.

COMPLAINTS BY THE INSTRUCTORS
Song Four
Let that young girl go
Let her go, I have given up on her
I try to speak to her
It's like speaking to a stone
A small stone like steel iron
The whiteman's steel iron.

Song Five
Are you the troublemaker, are you the cause of the storm?
Are you the stirrer of that dust-storm?
Are you the cause of the storm?
Let it build. Build up as me.
Are you the cause of the storm?

Translated by Leloba Molema and Nobantu Rasebotsa

Communal,
INTONJANE—XHOSA INITIATION SONGS
South Africa 1999   isiXhosa

In Xhosa society *intonjane* was and still is regarded as a sacred ritual performed to mark the development of a girl into womanhood when she first menstruates. During this time, the girl is secluded for about eight days in a hut prepared for the occasion, and tended by selected younger girls. Women and girls perform songs to celebrate the event. The observance of this ritual is so important that if a married woman experiences problems like those of infertility, she might have to return to her parents' home to have the ritual performed if it was not done before. During the time of seclusion, the girl is instructed in sexual matters by an experienced older woman, and especially on how to behave as a young woman. Although *intonjane* is no longer universally practiced, many rural communities still observe it.

In Xhosa culture the performance of song marks almost every social or ceremonial occasion that brings people together. Singing is accompanied by ululation and rhythmic movements such as the clapping of hands, stamping of feet on the ground, and shaking of the upper part of the body. Even the attire is specific to the occasion, and the words of the song also articulate the uniqueness of the event.

Some of the songs at *intonjane* are performed when the girl goes into seclusion; others when she comes out. Since both times are occasions of great joy and gratitude to the ancestors, the songs combine prayer and celebration. They may also convey a personal observation or comment on a particular issue in the village. Cryptic or metaphorical references to specific situations may obscure a song's meaning to all but the performers. This makes accurate translation difficult.

In *intonjane*, the lead singer usually sings every line twice or more, thus setting the pace, tune, and rhythm. In accompaniment, the other women sing "yho - yho - yho" for the duration of the song, and repeat the last word of each line after the lead singer. Certain songs, like the first, express a girl's coming of age and her readiness for initiation. Here the father, as in Song Five, is addressed as "father of the initiated girl"; this new status is likely to be a source of gratification to him—a "pleasing name." The girl's mother is also praised by being addressed through her clan name, MaJolinkomo. The singers express good wishes, praying for the protection of the girl against "whores" who might be jealous of her virginity. Toward the end of the first song (lines 11–13), the father's clan names are declaimed by one of the women, anticipating the future marriage and the cattle it will bring him.

Some songs, like the second, joyously invite the whole community to witness the girl's good behavior and growing maturity. Other songs, as in the third, admonish the girl to exercise self-control when she is sexually aroused—as a sign of maturity and a safeguard of her virginity. The fourth song glances wistfully at the women's own youthful days, and the fifth makes pointed critical comment on a particular issue within the village community. It was acceptable for a man to have a mistress who would be known by his wife and relatives. She would be expected to support the wife and to help the husband to care for his family. The sixth song thus reprimands Lekendlana's mistress for failing to live up to these expectations. The seventh song highlights the moral demand that the initiation ritual exacts on the initiates. The girl is probably no longer a virgin, but still needs her mother's guidance.

Songs One and Five were recorded in 1999 from the Xhosa radio station *Umhlobo Wenene* (True Friend) in Port Elizabeth. The other songs were performed by a group of women in April 1999, at KwaTuku B in Peddie, Eastern Cape, and recorded by Sisi Maqagi and Thandiwe Majola, the daughter of one of the performers, Nokwanda Majola.

Zingisa Guzana and V. M. Sisi Maqagi

✦

SONG ONE: THE GIRL HAS COME OF AGE
Iyho - yho - yho the girl has come of age
Father of the initiated girl is now called
with a pleasing name
Yho - yho - yho MaJolinkomo
Yho - yho - yho the girl has come of age
Father of the initiated girl
We have asked since yesterday, praying
These whores MaJolinkomo
Father of the initiated girl
Ha - la - a - a - a - la
Cattle of Mtika
Of Jotela
Of Mazeleni
You continue to act this way
Hoyi - ho - ho it is a wonder

SONG TWO: COME ALL
Come all, come and listen
Even you whores
You finally spoke
Pity you cry
You man
You will regret in the future
A selection has been made
Ho - ho - ho

SONG THREE: BE OF AGE GIRL
Be of age girl
Control yourself even if you are sexually aroused
It is the vagina which is like this
This thing is like this!

SONG FOUR: TODAY I THINK OF THE PAST
Today I think of the past
While the sun is going down

SONG FIVE: FATHER OF NTONJANE
Yho, yho father of ntonjane
Yho, yho father of ntonjane
Your child has come of age

SONG SIX: MISTRESS OF LEKENDLANA
Mistress of Lekendlana
Ha! Why are you behaving so badly?

SONG SEVEN: YHO YHO FATHER
Yho! yho! he! he! father
Yelele father ho! ho! ha!
I will remain behind
I am not going through with initiation
Ho! I behaved shamefully
I will still need my mother
Ho! he - ha - ha - ha

Translated by Zingisa Guzana

NyaMutango (Ntumba Machai),
MUTONDO—NYEMBA INITIATION SONGS

Namibia 1999   Nyemba

Songs and rituals restricted to female attendance are regarded as "women's secrets." One female ritual called *mutondo*, a generic word for tree, used to be performed when a girl had her first menstruation. Although *mutondo* is sometimes performed by women in western Zambia, it has probably become obsolete in Angola and Namibia. While many young men are still circumcised, *mutondo* is no longer performed. Most people cite the war in Angola and the growing influence of the churches as the reason for this disappearance. Elderly women may instruct young female relatives privately about sexuality. The women interviewed about their experience of *mutondo* complained that mothers these days only find out that their daughters have started menstruating when they come home pregnant.

The songs printed here emerged from three interviews held in 1999 in Kehemu, at the homestead of Ntumba Machai, called NyaMutango, and her family. NyaMutango, a Iauma speaker, was perhaps seventy years old, born by the Lomba River. She and her husband left for Zambia in 1971 and migrated to Namibia in 1995. Two older female relatives joined the first and second interviews. During the third interview with NyaMutango, her husband and son were present and also spoke. The three translators were younger relatives. I did the recordings. Before the interviews began, men and children were sent away and the interviews were held in whispers amid much laughter and giggling.

On the day a girl first menstruated, she would be taken into the bush by the elderly women of the community, most of them female relatives. The girl's mother did not participate. Around a mukula tree, or more exceptionally a muvulia tree, the ground was cleared. For every day the girl bled, the tree was cut so that its red fluid came out. As the girl drank this fluid, the initiation ceremony began and the women began to sing songs like "Here it comes, the *lingongo* of my daughter" (Song One). Ntumba Machai described *lingongo* as a big female chief with strong speeches, who burns all the bad things and brings good things. The oriole, which is addressed in the song, was called a chief; it always speaks the truth.

The initiate lived isolated in the bush for some time, assisted by an older woman, called *cilombolo*, who brought her food and other necessities. She instructed her about marriage, sexual life, and taboos. It was important that a girl learn correctly how to "dance" with her husband when having sex. The old women taught the initiate appropriate movements and they accompanied the movements with songs, as in Song Two below.

Women were not allowed to go anywhere near a male circumcision camp, and similarly, a man passing a women's *mutondo* was liable to be beaten severely. Part of the initiation ceremony was called *mukanda ua kutuka vamala* (the initiation camp to insult the men). Song Four is an example of a derisive song. On the last day of the ceremony the initiate admitted her limited knowledge and the necessity of being taught by elderly women about sexual matters (see Song Five). The older women then showed their private parts, but the girl was not supposed to look. The older women had become *makisi*—dancers with body-paint who represented the ancestors. The *makisi* lined up and the girl crawled between their legs while being beaten with whips made from branches. This experience taught the girl about the secret of the *makisi*.

When she returned to the village as a *muali* (a newly initiated girl), she was dressed and adorned beautifully and wore a veil. All her in-laws to-be would also come with gifts since she was now ready for marriage. The songs sung during the girl's return were sung by everyone and were accompanied with drumming. She was led into the center of the village where she and her future husband were seated on a reed mat. The girl's veil was lifted and her clothes were taken off until she was bare-breasted. She would stand as people around her sang songs about her return. These songs often used language with double meanings, thus the women present knew that *mbaka*, mostly used for "coastal lands" or "town" referred to menstruation. The girl then proceeded to the meeting-house, where she touched the beard of an old man. She would sing "Dance-dance" (Song Six), signifying that she was ready for sexual experiences. The girl and her husband-to-be withdrew into a hut, and the girl, under the supervision of the *cilombolo*, put her newly acquired skills into practice. After this, the girl climbed on top of her mother's hut, where a needle, symbolizing the penis, had been erected. She threw it away. Now, after having touched the beard of the man, she no longer feared such matters. This concluded the ceremonies.

Inge Brinkman

✦

SONG ONE

Here it comes, the *lingongo* of my daughter,
It comes to destroy the house.
Here it comes, the *lingongo* of my daughter,
It comes to destroy the house.
Here it comes, the *lingongo* of my daughter,
It comes to destroy the house.
Oriole, what has it carried?
Burning, burning.
Here it comes, the *lingongo* of my daughter,
It comes to destroy the house.

Song Two

A little, you turn your hips around
A big, you turn your hips around
A little, you turn your hips around
Child, let me tell you.
A little, a little, you turn your hips around.

Song Three

How did I give birth? The girdle.
How did I give birth? The girdle I tie around my waist.
How did I give birth? The girdle.
The whole day. The girdle I tie around my waist.
How did I give birth? The girdle.
Every night. The girdle I tie around my waist.
How did I give birth? The girdle.
[Turning to each other.] The girdle I tie around my waist.

Song Four

We found a man collecting honey, he had large testicles
We found a man collecting honey, he had large testicles
We found him climbing the tree with large testicles
We found a man collecting honey, he had a big penis
Chorus:
When we sing the penis dance
(repeats four times)

Song Five

Have you ever seen this big penis?
No, oh no, I just saw my first menstruation
Without knowing this, ee.
Have you ever seen this big vagina?
No, oh no, I just saw my first menstruation
Without knowing this, ee.

Song Six

Dance-dance
Oh, today, we will touch
Oh mother, mama, today I will touch
The beard of the lion.

Translated by Rebecca Kastherody, Dominga Antonio, and Sarah Machai

Communal, SETSWANA WEDDING SONGS

Botswana 1999   Setswana

Traditionally, brides in Botswana marry in their late teens and early twenties. Advice to them includes how to endure domestic hardship with fortitude and, on the other hand, hints at reasons for wanting to escape. The songs themselves are brief, but are performed over extended periods of time, with repetition and dance accompanied by percussion or other instruments. The examples provided here were written down from memory by Nobantu Rasebotsa and myself: we've heard them throughout our lives and performed them, communally, at the weddings of relatives and friends.

The first song, "Malala Swi," is included here as a significant narrative between a young woman and her maternal uncle in which she respectfully resists his amorous advances. In many ethnic communities in Botswana, a special relationship exists between a man and his sister's children. It is he who makes arrangements for their ritual initiation into adulthood, who contributes most of the cattle that make up their "bride-price," who provides his nephews with "seed capital" in the form of pregnant heifers, who often is much closer to his nieces and nephews than their biological father. This relationship is continuously strengthened by a constant exchange of gifts called *mashori* when made by the nieces and nephews, which their uncle then has to *tlhapisa* in reciprocation. Most commonly, when one slaughters a beast, one traditionally reserves the head of the beast as *mashori* for one's maternal uncle. Also, his own and his sister's children, being cross-cousins, are allowed to marry each other and to engage in overt, risqué verbal exchanges with each other. The uncle in Song One seems to be mistaking himself for one of his own children by making the sexual advance. That his niece rejects him is probably not a mark of feminism but of socially defined censure, indicating that uncles are not supposed to behave in this manner.

In the title of Song One, the root "lala" in "malala" means to sleep somewhere overnight. As the response to the narrator's call, "swi" not only punctuates the song but also allows her to exclaim at various points.

The wedding songs proper are sung and danced when the bride leaves her parents' home and arrives at the home of her parents-in-law. In recent times they contrast with the Christian hymns of church ceremonies and are sung when the bride and bridegroom arrive for luncheon and are escorted from their car to their table by the matrons of both families, carrying aloft baskets full of grain, stamping the ground with pestles, and sweeping it with brooms.

In Song Two, the word "cake" is a translation of Setswana "kuku," which comes from the Afrikaans "koek" and refers to female genitalia.

Leloba Molema

✦

Song One: Malala Swi

I went on a journey with my uncle, malala swi
After a while we rested, malala swi
He said, "Niece, where are the 'heads' due me?" malala swi
I said, "What do you mean, 'heads,' uncle?" swi, swi, swi
He said, "Everything is 'heads,' malala swi
   a thigh is also 'heads.'" swi, swi, swi
I said, "I'm not slept on whilst lying on my back, malala swi
   I'm young and will become pregnant,"
Swi, swi, swi, malala swi

Song Two: Sweep, Sweep, Sweep Girl

Sweep, sweep, sweep girl,
Sweep girl you will see wonders when we've gone
My aunt is a bully,
A bully of a woman
Sweep girl, you will see wonders.

Cakes are sweet,
Marriage is hard
Sweep girl, you will see wonders.

Song Three: Don't Say Oh!

Don't say oh! don't say oh! don't say oh!
You said that you love him.

Song Four: Come Out and See

Come out, come out, come out and see
The child is like a bright star.

Song Five: Look at the Sun

Look at the sun, they've placed it far away
The mothers, the women, have put it far away
There it is, look at it, they've put it far away
The mothers, the women, have placed it far away.

Translated by Leloba Molema

Elizabeth Dube, GOOD AS DEAD

Zimbabwe 2000   siNdebele

In 1980, Zimbabwe attained its independence after ninety years of colonial rule under the British. However, in Matabeleland, home to the Ndebele who make up 20 percent of Zimbabwe's population, peace was short-lived. In mid–1982, in order to deal with what was called a "dissident problem," Prime Minister Robert Mugabe unleashed the specially trained Fifth Brigade on the region (Mugabe's party had been defeated in Matabeleland, while winning the general election). He called this brigade *Gukurahundi*, which means "the storm that washes away the rubbish left over from the last harvest before the spring rains." People who experienced its brutality have never forgotten the horror inflicted by this brigade. In the space of a few weeks, thousands of innocent civilians had been massacred, their bodies dumped in mass graves, down mine shafts, or left to rot in the sun and be scavenged by animals. Thousands of others had been tortured and had their entire homesteads destroyed.

The killings continued off and on through the next several years until 1987. The families of those who suffered such a fate are still deeply pained by the memories and struggle to come to terms with the past. They believe that the spirits of their murdered dead are not at peace and continue to cause problems for the living. One of the hardest things for victims of those years is their inability to understand why they were targeted in this way. Dissidents were very few in number, and the vast majority of those who died were innocent. They understood the violence of the liberation war, but have never been able to explain to themselves the suffering of the *Gukurahundi* years.

Elizabeth Dube's family suffered five murders in the space of a few weeks in 1984. Her account of some of these murders and how they have affected her life comes from an interview I conducted as director of a Matebeland-based non-governmental organization, Amani Trust, which works exclusively with survivors of torture and organized violence with the aim of helping to mend the social fabric damaged by successive civil disturbances in this region of Zimbabwe.

Shari Eppel

✦

It is very painful, what happened to our family in 1984. God seemed to have decided that our family did not deserve to live, and directed all the torrent of His storm in our direction. It was as if a powerful river swept my family away, so many of the Dube family died. If I talk about it now, my heart beats faster and I have a blurred vision. I lose my breath with the pain. It was as if God had decided we were dirt that should be washed away.

All that I am about to describe happened before my eyes, and the eyes of my family. People died one after another; they were like leaves on the ground. We were all as good as dead then; there was no saying from one day to another who would die next. There was no order nor reason for whom they killed; there was no understanding nor explanation, even until today. This gave me the courage to do some of the things I am going to tell you all about—I was as good as dead in any case and my life, like all others, was worth nothing and could not be counted on. They came to try to kill us all, that was clear; they wanted to wipe us all out and start their own next generation in our place. So I thought of myself as dead at that time, and a dead person has courage to do things that a living person who values their life is too afraid to do. . . .

I would like to tell everyone the story of Busani and how he was beaten to death and thrown into a dam. The day that Busani died was a day like any other. Busani was my cousin, a young man and new to our community. I had asked for him to come and help me with the cattle herding, and he had not been there long. He arrived just before the Fifth Brigade began their terror in our community. I had realized by this time that young men in particular were at risk with this brigade. I had heard what they had done the previous week, when they had tied two young men from the village to a tree by their feet, and had then beaten them to death, like that, with their heads dangling near the ground. They were just any two boys—they had done nothing wrong. The whole village saw this happen, and many others were beaten on that day, women and school children too.

So I knew about the cruelty of those soldiers. They arrived at my homestead on the morning of this day, and began their abuse of me. "Where are the dissidents that you cook for?" They would ask such questions and then beat before you could even answer. You would just find yourself lying on the ground being kicked and beaten. I was made to take my cooking utensils out of the kitchen and into the bush to cook for the soldiers. I carried the pots out into the forest, and began to cook for these men, my heart beating with fear.

Then I saw Busani approaching, coming to herd the cattle into their pen. I was so afraid, I knew that if the soldiers saw him, they would do something terrible to him. I tried to warn him that the soldiers were nearby, that he should hide, but he was not paying me attention.

He started to come nearer, as he wanted to pick up his jersey. "Leave your jersey!" I was trying to warn him to run away, but he just kept on coming to pick up the jersey. It was a cream jersey; I can still see it. And as he picked up the jersey, the soldiers saw him and grabbed him. So really, you could say he died because he stopped to pick up that jersey on that day. Something as small as that could be the death of you then.

The soldiers picked up sticks and started to beat Busani. I could hear his cries and I was so full of fear and pain. I could no longer see properly and I was trying not to hear his cries. I could hear the blood rushing in my ears and in front of my eyes I could see nothing. While some soldiers beat him, others were telling me to dish their food. I was in such a terrible state and could not see properly, so I began to dish the soldiers' porridge onto the ground and not onto the plates. This made the soldiers angry. They shouted at me, but they stopped beating Busani. They said that the boy and I had to eat all the porridge that had been dished onto the ground. I could not eat anything, I was too afraid, but they made Busani eat it all, covered with soil and leaves.

Then they put handcuffs on Busani and took him away. That was the last time I saw him alive. But I heard from others that they led that poor boy through the bush, beating him and saying things like, "You are a dissident, where have you put your gun?" When you are in a situation like that, you will say anything to stop the beating, agree with all accusations if you think it will help. And Busani was saying, "Yes, I know the dissidents, I will show you their guns." Of course he could not, because there were no dissidents in our area. But he took them to the dam, saying he would find guns there, hoping to buy time, I suppose. Of course at the dam he could not find guns, and so they killed him and threw him into the water.

I was the one to find him, but that was seven whole days later. I was herding the cattle there to drink, and I noticed that they were very nervous of something, and they would not go down to the water. I was coming behind them, and suspected something. I, too, was afraid at that—the soldiers were still around and I was afraid they were at the water. My dog was whimpering and running to the water and back to me.

I knew I had to establish what was going on, so I went very carefully to the edge of the water. And then I could see that there was something floating in the water, out in the middle. At first I was confused, could not recognize what the object was—and then I identified that jersey, that cream jersey. It was Busani floating face down in the water, and all I could see was that jersey, the one that cost him his life, and the glint of handcuffs behind his back where he floated. That jersey floating, a pale shade of coffee—that is the image I can recall. I felt the blood rushing to my head and I felt faint. I did not know what to do. What could I do? A woman there on her own, and now I have discovered this poor dead child, who was my relative, and who had come to the region because I had requested him to herd my cattle.

I went straight home to bed. I stayed in my bed all night, but could find no rest. This boy was my responsibility—I was going to have to do something about this situation. He could not float there, rotting, and scaring the cattle forever. But everyone was so afraid, including me. I, too, was so afraid.

I realized that if I did not do something, he would float and decompose forever. So the next day, I went to tell the village head what I had found. "My child is in the dam. I know people are afraid, but we must take him out." Actually, the headman was very afraid. He said that if the soldiers caught us taking him from the water, then we would also be killed. I told him, if the soldiers want to kill anybody for doing that, they can kill me, I consider myself dead anyway. They had killed Busani for nothing; sooner or later they would kill me and they might then just as well kill me trying to bury Busani.

I think this made those men a bit ashamed, that I as a woman should be braver than them in this situation, and so they agreed to come with me. But they were not planning well—they were so scared. I told them to meet me at the water. I was the one who had to fetch a spade and some plastic bags and a blanket, and I took my dog with me as well. I went down to the water and there I had to wait for them to come. I sat on a rock next to the water's edge, and looked at poor Busani, floating swollen and rotten in the dam.

It was awful for the men. They waded out into the water to pull him to shore. The dam was not that deep, but the corpse was hard to handle. Busani had been many days in the water by then and was quite decomposed. As the men tried to steer him to shore and float his body to the edge, the flesh fell off the bones in their hands—that is how rotten he was. Their fingers just went straight through his flesh: he was disintegrating, still with the jersey and the handcuffs on.

While they rescued his body, I was looking for a place to bury him. There was an ant bear hole nearby, an animal's hole. Usually you only bury dogs in such a place, but the ground was very hard as it was a drought time, and we had to be quick. Nobody had time or energy to dig deep in such circumstances, so I took the spade and opened the animal den for Busani. I also collected big stones to cover the entrance in due course.

The men brought Busani out, and were in a state of nerves and were also shocked by the state of the body. They wanted to bury him then and there, as fast as they could, just shove him quickly in the hole and leave. But I had been thinking about the handcuffs. They did not belong to us and I was worried that if we buried Busani with the handcuffs, then in a few days' time the Fifth Brigade might come looking for them. They would beat us if they discovered that we had buried the handcuffs and might even force us to exhume the body to retrieve their property. Also, I did not want Busani to be buried in handcuffs.

So that is why I did it, the thing I did next. I told the men to lie Busani on his side, so that the handcuffs were visible. His flesh was shredding off, and the handcuffs had dug right into his arm, so that they were now partly buried in his flesh, which was soapy and sloppy and white with decay. I picked up a spade—like this—high in the air, and then hit his wrists as hard as I could with the blade of the spade. Although the flesh was soggy, the bones were hard, and I had to hit him several times to cut the hands right off. When I finally severed them, the impact of my blows meant that the hands shot away from him, they were displaced quite a distance from his arms, and the handcuffs dropped to the ground between the hands and the body.

The men were astonished at me doing this. But I was as good as dead then; fear was not an issue at that point. Actually I was angry too at what had happened, and did not want Busani to lie there in the handcuffs of the killers.

I picked up the hands which were falling to pieces and put them with the rest of the body in the blanket, and we rolled him all up together still in his coffee-coloured jersey, and buried him like that, his hands were buried along with the rest of him. The smell of the body was so bad that we had to work fast.

But as for the handcuffs, I picked them up and wrapped them in a plastic bag, all stinking and with bits of Busani's flesh still on them, and I took them away. I just thought to myself, I am a dead person now anyway, Busani died for nothing and now I feel dead too. I was a dead person at that moment.

And what did I do with those handcuffs? Having them made me angry; they reminded me of the fact that Busani died for nothing. When the Fifth Brigade called a meeting and made everyone attend, I went and I took the handcuffs with me. At the meeting, I just walked straight up to the soldiers, the ones I had been forced to cook for, and I just gave them the handcuffs, just like that, still wrapped in the plastic since the day we buried Busani. I just gave them straight to the soldiers. I wanted to ask them, why did they kill Busani, who was new to the area and knew nothing about dissidents? I did not have the words to ask them, but giving them the handcuffs was a way of telling them to their faces that I knew of their crime, I knew what they had done at the dam. Yes, the handcuffs were the proof of that and words were not necessary.

I thought they would kill me but I did not care. I was angry, but of course I was also so afraid. I expected blows to follow, but all the same, I just stood there in front of all those witnesses and gave them the handcuffs. But they did not hit me. They took the handcuffs from me and did not say one word. In silence, they took that pair of handcuffs and said nothing. There was nothing to say, they had no answer to the question that the handcuffs were asking. They could not say why they killed that child, and so they said nothing.

To this day, I think I am one of the few people in our region that did something that silenced those cruel men. For one minute, I think they had nothing to say because the handcuffs left them without words to justify Busani's murder and all their other crimes at that time.

I have never been able to forget that incident. I cannot forget it. . . .

My father and my brother were the next to die, a few weeks later. They were shot to death at night in their beds, in my homestead. My brother died with his stomach shot right out of him, his intestines hanging off the side of the bed to the floor. My father tried to cover his face with his hands as Fifth Brigade stood over him and shot him. The bullets went straight through his body and his head, and his fingers were blown to pieces by the bullets. His hands were shot off.

When I think of Busani now, I see him coming down the road towards me, looking for his jersey, and I am trying to warn him to leave the jersey and run away. My vision goes and I want to cry; I cannot see or think when I have that image, because I know what happens next. . . .

Busani's spirit is not at rest. People have seen his spirit—it wanders around the area, in the form of a pale light, near the ant bear hole where he is buried. He is not happy to be buried in such a place. He is not peaceful—he is lost. I feel so sad when I see that light, and remember how sorrowful

Busani is at what happened to him. What he wishes for is to be taken out of that place and to be given a decent funeral witnessed by all his family, as is everybody's right. I would like his body to be removed from that place, so that all can witness for themselves what happened to Busani, how he was murdered and had to have his hands amputated in order not to lie in handcuffs. All this needs to be witnessed. Then his spirit will be at peace, and I will be able to think of that time without this panic, without the deep pain that rests just here in my heart.

Transcribed by Shari Eppel
Translated by Shari Eppel and Nicholas Ndlovu

Unity Dow, CARING FOR THE DYING
Botswana 2000   English

Born in 1949, Unity Dow has distinguished herself in several areas. She cofounded the Women and Law in Southern Africa Research Project in 1989 and the Baobab Primary School in Gaborone, Botswana, in 1991. She also founded the Metlhaetsile Women's Center in 1990 and was its director until 1998, when she was appointed judge of the High Court, the first woman in Botswana to attain that position. She was also the first lawyer in Botswana to draw the attention of the courts to a law that discriminated against Botswana women who married foreign nationals (see the text "Citizenship: An Open Letter to the Attorney-General"). Married to an American, Dow personally struggled to gain the rights of Botswana citizenship for her children. She won the case, *Attorney General v. Unity Dow*, in 1990.

This excerpt from *Far and Beyon'*—Dow's first novel—offers a realistic view of HIV-AIDS. Set in Botswana during the rapid escalation of HIV-AIDS fatalities, the novel focuses on the distraught and desperate members of the community as they bury their dead, deal with their grief, and anticipate the imminent deaths of other loved ones.

Nobantu Rasebotsa

✦

She used to be a proud woman. Tall, poised, nose slightly turned up. Lips set in the permanent promise of a smile. She had been poor too. Materially poor, that is. But proud. She used to have a quiet dignity. A dignity some people are born with and others spend years trying to acquire. She was not any of these anymore. She was hardly human anymore. Mosa watched her as she lay under a tree, looking like something that had survived a fire. If what she had become could be described as survival under any circumstances. She was the colour of tar, an unhealthy black-grey, and her hair was thin and reddish.

Next to her sat her daughter Bibi, dazed. Although she was about two years old, she had stopped walking months ago and slid about on her bottom.

She moved very little. She had nowhere to go. Mosa thought she looked like some strange bird. Her neck was stretched and her mouth looked like a chopped off beak. Her neck was rigid. Her eyes occasionally swivelled from side to side, otherwise they were on her mother, as if she was afraid should she move away, or even look away, her mother might just disappear. It was perhaps a testimony to the power of the maternal bond that the little girl still saw, in this blackened, horizontal remnant of humanity, her mother.

Mosa was sitting on a wooden bench with two other women. They had come to see Cecilia, who had been moved out of the hot tin-roofed house for some air. Tears welled up as Mosa looked at this human being who was once so full of life. One of the women unable to hold back her tears stood up and left without a word. So much pain. So little hope. So many dying. So many children watching as their loved ones waste away and die. Many little faces full of fear and confusion. So little time to love the living as all emotions go into caring for the dying.

"I am sick, Mosa. I am sick," was all Cecilia could manage to whisper.

Mosa had nothing to offer in reply. She could not bring herself to offer any assurances about getting well soon. Her eyes moved from Cecilia's to the little girl's face. In response to her mother's words Bibi had moved closer to her and was now gripping her thumb. Cecilia's hands were no more than a collection of bones. Bones reaching for bones, thought Mosa as she watched the little girl's bony fingers wrap around her mother's bony thumb. Could the human warmth the child was seeking possibly be found in that lifeless hand?

"Do you want me to take her away for a while. To get her to play with other children?" Mosa asked.

"No, no. I have to see her. Do not take her away? She will not let you anyway. She will not agree to go." Her voice, though low, was clear. She began to cough, her sunken chest heaving and heaving, as if it would just split open right there.

"Can I talk to you, Mosa? I need to ask you a favour."

The other woman left the shade in response and went to join Cecilia's mother and other members of the family sitting under another tree some distance away.

"Will you go to Kagiso Office? You know the office for women and children. I want Bibi's father to pay child support. Before I die, I want to know someone will support her. Do you know anything about such things?"

Cecilia's voice was fading and Mosa had to move closer to listen. This meant sitting on the mat next to the dying woman. Mosa was quite sure Cecilia had TB but this was no time to think about personal dangers. Cecilia, lying on her side, grabbed Mosa's hand and Mosa was surprised, even alarmed, at the power in that grip. For a brief moment she panicked. What if I cannot get her to let me go?

"I have only been at the place once. But I do not know if they can help. Yes I will go and find out for you."

"You have to do it fast. I do not have a lot of time left. But I will not die until I am sure that something has been done. Please hurry." Having made her request, Cecilia let go of Mosa's hand and closed her eyes. Was she dead? Was she dying? But she seemed to be dozing off. Mosa stood up and bid the rest of the family farewell. She looked once more at little Bibi and then her tears came rolling down. She thought of the saying that one can return to all previous homes, except for the most precious of all, one's mother's womb. Bibi was indeed trying to be as close to that home as possible, laying her head on her mother's belly. Her eyes still closed, the mother winced with pain. But she did not push the child away. As if sensing Mosa's thoughts, she uttered, "Let her be. This pain cannot compare with the pain of leaving her behind."

Mosa hurried away, like the woman before her, leaving the yard with rigid shoulders, trying to hide the anguish she felt. The family had plenty to deal with and did not have the time to comfort those who had come offering comfort to begin with.

Mosa's anguish was compounded by her knowledge that similar scenarios were playing themselves out in many homes in the wards, villages and towns countrywide: young people dropping like kernels from a maize cob in the hands of a greedy man. Her own brothers' deaths had gone the same way.

Yvette Christiansë, GENERATIONS

South Africa 2001   English and Afrikaans

Yvette Christiansë was born in Doornfontein, Johannesburg, in 1954. Her family moved first to Swaziland in order to leave apartheid, then settled in Australia in the late 1970s. After training as a teacher and working as a journalist and editor, Christiansë graduated with a doctorate in English literature from the University of Sydney in 1998. In 1997 she joined Fordham University, New York, as an assistant professor. Her fiction and poetry (along with scholarly writing) has been published in Australia and the United States, and she has received one of Australia's highest honors for poetry, the Harri Jones Memorial Prize.

Christiansë began writing as a six year old, encouraged by storytelling from her grandmother, grandfather, and mother. At thirteen she recognized how sharply her experiences of the world differed from the writers read at school, and as a young woman in Sydney, she found the words to start writing about apartheid without the sensationalism it so readily offered through its spectacle of violence and cruelty. Graceful, courageous, and nuanced, her verse draws together the sacramental and the elemental, narratives of exploration and exile, the voices of emperors and slaves. Her first volume, *Castaways* (1999), opens on St. Helena, where her grandmother was born, and ends in the present, with a young woman's "voyage out," far from the slave past yet still "hungering for / steady ground." "Generations," hitherto unpublished and part of a longer work called "Requiem for a Republic," again reflects on journeys of desire, its voice both somber and sanguine.

Dorothy Driver

✦

Do not believe everything you hear

The dream holds here. It circles itself, holds
like talk that recalls two decades at the end of an evening
and those who have tried to find their Jerusalems
find, with each moment of rest, the way that the land
inhales them
    Heera, Vader van Genaade
    Gee my dag en klere
    Kinders maak ek myself [1]
Children who come here, come in troops
as if chained to a circus—their dear voices
are locked in the thrall of a song that will please
endless rows of the inner circle. We, we who are chained
to the walls of our childhood, salute you
and we give you our prayers while you surge ahead
like the storm of a ship that ploughs itself
into the distance of a new land, a land
your yesterdays can only imagine.
Do not forget us
    Ons het jou lief
    Ons onthou julle
    Ons onthou julle, hoor [2]
The point is that we speak softly.
We speak at gravesites where stone is,
implacably, the voice we cannot understand.
We carve ourselves into a lack of meaning
and we set off again. We press on,
deep into the destination of the past.
We sail, like vessels built for these waves.
And these waves are as if sand.
And we are like children ourselves, children
who have been told that the sand will overtake us,
like trees and other vegetation overtaken by dunes
at the edge of the waves.
    Bid vir ons. Versoek ons.
    O kinders van die toekomstig
    van die onbelowe, bid vir ons [3]
Extreme are our ways and our lives are blown
by the idea of horizons that lie deep in scriptures
that are the measure of dreams. *We beseech thee,*
we beseech thee and thy generations. For you are ours
and our lives have been laid down in the trenches
of the past as we chain ourselves to the wake

of such ships that storm seas, these seas
that ring and link themselves to such rhymes
that circle the world and clip the wings of birds.

1. Lord, Father of Mercy
   grant me strength and clothes
   children I'll make myself

2. We love you
   We remember you
   We remember you, hear

3. Pray for us. Entreat us
   O children of the future
   of the unbelievable, pray for us

CONTRIBUTORS

EDITORS

M. J. Daymond is professor and university fellow at the University of Natal, Durban. She has edited several volumes of fiction by Bessie Head, Lauretta Ngcobo, and Frances Colenso and co-edited the volume *South African Feminisms: Writing, Theory, and Criticism 1990–1994* (1996). She is an editor of the journal *Current Writing*.

Dorothy Driver is professor of English at the University of Cape Town, with an annual visiting appointment at the University of Chicago and an adjunct professorship at the University of Adelaide. She has edited books on Pauline Smith and Nadine Gordimer, and has published essays on Anne Barnard, Olive Schreiner, Bessie Head, Ellen Kuzwayo, Tsitsi Dangarembga, Yvonne Vera, Zoë Wicomb, and others. For twenty years she produced the *Journal of Commonwealth Literature*'s annual survey of South African English literature and literary criticism.

Sheila Meintjes is senior lecturer in political studies at the University of the Witwatersrand, Johannesburg. She currently serves as a member of South Africa's Commission on Gender Equality. In the 1980s she was active in anti-apartheid women's organizations in the Cape and in Natal, and later was a member of the Research Supervisory Group of the Women's National Coalition. She is co-editor of *The Aftermath: Women in Post-Conflict Transformation* (2002).

Leloba Molema is senior lecturer in the department of English at the University of Botswana and holds a Ph.D. in ethnology from Johannes Gutenberg University, Mainz, Germany. She is the editor of the academic journal *Marang* and co-editor, with Nobantu Rasebotsa, of *Women Creating the Future: An Anthology of Women's Writing in Southern Africa* (1998). Her present research interest is in anti-apartheid Afrikaans literature written by white South Africans.

Chiedza Musengezi is a founding member and director of Zimbabwe Women Writers, an organization that nurtures women's voices through writing. She studied at the University of Zimbabwe and has worked as a teacher and editor, in addition to serving as director of the Women and AIDS Support Network. Several of her short stories and poems have been published locally and internationally.

Margie Orford is an independent scholar whose interests span book publishing and film. She co-edited the anthology *Coming on Strong: Writing by Namibian Women* (1996) and subsequently worked with emerging women writers. Her film work includes the research and conceptualization of a series of documentaries on women, *Stories of Tenderness and Power*. She has written on Namibian literature and was awarded a Fulbright scholarship in 1999.

Nobantu Rasebotsa is senior lecturer in and former head of the department of English at the University of Botswana. She has published on the fiction of Alex La Guma and Nadine Gordimer, and also writes about African American literature. With Leloba Molema, she co-edited *Women Creating the Future: An Anthology of Women's Writing in Southern Africa* (1998). Her current research is on HIV-AIDS in African literature.

ASSOCIATE EDITORS

Heike Becker is senior lecturer in anthropology at the University of the Western Cape. She previously taught at the University of Namibia and has published extensively on gender in Namibian culture and history. Her current research interests are mainly in the field of war, violence, and memory in northern Namibia.

Devarakshanam Govinden completed her Ph.D. at the University of Natal, Durban, with a focus on Indian women's writing. She is former dean of the faculty of education of the University of Durban-Westville, and has presented papers locally and internationally on subjects ranging from education in South Africa to women's writing and women and peace.

Mary Lederer holds a Ph.D. from the University of California, Los Angeles, where she wrote a dissertation on the work of Bessie Head. She lectures in the department of English at the University of Botswana, and her current research focuses on English-language literature set in Botswana.

V. M. Sisi Maqagi lectures in the department of English at Vista University, South Africa. She is writing a doctoral dissertation on Bessie Head. She has published poetry in *Kotaz*, a Port Elizabeth magazine.

Virginia Phiri is a writer and art critic, as well as a human rights activist. She speaks seven languages and works in Harare, Zimbabwe, as an accountant and tax consultant.

Cristiana Pugliese is senior lecturer at the School of Languages at the University of Potchefstroom, South Africa. She is the author of *Author,*

Publisher and Gikuyu Nationalist: The Life and Writings of Gakaara wa Wanjau (1995) and serves on the board of directors of the journal *Englishes: Contemporary Literatures in English.*

TRANSLATORS AND HEADNOTE WRITERS

Yvette Abrahams completed her doctorate on the link between intellectual and other forms of violence against black women. Her future research projects include gender relations in Khoekhoe history, and surviving indigenous knowledge systems among women.

Tuzyline Jita Allan is associate professor of English at Baruch College, CUNY. She is the author of *Womanist and Feminist Aesthetics: A Comparative Review* (1995) and co-editor, with Thomas Fink, of the anthology *Literature Around the Globe* (1994). A collection of articles co-edited by Allan and Helen Mugambi, titled *African Masculinities in Literature and Film*, is forthcoming. Allan is currently writing a book on black transatlantic feminism.

Megan Biesele, Ph.D., has worked with Ju/'hoan San people in Namibia and Botswana since 1970 as both anthropological researcher and human rights activist. She serves as the president of the School of Expressive Culture in Austin, Texas, and as the coordinator for the Kalahari Peoples Fund, also in Austin. She co-authored *Healing Makes Our Hearts Happy: Spirituality and Transformation Among the Ju/'hoansi of the Kalahari* (1997) with Richard Katz and Verna St. Denis.

Maitseo Bolaane lectures in the history department at the University of Botswana. She is currently completing work for her Ph.D. at Oxford University, researching the comparative environmental history of East Africa and Botswana, and focusing on the relationship between local communities and wildlife conservation policy.

Inge Brinkman is a member of the department of African languages and cultures at the University of Ghent, Belgium. She is the editor of *Singing in the Bush: MPLA Songs During the War for Independence in South-East Angola (1966–1975)* (2001) and co-editor of *Grandmother's Footsteps: Oral Tradition and South-East Angolan Narratives on the Colonial Encounter* (1999).

Catherine Burns teaches in historical studies at the University of Natal, Durban. She researches the social and intellectual history of medicine, health, and women in Southern Africa, focusing on the nineteenth and twentieth centuries. She is currently working on two books, one of which is a biography of Louisa Mvemve.

Chandré Carstens is a graduate student and tutor in the department of English at the University of Cape Town. Her current research is in the field of Afrikaans cultural production.

Anthony Chennells is associate professor of English at the University of Zimbabwe and has published widely on Southern African literature, art, and religion. With Flora Veit-Wild he edited *Emerging Perspectives on Dambudzo Marechera* (1999).

Pam Claassen currently works at the University of Namibia as a research and publications officer, and resides in Windhoek, Namibia.

David Coplan is professor and chair in social anthropology at the University of the Witwatersrand, Johannesburg, and has published extensively on the anthropology of African performing arts. His publications include the groundbreaking study *In Township Tonight! South Africa's Black City Music and Theater* (1985).

Sarah Dupont-Mkhonza lectures at the University of Swaziland. She is a writer, activist, and journalist who has written poems, short stories, and plays in English and siSwati, as well as two novels, *Pains of a Maid* and *What the Future Holds*.

Ingrid de Kok, a poet and critic, is an associate professor in adult education at the University of Cape Town. She has edited books of cultural criticism and published two volumes of poetry. In addition her poems have appeared in numerous national and international journals and anthologies. (See the selection "Our Sharpeville," 1987, in this volume.)

Elizabeth Elbourne teaches in the department of history of McGill University, Montreal. Her forthcoming book is entitled *Blood Ground: Missions, Colonialism, and the Contest for Christianity in the Cape Colony and Britain, 1799–1853* and her research interests include the early nineteenth-century Cape Colony, women's history, and the history of religion.

Shari Eppel is a clinical psychologist, human rights historian, and the primary author of *Breaking the Silence, Building True Peace* (1997), the first historical account of the atrocities of the Mugabe government in Matabeleland post independence. She is director of the Amani Trust in Bulawayo, Zimbabwe, an organization devoted to helping victims of torture.

A. C. Fick teaches journalism and media studies at Rhodes University, South Africa. He has published on representations of subjectivity in South African literature.

Miki Flockemann teaches in the department of English at the University of the Western Cape. Her primary research interest is the comparative study of diasporic literatures and the aesthetics of transformation in both fiction and performance texts.

M. Furusa is a lecturer in the department of African Languages and Literature (Shona) at the University of Zimbabwe.

Pumla Dineo Gqola is a lecturer in the department of English and Classical Culture at the University of the Free State, South Africa.

Colette Guldimann has studied and taught at the Universities of Cape Town and London. Her research and publications focus on Southern African writing and culture.

Liz Gunner has written widely on African orature and literature. She is professor of English studies at the University of Natal, Pietermaritzburg. Her most recent book is *The Man of Heaven and the Beautiful Ones of God / UMuntu wasezulwini nabantu bahle bakaNkulunkulu: Writings from a South African Church* (2002).

Zingisa Guzana is a lecturer at Vista University, South Africa. Her research interests are in gender and the translation of women's writings.

W. Haacke is professor of African languages at the University of Namibia. He specializes in the linguistics of Khoekhoegowab (Nama/Damara).

Samukele Hadebe is a lecturer in the department of African Languages and Literature (Ndebele) at the University of Zimbabwe.

Werner Hillebrecht is a librarian and archivist. He compiled the Namibian bibliographic database NAMLIT and works at the National Archives of Namibia.

Kaleni Hiyalwa was born in northern Namibia and went into exile at age twelve. She is a published novelist, poet, and short story writer and lives and works in Windhoek, Namibia.

Janet Hodgson is a former lecturer in the department of Religious Studies at the University of Cape Town. Her publications include *The God of the Xhosa* (1982), *Princess Emma* (1987), and, with co-author Jay Kothare, *Vision Quest: Native Spirituality and the Church in Canada* (1990).

Diane Hubbard is the co-ordinator of the Gender Research and Advocacy Project at the Legal Assistance Centre, a public interest law firm based in

Namibia. Her publications include "The Many Faces of Feminism in Namibia," co-authored with C. Solomon, in Amrita Basu, ed., *The Challenge of Local Feminisms* (1995).

Heather Hughes teaches at the University of Lincoln, South Africa. She has co-authored a bibliography on South African women and is currently completing a biography of John Dube, the first president of the African National Congress.

Christopher Hurst is the penname used by Christopher John (M.A., Natal). He has worked with community theatre groups in Zimbabwe both as a teacher and a performer. In 1997 he joined the Drama and Performance Studies Program at the University of Natal, Durban, as lecturer. He was married to the late Elizabeth Ncube.

Fredricka Ndeshi Immanuel was born in Okaku, Namibia. She went into exile in 1977 and returned 1991 after independence. She is an educator whose work focuses on women and children.

Joyce Jenje-Makwenda is a visiting lecturer at the University of Zimbabwe. She is also an actress, published writer, and researcher. An accomplished film producer and director, she researched and directed *Zimbabwe Township Music*. She is currently working on a weekly television series with the Zimbabwe Broadcasting Corporation.

Ackson M. Kanduza is a graduate of the University of Zambia and holds a Ph.D. from Dalhousie University, Nova Scotia. He teaches the economic history of Southern Africa and gender studies at the University of Swaziland, where he is an associate professor of history.

Cons Uaraisa Karamata was educated in sociology and economics in Namibia and in Germany. He is a research assistant at the Multi-Disciplinary Research Centre at the University of Namibia.

Yahmillah Katjirua translates her mother tongue, otjiHerero, into English. She has worked for UNICEF in Namibia, and is currently employed at the Namibian Tender Board.

Kathryn Limakatso Kendall, Ph.D., spent two years at the University of Lesotho as a Fulbright Scholar and was the editor and amanuensis for Mpho 'M'atsepo Nthunya, the author of *Singing Away the Hunger: Stories of a Life in Lesotho* (1996).

Tselanngwefela Komerese completed his B.A. in humanities at the University of Botswana, majoring in history and English. He currently teaches social studies and English at Etsha Community Junior Secondary School in the Okavango region of Botswana.

Writing in Afrikaans, and later also in English, **Antjie Krog** has published nine volumes of poetry, one short novel, two children's books of verse, and a work of nonfiction stemming from her reporting on South Africa's Truth and Reconciliation Commission. (See the selection "The Birth of This Country's Language," 1998, in this volume.)

Desireé Lewis completed her Ph.D. at the University of Cape Town with a thesis on Bessie Head. She has written on feminist theory, Southern African writing, and popular culture, and has taught in the English departments at the University of the Western Cape and the University of Natal, Pietermaritzburg. She is presently working at the University of Cape Town's African Gender Institute.

Fiona Lloyd is one of the cofounders of WICSA: Southern African Women in Contemporary Culture. She currently works in Zimbabwe as a media trainer in conflict areas.

Rene Lotter has worked as a television producer, in Windhoek, Namibia, and has edited and translated many publications. She was a columnist for the newspaper *The Namibian* for several years, and now lives and works in Cape Town.

Lily Mafela is senior lecturer responsible for training secondary school history teachers in the Faculty of Education at the University of Botswana. Following her studies at the University of Botswana, University of Bristol, and Northwestern University, she did groundbreaking work on women's education in precolonial and colonial Botswana.

Born in Soweto in 1979, **Rirhandzu Mageza** is a final-year undergraduate student at the University of Cape Town, concentrating on political studies, as well as gender and women's studies.

James Mahlaule is a lecturer in the department of linguistics at the University of Zimbabwe. He lectures in Communication and Language for Specific Purposes.

Beauty Malope completed her B.A. in humanities at the University of Botswana, majoring in English and history, and currently teaches social studies at Maoka Community Junior Secondary School in Gaborone, Botswana.

Ntongela Masilela is professor of English and world literature at Pitzer

College in Claremont, California. He is also adjunct professor at the University of California, Irvine.

Mara Miller is a professional German/English translator. She lives and works in Windhoek, Namibia.

Alpheons Moroke received his B.A. in English from the University of Botswana and wrote a senior thesis on African American literature by women. He currently works as a journalist for the *Botswana Guardian*.

Thulisile Motsa-Dladla is the chief executive officer of an organization specializing in adult literacy in the Kingdom of Swaziland. She holds a master's degree in administration and has worked at various schools in the country as head of department, deputy head, and principal.

Levi Namaseb was born in the Namib Desert at Khori!gaos. One of six children, he was brought up by his mother in hunter-gatherer and oral culture. He is a lecturer in Khoekhoe literature and linguistics at the University of Namibia and wishes to promote the San languages after completing his Ph.D.

Nicholas Ndlovu is a project officer with the Amani Trust in Harare, Zimbabwe, a charity organization that rehabilitates torture victims. He works as a counselor and rehabilitation technician.

Lauretta Ngcobo was born and educated in KwaZulu-Natal, South Africa, went into exile in 1969, and returned to South Africa in 1992. She has published two novels, *Cross of Gold* (1981) and *And They Didn't Die* (1990), and edited a collection of essays on writing by "blackwomen" in Britain, *Let It Be Told* (1988). (See the selection "The Rending of the Veil," 1981, in this volume.)

Nepeti Nicanor is a mother and writer who is especially interested in the development of literature in Africa and the development of African languages. She lives with her daughters Leila and Megan in Windhoek, Namibia.

Abner Nyamende completed his Ph.D. at the University of Cape Town, where he is senior lecturer in Xhosa and African literature. His research on African-language literature includes a special interest in oral literature. Since 2001 he has served as president of the African Languages Association of Southern Africa. In addition to scholarly articles, he has published his poetry and fiction both locally and abroad, and co-wrote the Xhosa book *Imbongi Ijong' Exhantini* (1995).

Jeff Opland teaches at Charterhouse and at the School of Oriental and African Studies at the University of London. He is the author of books and articles on Anglo-Saxon and Xhosa literature, including *Anglo-Saxon Oral Poetry* (1980), *Xhosa Oral Poetry* (1983), and *Xhosa Poets and Poetry* (1998).

Candice Petersen studied at the University of Cape Town and in 1996 spent a year in Germany as an exchange student sponsored by Youth for Understanding. She is the first in her household to attend a tertiary institution, and her interests include television, the shifting forms of feminism, and the contradictory emotions evoked by racial definitions in varying political contexts.

Karen Press has published five collections of poetry, and her work has appeared in magazines and anthologies in South Africa, the U.K., the U.S., Canada, and France. She has also published children's stories, short fiction for adults, and science and mathematics textbooks. She lives in Cape Town. (See the selection "Krotoa's Story," 1990, in this volume.)

Terence Ranger, visiting professor of history at the University of Zimbabwe, has been researching and writing on Zimbabwean history for forty-five years. He has written seven books, including *Voices from the Rocks: Nature, Culture, and History in the Matopos Hills of Zimbabwe* (1999), *Revolt in Southern Rhodesia, 1896–97: A Study of African Resistance* (1984), and *Dance and Society in Eastern Africa, 1890–1970: The Bemi Ngoma* (1975).

Fiona Ross lectures in the department of social anthropology at the University of Cape Town. Her doctoral research, recently published by Pluto Press, reflects on women's testimonies before South Africa's Truth and Reconciliation Commission and on women's experiences of political activism.

Meg Samuelson is a Mellon fellow and Ph.D. candidate in the department of English at the University of Cape Town. Her dissertation is on gendered representations of the nation in post-apartheid South African narratives.

Esther Sbongile Sangweni is senior lecturer and assistant head in the department of English at the University of Zululand, South Africa.

A professor of African languages and literature at the University of Wisconsin-Madison, **Harold Scheub** has taught and conducted research in Eastern and Southern Africa. His most recent book is *A Dictionary of African Mythology: The Mythmaker as Storyteller* (1999).

Mary Simons is senior lecturer in the department of political studies at the University of Cape Town. A gender activist and labour and community mediator during the 1980s and 1990s, she was restricted under the Suppression of Communism Act (1976–1981) because of her anti-apartheid activity. She is currently a member of the Ministerial Advisory Committee to the Minister of Provincial and Local Government and recently co-edited *One Woman, One Vote: The Gender Politics of South African Elections* (2002).

Rosa Schneider has written on German settler women in Namibia during the German colonial period, and in particular, their autobiographical and fictional work. She is currently a freelance teacher in girls' and women's educational programs in Germany.

Gail Smith is contributing editor at *The Star* newspaper in Johannesburg and has worked in broadcast and print media internationally. A researcher and contributor on the documentary film *The Life and Times of Sara Baartman* (1998), she is now working on a documentary about the return of Baartman's remains to South Africa.

Irene Staunton is the former publisher of Baobab Books in Harare, Zimbabwe, and is now director of Weaver Press. She is also editor of the Heinemann African Writers Series.

Dianne Stewart completed her M.A. at the University of Natal, Durban, where she studied African languages and developed a special interest in women's issues. She is an author and freelance journalist whose books for children are widely translated.

Enamile Tlhobolo completed his B.A. in humanities at the University of Botswana, majoring in theology and religious studies. He teaches religious education at Masunga Senior Secondary School near Francistown, Botswana.

Philippa Tucker is an M.A. research student in the department of political studies at the University of the Witwatersrand, Johannesburg.

Elizabeth van Heyningen, Ph.D., is a research associate in the department of historical studies at the University of Cape Town. She has published on the social history of medicine and the history of Cape Town, as well as on colonial women in South Africa. She is co-author of *Cape Town in the Twentieth Century: An Illustrated Social History* (1999).

Wendy Urban-Mead is a doctoral candidate in African history at Columbia University and is completing a dissertation on the Brethren in Christ Church of Zimbabwe in the colonial period. Her article "'Girls of the Gate': Questions of Purity and Piety at the Mtshabezi Girls' Primary School in Colonial Zimbabwe, 1908–1940" was published in *Le Fait Missionaire* (August 2001).

Flora Veit-Wild is professor of African literatures at Humboldt University in Berlin. She lived for ten years in Zimbabwe and has published extensively on Zimbabwean literature. She is a cofounder of Zimbabwe Women Writers.

Nomfundo Walaza is the director of the Trauma Centre for Survivors of Violence and Torture in Cape Town. A clinical psychologist, she completed her training at the University of Cape Town. She has helped to shape a gendered response to South Africa's Truth and Reconciliation Commission.

Linda Waldman is a social anthropologist currently lecturing at Dublin Business School, Dublin. She has a long association with the towns and people of the Northern Cape and recently completed a Ph.D. on Griqua identity in South Africa. This research examines national and local identities, looking at the cultural dynamics of gender, status, religion, and politics.

Mary Watson is a Sainsbury fellow and graduate student in the department of English at the University of Cape Town. Her research involves popular forms of literature in postcolonial contexts.

Peggy Watson moved to Zimbabwe from England in 1980 and became one of the multiracial group of women who, in 1983, formed Women's Action Group. She is now a board member of that organization and authored a history of its formation and work, *Determined to Act* (1998). Professionally she has worked as a journalist, teacher, and social work adviser.

Melanie Yap, former journalist and general secretary of the Chinese Association of South Africa, is co-author of *Colour, Confusion and Concessions: The History of the Chinese in South Africa* (1996), the definitive history of the local Chinese community.

N. B. Zondi lectures in the isiZulu program at the University of Natal, Durban. Her teaching and research interests are in Zulu traditional literature.

PERMISSIONS ACKNOWLEDGMENTS AND SOURCES

For previously published texts not in the public domain, the rights holders are indicated below. Original texts published for the first time in this volume are copyrighted in the names of their authors. Except where noted below, the English-language translations contained in this volume were commissioned for this edition and are copyrighted in the names of their translators. Headnotes contained in this volume were commissioned for this edition and are copyrighted in the name of the Feminist Press. Archives and libraries that provided access to rare texts, or gave permission to reproduce them, are acknowledged below, and sources not indicated in the headnotes are listed.

In the case of oral materials, such as interviews and songs, every effort has been made to locate and gain permission to publish from the original speaker(s). Anyone who can provide information about copyright holders who have not been previously located is urged to contact the Feminist Press. Those seeking permission to reprint or quote from any part of this book should also contact the Feminist Press at the following address: Rights and Permissions, The Feminist Press at the City University of New York, The Graduate Center, 365 Fifth Avenue, Suite 5406, New York, NY 10016.

Anonymous, **AUNT, STRETCH OUT THE BLANKET**
Translation © 1994, reprinted by permission of David Coplan from: Coplan, David. 1994. *In the Time of Cannibals: World Music of South Africa's Basotho Migrants*. Johannesburg: Witwatersrand University Press.

Anonymous, **I AM A WAILING FOOL**
Translation © 1994, reprinted by permission of David Coplan from: Coplan, David. 1994. *In the Time of Cannibals: World Music of South Africa's Basotho Migrants*. Johannesburg: Witwatersrand University Press.

Anonymous, **A MOTHER PRAISES HER BABY**
Translation © 1966, reprinted by permission of Willard Trask from: Trask, Willard, ed. 1966. *The Unwritten Song*. London: Collier-Macmillan; New York: Macmillan.

Anonymous, **SONG OF THE AFFLICTED**
Translation from: Brown, John Croumbie. 1846. *Narrative of an Exploratory Tour to the North-East of the Colony of the Cape of Good Hope, by the Revs. T. Arbousset and F. Daumas of the Paris Missionary Society*. Cape Town: A. S. Robertson and Saul Solomon.

Anonymous, THE STORY OF NGANGEZWE AND MNYAMANA
Text courtesy of the National Library of South Africa, Cape Town.
[Carbutt, Mrs. Hugh Lancaster. 1879. "Ingangegwane: The Story of
Ngangezwe and Mnyamana." *Folk-Lore Journal* 1(4): 85–97.]

Anonymous, THE WAR IN ZULULAND
Text courtesy of the Campbell Collections of the University of Natal
(Killie Campbell Africana Library). [Inanda Seminary Papers, File 1a,
Killie Campbell Collections, University of Natal.]

Beh N!a'an, GIRAFFE SONG
Text from Biesele, Megan and Thomas Dowson. 1991. Videotape.
Courtesy of Witwatersrand University Film Unit, Johannesburg.

Susiwe Bengu, TESTIMONY OF A SCHOOL GIRL
Text courtesy of the Campbell Collections of the University of Natal
(Killie Campbell Africana Library). [Inanda Seminary Papers, File 1a,
Killie Campbell Collections, University of Natal.]

Hilda Bernstein (Tandi), DIARY OF A DETAINEE
Reprinted by permission of the publisher from: *Africa South in Exile* 5.2
(1961): 25–47.

Lily Changfoot, RETURN JOURNEY
Copyright © 1982 by Lily Changfoot. Reprinted by permission of the
author's estate from: Changfoot, Lily. 1982. *A Many-Coloured South African:
the Diary of a Non-Person.* St. Catherines, Ontario: Bonsecours Editions.

Jane Chifamba, THE WIDOW AND THE BABOONS
Reprinted by permission of the publisher from: Chifamba, Jane. 1982.
Ngano Dzepasi Chigare. Gweru: Mambo Press.

Yvette Christian, GENERATIONS
Copyright © 2002 by Yvette Christianë. Published by permission of
the author.

Communal, *BOJALE*—SETSWANA INITIATION SONGS
Reprinted by permission of the National Museum, Gaborone, (publisher)
from: Motlotle, Ntikwe. 1998. "*Bojale*—Girls Initiation School." *The Zebra's
Voice* 25.2: 19–21; and Motlotle, Ntikwe. 1998. "*Bojale* in Kgatleng." *The
Zebra's Voice* 25. 3–4: 22–25.

Communal, *INTONJANE*—XHOSA INITIATION SONGS
Copyright © 2002 by KwaTuku Women Singers Group. Published by
permission of the authors.

Communal, *IZISHO ZOKUSEBENZA*—WORK SONGS
Translation copyright © 1994, published by permission of Dianne

Stewart from: *Songs of Rural Zulu Women: Finding a Voice in a Transitional Society.* Unpublished M.A. Thesis. University of Natal, Durban.

Communal, SETSWANA WEDDING SONGS
Translation copyright © 2002, published by permission of Leloba Molema and Nobantu Rasebotsa.

Communal, SWAZI WEDDING SONGS
Translation copyright © 2002 by Thulisile Motsa-Dladla.

Tsitsi Dangarembga, THE LETTER
Copyright © 1985, reprinted by permission of the author from: 1985. *Whispering Land: An Anthology of Stories by African Women.* Stockholm: SIDA.

Jennifer Davids, POEM FOR MY MOTHER
Copyright © 1974, reprinted by permission of the publisher from: Davids, Jennifer. 1974. *Searching for Words.* Cape Town: David Philip, 1974.

Ingrid de Kok, OUR SHARPEVILLE
Copyright © 1987, reprinted by permission of the author from: *TriQuarterly* 69 (Spring/ Summer 1987).

Di//xao =Oma, OUR GOVERNMENT IS A GLOWING EMBER
Text from: Biesele, Megan. Unpublished Recording. Nyae Nyae, Namibia.

Paulina Dlamini, FLIGHT OF THE ROYAL HOUSEHOLD
Copyright © 1986, reprinted by permission of the publisher from: Bourquin, S., ed. 1986. *Paulina Dlamini: Servant of Two Kings.* Pietermaritzburg: University of Natal Press.

Unity Dow, CARING FOR THE DYING
Copyright © 2000, reprinted by permission of the publishers from: Dow, Unity. 2000. *Far and Beyon'.* Gaborone: Longman Botswana; and Dow, Unity. 2001. *Far and Beyon'.* Melbourne: Spinifex Press.

Elizabeth Dube, GOOD AS DEAD
Text courtesy of the Amani Trust Archives and Shari Eppel. [Eppel, Shari. 2000. Clinician interview. Harare.]

Federation of South African Women, WOMEN'S CHARTER
Text courtesy of FEDSAW. [FEDSAW. 1954. "Report of the First National Conference of Women."]

Nadine Gordimer, APRIL 27: THE FIRST TIME
Copyright © 1994, reprinted by permission of the author from: Brink, André, ed. 1994. *SA 27 April: An Author's Diary.* Cape Town: Queillerie.

Joan Hambidge, T.M.T. ♡ T.B.M.G.

Copyright © 1989, reprinted by permission of the author from: Hambidge, Joan. 1989. *Kriptonomie*. Cape Town: Human and Rousseau.

Hamsi (Marie Kathleen Jeffreys), THOUGH I AM BLACK, I AM COMELY
Copyright © 2002. Text courtesy of the National Library of South Africa, Cape Town. [Ref. MSC 64 / 1.1.]

Bessie Head, FOR "NAPOLEON BONAPARTE," JENNY, AND KATE
Copyright © 1990, reprinted by permission of the author's estate from: *Southern African Review of Books* (August/October 1990): 12–15.

Florence Nolwandle Jabavu, BANTU HOME LIFE
Copyright © 1928, reprinted by permission of the publisher from: Taylor, Rev. J. Dexter, ed. 1928. *Christianity and the Natives of South Africa: A Yearbook of South African Missions*. Alice: Lovedale Press.

Noni Jabavu, BUS JOURNEY TO TSOLO
Copyright © 1963, reprinted by permission of the author from: Jabavu, Noni. 1963. *The Ochre People: Scenes from a South African Life*. London: John Murray.

Ingrid Jonker, I DRIFT IN THE WIND
Copyright © 1966, reprinted by permission of the Ingrid Jonker Trust from: Jonker, Ingrid. 1966. *Kantelson*. Johannesburg: Afrikaanse Pers-Boekhandel.

Marevasei Kachere, WAR MEMOIR
Copyright © 2000, reprinted by permission of the publisher from: Zimbabwe Women Writers. 2000. *Women of Resilience*. Harare: Zimbabwe Women Writers.

Princess Magogo kaDinuzulu, BALLAD OF NOMAGUNDWANE
Translation © 1976, reprinted by permission of the estate of David Rycroft from: Rycroft, David. 1976. *African Language Studies* 16: 60 ff.

Mukwahongo Mekulu Ester Kamati, CHILDREN OF NAMIBIA
Copyright © 2002 by Mukwahongo Mekulu Ester Kamati. Published by permission of the author.

Kandjende's Sister, LETTER FROM KARIBIB
Text courtesy of the National Archives of Namibia, Windhoek. [Ref. NAN.ZBU W 111, p. 2 (2053).]

Andanette Kararaimbe, Gerhartine Kukuri, Gerhartine Tjituka, Natalia Kaheke, Andeline Kathea, and Sybil Bowker, MEETING OF HERERO WOMEN
Text courtesy of the National Archives of Namibia, Windhoek. [Ref. NAN.SWAA A50/119.]

Baboni Khama, Mmakgama Khama, Milly Khama, and Oratile Sekgoma, LETTER TO THE HIGH COMMISSIONER
Text courtesy of the Botswana National Archives and Records Service. [Doc. DLS 17/23.]

Khami, COURT RECORD
Text courtesy of the National Archives of Zimbabwe, Harare. [Ref. No. D3/19/5.]

Antjie Krog, THE BIRTH OF THIS COUNTRY'S LANGUAGE
Copyright © 1998, reprinted by permission of the publisher from: Krog, Antjie. 1998. *Country of My Skull*. Johannesburg: Random House.

Ellen K. Kuzwayo, AFRICAN WISDOM
Copyright © 1998, reprinted by permission of the publisher from: Kuzwayo, Ellen K. 1998. *African Wisdom: A Personal Collection of Setswana Proverbs*. Cape Town: Kwela Books.

!Kweiten ta //ken, WHAT THE MAIDENS DO WITH ROOI KLIP
Text courtesy of the University of Cape Town Libraries, Bleek Collection [No. 151; Lucy Lloyd Notebooks: 1874. *Bushman Notebook*, Vol. 6, No. 1: 3970–3974].

Keamogetswe Kwere and Lesie Kwere, WE WILL BE LEASING FOR OURSELVES
Translation © 1997–1998, published by permission of Maitseo Bolaane.

Queen Regent Labotsibeni, ADDRESS TO THE RESIDENT COMMISSIONER
Text from: National Archives of Swaziland, Mbabane. ["Installation of Sobhuza," Ref. RCS 756/20, folios 64–65 (22 December 1921).]

Eliza M., ACCOUNT OF CAPE TOWN
Text courtesy of the National Library of South Africa, Cape Town. ["A Kaffir Account of Cape Town," *King William's Town Gazette and Kaffriarian Banner* September 10, 1863. 3.]

Sindiwe Magona, STELLA
Copyright © 1991, reprinted by permission of the publisher from: Magona, Sindiwe. 1991. *Living, Loving and Lying Awake at Night*. Cape Town: David Philip and Northampton, Mass: Interlink Books..

Unangoroa Maherero, Louisa Kambazembi, Edla Maherero, Augusta Kambazembi, Magdalina Katjimune, and Hester Keha, NATION IS GOING TO RUINATION

Text courtesy of the National Archives of Namibia, Windhoek. [Ref. NAN: SWAA 1:49. 158/23/2.]

Thoko Remigia Makhanya, **A NOBLE WOMAN OF AFRICA**
Copyright © 1993, reprinted by permission of the publisher from: Rule, Peter, with Marilyn Aitken and Jenny van Dyk. 1993. *Nokukhanya: Mother of Light.* Johannesburg: The Grail.

Nise Malange, **I, THE UNEMPLOYED**
Copyright © 1986, reprinted by permission of Nise Malange from: Sitas, Ari, ed. 1986. *Black Mamba Rising: South African Worker Poets in the Stuggle.* Durban: COSATU.

Winnie Madikizela Mandela, **DETENTION ALONE IS A TRIAL IN ITSELF**
Text from: William Cullen Library, University of the Witwatersrand. [FEDSAW papers: A1985/F 2:4.]

Minnie Martin, **MOLIEGE'S VENGEANCE**
Text courtesy of the National Library of South Africa, Cape Town. [*The South African Magazine* (August 1906): 566–570.]

Cheche Maseko and Loice Mushore, **WAR FROM WITHIN**
Copyright © 1990, reprinted by permission of Irene Staunton from: Staunton, Irene, ed. 1990. *Mothers of the Revolution.* Harare: Baobab Books.

Sheila Masote, **TESTIMONY: TRUTH AND RECONCILIATION COMMISSION**
Reprinted by permission of the author from: www.truth.org.za. Human Rights Violation Hearings: Women's Hearings, Case no. JB04279/01 GTSOW.

Dorothy Masuka, **TWO SONGS**
Copyright © 1956, reprinted by permission of the author from: Galo Records. 1958–1959.

Charlotte Manye Maxeke, **SOCIAL CONDITIONS AMONG BANTU WOMEN AND GIRLS**
Text courtesy of the Africana Library, University of Fort Hare. [1930. *Christian Students and Modern South Africa: A Report of the Bantu-Europeans' Student Conference, Fort Hare, June 27th—July 3rd, 1930.* Fort Hare, Alice: Student Christian Association. 111–117.]

Cinikile Mazibuko and Makhosazane Nyadi, **TWO DREAM-MIRACLE STORIES**
Copyright © 1996, reprinted by permission of the publisher from: Muller, Carol. 1996. "Nazarite Women, Religious Narrative and the Construction of Cultural Truth and Power" in M. J. Daymond, ed. *South African Feminisms.* New York and London: Garland.

Louisa Mvemve, A "LITTLE WOMAN'S" ADVICE TO THE PUBLIC
Text courtesy of the National Archives of South Africa, Pretoria. [Ref. NTS 939 3/376 Part 1; 1915/1916.]

Helena Namases and Emma Narises, THE GIRL AGA-ABES
Copyright © 1994, reprinted by permission of Sigrid Schmid from: Schmid, Sigrid. 1994. *Tsi Tsi Ge Ge Hahe*. New Namibia Books.

Ellen Ndeshi Namhila, THE PRICE OF FREEDOM
Copyright © 1997, reprinted by permission of the publisher from: Namhila, Ellen Ndeshi. 1997. *The Price of Freedom*. Windhoek: New Namibia Books.

Native and Coloured Women of the Province of the Orange Free State, PETITION OF THE NATIVE AND COLOURED WOMEN OF THE PROVINCE OF THE ORANGE FREE STATE
Text courtesy of the National Archives of South Africa, Pretoria, Transvaal Archives Depot, National Archives Repository. [Ref: GG 1542 50/284 (Formerly: GG 1163 50/384).]

Elizabeth Ncube, PRAISE TO MBUYA NEHANDA
Copyright © 1993 by Elizabeth Ncube. Published by permission of the estate of Elizabeth Ncube.

Lassie Ndondo, PAST AND PRESENT
Copyright © 1963, reprinted by permission of the author from: Ndondo, Lassie. 1962. *Qaphela Ingane*. Pietermaritzburg: Natal Witness.

Lauretta Ngcobo, THE RENDING OF THE VEIL
Copyright © 1981 by Lauretta Ngcobo, reprinted by permission of the author and of Shelley Power Literary Agency from: Ngcobo, Lauretta. *Cross of Gold*. London: Longman.

Lilian Ngoyi, PRESIDENTIAL ADDRESS TO THE AFRICAN NATIONAL CONGRESS WOMEN'S LEAGUE, TRANSVAAL
Text from: William Cullen Library, University of the Witwatersrand. [Carter-Karis Microfilm of South African Political Materials, Reel 2B, Ref. 2:DA15: 30/11, Department of Historical Papers.]

Kaatje Nieuwveldt, TESTIMONY
Text from: National Archives of South Africa, Cape Town. [Item 1/UIT 14/37.]

Nosente of the Umgqwashe, THE STORY OF NOSENTE
Copyright © 1936, reprinted by permission of the trustees of the will of the late Dame Margery Perham from: Perham, Margery, ed. 1936. *Ten Africans*. London: Faber and Faber.

Phyllis Ntantala, **THE WIDOWS OF THE RESERVES**
Copyright © 1958, reprinted by permission of the publisher from: *Africa South in Exile* 2.3 (1958): 9–13.

Mpho 'M'atsepo Nthunya, **BEFORE THE BEGINNING**
Copyright © 1996, reprinted by permission of the author from: Nthunya, Mpho 'M'atsepo. 1996. *Singing Away the Hunger: Stories of Life in Lesotho*. Pietermaritzburg: University of Natal Press.

Regina Ntongana, **CROSSROADS**
Copyright © 1984, reprinted by permission of Beata Lipman from: Lipman, Beata, ed. 1984. *We Make Freedom: Women in South Africa*. London: Pandora.

NyaMutango (Ntumba Machai), *MUTONDO*—**NYEMBA INITIATION SONGS**
Copyright © 2002 by Ntumba Machai.

Karen Press, **KROTOA'S STORY**
Copyright © 1990, reprinted by permission of the author from: Press, Karen. 1990. *Bird Heart Stoning the Sea*. Cape Town: Buchu Books.

Ntebogang Ratshosa, **SPEECH TO THE BANGWAKETSE**
Text courtesy of the Botswana National Archives and Records Service. [Doc. S 601/20 and Doc. S. 5/5.]

Kristina Rungano, **THE WOMAN**
Copyright © 1984, reprinted by permission of the author from: Rungano, Kristina. 1984. *A Storm is Brewing*. Harare: Zimbabwe Publishing House.

Agnes Sam, **JESUS IS INDIAN**
Copyright © 1989, reprinted by permission of the publisher from: Sam, Agnes. *Jesus Is Indian and Other Stories*. London: Heinemann: 1994.

Olive Schreiner, **LEAVING THE FARM**
Copyright © 2002 by the estate of Olive Schreiner. Text courtesy of the Harry Ransom Humanities Research Center, the University of Texas at Austin.

Gasethata Segaise, Mmatsheko Pilane, and Motshabi Molefhe, **"LEND ME A DRESS": TESTIMONIES ON EDUCATION**
Copyright © 1991, 1999, published by permission of Gasethata Segaise.

Oratile Sekgoma, **INHERITANCE: TWO LETTERS**
Text courtesy of the Botswana National Archives and Records Service. [Doc. DCS 8/15 and Doc. S 48/5.]

Nehambo Magdalena Shamena, **EMERGENCY CALL FROM THE**

Text courtesy of the National Archives of Namibia, Windhoek. [Ref. NAN SWAA A50/119.]

Victoria Nombulelo M. Swaartbooi, **UMANDISA**
Copyright © 1957, reprinted by permission of the publisher from: Swaartbooi, Victoria Nombulelo M. 1957. *UMandisa*. Alice: Lovedale Press.

Gladys Thomas, **FALL TOMORROW**
Copyright © 1972, reprinted by permission of the author from: Matthews, James and Gladys Thomas. 1972. *Cry Rage!* Johannesburg: Spro-Cas.

Miriam Tlali, **THE HAUNTING MELANCHOLY OF KLIPVOORDAM**
Copyright © 1981, reprinted by permission of the author from: *Staffrider* 4.1 (April/May 1981): 13–16.

//Ukxa N!a'an, **THE OLD PEOPLE GIVE YOU LIFE**
Text from: Biesele, Megan. 1972. Recording. Dobe, Botswana.

!Unn/obe Morethlwa, **TOBACCO, SUGAR, ALCOHOL, AND COFFEE: THESE THINGS HAVE TURNED US INTO SLAVES**
Text from: Biesele Megan and Thomas Dowson. 1991. Videotape. Courtesy of Witwatersrand University Film Unit, Johannesburg.

Yvonne Vera, **WRITING NEAR THE BONE**
Copyright © 1997, reprinted by permission of the author from: *Neue Zürcher Zeitung*, 1997.

Zoë Wicomb, **ANOTHER STORY**
Copyright © 1990, reprinted by Permission of the publisher from: Lefanu, Sarah and Stephen Hayward, eds. 1990. *Colours of a New Day: Writing for South Africa*. Johannesburg: Ravan Press.

Doris M. Wisdom (Lessing), **THE CASE OF THE FOOLISH MINISTER**
Copyright © 1943, reprinted by permission of the author from: *Rafters* (Nov. 1943). Salisbury, Rhodesia.

Nongenile Masithathu Zenani, **A MAN HIDES FOOD FROM HIS FAMILY**
Copyright © 1992, reprinted by permission of the publisher from: Scheub, Harold, ed. 1992. *The World and the Word: Tales and Observations from the Xhosa Oral Tradition*. Madison: University of Wisconsin Press.

AUTHORS LISTED BY COUNTRY

BOTSWANA

Communal, Unity Dow, Opha Dube, Bessie Head, Baboni Khama, Milly Khama, Mmakgama Khama, "Banabotlhe Kwena," Keamogetswe Kwere, Lesie Kwere, Motsei Madisa, "Matshediso Moeng," "Segametsi Molefe," Motshabi Molefhe, Leloba Molema, Athaliah Molokomme, Ruth Motsete, Mmatsheko Pilane, Ntebogang Ratshosa, Gasethata Segaise, Oratile Sekgoma, Onalenna Selolwane, //Ukxa N!a'an, !Unn/obe Morethlwa

LESOTHO

Anonymous, Adèle Mabille, Mpho 'M'atsepo Nthunya

NAMIBIA

Emmillie Adams, Anonymous, Beh N!a'an, Sybil Bowker, Katrina de Klerk, Di//xao =Oma, Natalie Kaheke, Mekulu Mukwahongo Ester Kamati, Augusta Kambazembi, Louisa Kambazembi, Kandjende's Sister, Andanette Kararaimbe, Andeline Kathea, Magdalina Katjimune, Kambauruma Kazahendike, Urieta (Johanna Maria) Kazahendike, Hester Keha, Lissie Kisting, Sofia Kloete, Gerhartine Kukuri, Sofia Labau, Edla Maherero, Unangoroa Maherero, Helena Namases, Ellen Ndeshi Namhila, Emma Narises, NyaMutango (Ntumba Machai), Nehambo Magdalena Shamena, Nekwaya Loide Shikongo, Katrina Skeier, Katrina Stephanus, Gerhartine Tjituka, Sara van Wijk, Margarethe von Eckenbrecher, Magdalena Vries

SOUTH AFRICA

Anonymous, Susiwe Bengu, Hilda Bernstein (Tandi), Lily Changfoot, Yvette Christiansë, Communal, Jennifer Davids, Ingrid de Kok, Paulina Dlamini, Adelaide Charles Dube, Federation of South African Women, Eliza Feilden, Nadine Gordimer, Joan Hambidge, Hamsi (Marie Kathleen Jeffreys), Indian Women's Association, Tryn Isaac, Florence Nolwandle Jabavu, Noni Jabavu, Ingrid Jonker, Princess Magogo kaDinuzulu, Antjie Krog, Ellen K. Kuzwayo, !Kweiten ta //ken, Eliza M., Sindiwe Magona, Thoko Remigia Makhanya, Nise Malange, Winnie Madikizela Mandela, Minnie Martin, Sheila Masote, Charlotte Manye Maxeke, Cinikile Mazibuko, Fatima Meer, Nontsizi Mgqwetho, Gcina Mhlophe, MaMhlalise Mkhwanazi, Marion Morel (Marion Welsh), Louisa Mvemve, Native and

Coloured Women of the Province of the Orange Free State, Lauretta Ngcobo, Lilian Ngoyi, Kaatje Nieuwveldt, Nosente of the Umgqwashe, Phyllis Ntantala, Regina Ntongana, Makhosazane Nyadi, Karen Press, Agnes Sam, Emma Sandile, Olive Schreiner, Cherry Stephana Mogolo Sibeko, Joyce Sikhakhane, Maureen Kim Sing, Nokwanda Sithole, Mavis Smallberg, Victoria Nombulelo M. Swaartbooi, Gladys Thomas, Miriam Tlali, Noneko (Hannah) Toney, Lydia Umkasetemba , A. M. van den Berg, Zoë Wicomb, Nongenile Masithathu Zenani

SWAZILAND

Communal, Queen Regent Labotsibeni

ZIMBABWE

Jane Chifamba, Tsitsi Dangarembga, Elizabeth Dube, Hazel Hall, Marevasei Kachere, Khami, Angela Kotler, Cheche Maseko, Dorothy Masuka, "Thandiwe Mhlanga," Qedabakwabo Moyo, Maria Munsaka, Loice Mushore, Colette Mutangadura, Elizabeth Ncube, Lassie Ndondo, Kristina Rungano, Joyce Simango, Yvonne Vera, Doris M. Wisdom (Lessing)

INDEX